Classical FORTRAN statement	description	§
C This program...	comment	1.1
REAL*8 X	declare X a real variable	4.5
INTEGER*4 P	declare P an integer variable	4.5
COMPLEX*16 Z	declare Z a complex variable	4.6.1
LOGICAL*4 L	declare L a logical variable	4.6.2
CHARACTER*1 LTR	declare LTR a character variable	10.1
IMPLICIT NONE	require all variables to be typed	12.4.4
PARAMETER(T=2.D0)	replace each T by 2.D0	4.5
EQUIVALENCE(X,J)	overlay J on X in memory	4.6.3
COMMON /BLK/Q,R	define shared memory	8.2
BLOCK DATA	initialize variables in COMMON	8.6
EXTERNAL FCN	declare name FCN a parameter	7.2
END	this is the last source line	1.1
A=B+C-D*E/(F**G)	assignment	2.6
IF(A.LT.0.) A=B	logical IF	3.2
IF(A.LT.0.) THEN		
ELSE	} IF-THEN block	3.3
ENDIF		
GO TO 1	unconditional branch	3.2
STOP	return to operating system	1.1
DO 1 I=1,N		
1 CONTINUE	} DO loop	5.2
CALL SUB(I,J)	invoke subroutine SUB	6.1
SUBROUTINE SUB(I,J)	define subroutine SUB	6.1
FUNCTION FCN(X,Y)	define function FCN	6.3
RETURN	return to subprogram caller	6.1
READ *,B	free-format input	2.7
PRINT *,'A=',A	free-format output	1.1
READ(5,901) X	formatted input	9.1
WRITE(6,901) X	formatted output	9.1
901 FORMAT(F7.3)	format specification	9.1.1
OPEN(7,FILE='fyle')	open a file	9.4.1
CLOSE(7)	close a file	9.4.1
REWIND(7)	rewind a file	9.6
INQUIRE(UNIT=1,EXIST=OK)	find out about a file or unit	14.2.2

FORTRAN-90 statement	description	§
SAVE	save local variables	17.1
INTERFACE END INTERFACE	} subprogram interface	17.1.1
ALLOCATABLE A(:)	make array allocatable	17.1.2
ALLOCATE(A(N)) L=ALLOCATED(A) DEALLOCATE(A)	} array allocation	17.1.2
A=B+C-D*E/(F**G)	array assignment	17.1.1
X=A(:,1)	array section	17.1.1
T=TRANSPOSE(A)	$t_{i,j} = a_{j,i}$	17.1.1
P=MATMUL(B,C)	$p_{i,j} = \sum_k b_{i,k} c_{k,j}$	17.1.1
S=SUM(A)	$s = \sum_{i,j,\dots} [a_{i,j,\dots}]$	17.1.1
U=MAXVAL(A)	$u = \max_{i,j,\dots} [a_{i,j,\dots}]$	17.1.1
V=MINVAL(A)	$v = \min_{i,j,\dots} [a_{i,j,\dots}]$	17.1.1
XTY=DOT_PRODUCT(X,Y)	$x^\top y = \sum_j x_j y_j$	17.1.1
VEC=PACK(MAT,.TRUE.)	convert array to vector	17.1.1

parallel programming with MPI	§
INCLUDE 'mpif.h'	16.2.3
CALL MPI_INIT(RC)	16.2.3
CALL MPI_COMM_RANK(COMM,MYID,RC)	16.2.3
CALL MPI_COMM_SIZE(COMM,N,RC)	16.2.4
CALL MPI_SEND(DATA,COUNT,TYPE,DEST,TAG,COMM,RC)	16.2.3
CALL MPI_RECV(DATA,COUNT,TYPE,ORIG,TAG,COMM,STAT,RC)	16.2.3
CALL MPI_BCAST(DATA,COUNT,TYPE,ORIG,COMM,RC)	16.2.4
CALL MPI_FINALIZE(RC)	16.2.3

parallel programming with HPF	§
EXTRINSIC(HPF_LOCAL)	17.2.5
PURE FUNCTION R(Z)	17.2.5
CHPF$ PROCESSORS PROCS(2,3,4)	17.2.2
CHPF$ DISTRIBUTE E(*,BLOCK,CYCLIC) ONTO PROCS	17.2.2
CHPF$ ALIGN F(I,*) WITH G(I,*)	17.2.2
CHPF$ SEQUENCE V	17.2.5
CHPF$ INDEPENDENT,NEW(I)	17.2.2
FORALL(I=1:N,J=1:N,J.LE.I) G(I,J)=G(I,J)/G(I,I)	17.2.4
N=NUMBER_OF_PROCESSORS()	17.2.6

Second Edition

Classical
FORTRAN

**Programming for
Engineering and
Scientific Applications**

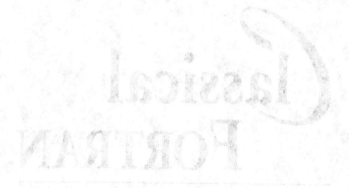

Second Edition

Classical FORTRAN

Programming for Engineering and Scientific Applications

Michael Kupferschmid

CRC Press
Taylor & Francis Group
Boca Raton London New York

CRC Press is an imprint of the
Taylor & Francis Group, an **informa** business

CRC Press
Taylor & Francis Group
6000 Broken Sound Parkway NW, Suite 300
Boca Raton, FL 33487-2742

First issued in paperback 2017

© 2009 by Taylor and Francis Group, LLC
CRC Press is an imprint of Taylor & Francis Group, an Informa business

No claim to original U.S. Government works

ISBN-13: 978-1-4200-5907-6 (hbk)
ISBN-13: 978-1-138-11643-6 (pbk)

Visit the Taylor & Francis Web site at
http://www.taylorandfrancis.com

and the CRC Press Web site at
http://www.crcpress.com

Contents

Preface

This book is a college text, self-study guide, and reference about programming computers in FORTRAN, the original and still most widely recognized language for engineering and scientific applications. It defines Classical FORTRAN, a simple subset of FORTRAN carefully chosen for its utility in numerical computing, and treats this language in progressively greater depth. In Chapters 1–6, just 87 pages, the reader gets a working introduction to the language; Chapters 7–10, 82 pages, cover the remaining topics that most engineers and scientists need for casual programming. Succeeding chapters provide in-depth treatment of memory management techniques; program design, documentation, and coding style; archaic, unusual, and dangerous usages (including the parts of FORTRAN-77 left out of the subset); program development in the UNIX™ environment; performance measurement and optimization; vector processing; parallel computation with the Message Passing Interface library; and selected features of Fortran-90 and High Performance Fortran. The book concludes with a collection of handy utility routines, an extensive bibliography, and a 36-page index. The emphasis throughout is on writing real programs for actual applications, with special attention to logical correctness, numerical accuracy, and run-time performance.

The student will discover in this book a conversational, classroom-proven style, based on the use of numerous examples and case studies, that makes it easy for readers whose main interest might *not* be computers or programming to quickly learn and use FORTRAN for real engineering and scientific applications. The book will be of special interest to graduate students whose research involves scientific computing, and to undergraduates studying or using numerical methods, but it should also be accessible to advanced high school students who know some science and mathematics. Students whose main focus is computers and programming *per se*, rather than applications, might find this book interesting too, especially if they have experience with other languages but little previous exposure to computing with floating-point numbers.

The teacher will find a small, clean subset language that restores the traditional elegant simplicity of FORTRAN and makes it fun to teach. The book starts very easy, so that even students who have weak backgrounds or a history of difficulty in other programming courses can find a toehold. Then it gradually leads through more difficult material to advanced topics (such as parallel processing) that are beyond the scope of most introductory programming textbooks. The coverage of number storage formats and IEEE floating-point arithmetic is unusually detailed, demystifying overflows, exceptions, roundoff errors, and other aspects of numerical computing with fixed word length. The discussion of program design, documentation, and programming style offers practical advice instead of abstract theories, and is timed to be of interest and value to students rather than seeming a pointless annoyance. The book dedicates a chapter to program development and debugging in UNIX™, but otherwise refers only incidentally to operating system issues, so it can be used for courses in which the students write programs in some other computing environment. There are 577 widely varied exercises to confirm the student's understanding of concepts. The exercises encourage the student to always be programming, some introduce special topics, and many are intended for assignment as programming projects. If you adopt this book for use in class you can get the *Solutions Manual,* which provides worked-out answers to about half of the exercises.

The engineer or scientist will see a compact review of basics, an easy way to get started with modern high-performance computing, expert advice about dealing with troublesome legacy codes, and an extended reference covering a wide spectrum of other topics. The comprehensive concept-driven index makes it easy to read the book out of order, and the bibliography points to further reading on many subjects. The final chapter of the book is a collection of general-purpose utility routines that may be of direct value to practitioners.

The merely curious will enjoy a colorful introduction to the FORTRAN programming subculture, and might possibly be persuaded to join it!

For a more thorough discussion of this book and its many intended audiences, please see §0.5.

0

Introduction

Colleges often invite faculty from other schools to evaluate the local curriculum. One such reviewer had almost finished his visit to a computer science department, and was about to give the dean of the school a favorable report, when someone carelessly mentioned having taught a course in numerical methods using FORTRAN. Incredulous, the visitor arched an eyebrow and looked down his nose with sudden contempt. "FORTRAN," he sneered, "is the language of *peasants!*"

I was not at the scene to enjoy this incident so I can only assume the report I heard was accurate, but true or apocryphal it makes a good story and several important points about FORTRAN programming. Hence the attitude of this book, and part of my motivation for writing it.

0.1 Why Study Programming?

Computing, as any teenager can tell you, is easy. You can play games and write reports for school. There are spreadsheet programs and database programs and programs that work like a hand calculator (all of these are referred to in the popular media as "*software programs,*" as though there were any other kind of program one might run on a computer). The vast communication utility that is the World Wide Web beckons anyone who has a network connection, some curiosity, and a few minutes (well, maybe more than a few minutes) to spare. On the Web you can buy almost anything, obtain copyrighted entertainment for free, proclaim your opinions in a personal "web log" [153], join total strangers in pointless, rambling conversations [182], or act the part of a fantasy character in a multi-player video game such as "World of Warcraft" [129]. On the Web shy people can [155] enjoy a vicarious social life

"Do your employees visit Web sites of this type when they should be working?"	companies surveyed responding "yes"
weather	2%
humor	2%
games	4%
travel	5%
shopping	6%
TV, radio, movies	10%
music	13%
sports	16%
sexually explicit	72%

ELRON SOFTWARE [123]

or [115] advertise for a mate without risking physical proximity to other human beings (but unintended physical proximity to people you meet on the Web can be risky). Developments in information retrieval from the Web are said [175] to presage an era of telosophy or "wisdom at a distance" (but seem already to have ushered in an era of widespread identity theft). Virtual reality is said [156] to "emphasize the experiential, creative side of people," becoming "the critical link in turning technology into a sustainable art form." There are even pictures of *naked girls* out there!

It's pretty obvious, looking at the countless applications that are already on the Web or available from your local PC store, that every important computing problem has now been solved once and for all, or will be shortly. And to get everything, effortlessly and *without having to know anything,* you just point and click. You can even get it all through your television or cellphone, just as you can watch TV or make phone calls on a personal computer. Soon, all three might be replaced by a single even simpler "information appliance" [167] [159].

It's not just teenagers who know about these things; you probably know all about this kind of computing, too. Except for a few old people, and many poor people [149], *everybody* knows all about this kind of computing. Some entrepreneurs have become famous and very rich [135] by being among the first to notice that the computer is the greatest household convenience of all time (but see [177]), the cure for every ill of public education (but see [168]), and the most addictive amusement ever devised [180]. Microsoft, maker of the most widely-used PC software, once famously claimed in anti-trust litigation that its Web browser is an *integral component* of its Windows operating system, so browsing the Web is clearly what they think computers are *for*.

Understanding the technical details of how a computer works inside is no help at all in this environment, and might even be a distraction that makes it harder for you to become "computer literate." To be a computer expert now means remembering minute details of *where* to point, and *what* to click, to make some popular programs and Web sites do whatever it is they do. That obnoxious whiz kid your boss brought in last month to fix the office network gets paid a thousand dollars a day mainly for making educated guesses about the undocumented idiosyncrasies of canned software that other people wrote.

Engineers and scientists use the computer as an information appliance just as everyone else does, and they depend on Internet services like email [160], on-line publication (at, e.g., www.arXiv.org), searching the Web for technical information [183], and remotely executing special-purpose technical software (e.g. www.ncbi.nlm.nih.gov/BLAST). But they also think up other uses for computers that are of zero interest to most consumers and therefore to most software manufacturers. General-purpose programs are available for some common technical applications, though telling them what to do often requires some sort of programming rather than just pointing and clicking. In many cases, however, engineering and scientific problems are so specialized that no existing program really fits. The engineer or scientist might be the only person who knows how the calculation should be performed, so nobody else could write a suitable program even if there were a market for one. In this context it is not very helpful to have an appliance that can do only set tasks chosen from a menu, even if the menu includes a great many choices.

When the problem you need to solve is one for which no program has yet been written, it is necessary instead to view the computer as a laboratory instrument that you use by programming it to do *whatever you want*. Computing of this sort is not so easy as the point-and-click variety, but it can be a lot more rewarding because it requires a lot more skill. The poet W. H. Auden anticipated computers when he remarked that "Machines are beneficial to the degree that they eliminate the need for labor, harmful to the degree that they eliminate the need for skill." Running a program that someone else wrote is to writing a program of your own as listening to the radio is to building a radio receiver, or as playing a CD is to playing the piano, or as flying tourist class is to flying *the plane*. Writing your own software requires some understanding of how computers actually work, rather than just a good memory for obscure facts about particular programs that can be bought or stolen. If the world of computing were a machine shop, software users would be the lathe tenders, turning stock into widgets, and programmers would be the millwrights who built the production line and the toolmakers who grind the bits that actually cut the metal. Programmers are above all consummate makers of tools.

Before the invention of the personal computer, people wrote letters longhand or with a typewriter. Banks, insurance companies, and payroll departments accounted for most of the tiny minority of people using computers, while engineers and scientists, doing numerical calculations too tedious for a slide rule, made up the rest. Today everybody uses computers to write letters (and so forth), the business people still use them to keep track of dollars and cents, and the engineers and scientists use them for numerical calculations too tedious for a hand calculator. Because the engineers and scientists now make up only a tiny fraction of computer users, it might seem that technical computing has faded away altogether. But the number of people who need computers for numerical calculations is actually *larger* than it was in the typewriter era, and they use them to do vastly more calculations.

Much of the software that everyone knows about is designed to improve the user's personal productivity, by making it easier to do things that could really be done in some other way with only a little more effort. I *could* turn around and look at the calendar hanging on my wall, rather than using the calendar program on my PC, or balance my checkbook by hand rather than using the computer to do the arithmetic. But many of the engineering and scientific calculations that I described above as "too tedious" really cannot practically be done *at all* except on a computer. For example, suppose we need to find the values of x where

$$\sin(x) = \tfrac{1}{2}x.$$

It's easy to see from the equation that $x = 0$ is one solution. It's also easy to see, from the graph, that there is another near $x = 2$, but its exact location can't be found by algebra. Finding that root precisely requires an iterative algorithm in which the answer is approximated with increasing accuracy by repeating some arithmetic calculations over and over. The simplest algorithm for this

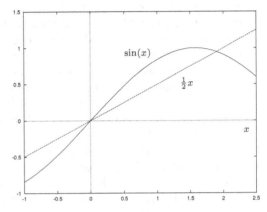

problem is **bisection**, which goes like this. First find an interval of x that is sure to contain the root, say $[\tfrac{1}{2}, 2\tfrac{1}{2}]$, and evaluate $f(x) = \sin(x) - \tfrac{1}{2}x$ at each end. Next find the midpoint of the interval by adding the end values together and dividing by 2, and evaluate $f(x)$ there. Determine which end of the interval gave an $f(x)$ value having the same sign as the value at the midpoint, and replace that end by the midpoint. Now repeat the steps until the interval is reduced in width to, say, 10^{-8}, and $f(x) \approx 0$. Doing that much arithmetic by hand would take a long time, and might wear out the buttons on your calculator before you finished. Bisection and other numerical algorithms, for solving nonlinear equations like our example and for doing many other technical calculations, are discussed in books such as [4].

Nonlinear equations have been studied for a long time so programs are available for solving them, but technical projects often give rise to the need for calculations that nobody has done before. It is only the new problems that are worth hiring people to think about, so it is essential for engineers and scientists to know how to write new programs for doing calculations not yet imagined. Most people, and even some self-styled "computer experts," can get along fine with software they buy at the corner store. But if you are an engineer or scientist, or hope to become one, then knowing how to program a computer is an important component of your basic professional literacy and a skill you will find it difficult to get along without.

0.2 The Evolution of FORTRAN

FORTRAN is ancient, as computing languages go, having had its first production run on Saturday, April 20, 1957 [128, p30]. The first widely-used version of the language was

FORTRAN-II, which evolved into FORTRAN-IV, later also known as FORTRAN-66 for the year in which it was described in a formal standard [120]. Further development yielded FORTRAN-77, then Fortran-90, Fortran-95, and Fortran-2000. Each new version of the language is a superset of the older versions, and there will surely be more; Fortran-08 is being defined as I write this. The eminent computer scientist Tony Hoare was prophetic, though widely disbelieved, when he quipped in 1984 [157, p13], "I don't know what the language of the year 2000 will look like but I know it will be called FORTRAN." Like the virus that causes the common cold, FORTRAN has survived in a hostile and constantly-changing world by periodic mutations. The changes have grown larger and more frequent starting with Fortran-90, so I will refer to Fortran-90 and its successors collectively as Modern Fortran. Most extant FORTRAN code falls between FORTRAN-66 and FORTRAN-77. This book is mainly about a subset of FORTRAN-77 (discussed in §0.4) that I will refer to as **Classical FORTRAN**.

IBM RESEARCH

FORTRAN was invented at International Business Machines (IBM) by engineers, not by computer scientists ("computer science" had not yet been named). The person who led the team was John Backus, pictured above. For his work he won the W. W. McDowell Award from the Institute of Electrical and Electronics Engineers, the A. M. Turing Award from the Association for Computing Machinery, several honorary doctorates, and in 1975 the National Medal of Science. He was also named an IBM Fellow, and in 1993 he was awarded the $375,000 Charles Stark Draper Prize of the National Academy of Engineering [117]. At least in the neighborhood where I grew up, these would not be considered bad wages for, among other things, thinking up a peasant language! Now perhaps even greater honors are paid to Backus by history, for his creation has outlived its author [132].

The name FORTRAN is an acronym for FORmula TRANslation, which is about the only thing the language is really good for. Classical FORTRAN forbids recursion and re-entry, uses static storage allocation, provides only primitive control and data structures, and is more easily abused than some modern programming languages. It is ill-suited to many tasks, and its extinction has been regularly predicted for many years. In the 1960s FORTRAN was destined to be supplanted by ALGOL, in the 1970s by PL1, in the 1980s by Pascal and then Modula-II and SISAL [95], and in the 1990s by Ada and C.

During the three years or so that it took me to write the first edition of this book, C++ advanced to the role of FORTRAN nemesis, reached its zenith, and began losing ground to Java [143] and Perl. Now Python and Ruby seem to be making some headway in numerical computing. Perhaps in the future FORTRAN will be doomed by Oz, or by some novelty yet undreamed of. FORTRAN contains no primitives for graphics, so languages that do, such as Visual BASIC, are strong contenders for some applications. Every language is interesting and appropriate for something, so in addition to FORTRAN you should try to learn the ones that happen to be in vogue at the moment. Plan to absorb the culture and mindset of each language *du jour* that you study, in addition to its rules. But when you've picked one to learn, don't put it off! Programming languages seldom disappear altogether but they do wax and wane in popularity and importance. Over the many years that people have been using FORTRAN several of its supposed successors have themselves become effectively, if not quite literally, extinct.

FORTRAN passed from being merely old-fashioned to being politically incorrect during the great structured programming debate of the 1970's. It all started with the publication of a letter [138] in which Prof. Dr. Edsger W. Dijkstra denounced explicit branching statements, on rather abstract philosophical grounds and without citing empirical evidence or mentioning any particular language. Later [139] he made it clear that it was FORTRAN he had in mind, called the language "infantile," and declared it too risky to use. In another famous paper [110], Niklaus Wirth, inventor of the toy language Pascal, condemned FORTRAN as singularly unsuited to the clear expression of program structure. Other computer scientists applauded, contradicted [78], or sought to temper these opinions. Everyone had seen lurid examples of code rendered incomprehensible by the abuse of GO TO statements, and everyone had also seen GO TO used in clear and harmless ways, so there began a vigorous and sometimes heated public argument, among personages of greater and lesser eminence, that still flares up every so often both in print [174][163][187][142] and on-line (in, for example, the sci.math.num-analysis newsgroup). Most Classical FORTRAN programmers view this residual skirmishing with bemusement, but each round finds fresh combatants ready to inject the old issue with new venom. While savants debate, the C language and its many derivatives now most in fashion boast control structures that make FORTRAN's humble GO TO seem the very soul of prudence.

Structured programming constructs similar to those advocated by Wirth and Dijkstra became part of FORTRAN-77, but by then there had been other advances in language design and a shift of interest among academic computer scientists to non-numerical computing problems, and FORTRAN never regained their respect. There were probably also social aspects to the rejection of FORTRAN by many computer scientists. For a long time the language was seen as a creature of IBM, whose authoritarian corporate culture was philosophically repugnant to the rebellious and free-thinking university community of the 1960's and 1970's. For many young faculty of that era FORTRAN conjured up the hateful image of obedient organization men, company drones in identical brush cuts and button-down collars, mindlessly polishing desk signs that said THINK. Because of its use for mere engineering calculations, FORTRAN was widely regarded as humdrum and embarrassingly lowbrow by the new academic discipline, which was worried about establishing its credibility as an independent field of science and wanted very much to shed the widespread early perception that it was mainly about the systematic study of programming. Some computer science departments came to regard it as beneath their dignity to teach their students how to program in *any* language, and many now content themselves with instead teaching *about* programming. In this atmosphere it is no surprise that some computer scientists, such as the one in the anecdote about FORTRAN given at the beginning of this chapter, consider it vulgar even to mention that particular "F word."

Another development that has been thought to spell the end of FORTRAN, and indeed of all technical programming languages at a similar level of abstraction, is the emergence of higher-level scientific computing environments such as MATLAB and Maple. These and other packages support programming in terms of larger mathematical operations, such as matrix algebra and calculus, rather than the scalar arithmetic of Classical FORTRAN. A science dean in my acquaintance once suggested [137] that because of the availability of high-level programming environments it might now be appropriate to teach FORTRAN only in the history department.

0.3 Why Study FORTRAN?

FORTRAN, as any browser of the *New York Times* classified section can tell you, is indeed history and has been for a long time. There are, after all, hundreds of ads for programmers each Sunday, and not one of them ever mentions FORTRAN.

Yet not long ago a compiler marketing study [186] found that about 370,000 programmers worldwide, some 32% of all users of engineering and scientific workstations, were writing in FORTRAN! It identified the biggest user communities as those engaged in "software engineering," "scientific research," "design engineering and analysis," and "classified defense," but many other sectors are also represented. Even if there is some wishful thinking in this report, it seems that FORTRAN is still used quite a bit despite the agreement of a great many armchair experts that it is only a fading memory. Proprietary compilers are marketed by several manufacturers [34] and the free g77 compiler is standard in the Linux [127] [106] operating system and in the cygwin UNIX™ emulator for Windows. Two different free compilers, g95 and gfortran, are available now (and under continuing development) for Modern Fortran. An impartial observer of these facts might say about FORTRAN, as Mark Twain did after reading his own obituary in a newspaper, "The rumors of my death have been greatly exaggerated."

Why should *anybody* still be interested in FORTRAN, fifty years after it was invented and long after it was consigned to oblivion by the academic computer science community? How can this dinosaur of a language insult the most famous and venerated authorities on the philosophy of programming by going on, decade after decade, heedless of its own egregious defects? And how can Classical FORTRAN persist as it does in the face of Modern Fortran, which is at least the deliberate product of an expert committee and therefore less rife with doctrinal error? Why not use some other language, or one of those high-level programming environments, instead?

There are in fact several very good reasons for the resilience of FORTRAN, and of Classical FORTRAN in particular.

Some of the special-purpose packages, such as MATLAB, are actually quite general, but their primitives are higher-level than those of FORTRAN and thus inevitably support best the particular kinds of calculations for which they were originally designed. This can make them a poor fit to problems that are really new, so while they can be made to work it might be a **kludge**, a clumsy adaptation, like using the sharp end of an oboe to pry the lid off a can of paint. Package users understandably favor projects they know the package can do, whereas the idea of programming is to let the engineering or science dictate what calculation is needed. A low-level description of some problems can be easier to understand, and a FORTRAN program almost always executes much faster than the same calculation performed by a high-level package. FORTRAN and MATLAB can invoke one another, so the two are sometimes used together.

Compared to many other low-level languages, Classical FORTRAN is conceptually simple, intuitive, and easy to use. Classical FORTRAN uses the same operators (+, -, *, /, and **) to do arithmetic with both integer and real numbers, but there are only a few other instances where a symbol means different things depending on the context in which it is used. Classical FORTRAN treats side effects as undesirable, rather than relying on them in standard usage as some languages do. Even the character set is small and familiar. FORTRAN is easy enough to learn so that engineers and scientists whose main focus is *not* computer programming can teach it to themselves, by trial and error and by reading books like this one, just as they did at the dawn of computing before courses in programming were introduced [162].

FORTRAN is close to algebra and is therefore very convenient for numerical computing. Some languages provide abstractions, such as recursively-defined data structures and object orientation, that are ideal for solving operating system, database, and even a few numerical computing problems, but Classical FORTRAN's simpler data and control structures are a much closer fit to the vast majority of engineering and scientific applications. Although Classical FORTRAN lacks primitives for operations on whole matrices and vectors, representing them and passing them to subprograms is straightforward and does not require the manipulation of pointers. Most FORTRAN compilers provide for automatic run-time checking of array subscripts. FORTRAN is modular, providing for separate compilation and encouraging the construction of libraries. Classical FORTRAN is standard and widely available, so programs written in it are usually easy to port from one machine or computer installation to another.

After such a long period of development, Classical FORTRAN compiler technology is very mature and robust. This, combined with the simplicity of the language and the closeness of FORTRAN constructs to the hardware of actual computers, makes it possible for optimizing compilers to generate extremely efficient machine code. The simplicity of Classical FORTRAN data structures makes programs easy to vectorize and parallelize. Its strong compiler optimization and affinity for vector and parallel processing give Classical FORTRAN a big advantage over most other programming environments for applications where execution speed is important. Rewriting a spreadsheet program in FORTRAN, for example, can reduce its running time from hours to minutes [169].

These desirable attributes make FORTRAN the language of choice for many new engineering and scientific computing projects. Programming is a young person's game just because most senior engineers and scientists manage other people rather than doing technical work themselves, so of the many people who are today FORTRAN programmers the majority are engineers and scientists in the most productive stage of their careers, writing fresh code for new uses. Most operating systems support mixed-language programming, so even if some parts of a program are most easily written in another language the parts that do numerical calculations can still be coded in FORTRAN.

Finally, there is an enormous installed base of specialized application programs written in Classical FORTRAN. This **legacy code** is essential to the everyday functioning of industry and government, and rewriting it all in other languages, even if that made technical sense, would require vast investments of money and skilled labor over a period of many years. Most of these applications still belong in FORTRAN, so they will probably be maintained and improved for the foreseeable future rather than being replaced by programs written in other languages. After 20 years of concerted effort to recode all of its applications in the Ada programming language (and of actively discouraging the use of other languages for new projects), the US Department of Defense reported in 1995 [150] that it still had about 20 million source lines in FORTRAN, compared to about 60 million source lines recoded into Ada from more than 450 different languages, including FORTRAN, over that period. Many old programs for nontechnical applications were rewritten before (or soon after) January of the year 2000 because they used two-digit dates and it was cheaper to replace than to revise them. But most engineering and scientific applications do not involve the manipulation of dates, so very few legacy FORTRAN programs had to be recoded into other languages on account of the "millennium bug." Because FORTRAN is now usually taught only surreptitiously, knowing how to deal with legacy codes is an uncommon skill that can give you a big advantage in getting, doing, and keeping your job as an engineer or scientist.

Some legacy FORTRAN programs are ugly, wrong, and impossible to understand or maintain, just as the critics of FORTRAN have always charged. But that is because they were written (and perhaps revised many times) before people knew much about programming in *any* language, not because they were written in FORTRAN. It is in fact eloquent testimony to the durability of the language that many old applications have remained in use, sometimes despite worsening infirmities, for longer than most of their critics have been alive. Now, as in the past, many of FORTRAN's most ardent detractors are programmers who have never actually used the language, and some are merely computer users who never wrote a significant program in *any* language.

Every so often someone sends me a new list of funny comparisons between programming languages and cars (see for example [176]). Assembler language is always likened to a racing car because both are very fast but hard to drive and expensive to maintain. Classical FORTRAN is usually described as a Model T Ford, simple and reliable but not too exciting, revolutionary in its time but, of course, quaintly antique now. I think a more accurate automotive metaphor would be the sturdy little 1957 Willys Jeep. It looks strange, rides rough, and has a standard transmission, but with just a few minor repairs along the way it's been running fine all these many years. It still starts right up every morning, doesn't use much gas, and gets me where I need to go even if that happens to be off the paved road.

The best analogy, though, is the one we got from the pompous professor quoted at the front of the chapter. FORTRAN is, after all, not a car but a *language*. The language of peasants, unpretentious country people, is typically plain and direct. Yet it can be richly expressive out of all proportion to its simplicity, and occasionally [185] such a language sustains a magnificent literature of enduring beauty. Apt though it is, this analogy is imperfect too, because while the number of people who speak most peasant languages is declining [165], the community of FORTRAN users is probably about the size now that it was before the invention of the personal computer. But if there is a language in your experience that was originally spoken by peasants, such as Yiddish or Gaelic, it might help to think of FORTRAN like that. Nu?

0.4   Classical FORTRAN

Most old textbooks on FORTRAN programming tried to cover *every* statement and feature of FORTRAN-66 or FORTRAN-77, and many new ones carry on that tradition by discussing *all* aspects of Modern Fortran. To judge these books by their covers, it must be important in marketing a programming text that the name of the very latest language version appears explicitly in the title, to reassure prospective buyers that they will be reading about the most recent innovations. To judge these books by their contents, it must be that the only authoritative reference is an exhaustive language manual regurgitating this morning's revision of the official standard.

But most programmers who write real engineering and scientific applications in FORTRAN actually use only a tiny subset of the language, carefully chosen from all the many features on offer. Reckless newcomers are apt to try everything, but those who stay soon discover that only a few statements are needed while most of the rest are confusing or dangerous. It would be nice to believe that technology in general and FORTRAN in particular evolve in a rational way that results in more or less continuous improvement, but history seems to have other plans! New versions of FORTRAN must be **upward compatible**, so that old programs and old programming styles continue to work, and that means that when new features are added none of the old ones are really taken out (though they might be officially designated beneath contempt). Because of this the language is full of lunatic ideas that seemed promising at the time they were introduced, but which fortunately never caught on. Successful FORTRAN users always turn out to be ruthlessly discriminating about which language features they adopt.

Not only do seasoned programmers tend to use rather *small* working FORTRAN vocabularies; most of them seem to use pretty much *the same* subset of statements. At first this may be surprising, but perhaps it is just because there are only a few ways to pick a small subset of FORTRAN that contains all the functionality needed for engineering and scientific applications. As the FORTRAN defined by the standards has grown over the years, so has this common subset that people really use, but the subset changes much more gradually, never includes everything, always includes extensions that are widely available but have not yet been officially sanctioned, and pays no homage to any particular version of the language standard. What most people mean by "FORTRAN" is that common subset, so it is what most of this book is about. To distinguish this living tongue from the desiccated fiction of the standards documents, I call it **Classical FORTRAN**. To teach the everyday speech of FORTRAN programmers and provide an effective introduction to their computing culture, a textbook must first of all recognize the existence of this language and respect it in its own right.

I do not mean to suggest that standards are evil or useless; to the contrary, they are very important because they delimit for compiler manufacturers just what a FORTRAN language implementation must do (though lately the implementations have mostly not kept up with the evolution of the standard). But FORTRAN, like English, is defined operationally by the way its writers use it, rather than by the proclamations of self-anointed expert committees. The FORTRAN standard is dreamed up by language theorists, compiler designers, and government bureaucrats, possibly influenced by suggestions from a few vocal and very sophisticated users. Yet standard practice is by definition not what the standards documents *say*, but what the vast majority of ordinary professional programmers *do* in their daily work of writing real programs. The clearest and most graceful authors of English are certainly expert in the syntax and grammar of the language, and they might have read a book like Strunk and White's *The Elements of Style* [179], but they don't spend much time consulting rule books and sometimes they even break the rules on purpose. Mocking the rule that a sentence should not end with a preposition, Winston Churchill is supposed to have said "This is the sort of English up with which I will not put." Programmers have always, and with equal justification, had that attitude about the FORTRAN standard. As a colleague once remarked to me [172] "One person's standard is another person's problem." So this book is *not* about everything in ISO/IEC 1539[118].

The standard changes from time to time and older versions of the language are declared obsolete (most recently FORTRAN-77, officially pronounced dead on June 5, 1997), but people just go right on using the language as they know and love it. Classical FORTRAN includes many statements that have been in the language ever since FORTRAN-II, and others selected from those that were introduced to make FORTRAN-66 and FORTRAN-77. Eventually there will be some additions from more recent versions, but the language presented in §1–§16 and §18 of this book does not include any. The Fortran-90 innovations that I am hoping will someday be adopted by the engineering and scientific programming community are discussed in §17.1.0–§17.1.4, and the other added features of Fortran-90, which I predict will seldom be used, are listed in §17.1.5. There are a few numerical computing problems, notably the integration of stiff partial differential equations using finite-element meshes that evolve over time, for which abstract data types, recursion, pointers, and other advanced features of Modern Fortran seem appropriate, but if you really need object-oriented programming [148] the more stable and widely-used C++ language might be a better choice.

Even in the unlikely event that *all* of Modern Fortran comes to be widely used, the Classical FORTRAN of today will of course still be in it. When someone announces, usually in a slightly superior tone, "Oh, I'm using Fortran-[fill in latest version number]" it often just means "I'm compiling a program written in (or very nearly in) Classical FORTRAN with a Fortran-[fill in latest version number] compiler."

The earlier versions of the language are nested subsets of Modern Fortran, so if you're writing Classical FORTRAN you're writing Modern Fortran. To paraphrase an oft-quoted disparagement of Classical FORTRAN and its users, a determined programmer can write FORTRAN (or code that looks like it) in any language, *even* in Modern Fortran.

Just what constitutes Classical FORTRAN, as I have described it above? It would be interesting to perform a rigorous statistical analysis of all the engineering and scientific programs that have ever been written, to discover what statements and language features are most often used *in the ones that work,* but it is hard to imagine how such an exhaustive survey could ever be conducted. Any practical estimate must be based on a sample, and mine is the few thousand programs that I have encountered as a programming consultant. My judgement about what statements should be considered part of Classical FORTRAN is doubtless also colored by the personal tastes that I have developed in my own experience as a programmer. The table below summarizes my selection.

The Statements of Classical FORTRAN

statement example	description	§
C This program...	comment	1.1
REAL*8 X	declare X a real variable	4.5
INTEGER*4 P	declare P an integer variable	4.5
COMPLEX*16 Z	declare Z a complex variable	4.6.1
LOGICAL*4 L	declare L a logical variable	4.6.2
CHARACTER*1 LTR	declare LTR a character variable	10.1
IMPLICIT NONE	require all variables to be typed	12.4.4
PARAMETER(T=2.D0)	replace each T by 2.D0	4.5
EQUIVALENCE(X,J)	overlay J on X in memory	4.6.3
COMMON /BLK/Q,R	define shared memory	8.2
BLOCK DATA	initialize variables in COMMON	8.6
EXTERNAL FCN	declare name FCN a parameter	7.2
END	this is the last source line	1.1
A=B+C-D*E/(F**G)	assignment	2.6
IF(A.LT.0.) A=B	logical IF	3.2
IF(A.LT.0.) THEN		
ELSE	} IF-THEN block	3.3
ENDIF		
GO TO 1	unconditional branch	3.2
STOP	return to operating system	1.1
DO 1 I=1,N		
1 CONTINUE	} DO loop	5.2
CALL SUB(I,J)	invoke subroutine SUB	6.1
SUBROUTINE SUB(I,J)	define subroutine SUB	6.1
FUNCTION FCN(X,Y)	define function FCN	6.3
RETURN	return to subprogram caller	6.1
READ *,B	free-format input	2.7
PRINT *,'A=',A	free-format output	1.1
READ(5,901) X	formatted input	9.1
WRITE(6,901) X	formatted output	9.1
901 FORMAT(F7.3)	format specification	9.1.1
OPEN(7,FILE='fyle')	open a file	9.4.1
CLOSE(7)	close a file	9.4.1
REWIND(7)	rewind a file	9.6
INQUIRE(UNIT=1,EXIST=OK)	find out about a file or unit	14.2.2

Declarations and other non-executable statements are listed above the line, and executable statements below. The section numbers tell where each statement is first introduced. The statements and language features of FORTRAN-77 that are omitted from this table are mentioned in the **Omissions** Section of each chapter, and most are further discussed in §13. In §16.2 I concede under duress the necessity of introducing the INCLUDE statement, but as this is a requirement only of MPI I have not listed it here as a part of Classical FORTRAN (also see §13.1.4).

0.5 About This Book

Anybody can read a manual, and something like one is available for every FORTRAN compiler. Why is a textbook needed at all, and why did I think it necessary to write this one when there are already several other FORTRAN programming books in print? What is it that makes this book different from the others, and is it the right one for you?

0.5.1 Motivation and History

My job as consultant at a university computing center is to help graduate students and research faculty write programs that perform numerical calculations. Until about 1990 new graduate students in engineering and science always arrived knowing at least some FORTRAN, either because it was part of their long-ago undergraduate curriculum or because they picked it up on their own by reading a textbook like the classic that I myself learned from [87]. Now most incoming students admit to having had an undergraduate computer science course, usually using the C++ language, but then they hasten to add that it did *not* teach them how to program! They explain to me that what they really need to learn for their research project is FORTRAN, and that from the books they have found on the language this seems like a daunting task. Do I know of a course they could take, or of a single book they could read, that would get them started quickly? Alas, in 1990 I did not. It seemed to me that all of the recent books covered too much of the language, that some used FORTRAN merely as a vehicle for teaching about programming in general rather than as an end in itself, and that most left out topics (such as parallel processing) that are now often important for engineering and scientific applications.

To satisfy this demand from my consulting clients, and to make my job easier by helping them get their programs right, in January of 1994 I began offering a zero-credit three-day intensive short course on FORTRAN programming. The course was immediately oversubscribed, and for the next three years I taught it twice each year, usually to 20 or 30 students each time, during the January and May vacation periods between our academic terms. In 1997 and 1998 the short course was spread over a full semester as part of a graduate course called *Computer Methods in Electric Power Engineering*, with students who wanted only the FORTRAN component admitted to those classes for the short-course fee. Several professors in other departments then wondered about the possibility of recommending the FORTRAN course as a pre- or co-requisite for courses they taught in computational fluid dynamics, optimal control theory, and the numerical solution of partial differential equations. In response to their interest, our School of Engineering introduced in spring of 1999 a new one-credit upper-division elective called FORTRAN *Programming,* and invited me to teach it.

To provide a way for students who could not schedule my course (or who could not wait for the next occurrence) to learn its contents on their own, I began in January of 1996 to write up my class notes in the form of a text, and after that the book developed along with the course.

First Edition By January of 1999 the book was essentially finished, and I began selling a prepublication edition in our campus bookstore. To my delight many people besides my students bought the book, and some of them also sent me corrections and suggested improvements. Professor Alyce Brady used Chapter 4 in a computer architecture course at Kalamazoo College. The enthusiasm of my readers, as reflected particularly in anonymous course evaluations, and the popularity of the text with bookstore browsers, encouraged me to find a commercial outlet, and in December of 2000 I accepted an offer from Marcel Dekker Inc. to publish the book. Thanks largely to the skillful work of my editors B. J. Clark and Brian Black, the first edition appeared in 2002.

Second Edition   In January of 2004 Marcel Dekker was acquired by Taylor & Francis Books, Inc., and *Classical* FORTRAN was assigned to its CRC Press division. In June of 2006 CRC invited me to prepare a Second Edition and that is the book you are reading now. In addition to reformatting the text in the Taylor & Francis style I have made numerous revisions to the content, among which the most significant are itemized below.

- Several typographical errors that affected the meaning of the text (and which were previously reported in the usenet news group `comp.lang.fortran`) have been fixed, along with many others that were merely distracting.

- The discussions of Classical FORTRAN and Modern Fortran in this chapter and in §17.3 have been updated to account for developments in the language standard and in my perception of the FORTRAN programming culture.

- When compilers and operating systems are mentioned (mainly in this chapter and in §14) the exposition now assumes more freely that the reader might be using `g77` under Linux.

- Chapter 9 now includes an additional case study (§9.7) about file I/O.

- Three new sections (§18.5.3, §18.5.4, and §18.5.5) have been added to clarify some details about the `TIMER` routine and to present an alternate version that uses Pentium cycle counts.

- The Index and Bibliography have both been revised and slightly enlarged.

0.5.2   Audience

Some people prefer a compiler manual to a textbook, and if you are one of them perhaps you should learn FORTRAN in that way rather than by reading this book. Once you know all of the statements and features of the language you can probably figure out ways of using them to accomplish your goals. Unfortunately, a compiler manual includes *everything,* whereas I have pointed out in §0.4 that in using FORTRAN one key to success for most people is knowing which statements and features *not* to use. Another shortcoming of compiler manuals is that while they are filled with *what* the language can do and *how* to do it, they are typically almost silent about *why.* Getting programs of useful size to actually work requires an approach, discussed at length in §12, that is informed by an understanding of why one might want to use each language statement and feature. By reading this book you can learn what statements and features not to use, and why and where to use the others, without having to make all the mistakes that I made in the process of becoming an experienced FORTRAN programmer. Although this book describes mainly Classical FORTRAN it is, in its target audience, coverage of topics, organization, pedagogical approach, and programming style, emphatically *not* your father's textbook.

Anyone of normal intelligence can learn to program computers in FORTRAN, but success as a writer in any language, including FORTRAN, requires above-average imagination, curiosity, industry, and common sense. To learn anything, including programming, requires a degree of intellectual openness and a willingness to temporarily suspend your disbelief and defer value judgements about the material. So this book is addressed to creative people who think for a living but aren't convinced that they already know it all.

If you see yourself as a dummy and enjoy being talked down to and patted on the head, or if you think of computing professionals as nerds and geeks rather than as people, or if you're convinced that the world of computing is defined by Microsoft, then you might be happier running applications you bought at the store instead of learning to write programs of your own. On the other hand, if you suspect that the human sex drive is just a repressed form of the natural urge to program, this book might not be for you either. I've tried to be relentlessly practical, teaching things that the student can actually use to write real engineering and scientific applications, so the focus of the book is on that end result rather than on programming for amusement. If you're a computer scientist who works at the bleeding edge of technology on massive software projects, this book is also probably not for you. Although the language and programming techniques I discuss can be used for projects of any size, my interest here is not in advancing the state of the art but in teaching people who aren't computer experts how to write straightforward programs for ordinary technical calculations.

Here are some categories of readers for whom this book definitely *is* intended.

- Engineers and scientists who once learned some FORTRAN and want to brush up and modernize their old skills because they unexpectedly need to do some serious numerical calculations.

- Programmers who have been using FORTRAN right along but suspect they are missing certain tricks of the trade that would help them get their programs right with less effort.

- Programmers who are comfortable with Classical FORTRAN but occasionally need to consult a handy reference book.

- Programmers who want to translate Classical FORTRAN code into some other language, but first need to learn enough about FORTRAN to understand what the program does.

- Desperate individuals who know nothing about FORTRAN but find themselves suddenly responsible for looking after a Classical FORTRAN application and therefore need to learn, quickly, just enough to get by.

- Graduate students in engineering or science who got only minimal instruction in programming and either never studied FORTRAN or forgot enough of it so that now they can't complete their M.S. or Ph.D. project unless they learn or re-learn the language. Often these readers have found MATLAB or Excel too slow.

- Computer science students or recent graduates who have discovered that their degree program taught them nothing about computing for real engineering and scientific applications, and now wish to correct that omission.

- Undergraduates in engineering and science who are looking for an easier way to do their numerical computing projects.

- Precocious high school students who have a serious interest in math, science, or engineering and want to find out what there is about computing that makes it different from watching television.

- Curious bystanders who want to know something about FORTRAN, even though they don't have an immediate use in mind, just to broaden their perspective on programming languages.

- Computer science faculty members who hope to scandalize their colleagues by being seen with a faintly heretical book.

- Self-styled authorities on Fortran who just want to verify their suspicion that everything I have to say is either irrelevant or wrong.

- Managers who don't really *want* to know *anything* about FORTRAN, but who expect to be leading people who do and therefore *need* to know *something* about the language and the programming process.

Talking about FORTRAN without mentioning mathematics would be like talking about cooking without mentioning food, so there are many places where I have found it necessary to assume that the reader knows some algebra or calculus, and several of the examples involve elementary numerical methods. If you're worried that you don't know enough about these subjects to understand a book about FORTRAN, my advice is to continue reading and see how it goes. You can learn a lot about FORTRAN programming if you know even a little about math, and in the process you'll learn a lot more about math.

0.5.3   Organization

This is a big book, but you don't have to read it all at once; the diagram below shows one convenient division into parts. Many FORTRAN programmers eke out their code knowing only the material covered in §1–§6, and that's less than one hundred pages. If you're willing to read about that much more, §7–§10, you can learn all of the remaining language elements you will probably ever need in programming numerical calculations for engineering and scientific applications.

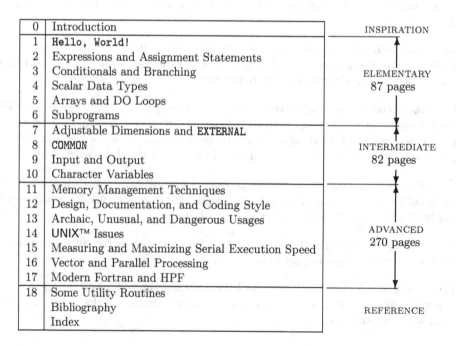

0	Introduction	INSPIRATION
1	`Hello, World!`	
2	Expressions and Assignment Statements	
3	Conditionals and Branching	ELEMENTARY
4	Scalar Data Types	87 pages
5	Arrays and DO Loops	
6	Subprograms	
7	Adjustable Dimensions and `EXTERNAL`	
8	`COMMON`	INTERMEDIATE
9	Input and Output	82 pages
10	Character Variables	
11	Memory Management Techniques	
12	Design, Documentation, and Coding Style	
13	Archaic, Unusual, and Dangerous Usages	
14	UNIX™ Issues	ADVANCED
15	Measuring and Maximizing Serial Execution Speed	270 pages
16	Vector and Parallel Processing	
17	Modern Fortran and HPF	
18	Some Utility Routines	
	Bibliography	REFERENCE
	Index	

Eventually you'll probably want to continue with §11–§17, which discuss how the language is, should, and should not be used, how to develop applications under UNIX™, and how to make programs run faster. Memory management, performance tuning, and parallel processing are all important once you have mastered the basics. The programming approach that is illustrated throughout the book and discussed in §12 is enlightening to many students, and if you have to deal with a legacy code you will probably find the suggestions in §13 helpful. A subset of Fortran-90's new features are introduced in §17.1, chosen because they are natural extensions to Classical FORTRAN or are needed for the introduction to High Performance Fortran in §17.2.

Several library routines are described in §18, to serve as extended examples of working code and because they are referred to earlier in the book. I've tried to make the Index very thorough, so that by using it and the Table of Contents you will be able to find what you're looking for without reading the whole book. On the other hand, in case even this book doesn't contain enough detail for you, some suggestions for further reading are listed in the first section of the Bibliography.

Each chapter freely assumes that you've read the ones that come before it, and several important conceptual threads carry through multiple chapters. For example, the way in which arrays are stored and passed to subprograms is developed gradually as the exposition progresses from §5 to §6, §7, §11, and §17. You will probably notice other ideas that reappear several times after they are first introduced. Many of the threads can be traced by using the Index.

As I mentioned in §0.4, each chapter uses a section entitled Omissions to list FORTRAN features that might reasonably have been included there but which I chose not to discuss. These sections also mention related topics that are just over the fuzzy border between the chapter and adjacent subjects. Many of the omissions are discussed later, in §13 or elsewhere, and those are listed in *slanting type;* some that are not discussed in this book might interest you as subjects for further study using other sources. If you begin this book not knowing much FORTRAN you will want to pay close attention to what I say, but if you already know quite a lot of FORTRAN it might be most helpful to see from the Omissions what I've left out of each chapter, and to understand from §13 *why.*

Throughout the book I have tried to clearly identify Classical FORTRAN's limited region of special competence, and sometimes I suggest alternatives for tasks that are beyond it.

0.5.4   Pedagogical Approach

It is sometimes possible to prove by mathematical logic that a computer program is correct in the sense that it satisfies a formal specification [38], and it is occasionally useful to think of a program as itself being a constructive proof of some theorem. A few computer scientists, most notably our old friend Dijkstra [140], have therefore advocated the use of correctness proofs and similar **formal methods** as the basis for all program design, and as the best starting point for teaching students how to program. Unfortunately, even very meticulous specifications usually turn out to have been imprecise or inappropriate and to require adjustment as the program they define takes shape, so proof-based formal methods have been challenged on philosophical grounds [134] and have turned out to be of limited practical value [130]. Even if proof-based formal methods were more useful in practice, I believe they are far too abstract to be useful in teaching beginners. (Starting with a rigorous mathematical formalization has failed before, as when the "new math" debacle of the 1970s left a generation of school children unable to make change.) Some related but less-formal methods, however, such as structured programming and successive refinement [109], do play a role in this book.

Another important philosophical influence on the teaching of programming has been the discipline of **software engineering**. Since the dawn of computing, programmers have been skilled artisans laboriously trained by apprenticeship. To become an artisan of any sort requires natural talent and the guidance of a mentor, so there are never enough expert programmers and the few there are command high wages. Also, artisans produce hand-made products lacking the uniformity of production-line goods. From the perspective of the software manufacturing industry, it would be very desirable to mechanize and deskill the programming function so that more people could do it, the cost could be reduced, and the quality of the finished product could be more easily regulated. Software engineering uses project management techniques from other branches of engineering, some of the formal methods mentioned above, a few ideas from cognitive psychology, and software development tools, all in an attempt to make the programming process more routine and less of an art. There are some huge undertakings for which software engineering is really necessary, but most routine technical computing projects are small enough to be hand-made works of craftsmanship. The main target audience of this book is individual engineers and scientists who need to write relatively modest programs for their own use, so although several ideas from software engineering appear in §12 I have mostly taken the attitude that I am mentoring artisans rather than training software engineers.

Thus, while students who learn to program by using this book will gain some necessary background (and perhaps also the motivation) to study formal methods or software engineering later on, those subjects will not be our focus here. Instead, *this book treats computer programming as a kind of expository writing.*

The way people get to be good at creative writing in a natural language like English is by learning some grammar in grade school, reading the works of great authors, and using the language for a long time. It's only after these preliminaries that the student is able to distinguish a graceful sentence from a clumsy one, or to appreciate a good polemic (how am I doing?) or to participate in a discussion about writing style. It is the current fashion in teaching programming to introduce style as early as possible, so as to prevent the student from falling into any bad habits, something like very early toilet training to keep children from ever getting dirty. One successful textbook [90] that introduces design at the very beginning argues for the importance of advance planning by quoting Aldous Huxley as having said "People always get what they ask for; the only trouble is that they never know, until they get it, what it actually is that they have asked for." The second part of this statement is often true but, at least in computer programming, the first part unfortunately is not. Beginning programmers in fact *hardly ever* get what it was they asked for, even when they know quite clearly what that was, because they don't yet know how to ask. One way to be sure of *not* getting the program you want is to base your design on abstract concepts that are introduced before they can be fairly illustrated. It would save a lot of bother if we could be born old and experienced and then youthen, like Merlin, so as to benefit from mature wisdom throughout our lives. Unfortunately, people just don't grow that way, and neither do programmers. Haranguing students about design is a pointless distraction until they know enough about programming to appreciate the importance of thinking things through ahead of time. So I have put off program design, documentation, and coding style until §12, after the reader has had enough experience struggling with actual programs to understand how hard it can be to get them right.

Natural languages are strongly idiomatic, so fluency requires a knowledge of much more than just vocabulary words and rules of grammar. The rest of the world has a tough time understanding American baseball fans who talk about "the bottom of the ninth" or Marines who use the motto "semper fi." In a similar way, fluency in Classical FORTRAN requires a knowledge of its social conventions and figures of speech, so I've tried to teach those things along with the syntax and semantics of the language. This cultural context is especially obvious in §11–§14, but it is everywhere in the book.

The only way most people learn anything is by example, so this book is filled with examples. Usually I introduce a new topic not by explaining it but by presenting an example that is designed to help the reader discover the key insight *before* being told what it is. FORTRAN is for numerical calculations, so except in §10 and §18 that is what most of the examples are about. (In particular, the book does *not* begin, as many others do, with examples of text processing.) After I've introduced a few major new ideas, I often use a case study, which is a significant example followed by a list of easily-generalizable observations, to combine and further illustrate the ideas and to introduce related new material of a more detailed nature. A few standard utility routines are used and referred to repeatedly in §9–§15, and they are discussed in detail in §18.

The process of compiling, running, and debugging programs is mentioned in §1 and described in somewhat more detail in §14, but this book is really about the FORTRAN language and how to write programs in it, rather than about computers or computing in general. I have intentionally omitted or given short shrift to many topics that would be expected in, say, a freshman-level textbook about computer science. On the other hand, some topics are treated in much more depth than is usual for an introductory book. A FORTRAN compiler artfully translates the pleasant myth of our source text into the gritty reality of object code, mostly sustaining the illusion that the machine executes FORTRAN statements operating on FORTRAN data structures, but there are a few places where the illusion fails, or is at least imperfect. Then it is necessary to look beyond the source-code model of computing to understand what is really happening. Computer numbers have limited range and precision, FORTRAN arrays are mapped to a line for storage, addresses rather than values are passed as FORTRAN subprogram parameters, and the architectural details of the hardware matter very much in vectorization, parallel processing, and performance tuning. Most textbooks about computer programming (except of course those about assembler language, just one step removed from machine code) are loath to discuss these embarrassing gaps in the scenery, and I too favor the FORTRAN model of what the computer does. But where it is necessary in order to avoid hand-waving or appeals to magic, I have without apology described some of what goes on behind the scenes in the machine code. To neglect these details altogether would leave the reader with a subtly flawed and dangerously incomplete understanding of FORTRAN, so I have tried to integrate them seamlessly into the exposition.

The exercises are collected at the end of each chapter, but they are *not* an afterthought! Some of the exercises are easy tests of your recall or surface comprehension of the reading, but most are more deviously contrived to really test your understanding, many add little grace notes to the material presented in the text, and a few in each chapter are big enough to serve as programming projects. Even if you are reading the book for self-study, you should try some of the exercises in each chapter. (If you think you might not need to read some chapter, you can try the exercises as a way of finding out.) In working the exercises you will discover that it is often helpful to write a FORTRAN program, even if that is not explicitly requested, and you should use the machine whenever you can. Instructors who adopt this book for a course can request the *Solutions Manual*, which provides detailed explanations for about half of the exercises.

0.5.5 Typographical Conventions

It will help in reading this book to know about some typographical conventions that I have followed.

Section References A single number following the symbol "§" denotes a chapter, two numbers separated by a dot denote a section, and three numbers separated by dots denote a subsection. In the narrative, chapters are called "chapter," and both sections and subsections are called "section." The book contains many crossreferences to particular sections, which you can find in the Table of Contents. I also often use "above" or "earlier" to mean appearing before here in the book (on or before this page) and "below" or "later" to mean appearing after here in the book (on or after this page).

Fonts   TYPEWRITER TYPE is used for FORTRAN source code and terminal-session excerpts; *slanting type* is used in the narrative for points of an enumeration and in Omissions to indicate topics that are discussed later; and *italic type* is used for emphasis. **Boldface** is used for chapter, section, subsection, and item headings and, within the text, to denote the first or defining use of a word or phrase that has a special technical meaning (these words, among others, are listed in the Index). In mathematical formulas, matrices are denoted by upper-case bold letters and vectors by lower-case bold letters, as in $\mathbf{y} = \mathbf{Ax}$, and the elements of a vector or matrix are denoted by the corresponding lower-case letter with the appropriate number of subscripts, as in y_j or $a_{i,j}$.

Code Segments   FORTRAN statements embedded in the text, and displayed code segments, are printed in TYPEWRITER TYPE. In program listings, the character : is used as a vertical ellipsis, to show the omission of some lines that are unimportant to the example; sometimes such omitted lines are replaced by a description in [square brackets]. Similarly, the pattern ... is used as a horizontal ellipsis to show the omission of characters. Code segments are often printed side-by-side; it will be clear from the context whether they are alternatives to be compared or different parts of a single program. Some listings are printed with sequence numbers (in §13.11) or line numbers (in §18), and in those places lines of code are referred to in the text by giving their numbers in boxes. Thus 10 refers to the line numbered 10 in a listing (it will be clear in context that this is not to be confused with *statement* number 10, if there happens to be one of those too).

Terminal-Session Excerpts   A conversation between an interactive user and the UNIX™ operating system is shown as a transcript, like this.

```
unix[1] this is what the user types
this is what gets typed back
```

Here the first line consists of the prompt unix[1], which is typed by the operating system, followed by this is what the user types, which is entered by the user. The second line shows what gets typed back, by the operating system or perhaps by a program that is run by the user's command. You should assume that each line of input entered by the user is terminated by pressing the ENTER or carriage return key. When it is necessary to show this explicitly, such as when a user's input consists *only* of pressing ENTER, that is shown in the transcript by the symbol ⏎R. Similarly, when the user sends a "control-D" by holding down the CTRL key while pressing D or d, that is shown in the transcript as ^D, and a "control-C" is shown as ^C (the meanings and uses of these signals are explained in the text). The number inside the unix[ ] prompt increments through the book so the next one, which occurs in §1.3, will be a 2.

Other Symbols   In the narrative, a number in square brackets like [37] is a citation to the bibliography entry having the given number; within a citation, § and p. denote a section or page *in the work cited.* In case studies, the observations are denoted thus 1⟳, and if this observation occurs in §4.5 it might be referred to elsewhere in the book as 4.5⟳1. The symbol ☠ is used in §13 to flag dangerous usages. The symbol ␣ denotes a blank.

In Exercise 4.10.39 I use the symbol j to represent $\sqrt{-1}$, in keeping with the convention from electrical engineering, but elsewhere $\sqrt{-1}$ is denoted i. When i or I is also used as an index, the text clarifies what is meant if that is not obvious from context.

I, You, We, and They   You have probably noticed that I refer to myself as "I" or "me" and to you as "you" rather than using passive voice or some other awkward device to avoid mentioning the author and reader of this book. I will also sometimes write "we" or "us." In doing this I do not mean to invoke the royal We, as though I were a king or a pope, but merely to include both the author and the reader. Thus, for example, when I say in §2.4 "Many functions are built into FORTRAN, and as *we* shall see in §6.3 you can also write your own." I mean to suggest that you imagine the two of us working through the text together.

To illustrate certain things it will be convenient to talk about a couple of other programmers, so I have invented two of them, named David A. Scientist (UNIX™ user ID david) and Sarah N. Engineer (sarah). I sincerely hope that these are not the names of any real people.

0.5.6   Computing Environment Dependencies

FORTRAN compilers are available for almost every machine, from PCs to supercomputers, and the Classical FORTRAN language described in this book works about the same on all of them. The differences between environments are mainly in the interface that a program can use to obtain operating system services (the "system calls") and in the facilities that you can use in developing programs. In several places I will offer advice about making FORTRAN programs easily portable from one environment to another, so that even these unavoidable variations will not be very troublesome. Thus, except for the material in §14, almost everything in this book is relevant and true for almost all FORTRAN environments.

There are, however, many places here and there in the narrative where it is convenient to be specific about the computing environment when explaining something about how to use FORTRAN, and in order to discuss debugging and the other topics of §14 it is essential to assume that we are using some particular environment. This is unfortunate, because systems differ superficially in how the compiler is invoked, how an executable gets run, how FORTRAN logical I/O units are assigned to logical devices, what the system routines look like, and how to use the debugger. On the other hand, most systems are similar enough in what they do, and different systems use few enough general approaches to doing those things, that a programmer who knows one system can usually figure out any of the others just by reading some manuals. I am therefore optimistic that you will have no difficulty interpreting error messages that are formatted differently from those given here or otherwise negotiating the departures of your computing environment from the one I discuss. Of course, no translation will be required if you happen to be using exactly the environment this book assumes.

Most readers have used personal computers running the Microsoft Windows operating system so that might seem a natural choice. Unfortunately, Windows is rarely (but see [111]) an ideal platform for writing FORTRAN programs. As discussed in §0.1, the default expectation in the PC culture is that the problem you want to solve is one for which a program has already been written, not that you will want to write a new program. The several FORTRAN program development environments that are available for Windows look quite different from one another, and no single one is used by enough people to be considered the exemplar. Windows compilers are apt to adhere blindly to the language standard and to omit some extensions so common in other compilers that I have here regarded them as de facto standards and included them in Classical FORTRAN. (The places where Windows

DILBERT by S. Adams, reprinted by permission of United Feature Syndicate, Inc.   © 11/9/93 United Feature Syndicate

compilers most often depart from common practice are in not allowing data initializations in
a type declaration and in certain syntactical details of FORMAT statements; some workarounds
for these problems are mentioned in §13.) The graphical user interfaces of some Windows
Fortran packages are sufficiently complex that describing or illustrating how to use one
would require not a separate chapter but a separate book.

UNIX™ is, for better or for worse, by far the most widely used single computing environment for engineering and scientific programming today, so that is the environment I assume.
The book does not expect the reader to have any prior UNIX™ *knowledge or experience,* and
it thoroughly covers the few little parts of UNIX™ we will need. UNIX™ has vitriolic critics
[145] [166] [125] and I confess that it is not my personal favorite (that would be MTS, now
extinct) but it does have some endearing attributes. UNIX™ runs about equally badly on
a wide variety of machines, it is available in both proprietary vendor-supported versions
and free open-source versions such as Linux [127] [106] and cygwin, and it is so pervasive
in the technical computing community that, like Classical FORTRAN, it will probably never
die. UNIX™ is the base operating system for Apple Macintosh computers. In contrast to
Windows, UNIX™ makes the default assumption that you will want to write a program to
solve each new problem, and then it dedicates its entire existence to making that possible.
Non-programmers always hate UNIX™ but programmers almost always love it. Even if you
intend to write programs that will ultimately run under Windows, you might decide to use
a UNIX™ workstation or a Mac or PC running UNIX™ as your development platform.

Many different UNIX™ FORTRAN compilers are available, including the ones supplied by
workstation manufacturers, several from companies that make only software, and the Gnu
Project [116] compilers g77, g95, and gfortran. The Gnu compilers come as part of Linux
and cygwin, as I mentioned in §0.3, and can also be downloaded free for Windows. Compilers differ in their cost and cleverness, but most just translate source code and link an
executable (as explained in §1.2) rather than being buried in larger program development
packages, so they look and work about as described here. To use a Modern Fortran compiler to compile Classical FORTRAN programs it might be necessary to specify options that
identify the source code as fixed form. I wrote this book using several different UNIX™
workstations and FORTRAN compilers made by Sun Microsystems and IBM. Most of the
examples showing user interactions with UNIX™ or a compiler were generated on a Sun.

It will turn out to be handy on some occasions for us to assume in addition to UNIX™ that
we are using the bash interactive shell. I will always assume that we are communicating
with UNIX™ by typing commands and reading typed replies rather than by clicking buttons
or selecting menu items on a graphical user interface.

Throughout the book I assume that the computer's floating-point arithmetic complies
with IEEE Standard 754 [19] and that the rightmost byte of a word is least significant, but

these things make an important difference only in the discussion of number storage formats in §4.

0.6 Advice to Instructors

This book can be used as the text of a FORTRAN programming course in several different ways depending on the time available, the format, and the audience.

One Day One full day, including about 6 hours of class, is long enough to present a significant example and a chapter summary for each of §1–§6. In §0.5.3 these chapters are identified as the ELEMENTARY part of the book. A short course of this duration and intensity is suitable only for professional programmers who already know other languages, and who afterwards study the chapters in the text, read further on their own, and immediately begin using the language in their work.

15 Hours In three full days each including about 5 hours of class, or in a semester-long course including 1 hour of class per week for 15 weeks, it is possible to present a significant example and a chapter summary for each of §1–§12 and perhaps some additional material selected from the remaining chapters. The short-course format is again appropriate only for professionals, but the semester-long format is suitable for undergraduates who read each chapter before it is presented in class and do programming projects throughout the course.

30 Hours In a semester-long course including 2 hours of class per week for 15 weeks, or in a 2-semester course of 1 hour per week, it is possible to recapitulate in class the book's development of the material in §1–§12, rather than just presenting summaries, and perhaps to discuss additional topics from the remaining chapters.

45 Hours In a semester-long course including 3 hours of class per week for 15 weeks, it is possible to cover the entire book or to include a mentored weekly programming laboratory in addition to regular classroom meetings.

Studio Course or Self-Study This book could serve as the basis for an all-laboratory studio course in which the students run most examples and case studies and work some programming exercises in class, along with reading the text, in a process of active discovery of the material. Working through the book with a computer is also a good strategy for readers who wish to learn FORTRAN programming outside of a classroom setting.

I expect §0 to be read by interested students on their own and §18 to be consulted for reference, rather than these being taught in class.

0.7 About The Author

I was born in the year the first general-purpose electronic computer was built, but I suppose that might not be enough to convince you to read this book. What makes me think I can teach you this stuff, anyhow?

First, I have had some success as a FORTRAN programmer. I learned the language in the spring of 1966 when I was a college sophomore and have used it more or less constantly ever since, as an undergraduate engineering major, as an engineer in industry, as a graduate student, in my dissertation research project, and as a computing center staff member. Since 1981 my full-time job has been to help research faculty and their graduate students in engineering and science with numerical computing projects, almost all of which are in FORTRAN. I also use FORTRAN in my own

Kupferschmid, Michael, 1946– National Merit Scholar 1964; B.S. electrical engineering 1968, M.Eng. feedback control systems 1972, M.S. operations research and statistics 1980, Ph.D. numerical optimization 1981, all from Rensselaer Polytechnic Institute; Professional Engineer 1973 Connecticut license #9131; Diaz Prize for research in mathematics 1981; $\tau\beta\pi$, $\eta\kappa\nu$, $\pi\mu\epsilon$, and $\Sigma\Xi$ honor societies. 1968–1971 design engineer for military helicopter autopilots, Sikorsky Aircraft; 1972–1974 Teaching Fellow, Yale University; 1974–1976 control systems designer, Devices Inc.; 1976–1978 Design Supervisor, J. R. Clancy Inc.; since 1981 Scientific Programming Consultant and adjunct faculty at Rensselaer. Co-author, *Introduction to Operations Research,* Wiley 1988 [53].

research, publishing papers about methods and applications of nonlinear optimization and about the experimental study of algorithm performance, and supervising thesis projects for M.S. and Ph.D. students in applied mathematics. I have written numerical software for research contracts, and often work as a private consultant to industry on technical computing problems. During my programming career I have learned and used several other languages, including IBM System/370 Assembler Language (my personal favorite), PL1, Pascal, C, and the simulation languages Simscript, GPSS, Dynamo, and ACSL, but the language almost all of my consulting clients and students use, and the one I use most of the time, is FORTRAN. What works for me, and for them, is what I talk about in this book.

Second, my students seem to have success as FORTRAN programmers. I've taught college courses in computer programming and numerical methods on and off since 1972, and I've used the material in this book since 1994 in both regular courses and 3-day intensive short courses. Outside the classroom, I've taught FORTRAN one-on-one to dozens of consulting clients. I also teach college courses in calculus and operations research, and in 1988 co-authored a textbook [53] that is still available in its third printing. The teaching style that works in class, and in the other text, is the style I've tried to use in writing this book.

0.8 Acknowledgements

FORTRAN has been an indispensable tool in my professional life, so some of the people I need to thank for helping me with this book really deserve credit for much more. I learned how to program from Jack Gelb, who as a graduate student taught the FORTRAN component of my first course in numerical methods, and from the textbook we used, Daniel D. McCracken's 151-page *A Guide to Fortran IV Programming,* first edition [87]. The papers of David Parnas on information hiding [94], and the book *The Elements of Programming Style,* by Brian W. Kernighan and P. J. Plauger [8], profoundly influenced my approach to programming. The Michigan Terminal System [40] and its software development utilities, including John Stevens' remarkable interactive FORTRAN processor *IF, were the ideal computing environment in which to become a mature programmer. Over the years my many consulting clients have provided the opportunity for me to read and write lots of FORTRAN programs, and thus to learn a great deal from them, as I was having fun working on their problems. I thank them all.

I am equally grateful to the hundreds of students who have studied programming with me, for insisting that I write this book and for giving me their feedback on separate chapters as they used them in class. Many people who were not students in my classes also read this book in draft, and I am grateful to all of them as well. A succession of managers in Rensselaer's Alan M. Voorhees Computing Center have supported and encouraged me in this work, including Bob Gallagher, Richard Alexander, Sharon Roy, and Mark Miller, as have Rensselaer administrators Gary Judd and John Kolb. The opinions expressed in this book are of course not necessarily theirs (in some cases this may be an understatement) or those of my employer. Some of the chutzpah I have needed to pursue this project came from watching in awe as Aaron Lansky, against formidable odds, built the National Yiddish Book Center.

Harriet Borton, whose patience and good humor are apparently without limit, supplied vast amounts of expert help with LaTeX 2_ε. Garance Drosehn helped me understand some of the variations in memory architecture described in §4.8, and has over the years taught me many things about operating systems. Randy Scarborough read §15 and suggested improvements. Lou Ellen Davis gave me corrections to a public-domain version of her poem "The Perfect Program," and several other authors and publishers granted permission to use copyrighted work, as indicated throughout the book in figure credits and literature citations. Jessica Kilmer beat several photocopying machines into submission, including at least one known to contain an actual devil, in the course of duplicating draft chapters for use in my classes.

Finally, and most of all, I am deeply grateful to the following referees for their careful reading, critical review, and useful discussions of the original manuscript: Professor M. S. Krishnamoorthy, Dr. Chris Ettles, Professor Laura Gross, Dr. Terrence K. Kelly, Dr. Darryl Ahner, Dr. Eric Johnson, Bill Emge, and Donna Dietz. Their wisdom was of great value to me in more ways than they can know, and their numerous suggestions significantly improved the book. I also got some good ideas from a few naysayers who think I should have written a different book altogether. Being lectured like a schoolboy on the conventional wisdom helped remove any last vestige of doubt that I might have had about the correctness of the *unconventional* approach I have taken in teaching FORTRAN programming and in writing this book.

Often my readers were not unanimous in their opinions and sometimes I ignored their advice altogether, so while all of these people helped me and deserve a share of the credit for whatever you might like about this book, I must take the blame for any failures of judgement or other mistakes you find. I shall of course be very happy to receive corrections or comments from you, so that the book can be improved if there is someday a Third Edition.

0.9 Disclaimers

Most of the source code in this book appears in short fragments, each meant to illustrate some little idea about FORTRAN programming rather than to perform a whole calculation or to serve by itself as a model for production code. But among the examples and case studies, there happen to be a few complete programs that you might be tempted to modify or imitate for solving the typical problems they address, and there are a few subprograms that are potentially useful with little or no revision. The routines of §18, if we are to believe the title of that chapter, might be of even wider utility. The table on the next page lists all of these programs and subprograms. Some exercises also contain programs, subprograms, or code fragments, but none of those are listed because many are *wrong on purpose*.

purpose of routine	name	§§
find the hypotenuse of a right triangle		2
solve a quadratic equation		3
approximate the sine of an angle		4.5
approximate the log of a number		4.6.2
multiply matrices		5.6, 17.1.4
compute descriptive statistics		9.2, 9.5
merge files		9.7
plot $f(x)$ versus x		10.7.1
plot contours of $f(x, y)$		10.7.2
find a symmetric-matrix-vector product		11.5
find a sparse-matrix-vector product		11.6.2
sort using a linked list		11.7
integrate by the rectangle rule		16.2.4, 17.2.6
transpose a matrix	MATRNS	6.1, 7.1.2
find the dot product of two vectors	DDOT	6.3, 7.1.1
solve $f(x) = 0$ for x	BISECT	6.4, 7.2.2, 8.2, 12.3.2
find the length of a string	LENGTH	10.2
translate a string	UPSTR	10.3
shift a string left	SHIFTL	10.3
prompt for input from the keyboard	PROMPT	10.4
ask a yes-or-no question	QUERY	10.5
convert numerals to an integer	BTD	18.1.1
convert an integer to numerals	DTB	18.1.2
insert an integer into a string	INTINS	18.2.1
insert a string into a string	STRINS	18.2.2
attach a file to a unit	GETFIL	18.3
add two-part values	TPVADD	18.4.1
subtract two-part values	TPVSUB	18.4.1
normalize a two-part value	TPVNML	18.4.2
convert a two-part value to a REAL*8	TPV2R8	18.4.3
convert a REAL*8 to a two-part value	R82TPV	18.4.3
scale a two-part value	TPVSCL	18.4.4
estimate CPU time	TIMER	18.5

It is my intention not to provide a course on numerical methods or a ready-made library of source code, but only to teach you how to write *your own* code, so all of these routines are present, as it were, merely by accident. Most of them have sparse comments or none at all, few of them are bulletproof against bad inputs, and in many of them I have intentionally sacrificed robustness, generality, or ease of use for brevity and aptness in illustrating several language features at once. So while you are welcome to all of this code, please remember its shortcomings and that you will be using it *at your own risk.* I make no warranties, express or implied, that the code contained in this book, whether it is listed in the table above or not, is free of error, or is consistent with any particular standard of merchantability, or that it will be suitable for any particular purpose. None of it should be relied on for solving a problem whose incorrect solution could result in injury to a person or destruction of property. Both I and the publisher disclaim all liability for direct or consequential damages resulting from use of the code or anything else you find in this book.

This book reflects my imperfect knowledge, questionable taste, and personal experience. I have tried very hard not to say anything that is *untrue,* but in many places I have been intentionally *imprecise,* especially at the beginning of a topic, so as to convey the general idea before filling in the details later. I advocate some usages that are widely practiced and that I have found good but that are not guaranteed by the FORTRAN language standard to be recognized by all compilers, while in other places I condemn things that I have found to be bad partly *because* they are not recognized by all compilers. Occasionally I use technical terms and literary or cultural allusions that are far outside the scope of the book, and except when they are essential to the continuity of the exposition I do so without warning or explanation. I don't expect each reader to agree with every technical judgement or nuance of opinion expressed here, and not everybody likes my style. It isn't necessary to love this book in order to learn from it. But I do hope that it isn't boring, and that it will help even people who are not really interested in computing learn how to write programs that work.

This book was written in 1996–98 and last revised in 2008, so it reflects my understanding of the subject during that interval. Between then and now, the moment you are reading these words, computing has doubtless continued its reckless haphazard evolution, and many things have changed in significant ways. I have tried to focus on concepts that will outlast mere shifts in programming fashion, but any practical treatment unavoidably depends on particulars that sooner or later become obsolete. It would be wrong to say that I regret any anachronisms that have resulted from actual improvements in the art, but I do hope that some of what I have written will continue to be useful for a long while. One indication that this might be possible is Classical FORTRAN itself, which has survived dramatic changes in computer hardware, operating systems, and programming practice.

0.10 Exercises

0.10.1 A widely believed postmodernist deconstruction of computing history goes something like this (but also see [182]). *Before the invention of the PC, computing was the exclusive preserve of scientists, all of them arrogant and most a little mad, working in the antiseptic isolation of glass-walled rooms on harmful secret projects beyond the understanding or control of ordinary citizens. With the introduction of personal computers this dangerous cabal was demystified and finally destroyed, and common people assumed their rightful place as the owners and beneficiaries of this technology. Making computing accessible to the rest of us has transformed it from a sinister threat into an instrument of social progress, and exposed its former technical users, and uses, as ridiculous and obsolete.* (a) Who were the people using the mainframe computers of the pre-PC era, and what were the machines actually doing? (b) Were these activities mostly harmful to people, or mostly beneficial? (c) Were mainframe computers kept in antiseptic glass-walled rooms for the purpose of excluding people who did not belong to a cabal? Are today's PC hackers uniformly welcoming of people from outside their peculiar culture? (d) Has the introduction of the PC made computing an instrument of social progress? (e) Has the need for technical computing to solve engineering and scientific problems been eliminated by the popularization of the personal computer as an information appliance?

0.10.2 As a wise old wizard once observed [181, p258-259], "Perilous to us all are the devices of an art deeper than we possess ourselves." What might this have to do with learning to program? Describe some perils of using computers without understanding something about how they work.

0.10.3 Computers are good for processing information, and a large amount of information is available on the World Wide Web because anybody can post anything there. (a) Would you expect the information posted on the Web to be uniformly true and accurate? (b) Is information the same thing as knowledge? If not, explain the difference between the two. (c) Is knowledge the same thing as wisdom? If not, explain the difference between the two.

0.10.4   Describe the rabble for whom computer programming is a useful skill, and explain why it is insufficient for them to be merely sophisticated users of software that is written by others. Is there any reason this book might be of interest to a manager, or to a management student?

0.10.5   Using a hand calculator to do the arithmetic, perform a few iterations of the bisection algorithm described in §0.1 to approximate the positive solution of $\sin(x) - \frac{1}{2}x = 0$. How precise is your answer?

0.10.6   Outline the history of FORTRAN and explain its rejection by the academic computer science community. Is there any reason this book might be of interest to someone who is a computer scientist, or is studying to become one?

0.10.7   Why might FORTRAN be preferable to MATLAB for certain calculations? Why do most engineers and scientists find it necessary to know how to program computers in a language like FORTRAN? Why is FORTRAN often preferable to other languages on its level for typical engineering and scientific calculations?

0.10.8   A wag in my acquaintance once told me that C is The Language of the Proletariat and Lisp is The Language of the Bourgeoisie. (a) Why do I think it is appropriate for FORTRAN to be known as The Language of Peasants? (b) Why might the artificial intelligence (AI) research community embrace Lisp, a special-purpose language for AI research, while heaping scorn on FORTRAN, a special-purpose language for numerical computing?

0.10.9   If FORTRAN is used, as I claim in §0.3, why is it not mentioned in more employment ads in the *New York Times*? Do ads for jobs in engineering and science typically contain an explicit requirement that applicants should be familiar with calculus? Is Lisp ever mentioned as a required skill in newspaper employment ads?

0.10.10 Your corner gas station probably doesn't sell aviation fuel. Why do you suppose that is? Does it mean that nobody flies anymore? Several of the Fortran compilers available for personal computers are commercial products. Why doesn't your neighborhood PC store stock them?

0.10.11 Summarize and critique the explanation given in §0.3 for the survival of Classical FORTRAN. Why does this book cover mainly that subset, rather than all of Modern Fortran? How does Classical FORTRAN change over time? Is a Classical FORTRAN program also a Modern Fortran program? Explain.

0.10.12 The programming language most commonly used today, C, has 32 "keywords" or statements. How many statements (or combinations of statements that we will always use together, such as DO–CONTINUE) are included in the Classical FORTRAN discussed in §1–§16 and §18 of this book?

0.10.13 As we shall see in later chapters, the symbol * can be used in FORTRAN in specifying the type of a variable, or in describing the size of an array argument to a subprogram, or for the repetition of data-initialization values, as well as to denote ordinary multiplication. Similarly, / is used in naming COMMON blocks and in compile-time data initialization, as well as to denote either floating-point or integer division. This is called **overloading**, and many other languages do much more of it than Classical FORTRAN does. (a) Can you think of any advantages to this practice? List them. (b) Are there any drawbacks? List them.

0.10.14 Why is it easier for most people to learn a programming language from a textbook than from a compiler manual?

0.10.15 This book does not rely much on formal methods or software engineering. What approach does it take to teaching computer programming? Why does it put off a discussion of programming style until §12?

0.10.16 How much does this book expect the reader to know about mathematics and numerical methods? How much does it expect the reader to know about UNIX™?

0.10.17 How much of this book must you read in order to learn elementary FORTRAN? Intermediate FORTRAN? What chapter contains advice about dealing with legacy codes? Where is the list of suggested reading?

0.10.18 What is the purpose of the Omissions Section in each chapter? Where can more information be found about omitted topics that are listed in *slanting* type?

0.10.19 If you notice a **boldface** word in the text but then forget where it was, how can you easily find it again?

0.10.20 In this book, what does a reference like §1 mean? §1.2? §1.2.3?

0.10.21 What does a number like $\boxed{23}$ mean in this book? What do ⌐R, ^C, and 3⇨ mean? Whose UNIX™ user ID is **sarah**?

0.10.22 Can the FORTRAN language discussed in this book be used in a variety of hardware and operating system environments, or only on UNIX™ workstations? Why have I chosen UNIX™ as the computing environment to assume in this book? Can UNIX™ be run on personal computers?

0.10.23 What sort of warranty comes with the code segments in this book? Where can you find a code segment that illustrates contour plotting?

1

Hello, World!

A computer can do arithmetic, perform logical operations such as comparisons, move information from place to place in its memory, and communicate with its user by reading inputs and writing outputs. To coordinate these elementary operations to perform a useful task, the machine must be given a set of directions called a **program**.

1.1 Case Study: A First FORTRAN Program

In FORTRAN and other **procedural languages**, a program is a list of directions that are executed one at a time from first to last in the order they are encountered. A very simple program is listed below.

```
C
Code by David A. Scientist
C
C     This program says hello.
C
      PRINT *,'Hello, world!'
      STOP
      END
```

It's easy to guess from the ordinary meanings of the English words PRINT and STOP that this program just prints the message Hello, world! and stops. The interesting things about the program have to do not with its behavior but with its typographical layout. Here are some observations about that.

1➪   The program is just text, made up of ordinary typewriter characters, and the spaces are ordinary blanks. It is necessary to use an editor (such as vi or emacs in UNIX™) to type the text into a file on the computer where it will be used. The text of a FORTRAN program is referred to as **source code**.

2➪   The program consists of **comments**, which are denoted by a C in column 1, and **statements**. Comments are *not* directions to the computer and are written by the programmer only to explain to himself or herself, and to other humans, what the program is supposed to do. Some FORTRAN statements, such as PRINT and STOP in this program, are **executable**, because they make the computer do something. Others, such as END, are nonexecutable and provide information that is used in processing the source code (as described below in §1.3). An END statement marks the end of the source code, and must be the last statement in every FORTRAN program.

3⮕ Comments and character strings (such as `Hello, world!` in our example) can contain any character on your keyboard, but in FORTRAN statements we will use only the following **character set**:

```
ABCDEFGHIJKLMNOPQRSTUVWXYZ
1234567890
+-*/=.,:()'
```

The quote mark (`'`) used in FORTRAN is the forward quote or apostrophe, and the parentheses are (round), not [square brackets] or {curly braces}.

4⮕ Classical FORTRAN uses a **fixed source form** in which each line is divided into **fields** that have different uses. Comments must begin with a `C` in column 1 but can then extend as far to the right as desired. Statements must begin in or to the right of column 7, and must end in or to the left of column 72. The end of a line denotes the end of a statement, unless the statement is continued (as described in §3.4). Comments cannot be continued; each comment line must begin with a `C`.

5⮕ FORTRAN statements must conform to certain rules of **syntax**, or typographical construction. Thus, for example, it would be wrong to omit the comma from the `PRINT` statement in our example, or to place it in front of the `*`. On the other hand, it usually doesn't matter how many blanks you use between words and symbols, so we could have written `PRINT* ,` instead of `PRINT *,`. The language elements introduced in §2–§9 are mostly simple enough that you will be able to write syntactically correct statements just by imitating the examples. You already know how to write the `STOP` and `END` statements. Our main focus will be on the meaning or **semantics** of the statements, and on how and why to use them to describe the calculation you have in mind.

1.2 Compiling the Program

Although it might be possible in principle to build a computer that could directly execute FORTRAN source code, that is never done in practice. The list of directions we actually provide to a computer must be written not in FORTRAN but in whatever **machine language** is native to the computer's **processor**. It is possible to code directly in machine language, or in the equivalent but slightly more symbolic **assembler language** of a processor, but that is noticeably more difficult than writing in FORTRAN and yields a program that can be run on only one kind of machine. Instead we will automatically translate our FORTRAN source code into appropriate machine language instructions chosen from the **instruction set** of the processor we are using. The resulting list of machine language instructions is called **object code**.

The various operating system services that FORTRAN programs require, such as input and output operations, are typically provided by **system routines**. These fragments of machine code are stored in a **system library** and must be inserted into the object code for a program before it can be executed. The insertion of library routines is called **linkage editing**, and is performed on computers running the UNIX™ operating system by a program called the **loader** (but known to UNIX™ as `ld`). The result of linking the necessary system routines into the object code for a program is called an **executable**, and it is only an executable that can be **run**.

In UNIX™ systems, the translation of FORTRAN source into object code and the invocation of ld to link in the system routines are both performed by a program called the FORTRAN **compiler** (known as f77). The compilation process is pictured below.

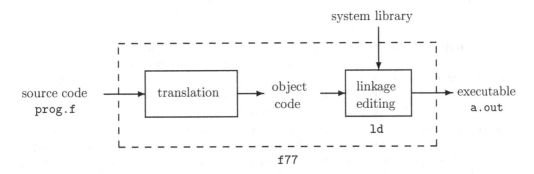

The executable program is stored in a file having the default name a.out, as shown in the diagram. The machine code is not readable as text, so you can't view it with an editor.

1.3   Running a Program in UNIX™

If our source code is in a file named prog.f, as shown in the diagram, we might have this exchange with UNIX™ to compile and run the program.

```
unix[2] f77 prog.f
unix[3] a.out
 Hello, world!
unix[4]
```

Recall from §0.5.5 that UNIX™ command prompts are denoted unix[ ] and numbered consecutively in the examples of this book. The prompts are written by the operating system; the commands f77 prog.f (to compile the program) and a.out (to run the executable) are typed by the user, and the output line Hello, world! is printed by the executable when it runs.

If there are syntax errors in the source code, the compiler will print messages about them and not generate an executable. If there are errors in the logic of the program the executable might do something that causes the operating system to interrupt it when a.out is run, in which case UNIX™ will print a message. Using the compiler, interpreting error messages, and finding mistakes (euphemistically called **bugs**) are all discussed at length in §14.

What happens inside the machine when you run an executable is complicated in detail but not difficult to understand in broad overview. The processor is made of electronic devices such as transistors and resistors, etched into a chip of silicon along with wires that connect the components to form circuits such as logic gates and flipflops. These circuits make up the central processing unit or **CPU** of the computer and its random-access memory or **RAM**. One of the circuits is an internal clock that changes the voltage on a **clock wire** between two values, low to high and back to low, once every clock cycle. If your computer has a 2 GHz clock, the period of the clock signal is $\frac{1}{2} \times 10^{-9}$ seconds. Another circuit is a **program counter** that always contains the address in memory of the next machine instruction to be executed. In each clock cycle (or perhaps over a few cycles) a machine instruction is fetched from memory and interpreted by decoding circuits, and the program counter is changed to point to the instruction that will be fetched in the next cycle. According to this cycle's instruction and its operands, the decoder changes the pattern of high and low voltages on **control wires** that govern the operation of the other circuits in the processor. The control wire settings determine what those circuits do at the next clock transition, to accomplish the arithmetic calculation or logical operation or data movement that is required. In the end this chain of events results in changes to the contents of memory. *Computer programs work by changing the contents of memory.* Other circuits can copy the contents of memory to the display of your workstation, or translate your keystrokes into values in memory.

When you issue the UNIX™ command `a.out`, the operating system opens that file and copies the machine instructions it contains into memory. Then it puts the starting address of those instructions in the program counter so that, on the next transition of the processor's clock, they begin to execute one by one. *Your program is now controlling the computer.* When your program executes the machine code that corresponds to a FORTRAN STOP statement, the address in memory of the next machine instruction in the operating system is placed in the program counter, which returns control to UNIX™. Your program shares the machine with various operating system processes and perhaps with programs being run by other people, so it might be temporarily interrupted to give them a chance at the processor, but UNIX™ arranges for this timesharing to be invisible to your program.

Different processors have different instruction sets, so an executable compiled for one will not run, nor even be recognized as machine language, on another. Over the years a few series of computer models using the same instruction set have been designed to share executables, but usually even machines that use the same processor type cannot run each other's object code (because of differences in such things as the format of executable files). In that case it is necessary to recompile your FORTRAN program when you move it to a new machine. As mentioned in §0.3, a FORTRAN compiler is available for almost every computer, and the Classical FORTRAN discussed in this book can be compiled without change by most of them.

It might seem that recompilation is a big nuisance, but it is a whole lot less trouble than rewriting the program for each computer. If we code our applications in machine language or assembler language, then for M processors we need M different programs, and for N applications that would mean $N \times M$ programs. If we write in a platform-independent language such as FORTRAN and translate to machine code on each processor, we need only $N + M$ programs, the N applications and a compiler for each processor. It would be convenient if every computer used the same instruction set, but the continuous development of microprocessors makes standardization at that level unlikely for the foreseeable future.

1.4   Omissions

Some programming textbooks begin with an explicit discussion of problem formulation and program design, but as explained in §0.5.4 I have elected to discuss problem formulation as we go along and to put off a formal treatment of program design until §12. A discussion of errors and debugging is similarly deferred, as mentioned above, until §14. Among the FORTRAN-77 language features that could have been introduced in this chapter, but which are not parts of the Classical FORTRAN discussed in this book, are *the PROGRAM statement; free-form source, mixed case, and other typographical extensions; sequence numbers; programs without a STOP statement;* PAUSE; *and the EXIT system routine.* As mentioned in

§0.5.5, omissions that are listed in *slanting* type are discussed at least briefly somewhere else in the book (you can find out where by consulting the Index). Many other things that might reasonably have been mentioned here, such as *other fields of a statement,* I have put off until we need them.

In order to actually write and run programs, as called for by many of the exercises, you will need to know how to obtain access to a computer, how to operate its hardware, and how to enter text into a file. If the machine you use is not a UNIX™ workstation, you will also need to find out how to use its operating system and how to invoke its FORTRAN compiler. Unfortunately, all these things are specific to your computing environment and therefore can't be covered here.

A thorough discussion of computer architecture and code translation is also outside the scope of this book.

1.5   Exercises

1.5.1   Define the following terms. (a) syntax; (b) semantics; (c) source code; (d) object code; (e) linkage editing (f) executable.

1.5.2   What is the character set used for FORTRAN statements in this book?

1.5.3   Where can blanks be inserted without changing the meaning of a FORTRAN statement?

1.5.4   State the rules for writing FORTRAN (a) comments and (b) statements. (c) What happens to statement text that extends beyond column 72? (d) Can a comment be continued? (e) Can a statement begin in column 8?

1.5.5   Explain the difference between comments, executable statements, and non-executable statements in a FORTRAN program.

1.5.6   List the three FORTRAN statements that were introduced in this chapter. What does each do?

1.5.7   Explain the difference between STOP and END. Can a program have more than one STOP statement? More than one END?

1.5.8   Give two reasons in favor of coding in FORTRAN rather than in machine language or assembler language.

1.5.9   The FORTRAN compiler performs two main tasks. What are they?

1.5.10   If a FORTRAN source program is in a file named source.f, what UNIX™ commands could be used to compile and run it?

1.5.11   The FORTRAN compiler is itself a program, usually written in the C language. Could a FORTRAN compiler be written in FORTRAN? How could such a program be compiled?

1.5.12   Is it likely that an executable prepared on one kind of computer can be run on a computer of a different kind? Why, or why not? What must be done to move a FORTRAN program from one machine to another of a different kind?

1.5.13   Enter the example source program from this chapter into a file on your computer, compile it, and run it to obtain the output shown in the text.

1.5.14 Use the Index to find out where in the book the `PROGRAM` statement is mentioned, and read the article about it. Now explain why that statement was omitted from this chapter, and is not included in the table of §0.4 as part of the Classical FORTRAN language we will study.

2

Expressions and Assignment Statements

The `Hello, world!` program of §1 served to illustrate the typographical layout of FORTRAN source code, but it did no useful work. Here is a slightly more exciting example that computes a numerical result using the Pythagorean theorem.

```
C
Code by Sarah N. Engineer
C
C     This program finds the hypotenuse of a right triangle.
C
C     variable  meaning
C     --------  -------
C     A         length of one side
C     B         length of perpendicular side
C     HYP       length of hypotenuse
C     SQRT      Fortran function for square root
C
C ------------------------------------------------------------------
C
C     assign the lengths of the sides
      A=7.0
      B=5.0
C
C     compute the diagonal
      HYP=SQRT(A**2 + B**2)
C
C     report the result
      PRINT *,HYP
C
      STOP
      END
```

This program is more elaborate than the first one in several ways. We will discuss its executable statements in a moment, but first consider only the comments. Like the first program, this one says who wrote it. Then there is a brief description of what the program does, followed by an alphabetical list of names with descriptions of what they stand for, and then a line dividing this **preamble** from the **body** of the code. The statements in the body of the program are separated into **stanzas** by blank comments, and each stanza carries a comment describing what it does.

All of your programs should contain comments like these to explain, to others who read the code but most of all to you yourself, what is going on and why. We will study the internal documentation of FORTRAN programs in great detail in §12.3.2. Until then, however, I will use comments only occasionally. This is not because they are unimportant but because in many cases the code fragments we look at will not be complete programs, and because the text itself will be devoted to explaining them so additional comments would be repetitious.

Also, while you are learning the statements of FORTRAN I want you to focus mainly on the code itself rather than on the applications I use to illustrate the language features. Try to remember between now and §12 that comments are essential to a real program, and that I will have more to say about them after you know some FORTRAN.

2.1   Constants

The statements of the hypotenuse program involve the numbers 7.0 and 5.0 (with decimal points), and 2 (*without* a decimal point). These are examples of two basic FORTRAN **data types,** "real" and "integer."

A **real constant** is a number having a fractional part. Here are some examples of real constants.

1.0	a number with a fractional part of zero
-3.141593	an approximation of $-\pi$
6.02E+23	6.02×10^{23}
0.0	a real zero

The numbers 7.0 and 5.0 in the program are real constants, involved in calculations that we expect to yield numbers having fractional parts. Real numbers are stored inside the computer using a fraction-exponent form (described in §4.2), so most values are represented only approximately.

An **integer constant** is a number having no fractional part. Some examples of integer constants are given below.

1	a number having no fractional part
-3141593	a large negative integer
0	an integer zero

The numbers 2 in the program are integer constants, denoting whole-number exponents (as discussed below in §2.3). Integer numbers are stored exactly, but have a more limited range than reals (as described in §4.1). There is no syntax for integer constants similar to the E notation for reals.

In FORTRAN, numerical constants are never written with commas. The compiler would complain that an integer constant such as -3,141,593 contains syntax errors.

2.2   Variables and Variable Names

We also find in the hypotenuse program several **variables,** A, B, and HYP, which are reminiscent of those used in algebra to represent quantities that are unknown or arbitrary. In FORTRAN, *a variable is the name of a location in memory.* Recall from §1.3 that programs work by changing the contents of memory, so FORTRAN programs work by changing the values of variables.

Variable names in Classical FORTRAN consist of 1 to 6 characters, the first of which is a capital letter and the remainder of which are capital letters or numerals.

The first letter of a variable name denotes the type of value the variable can store. Names beginning with the letters I, J, K, L, M, or N are for integer values, and names beginning with any other letter are for real values. Here are some legal and illegal variable names.

A	a real variable
B	a real variable
HYP	a real variable
PI	a real variable
INDEX	an integer variable
K9	an integer variable
HYPOTEN	too long
9K	does not start with a letter
X_Y	_ is not a letter or a numeral

Try to pick variable names that describe the quantities they represent.

2.3 Arithmetic Operators

Besides constants and variables, our example program also uses the arithmetic **operators** + and **. Here is a complete list of the arithmetic operators in Classical FORTRAN.

+	add
−	subtract, or negate
*	multiply
/	divide
**	exponentiate

The minus sign − can be used either as a binary operator, to subtract one value from another, or as a unary operator to change the sign of a value. It is also permissible to use the plus sign + as a unary operator (perhaps to emphasize for a human reader that a constant is positive). The quantities involved in a binary operation should be of the same type, integer or real, except that a whole number exponent should always be an integer. When one integer is divided by another, the result is the integer part of the quotient, obtained by **chopping** off and throwing away the fractional part (not by rounding). Here are some examples, showing FORTRAN on the left and algebra on the right, to illustrate the meanings of the arithmetic operators.

3+2	5
−Z	$-z$
X*Y	xy
29/5	5
−29/5	-5
29./5.	5.8
A**2	a^2
B**2.2	$b^{2.2}$

2.4 Function References

In addition to constants, variables, and operators, our program also contains a **function reference** to SQRT, which returns in its name the positive square root of its argument. The naming rules for functions are the same as for variables, so SQRT returns a real result. It also expects a real argument, but there are other functions for which the type of the argument does not match the type returned. Many functions are built into FORTRAN, and as we shall see in §6.3 you can also write your own. Some of the built-in functions have more than one argument. Here are a few of the ones that perform familiar mathematical operations.

SQRT(X)	$\sqrt{x}$
EXP(X)	e^x
ERF(X)	$\frac{2}{\sqrt{\pi}} \int_0^x e^{-y^2} dy$
MOD(N,M)	remainder of the division N/M

The syntax of a FORTRAN function reference is meant to recall the standard mathematical notation in which $f(x)$ means a function of x.

2.5 Expressions

A FORTRAN **expression** is made up of constants, variables, operators, function references, and **parentheses**, and specifies a rule for computing a (scalar) value. We saw some expressions earlier, in §2.3, where they were used to illustrate the meaning of the arithmetic operators. Here are some more FORTRAN expressions. As shown by the first two examples, a constant or a variable is by itself an expression.

```
3.0
X
X+3.0
(-B+SQRT(B**2-4.0*A*C))/(2.0*A)
1 + 3*7/4 - 3*(7/4)
```

What is the value of the last expression listed above? In order to be certain, it is necessary to know the order in which the operations are performed, which is summarized in the **precedence** table below.

( )	from inside out, and function references
**	from right to left
* and /	from left to right
+ and -	from left to right, and unary negation

Quantities in parentheses are found first, just as in algebra. If the argument of a function is known, rather than itself being an expression, then evaluating the function also has the highest precedence. Then come the other operations, in the order shown. Notice that the order in which successive exponentiations are performed is right to left, while successive multiplications and divisions, and successive additions and subtractions, are performed left to right. In FORTRAN it is not permitted to write operators adjacent to one another, so an expression such as 2*-3 is not allowed even though -3 by itself is a legal unary negation. The exponentiation operator ** is regarded as one symbol rather than as adjacent multiplication operators. Here are some more expressions, with their meanings.

2*(-3)	$2 \times -3 = -6$
2**2**3	$2^{(2^3)} = 2^8$
(2**2)**3	$(2^2)^3 = 2^6$
X/Y/Z/W	X/(Y*Z*W)
X*Y/Z*W	X*(Y/Z)*W
(X+3.)**(-1)	1./(X+3.)

The first three meanings are given algebraically, the last three by equivalent but simpler or less ambiguous FORTRAN expressions. Try to write expressions in such a way that they are easy to understand without having to remember the precedence order of the operations.

2.6 Assignment Statements

Several statements in our example code are of the form *variable = expression*, but they are *not* equations. In FORTRAN, the equals sign is the **assignment operator**. An assignment always has a variable on the left-hand side and an expression on the right-hand side, and it says to evaluate the expression and then give its value to the variable. You learned earlier that a FORTRAN variable is the name of a storage location in memory, so the effect of an assignment is to store the value of the expression into the memory location named by the variable. This is quite different from an equation in algebra, which is a logical assertion that two quantities are equal rather than a command to change the value of a variable. Computer programs work by changing the contents of memory, so it is assignment statements that do the work of FORTRAN programs.

Because the expression on the right-hand side of an assignment statement is evaluated before the variable on the left-hand side gets its value replaced, the same variable name can appear on both sides of the equals sign. Thus, we can write the following program in FORTRAN even though the sequence of assignments would not be meaningful if they were equations in algebra.

```
X=1.
X=3.
X=X+4.
STOP
END
```

The first statement gives the variable X the value 1.. The quantities appearing on the two sides of an assignment statement should be of the same type, real or integer, and since X is a real variable the constant is written with a decimal point to show that it is also real. The second statement replaces the earlier value of X with the new value 3.. The third assignment evaluates the expression X+4. using the current value of X (which we just said was 3.) and assigns the result, 7., to X. Before the execution of the first assignment, X is *undefined,* and cannot be assumed to have any particular value.

2.7   READ and PRINT

The only things in our example program that remain to be discussed are the PRINT, STOP, and END statements. These were all introduced in §1 and there is only a little more to say about them here. In the Hello, world! program we printed a character string, whereas here we print the value of the variable HYP. Several character strings and values can be printed with one PRINT statement, so we could have written our example like this.

```
A=7.0
B=5.0
PRINT *,'A=',A,' B=',B
HYP=SQRT(A**2 + B**2)
PRINT *,'HYP=',HYP
STOP
END
```

The character strings serve to label the variable values that are printed, so the output from the program is easier to interpret.

```
 A= 7.000000000 B= 5.000000000
 HYP= 8.602325439
```

The items in the variable list of a PRINT statement can actually be expressions, so we could have written this instead.

```
A=7.0
B=5.0
PRINT *,'A=',A,' B=',B
PRINT *,'HYP=',SQRT(A**2 + B**2)
STOP
END
```

There is a READ statement corresponding to PRINT, which we could use in our example program as follows.

```
READ *,A,B
PRINT *,'A=',A,' B=',B
HYP=SQRT(A**2 + B**2)
PRINT *,'HYP=',HYP
STOP
END
```

When it is run, this program waits for the user to enter two values followed by a ⌇R. Reading in A and B rather than assigning them fixed values allows the executable of this program to be used for many different triangles. Until we get around to a thorough study of FORTRAN input and output in §9, these simple PRINT and READ statements will meet the communication needs of our programs.

2.8 Omissions

Other data types, type declarations, and type conversions; compile-time initialization of variables; the PARAMETER statement; mixed-mode expressions; most of the built-in functions; program design, documentation, and coding style.

2.9 Exercises

2.9.1 Could any of the statements in the hypotenuse program be interchanged without affecting the behavior of the program?

2.9.2 Is GOD real? Explain.

2.9.3 Must the value of a FORTRAN variable vary during the execution of a program? Write down the letters that begin names of variables that FORTRAN considers integers by default. Can variables have first and last names, such as "ITEM A"? Is it legal to use the same variable name for more than one quantity?

2.9.4 Simplify these expressions. (a) EXP(1.0)**3.2 (b) EXP(3.2)**3.2 (c) EXP(3.2**2) (d) EXP(ALOG(A)+ALOG(B)). The ALOG function computes the real natural logarithm of its real argument.

2.9.5 In §2.5 we saw that X/Y/Z/W is equivalent to X/(Y*Z*W), where X, Y, Z, and W are real variables. Is it also true that I/J/K/L is equivalent to I/(J*K*L), where I, J, K, and L are integer variables? Remember that integer division chops. If the two expressions are *not* equivalent, give an example to show that they can yield different results. If the two expressions always yield the same result, prove it.

2.9.6 Explain the difference between a FORTRAN assignment statement and a mathematical equation.

2.9.7 Correct the following FORTRAN "statements." Explain your answers, and state any assumptions you find it necessary to make.

```
-J=5
A*X**2+B*X+C=0
```

2.9.8 Explain the difference, if any, between the following statements.

```
A=-B
A=-1.0*B
```

2.9.9 If I=7 and X=3. before the following assignments, to what values are I and X changed? Add more parentheses to make the assignments unambiguous. (a) I=I+1/I-3 (b) X=X/(X-1.)**2**(-1)-1.

2.9.10 What is printed by this program? Explain why, and confirm your answer by experiment. How can you revise the program so it prints a better approximation to the sine of 1 radian?

```
X = 1.
Y = SIN X
PRINT *, Y
STOP
END
```

2.9.11 Revise the final program in §2.7 to prompt for A, read A, prompt for B, and read B, rather than waiting silently for the user to enter the values.

2.9.12 The following poem is attributed to John Saxon, who was an author of math textbooks [173].

> A Dozen, a Gross, and a Score
> plus three times the square root of four,
> divided by seven
> plus five times eleven,
> equals nine squared and not a bit more.

Write a FORTRAN program to verify this claim numerically. Compute the quantity described, and print the difference between it and 9^2 to show that it is not a bit more.

2.9.13 Write a program to find the angles in an arbitrary triangle, given the lengths of the three sides. If you use the law of cosines you will find it helpful to know that the built-in function ACOS(X) returns the angle, in radians, whose cosine is X.

3

Conditionals and Branching

The programs of §1 and §2 are examples of **straight-line code**, in which the executable statements are performed exactly once, in order from first to last. If we think of each FORTRAN statement as being in control of the processor for the duration of its execution, then the progress of execution from one statement to the next can be regarded as a **flow of control** through the program. In straight-line programs, the flow of control is strictly from top to bottom.

Some useful tasks, such as the hypotenuse calculation of §2, can be performed by straight-line programs. However, most algorithms require the sequence of statements that are executed to be conditional on the values of input data or the results of intermediate computations. Depending on the result of a **test**, control might be transferred from one statement to another statement that does not immediately follow the first in the top-to-bottom order of the program listing. This change in the flow of control is called a **branch**.

To see how FORTRAN provides for testing and branching, we will consider the problem of finding the roots of the quadratic equation $ax^2 + bx + c = 0$ by evaluating the formula

$$x = \frac{-b \pm \sqrt{b^2 - 4ac}}{2a}.$$

This is actually not a very good way to solve a quadratic equation numerically [5, §2.6], but it makes a good example because the formula is widely known and easy to evaluate by hand.

The quantity under the radical, $b^2 - 4ac$, is called the **discriminant** of the quadratic, because it determines whether there will be one real root, two real roots, or a conjugate pair of complex roots. We will name the discriminant d, and to keep things simple we will assume that all of the coefficients a, b, and c are nonzero.

3.1 Flowcharting

Now imagine performing the calculation with a pencil and paper, and writing down the steps of the process (that is, the algorithm) in a letter to a friend who lives in another state. Because there are decisions in the algorithm depending on the value of d, a straight-line list of formulas won't do. What *would* do is a **flowchart** like the one on the next page, which puts each step in a box and uses arrows to show the flow of control between them.

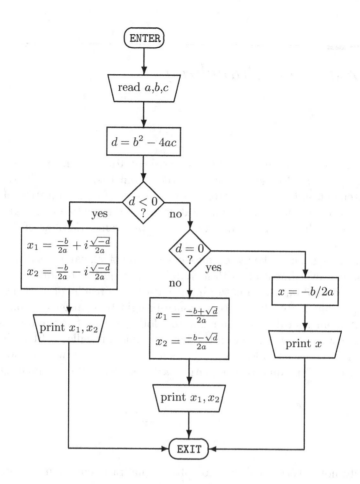

The shape of each flowchart box indicates the kind of operation it represents, with ovals for entry and exit, trapezoids for input and output, rectangles for calculations, and diamonds for decisions. Think of control entering the diagram at the top, at ENTER, and flowing down through the boxes, finding a unique path to EXIT. Control always flows through the boxes for reading the coefficients and computing the discriminant. Then there is a test whether d is negative. If it is, control follows the left branch on the diagram and reaches the box for finding a complex conjugate pair of roots. (Here $i = \sqrt{-1}$, which we have factored out of the square root so that the quantity under the radical is $-d$ and therefore positive.) If it turns out that d is *not* negative, then it must be either zero or positive. If $d = 0$, control follows the right branch from the second test and reaches the box for finding a single real root. In the final case where d is positive, we end up at the box for finding two real roots. Whichever path the control flow takes, it goes through some box that prints the root or roots that we found. The flowchart unambiguously defines the algorithm.

Notice that the entries in the boxes of the flowchart are algebra, not FORTRAN. In other problems it might be more appropriate to describe the steps in English prose, rather than in formulas. In any event, the text in the boxes should be phrased in terms of the problem being solved rather than in terms of the program we are planning to write. As we shall see, several different FORTRAN programs can be written to implement the algorithm described by this flowchart (as could programs written in languages *other* than FORTRAN).

3.2 The GO TO Statement

Here is a literal implementation of the algorithm described by our flowchart.

```
      READ *,A,B,C
      D=B**2-4.*A*C
      IF(D.LT.0.) GO TO 1
      IF(D.EQ.0.) GO TO 2
      X1=(-B+SQRT(D))/(2.*A)
      X2=(-B-SQRT(D))/(2.*A)
      PRINT *,'X1=',X1,' X2=',X2
      STOP
    1 E=-B/(2.*A)
      F=SQRT(-D)/(2.*A)
      PRINT *,'X1=',E,'+i',F,' X2=',E,'-i',F
      GO TO 3
    2 X=-B/(2.*A)
      PRINT *,'X=',X
    3 STOP
      END
```

The first two statements do just what the corresponding flowchart boxes call for. In the formula for D we have used an integer for the whole-number exponent in B**2, but a real constant 4. to avoid mixing types in the arithmetic.

Next comes the first test, which is implemented by a **logical IF** statement. The syntax of a logical IF is

        IF(logical expression) statement

in which the condition expressed by the `logical expression` can be true or false, and the `statement` gets executed only if the condition is true. The logical expression D.LT.0. is true only if D is Less Than zero. We have used a real zero, 0., to avoid mixing types in the comparison. Here are all the **logical operators**, arranged in their precedence order.

( )	inside out, and function references
.NOT.	left to right
.AND.	left to right
.OR.	left to right
.EQ. .NE. .GT. .LT. .GE. .LE.	left to right

The `statement` part of the first logical IF in our program is a GO TO, but it could be any executable FORTRAN statement except another IF or a DO (which we will take up in §5). If the expression D.LT.0. is true, control is transferred to the statement E=-B/(2.*A), which carries the **statement number** 1. A statement number is an unsigned integer appearing in the **statement number field** of an executable statement. We will always right-justify statement numbers in columns 2 through 5 inclusive. A transfer of control caused by a GO TO statement is a branch, and the numbered statement to which control is transferred is called the **branch target**.

Statement 1 corresponds to the leftmost box of formulas in the flowchart, for computing complex conjugate roots. Suppose for the moment that D is negative and we have taken the branch to 1. The program introduces the variables E and F, which aren't mentioned in the flowchart, to hold the real and imaginary parts of the complex roots. Because D is negative, -D is positive and we can calculate the square root. The PRINT statement intersperses character strings with the numerical values it prints, so that the output can be read as two complex numbers. If the user enters the values 1, 2, and 3 for A, B, and C, for example, the conversation might go like this.

```
unix[5] a.out
1 2 3
 X1= -1.000000000 +i 1.414213538  X2= -1.000000000 -i 1.414213538
unix[6]
```

As we shall see in §4.6.1, FORTRAN can represent complex numbers directly, but this program avoids needing to do that by treating the real and imaginary parts separately.

After the PRINT statement the flow of control encounters another branch, this time an unconditional GO TO 3 which takes it to a STOP statement. So the sequence of program statements corresponding to the leftmost path through the flowchart is

```
      READ *,A,B,C
      D=B**2-4.*A*C
      IF(D.LT.0.) GO TO 1
    1 E=-B/(2.*A)
      F=SQRT(-D)/(2.*A)
      PRINT *,'X1=',E,'+i',F,' X2=',E,'-i',F
      GO TO 3
    3 STOP
```

I could just as well have written another STOP statement in place of the GO TO 3, but I wanted to illustrate an unconditional GO TO.

Now consider what happens in the program if it turns out that D is not negative. The logical condition D.LT.0. evaluates to false this time, so the GO TO 1 statement doesn't get executed. Instead, control **falls through** to the second test. If D.EQ.0. that results in a branch to statement 2, which corresponds to the rightmost formula box in the flowchart. Here a single real root called X is calculated and printed out, and the flow of control reaches the STOP statement numbered 3 again. In the program, that STOP statement serves for both the case when D.LT.0. and the case when D.EQ.0..

If D turns out to be positive, so that the second test fails, then control falls through to assignments for X1 and X2, the formulas for two real roots. After these values are printed out, the flow of control encounters a different STOP statement (the one without a number). In place of this STOP we could just as well have coded another GO TO 3. A program can contain as many STOP statements as you find it convenient to use, or only one that is reached by all the possible paths of control flow through the program.

3.3   The IF-THEN Construct

Although the program of §3.2 has the virtue that its statements are in one-to-one correspondence with the blocks of the flowchart, it is confusing and clumsy to read *without* the flowchart. Especially with no comments, the code is hard to understand. The program at the top of the next page uses a different construct for conditional execution to achieve a slightly more graceful expression of the algorithm.

```
      READ *,A,B,C
      D=B**2-4.*A*C
      IF(D.LT.0.) THEN
          E=-B/(2.*A)
          F=SQRT(-D)/(2.*A)
          PRINT *,'X1=',E,'+i',F,' X2=',E,'-i',F
      ELSE
        IF(D.EQ.0.) THEN
          X=-B/(2.*A)
          PRINT *,'X=',X
        ELSE
          X1=(-B+SQRT(D))/(2.*A)
          X2=(-B-SQRT(D))/(2.*A)
          PRINT *,'X1=',X1,' X2=',X2
        ENDIF
      ENDIF
      STOP
      END
```

The first two statements are the same as they were before. Next, however, instead of logical IF and GO TO statements this program uses the IF-THEN **construct**, also called an IF-THEN **block**, which has the following general form.

```
      IF(logical expression) THEN
        what to do if the logical expression is true
      ELSE
        what to do if the logical expression is false
      ENDIF
```

The ELSE and the statements telling what to do if the logical expression is false are optional and may be omitted, but if they are included the ELSE *must be on a line by itself.* It is a common error, easy to make when the ELSE clause contains a single statement, to put that statement on the same line with the ELSE.

Because our algorithm needs two tests, the program **nests** one IF-THEN construct inside another, as emphasized by the indentation of the source text. Recall from §1.1 that statements begin in *or to the right* of column 7, so indentation can always be used like this to clarify the logical structure of a program.

If D.LT.0., then this code executes the same statements we ran into before when D.LT.0., but now they are located immediately after the test (rather than being far away at statement 1), and most people think that makes them easier to find. If D.LT.0. is false, we do the ELSE clause of the first IF-THEN construct, which here turns out to be another IF-THEN construct. The inside IF-THEN distinguishes between the cases D.EQ.0. and not, executing in each case the same statements we saw in the first program. This program needs no statement numbers, and the three logical cases distinguished by the algorithm are easy to spot in the code.

Another approach when there are nested logical conditions is to code separate IF-THEN blocks rather than using ELSE at all, as shown on the next page. In reading this code it is necessary to keep in mind only one alternative at a time. Which style is easiest to understand is a judgement call that must be made by the programmer depending on the situation.

```
IF(y) THEN
   statements a
ENDIF
IF(.NOT.y .AND. z) THEN
   statements b
ENDIF
IF(.NOT.y .AND. .NOT.z) THEN
   statements c
ENDIF
```

3.4   The Logical IF Statement

In our first implementation we encountered the logical IF statement with GO TO as its predicate, but there I pointed out that the statement part of a logical IF can be something other than a GO TO. This suggests using logical IF statements to select actions directly, rather than to select transfers of control, which leads to this third version of the quadratic formula program.

```
READ *,A,B,C
D=B**2-4.*A*C
E=-B/(2.*A)
F=SQRT(ABS(D))/(2.*A)
IF(D.LT.0.) PRINT *,'X1=',E,'+i',F,
;                     'X2=',E,'-i',F
IF(D.EQ.0.) PRINT *,'X=',E
IF(D.GT.0.) PRINT *,'X1=',E+F,' X2=',E-F
STOP
END
```

Now in addition to D we always calculate the two terms of the formula

$$x = -\frac{b}{2a} \pm \frac{\sqrt{b^2 - 4ac}}{2a}$$

calling the first term E and the second F. Earlier we took the square root of D if D was positive, or the square root of -D if D was negative, but that amounts to taking the square root of |D| so that's what we do here in finding F. The built-in function ABS returns the real absolute value of its real argument.

According to the sign of D, the appropriate PRINT statement is used to assemble E and F into a complex conjugate pair of roots, or a single real root, or a pair of real roots. If we had noticed earlier that E and F can be computed the same way for all three cases, we could have simplified the other programs, too.

Normally the end of a statement is the end of the line, but the first PRINT statement in this program is continued to a second line by the presence of a **continuation character** in column 6 of the second line. We will always use a semicolon ; for the continuation character. It is a common typographical error to put a continuation character in the wrong column, or to put something else in the continuation column, so it is important to count carefully and keep things lined up. Blank spaces don't matter between the elements of the variable list in a PRINT statement, so in this example I indented the continued text to be under the text on the first line of the statement; this makes it clear at a glance that X2 is just the complex conjugate of X1.

3.5   Flowcharting Reconsidered

Our first program, using GO TO statements, was a direct translation of the quadratic formula flowchart into FORTRAN. The second, using IF-THEN blocks, implemented the algorithm more clearly but with statements that are harder to put into one-to-one correspondence with the boxes of the flowchart. The last program, which is arguably the simplest and easiest to understand of the three, hardly follows the flowchart at all. It is not uncommon that the clearest code turns out to be quite different from the most obvious flowchart for an algorithm.

After studying this example, and especially after seeing the third program, it has probably occurred to you that when viewed in the right way this calculation is simple enough to be understood without using a flowchart at all. If an algorithm is so complicated that a flowchart is indispensable for understanding it, then code to implement it is probably going to be hard to write, hard to understand, and hard to get correct. In §12 we will study ways of decomposing a problem into pieces so that each piece is small and simple enough to get right without resorting to flowcharts.

Flowcharts are of great value to beginning students of FORTRAN, and even experienced programmers occasionally use them in working out the logic of an algorithm. You should use them for as long as they help you to understand what you are doing. But because they are seldom really needed by any but the most novice programmers, and sometimes suggest clumsy approaches to programming, I will use them only sparingly after this chapter.

3.6   Additional Examples

Often there are several different but logically equivalent ways to code a calculation involving a test, and sometimes it turns out that an explicit test is not required. Here are some examples to exercise your understanding of the statements discussed in this chapter.

First consider the code segment on the left below, and describe to yourself in plain language what it does.

```
      IF(X.LT.0.) GO TO 1          IF(X.LT.0.) THEN
      Y=X                             Y=-X
      GO TO 2                      ELSE
    1 Y=-X                            Y=X
    2 ...                          ENDIF
```

The code sets Y to X if X is positive or to -X if X is negative. An easier way of saying this is with the code on the right. The version on the left below is shorter; as we saw earlier it is often possible to simplify code by using a logical IF with a predicate that does something.

```
      Y=X                          Y=ABS(X)
      IF(Y.LT.0.) Y=-Y
```

Now Y is unconditionally assigned the value of X, and then its sign is changed if necessary. But the code can be simplified still further, as on the right above, by using the built-in function ABS that we first encountered in §3.4. After all, the absolute value of X is X if X is positive and −X if X is negative. For example, |3| = 3 because 3 is positive, but because −3 is negative we compute its absolute value as |−3| = −(−3) = 3.

The next example is typical of code for bounding a variable between permissible values.

```
      IF(I.LT. 0) GO TO 1              IF(I.LT.0) THEN
      IF(I.GT.10) GO TO 2                 I=0
      GO TO 3                          ELSE
    1 I=0                                 IF(I.GT.10) THEN
      GO TO 3                                I=10
    2 I=10                                ENDIF
    3 ...                              ENDIF
```

We can clarify the code on the left by replacing its GO TO statements with IF−THEN constructs as on the right above. A still simpler expression of the same idea uses the logical IF statements on the left below.

```
      IF(I.LT. 0) I= 0                I=MINO(10,MAXO(I,0))
      IF(I.GT.10) I=10
```

As in the previous example it turns out that this calculation can be performed using built-in functions. In the code on the right above, MINO and MAXO return for their integer values respectively the smaller and the larger of their integer arguments. (That's a zero at the end of each function name, not an oh.) Thus MAXO(I,0) is I if I is greater than zero, or zero otherwise, and the assignment sets I to the smaller of that value and 10. Although the final version is the most terse it requires some analysis to figure out, so the code on the left above, using the logical IF statements, is probably the best of the alternatives.

Finally, consider the loop on the left below, which would be a little mysterious without the comment. Before reading on you should try to convince yourself that it really does add up the integers from 1 to N.

```
C     find J=1+2+...+N            C     find J=1+2+...+N
      J=0                               J=0
      I=1                               I=1
    2 J=J+I                        1 IF(I.LE.N) THEN
      IF(I.EQ.N) GO TO 1                J=J+I
      I=I+1                             I=I+1
      GO TO 2                           GO TO 1
    1 ...                              ENDIF
```

We can try to make this calculation clearer by replacing the GO TO statements by the IF−THEN construct on the right above, but that isn't much of an improvement. However, it is not hard to show that

$$\sum_{i=1}^{n} i = \tfrac{1}{2}n(n+1)$$

so the whole loop could be replaced by the following statement.

```
      J=N*(N+1)/2
```

I will have more to say about using formulas in place of iterative processes in §15.2.1.

Clarity and simplicity are hallmarks of good writing in FORTRAN just as in any other language. Work hard to find the best way of expressing each calculation. When you are editing code, whether it was written by you or by someone else, figure out what each code segment does and then write a new version, if necessary, that gives the same result. Coding style is discussed at length in §12.4.

3.7 Omissions

Flowcharting was at one time something of a cottage industry, involving special forms printed on large paper, manuals explaining the technique, plastic templates for drawing the boxes, and a more extensive catalog of standard box shapes than I have mentioned here. I have also refrained from discussing the programs that were commonly used years ago for constructing flowcharts from a coded description or from FORTRAN source.

FORTRAN provides other mechanisms for conditional execution in addition to the ones I have explained here, including *ELSE IF,* the *assigned GO TO,* the *computed GO TO,* and the *arithmetic IF*.

3.8 Exercises

3.8.1 From memory, describe the behavior of (a) all the FORTRAN statements introduced so far; (b) all the built-in functions mentioned so far.

3.8.2 Explain why it can sometimes be helpful to flowchart an algorithm, and describe the drawbacks and limitations of flowcharting. Is there always a simple correspondence between the boxes of a flowchart and the statements in a FORTRAN program that implements the algorithm?

3.8.3 This chapter introduced four standard box shapes for flowcharting. Describe them and explain how they are used. What should be written inside flowchart boxes?

3.8.4 In §3.2, the sequence of program statements corresponding to the leftmost path through the flowchart is given. Write down the sequence of statements corresponding to (a) the middle path; (b) the rightmost path.

3.8.5 In the quadratic formula example we assumed that none of the coefficients is zero (so that, for example, we can divide by a). (a) Modify the flowchart to account for the possibility that any or all of the coefficients could be zero. (b) From the flowchart, write a FORTRAN program implementing the more general algorithm.

3.8.6 Show that $\sum_{i=1}^{n} i = \frac{1}{2}n(n+1)$.

3.8.7 What is the biggest statement number allowed? Are there any drawbacks to using numbers that large? Can two statements have the same number? How should statement numbers be justified in their field? Why?

3.8.8 Explain the syntactical difference between the logical IF statement and the IF-THEN construct.

3.8.9 The program below tests whether the input value I is equal to either 2 or 3. Unfortunately, it elicits an error message from the compiler. (a) Explain what is wrong with this code. (b) Fix the program, compile it, and run the executable to verify your correction.

```
READ *,I
IF(I .EQ. (2 .OR. 3)) PRINT *,I
STOP
END
```

3.8.10 What FORTRAN statements are *not* permitted as the predicate of a logical IF?

3.8.11 What gets printed by this program? Explain why.

```
J=-4
IF(-J.LE.1-J .AND. J**J.GT.1) J=-J/J
PRINT *,J
STOP
END
```

3.8.12 Consider the following code segment.

```
IF(N-2*(N/2) .EQ. 0) THEN
    IXHZ=N/2
ELSE
    IXHZ=N/2 + 1
ENDIF
```

(a) What does this code segment compute? Is there a succinct mathematical description of how IXHZ is related to N? Hint: what possible values can the expression N-2*(N/2) take on? (b) Replace this code segment with a single assignment statement that sets IXHZ to the correct value without having to do any test. Which version of the code do you think is easier to understand?

3.8.13 The following program actually prints L=0 X=0. if the value read for K is 1, but L=2 X=2. if the value read for K is 0.

```
L=2
X=2.
READ *,K
IF(K.EQ.1) THEN
    L=0
    X=0.
ELSE L=1
ENDIF
PRINT *,'L=',L,' X=',X
STOP
END
```

(a) If the author intended the output for K=0 to be L=1 X=2., what is wrong with the program? Remember that FORTRAN ignores most blanks in statements. (b) Add to the PRINT list a variable named ELSEL. What value is printed for it? (c) Correct the program to obtain the intended behavior.

3.8.14 State the argument and return types for each of these built-in functions, and explain how the returned value depends on the argument value or values: (a) ABS(), (b) MAXO(), (c) MINO().

3.8.15 Based on the exposition in this chapter, is it better to make difficult code easier to understand by adding comments, or by finding a clearer way to express the calculation in FORTRAN? In which chapter of this book is program design and documentation discussed further?

3.8.16 In what column must a continuation character appear? What continuation character is used in this book? Determine by experiment whether your FORTRAN compiler permits comments *between* the lines of a continued statement.

3.8.17 Simpson's Rule [4] approximates a definite integral as

$$\int_a^b f(x)dx \approx \frac{h}{3}[f(a) + 4f(a+h) + 2f(a+2h) + 4f(a+3h) + \cdots + 4f(b-h) + f(b)]$$

where $h = (b-a)/n$ and $n \geq 2$ is even. (a) Flowchart an algorithm to evaluate this sum. (b) Write a FORTRAN program implementing your algorithm for $f(x) = \ln(x)/x$, $a = \frac{1}{2}$, and $b = 3$, and use it to confirm that the integral is about 0.3632479734471903 (c) Plot a graph showing how the error in the approximation varies with n.

3.8.18 An amortized mortgage is repaid in equal installments each consisting of interest and principal. The interest is that due on the outstanding balance for the preceding period, and the remainder of the installment is repayment of principal. If the loan amount is P, the interest rate is $100i\%$ per month, and there are n monthly payments, then each payment is

$$A = P\frac{i(1+i)^n}{(1+i)^n - 1}.$$

(a) Flowchart the calculation of an amortization table listing the number of each payment, the interest and principal it contains, the remaining balance, and the aggregate interest and principal paid so far. (b) Write a FORTRAN program to implement the flowchart. Use a real variable to store the value of i. (c) Prove the formula for A.

3.8.19 Three real numbers a, b, and c are to be sorted into increasing order. (a) Flowchart an algorithm that does this using as few comparisons as possible. (b) Write a FORTRAN program to test your algorithm.

3.8.20 Three people and a monkey were shipwrecked on a desert island and spent the first day gathering coconuts for food. The sun set before they could divide them, so they agreed to wait until the next morning. During the night, the first person awoke and thought "There is going to be an argument about dividing the coconuts tomorrow, so I'll just take my third now." She divided the pile into 3 equal parts and had one coconut left over, which she gave to the monkey. She hid her third in the bushes and put the other two thirds back together, and went back to sleep. Later in the night, the second person did exactly the same thing, and just before morning the third person did too. When dawn broke they divided the coconuts that were left, and each person got one third of those with none left over for the monkey. How many coconuts were there? (a) Write a FORTRAN program to find the *two* smallest possibilities. (b) Modify your program to read in the number p of shipwrecked people and to solve the problem assuming each wakes up in turn and divides the pile into p parts with one left over for the monkey, with the final division in the morning still coming out even. Verify that when $p = 3$ this program yields the same results as the first one. (Adapted from [144]).

3.8.21 The flowchart on the next page precisely specifies a version of the bisection algorithm, first described in §0.1, for solving an algebraic equation of the form $f(x) = 0$. The quantity ϵ mentioned in the flowchart is called a **convergence tolerance**. (a) Using only the language elements presented so far, write a FORTRAN program that implements the

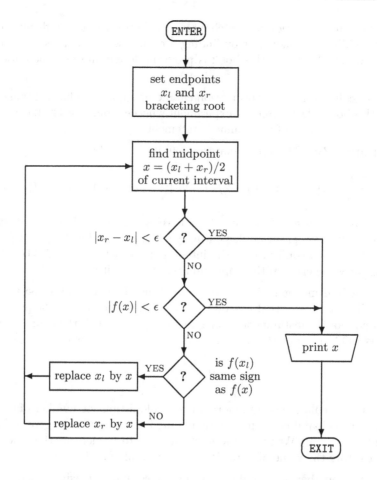

algorithm for $f(x) = \sin(x) - \frac{1}{2}x$. (b) Run the program on your computer using $\epsilon = 10^{-3}$ and confirm that it gives approximately the correct answer. (c) Here are two common approaches to testing whether two variables, say F and FL, have the same sign.

```
IF(F*FL .LT. 0.) GO TO 1
IF((FL.GT.0..AND.F.LT.0.).OR.(FL.LT.0..AND.F.GT.0.)) GO TO 2
```

Explain how each test works, and discuss its advantages and drawbacks.

3.8.22 Each code segment below performs the statements in [body of loop] ten times, and each contains an explicit branch GO TO 1.

```
      KMAX=10                        KMAX=10
      K=1                            K=1
    1 IF(K.LE.KMAX) THEN          1 [body of loop]
      [body of loop]                 K=K+1
      K=K+1                          IF(K.LE.KMAX) GO TO 1
      GO TO 1
      ENDIF
```

The code on the left also contains an *implicit* branch, when the IF statement fails, to the statement following the ENDIF. In the code on the right, control simply falls through when the IF fails. Which version do you think is easier to understand, and why?

4

Scalar Data Types

So far we have distinguished FORTRAN variables and constants as being either integer or real. Recall from §2.2 that variables whose names begin with I, J, K, L, M, or N store integer values, while those beginning with any other letter are for real values. FORTRAN also provides several other data types, and permits the explicit declaration of a variable's type to override the default naming rules.

4.1 Integers

Computers store and manipulate numbers in **binary** form, that is, represented in base 2 using the symbols 0 and 1. The binary number system, like the familiar decimal system, uses **positional notation**, in which the rightmost place in an integer is the units place. In decimal, successive places to the left have values of 10, 100, and so on, while in binary the places to the left have values of 2, 4, and so on. Thus, for example,

$$19_{10} = 1 \times 10^1 + 9 \times 10^0 = 19$$
$$10011_2 = 1 \times 2^4 + 0 \times 2^3 + 0 \times 2^2 + 1 \times 2^1 + 1 \times 2^0 = 19$$

so $19_{10} = 10011_2$. Just as each symbol in a decimal number is called a digit, each symbol in a binary number is called a **bit**.

Variables and constants of the type we have been referring to as "integer" are stored in memory as a contiguous sequence of 32 bits called a **word** or **fullword**. The bits of a word are grouped into four 8-bit **bytes**, as shown in the diagram below.

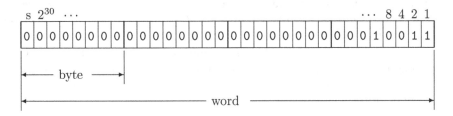

Some of the bit positions in the diagram have their values marked above them. Because a fullword integer is 4 bytes long, Classical FORTRAN names that data type INTEGER*4. So what we have been casually referring to as the type "integer" is more formally INTEGER*4.

The leftmost bit, marked "s" in the diagram, is the **sign bit**. The sign bit is 0 for a positive number or 1 for a negative number. If the number is positive, as in the example shown, the rightmost 31 bits represent the binary value of the integer. If the number N is

negative (so that -N is positive), then all 32 bits (including the sign bit of 1) represent the
2's complement of -N, which is $2^{32} + N$ (and hence positive).

The largest positive value that can be stored in an INTEGER*4 has the bit pattern
01111111111111111111111111111111, a zero followed by 31 1's, representing the value

$$2^{30} + 2^{29} + 2^{28} + \cdots + 2^1 + 2^0 = 2^{31} - 1 = 2147483647 \approx 2 \times 10^9$$

or about two billion. Values bigger than this *won't fit* in an INTEGER*4 variable, and can't
be declared as INTEGER*4 constants. To see what happens when an INTEGER*4 gets too
big, consider the following program.

```
I=2147483647
I=I+1
PRINT *,'2147483647+1=',I
STOP
END
```

This sets I to the largest representable value and then adds 1 to it, producing the output
shown below.

```
 2147483647+1= -2147483648
```

It is disconcerting to find that adding 1 to a positive number can yield a negative number,
but that is precisely the result of a **fixed-point overflow**. Here is the bit pattern produced
by the addition:

$$
\begin{array}{r}
01111111111111111111111111111111 \\
+1 \\
\hline
10000000000000000000000000000000
\end{array}
$$

The sign bit has become a 1, which means the bit pattern is the 2's complement of some
negative number. The value of the bit pattern is 2^{31} and this is 2^{32} plus the number
represented, so the value of the number itself is $2^{31} - 2^{32} = -2^{31} = -2147483648$, as
reported by the program.

Until now you might have assumed that computers could be relied upon always to do
integer arithmetic correctly, but the calculation discussed above shows that fixed-point overflows can make the answers wrong if any of the numbers involved in a calculation get too
big. No warning message is produced when an integer overflows, and if the trouble happens
at some intermediate step of a long program the eventual output might have the correct sign
and look plausible even though it is dead wrong. Two billion is a large number, but computers count very fast and it is not uncommon for programmers to underestimate how big an
integer will get. Fixed-point overflow is thus a serious potential problem that must always
be worried about and guarded against. It has nothing to do with FORTRAN in particular,
because all non-symbolic programming languages use the same machine representation for
integers, so switching to C or Pascal or assembler language won't help. All you can do is
remember to *avoid using integer variables to store values that will get too big.*

4.2   Reals

A real number, as you will recall from §2.1, has a fractional part (which might be zero). Modern computers store real values using bit patterns that are specified in the **IEEE floating-point standard** [19] [11]. The data type that we have been referring to as "real" is known to FORTRAN as REAL*4 and is represented in IEEE arithmetic by the bit pattern shown below.

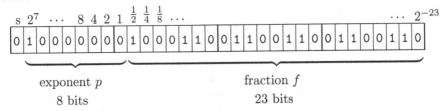

As indicated by the name of the data type, a REAL*4 value is stored in a fullword of 4 bytes just as an INTEGER*4 is, but now the bits have different meanings. The first bit still denotes the sign, but the next 8 bits are the binary value of a **biased exponent** p and the last 23 bits are a **binary fraction** f. The number r represented by the bit pattern is

$$r = (-1)^s \times 2^{p-127} \times (1 + f)$$

where the first term $(-1)^s$ accounts for the sign of the number and the 127 in the second term is the **exponent bias**. The 8 bits of exponent can represent values p from zero through 255, so the value of the second term can vary from 2^{-127} to 2^{+128}. Biasing the exponent thus permits the representation of positive and negative exponents without using a bit to explicitly denote the exponent sign. For the example shown,

$$p = 10000000_2 = 2^7 = 128$$

The value of the binary fraction f can be decoded from positional notation, just as we read other binary numbers, but now the bit positions must be thought of as being to the right of a binary point and thus correspond to negative rather than positive powers of 2. As shown in the diagram, the leftmost bit position in f has the value $2^{-1} = \frac{1}{2}$, the next $\frac{1}{4}$, and so on down to the least significant bit which has the value $2^{-23} = \frac{1}{8388608}$. For the example shown,

$$f = .10001100110011001100110_2$$
$$= \frac{1}{2} + \frac{1}{32} + \frac{1}{64} + \frac{1}{512} + \frac{1}{1024} + \cdots + \frac{1}{4194304}$$
$$\approx .5498$$

Putting the pieces together, we find for the example that

$$r = (-1)^0 \times 2^{128-127} \times (1 + .5498\cdots) \approx 3.1$$

To add real values that have different exponents when represented in this way, we would move or float the binary point in the smaller number to the left until the exponents were the same before adding the fractions. Because of this process, real numbers are also referred to as **floating-point** numbers. A floating-point number is said to be **normalized** when $p > 0$, or unnormalized when $p = 0$ and f is nonzero. The results of floating-point arithmetic are always normalized by the processor, if possible, before they are used or stored.

Normalized REAL*4 numbers of either sign can range in magnitude from about 1.2×10^{-38} to about $3.4 \times 10^{+38}$. The large range of real numbers makes them suitable for storing not only values with fractional parts but also some whole numbers that are too large to be represented as INTEGER*4s. However, because f is a finite sum of negative powers of 2, only certain real values can be represented exactly. The value 1.5 is $2^0 \times (1 + \frac{1}{2})$, so it can be represented exactly. But when the value 3.1 is written in the REAL*4 format its fraction $.1000\overline{1100}$ has a part that repeats, and we can fit only 23 bits of it into f so in our example above the representation is inexact. The "real" numbers in FORTRAN are actually just a finite set of fractions, lacking the continuity and extent of the real numbers $\mathbb{R}^1$ in mathematics. A real value (in the mathematical sense) that does not happen to be represented exactly in a REAL*4 FORTRAN variable is approximated to a precision of 6 or 7 decimal digits, rarely 8, depending on the value.

In addition to REAL*4, FORTRAN also provides the data types REAL*8 (also called **double precision**) and REAL*16 (also called quadruple precision or **extended precision**), which occupy respectively 8 bytes or one **doubleword** and 16 bytes or two doublewords in memory. The IEEE bit patterns for these types are similar to the one for REAL*4 except that they have more exponent bits, more fraction bits, and different exponent bias values, as summarized in the table below. (The bit pattern for REAL*16 quantities is only suggested by the IEEE standard, not required, and some computer vendors do not follow the standard.)

type name	exponent bits	fraction bits	exponent bias	range normalized	precision digits
REAL*4	8	23	127	$10^{\pm 38}$	6-8
REAL*8	11	52	1023	$10^{\pm 308}$	15-17
REAL*16	15	112	16383	$10^{\pm 4932}$	33-34

The table also shows the order of magnitude of the largest and smallest normalized numbers that can be represented in each type, and the decimal precision. FORTRAN variables that are real because of the default naming rules, and constants written with a decimal point, are assumed by the compiler to be REAL*4. We shall see in §4.5 how to declare variables and constants that are of the other real types.

In §4.1 we saw how calculating a value that is too large to store in an INTEGER*4 causes a fixed-point overflow and yields an incorrect result. It is also possible to overflow real variables, but in IEEE arithmetic instead of getting a wrong number we get a special bit pattern that is recognized as $+\infty$ or $-\infty$. Subsequent calculations involving the variable use the infinite value, and in some circumstances that leads to sensible results (for example, dividing a finite value by a variable that has been set to a bit pattern for $\pm\infty$ yields zero). A warning message is also written when the program stops so that you can tell, even if it isn't obvious from the program's output, that an overflow occurred sometime during the run. IEEE arithmetic includes another special bit pattern called a **NaN**, which stands for "not a number" and results from asking for something like 0./0. or SQRT(-1.). NaNs, infinities, and other **IEEE exceptions** are discussed further in §14.3.2.

It is quite common for floating-point calculations to **underflow**, producing a result smaller than the smallest nonzero value the data type can represent (the least possible *un*normalized value, which for a REAL*4 is about $\pm 1.4 \times 10^{-45}$). Then FORTRAN sets the result to zero. The bit patterns for zero, unnormalized values, NaN, and $\pm\infty$ cannot be decoded by using the formula for r given above (but see [11]). Bit patterns for some special values are given in §4.7.

4.3 Roundoff Errors

We have seen that most real values (like 3.1) can't be represented exactly using IEEE numbers. Conversely, the decimal equivalent of a binary floating-point value might be truncated when it is written out using a fixed number of digits. Something is usually lost in translation when you use a decimal number in FORTRAN source code, or read one in as data, or when your program writes its answer in decimal form. The graininess of computer numbers is one source of error in floating-point calculations, but it is unfortunately not the only one.

Other imprecisions creep in by way of arithmetic. Computers use binary numbers, but suppose for the sake of illustration we have a machine that does decimal arithmetic and retains 3 significant digits in each result. What happens if we have it find this sum?

$$1.00 + \underbrace{.001 + .001 + \cdots + .001}_{1000 \text{ terms}}$$

The result of 1.00+.001 is 1.001, but there aren't enough digits in the computer's representation of the numbers to store the final 1, so there is a loss of significance and only 1.00 is kept. The same thing happens at each successive addition, and we get 1.00 for the answer. If the numbers are added in the opposite order, we get a different answer.

$$\underbrace{.001 + .001 + \cdots + .001}_{1000 \text{ terms}} + 1.00$$

Now the first result is .001+.001=.002, and all the digits can be kept. Then the second addition yields .002+.001=.003 and so on, until the final sum is 1.00+1.00=2.00, the correct answer. The terms in this sum are all positive, but the same thing can happen with subtraction. The sort of error illustrated by this example can be minimized by adding the terms in increasing order of their absolute values, but that is seldom practical unless the relative sizes of the terms are known in advance; sorting takes a lot of machine time.

There is also a loss of significance when finding the difference between quantities that are almost the same, as in this example.

```
  1.23
 -1.22
 -----
   .01
```

The operands both have 3 significant digits, but the difference has only 1 significant digit. This is sometimes called a **cancellation error**, perhaps because the leading digits that are identical seem to cancel each other out in the answer.

Multiplication and division lead to a loss of precision when the exact result, which usually has more bits than the operands, is rounded to the length of the operands. This is a less important source of error than those illustrated above, so multiplication and division can be expected to produce a smaller loss of accuracy than addition and subtraction [9, §4.2.2]. However, multiplication and division can also underflow to zero.

On a decimal computer where the smallest representable value greater than zero is .001, the calculation below yields a wrong answer.

$$\underbrace{\frac{.001}{10.0} + \frac{.001}{10.0} + \cdots + \frac{.001}{10.0}}_{\text{1000 terms}}$$

Each division produces .001/10.0=.0001, which is too small to represent and underflows to zero. If we instead add up the numerator terms first, which can be done without loss of precision, and then divide we get 1.00/10.0=.100, which can be represented.

Imprecisions in the representation of numbers, loss of significance, the shortening of long products and quotients, and the effects of underflows are together referred to as **roundoff errors**. Like fixed-point overflows and floating-point exceptions, roundoff errors are not a failing of FORTRAN but an unavoidable and language-independent hazard of machine arithmetic, resulting from the way in which computers store and manipulate numbers. Roundoff errors accumulate as arithmetic is performed and depend on the relative magnitudes of the numbers involved, and their effect on your answers depends on how errors made in each step of a calculation propagate through subsequent steps [107]. These things in turn all depend on the algorithm, so it is important to use numerically stable methods that are appropriate to the calculation you have in mind [5, §2]. Roundoff errors decrease as the length of the floating-point numbers (and hence the amount of memory they occupy) increases. Even after a good algorithm has been chosen, it often turns out that REAL*4 variables lack the precision (and range, to avoid underflows) necessary to yield precise answers. When numerical analysts are showing off they sometimes brag to each other about having solved some hard problem in single precision [151] but in practice most serious numerical computing calls for REAL*8 numbers. In a few situations, such as accumulating the dot product of two vectors or finding the correction to use in solving a linear system with iterative refinement, it is prudent to use REAL*16 variables. A simple sanity check on the numerical stability of a calculation is to repeat it using a different level of precision. Getting dramatically different answers when you switch from REAL*4 to REAL*8 or from REAL*8 to REAL*16 is prima facie evidence of a problem with roundoff errors.

The choice of an algorithm often determines the accuracy of a calculation in another way besides through the algorithm's indirect effect on the generation and propagation of roundoff errors. Many numerical methods approximate a result by adding up the leading terms from an infinite series, or by making a step size merely very small when it really should be going to zero, or by some other limiting process that can't be carried to completion because of the finite nature of machine computation. These mathematical shortcomings of the algorithm introduce **truncation errors**, which would be present even if the arithmetic could be carried out to infinite precision. It is a heartbreaking irony of numerical computing that reducing the truncation error of an algorithm by changing the number of terms, or the step size, or whatever, almost always *increases* the roundoff error. In that case there is an optimal choice about what to do, yielding a total error below which it is impossible to get. Truncation errors are the province of numerical analysis and therefore beyond the scope of this text, but it is important to realize that attempts to control them will also affect roundoff error.

Roundoff errors occur only in floating-point calculations, and most programmers who write in languages other than FORTRAN don't do many of those. But floating-point arithmetic is our stock in trade, so we will have some slight ongoing interest in roundoff errors throughout the remainder of this book.

4.4 Type Conversions

Often it is necessary to use the whole number in an integer variable as a real value with a fractional part of zero, or to give a REAL*8 variable the rounded-off value of a REAL*16. As we have seen, the bit patterns used to represent these data types are different, so they can't just be used interchangeably. To convert between them, FORTRAN provides built-in functions that accept an argument of one type and return the value in another type. The table below lists the ones we will use most often; some others are mentioned in §4.6.

function	returns	from argument
X=FLOAT(I)	REAL*4	INTEGER*4
Y=DFLOAT(I)	REAL*8	INTEGER*4
X=SNGL(Y)	REAL*4	REAL*8
Y=DBLE(X)	REAL*8	REAL*4
Z=QEXTD(Y)	REAL*16	REAL*8
Y=DBLEQ(Z)	REAL*8	REAL*16
I=IFIX(X)	INTEGER*4	REAL*4

If a REAL*8 value is too big to fit in a REAL*4, or if a REAL*16 is too big to fit in a REAL*8, then the result of the conversion is the bit pattern for the correctly-signed ∞. If a REAL*4 value is too big to fit in an INTEGER*4, then the result of the conversion is the largest integer of the appropriate sign. The IFIX function truncates or **chops** off the fractional part of its argument, rather than rounding, so IFIX(2.1) and IFIX(2.9) both return the integer value 2.

To see how the type conversion routines can be used, consider the problem of finding the integer closest to the real ratio of the positive whole numbers represented by two integers. For example, if I=7 and J=4 are integers, we want to find the integer L that is closest to $\frac{7}{4} = 1.75$, or 2. The simple integer division L=I/J won't do the job because 7/4 chops to 1. This can be fixed up by adding 1 when necessary (see Exercise 4.10.31), but the resulting code is unobvious and several statements long. Here is a less subtle solution.

```
L=IFIX(0.5+SNGL(DFLOAT(I)/DFLOAT(J)))
```

As you will recall from §2.5, the expression on the right-hand side of this assignment gets evaluated from the inside out, function evaluations before arithmetic. The whole numbers in I and J get converted to REAL*8 values first, so that the division will yield the ratio as a REAL*8. That's the argument of the SNGL function, which converts it to a REAL*4.

Next we add 0.5, which has the effect that when the result is chopped back to an integer by the IFIX function, the ratio will have been *rounded* to the nearest whole number. For the example above, 1.75+0.5=2.25, which chops to 2 as desired. If the starting integers had instead been, say, I=9 and J=4, so the ratio was 2.25, then adding 0.5 would yield 2.25+0.5=2.75, which also correctly chops to 2. So IFIX can be used to round as well as to chop; *to round a positive value to the nearest integer, add one half and then chop.*

4.5   Case Study: Computing the Sine

To illustrate the use of some different data types, and to introduce a few other features of FORTRAN, we will study a program that computes $\sin(x)$. There are built-in functions for this (SIN() for REAL*4 values, DSIN() for REAL*8, and QSIN() for REAL*16), but how do they work? Computers can do arithmetic, but there is no circuit in the hardware for finding the sine of an angle. It must be calculated using an algorithm.

A naïve approach to evaluating the sine function uses its power series expansion. As you might recall from your calculus course,

$$\sin(x) = \frac{x^1}{1!} - \frac{x^3}{3!} + \frac{x^5}{5!} - \frac{x^7}{7!} + \cdots = \sum_{i=1}^{\infty} \frac{(-1)^{i+1} x^{2i-1}}{(2i-1)!}$$

This is an infinite series, but the factorial function grows faster than any polynomial so eventually the terms get smaller and smaller. It should therefore be possible to approximate the function by adding up a finite number of terms, and each of them can be calculated using only arithmetic. Here is some code that does it.

```
      REAL*8 X,Y,F,NUMER,PI
      INTEGER*4 DENOM,I/1/
      PARAMETER(PI=3.1415926535897932D0)
      READ *,Y
      X=(PI/180.D0)*Y
      NUMER=X
      DENOM=1
      F=NUMER/DFLOAT(DENOM)
      NTERM=8
    1 I=I+1
        NUMER=NUMER*(-X**2)
        DENOM=(2*I-1)*(2*I-2)*DENOM
        F=F+NUMER/DFLOAT(DENOM)
      IF(I.LT.NTERM) GO TO 1
      PRINT *,'approximate=',F,' exact=',DSIN(X)
      STOP
      END
```

There are many observations (not all of them flattering) to be made about this little program.

1⟹   The first two statements are **type declarations**, which override the default naming rules for variables. The first line declares all of the real variables in the program to be REAL*8, and the second line declares all of the integer variables except NTERM to be INTEGER*4. Because NTERM is not explicitly typed, its type is determined by the default naming rules to be also INTEGER*4. If DENOM were not explicitly typed, it would be a REAL*4; if NUMER were not explicitly typed it would be an INTEGER*4.

2⟹   The variable I, which counts the terms in the series, is given a **compile-time initialization** to the value 1. When the loader copies the executable for this program into memory, the location named by I will be given the value 1 before the program begins to run. I remains an ordinary variable, and its value can be changed later; it gets incremented at statement number 1. In this program we could just as well have given I its initial value with an assignment statement, but in §6.5 we will encounter a situation in which compile-time initialization is essential.

3⟹ The PARAMETER statement initializes PI by making it a **parameter constant**. This causes the compiler to substitute the numerical value for the name PI everywhere else in the program, *before translating the source code into machine instructions*. It wouldn't make sense to try changing the value with an assignment statement, because something like PI=4.D0 would end up 3.1415926535897932D0=4.D0, which doesn't make any sense. Parameter constants are used for quantities that should never change, such as constants of geometry. Some high-level languages such as Maple know the values of constants like π, but FORTRAN has to be told.

4⟹ The value of PI is given to 17 significant digits, which is as much precision as can be stored using a REAL*8. The string of digits ends with D0 (that's a zero), to mark the number as a REAL*8 constant. This is similar to the way we declared REAL*4 constants with an E-type exponent in §2.1, and is necessary to ensure that the compiler will use all of the digits. Here are some more examples.

$$
\begin{aligned}
180.\text{D0} &= 180 \\
-57.\text{D-02} &= -.57 \\
6.02\text{D}+23 &= 6.02 \times 10^{23} \\
0.\text{D0} &= 0 \\
1.\text{D0} &= 1
\end{aligned}
$$

Even simple values like zero and one should have D0 appended to tell the compiler they are to be treated as REAL*8 quantities. To denote a REAL*16 constant, replace the D with a Q.

5⟹ The type declarations and the PARAMETER definition are non-executable statements that go *before* the first executable statement.

6⟹ The action begins with the READ, which gets from the user an angle Y measured in degrees of arc. This isn't suitable for our power series formula, which assumes the angle will be measured in radians, so the program next converts the angle to radians (recall that there are π radians in 180 degrees).

7⟹ Now we're ready to add up terms of the series, beginning with $x^1/1!$. If we keep track of the numerator and denominator of each term, we can use those values to find the numerator and denominator of the next term. To start the process, we initialize NUMER and DENOM for the first term, and use them to initialize the sum, F. NUMER is REAL*8, but DENOM was declared to be an INTEGER*4, so to avoid mixing types we must use the DFLOAT function to **float** or convert DENOM to a REAL*8 before dividing to find F. Declaring DENOM to be INTEGER*4 made this code more interesting, but the calculation would have been easier if DENOM had been REAL*8 instead.

8⟹ Next there is a loop, beginning with statement 1 and ending with the IF. Before entering the loop we set NTERM, the number of terms to be used. The term counter I, which was initialized at compile time to 1, gets incremented to 2 right away because we have already found the value of the first term. The test at the bottom of the loop sends the flow of control back to statement 1 until I has reached NTERM.

9⟹ Each term's numerator can be obtained by multiplying the previous term's numerator by $-x^2$, and each term's denominator is (convince yourself) just the previous one multiplied by $(2i-1)(2i-2)$. So the body of the loop consists of finding the next numerator and denominator, dividing to compute the term, and adding it to F. The updating of DENOM uses integer arithmetic, because DENOM is an INTEGER*4.

10⇨ When the test fails, control falls through to the PRINT statement, which reports the approximation F and also the value returned by the library function for the sine of a REAL*8. A function reference like DSIN(X) can appear in the variable list of a PRINT statement just like any other expression.

11⇨ FORTRAN elementary mathematical functions all use the same naming scheme to indicate their precision, so just as DSIN takes a REAL*8 argument and returns a REAL*8 result, we would use DLOG10 for the common log of a REAL*8, QSQRT for the square root of a REAL*16, and so on (see §6.6.1).

Running our program produces the following results.

```
unix[7] a.out
45
 approximate= 0.707106781188698075 exact= 0.707106781186547573
unix[8]
```

The 45 is the angle in degrees, entered by the user and read into Y, and the next line is the output showing F and DSIN's value for the sine.

The sine of 45° is actually .707106781186547524 correct to 18 digits, but we probably introduced some roundoff error in converting the angle to radians. FORTRAN library routines typically implement more sophisticated algorithms than adding up a series [23][85], and almost always return answers that are correct in every bit position, so the **exact** value printed above is probably indeed exact for the angle we actually used. On the other hand, PRINT decided to give us 18 decimal digits when we know from §4.2 that no more than 17 of them (and perhaps as few as 15) can be trusted because of imprecisions in the floating-point number representation. And the answer from DSIN does agree with the correct value to 16 digits.

The larger discrepancy between our approximation and the DSIN answer (they disagree in the 11th digit) is due to the truncation error we introduced by using only 8 terms of the infinite series, and to roundoff errors in our calculation of the terms and their sum.

4.6   Other Data Types

In addition to the integer and real data types introduced so far, we will also need types for representing complex and logical values. Character variables are discussed in §10.

4.6.1   Complex Numbers

To do arithmetic on complex numbers by hand, it is necessary to manipulate the real and imaginary parts separately as in the calculation below.

$$
\begin{aligned}
(1 + 2i) + (3 + 4i)(5 + 6i) &= 1 + 2i + 15 + 18i + 20i + 24i^2 \\
&= (1 + 15 + 24(-1)) + (2 + 18 + 20)i \\
&= -8 + 40i
\end{aligned}
$$

First we find all the cross products. Then, remembering that $i^2 = -1$, we collect real and imaginary terms and simplify. We could do this calculation in a similar way with FORTRAN, using the data types that have already been introduced, by processing the real and imaginary parts separately (as we did in the quadratic equation example of §3). However, FORTRAN also permits complex variables and constants, which can be manipulated using ordinary arithmetic operators and complex versions of the built-in mathematical functions. Usually, this is much more convenient than dealing with the real and imaginary parts separately.

FORTRAN represents a complex number $a + bi$, where $i = \sqrt{-1}$, by storing a and b as two real numbers adjacent in memory. The a and b parts are of the same real type, and that real type determines the complex type as shown in the table below.

complex type	type of parts
COMPLEX*8	REAL*4
COMPLEX*16	REAL*8
COMPLEX*32	REAL*16

Thus, for example, $1 + 2i$ is stored in the COMPLEX*16 data type as two adjacent REAL*8 values 1.D0 and 2.D0. Here is a program that uses COMPLEX*16 numbers to perform the calculation we did by hand above.

```
COMPLEX*16 A/(1.D0,2.D0)/,B,C,D
REAL*8 X/5.D0/,Y/6.D0/
B=(3.D0,4.D0)
C=DCMPLX(X,Y)
D=A+B*C
PRINT *,D
STOP
END
```

The program begins by declaring A, B, C, and D, using a compile-time initialization to set A to the COMPLEX*16 constant (1.D0,2.D0). The parentheses tell the compiler that the values are the real and imaginary parts of a complex number (in that order), signifying $1.D0 + 2.D0i$. Then X and Y are declared REAL*8 and initialized. Next B is set to $3.D0 + 4.D0i$, and the built-in function DCMPLX is used to set C=X+iY. The parentheses notation for a complex constant works only for combining literal numbers or (what is the same thing) parameter constants, not variables, so we could *not* have written C=(X,Y).

With the data on hand, we now find D=A+B*C using the same statement we would use for ordinary real variables, and output the result. Running the program produces the same answer we found by hand, $-8 + 40i$.

```
unix[9] a.out
 (-8.00000000000000000,40.0000000000000000)
```

PRINT * outputs complex numbers, and READ * reads them, in the same parenthesized form that is used for defining complex constants in FORTRAN source code.

Just as real values can be combined to make a complex number, the real and imaginary parts of a complex number can be extracted using built-in functions. These operations can all be viewed as type conversions, and are summarized in the table at the top of the next page.

function	returns	from argument(s)
C=CMPLX(X,Y)	COMPLEX*8	REAL*4
X=REAL(C)	REAL*4	COMPLEX*8
Y=AIMAG(C)	REAL*4	COMPLEX*8
C=DCMPLX(X,Y)	COMPLEX*16	REAL*8
X=DREAL(C)	REAL*8	COMPLEX*16
Y=DIMAG(C)	REAL*8	COMPLEX*16
C=QCMPLX(X,Y)	COMPLEX*32	REAL*16
X=QREAL(C)	REAL*16	COMPLEX*32
Y=QIMAG(C)	REAL*16	COMPLEX*32

The complex versions of the built-in mathematical functions have names that begin with C, as in this program.

```
COMPLEX*16 C,D
REAL*8 PI/3.1415926535897932D0/,X,Y
C=DCMPLX(0.D0,PI)
D=CDEXP(C)
X=DREAL(D)
Y=DIMAG(D)
PRINT *,'exp(pi*i)=',X,' + i',Y
STOP
END
```

The function CDEXP accepts an argument that is COMPLEX*16 (a Complex Double) and returns its exponential as a COMPLEX*16. The program produces the output

```
unix[10] a.out
 exp(pi*i)= -1.00000000000000000  + i 0.122464679914735321E-15
```

which is within roundoff error of the correct result $e^{\pi i} = -1$.

4.6.2   Logicals

We have been using logical conditions in IF statements since §3. In this one

```
    IF(A.GT.B) X=Y
```

the logical expression A.GT.B evaluates to either true or false. Often it is convenient to store and manipulate logical values explicitly, in addition to using them in IF statements, so FORTRAN provides the LOGICAL*4 data type.

Some uses of logical variables and logical constants are illustrated by the program at the top of the next page, which adds up terms of the alternating series

$$x = 1 - \frac{1}{2} + \frac{1}{3} - \frac{1}{4} + \cdots = \sum_{i=1}^{\infty} \frac{(-1)^{i+1}}{i} = \ln 2$$

stopping when either the absolute value of the difference between successive approximations to x is less than .01, or 100 terms have been computed.

The program begins by declaring DONE and EVEN to be of type LOGICAL*4, and a compile-time initialization is used to set DONE to the logical value false. Notice that the logical

```
      LOGICAL*4 DONE/.FALSE./,EVEN
      EVEN=.TRUE.
      I=0
      X=0.
    1 IF(DONE) THEN
        PRINT *,X
        STOP
      ELSE
        I=I+1
        XOLD=X
        EVEN=.NOT.EVEN
        IF(    EVEN) X=X-1./FLOAT(I)
        IF(.NOT.EVEN) X=X+1./FLOAT(I)
        DONE=(ABS(X-XOLD).LT.0.01) .OR. (I.GE.100)
        GO TO 1
      ENDIF
      END
```

constant .FALSE. includes the periods on either end of the word. In the next statement EVEN gets assigned the value of .TRUE., the other logical constant. In some programs it is helpful to put the true and false values into parameter constants having more convenient names, like this.

```
      LOGICAL*4 T,F
      PARAMETER(T=.TRUE.,F=.FALSE.)
```

Next we initialize I and X, and enter the loop that starts at statement 1. On the first iteration DONE is false because of its compile-time initialization, so we do the ELSE clause. This increments the loop counter I, saves the previous value of the sum in XOLD, and adds minus or plus the next term of the series according to whether it is an even-numbered or odd-numbered term. Before each term is added to the sum, EVEN=.NOT.EVEN reverses the logical sense of EVEN. This makes EVEN false for the first term, which has the odd index value I=1. DONE gets the value of the logical expression on the right-hand side of its assignment, which is true if either or both of the stopping criteria are satisfied. The logical expression uses parentheses to remove any ambiguity about the order of the operations, and to make the test a little easier to read. Successive values of X will be alternately higher and lower than the previous value, so the first convergence test must use the absolute value of the difference.

At first it might seem that tests involving logical variables should compare them to the logical constants. For example, in place of statement number 1 we could have written

```
    1 IF(DONE.EQ..TRUE.) THEN
```

This test would also yield the desired result, because if DONE is true then the logical expression DONE.EQ..TRUE. is also true, but the comparison is unnecessary. The condition in an IF must be a logical expression, something that evaluates to true or false, and the variable DONE fits that description all by itself.

4.6.3 Bits and Hexadecimal Numbers

Even though only a single bit is needed to represent a value that is true or false, a LOGICAL*4 quantity occupies a fullword in memory. As discussed in §15.2.2, this inefficient use of space is usually justified because the processor can access the bit at the beginning of a word more quickly than some other bit. However, occasionally it is necessary or convenient to store true or false values in the different bits of a word, or to separately manipulate the individual bits of a numerical value. To permit such **bitwise logical operations**, FORTRAN provides the built-in functions specified in the US Department of Defense document MIL-STD-1753 [24, §2.6.1]. The ones we will use are listed in the table below.

Each of the bitwise logical functions has an argument or arguments of type INTEGER*4 and returns an INTEGER*4 result, but instead of thinking of these values as integers we can regard them as strings of 32 bits. Each bit position in a function value is the result of performing the given operation on the bit(s) from the corresponding position in the argument(s).

function	returns
L=NOT(I)	bitwise NOT
L=ISHFT(I,NBITS)	I shifted left by NBITS bits
L=IAND(I,J)	bitwise AND
L=IOR(I,J)	bitwise OR
L=IEOR(I,J)	bitwise exclusive OR

NOT(I) has a 1 bit wherever I has a 0 bit, and a 0 bit wherever I has a 1 bit. The ISHFT function shifts the argument bit pattern left or right by NBITS bits (or not at all) depending on whether NBITS is positive or negative (or zero), and fills the vacated bit positions with 0 bits. The other functions behave as summarized in this table.

bit in		corresponding bit in		
I	J	IAND(I,J)	IOR(I,J)	IEOR(I,J)
0	0	0	0	0
0	1	0	1	1
1	0	0	1	1
1	1	1	1	0

In the example above we used the logical condition ABS(X-XOLD).LT.0.01 to test for convergence of the log series. This kind of **absolute error** test works fine if we know ahead of time how big the quantities X and XOLD will be because we can use that knowledge in selecting the tolerance. When X and XOLD are on the order of 1, comparing their difference to .01 means "stop when the answer changes by less than about 1%." If X and XOLD were on the order of .001 instead, then asking for a difference less than .01 would not ensure that we got anywhere near the right answer. When the magnitudes of the quantities being compared are not known in advance, a convergence test must be something like ABS((X-XOLD)/X).LT.0.01, based on the **relative error**. Unfortunately, this approach is perilous on account of the division. What if X and XOLD both tend towards zero?

Perhaps these difficulties can be circumvented by using the bitwise logical functions to compare the binary representations of two values directly. In the program at the top of the next page, X and Y are considered close enough if their signs and exponents are the same, and if they agree in the most significant 13 bits of their fractions. This test is insensitive to the scale of the numbers, and cannot fail because of division by zero. The idea is to compare the bits of X and Y, but those are REAL*4 variables and the compiler expects bitwise logical functions to be invoked with INTEGER*4 arguments. The EQUIVALENCE statement at the beginning of the program causes the INTEGER*4 variable I and the REAL*4 variable X to identify the same fullword in memory, so that I has the same bit pattern as X. Similarly,

```
      EQUIVALENCE(I,X),(J,Y)
      INTEGER*4 MASK/Z'FFFFFC00'/
      LOGICAL*4 CONVRG
      X=123.001
      Y=123.002
      K=IEOR(I,J)
      L=IAND(K,MASK)
      CONVRG=(L.EQ.0)
      PRINT *,CONVRG
      STOP
      END
```

J is an INTEGER*4 name for the bit pattern stored in Y. The EQUIVALENCE statement has only a few safe uses, and after this example we won't need it much until §10.

In the IEEE floating-point representation described earlier, the bit patterns for X (that is, I) and Y (otherwise known as J) turn out to be as follows.

```
X=I=01000010111101100000000010000011
Y=J=01000010111101100000000100000110
  K=00000000000000000000000110000101
```

To find where these words disagree, the program uses the exclusive-OR function IEOR, which yields an output bit of 1 wherever the input bits differ. This gives K the value shown above. Only the sign, the 8-bit exponent, and the leftmost 13 fraction bits matter in our comparison, so we need to ignore the rightmost 10 bits in the difference. To do this we use the IAND function between K and a **bit mask**, as follows.

```
   K=00000000000000000000000110000101
MASK=11111111111111111111110000000000
   L=00000000000000000000000000000000
```

The differences between I and J are all in the last 10 bit positions, so the result of the IAND is L=0. This makes the logical expression L.EQ.0 true, so true is the value printed for CONVRG. If there had been a difference farther to the left (such as if K had ended with the pattern 10110000101), then some 1 bit in the difference would have overlapped with a 1 bit of the mask, L would not have come out zero, and CONVRG would have ended up false.

The only thing left to explain about our example program is the peculiar compile-time initialization of MASK. The constant appearing there, Z'FFFFFC00', is a **hexadecimal** or base-16 number. We could have used an ordinary integer instead, but because of the intimate relationship between hex and binary it is easier to set a bit pattern using hex than it is using a decimal value. Hexadecimal numbers are also sometimes used to represent **byte codes** for characters, as we shall see in §10.1. Instead of digits or bits, hexadecimal numbers have **hexits**, which are shown with their decimal equivalents and binary bit patterns in the table on the next page. Stringing together the binary equivalents of the hexits FFFFFC00 yields the bit pattern given above for MASK. The syntax Z' ' tells the compiler that what follows is a hex constant. Each hexit specifies 4 bits, so it takes 2 hexits to specify a byte. Because MASK is an INTEGER*4 variable, the constant used to initialize it is 8 hexits long.

Alas, like the other convergence tests we considered, this one suffers from a fatal flaw (see Exercise 4.10.47). There is no single sure-fire way to test whether two unequal floating-point values are close enough.

hex	decimal	binary
0	0	0000
1	1	0001
2	2	0010
3	3	0011
4	4	0100
5	5	0101
6	6	0110
7	7	0111
8	8	1000
9	9	1001
A	10	1010
B	11	1011
C	12	1100
D	13	1101
E	14	1110
F	15	1111

4.7   Some Special Values

In §4.1 and §4.2, I described the computer representation of integers and real numbers but did not give the bit patterns that are used for floating-point zero, $+\infty$, $-\infty$, and NaN. Now we can finish that story with the table below, which summarizes those and some other special values that FORTRAN programs occasionally need to set or test [27, p9,11].

quantity		hexadecimal	decimal
INTEGER*4	zero	00000000	0
	+1	00000001	1
	−1	FFFFFFFF	−1
	largest +	7FFFFFFF	2147483647
	largest −	80000000	−2147483648
REAL*4	+0	00000000	0.0
	−0	80000000	−0.0
	+1	3F800000	1.0
	−1	BF800000	−1.0
	largest	7F7FFFFF	3.4028235E+38
	smallest normal	00800000	1.1754944E−38
	smallest subnormal	00000001	1.4012985E−45
	infinity +	7F800000	$+\infty$
	infinity −	FF800000	$-\infty$
	NaN	7FFFFFFF	not a number
REAL*8	+0	0000000000000000	0.D0
	−0	8000000000000000	−0.D0
	+1	3FF0000000000000	1.D0
	−1	BFF0000000000000	−1.D0
	largest	7FEFFFFFFFFFFFFF	1.7976931348623157D+308
	smallest normal	0010000000000000	2.2250738585072014D−308
	smallest subnormal	0000000000000001	4.9406564584124654D−324
	infinity +	7FF0000000000000	$+\infty$
	infinity −	FFF0000000000000	$-\infty$
	NaN	7FFFFFFFFFFFFFFF	not a number

The decimals given for the largest and smallest floating-point numbers are of course only approximate, so to specify them you should use their hex values instead. Some compilers require an option to be specified if they are to recognize hexadecimal values in compile-time initializations (g77 is one; see §14.1).

4.8   Architectural Variations

The storage formats I have described in this chapter are the most common by far in modern scientific computers, but they are not the only ones in use. A small fraction of the processors now being manufactured have words longer or shorter than 32 bits, or bytes containing fewer or more than 8 bits. The IBM S/390 architecture, which is still being made and is used by many older machines that remain in service, has a floating-point number format (mentioned in §13.4.2) different from the IEEE standard, and some Cray computers use yet another floating-point format. The Intel Pentium series of processors use an extended-precision number format that is less than 16 bytes long, and because of this some compilers that are used mainly on PC hardware, such as g77, do not support the REAL*16 and COMPLEX*32 data types at all. Thus, although the basic concepts outlined in this chapter hold true for virtually all computers, some of the details might not hold true for your processor if it has an architecture different from the one I have assumed.

A far more common variation is in the ordering of the bytes within the word or doubleword representing a numerical value. The bit patterns shown in §4.1, §4.2, and §4.6.3 don't really specify the order in which the bytes are stored in memory, but to readers of English they probably suggest that the most significant byte, on the left, is at the lowest memory address. This format is called **big-endian**. In a **little-endian** architecture, the byte order is reversed (but *within* each byte the most significant bit is still at the lowest address). This means that scalar data objects longer than one byte are stored differently in memory on machines of differing endian-ness. Characters, as we shall see in §10, are stored one byte at a time, so the first character in a string is at the low-address end on any machine. Integers and real numbers, however, are stored big-end first in big-endian machines and little-end first in little-endian ones. Thus, for example, the value

```
REAL*8 NAN/Z'7FFFFFFFFFFFFFFF'/
```

which represents not-a-number on either architecture, is actually stored as 7FFFFFFFFFFFFFFF on big-endian machines and as FFFFFFFFFFFFFF7F on little-endian ones.

Almost always, the order in which bytes are stored doesn't matter to a FORTRAN programmer, because the compiler knows the architecture it is translating for and makes everything consistent. For example, the compile-time initialization above is coded as shown whether the program is to be run on a big-endian machine or a little-endian machine. But byte order *can* make a difference when characters are stored in variables of other types (discussed in §13.10.1) or when a calculation involves bit manipulations that depend on a particular byte ordering (see Exercise 5.8.35), or when binary data from an unformatted write (discussed in §9.8) are moved between machines that differ in endian-ness. Remembering that byte order can vary between machines and knowing how numbers are actually represented in memory will help you recognize and understand any inconsistencies that may arise in those and other unusual circumstances.

4.9   Omissions

The standard variable types *INTEGER*2* and *LOGICAL*1*; *character variables; non-standard variable types; IMPLICIT; two-part values;* ways to get more precision than REAL*16, such as Brent's Multiple Precision library; IEEE directional rounding; alternate bit patterns for NaN's; IBM S/390, CDC 7600, and other non-IEEE floating-point number representations; other integer number representations; the bit patterns used for LOGICAL*4 variables; interval arithmetic; other built-in type conversion routines; other MIL-STD-1753 bit manipulation routines; implied DO in compile-time data initializations; the algorithms actually used for elementary functions such as $\sin(x)$.

4.10   Exercises

4.10.1   From memory, write down all of the FORTRAN statements introduced so far and describe what each one does.

4.10.2   Some storage increments are defined in §4.1. (a) Others not mentioned there include the **crumb**, which is 2 bits, and the **nybble**, which is 2 crumbs. Starting with bit, crumb, and nybble, list the names of all the memory increments you know corresponding to successive doublings from the bit. (b) A **kilobyte** (KB) is $2^{10} = 1024$ bytes, and a **megabyte** (MB) is 1024 KB. How many bits are in a megabyte?

4.10.3   Computer random-access memory or RAM is now cheap, but the first large memories were very expensive; an early IBM mass storage unit had a capacity of one megabyte and sold for one million dollars. In contrast, haircuts are now expensive, but they used to be cheap; an old song advertises "Shave and a haircut, two bits." (a) Based only on this information, what should have been the actual cost of a shave and a haircut back then, in cents? (b) How much money do people usually mean when they say "two bits?" (c) About how much does RAM cost today, per byte? Explain how you got your answer.

4.10.4   What is the largest positive value that can be stored in an INTEGER*4 variable?

4.10.5   Run the following program and explain its output.

```
I=IFIX(2.E+9)
J=150000000
K=I+J
PRINT *,K
STOP
END
```

4.10.6   As explained in §4.1, a negative integer N is represented by the 2's complement of -N, which is $2^{32}+N$. Show that the 2's complement of a binary number can also be obtained by flipping all of the bits and then adding 1.

4.10.7   Find the bit pattern and the numerical value resulting from each of the following INTEGER*4 calculations: (a) -2147483648+(-2147483648); (b) 2147483647+2147483647.

4.10.8 The bit pattern 10111101110000000000000000000000 defines a normalized **REAL*4** quantity. (a) What is the value represented? (b) How many decimal digits of precision are represented?

4.10.9 A bit pattern must be interpreted in different ways depending on the type of data it represents. (a) The integer value 19 has an **INTEGER*4** bit pattern given in §4.1. If this bit pattern is interpreted as a **REAL*4** number, what is its value? (b) Interpret the **REAL*4** bit pattern for the number 3.1 as an **INTEGER*4**.

4.10.10 In §4.2 it is explained that the bit pattern for a **REAL*8** is similar to that for a **REAL*4** except for having more exponent bits, more fraction bits, and a different exponent bias. Diagram the bit pattern for a **REAL*8** value.

4.10.11 Find the bit pattern that represents 5.5 as a normalized IEEE **REAL*4** number.

4.10.12 Write a program to verify the correctness of the hex codes given in the table of §4.7.

4.10.13 When the following statement is executed,

```
IF(X .GT. 0.D0) GO TO 1
```

is the branch taken if **X** turns out to be a **REAL*8** NaN? If so, explain why; if not, explain why not.

4.10.14 A constant that is written without a D is regarded by most FORTRAN compilers as a **REAL*4** value even if it is stated with more than 7 significant digits. Inadvertently omitting the D can therefore result in an unintended loss of precision called a **precision leak**. (a) Running the program on the left on a certain computer yields the output shown on the right. Explain why the first two values are correct to only 8 digits.

```
REAL*8 PI
PI=3.1415926535897932
PRINT *,PI                          3.14159274101257324
PI=DBLE(3.1415926535897932)
PRINT *,PI                          3.14159274101257324
PI=3.1415926535897932D0
PRINT *,PI                          3.14159265358979312
```

(b) In the last number printed out, does the trailing 2 mean anything? Why is the next digit to the left a 1 rather than a 2? Explain. (c) Run the program on your computer to see how your compiler treats constants without a D. If it happens to be smart enough to use all the digits you supply, does that mean that you can stop worrying and leave out the D? Explain.

4.10.15 It is desired to calculate the quantity

$$z = \frac{98000xy}{xy + 1000}$$

Does the following FORTRAN statement, which is syntactically correct, perform the desired calculation?

```
Z=(9.8D+04*X*Y)/(X*Y+1.D0+03)
```

If so, confirm it by experiment for $x = 3.1$ and $y = -4.5$; if not, explain why not and correct the code.

4.10.16 A and B are defined below [86, §1.2] for $x \neq 0$ and $\cos(x) \neq -1$.

$$A = \frac{1 - \cos(x)}{x^2} \qquad B = \frac{\sin^2 x}{x^2[1 + \cos(x)]}$$

(a) Show that, algebraically, $A = B$. (b) Find $\lim_{x\to 0} A = \lim_{x\to 0} B$ and $\lim_{x\to\pi} A = \lim_{x\to\pi} B$ analytically. Hint: use L'Hospital's Rule. (c) Write a FORTRAN program that uses REAL*4 calculations to find A and B for $x = 0.1, 0.01, \ldots, 0.00000001$, and print A and B side by side. What happens as x gets smaller, and why? (d) Repeat the comparison for $x = \pi + 0.1, \pi + 0.01, \ldots, \pi + 0.000001$, and contrast the output to that obtained before. (e) Rewrite the program to use REAL*8 calculations. Now what happens?

4.10.17 Solve Exercise 3.8.17 parts (b) and (c) using REAL*8 arithmetic. How does the graph of the error in the approximation versus n compare with the graph you got using REAL*4 arithmetic?

4.10.18 Write a program that uses the quadratic formula to solve the equation $ax^2 + bx + c = 0$ for x, with $a = 1$, $b = 100.01$, and $c = 1$. How closely do the x values you found satisfy the equation? Compare the results using REAL*8 calculations to those you get using REAL*4.

4.10.19 Show that, as claimed in §4.5, the denominator of the i'th term in the sine series is the previous denominator multiplied by $(2i - 1)(2i - 2)$.

4.10.20 Modify the sine example to print out its successive approximations to the function value. (a) Can you get an answer closer to the correct function value by increasing the number of terms used? If not, why not? (b) Further modify the program to make DENOM a real variable. Can you get a more accurate answer now? (c) Study the behavior of the program when the value read in for Y is 1350 degrees of arc. How can you modify the code to work better for large angles?

4.10.21 The following function is defined for $\alpha \leq 1$.

$$\phi = \left(1 - \alpha + \frac{1}{2\pi} \sin(2\pi\alpha)\right)^{3/2}$$

(a) Write a program that evaluates ϕ at 101 values of α evenly spaced from -1 to $+1$, and writes out each value of α and the corresponding value of ϕ. Use REAL*8 arithmetic for all the floating-point calculations. You might find it handy to use built-in functions such as DFLOAT and DSIN. (b) At $\alpha = 1$, the quantity inside the outer parentheses in the formula for ϕ might turn out to be slightly negative on account of roundoff errors. Modify your program so that this artifact of floating-point arithmetic does not result in the program reporting a NaN for the final value of ϕ.

4.10.22 It has been observed [71] [9, §4.2.4B] that in many collections of naturally occurring numerical values, such as tables of physical constants or stock prices, the frequency of occurrence of the leading digit d is closely approximated by **Benford's Law**, $\log_{10}(1 + \frac{1}{d})$, $d = 1, \ldots, 9$. Thus the leading digit 1 occurs more frequently than the leading digit 2, and so on. (a) Write a FORTRAN program to print a table of these digit frequencies and check whether they add up to approximately 1. (b) Prove or disprove that

$$\sum_{d=1}^{9} \log_{10}\left(1 + \frac{1}{d}\right) = 1$$

4.10.23 The exponential function e^x has a series expansion $e^x = \sum_{k=0}^{\infty} x^k/k!$. (a) Write a program to evaluate e^x by adding up terms of the series until the answer stops changing.

Use REAL*8 numbers throughout. (b) Run your program to approximate e^{-10}, and compare the result to that returned by the built-in function DEXP. Can you explain the discrepancy? (c) Try using REAL*4 and REAL*16 numbers instead, and compare the results to those you obtained using REAL*8. Is there a roundoff error problem with this calculation? (d) Now try finding e^{+10} and taking its reciprocal. Can you explain why this works better?

4.10.24 The n'th **harmonic number** is defined as $\sum_{i=1}^{n} 1/i$. Write a program to find the first harmonic number greater than 10. Does your answer depend on the order in which you add up the terms?

4.10.25 There is no built-in FORTRAN function for $\log_2 x$. (a) Write a code segment to compute $Y = \log_2(X)$ assuming X and Y are REAL*8. (b) Write a code segment using floating-point calculations to compute $L = \lfloor \log_2(I) \rfloor$ where I and L are INTEGER*4 variables and $\lfloor y \rfloor$ is the largest integer less than or equal to y. (c) Write a code segment to compute $L = \lfloor \log_2(I) \rfloor$ *without* using any floating-point calculations.

4.10.26 Write a program to approximate the largest value of EPS, a REAL*8 quantity, such that 1.D0+EPS evaluates to 1.D0.

4.10.27 If the result of an IEEE floating-point operation is too big to store, it gets set to the bit pattern for the correctly-signed infinity and execution of the program continues. This behavior might be desirable for most of the arithmetic operations in a program but unwanted in some cases. Assuming REAL*8 variables, write code segments to (a) output an error message and stop the program if the calculation of C=A+B is about to overflow; (b) set the result to the bit pattern for the correctly-signed maximum value and continue, if F=D/E is about to overflow.

4.10.28 Exercise 3.8.21 suggests two different ways of determining whether the real variables F and FL have the same sign:

```
IF(FL*F .LT. 0.) GO TO 1
IF((FL.GT.0..AND.F.LT.0.).OR.(FL.LT.0..AND.F.GT.0.)) GO TO 2
```

For what values of F and FL are these tests precisely equivalent?

4.10.29 Which result, F or G, most closely approximates $\frac{ac}{bd}$? Explain.

```
REAL*4 A/1.E-23/,B/2.E+23/,C/3.E+19/,D/4.E-19/
F=(A/B)*(C/D)
G=(A*C)/(B*D)
```

4.10.30 The average $\bar{x}$ of N numbers x_i can be found from $\bar{x} = \frac{1}{N} \sum_{i=1}^{N} x_i$, or [9, p216] by using **Knuth's recursion** $\bar{x} \leftarrow \bar{x} + (x_i - \bar{x})/i$, $i = 1, \ldots, N$. (a) Write a FORTRAN program that implements Knuth's recursion and test it to prove that it computes the average correct to within roundoff. (b) What are the advantages of using Knuth's recursion? What are the drawbacks? (c) Derive the recursion.

4.10.31 In §4.4 we used type conversion routines to compute the integer closest to the positive ratio of the whole numbers represented by two integers. (a) Write a code segment that uses only integer arithmetic and comparisons to accomplish this task. (b) Modify the code given in §4.4 so that it works no matter what sign the ratio has.

4.10.32 Write FORTRAN statements to convert (a) a REAL*8 variable to an INTEGER*4; (b) a COMPLEX*8 variable to a COMPLEX*16.

4.10.33 The FORTRAN program below adds up dollar amounts using real variables.

```
      SUM=0.
    1 PRINT *,'enter the next value'
      READ *,V
      IF(V.NE.0.) THEN
         SUM=SUM+V
         GO TO 1
      ELSE
         PRINT *,SUM
         STOP
      ENDIF
      END
```

(a) Explain why this program does not always yield results that are accurate to the penny.
(b) Suggest a way of rewriting the calculation so that the results are always correct.

4.10.34 Sometimes code involving complex numbers can be made typographically simpler and more obvious by defining a constant I to have the value $\sqrt{-1}$. (a) What is printed by the following program, and why?

```
      COMPLEX*16 I,Z
      PARAMETER(I=(0.D0,1.D0))
      Z=2.D0+3.D0*I
      PRINT *,Z,I*I
      STOP
      END
```

(b) Does this program violate our rule against mixing types in an expression? Explain.
(c) Recode the program to perform the same calculations and write the same output, *without* using a constant set to the value $\sqrt{-1}$.

4.10.35 Write a program to compute i^i, where $i = \sqrt{-1}$.

4.10.36 The three cube roots of 1 are 1, $\frac{1}{2}(-1 + i\sqrt{3})$, and $\frac{1}{2}(-1 - i\sqrt{3})$, where $i = \sqrt{-1}$. Confirm this by writing a FORTRAN program that raises each of the last two expressions to the third power.

4.10.37 Write a code segment to find the complex conjugate $a - bi$ of the value $a + bi$ in a COMPLEX*16 variable named Z.

4.10.38 Write a code segment to compute $(a + bi)/(c + di)$, where $i = \sqrt{-1}$, *without* using any complex variables.

4.10.39 The transfer function of a second-order linear dynamic system is

$$H(j\omega) = \frac{\omega_0^2}{-\omega^2 + 2j\zeta\omega_0\omega + \omega_0^2}$$

where $j = \sqrt{-1}$ (in electrical engineering, j rather than i is used for the imaginary unit). The **magnitude** of a complex number $a + jb$ is

$$|a + jb| = \sqrt{a^2 + b^2}$$

Write a program that outputs $|H(j\omega)|$ for $\zeta = 0.05$ and values of the ratio $\omega/\omega_0 = 0.1, 0.2, \ldots, 10$. This data could be used in making a frequency-response or **Bode plot** for the linear system.

4.10.40 The quadratic formula program of §3.4 handles the real and imaginary parts of a complex root separately. (a) Rewrite the program to use complex variables instead. (b) Generalize the program to accept complex values for the coefficients a, b, and c, and test it using an example whose solution you can find analytically.

4.10.41 Modify the logarithm example of §4.6.2 to eliminate the logical variable EVEN, and to use REAL*8 floating-point values.

4.10.42 Simplify the following statements.

```
IF(.TRUE.) X=Y
IF(A.GT.B.OR.(.NOT..FALSE.)) B=A
```

4.10.43 The **exclusive-OR** of two logical values A and B is true if A is true and B is false, or if B is true and A is false. If neither A nor B is true, or if both are true, then their exclusive-OR is false. (a) Write a FORTRAN statement that uses the logical operators .AND., .OR., and .NOT. to set the LOGICAL*4 variable EXOR to the exclusive-OR of the LOGICAL*4 variables A and B. (b) If I and J contain the bit patterns your compiler uses to represent logical values, does IEOR(I,J) happen to return a bit pattern that corresponds to the logical value of their exclusive-OR?

4.10.44 The bit pattern 10101010101010101010101010101010 could be defined by what hex constant? What decimal value could be used to initialize an INTEGER*4 to this bit pattern?

4.10.45 Write a code segment that sets the LOGICAL*4 variable NML to .TRUE. if the REAL*4 value in X is normalized, and to .FALSE. otherwise.

4.10.46 To study how the numerical accuracy of a certain algorithm varies with the precision of the calculations, it is desired to degrade the precision of a particular variable in the algorithm from 52 fraction bits (REAL*8 precision) to 37 fraction bits (about halfway between REAL*8 and REAL*4). Write a code segment to illustrate how this can be done by using bitwise logical operations to set the least-significant 15 bits of the fraction to zero.

4.10.47 (a) What is the fatal flaw in the bit-comparison approach to testing whether two real numbers are close enough? Hint: are the smallest normalized positive value and the smallest normalized negative value close to each other? (b) Another error measure that tries to avoid the problems of the absolute and relative measures is

$$\frac{|x - x_{old}|}{1 + |x|}$$

This measure behaves like relative error when $|x|$ is large and like absolute error when $|x|$ is small. Are there circumstances in which it is also misleading?

4.10.48 On a computer that is working properly any calculation starting from fixed input data yields results that are entirely deterministic and repeatable, so a program cannot be used to generate numbers that are truly random. However, it *is* possible to generate a sequence of **pseudorandom numbers** that is statistically indistinguishable from a truly random sequence, and the numbers in such a sequence are often referred to loosely as random numbers. A simple and often-used method of generating pseudorandom numbers is [9, §3.2.1] the **mixed congruential algorithm** $x \leftarrow (ax + b) \bmod 2^{31}$, where x, a, and b are all integers. The result of $i \bmod j$ is just the remainder from whole-number division, so for example 17 mod 3 = 2. The algorithm thus computes each number in the pseudorandom sequence by multiplying the previous number by a, adding b, and then finding the remainder when the result is divided by 2^{31}. Good results are said [5, p246] to be obtained by using

$a = 843314861$ and $b = 453816693$. The starting value of x or **seed** should be a large positive odd integer. (a) Within what range of values will iterates be generated by the mixed congruential algorithm? (b) If a fixed-point overflow occurs in computing a product or sum of INTEGER*4 quantities, how is the result related to the true product or sum modulo 2^{31}? Explain how $(ax + b) \bmod 2^{31}$ can be found by using ordinary integer arithmetic and without explicitly invoking a modulus function. Hint: the bitwise logical AND of the byte pattern 7FFFFFFF with an integer sets the sign bit to zero but leaves the other bits alone. (c) Write and run a FORTRAN program that uses the algorithm to compute integers in the pseudorandom sequence beginning with the seed 123457. (d) How many numbers are generated before the sequence repeats? This is called the **period** of the generator. Does the starting value 123457 repeat?

5

Arrays and DO Loops

The variables and constants we have used so far have all been **scalars**, single values. Many engineering and scientific calculations also involve vectors and matrices, which are rectangular arrays of numbers. For representing vectors and matrices, FORTRAN provides a data structure called the **array**. An array is an ordered list of scalar **elements**, each of which can be referred to by its location in the array. Arrays follow the usual variable naming rules.

The manipulation of arrays typically requires looping to perform the same operation on a sequence of elements. In earlier chapters we saw several examples of looping, and in all of them the repetition was controlled by initializing a loop counter, incrementing and testing its value, and transferring control back to the top of the loop until no more iterations remain to be done. A **free loop** of that kind is necessary in a few circumstances, but FORTRAN provides another construct called the DO **loop** that is simpler and easier to use most of the time.

5.1   Vectors

The elements of an array must all have the same scalar data type, and that is the type of the array. This program uses an array to represent a vector.

```
      REAL*8 X(5),SUM
      READ *,X
      SUM=0.D0
      I=1
1     SUM=SUM+X(I)
      I=I+1
      IF(I.LE.5) GO TO 1
      PRINT *,SUM
      STOP
      END
```

The program adds up the elements of the vector X. The first line declares the size or **dimension** of the vector by appending "(5)" to the name given in the type statement. There are 5 elements in X, each a REAL*8 scalar. The READ expects the user to enter 5 values, in order from element 1 through element 5. Then the SUM is initialized to zero.

Next we find a loop. The counter I is initialized to 1, incremented by the assignment I=I+1 at the end of each iteration, and tested at the IF statement to determine whether enough iterations have been done. In each iteration, the Ith element of X is added to SUM, so when the loop control test fails SUM will contain X(1)+X(2)+X(3)+X(4)+X(5). The Ith element of X is referred to in the executable part of the code as X(I). In this example the **subscript** of X is the loop counter I, but any integer expression is permissible as a subscript.

In the declaration of the array, X(5) means the vector has 5 elements, but in the executable code of the program X(5) would refer to the single 5th element of X.

In Classical FORTRAN the elements of an array are stored in contiguous memory locations, so X occupies a total of 5 adjacent doublewords. An element outside the dimensions of an array, such as X(0) or X(6) in our example, is a memory location that is probably occupied by some other variable in the program or by the machine code for the executable statements themselves (or perhaps even by something that belongs to the operating system or another user). If your program inadvertently tries to use array elements outside the dimensioned size of the array, then depending on what those memory locations contain and who owns them you might get a nasty message from UNIX™ or just incorrect results without any indication that something went wrong. Such array **subscript overflows** must therefore be zealously guarded against by carefully checking the array-indexing logic of your code. *Don't refer to elements outside the dimensioned size of an array.* As discussed in §14.1.2, many FORTRAN compilers have an option that enables automatic run-time checking of array subscripts.

5.2   The DO Loop

To initialize, increment, and test the index of a free loop takes three FORTRAN statements, and some care is needed to get the branching logic right. This seems like a lot of trouble when in our example all we wanted to do was make I count 1, 2, 3, 4, 5.
Many free loops follow the same pattern as ours,

```
      initialize loop counter
   1     body of loop
      increment loop counter
      if(not done yet) GO TO 1
```

or one that is logically equivalent. The DO **loop** is a FORTRAN construct that implements this pattern in a concise and convenient way. Using it, the program of §5.1 can be rewritten like this.

```
      REAL*8 X(5),SUM
      READ *,X
      SUM=0.D0
      DO 1 I=1,5
          SUM=SUM+X(I)
    1 CONTINUE
      PRINT *,SUM
      STOP
      END
```

The loop now begins with the DO 1 and extends through the 1 CONTINUE, which match up because the 1 in the DO 1 is the statement number in the 1 CONTINUE. The **body** of this loop is the single statement SUM=SUM+X(I), but a DO loop can have any number of statements in its body. The DO, the body, and the CONTINUE together make up the **range** of the loop.

Each statement in the range of the loop is executed repeatedly with the DO variable or **index**, I, equal to 1, 2, 3, 4, and 5 successively. The part of the DO statement that says "I=1,5" specifies that the index I starts at the **lower limit** of 1 and cannot exceed the **upper limit** of 5.

The amount that is added to the index on each iteration is called the **increment** of the loop. A loop increment can be specified by appending a comma and the increment value to the DO statement, so our example would do the same calculation if we wrote DO 1 I=1,5,1 instead. If the increment is not specified it defaults to 1. If we had wanted to compute X(1)+X(3)+X(5) we could have written DO 1 I=1,5,2 to specify an increment of 2. In Classical FORTRAN the DO variable, lower limit, upper limit, and increment must all be integers. The index must be a scalar variable, but the limits and increment can be constants, variables, or expressions and may be or involve array elements that are not changed in the loop.

When the increment of a DO loop is not 1, the index might never take on the value of the upper limit. If we had said DO 1 I=1,5,3 then I would have taken on only the values 1 and 4, because adding the increment again would make I bigger than the upper limit. If the lower limit is bigger than the upper limit, the increment can be negative, in which case the loop counts down instead of up. If we had written DO 1 I=5,1,-1 then I would have taken on the values 5, 4, 3, 2, 1. The increment of a DO loop can't be zero.

If the increment is positive and the upper limit is less than the lower limit, then the behavior of the DO loop depends on which version of the language standard your compiler obeys. Most FORTRAN-66 compilers generate machine code that does one iteration or **pass** of the loop; code from a FORTRAN-77 compiler skips the loop entirely. Some badly-written old programs depend on the FORTRAN-66 behavior, so all modern compilers provide a switch to get it instead of the FORTRAN-77 behavior. Negative DO increments were not allowed by FORTRAN-66, so if a loop increment is negative and the lower limit is less than the upper limit, the programmer probably intended the loop to be skipped. Whenever you are writing new code in which the loop limits might be out of order, test them before the loop so that you can do the right thing independently of which convention the compiler happens to follow.

Free loops, because they are hand-wrought and therefore dependent on the programmer to get the branching logic right, sometimes turn out to be **endless loops**, like the one shown below.

```
      REAL*8 X(5),SUM
      READ *,X
      SUM=0.D0
      I=1
    1    SUM=SUM+X(I)
      I=I-1
      IF(I.LE.5) GO TO 1
      PRINT *,SUM
      STOP
      END
```

This is just our first program damaged by a typo that turned a plus sign into a minus sign. Now I becomes negative, and the IF never fails. (Well, not quite never; see Exercise 5.8.26.) It is much more difficult to get a DO loop wrong in such a way that it is endless, so a DO loop is effectively **bounded** by its limits. *Never use a free loop when you can use a* DO *loop instead.*

5.3   Matrices

To represent a matrix, FORTRAN uses an array having two dimensions. The code below fills up the array MAT, giving each element a different value.

```
      INTEGER*4 MAT(2,3)
      DO 1 J=1,3
          DO 2 I=1,2
              MAT(I,J)=(5*I)+(7*J)
  2       CONTINUE
  1 CONTINUE
      :
```

The array's size is again specified in parentheses after its name in the type declaration, but now there are two dimensions. The number of rows in MAT is the leftmost number, 2, and the number of columns is the second dimension, 3. Arrays having more than two dimensions can be specified simply by using a longer comma-separated list (all compilers recognize at least 3 dimensions, and most up to 7), but in engineering and scientific computing 3 dimensions are needed only rarely and more than 3 almost never.

The number of dimensions an array has is called its **rank**, the number of elements in a dimension is called the dimension's **extent**, the product of an array's extents is its **size**, and an ordered list of the extents can be used to describe the array's **shape**. In the example above, MAT has rank 2, extents of 2 and 3, a size of 6 elements, and the shape (2,3). The parenthesized list we append to the array name in order to declare its dimensions is technically just the array's shape.

The DO 1 loop has for its body the DO 2 loop, so the DO 2 loop is said to be **nested** inside the DO 1 loop. The entire I loop gets repeated 3 times, first with J equal to 1, then with J equal to 2, and finally with J equal to 3. Each time the DO 2 loop is executed, I runs from 1 to 2 all over again. When loops in a nest have adjacent CONTINUE statements, a single CONTINUE can be used instead, like this.

```
      INTEGER*4 MAT(2,3)
      DO 1 J=1,3
      DO 1 I=1,2
          MAT(I,J)=(5*I)+(7*J)
  1 CONTINUE
      :
```

This code is precisely equivalent to the first version; the nesting works just the same whether we use separate CONTINUE statements or a shared one. Although the DO statements now refer to the same statement number, the inside one is still repeated 3 times with J equal to 1, then 2, and finally 3.

Either code segment assigns the elements of MAT in the same order as if we had instead written the sequence of assignment statements shown on the right below, and yields the matrix shown on the left.

$$MAT = \begin{bmatrix} 12 & 19 & 26 \\ 17 & 24 & 31 \end{bmatrix}$$

```
MAT(1,1)=5*1+7*1
MAT(2,1)=5*2+7*1
MAT(1,2)=5*1+7*2
MAT(2,2)=5*2+7*2
MAT(1,3)=5*1+7*3
MAT(2,3)=5*2+7*3
```

Computer memory is strictly linear, with one byte following another like the boxcars in a railroad train, so there is no natural way to store two-dimensional data. The elements of a matrix (or of an array having more than two dimensions) must be stored in a one-dimensional sequence of consecutive memory locations. The six adjacent fullwords that MAT occupies in our example are thus arranged side by side in a line, *not* in the rectangular pattern suggested by the mathematical notation on the left above.

FORTRAN stores arrays in **column-major order**, with the top of the first column at the lowest memory address, the top of the second column head-to-toe after the bottom of the first column, and so forth. In our example the elements of MAT are stored like this.

MAT(1,1)	MAT(2,1)	MAT(1,2)	MAT(2,2)	MAT(1,3)	MAT(2,3)	
12	17	19	24	26	31	
3492	3496	3500	3504	3508	3512	3516

Here we see a six-word piece of memory where MAT is stored, beginning at the hypothetical address 3492 (bytes). The second element of the array starts 4 bytes later, at 3496, and subsequent elements follow in successive fullwords. The three columns of the array are transposed and laid out one after another, which arranges the elements in the order that would be obtained by stepping through the array subscripts with the *inner subscript varying most rapidly,* as in the code segments shown above.

5.4   The Rules of DO Loops

The syntax of DO loops should be clear by now from the discussion in §5.2 and from the examples, but there are some important facts about the semantics of the construct that need further explanation.

Loops may nest, but must not cross. In the previous section we saw an example of nested loops. The code on the left below is legal, but that on the right is not.

```
C     this is a nest of loops          C     this is nonsense
      DO 1 J=1,3                              DO 1 J=1,3
      DO 2 I=1,2                              DO 2 I=1,2
          MAT(I,J)=0                              MAT(I,J)=0
    2 CONTINUE                             1 CONTINUE
    1 CONTINUE                             2 CONTINUE
```

Branches out are allowed, but not branches in. The code on the left below terminates the loop prematurely by branching out when a negative value is found.

```
C     this is ok                        C     this is illegal
      DO 3 K=1,10                              IF(A.EQ.1.) GO TO 5
          IF(NDX(K).LT.0) GO TO 4                B=3.
          NDX(K)=3                               DO 6 J=1,3
    3 CONTINUE                             5         X(J)=B
    4 ...                                  6 CONTINUE
```

On the right, the test can branch into the body of the loop from outside, in which case control does not flow through the DO statement and the value of J is undefined. The branch on the left below just skips to the next value of L if IDY(L) is negative, but the one on the right is into the range of the loop.

```
C     this is ok              C     this is illegal
      DO 7 L=3,7,2                  IF(A.EQ.1.) GO TO 6
          IF(IDY(L).LT.0) GO TO 7   B=3.
          S=S-IDY(L)                 DO 6 J=1,3
    7 CONTINUE                          X(J)=B
                                     6 CONTINUE
```

A branch to the CONTINUE statement of a loop is permitted from within the body of the loop, but not from outside.

The DO index is undefined outside the loop. The code on the left below assumes that after the loop J will have the last value that it took on in the loop, N. Depending on how the compiler implements the test-and-branch for controlling the loop, J might actually be N+1 or even zero, so it cannot safely be assumed to have any particular value.

```
C     this is risky           C     this works for sure
      T=0.D0                         T=0.D0
      DO 8 J=1,N                     DO 8 J=1,N
          T=T+X(J)                       T=T+X(J)
    8 CONTINUE                     8 CONTINUE
      AVG=T/DFLOAT(J)                AVG=T/DFLOAT(N)
```

The code on the right above avoids this ambiguity and also makes it more obvious what the programmer had in mind. The DO index must also be assumed to become undefined after branching out of the range of a loop, as in the code on the left below. On the right, M is copied into the non-index variable MSAVE, which retains its value outside the range of the loop.

```
C     this is risky           C     this works for sure
      DO 9 M=1,N                     DO 9 M=1,N
          IF(X(M).GT.P) GO TO 8          MSAVE=M
    9 CONTINUE                            IF(X(M).GT.P) GO TO 8
    8 I=M+3                        9 CONTINUE
                                   8 I=MSAVE+3
```

The DO index must not be modified in the body of the loop. In using a DO rather than a free loop, we relinquish not only responsibility for managing the counter but also the right to change it. The code on the left below has unpredictable behavior and is disallowed by most compilers.

```
C     index is changed in the body   C     index is only used
      DO 10 M=1,4                           DO 10 M=1,3,2
          Y(M)=A                                Y(M)=A
          M=M+1                                 Y(M+1)=B
          Y(M)=B                       10 CONTINUE
   10 CONTINUE
```

The intent of the code on the left is apparently to assign Y(1)=A, Y(2)=B, Y(3)=A, Y(4)=B. The code on the right does that, without modifying M. The limits and increment also must not be modified in the body; these are part of the loop control logic and off limits just like the index.

5.5 Array Dimensioning

All the array declarations we have used so far simply specified the number of elements in each dimension. For example,

```
REAL*8 BIG(100)
```

describes a vector of 100 elements, which are assumed to be numbered starting with 1. We can refer to these elements as BIG(1), BIG(2), ..., BIG(100).

Occasionally it is more natural to number array elements starting with a value other than 1. To permit this, FORTRAN provides a different syntax for specifying the range of index values in each dimension. If we would rather number the elements of BIG from 0 to 99, we can instead declare

```
REAL*8 BIG(0:99)
```

Now the elements are BIG(0), BIG(1), ..., BIG(99). The subscript limits can be any integers, as long as the maximum value is not less than the minimum. Here are some more examples.

```
REAL*4 WEIRD(100,-37:5)
INTEGER*4 LMN(1:10)              INTEGER*4 LMN(10)
```

The top declaration makes WEIRD a two-dimensional array whose first index varies from 1 to 100 and whose second index has values −37, −36, ..., 5. The second declaration is equivalent to the simpler version on the right.

Classical FORTRAN allocates the storage for arrays at the time an executable is loaded into memory, before the program begins running. That means *the size of an array is fixed at compilation* and cannot be made to depend on a value that is determined at run time. For example, the code on the left below is illegal.

```
C     this is forbidden          C     do this instead
      READ *,N                          INTEGER*4 VARIES(1000)
      INTEGER*4 VARIES(N)               READ *,N
         :                               IF(N.GT.1000) STOP
                                            :
```

The array declaration is not executable and should appear typographically *before* the READ statement in the source text, so the program on the left is syntactically incorrect. It is also semantically wrong, because the space for VARIES must be determined temporally *before* N becomes known. If the size of an array depends on input data, the array must be dimensioned big enough for the largest problem that is contemplated, as shown on the right above. Then, before undertaking to solve each problem it is prudent to test whether the input data are going to fit in the array.

A fixed allocation of storage can be shared among several different arrays that individually vary in size, as we shall see in §11.2, and Fortran-90 provides for dynamic memory allocation as discussed in §17.1.2, but simple programs written in Classical FORTRAN typically fix the dimensions of each array. If a program contains several arrays whose dimensions must be changed (we hope infrequently) to accommodate problems of different sizes, editing the source text can be tedious and error-prone. The code on the left below works for problems having N no more than 10. To make it accommodate problems having N up to 100 requires some hand calculation and the revision of three dimensions, and comments are needed as a reminder of how the various array dimensions depend on the maximum value allowed for N.

```
C              N      2N                    PARAMETER(N=10)
      REAL*8 X(10),Y(20)                    PARAMETER(M=2*N,L=N*(N+1)/2)
C                   N(N+1)/2                REAL*8 X(N),Y(M)
      INTEGER*4 Z(55)                       INTEGER*4 Z(L)
          :
```

In the code on the right the second PARAMETER statement computes the dimensions that depend on N, so the program can be resized by changing only the value of N itself. Recall from §4.5 that parameter constants such as N, M, and L in this example are replaced by their numerical values during compilation, so by the time the code on the right gets translated into machine language the dimensions of the arrays are numbers.

5.6   Case Study: Matrix Multiplication

To illustrate the use of arrays and DO loops, we will calculate this matrix product:

$$\begin{bmatrix} 1 & 4 & 7 \\ 2 & 5 & 8 \\ 3 & 6 & 9 \end{bmatrix} \begin{bmatrix} 4 & -1 \\ -2 & 5 \\ 6 & -3 \end{bmatrix} = \begin{bmatrix} 38 & -2 \\ 46 & -1 \\ 54 & 0 \end{bmatrix}$$

If $\mathbf{A}$ is a matrix with m rows and n columns having elements $a_{i,k}$, and $\mathbf{B}$ is a matrix with n rows and p columns having elements $b_{k,j}$, then the product matrix $\mathbf{C} = \mathbf{AB}$ has elements

$$c_{i,j} = \sum_{k=1}^{n} a_{i,k} b_{k,j}, \quad i = 1, \ldots, m, \ j = 1, \ldots, p$$

You should convince yourself that you understand how this formula yields the result matrix shown above. Here is a program that does the calculation.

```
      INTEGER*4 P
      PARAMETER(M=3,N=3,P=2)
      REAL*4 A(M,N)/1.,2.,3.,4.,5.,6.,7.,8.,9./
      REAL*4 B(N,P)/4.,-2.,6.,-1.,5.,-3./,C(M,P)/6*0.0/
      DO 1 I=1,M
      DO 1 J=1,P
          DO 2 K=1,N
              C(I,J)=C(I,J)+A(I,K)*B(K,J)
    2     CONTINUE
    1 CONTINUE
      PRINT *,C(1,1),C(1,2)
      PRINT *,C(2,1),C(2,2)
      PRINT *,C(3,1),C(3,2)
      STOP
      END
```

1⇨ The same values must be used as both array extents and DO limits, so they are defined as the parameter constants M, N, and P rather than as integer literals. The first dimension of A is supposed to have the same value as the limit on the I loop, and using the symbol M for both, rather than numbers, ensures that a typographical mistake won't leave the values different; likewise for the repeated uses of N and P. Using parameter constants also distinguishes M from N even though they happen to have the same value, which makes it easier to verify that the array dimensions and program logic make sense. The default naming rules would consider P a real number, so it must be declared INTEGER*4.

2⇨ Compile-time initializations are used to get the problem data into arrays A and B. The values must be listed in the same column-major order that will be used to store them in memory. The result array C is set to zeros with a compile-time initialization that uses a **repetition factor** 6* rather than writing out 0.0,0.0,0.0,0.0,0.0,0.0.

3⇨ The calculation of the C(I,J)s is performed by a nest of three DO loops. The I and J loops share a CONTINUE because it is convenient to think of them as working together to step I and J through all possible combinations, addressing the elements of C one by one. The DO 1 statements could be exchanged without affecting the results because the calculation does not depend on the *order* in which the elements of C are found. (As we shall see in §15.2.7, however, the order in which array elements are accessed can affect the speed of a program's execution.)

4⇨ The K loop accumulates the terms in the sum for each C(I,J) according to the formula given above. For each combination of I and J the inside loop runs K from 1 to N, working down the Jth column of B and across the Ith row of A.

5⇨ When the nest of loops is finished, the PRINT statements output the rows of the result matrix C. The whole matrix could have been written out using   PRINT *,C   but then the elements would all appear on one line, in column-major order.

5.7   Omissions

Column major order for arrays having more than 2 dimensions; *arrays having non-numeric data types;* DO *targets other than* CONTINUE*; the use of* CONTINUE *as other than a* DO *target;* non-integer DO indices; implied DO loops in compile-time data initializations.

5.8   Exercises

5.8.1   From memory, write down all of the FORTRAN statements introduced so far and describe what each one does.

5.8.2   Can an array have some elements of one type and some of another? Can some rows of an array have more elements than others?

5.8.3   What is printed by this program? Explain why.

```
    INTEGER*4 I(10)/10,9,8,7,1,2,3,4,5,6/
    PRINT *,I(I(I(3)))
    STOP
    END
```

5.8.4   What is printed by this program? Explain why.

```
    INTEGER*4 Q(3,3)/7,1,2,2,3,3,1,5,6/
    PRINT *,Q(Q(1,2),Q(Q(3,1),2))
    STOP
    END
```

5.8.5   If an array is dimensioned X(0:2,-1:3,5,7) what are its (a) rank; (b) extents; (c) size; (d) shape?

5.8.6   Exercise 4.10.45 asks for a code segment that sets the LOGICAL*4 variable NML to .TRUE. if the REAL*4 value in X is normalized, and to .FALSE. otherwise. Write a code segment that does this when X is REAL*8. Hint: use EQUIVALENCE to overlay a 2-element INTEGER*4 vector on X.

5.8.7   Revise the following program segment to protect against array subscript overflow (a) without using a DO loop; (b) using a DO loop.

```
      INTEGER*4 VALS(100)
      I=1
    2 READ *,VALS(I)
      IF(VALS(I).EQ.0) GO TO 1
      I=I+1
      GO TO 2
    1 ...
```

5.8.8   What is printed by this code segment? Explain why.

```
      DO 1 K=-9,37,12
          PRINT *,K
    1 CONTINUE
```

5.8.9   What is printed by this program? Explain why.

```
      DO 1 I=1,4
      DO 1 J=I,4
      DO 1 K=J,4
          PRINT *,K
    1 CONTINUE
      STOP
      END
```

5.8.10 Flowchart a code segment that simulates the action of a DO loop. Is there any way to tell by looking at the flowchart whether the code that implements it will be written using a DO loop or a free loop?

5.8.11 Explain why it is better to use a DO loop rather than a free loop whenever that is possible. Can you think of an example to show that a free loop sometimes cannot be replaced by a DO loop?

5.8.12 When does a DO loop whose starting index is greater than its ending index have its body executed? Add a test or tests before this loop to ensure that no iterations are performed if the loop limits are out of order.

```
      DO 2 I=N,M,L
          [loop body]
    2 CONTINUE
    3 ...
```

5.8.13 Consider the following program.

```
      INTEGER*4 N(7)/4,7,2,1,2,10,4/
      DO 1 J=N(1),N(2),N(3)
          N(J)=N(J-1)+J
    1 CONTINUE
      PRINT *,N
      STOP
      END
```

(a) Is the loop legal? (b) What is printed? (c) Rewrite the program so that whether the loop is legal does not depend on the initial data in N.

5.8.14 Determine by experiment how your FORTRAN compiler handles a DO loop with a zero increment.

5.8.15 What is the maximum number of iterations that can be performed by a DO loop? Write and test a program that counts iterations, to illustrate your answer.

5.8.16 Code a DO loop whose index I counts up from 1 to N but which contains a variable J that counts down from N to 1.

5.8.17 In the matrix multiplication program of §5.6, the 2 CONTINUE is adjacent to the 1 CONTINUE. Rewrite the program to use a single CONTINUE. Does this make the code easier, or more difficult, to understand?

5.8.18 Simplify the following program.

```
      INTEGER*4 M/1/,N/3/,P/1/
      REAL*8 A(1,3),B(3,1),C(1,1)
      READ *,A,B
      DO 1 I=1,M
      DO 1 J=1,P
          C(I,J)=0.D0
          DO 2 K=1,N
              C(I,J)=C(I,J)+A(I,K)*B(K,J)
    2     CONTINUE
    1 CONTINUE
      PRINT *,C
      STOP
      END
```

5.8.19 Rewrite the following programs to use DO loops instead of free loops: (a) the bisection program of Exercise 3.8.21; (b) the Simpson's Rule program of Exercise 3.8.17; (c) the mortgage calculation of Exercise 3.8.18; (d) the coconut programs of Exercise 3.8.20; (e) the sine program of §4.5; (f) the ln (2) program of §4.6.2; (g) the roundoff error study of Exercise 4.10.16; (h) the $\phi(\alpha)$ program of Exercise 4.10.21; (i) the Benford's Law program of Exercise 4.10.22; (j) the e^x program of Exercise 4.10.23; (k) the harmonic number program of Exercise 4.10.24; (l) the Knuth's recursion program of Exercise 4.10.30; (m) the transfer function program of Exercise 4.10.39.

(n) Would it improve the money-adding program of Exercise 4.10.33 to replace its free loop with a DO loop?

(o) Can the endless loop of §5.2 be rewritten to use a DO loop instead of a free loop?

5.8.20 Suppose **A** is a square matrix having n rows and columns. (a) Write a code segment to print out only the diagonal elements $a_{i,i}$. (b) Write a code segment to print out only the elements above the diagonal.

5.8.21 Write a program that reads 10 numbers into a real array A, sorts the values in increasing order, and prints out the sorted list (a) *without* using DO loops and (b) using DO loops. There are lots of ways to sort a list of numbers, and many textbooks describe various algorithms in detail, but don't research the problem anywhere; just come up, on your own, with some way that works.

5.8.22 The input data to the following program are entered in row-major order, beginning 1 5 9 13 2 ....

```
      INTEGER*4 MR(4,4),M(4,4)
      READ *,MR
      :
      [missing code]
      :
      PRINT *,M
      STOP
      END
```

$$M = \begin{bmatrix} 1 & 5 & 9 & 13 \\ 2 & 6 & 10 & 14 \\ 3 & 7 & 11 & 15 \\ 4 & 8 & 12 & 16 \end{bmatrix}$$

Fill in the missing code to rearrange the data so that M has the contents shown on the right. What is the mathematical term for the required matrix operation? How are the data printed back out?

5.8.23 If in the matrix multiplication program of §5.6 the three PRINT statements were replaced by the single statement   PRINT *,C   what output would be produced?

5.8.24 Fix the following code segment

```
      REAL*4 A(10)
      DO 1 I=0,9
          A(I)=0.
    1 CONTINUE
      :
```

(a) by changing the DO statement, leaving the array declaration alone; (b) by changing the array declaration, leaving the DO statement alone.

5.8.25 Is the following code legal FORTRAN, according to this chapter?

```
    DO 1 I=1,100,I
        PRINT *,I
  1 CONTINUE
```

If it is, what output is printed? If it is not, write a legal code segment to accomplish what the programmer apparently intended.

5.8.26 In §5.2 an example is given of an endless loop. Even if addressing array elements outside the dimensioned size of X does not stop the program, the loop is not really endless because the IF eventually fails and the program stops. (a) Why? (b) How many iterations have been performed by then?

5.8.27 Column-major order corresponds to varying the inner or leftmost subscript most rapidly. In the following program, how are the elements of TREDEE laid out in memory? What gets printed?

```
    REAL*4 TREDEE(2,2,2)
    L=0
    DO 1 I=1,2
    DO 1 J=1,2
    DO 1 K=1,2
        L=L+1
        TREDEE(I,J,K)=FLOAT(L)
  1 CONTINUE
    PRINT *,TREDEE
    STOP
    END
```

5.8.28 Consider repeating the following calculation: if n is even, halve it; if n is odd, multiply it by 3 and add 1. If the starting value is 5, this iteration generates the sequence 5, 16, 8, 4, 2, 1, 4, 2, 1, ... After the first 1 is generated, the pattern 1, 4, 2, repeats over and over. For a starting value of 5 there are six numbers in the sequence up to and including the first 1, but for other starting values more or fewer numbers might be generated before finding a 1. A conjecture in number theory [152] is that no matter what starting value we use, the iteration will eventually generate a 1. (a) Write a program to confirm that the algorithm eventually generates a 1 for each starting value between 1 and 100. (b) For each starting value, print out how many values are generated (but not the generated values themselves) until a 1 appears, counting the starting value and the 1.

5.8.29 Two five-digit integers are to be constructed using each of the digits 0-9 exactly once (a leading zero is allowed). Write a program to find the numbers so that their absolute difference is (a) as large as possible; (b) as small as possible.

5.8.30 Each row of seats in an auditorium should be higher than the previous row so that the spectators can see over the heads of the people in front of them. If the average distance from a person's eye to the top of his or her head is h, the distance from the stage to the first row of seats is D, and the distance between rows is d, the eye height of a spectator in the n'th row needs to be at least

$$H_n = \frac{(H_{n-1} + h)(D + (n-1)d)}{D + (n-2)d}.$$

Assuming that $H_1 = 0$, $h = 3.6$ inches, $D = 10$ feet, and $d = 42$ inches, write a program to compute $H_2, \ldots, H_{30}$.

5.8.31 The deflection y of a uniformly-loaded cantilever beam of length l, measured a distance x from the fixed end, is given by

$$y = \frac{w}{2EI}\left(\frac{l^2 x^2}{2} - \frac{l x^3}{3} + \frac{x^4}{12}\right)$$

where w is the load per unit length, E is the elastic modulus of the beam material, and the moment of inertia $I = ab^3/12$ for a rectangular beam of width a and height b. If $w = 320/l$ pounds per foot, $l = 6$ feet, $E = 1600000$ pounds/inch^2, $a = 1.625$ inches, and $b = 8.25$ inches, write a program that computes y for 20 values of x between 0 and l.

5.8.32 The ellipsoid algorithm for nonlinear optimization [53, p315-322] generates a sequence of n-dimensional ellipsoids whose volumes decrease in a geometric series with ratio

$$q(n) = \sqrt{\frac{n-1}{n+1}}\left(\frac{n}{\sqrt{n^2-1}}\right)^n.$$

(a) Write a program that computes values of $q(n)$ for $n = 2, \ldots, 10$ and prints out a table listing n in the first column and $q(n)$ in the second column. Label the columns appropriately. (b) Find analytically $\lim_{n \to 1} q(n)$, and modify your program to report the correct value for $q(1)$. (c) Write a program to investigate experimentally what happens to $q(n)$ as n becomes arbitrarily large. (d) Find analytically $\lim_{n \to \infty} q(n)$. Does this result agree with what you observed?

5.8.33 The steady-state temperature distribution $u(x, y)$ in a thin plate is described by the **Laplace equation** [4, p692ff.]

$$\frac{\partial^2 u}{\partial x^2} + \frac{\partial^2 u}{\partial y^2} = 0.$$

If fixed values of u are specified along the boundaries of a square domain, the solution of Laplace's equation can be approximated in the interior of the domain by dividing the domain into cells as shown in the figure on the left below and using the iteration given on the right.

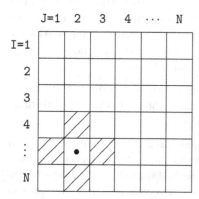

$$u_{i,j} \leftarrow \tfrac{1}{4}(u_{i-1,j} + u_{i+1,j} + u_{i,j-1} + u_{i,j+1})$$

The value of u at each interior cell (such as •) is found by averaging the values in the adjacent 4 cells (crosshatched) and this process is repeated until the values stop changing.

(a) Write a program to find the steady-state temperature distribution in a square plate. Represent the grid of cells by a square array, and set u in the edge cells to fixed values of your choice. Then apply the given iteration to update the value of u in each of the interior cells, in any order you like. Repeat the process of updating all the interior cells until the temperatures there don't change much any more. (b) Describe all the decisions you needed to make in writing your program. How do your results vary with the number of cells you use? With the order in which you use the iteration formula to update the interior cells? (An example involving integration of the Laplace equation on a more complicated domain is given in [87, p97-100].)

5.8.34 The factorial function is defined by $n! = n(n-1)!$ and $0! = 1$, so for $n > 0$, $n! = 1 \times 2 \times \cdots \times n$. (a) Write and test a program that reads an integer n and uses integer arithmetic to compute $n!$ exactly. What is the largest value of n for which the program can be used? (b) Revise the program to use REAL*8 arithmetic. Now what is the largest n that can be used? Are the $n!$ values still exact? (c) Rewrite the program to do the calculation in a different way so that it works for values of n from 0 to at least 2000. Hint: $a \times b = 10^{\log_{10}(a) + \log_{10}(b)}$.

5.8.35 The order in which FORTRAN array elements are stored in memory is the same no matter what endian-ness the processor has. However, as discussed in §4.8, the endian-ness of the processor *does* affect the order in which the bytes are stored *within* a word or doubleword, and in certain rare circumstances that can have surprising consequences. Consider the following program, in which compile-time initializations are used to set the elements of I to the hexadecimal values shown.

```
REAL*8 DW
INTEGER*4 I(2)/Z'3FF00000',Z'00000000'/
EQUIVALENCE(DW,I)
PRINT *,DW
STOP
END
```

The EQUIVALENCE overlays the two-element INTEGER*4 vector I on the memory occupied by DW, so it appears that DW will contain 3FF0000000000000, which represents the REAL*8 value 1.D0 according to the table in §4.7. When the program is run on a big-endian machine its output is

1.

but when it is run on a little-endian machine it prints

5.29980882E-315

(a) Explain in detail why this happens. (b) How should the compile-time initialization of I be changed so that DW is initialized to the value 1.D0 on a little-endian machine? (c) The following program prints 1. on both big-endian and little-endian machines.

```
REAL*8 DW/Z'3FF0000000000000'/
PRINT *,DW
STOP
END
```

Why doesn't this initialization depend on the endian-ness of the processor?

5.8.36 To debug a program that gives incorrect results, a programmer adds a PRINT statement to write out some variables. To his surprise and annoyance, this causes the bug to disappear! Now the output is correct, but removing the PRINT statement makes it wrong again. Can you suggest a possible explanation for this? Do you suppose the same thing might also happen to programmers writing in languages other than FORTRAN?

6

Subprograms

Suppose we know the values of $\mathbf{F}$ and $\mathbf{G}$ and want to find $\mathbf{D}$ from the formula below, in which all of the variables are 10×10 matrices. Matrix calculations are necessary in many fields of engineering and science. How might we code this one in FORTRAN?

$$\mathbf{D} = \mathbf{G}^\top (\mathbf{I} - \mathbf{G}\mathbf{F}\mathbf{F}^\top\mathbf{G}^\top)^{-1}\mathbf{G}$$

Recall that the transpose of an $m \times n$ matrix $\mathbf{A}$ is the $n \times m$ matrix $\mathbf{A}^\top$ whose (i,j)th element is $a_{j,i}$, the (j,i)th element of $\mathbf{A}$. Matrix multiplication works as described in §5.6 so, for example, $\mathbf{GF}$ in the above expression is a matrix whose (i,j)th element is $\sum_{k=1}^{10} g_{i,k} f_{k,j}$. The inverse of a nonsingular square matrix $\mathbf{A}$ is the matrix $\mathbf{A}^{-1}$ such that $\mathbf{A}\mathbf{A}^{-1} = \mathbf{I}$, where $\mathbf{I}$, the identity matrix, has diagonal elements all equal to 1 and zeros everywhere else. Finding the inverse of a matrix is quite a bit more complicated than finding a transpose or a matrix product, but it still involves only arithmetic.

A straightforward way of calculating $\mathbf{D}$ would be to build up the result by the following sequence of operations.

> multiply to get $\mathbf{GF}$
> transpose to get $\mathbf{F}^\top$
> multiply to get $[\mathbf{GF}]\mathbf{F}^\top$
> transpose to get $\mathbf{G}^\top$
> multiply to get $[\mathbf{GFF}^\top]\mathbf{G}^\top$
> subtract to get $\mathbf{I} - [\mathbf{GFF}^\top\mathbf{G}^\top]$
> invert to get $[\mathbf{I} - \mathbf{GFF}^\top\mathbf{G}^\top]^{-1}$
> multiply to get $\mathbf{G}^\top[(\mathbf{I} - \mathbf{GFF}^\top\mathbf{G}^\top)^{-1}]$
> multiply to get $\mathbf{D} = [\mathbf{G}^\top(\mathbf{I} - \mathbf{GFF}^\top\mathbf{G}^\top)^{-1}]\mathbf{G}$

Each of these steps could be performed by some DO loops, as shown in the listing on the next page. The listing is incomplete, because only the first page of code is shown and by the end of it we have gotten through only the subtraction step in our outline of the calculation. To write out the remaining steps would take several more pages, but we've already seen enough to draw several important conclusions.

This kind of source text is called **open code**, because every detail is immediately visible. Usually it is a good thing in programming, as elsewhere in life, to have things out in the open rather than hidden from view, but the price we pay for being able to see everything in this program is that there is too much to look at. The code goes on and on, like the ocean stretching from horizon to horizon as seen from a life raft in the middle of the Pacific.

The code is also about as boring as the open ocean because, at least to judge from the part we can see, it repeats a few patterns over and over. One matrix multiplication or transposition looks pretty much like another (and after the inversion is over we can look forward to two more multiplications). This calculation uses only one matrix inverse, but tomorrow we might need to evaluate a formula containing several, and then we would have to copy pages of code for each inversion. The only important thing that changes from one instance of multiplication or transposition or inversion to the next is the variables involved, except of course for the mistakes we are likely to make in copying the code.

```
C       This program computes the matrix result D.
        REAL*8 D(10,10),F(10,10),G(10,10),I(10,10)
        REAL*8 GF(10,10),FT(10,10),GFF(10,10),GT(10,10),GFFG(10,10)
        REAL*8 A(10,10),[other declarations]
C       :
        [code to read in values for F and G]
        [code to set I to the 10 x 10 identity matrix]
C       :
C       multiply
        DO 1 J=1,10
        DO 1 L=1,10
            GF(L,J)=0.D0
            DO 2 K=1,10
                GF(L,J)=GF(L,J)+G(L,K)*F(K,J)
    2       CONTINUE
    1 CONTINUE
C
C       transpose F
        DO 3 J=1,10
        DO 3 L=1,10
            FT(L,J)=F(J,L)
    3 CONTINUE
C
C       multiply
        DO 4 J=1,10
        DO 4 L=1,10
            GFF(L,J)=0.D0
            DO 5 K=1,10
                GFF(L,J)=GFF(L,J)+GF(L,K)*FT(K,J)
    5       CONTINUE
    4 CONTINUE
C
C       transpose G
        DO 6 J=1,10
        DO 6 L=1,10
            GT(L,J)=G(J,L)
    6 CONTINUE
C
C       multiply
        DO 7 J=1,10
        DO 7 L=1,10
            GFFG(L,J)=0.D0
            DO 8 K=1,10
                GFFG(L,J)=GFFG(L,J)+GFF(L,K)*GT(K,J)
    8       CONTINUE
    7 CONTINUE
C
C       subtract from the identity
        DO 9 J=1,10
        DO 9 L=1,10
            A(L,J)=I(L,J)-GFFG(L,J)
    9 CONTINUE
        :
```

6.1 SUBROUTINE **Subprograms**

To avoid the need for repetition of the kind we used above, FORTRAN provides a simple and elegant way to execute a code segment repeatedly with different data. The way to do it is by turning the code segment into a **subprogram**.

There are three kinds of subprograms in FORTRAN: **subroutines, functions**, and BLOCK DATA subprograms. A program that is not a subprogram is referred to as a **main program** to distinguish it from any subprograms it might invoke, so all the complete programs we saw in §1–§5 were main programs. A main program or a subprogram of any kind can also be referred to simply as a **routine**. We will take up functions in §6.3 and BLOCK DATA in §8.6. The matrix calculation above can be simplified using subroutines.

A subroutine performs an action. If we use a subroutine for each of the actions – multiplication, transposition, subtraction, and inversion – we can code the entire calculation of **D** as follows.

```
C     This program does the calculation using subroutines.
      REAL*8 D(10,10),F(10,10),G(10,10),I(10,10)
      REAL*8 GF(10,10),FT(10,10),GFF(10,10),GT(10,10),GFFG(10,10)
      REAL*8 A(10,10),AINV(10,10),GTAINV(10,10)
C     :
      [code to read in values for F and G]
      [code to set I to the 10 x 10 identity matrix]
C     :
C     calculate D
      CALL MATMPY(G,F, GF)
      CALL MATRNS(F, FT)
      CALL MATMPY(GF,FT, GFF)
      CALL MATRNS(G, GT)
      CALL MATMPY(GFF,GT, GFFG)
      CALL MATSUB(I,GFFG, A)
      CALL MATINV(A, AINV)
      CALL MATMPY(GT,AINV, GTAINV)
      CALL MATMPY(GTAINV,G, D)
C     :
      [code to print out or use D]
C     :
      STOP
      END
```

Here are some observations about this version of the program.

1▷ Unlike the earlier program, this code is short enough to be seen at a glance. The whole calculation of **D** takes only 9 statements, each subprogram invocation corresponding to one of the 9 steps outlined at the beginning of the example. This is much easier to understand, and more likely to be correct, than the open-code version.

2▷ I named the subroutines MATMPY (for matrix multiply), MATRNS (for matrix transpose), MATSUB (for matrix subtract), and MATINV (for matrix invert). There is nothing special about these names, and I could have chosen others instead. Subroutine names follow the same rules as variable names, but a subroutine name carries no value and thus has no type or dimensions. The different subprograms used in a main program must have different names.

3⇨   A subroutine is invoked by the CALL statement. A CALL is a kind of branch, transferring control to the first statement of the subroutine. When a subroutine is finished it returns control to the next statement after the CALL that invoked it.

4⇨   The variables that are to be used in each subroutine invocation are **passed** to the routine in a parenthesized list. The variables in the list are referred to as **arguments** or **formal parameters**. In the CALL statement, a parameter is also referred to as an **actual parameter**. For typographical clarity I have arranged the parameter lists so that inputs come first and are separated from results by a space.

Writing open code to complete the calculation of **D** would be a major project, but coding the subroutine calls is very little work. If we happen to have the necessary subroutines already on hand then we need to know only how to call them, not the intimate details of how they work internally. Even if we have to write all of the subroutines from scratch, that is less work than the open coding because MATMPY is used five times and MATRNS twice. And, of course, writing the subroutines for this project means that we *will* have them on hand for the next project in which they can be used.

To write each of the subroutines we need only reproduce the appropriate segment of open code in a separate place (usually at the end of the .f file containing the main program, or in a .f file containing only the subroutine), surround it with statements marking the beginning and end of the subroutine, and repeat any declarations that are needed to specify the types and dimensions of the parameters. Doing that for MATRNS yields this code.

```
      SUBROUTINE MATRNS(A, AT)
      REAL*8 A(10,10),AT(10,10)
      DO 1 J=1,10
      DO 1 I=1,10
          AT(I,J)=A(J,I)
    1 CONTINUE
      RETURN
      END
```

Here are some observations about the routine.

1⇨   The beginning of the subroutine is identified by the SUBROUTINE statement. The name MATRNS given here must of course match the name given in the CALL statements that invoke the routine.

2⇨   When MATRNS is invoked, the CALL transfers control to the first executable statement inside the subroutine, which is DO 1 J=1,10 . At the end of the calculation, the RETURN statement transfers control back to the first statement after the invoking CALL. Every subprogram must execute a RETURN (or a STOP, which returns control to the operating system).

3⇨   Like every main program, every subprogram must have END for its last statement to tell the compiler there are no more source lines in the routine. The source code of several routines might be stored in one .f file, so the compiler cannot use the top and bottom of the file itself to delimit a routine.

4⇨   The parameters listed in the SUBROUTINE statement must match in number, order, and type the parameters appearing in the CALL statements that invoke the routine, but *the names of the variables need not be the same as the names in the calling routine.* This is essential if the subroutine is to be called repeatedly with different actual parameters. The variables listed in the SUBROUTINE statement are called **dummy parameters**, because *their names are unrelated to those of variables in other routines,* including the calling routine. On the first call of MATRNS, the main program passes in the array it names F, which is referred to inside the subroutine as A, and the subroutine returns AT, which is known to the main program as FT. During the second call, the actual parameter G corresponds to the dummy parameter A, and GT corresponds to AT. The subroutine variable A has nothing to do with the variable A in the main program. The dummy parameters A and AT must be typed and dimensioned inside the subroutine.

5 ⇨ The subroutine variables I and J are local to MATRNS and *they have nothing to do with variables having the same names in other routines,* including the calling routine. Inside MATRNS, I is used as an integer DO index and array subscript. In our main program, I is the REAL*8 10 × 10 identity matrix. These are completely separate variables, naming different storage locations in memory.

6 ⇨ The local variables of a subprogram are saved across invocations, so upon entry they have the values they had at the previous RETURN from the subprogram. (A few compilers for Classical FORTRAN, such as g77, depart from this usual behavior by requiring an option to be specified if subprogram local variables are to be saved; see §14.1.3.) In our example and in most cases it doesn't matter, but as we shall see in §6.5 it is occasionally desirable for a subprogram to remember something about its previous invocations.

7 ⇨ The main program and the subroutines it calls are each compiled separately, one at a time. This **separate compilation** is the reason why the names of dummy parameters and local variables in each routine have nothing to do with the names of variables in other routines. While the compiler is translating each routine into machine language it has no way of knowing about any other routines that might be used in the program. Only the loader knows about all the pieces that must be linked together in making the executable, and by the time it gets them the variable names have all been translated into memory addresses. Separate compilation is one of FORTRAN's great strengths, because as we shall see in §14.4 and §14.5 it permits the construction and use of object-code libraries. It has many consequences for the semantics of the language, which I will point out as we encounter them.

8 ⇨ Subprograms can invoke other subprograms to any depth. Thus, if a program consists of a main and the subroutines P, Q, R, and S, it could have a structure like this.

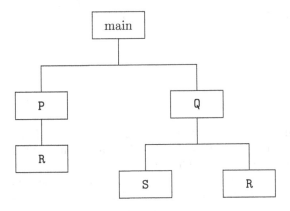

However, as mentioned in §0.2, Classical FORTRAN forbids recursion, so no routine may directly or indirectly invoke itself. It would not be permissible for subroutine R in the above diagram to in turn call subroutine P. Although the tree structure of subprogram invocations in a FORTRAN program reflects a hierarchical logical organization, each subprogram is an independent routine and thus is not syntactically or semantically contained within the routine or routines that invoke it.

6.2   Call By Reference

After subroutine MATRNS in the example of §6.1 has returned control to its caller, the actual parameter corresponding to its dummy parameter AT will have been replaced by a new value. The precise moment at which that happens doesn't matter in this program, but in some situations it can.

You might suppose that a subprogram would copy the actual parameters it receives into its dummy parameters upon entry, perform its calculation, and copy the resulting new dummy parameter values back into the actual parameters upon return, but that would waste both memory and machine time. Instead, FORTRAN arranges for subprograms to manipulate their actual parameters directly, by addressing the memory locations *where the parameters are stored in the routine that originally allocated them*. This is known as **call by reference** or **call by name**, because what gets passed to the subprogram is the memory location of the actual parameter rather than its value. (Address calculations take place entirely behind the scenes, so the memory location that is passed for each parameter is not itself accessible to you as a FORTRAN programmer and cannot be manipulated by statements in your source code. FORTRAN statements refer to the *values* of variables, not to the addresses where those values are stored.) If a parameter is an array, its location is the address of the first element, and the machine code that the compiler generates for the subprogram figures out the locations of the other array elements based on this starting address and the size in bytes of each element.

If a subprogram changes the value of a dummy parameter, the value of the actual parameter gets changed *immediately*. Because of this, passing the same variable for more than one actual parameter can have surprising consequences. Here EXCH returns in L the elements of K in opposite order.

```
INTEGER*4 I(2),J(2)             SUBROUTINE EXCH(K,L)
I(1)=1                          INTEGER*4 K(2),L(2)
I(2)=2                          L(1)=K(2)
CALL EXCH(I,J)                  L(2)=K(1)
PRINT *,J(1),J(2)               RETURN
I(1)=1                          END
I(2)=2
CALL EXCH(I,I)
PRINT *,I(1),I(2)
STOP
END
```

The first PRINT prints 2 1, as expected, but the second prints 2 2. When I is passed for both parameters, K and L are **aliased**. The first assignment in EXCH replaces L(1) by K(2)=I(2)=2, which sets I(1) to 2. The second then replaces L(2) by K(1), which is I(1) and now equal to 2, so I(2) becomes 2. To avoid this sort of confusion, *don't pass the same actual parameter for two dummy parameters if either dummy parameter gets changed.*

Call by reference is safe except in the situation just illustrated, and you never need to worry about it if you don't pass the same actual parameter for two dummy parameters one of which changes. Of course, it is desirable if possible to design a subprogram so that disaster will not ensue even if you violate the rule by mistake (see Exercise 6.8.9).

Sometimes it is convenient to eliminate the possibility of aliasing by using only one parameter, as in the code at the top of the next page. Subprograms like this version of EXCH are said to work **in-place**. Routines for numerical linear algebra often work in-place to

```
      INTEGER*4 I(2)                 SUBROUTINE EXCH(K)
      I(1)=1                         INTEGER*4 K(2),TEMP
      I(2)=2                         TEMP=K(1)
      CALL EXCH(I)                   K(1)=K(2)
      PRINT *,I(1),I(2)              K(2)=TEMP
      STOP                           RETURN
      END                            END
```

save memory, overwriting an input matrix with the result [26]. In the introductory example of this chapter, we could have specified that MATINV should overwrite its input matrix with the inverse, rather than returning the separate parameter AINV.

6.3 FUNCTION Subprograms

Ever since §2.4 we have been using functions that are built into FORTRAN, such as SQRT. Functions that you write for yourself can be used in the same way. A function is like a subroutine in that each is a separately-compiled code segment that can be invoked repeatedly, for different arguments, wherever it is needed. But whereas a subroutine returns its results (if any) to the calling routine only by changing its actual parameters, *a function also returns a scalar value in its name*. A subroutine is invoked by the CALL statement, but a function is invoked by mentioning it in an expression. A subroutine is allowed to not have a parameter list, but in Classical FORTRAN a FUNCTION subprogram *must* have at least one parameter.

The compiler knows the types of FORTRAN's own built-in functions, even when they do not follow the default naming rules for variables. For example, it knows that DSQRT returns a REAL*8 value. But any function *you* write is typed according to the default naming rules unless you explicitly declare its type both in the routine that invokes it and in the function itself. This function returns in DDOT the dot product $x^\top y = \sum_{j=1}^{10} x_j y_j$.

```
      FUNCTION DDOT(X,Y)
      REAL*8 DDOT,X(10),Y(10)
      DDOT=0.D0
      DO 1 J=1,10
          DDOT=DDOT+X(J)*Y(J)
    1 CONTINUE
      RETURN
      END
```

Here are some observations about DDOT.

1⟩ The function begins with a FUNCTION statement and ends with an END statement, just as MATRNS began with SUBROUTINE and ended with END.

2⟩ The dummy parameters of a function, like those of a subroutine, must be typed if they do not follow the default naming rules, and must be dimensioned if they are arrays. Here the vectors X and Y are declared inside the function. Parameters are passed to a function the same way they are passed to a subroutine, by reference.

3⟩ The function name DDOT returns a REAL*8 value, so it does not follow the default naming rules and therefore must be typed inside the function. A function can have any scalar data type. Functions in Classical FORTRAN can return only scalar values, so the name of a function must not be dimensioned.

4⇨ The function name *must* be assigned a value within the subprogram, and your compiler should complain if it is not.

5⇨ Functions and subroutines can invoke other functions and subroutines in any combination, so long as there is no recursion.

6⇨ A function must be invoked by using its name in an expression. Here is a program that invokes DDOT.

```
REAL*8 Z,DDOT,X(10),Y(10)
READ *,X,Y
Z=DDOT(X,Y)
PRINT *,Z
STOP
END
```

Notice that DDOT is declared in the invoking routine as well as inside the function itself.

6.4   Case Study: Bisection

As an example of how subroutine and function subprograms can be used together, we will next consider the bisection algorithm for solving a single algebraic equation of the form $f(x) = 0$. This important numerical method was described in §0.1 and flowcharted in Exercise 3.8.21. Those discussions were about finding the value of x where $\sin(x) = \frac{1}{2}x$, which is where $f(x) = \sin(x) - \frac{1}{2}x = 0$, so that particular $f(x)$ was built into the code. Now we would like to implement the algorithm in a general way, so the same code can be used to find a zero of any arbitrary function that has one. Here is a subroutine that does the calculation, and some observations about it.

```
      SUBROUTINE BISECT(XL,XR, X,F)
      REAL*8 XL,XR,X,FCN,FL,FR,F
      FL=FCN(XL)
      FR=FCN(XR)
      DO 1 I=1,10
          X=0.5D0*(XL+XR)
          F=FCN(X)
          IF(F*FL .LT. 0.D0) THEN
              XR=X
              FR=F
          ELSE
              XL=X
              FL=F
          ENDIF
    1 CONTINUE
      RETURN
      END
```

1⇨ For simplicity this routine always does 10 bisections rather than testing for convergence to a root, and it ignores the possibility that the function has no zero between the starting values of XL and XR. Less primitive versions of this routine will be used to illustrate various things in §7.2, §8, and §12.3.

2⇨ The values of the function $f(x)$ are calculated by a FUNCTION subprogram named FCN. Here's what FCN might look like for $f(x) = \sin(x) - \frac{1}{2}x$.

```
FUNCTION FCN(X)
REAL*8 FCN,X
FCN=DSIN(X)-0.5D0*X
RETURN
END
```

Notice that FCN must be declared REAL*8 both inside the function subprogram and in BISECT.

3⇨ To use BISECT we must call it from a routine that sets the initial values of XL and XR and uses the results that are returned, like this main program.

```
REAL*8 XL,XR,X,F
XL=0.5D0
XR=2.5D0
CALL BISECT(XL,XR, X,F)
PRINT *,X,F
STOP
END
```

4⇨ Neither BISECT nor the main program knows anything about what is inside of FCN, so to change $f(x)$ it's necessary to revise only FCN. Of course the main does specify the initial interval by giving values to XL and XR, and those might need to be changed to enclose a zero of the new function.

5⇨ Looking only at the main program, it might seem that we could pass the literal constants 0.5D0 and 2.5D0 to BISECT for its first two actual parameters, rather than the variables XL and XR. After all, we commonly invoke FORTRAN built-in functions with literal arguments, as in Y=DSQRT(5.D0), so why not CALL BISECT(0.5D0,2.5D0, X,F)? In later chapters you will see me use literals as subprogram arguments in some cases. A glance at BISECT, though, reveals that it *changes* the dummy parameters XL and XR, so it wouldn't make sense for the actual parameters to be constants. Passing a literal or PARAMETER constant for an actual parameter that gets changed by the subprogram can have strange consequences (as discussed further in §13.6.3), and because of separate compilation it can't be detected by the compiler. If you're not sure whether a subprogram changes an input parameter, put the value in a variable and pass that instead of a constant.

6.5 Detecting First Entry

Occasionally it is necessary or convenient to execute part of a subprogram only once, the first time the routine is invoked. In the top example on the next page, function PM returns the dot product of vector A, which is passed in, with another vector B that it generates and

```
      FUNCTION PM(A)                    REAL*8 X(100),Y(100),PM
      REAL*8 PM,A(100),B(100)          READ *,X
      B(1)=1.D0                        PRINT *,PM(X)
      B(2)=1.D0                        READ *,Y
      DO 1 I=3,100                     PRINT *,PM(Y)
          B(I)=B(I-1)+1.D0/B(I-2)      STOP
    1 CONTINUE                         END
      PM=0.D0
      DO 2 I=1,100
          PM=PM+A(I)*B(I)
    2 CONTINUE
      RETURN
      END


      FUNCTION PM(A,NC)                 REAL*8 X(100),Y(100),PM
      REAL*8 PM,A(100),B(100)          NC=0
      IF(NC.EQ.0) THEN                 READ *,X
         B(1)=1.D0                     PRINT *,PM(X,NC)
         B(2)=1.D0                     READ *,Y
         DO 1 I=3,100                  PRINT *,PM(Y,NC)
             B(I)=B(I-1)+1.D0/B(I-2)   STOP
    1      CONTINUE                    END
      ENDIF
      PM=0.D0
      DO 2 I=1,100
          PM=PM+A(I)*B(I)
    2 CONTINUE
      NC=NC+1
      RETURN
      END


      FUNCTION PM(A)                    REAL*8 X(100),Y(100),PM
      REAL*8 PM,A(100),B(100)          READ *,X
      LOGICAL*4 FIRST/.TRUE./          PRINT *,PM(X)
      IF(FIRST) THEN                   READ *,Y
         B(1)=1.D0                     PRINT *,PM(Y)
         B(2)=1.D0                     STOP
         DO 1 I=3,100                  END
             B(I)=B(I-1)+1.D0/B(I-2)
    1      CONTINUE
         FIRST=.FALSE.
      ENDIF
      PM=0.D0
      DO 2 I=1,100
          PM=PM+A(I)*B(I)
    2 CONTINUE
      RETURN
      END
```

stores internally. The vector B ends up containing the same values every time, so it is a waste of effort to find it more than once. That could be avoided by moving the calculation of B to the main program and passing B as a second parameter to PM, but maybe PM is to be used from other main programs too, and we want to code the calculation of B only once.

The second program solves this problem by adding the parameter NC, a **call counter** that counts the invocations of the function. When PM is invoked the first time, NC=0 so PM calculates B before using it. PM increments NC before it returns, so on its second invocation NC=1 and the calculation of B is skipped.

Sometimes it is not possible to pass a call counter, because we can't change the invoking routine. In that case a compile-time initialization can be used to set a call counter or logical flag that is local to the subprogram, as in the third program. The logical variable FIRST has its initial value of .TRUE. when PM is entered for the first time, so B gets calculated. Then FIRST gets set to .FALSE., so on subsequent invocations the calculation of B is skipped. Some other situations in which it is necessary to detect first entry are mentioned in Exercises 10.9.39 and 11.9.32.

6.6 FORTRAN, System, and Library Routines

Many subprograms turn out to be useful in a variety of projects, and some, like SQRT, are needed so often that they are built into FORTRAN. The UNIX™ operating system provides a set of **system routines** that can be invoked from FORTRAN programs to obtain operating system services such as finding out today's date. An assortment of commercial and public-domain **subprogram libraries** are available, containing routines for a wide spectrum of common numerical computing tasks, and a few handy subprograms are described in §18. The FORTRAN compiler knows where to find its built-in functions and the UNIX™ system routines; §14.5 explains the mechanics of building your own subprogram libraries and linking routines from them into your programs.

This section is a survey of the subprograms that are available in FORTRAN, UNIX™, and some widely-used numerical libraries.

6.6.1 FORTRAN Built-In Functions

So far we have encountered the type conversion functions listed in §4.4 and §4.6.1, the bitwise logical functions listed in §4.6.3, and a few mathematical functions such as SQRT. The table on the next page summarizes all the mathematical functions that we will consider part of Classical FORTRAN.

In this table Y, X and S are REAL*8 quantities, I, J, and K are INTEGER*4, and Z and W are COMPLEX*16. For each function that returns a real value, only the name of the REAL*8 version is listed. The procedure for forming the name of a corresponding function having some other type depends on whether removing the leading D leaves a name that is REAL*4 according to the default naming rules. The examples below illustrate the two cases.

REAL*4	REAL*8	REAL*16	COMPLEX*8	COMPLEX*16	COMPLEX*32
ABS	DABS	QABS	CABS	CDABS	CQABS
ALOG	DLOG	QLOG	CLOG	CDLOG	CQLOG

The COMPLEX*8 and COMPLEX*32 versions of DCONJG are named CONJG and QCONJG respectively. Implementations differ in the thoroughness of their coverage of the REAL*16 and complex versions of the built-in functions. If your compiler's elementary function library provides complex versions of DATAN2 or DGAMMA, whose names would become longer than six characters if they followed the example above, consult the manual to find out what names the implementor has chosen.

function	returns	name
Y=DSQRT(X)	$y = \sqrt{x}$	square root
Y=DEXP(X)	$y = e^x$	exponential
Y=DLOG(X)	$y = \log_e(x) = \ln(x)$	natural logarithm
Y=DLOG10(X)	$y = \log_{10}(x)$	common logarithm
Y=DCOS(X)	$y = \cos(x)$	cosine
Y=DACOS(X)	$y = \arccos(x) = \cos^{-1}(x)$	arc cosine
Y=DSIN(X)	$y = \sin(x)$	sine
Y=DASIN(X)	$y = \arcsin(x) = \sin^{-1}(x)$	arc sine
Y=DTAN(X)	$y = \tan(x)$	tangent
Y=DATAN(X)	$y = \arctan(x) = \tan^{-1}(x)$	arc tangent
Y=DATAN2(X,S)	$y = \arctan(x/s) = \tan^{-1}(x/s)$	arc tangent
Y=DSINH(X)	$y = \sinh(x) = (e^x - e^{-x})/2$	hyperbolic sine
Y=DCOSH(X)	$y = \cosh(x) = (e^x + e^{-x})/2$	hyperbolic cosine
Y=DTANH(X)	$y = \tanh(x) = \sinh(x)/\cosh(x)$	hyperbolic tangent
Y=DERF(X)	$y = \mathrm{erf}(x) = \frac{2}{\sqrt{\pi}} \int_0^x e^{-t^2} dt$	error function
Y=DGAMMA(X)	$y = \Gamma(x) = \int_0^\infty t^{x-1} e^{-t} dt$	gamma function
Y=DABS(X)	$y = \lvert x \rvert$	absolute value
J=IABS(I)	$j = \lvert i \rvert$	absolute value
S=DMAX1(X,Y)	$s = \max(x, y)$	highest value
K=MAX0(I,J)	$k = \max(i, j)$	highest value
S=DMIN1(X,Y)	$s = \min(x, y)$	lowest value
K=MIN0(I,J)	$k = \min(i, j)$	lowest value
Y=DMOD(X,S)	$y = x \bmod s$	modulus
J=MOD(I,K)	$j = i \bmod k$	modulus
Y=DSIGN(X,S)	$y = [\text{sign of } s] \times x$	transfer of sign
J=ISIGN(I,K)	$j = [\text{sign of } k] \times i$	transfer of sign
Z=DCONJG(W)	$z = x - y\sqrt{-1}$ if $w = x + y\sqrt{-1}$	complex conjugate

The complex versions of ABS return the real magnitude of their argument; if $z = x + y\sqrt{-1}$ then CDABS(Z) returns $\sqrt{x^2 + y^2}$. The sine, cosine, and tangent functions expect their arguments to be angles measured in radians (recall that π radians $= 180°$). DATAN2(X,S) and DATAN(X/S) give the same result, but the two-argument function avoids a division by zero, and a corresponding IEEE exception message, in the event that S is zero.

Some built-in functions are defined only over a limited range of argument values, either because of the properties of the mathematical function being approximated or because of the limited range of floating-point numbers. The limits for the REAL*8 versions are summarized in the table below.

function	range of definition
Y=DSQRT(X)	$0 \le X$
Y=DEXP(X)	$X \le +\ln(R_{max})$
Y=DLOG(X)	$0 < X$
Y=DLOG10(X)	$0 < X$
Y=DACOS(X)	$-1 \le X \le +1$
Y=DASIN(X)	$-1 \le X \le +1$
Y=DSINH(X)	$-\ln(R_{max}) \le X \le +\ln(R_{max})$
Y=DCOSH(X)	$-\ln(R_{max}) \le X \le +\ln(R_{max})$
Y=DTANH(X)	$-\ln(R_{max}) \le X \le +\ln(R_{max})$

The argument limits for the exponential and hyperbolic functions are given in terms of $\ln(R_{max})$, where R_{max} is the largest representable real value. According to §4.2 the largest

REAL*8 is of order 10^{308} and the natural log of 10^{308} is about 710, so for the functions listed $\ln(R_{max}) \approx 710$. Because the largest real value depends on the precision used, the argument limits have other values for the REAL*4 and REAL*16 versions of the functions. The complex versions of some functions are defined for argument values that would be out of range for the real versions; for example, CDSQRT((-1.D0,0.D0))$= 0 + 1i$. If any of the floating-point functions is invoked with an out-of-range argument it will return a NaN as described in §4.2. The DMOD(X,S) and MOD(I,K) functions are defined only for S and K not equal to zero, and DSIGN(X,0.D0) and ISIGN(I,0) return $|X|$ and $|I|$ respectively. Consult your compiler manual for the ranges of definition of built-in functions not listed above.

6.6.2   UNIX™ System Routines

Some FORTRAN compilers provide built-in routines for interrogating or changing the world beyond your program, but these vary from one implementation to another so it is safer to rely on operating-system routines for those services. The table below gives a representative list of useful system routines that are usually available to FORTRAN programs running under UNIX™. Many of these routines are discussed in detail later, in the sections indicated.

name	purpose	§
ETIME	measure elapsed CPU time	15.1.3
EXIT	stop the program with a specified return code	14.2.6
FDATE	get the current date and time of day	14.2.1
FLUSH	cause an output buffer to be written	14.2.2
FSTAT	get information about a file attached to a given unit	14.2.2
GETARG	get command-line arguments as character strings	14.2.4
GETCWD	get the name of the current UNIX™ directory	
GETENV	get the value of a UNIX™ environment variable	14.2.3
IARGC	get the number of command-line arguments given	14.2.4
IDATE	get the current date	14.2.1
IOINIT	change FORTRAN I/O initializations from defaults	
IRAND	generate pseudorandom integers	
ITIME	get the current time of day	14.2.1
SLEEP	suspend execution for a given interval of time	
STAT	get information about a file having a given name	14.2.2
SYSTEM	execute UNIX™ commands from within the program	14.2.5
UNLINK	remove a file	14.2.2

6.6.3   Subprogram Libraries

After you know all about subprograms, most of the code you write should be in the form of functions and subroutines that can be used repeatedly by you and anyone you share them with. For several decades, countless FORTRAN programmers before you have recognized the value of reusable code and written handy routines for doing all sorts of things. Thanks to their extravagant labors there is now a vast literature of numerical subprograms you can use. Some of this code is in commercial libraries, and more is in the public domain.

Commercial Subprogram Libraries   The most widely available and commonly used general-purpose commercial libraries are the **IMSL Library** [20], distributed by Visual Numerics, and the **NAG Library** [26], distributed by The Numerical Algorithms Group. These libraries provide similar encyclopedic coverage of topics in basic numerical and statistical computing, including those listed on the next page.

Topics Covered by General-Purpose Libraries

approximation of special functions
determinants
eigenvalues and eigenvectors
Fourier and Laplace transforms
integral equations
integration and differentiation
interpolation and approximation
least squares problems
line printer graphics
linear, nonlinear, and integer optimization
mathematical constants
matrix arithmetic, inversion, and orthogonalization
nonlinear algebraic equations
ordinary and partial differential equations
pseudorandom number generation
simultaneous linear algebraic equations
sorting
summation of series
zeros of polynomials

analysis of variance
categorical and discrete data analysis
cluster analysis
contingency table analysis
correlation and regression analysis
covariance structures and factor analysis
density and hazard estimation
descriptive statistics
discriminant analysis
multidimensional scaling
multivariate statistics
nonparametric statistics
probability distribution functions and their inverses
sampling
smoothing
survival analysis
tests of goodness of fit and of randomness
time series analysis and forecasting

There are other commercial libraries, notably the **Harwell Library** [17] and the IBM Engineering and Scientific Subroutine Library [15] or **ESSL**, that are best known for their special-purpose subprograms. The Harwell Library covers a variety of topics, including some of those listed for the general-purpose libraries, but it also includes a famous few routines that solve sparse systems of linear algebraic equations. ESSL also covers part of the general-purpose list with routines for linear equations, eigenvalues and eigenvectors, Fourier transforms, sorting and searching, interpolation, integration, and pseudorandom number generation, but its unique virtue is extremely fast execution on certain IBM computers.

Commercial code usually implements the best known algorithms, runs fast, is thoroughly validated for correctness, and reliably gives accurate results. It is a big convenience to get a wide assortment of numerical software in one library, rather than having to search in many places for individual routines that do what you need, and most vendors give their customers a phone number to call for help. On the other hand, whether they are rented or sold, commercial libraries come in object-code form, and their FORTRAN source is usually available only for an extra license fee or not at all. Without the source code, it can be difficult to debug programs that use a library and impossible to find out in detail how the library routines actually work. Also, many of the routines in commercial libraries are just proprietary versions of software that is already available for free elsewhere.

Public-Domain Software   The best-known repository of public-domain numerical software is Netlib, maintained by the US Department of Energy at Oak Ridge National Laboratory. You can find out about it by sending email to `netlib@ornl.gov` with the single word `help` as the content of the message. This will elicit a computer-generated response explaining what to do next. By exchanging further messages with the server machine, you can locate software by name or purpose and retrieve the FORTRAN source code for any routines you want. Netlib is also accessible via the World Wide Web at `http://www.netlib.org/index.html`. From there you can search for what you want and use your web browser to download the appropriate files. There is no charge for accessing Netlib; you pay only the network access fees you normally incur, if any, to send and receive email or to browse the web.

The best-known subprogram library in Netlib is **LAPACK** [37], which contains routines for factoring and inverting matrices, estimating condition numbers and error bounds, solving least-squares problems and systems of linear equations, and finding eigenvalues, eigenvectors, and singular-value decompositions. LAPACK invokes routines from another library, the Basic Linear Algebra Subprograms or **BLAS**, to perform matrix arithmetic calculations such as dot products. The BLAS comes with LAPACK, or can be obtained separately from Netlib. One of the BLAS routines, `D1MACH`, contains information about the floating-point number systems used by various computer architectures, including those of many older machines that did not conform to the IEEE standard described in §4.2, and this routine is used by some of the other software packages that are available from Netlib. LAPACK is the descendant of two famous earlier subprogram libraries, **LINPACK** and **EISPACK**, which are also in Netlib and also invoke routines from the BLAS. If you are working with an old program you might discover that it uses routines from those libraries.

Other Netlib offerings of wide interest are the **ToMS Library**, which contains routines implementing the collected algorithms from *Transactions on Mathematical Software,* a journal published by the Association for Computing Machinery (ACM), and the general-purpose **SLATEC Library**.

Another important code repository is the book *Numerical Recipes in FORTRAN* [12], which includes source listings of "well over 300" routines, of somewhat variable quality, covering many of the topics found in general-purpose libraries. This code can also be obtained in machine-readable form at modest cost by following ordering instructions given in the book. Some other textbooks on numerical methods also contain listings of FORTRAN source code to implement the algorithms they discuss, or pseudocode that can be readily translated into FORTRAN. For example, [45] includes cubic spline routines that are so widely used as to be practically standard.

In using public-domain software it is important to remember that "Anything free comes with no guarantee!" and this adage is in fact included as a reminder in every file sent by Netlib. However, the routines that are available from Netlib, and those printed in *Numerical Recipes* and most other textbooks, are in fact generally recognized by the numerical computing community as safe and useful. There are many sources of public-domain numerical software besides those mentioned here, and your web browser's search engine might find some of them if you give it the right keywords to describe what you need. But you should never use free software from any origin you're not sure of unless you first study the source code carefully to verify that it is safe to use and actually does what you want. Any software you get from somebody else could potentially be a **Trojan horse**, containing code that will, when you run it, corrupt your files or otherwise vandalize your computing environment.

6.7   Conclusion and Omissions

In this chapter we have encountered subprograms for doing matrix arithmetic, solving non-linear equations, computing elementary mathematical functions, getting operating system services, and implementing all the standard numerical methods. The next two chapters are devoted to some features of FORTRAN that can be used to make the subprograms you write more general, so that a single routine can be used for a wider variety of problems. After that, our study of programming will involve subprograms so often and so integrally that you might think writing and using subprograms is what the rest of the book is really all about.

Subprograms are the movable type of computer programming, enormously multiplying our productivity and creative power by letting us write code once and use it many times. Professional programmers write main programs that consist, like our example in §6.1, of little more than some data declarations and a series of subprogram invocations. As discussed further in §12.2.2, what they spend their time and effort on is writing subroutines and functions that can be used in lots of different main programs.

I have intentionally omitted from this chapter several language features that are not part of Classical FORTRAN and a few other topics of mainly cultural interest, including these:

> *ENTRY; alternate returns; SAVE; call by value; statement functions;* other built-in mathematical functions, including the complementary error, log gamma, cotangent, degree trigonometric, positive difference, and type-changing maximum and minimum functions; the GAMS catalog and software classification system; the IBM Scientific Subroutine Package, precursor to the IMSL Library; the use from FORTRAN of routines written in other languages, and the use from other languages of routines written in FORTRAN.

6.8   Exercises

6.8.1   What are the advantages of using subprograms instead of writing open code for everything? Write down as many as you can think of.

6.8.2   What are the three kinds of subprograms in Classical FORTRAN, and where in this book is each of them first discussed in detail?

6.8.3   List the differences between SUBROUTINE subprograms and FUNCTION subprograms. Can a FUNCTION subprogram change the values of its parameters?

6.8.4   In the open code of the introductory example in §6.1, is it really necessary to transpose F or G? Explain. Are the transpositions necessary when the program is rewritten using subroutines?

6.8.5 Is it permissible for a subprogram's dummy parameters to have the same names as the actual parameters in the invoking routine? For example, if a subroutine is invoked using `CALL ABCD(X,Y)` could `ABCD` begin with the statement `SUBROUTINE ABCD(X,Y)`? Explain.

6.8.6 The introductory example of §6.1 contemplates evaluation of the matrix expression $\mathbf{D} = \mathbf{G}^\top(\mathbf{I} - \mathbf{G}\mathbf{F}\mathbf{F}^\top\mathbf{G}^\top)^{-1}\mathbf{G}$ by explicit inversion of the matrix $(\mathbf{I} - \mathbf{G}\mathbf{F}\mathbf{F}^\top\mathbf{G}^\top)$. Numerical analysts will find this an unappetizing prospect [73, p108] on account of the large number of operations involved, and the consequent growth of roundoff errors, in computing the matrix inverse. (a) Show how the inversion can be avoided by solving two triangular systems of matrix equations. Hint: factor $(\mathbf{I} - \mathbf{G}\mathbf{F}\mathbf{F}^\top\mathbf{G}^\top) = \mathbf{L}\mathbf{U}$, where $\mathbf{L}$ and $\mathbf{U}$ are respectively lower and upper triangular matrices. Matrix factorization is discussed in numerical methods textbooks such as [4]. (b) What subroutines might be useful in doing the calculation this way?

6.8.7 FORTRAN routines are compiled separately. What are some consequences of this?

6.8.8 Write a `MATMPY` subroutine that implements the algorithm of §5.6 to find the product of two 10×10 matrices.

6.8.9 Consider the following program.

```
L=37                          SUBROUTINE SETPRT(I,J)
CALL SETPRT(K,L)              I=2
K=54                          PRINT *,J
CALL SETPRT(K,K)              RETURN
STOP                          END
END
```

(a) Describe in words what `SETPRT` does. (b) What is printed by the program? Verify your answer by experiment. (c) Revise `SETPRT` so that it does what you described even if it is passed the same actual parameter for both of its dummy parameters. Now what does the program print?

6.8.10 In the introductory example of §6.1 the matrix `F` is not needed after its inverse `FT` has been found. It is therefore proposed to eliminate the array `FT` and let the first call to `MATRNS` simply overwrite `F` with its transpose. (a) Does writing `CALL MATRNS(F, F)` yield the correct transpose in `F`? If not, explain why not. (b) Rewrite `MATRNS` so that it has the calling sequence `CALL MATRNS(F)` and transposes `F` in-place.

6.8.11 Write a `FUNCTION` subprogram `ANGL(Z)` to return the angle in degrees between the real axis of the complex plane and a line connecting the origin to the point representing `Z`.

6.8.12 Can the same array be passed for both actual parameters to the routine below? Why or why not? What must be true of a subprogram in order for its behavior to change when it is passed the same variable for more than one actual parameter?

```
      SUBROUTINE TWICE(A,B)
      REAL*8 A(3,3),B(3,3)
      DO 1 I=1,3
      DO 1 J=1,3
          B(I,J)=2.D0*A(I,J)
    1 CONTINUE
      RETURN
      END
```

6.8.13 Write a FUNCTION subprogram named THREE that returns the value 3.D0. According to §6.3, does this routine require a parameter? If so, what is its purpose? Is this a good way to specify the value 3.D0 in a program? Would it be a good way to specify an approximation to π?

6.8.14 Write FUNCTION subprograms (a) DTR(DEG) to return the angle in radians corresponding to a given angle DEG in degrees; and (b) RTD(RAD) to return the angle in degrees corresponding to a given angle RAD in radians. Use REAL*8 variables everywhere. (c) Confirm by experiment that DTR(RTD(RAD)) gives back RAD, and that RTD(DTR(DEG)) gives back DEG. If these results are not exact, explain why.

6.8.15 What does this program print out? Why?

```
      PRINT *,KF(3)              FUNCTION KF(N)
      STOP                      KF=0
      END                       DO 1 I=1,N
                                   CALL KS(I,KF)
      SUBROUTINE KS(L,M)      1 CONTINUE
      M=M+L                     RETURN
      RETURN                    END
      END
```

6.8.16 Classical FORTRAN does not permit recursion, which is a subprogram directly or indirectly invoking itself. Is the statement Y=DEXP(DEXP(X)) an example of recursion? If not, write code that does provide an example of recursion.

6.8.17 Consider the following program, in which subroutine SUB changes the value of I.

```
      DO 1 I=1,10               SUBROUTINE SUB(J)
         CALL SUB(I)            PRINT *,J
    1 CONTINUE                  J=J+1
      STOP                      RETURN
      END                       END
```

(a) Is it legal for the code in the body of a DO loop to change the value of the loop counter? (b) Can the compiler detect that the value of I will be changed in the body of the loop? If not, explain why not. (c) What values get printed out? Confirm your answer by experiment.

6.8.18 When is it permissible for the actual parameter that is passed to a subprogram to be a literal constant, such as 3.7D0 or 8?

6.8.19 Write a subroutine that only prints the message

```
Good bye, cruel world.
```

and stops. Does this subroutine need any parameters? Does it return any value? Does it perform an action?

6.8.20 Exercise 4.10.48 introduced the mixed congruential algorithm for generating pseudorandom numbers. Use that algorithm to write SUBROUTINE MYRAND(ISEED) that replaces ISEED by the next iterate in the pseudorandom sequence. Use the main program at the top of the next page to test your routine.

```
      INTEGER*4 ISEED/123457/
      DO 1 K=1,100
          CALL MYRAND(ISEED)
          PRINT *,ISEED
    1 CONTINUE
      STOP
      END
```

6.8.21 The **Riemann Zeta function** is defined as

$$\zeta(x) = \sum_{i=1}^{\infty} 1/i^x$$

(a) Write a FUNCTION subprogram to return the REAL*8 value of this function when it is evaluated for REAL*8 values of x, and confirm by experiment that it correctly approximates the exact value $\zeta(2) = \frac{1}{6}\pi^2$. (b) Revise your function to accept COMPLEX*16 values of x and return COMPLEX*16 function values. Does it still give the right answer if $x = 2+0\sqrt{-1}$? Confirm that it correctly approximates $\zeta(2+2\sqrt{-1}) \approx .8673518296359931 - .2751272388078576\sqrt{-1}$.

6.8.22 A series expansion for the **error function** is [35, §7.1.5]

$$\text{erf}(x) = \frac{2}{\sqrt{\pi}} \sum_{n=0}^{\infty} \frac{(-1)^n x^{2n+1}}{(2n+1)n!}$$

where x is a real variable. One way of finding erf(z), where $z = x + y\sqrt{-1}$, is simply to evaluate this series using complex arithmetic. If the elementary function library used by your FORTRAN compiler provides a routine for approximating erf(z) for COMPLEX*16 arguments z then (according to §6.6.1) it will be called CDERF(Z), but some libraries do not include such a routine. (a) Does your compiler recognize CDERF(Z) as a built-in function? (b) Write a FUNCTION subprogram CDERF(Z) that approximates the COMPLEX*16 value using the series given above. What is the largest number of terms that can be used? (c) Verify that your routine returns an answer close to erf($1+\sqrt{-1}$) $\approx 1.3161512816979477 + 0.19045346923783471\sqrt{-1}$.

6.8.23 In the example of §6.5, we want to initialize B only once. The solutions proposed there make the initialization conditional on a call counter or logical flag indicating whether this is the first invocation of PM, but other approaches might also work. Discuss the virtues and drawbacks of instead (a) using a compile-time initialization for B; (b) moving the initialization of B to a separate subroutine that can be called before the first invocation of PM, and passing the B returned by that subroutine into PM.

6.8.24 Describe how a call counter could be used to make a subroutine return immediately *every other* time it is called. What happens if a fixed-point overflow occurs in incrementing a call counter?

6.8.25 What is the name of the REAL*4 version (a) of DEXP? (b) Of DMOD?

6.8.26 Write a FUNCTION subprogram CSNGL(Z) that converts a COMPLEX*16 argument Z into a COMPLEX*8 return value.

6.8.27 A FUNCTION subprogram can be of any scalar data type, including LOGICAL*4. (a) Write FUNCTION EXOR(A,B) that returns a logical value equal to the exclusive-OR of the logical values A and B. The exclusive-OR operation is defined by the **truth table** at the top of the next page, in which the entries are the values of A exclusive-OR B.

	A=0	A=1
B=0	0	1
B=1	1	0

Is the *bitwise* exclusive-OR function IEOR described in §4.6.3 of any help in solving this problem? (b) Write FUNCTION LOGIC(A,B,TABLE) that returns .TRUE. or .FALSE. according to the values of the logical variables A and B and a truth table contained in the INTEGER*4 parameter TABLE. Hint: the most general solution is also the simplest, and does not explicitly consider separate cases to account for all 16 possible 2 × 2 truth tables.

6.8.28 The statement J=MOD(I,K) assigns to J the remainder from the integer division I/K. (a) Assuming I and K are positive, write a code segment to accomplish the same result without using any built-in functions. (b) Is the MOD function defined for values of I or K that are zero or negative? Confirm your answer by experiment. (c) Revise your solution to part (a) so that it gives the same results as the MOD function even if I or K or both are zero or negative.

6.8.29 Tests similar to the one below are commonplace in legacy FORTRAN programs.

```
IF(I-5*(I/5).EQ.2) GO TO 1
```

(a) If I is a positive integer, what does the expression I-5*(I/5) represent? Explain what the statement does. (b) Recode the statement, using the MOD function to achieve the same effect. (c) Which version do you think is easier to understand? Justify your opinion.

6.8.30 An integer is **prime** if it is evenly divisible only by itself and 1. (a) Write FUNCTION PRIME(N) that returns the LOGICAL*4 value .TRUE. if |N| (the absolute value of N) is a prime number, or .FALSE. if |N| is **composite** (that is, not prime). (b) Use your function in a program that determines whether 123457 is a prime number. (c) Use your function in a program that prints the first 100 primes.

6.8.31 One of the built-in functions mentioned in the table of §6.6.1 is DMOD(X,S), which returns $x \bmod s$ when x and s are REAL*8 numbers. The mathematical definition of this function is $x \bmod s = x - s \times \lfloor x/s \rfloor$, where $\lfloor q \rfloor$, called the **floor** of q, means the largest whole number less than or equal to q. (a) Write a program that prints out the values of DMOD(5.D0,1.D0) and DMOD(0.5D0,0.1D0), and compare its output to the values you get using the definition given above. (b) Is it necessary to perform a great many arithmetic operations in order for small errors in the machine representation of floating-point numbers to have a significant effect? Explain.

6.8.32 The statement J=ISIGN(I,K) sets J to the absolute value of I with the sign of K. To what does J get set on your computer if K=0?

6.8.33 As mentioned in §6.6, some built-in functions are defined only for a limited *range* of argument values. The function Y=DEXP(X) is defined only for X less than or equal to $\ln(R_{max})$, the natural logarithm of the largest number representable as a REAL*8 value. (a) Explain *why* X must be less than $\ln(R_{max})$. (b) Determine, by experiment or calculation, a value for $\ln(R_{max})$ more precise than "about 710."

6.8.34 What is the *domain* over which the values of the following functions can vary? In other words, if X is a REAL*8 value in the range over which the function is defined, how big or small can Y become if (a) Y=DSQRT(X); (b) Y=DLOG(X); (c) Y=DGAMMA(X)?

6.8.35 What is the most negative value of X for which DEXP(X) returns a nonzero value?

6.8.36 Write a program that prints out $\Gamma(\mathrm{erf}(\ln(x)))$ and use it to verify that

$$\Gamma(\mathrm{erf}(\ln(\pi))) \approx 1.0730819520232482$$

6.8.37 What UNIX™ system routine returns (a) the current date and time of day? (b) Pseudorandom numbers?

6.8.38 Where can you find subprograms ready-made to use in your programs? Where in this book is it described how to link library subprograms into your executables?

6.8.39 Name four libraries in which you might find routines for computing the eigenvalues of a matrix.

6.8.40 List some advantages and drawbacks of using commercial and public-domain software.

6.8.41 How do you find software in, and acquire it from, Netlib?

6.8.42 The subprograms you write for a single program should have names that differ from one another and from the names of FORTRAN built-in functions and operating system routines. Determine by experiment what your FORTRAN compiler does with the following program, which violates this rule.

```
REAL*8 DSQRT
PRINT *,DSQRT(2.D0)
STOP
END
FUNCTION DSQRT(X)
REAL*8 DSQRT,X
DSQRT=X**2
RETURN
END
```

7

Adjustable Dimensions and EXTERNAL

The matrix arithmetic subprograms we discussed in §6.1 and §6.3 were for 10×10 matrices and 10-element vectors, so the MATRNS and DDOT routines we wrote dimensioned their dummy arguments that way. If tomorrow we need to transpose an array that is, say, 20×30 instead, or to find the dot product of 50-element vectors, we can simply modify the source code of the affected routine to use the new dimensions, and recompile it. However, if in a single program we want to use MATRNS or DDOT repeatedly to process arrays having several different sizes, we need some way to have the dimensions inside the subprogram change from one invocation to the next. In this chapter we will see how FORTRAN makes that possible.

It is often necessary for one subprogram to use another, as in the case study of §6.4 where BISECT invoked FCN. If we wanted to replace FCN with a different function subprogram, we could just modify the source code of BISECT to invoke the new routine instead, and recompile. But if in a single program we wanted to have BISECT use FCN1 on one occasion and FCN2 on another, we would need some way of specifying in each call of BISECT the *name* of the subprogram that it should invoke this time. We will also see in this chapter how FORTRAN makes that possible.

Both these generalizations are essential if our subprograms are to be useful for solving many different problems rather than just particular special cases.

7.1 Adjustable Dimensions

To see how the array dimensions in a subprogram can be adjusted, we will begin by reconsidering the DDOT function of §6.3. The source code we wrote there is shown again on the left below. It assumes that X and Y are 10 elements long.

```
      FUNCTION DDOT(X,Y)              FUNCTION DDOT(X,Y,N)
      REAL*8 DDOT,X(10),Y(10)         REAL*8 DDOT,X(N),Y(N)
      DDOT=0.DO                       DDOT=0.DO
      DO 1 J=1,10                     DO 1 J=1,N
          DDOT=DDOT+X(J)*Y(J)             DDOT=DDOT+X(J)*Y(J)
    1 CONTINUE                      1 CONTINUE
      RETURN                          RETURN
      END                             END
```

The code on the right receives the INTEGER*4 variable N as a subprogram parameter and uses it as an **adjustable dimension** for X and Y. It also uses N as the DO limit, so this DDOT works for vectors of arbitrary length. In the code at the top of the next page, the new version is invoked twice with different values of N.

```
REAL*8 U(5),V(5),UV,W(1000),Z(1000),WZ,DDOT
:
UV=DDOT(U,V,5)
WZ=DDOT(W,Z,1000)
```

An array argument can be adjustably dimensioned *only* if both it and the adjustable dimensions are passed as parameters to the subprogram.

We can revise MATRNS in a similar way, passing both dimensions of the matrix to be transposed. The old code from §6.1 is shown on the left below, and a version with adjustable dimensions is on the right.

```
      SUBROUTINE MATRNS(A, AT)            SUBROUTINE MATRNS(A,M,N, AT)
      REAL*8 A(10,10),AT(10,10)           REAL*8 A(M,N),AT(N,M)
      DO 1 J=1,10                         DO 1 J=1,M
      DO 1 I=1,10                         DO 1 I=1,N
          AT(I,J)=A(J,I)                      AT(I,J)=A(J,I)
    1 CONTINUE                         1 CONTINUE
      RETURN                              RETURN
      END                                 END
```

With adjustable dimensions we can use MATRNS for matrices of arbitrary size. In the code below, the new version is called twice with different values of M and N.

```
REAL*8 R(3,2),RT(2,3),S(10,10),ST(10,10)
:
CALL MATRNS(R,3,2, RT)
CALL MATRNS(S,10,10, ST)
```

7.1.1 Assumed-Size Arrays

The adjustable dimensioning scheme illustrated above can actually be simplified slightly because of the way that FORTRAN stores arrays in memory. Recall from §5.3 that the elements of an array are laid out by column-major order in successive memory locations starting at the address that corresponds to the name of the array. Thus, in the DDOT example we considered earlier, the vector U is stored like this.

U(1)	U(2)	U(3)	U(4)	U(5)	
65608	65616	65624	65632	65640	65648

Parameters are passed by reference, as explained in §6.2, so when an array is passed to a subprogram what the machine code of the subprogram actually receives is the array's starting address. In the picture of memory shown above, the vector U is assumed to have the starting address 65608. If U is passed to DDOT for the dummy parameter X, then DDOT uses the name X to refer to those same storage locations, like this.

X(1)	X(2)	X(3)	X(4)	X(5)	
65608	65616	65624	65632	65640	65648

When the FORTRAN compiler translates the source code of DDOT, it must generate machine instructions for calculating the actual memory addresses where the elements of X are stored. For an array having one dimension, the only things that are needed to do this are the starting address and the size in bytes of each element. The address of X(J) is just the starting address passed in for X, plus $(J-1)$ times the size in bytes of each element. The type declaration in DDOT tells the compiler that X has elements 8 bytes long, so it can find X(2) at the starting address plus 8 bytes, X(3) at the starting address plus 16 bytes, and so on.

Thus, in DDOT the compiler really needs to be told only that the vector parameters are vectors, not how long they are. Because of this, rather than using N as an adjustable dimension we could instead dimension X and Y as shown below.

```
        FUNCTION DDOT(X,Y,N)
        REAL*8 DDOT,X(*),Y(*)
        DDOT=0.D0
        DO 1 J=1,N
            DDOT=DDOT+X(J)*Y(J)
    1   CONTINUE
        RETURN
        END
```

The asterisk in X(*) and Y(*) is called an **assumed-size** dimension. It tells the compiler that X and Y are 1-dimensional arrays *without* saying how many elements they were declared to have, back in the routine where they were allocated. In using an assumed size, we reassure the compiler that *we* know how long the array actually is, even though *it* doesn't know, and we promise that we will not refer to elements beyond that dimensioned size.

For arrays with two dimensions, the situation is more complicated. Recall from §5.3 that column-major order puts the top of the first column at the starting address of the array, the top of the second column head-to-toe after the bottom of the first column, and so forth. Thus, in the MATRNS example of §7.1 the matrix R, which has 3 rows and 2 columns, is stored like this.

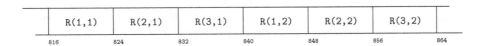

R(1,1)	R(2,1)	R(3,1)	R(1,2)	R(2,2)	R(3,2)	
816	824	832	840	848	856	864

What does the machine code of MATRNS need to know in order to calculate the address of, say, R(2,2)? The offset of R(2,2) from the beginning of the array must be, just as in the case of a one-dimensional array, the number of bytes in each element times the number of elements coming before R(2,2). Now, however, R(2,2) has the whole first column in front of it as well as the first element R(1,2) of the second column, putting it $8[3+1] = 32$ bytes past the starting address 816. In general, R(I,J) comes after $(J-1)$ preceding columns (each of length 3) and $(I-1)$ elements in column J, so its address is the starting address plus $8[(J-1)\times3+(I-1)]$. Thus, to find the address of a given element in a two-dimensional array, we need to know not only its starting address and the number of bytes in each element, but also *the length of the columns* (i.e., the number of rows, here 3). But the length of the rows (the number of columns, here 2) doesn't enter into the calculation so it can be an assumed-size dimension in MATRNS, like this.

```
      SUBROUTINE MATRNS(A,M,N, AT)
      REAL*8 A(M,*),AT(N,*)
      DO 1 J=1,M
      DO 1 I=1,N
          AT(I,J)=A(J,I)
    1 CONTINUE
      RETURN
      END
```

Similarly, the declaration of AT must give the actual number of its rows (here N) but can specify an assumed size for the number of its columns.

If an array having more than two dimensions is passed as a subprogram parameter, only the final dimension can be declared assumed-size in the subprogram. The dimensions of an array other than the rightmost dimension are called the array's **leading dimensions**. The actual values of the leading dimensions are needed in the addressing calculations.

Because a subprogram uses the number of bytes in each element of an array parameter to calculate the addresses of the elements, disaster will ensue if the array is typed differently in the subprogram and in the routine where the array was allocated. For example, suppose we erroneously write this.

```
C     these are the wrong type
      REAL*4 E(3,3),ET(3,3)
      CALL MATRNS(E,3,3, ET)
      :
```

MATRNS will still calculate the addresses of elements in A and AT assuming each element is 8 bytes long rather than 4, eventually attempting (perhaps successfully) to use and change quantities in memory far outside the storage reserved for E and ET. Because the element index values never exceed 3, this mistake will *not* be detected as an array bounds violation even if a compiler option is used to enable subscript checking (as described in §14.1.2).

Assumed-size dimensions are convenient in cases when the trailing dimension of an array parameter is not also passed as a subprogram parameter and therefore cannot be used as an adjustable dimension (also see §13.7.1). If the actual value of a trailing dimension *is* passed, however, as in MATRNS above, it should be used in preference to * so that the code is easier for humans to understand. The main reason for learning how assumed-size dimensions work is so that it will be easier to see what happens when a subprogram uses only part of an array parameter, as discussed next.

7.1.2   Passing Leading Dimensions

In the examples we have seen so far the adjustable dimensions passed to subprograms were always the actual sizes of the arrays, but that is not always convenient. Because Classical FORTRAN uses static memory allocation, it is necessary to make arrays big enough for the largest problem instance that a program will be used to solve. This is done by declaring each array with big enough constant dimensions where it is allocated, in the main program or in the subprogram where the array first appears. Problems smaller than the maximum size will use only part of such an array, and subprograms that receive the array as a parameter must also be told the actual size of the problem. This introduces a complication that is illustrated by the following program.

```
      INTEGER*4 K(3,4)/1,2,3,4,5,6,7,8,9,10,11,12/
      CALL SUB(K,2,3)
      STOP
      END
C
      SUBROUTINE SUB(L,M,N)
      INTEGER*4 L(M,N)
      PRINT *,L(1,1),L(1,2),L(1,3)
      PRINT *,L(2,1),L(2,2),L(2,3)
      RETURN
      END
```

$$K = \begin{bmatrix} 1 & 4 & 7 & 10 \\ 2 & 5 & 8 & 11 \\ 3 & 6 & 9 & 12 \end{bmatrix}$$

The main uses a compile-time initialization to give K the contents shown on the right. What does the subroutine print? The dummy parameters M and N receive the values 2 and 3 respectively, so inside of SUB the array is adjustably dimensioned as L(2,3). It might seem that this should correspond to the upper left 2×3 submatrix of K, but instead the program prints the following output.

```
 1 3 5
 2 4 6
```

This behavior, which might strike you as counterintuitive, can be explained by recalling how the compiler arranges the elements of K, and how it assumes the elements of L must be arranged, according to column-major order.

In the main program, where the memory locations for K are allocated by the compiler, the matrix gets laid out as shown below.

K(1,1)	(2,1)	(3,1)	(1,2)	(2,2)	(3,2)	(1,3)	(2,3)	(3,3)	(1,4)	(2,4)	(3,4)
1	2	3	4	5	6	7	8	9	10	11	12
5184	5188	5192	5196	5200	5204	5208	5212	5216	5220	5224	5228	5232

When the subroutine is called, the address of the first element of K, here 5184, is as usual passed for the dummy parameter L. Because of separate compilation, the compiler cannot know how the actual parameter corresponding to L was originally dimensioned. The adjustable dimensions are M = 2 and N = 3, so SUB interprets the data *as though it were laid out in column-major order for a 2×3 matrix instead.* So what the subroutine sees for L is this, and the PRINT statements produce the output shown above.

L(1,1)	(2,1)	(1,2)	(2,2)	(1,3)	(2,3)
1	2	3	4	5	6	7	8	9	10	11	12
5184	5188	5192	5196	5200	5204	5208	5212	5216	5220	5224	5228	5232

If it is the upper left submatrix of K that we really want to be using when we refer in the subroutine to L, then we must provide the subroutine's machine code with the information that it needs to compute the addresses of elements in K. As explained in §7.1.1 that means the starting address (passed for L), the length of each array element (declared to be 4 bytes), and *the length of the columns in* K. In other words, we must pass the actual leading dimension of K, so the compiler will know that the columns of the array are 3 elements long even though we are using only 2 rows.

Here is a revised version of the program in which SUB uses the leading dimension LDL of the actual parameter corresponding to L.

```
      INTEGER*4 K(3,4)/1,2,3,4,5,6,7,8,9,10,11,12/
      CALL SUB(K,3,2,3)
      STOP
      END
C
      SUBROUTINE SUB(L,LDL,M,N)
      INTEGER*4 L(LDL,*)
      PRINT *,L(1,1),L(1,2),L(1,3)
      PRINT *,L(2,1),L(2,2),L(2,3)
      RETURN
      END
```

$$K = \begin{bmatrix} 1 & 4 & 7 & 10 \\ 2 & 5 & 8 & 11 \\ 3 & 6 & 9 & 12 \end{bmatrix}$$

The second dimension of L doesn't matter, and we have made it assumed-size because none of the subroutine parameters give the actual second dimension of K. Now the program prints this output.

```
 1  4  7
 2  5  8
```

Of course if K and L had d dimensions instead of two, we would have to pass $d - 1$ leading dimensions. The general principle to be drawn from this example is that if you pass an array to a subprogram and you want element (I,J) to refer to the same storage location from within the subprogram that it does in the routine where the array was allocated, you must *pass the leading dimensions* and use them as adjustable dimensions inside the subprogram.

As a further illustration of this idea, here is a program that passes the leading dimensions of A and AT to MATRNS.

```
      REAL*8 H(10,10),HT(10,10)
      H(1,1)=1.D0
      H(2,1)=2.D0
      H(1,2)=3.D0
      H(2,2)=4.D0
      CALL MATRNS(H,10,2,2, HT,10)
      PRINT *,HT(1,1),HT(1,2)
      PRINT *,HT(2,1),HT(2,2)
      STOP
      END
C
      SUBROUTINE MATRNS(A,LDA,M,N, AT,LDAT)
      REAL*8 A(LDA,*),AT(LDAT,*)
      DO 1 J=1,M
      DO 1 I=1,N
          AT(I,J)=A(J,I)
    1 CONTINUE
      RETURN
      END
```

This version of MATRNS can be used for problems of arbitrary size in which the matrices are stored in arrays that might be larger than the problem size.

7.2   EXTERNAL

In the case study of §6.4, we used the BISECT subroutine once. Now suppose that in a single main program we need to call BISECT twice, first to solve $\sin(x) - \frac{1}{2}x = 0$ and then to solve $e^{-x} - x = 0$. The version of BISECT in §6.4 invokes only a single function subprogram, so for BISECT to use two different functions we will have to modify it somehow.

7.2.1   Fixed Subprogram Names

One way of making BISECT use different functions is to add a parameter to its calling sequence telling which formula to use. Then BISECT can pass that information on to FCN, which will evaluate the right formula. Here is some code that implements this idea.

```
      SUBROUTINE BISECT(NF,XL,XR, X,F)        FUNCTION FCN(NF,X)
      REAL*8 XL,XR,X,FCN,FL,FR,F              REAL*8 FCN,X
      FL=FCN(NF,XL)                           IF(NF.EQ.1) FCN=DSIN(X)-0.5D0*X
      FR=FCN(NF,XR)                           IF(NF.EQ.2) FCN=DEXP(-X)-X
      DO 1 I=1,10                             RETURN
          X=0.5D0*(XL+XR)                     END
          F=FCN(NF,X)
          IF(F*FL .LT. 0.D0) THEN
              XR=X
              FR=F
          ELSE
              XL=X
              FL=F
          ENDIF
    1 CONTINUE
      RETURN
      END
```

The integer NF, which must be set in the main program and passed to BISECT, tells which formula to use. It is BISECT that invokes FCN, so the only way we can get NF into FCN is through BISECT. We could add more formulas by simply modifying FCN to recognize more values of NF.

Another approach would be to define each function with a different subprogram and test NF in BISECT to determine which one to invoke, as shown at the top of the next page. To accommodate more functions with this scheme we would need to further modify BISECT to recognize more values of NF. Even with only two choices, our formerly-simple BISECT code is now clogged with IF statements. On the other hand, the functions FCN1 and FCN2 of this solution are each simpler than the FCN that receives NF.

Both of these methods require the function subprograms to have particular names. A subprogram name like FCN or FCN1 in this example is referred to as a **magic name**, because it has been given a special status by being fixed or **hard-coded** into the program. Magic names often turn out to be a nuisance, as they would in this example if we wanted to use the name FCN or FCN1 for some other purpose in the program that calls BISECT. For example, suppose our main program also needs to evaluate $\int_0^1 e^{\sqrt{x}}dx$ by calling an integration subroutine that uses the magic name FCN or FCN1 to define the integrand. It wouldn't make sense to have two different function subprograms with the same name, so we will have to change either BISECT or the integration routine to make the magic names different. In a

```
      SUBROUTINE BISECT(NF,XL,XR, X,F)        FUNCTION FCN1(X)
      REAL*8 XL,XR,X,FCN1,FCN2,FL,FR,F        REAL*8 FCN1,X
      IF(NF.EQ.1) FL=FCN1(XL)                 FCN1=DSIN(X)-0.5D0*X
      IF(NF.EQ.2) FL=FCN2(XL)                 RETURN
      IF(NF.EQ.1) FR=FCN1(XR)                 END
      IF(NF.EQ.2) FR=FCN2(XR)
      DO 1 I=1,10                             FUNCTION FCN2(X)
          X=0.5D0*(XL+XR)                     REAL*8 FCN2,X
          IF(NF.EQ.1) F=FCN1(X)               FCN2=DEXP(-X)-X
          IF(NF.EQ.2) F=FCN2(X)               RETURN
          IF(F*FL .LT. 0.D0) THEN             END
              XR=X
              FR=F
          ELSE
              XL=X
              FL=F
          ENDIF
    1 CONTINUE
      RETURN
      END
```

big program involving many subprograms it might take a lot of work to resolve such name conflicts. If we are using library routines, we might not be able to change the names (because we don't have access to the source code) or want to (because other programs might be using the routines, and depend on those magic names).

7.2.2 Passing Subprogram Names

To avoid the need for magic names, and all the problems they can cause, FORTRAN provides a much simpler and more elegant solution to the problem of specifying what subprogram to invoke: it is possible to pass the name of one subprogram to another as a parameter. To let the compiler distinguish between the name of a subprogram and the value of an ordinary variable, it is necessary to declare routine names that are passed in this way as EXTERNAL.

The code at the top of the next page uses this approach to call BISECT twice, first for FCN1 and then for FCN2 (these are the routines we defined above in §7.2.1). Here are some observations about the program.

1⇨ In BISECT, the name FCN is a dummy parameter. Just as XL in the subroutine corresponds to the actual parameter A on the first call of BISECT and to C on the second call, references to FCN are really references to FCN1 during the first call and to FCN2 during the second.

2⇨ The EXTERNAL statement in the main program tells the compiler that the symbols FCN1 and FCN2 are subprogram names. Because of separate compilation, it would otherwise assume they were scalar variables passed to BISECT (even if there were other evidence to the contrary, such as an invocation of each function in the main program).

3⇨ In BISECT, it is clear that FCN is a function because it is used with a parenthesized argument list and is not dimensioned as an array. Furthermore, FCN appears as a dummy parameter of the subroutine, so if it is a function it must be one whose actual name is being passed in. Most compilers can therefore deduce that FCN is an external symbol even if it is not declared that way in the subroutine. Unfortunately, some few compilers *do not*. If you want your code to work everywhere, then every routine name that is passed as a parameter must be declared EXTERNAL in the routine that receives it as well as in the calling routine.

```
REAL*8 A,B,C,D,X,F                 SUBROUTINE BISECT(FCN,XL,XR, X,F)
EXTERNAL FCN1,FCN2                 EXTERNAL FCN
A=0.5D0                            REAL*8 XL,XR,X,FCN,FL,FR,F
B=2.5D0                            FL=FCN(XL)
CALL BISECT(FCN1,A,B, X,F)         FR=FCN(XR)
PRINT *,X,F                        DO 1 I=1,10
C=0.D0                                 X=0.5D0*(XL+XR)
D=1.D0                                 F=FCN(X)
CALL BISECT(FCN2,C,D, X,F)             IF(F*FL .LT.0.D0) THEN
PRINT *,X,F                                XR=X
STOP                                       FR=F
END                                    ELSE
                                           XL=X
                                           FL=F
                                       ENDIF
                                 1 CONTINUE
                                   RETURN
                                   END
```

4⟹ Subroutine names can be passed just like the names of function subprograms, and either can be passed to both subroutines and functions.

5⟹ In this example FCN1 and FCN2 are not actually invoked in the main program, so they return no values to the main program and don't need to be typed there. Inside the subroutine, FCN does return values, so it must be typed there.

A function subprogram need not be declared EXTERNAL if only its *value*, rather than its *name*, is passed. For example, if SUB is a subroutine and G is a function, then a statement such as the one on the left below

```
CALL SUB(G(X))                     VALUE=G(X)
                                   CALL SUB(VALUE)
```

evaluates G(X) first and then passes the resulting numerical value to SUB as an ordinary scalar, exactly as though the code had been written as on the right. Conversely, if we intended to pass the *name* G to SUB, so that SUB could invoke the function G for itself, then it would be an error to code the call as shown on the left (even if G is declared EXTERNAL). Inappropriate uses of EXTERNAL are discussed further in §13.7 and §14.3.2.

7.3 Summary and Omissions

When you pass an array parameter to a subprogram, always pass its declared leading dimensions as well, and use them as adjustable dimensions inside the subprogram. If the declared trailing dimension of the array happens also to be passed in as a parameter, use it as an adjustable dimension inside the subprogram too, so that a compiler option can be given to detect array subscript overflows. If the trailing dimension is not passed as a parameter, make it assumed size by coding it as *.

When you pass the name of one subprogram to another, declare it to be EXTERNAL in both the calling routine and the called routine.

Here are some topics relating to adjustable dimensions and `EXTERNAL` that I have intentionally omitted from this chapter.

Arrays dimensioned 1; use of integer expressions, rather than simple variables, as adjustable dimensions; use of `EXTERNAL` to substitute your own routine for a FORTRAN built-in function; `INTRINSIC`, and passing the names of built-in functions.

7.4   Exercises

7.4.1   Is it sometimes desirable simply to give an array the same fixed dimensions in all of the routines where it appears? Why is this often inconvenient? Is it ever impossible?

7.4.2   In Classical FORTRAN, can an adjustable dimension or an assumed-size dimension be used in declaring an array where it is originally allocated, such as in a main program? If so, devise an example; if not, explain why not.

7.4.3   In Classical FORTRAN, can an adjustable dimension be used in declaring a local array, as in this example?

```
      SUBROUTINE NBRAVG(M,N)
      INTEGER*4 M(N),TEMP(N)
      :
```

If not, explain why not. If so, read §17.1.2.

7.4.4   This code implements the algorithm of §5.6 to find the product of two 10×10 matrices, as required for Exercise 6.8.8.

```
      SUBROUTINE MATMPY(A,B, C)
      REAL*8 A(10,10),B(10,10),C(10,10)
      DO 1 I=1,10
      DO 1 J=1,10
          C(I,J)=0.D0
          DO 2 K=1,10
              C(I,J)=C(I,J)+A(I,K)*B(K,J)
    2     CONTINUE
    1 CONTINUE
      RETURN
      END
```

Revise the routine to use adjustable dimensions so that it can multiply matrices of various sizes, stored in arrays that might be larger than needed. It should be impossible in calling the revised routine to specify a product that is not conformable.

7.4.5   A 3-dimensional array is passed to a subprogram. Which of its dimensions can be given as * when the array is declared within the subprogram? Why? $\boxed{\text{A}}$ The first. $\boxed{\text{B}}$ The last. $\boxed{\text{C}}$ All but the first. $\boxed{\text{D}}$ All but the last. $\boxed{\text{E}}$ None.

7.4.6 In the following program the vector L is dimensioned (5:10) in the main but (1:6) in TRYDIM.

```
INTEGER*4 L(5:10)/1,2,3,4,5,6/     SUBROUTINE TRYDIM(L)
CALL TRYDIM(L)                     INTEGER*4 L(1:6)
STOP                              PRINT *,L(5)
END                               RETURN
                                  END
```

(a) What value gets printed? Explain why. (b) Change the dimensioning in TRYDIM to L(*). What gets printed now?

7.4.7 Revise the following routine, *without using adjustable dimensions*, so that it can be used with vectors of arbitrary length.

```
    SUBROUTINE ADDVEC(X,Y, Z)
    REAL*8 X(10),Y(10),Z(10)
    DO 1 K=1,10
        Z(K)=X(K)+Y(K)
  1 CONTINUE
    RETURN
    END
```

Is the single dimension of a vector a leading dimension, or the trailing dimension? Explain.

7.4.8 In the following code, what is the largest value of N that can safely be passed into SUB from its caller?

```
    SUBROUTINE SUB(N)                FUNCTION ISMSQ(Z,N)
    INTEGER*4 Z(5)/1,2,3,5,8/        INTEGER*4 Z(*)
    PRINT *,ISMSQ(Z,N)               ISMSQ=0
    RETURN                           DO 1 J=2,N+1
    END                                    ISMSQ=ISMSQ+Z(J)**2
                                   1 CONTINUE
                                     RETURN
                                     END
```

If a larger value of N is inadvertently passed to SUB, will the error be detected if the -C (or -fbounds-check) compiler option was given? Revise the code listed above to write a message and stop if N is too large.

7.4.9 An $n \times n$ matrix A is **symmetric** if $a_{i,j} = a_{j,i}$ for all $i = 1, \ldots, n$ and $j = 1, \ldots, n$. (a) Write a FUNCTION subprogram to determine whether a square matrix is symmetric. Your subprogram should return the LOGICAL*4 value .TRUE. if the matrix is symmetric, and .FALSE. if it is not. It should be possible to use your routine to check matrices of arbitrary size, and to check matrices that are stored in the upper-left corner of an array that is dimensioned bigger than it needs to be in the invoking program. (b) Would it sometimes make sense to identify as symmetric a matrix in which the largest difference between $a_{i,j}$ and $a_{j,i}$ is, say, 10^{-14}? Make it possible for the invoking routine to tell your function how close the compared elements have to be in order for the array to be considered symmetric.

7.4.10 In the following code, what is the largest value of N that can safely be used?

```
REAL*8 A(10)                          SUBROUTINE XYZ(A)
CALL XYZ(A)                           REAL*8 A(20)
PRINT *,A                             READ *,N
STOP                                  DO 1 I=1,N
END                                          A(I)=DFLOAT(I)
                                    1 CONTINUE
                                      RETURN
                                      END
```

Justify your answer, and correct the typographical error in XYZ.

7.4.11 Revise the following routine so it can be called with arrays of arbitrary size, if the upper left subarray of B that is used has M rows and N columns.

```
    SUBROUTINE EVEN(A, B)
    REAL*8 A(20,30),B(10,30)
    DO 1 J=1,30
    DO 1 I=1,10
        B(I,J)=A(2*I,J)
  1 CONTINUE
    RETURN
    END
```

Assume that in the calling routine, where A and B are originally allocated, B might be dimensioned larger than M × N and A might be dimensioned larger than 2M × N.

7.4.12 A program containing the array declaration INTEGER*4 LMN(12,37) is compiled, and when the executable is loaded into memory the first element of LMN happens to be located at the address 4936. At what address is the element LMN(7,23) located?

7.4.13 This problem is about when to make an array dimension assumed-size and when to make it adjustable.

(a) The code on the left below is the beginning of a main program that calls ABC, and the code on the right is the beginning of the subroutine.

```
REAL*8 X(10)                          SUBROUTINE ABC(X,N)
READ *,N                              REAL*8 X(?)
CALL ABC(X,N)                         DO 1 I=1,N
  :                                     :
```

In ABC, should the question mark ? be replaced by *, or by N? Explain why.

(b) Now consider the main program on the left below.

```
PARAMETER(N=10)                       SUBROUTINE ABC(X,N)
REAL*8 X(N)                           REAL*8 X(?)
CALL ABC(X,N)                         DO 1 I=1,N
  :                                     :
```

In ABC, should the question mark ? be replaced by *, or by N? Explain why.

(c) If ABC is a library routine that might be called from main programs like either of the examples above, how should X be dimensioned in the subroutine?

(d) If the calling sequence of ABC can be changed, how could the program of part (a) be revised so that X is adjustably dimensioned to the correct size even though N varies?

7.4.14 The following program is the revised version of the example about leading dimensions from §7.1.2, but with a mistake. Instead of passing a leading dimension of 3 to SUB, this main program erroneously passes a leading dimension of 4. What does the program print? Why?

```
      INTEGER*4 K(3,4)/1,2,3,4,5,6,7,8,9,10,11,12/
      CALL SUB(K,4,2,3)
      STOP
      END
C
      SUBROUTINE SUB(L,LDL,M,N)
      INTEGER*4 L(LDL,*)
      PRINT *,L(1,1),L(1,2),L(1,3)
      PRINT *,L(2,1),L(2,2),L(2,3)
      RETURN
      END
```

7.4.15 Consider the following program.

```
      INTEGER*4 A(10,10)/100*0/        SUBROUTINE PRT22(A)
      N=3                              INTEGER*4 A(10,10)
      DO 1 I=1,N                       PRINT *,A(2,2)
      DO 1 J=1,N                       RETURN
          A(I,J)=J+N*(I-1)             END
    1 CONTINUE
      CALL PRT22(A)
      STOP
      END
```

(a) What does the program print? Why? (b) Revise PRT22 to not use fixed dimensions for A; in the main program, change only the CALL. Run your revised program and confirm that it prints the same output as before.

7.4.16 The program below is supposed to print the sum of the diagonal elements, or **trace**, of the matrix

$$M = \begin{bmatrix} 5 & 1 \\ 3 & 8 \end{bmatrix}.$$

Fix the coding mistakes so that TRACE works correctly for arrays of arbitrary size. Then confirm that the program works, by compiling and running it to print the result 13.

```
      INTEGER*4 M(10,10),TRACE         FUNCTION TRACE(A,N)
      M(1,1)=5                         INTEGER*4 A(N,N)
      M(2,1)=3                         K=0
      M(1,2)=1                         DO 1 I=1,N
      M(2,2)=8                             K=K+A(I,I)
      PRINT *,TRACE(2,M)             1 CONTINUE
      STOP                             END
      END
```

7.4.17 To which subroutine, SUBA or SUBB, does this main program pass the subprogram name T? What kind of a subprogram is T?

```
EXTERNAL T
REAL*8 T
CALL SUBA(T(5.D0))
CALL SUBB(T,5.D0)
STOP
END
```

7.4.18 What is a magic or hard-coded subprogram name, and why are they undesirable?

7.4.19 Explain why a subprogram name that is passed as a parameter to another subprogram must be declared EXTERNAL.

7.4.20 What is printed by this program?

```
EXTERNAL H                          FUNCTION NZ(P,K)
PRINT *,NZ(H,2)                     EXTERNAL P
STOP                                CALL P(3,NZ)
END                                 RETURN
                                    END

SUBROUTINE H(K,L)
L=K+2
RETURN
END
```

Describe the flow of control.

7.4.21 If $y = f(x)$ is a monotone function for $x \in [a, b]$, then the inverse function $f^{-1}(y)$ is the value of x for which $f(x) = y$. (a) Write a FORTRAN FUNCTION with the calling sequence X=FINV(F,A,B,Y) to return $f^{-1}(y)$. Here F is the name of a function subprogram having the calling sequence F(X) and returning $f(x)$, A and B are the endpoints of the interval $[a, b]$, and Y is the function value y at which the value of the inverse function is desired. Use the function $f(x) = x^2$ and $y = 2$ to test your code. What does your code do if there is no x at which $f(x) = y$? (b) Can you find a way to accomplish this calculation by calling BISECT within FINV? If not, explain why not.

7.4.22 Consider the following program.

```
EXTERNAL K                          SUBROUTINE SUB(L,I,J)
I=2                                 EXTERNAL L
CALL SUB(K,I,J)                     J=L(I)
PRINT *,J                           RETURN
STOP                                END
END

                                    FUNCTION K(I)
                                    K=I+1
                                    RETURN
                                    END
```

(a) What gets printed? Explain why, describe the flow of control, and confirm your answer by experiment. (b) What happens if the EXTERNAL in the main program is omitted? Explain why, describe the flow of control, and confirm your answer by experiment. (c) What happens if the EXTERNAL in SUB is omitted? The answer to this part might vary with the compiler you use.

7.4.23 The NAG library routine D02BAF can be used to integrate ordinary differential equations with given initial conditions. Here is an example of such an **initial value problem**.

$$\frac{dy}{dx} = -ax, \qquad y(0) = 5$$

The subroutine's calling sequence is

```
CALL D02BAF(X,XEND,N,Y,TOL,FCN,W,IFAIL)
```

in which N and IFAIL are INTEGER*4 and the other parameters are all REAL*8. X must be set to the initial value of x (zero in the example problem above) before D02BAF is called, and has the same value as XEND when the subroutine returns. XEND specifies the value of x at which Y is to be found. N is the number of equations (1 in the example problem). Y is a vector of N dependent variables (so it's just a scalar for the example problem). Y must be set to the initial value of y (5 in the example problem) on entry, and it contains the value $y(\text{XEND})$ on return. TOL is the error tolerance that D02BAF is to use, and FCN is the *name* of a subroutine subprogram described below. W(N,7) is a work array. IFAIL should be set to zero on entry, and will be zero on return unless D02BAF detected an error.

The subroutine FCN has this calling sequence, in which all the variables are REAL*8.

```
SUBROUTINE FCN(X,Y,F)
```

This routine must return in F the value of dy/dx at X.

(a) Write a main program and an FCN subroutine that could be linked with D02BAF to integrate the example problem given above and print out $y(10)$ for $a = 2$. (b) If you have access to the NAG library, run your program and verify that the value it reports for $y(10)$ is correct.

8

COMMON

In the case study of §6.4 we called a version of the BISECT subroutine to solve $f(x) = 0$, where $f(x) = \sin(x) - px$ and $p = \frac{1}{2}$. Here is the subprogram we used to define the function $f(x)$, revised slightly to store the constant $\frac{1}{2}$ in a variable named P instead of coding the literal 0.5D0 directly in the formula.

```
FUNCTION FCN(X)
REAL*8 FCN,X,P/0.5D0/
FCN=DSIN(X)-P*X
RETURN
END
```

If we want to solve $f(x) = 0$ for some other value of p, we can just change the initialization of the variable P in FCN, and recompile.

Now suppose that, during a single run of the program, we need to solve the equation for several *different* values of p. To do this the main program will have to call BISECT repeatedly, and during each call FCN will have to use whatever value of P the main program has set. But it is BISECT, not the main program, that invokes FCN. Using the language features that you have learned so far, the only way a value of P can get from the main program into FCN is through BISECT.

8.1 Passing Data Through

The program below solves $\sin(x) - px = 0$ for $p = 0.4$ and $p = 0.5$ by setting the value of p in the main and passing it through BISECT and on to FCN.

```
      REAL*8 XL,XR,X,F,Q                SUBROUTINE BISECT(XL,XR,R, X,F)
      DO 1 IQ=4,5                       REAL*8 XL,XR,X,FCN,FL,FR,F,R
          XL=0.5D0                      FL=FCN(XL,R)
          XR=2.5D0                      FR=FCN(XR,R)
          Q=DFLOAT(IQ)/10.D0            DO 1 I=1,10
          CALL BISECT(XL,XR,Q, X,F)         X=0.5D0*(XL+XR)
          PRINT *,Q,X,F                     F=FCN(X,R)
    1 CONTINUE                              IF(F*FL .LT. 0.D0) THEN
      STOP                                      XR=X
      END                                       FR=F
                                             ELSE
      FUNCTION FCN(X,P)                          XL=X
      REAL*8 FCN,X,P                             FL=F
      FCN=DSIN(X)-P*X                        ENDIF
      RETURN                        1 CONTINUE
      END                                 RETURN
                                          END
```

Because of separate compilation, the variable name used to store p need not be the same in the different routines, and as a reminder of that fact I have called the coefficient Q in the main program and R inside BISECT.

Unfortunately, passing the coefficient in this way makes BISECT rather specialized. Now it is useful for problems in which the calling routine needs to send exactly one REAL*8 scalar on to FCN, but if tomorrow we need to send two values we will have to revise BISECT again. If we pass several different EXTERNAL function names into BISECT in a single program, as described in §7.2, each function might require different types and quantities of data to be set in the main program and passed on, possibly resulting in a complicated mess of extra parameters to BISECT and FCN only some of which would be used in each case. None of these complications can be tolerated in a library routine, which must be useful in the widest possible variety of situations. If BISECT were a library routine that somebody else wrote, we might not even have the source code for it and then *could not* change it as proposed above. Often it is necessary for a program that calls a library routine to communicate data to another subprogram that the library routine invokes, but it is impossible to modify the library routine to pass the data through.

8.2   Passing Data Around

To solve this problem FORTRAN provides a way for routines to share storage locations in memory, and this allows two routines to exchange data even when one does not invoke the other. As I explained in §6.1, a quantity that is not passed as a subprogram parameter is strictly local to the main program or subprogram in which it is used. Allowing two routines to have certain memory locations in common makes the values stored there accessible from either routine. The code below is our earlier example rewritten to store p in a COMMON **block** that is shared by the main program and FCN.

```
      REAL*8 XL,XR,X,F,Q                SUBROUTINE BISECT(XL,XR, X,F)
      COMMON /SLOPE/ Q                  REAL*8 XL,XR,X,FCN,FL,FR,F
      DO 1 IQ=4,5                       FL=FCN(XL)
          XL=0.5D0                      FR=FCN(XR)
          XR=2.5D0                      DO 1 I=1,10
          Q=DFLOAT(IQ)/10.D0                X=0.5D0*(XL+XR)
          CALL BISECT(XL,XR, X,F)           F=FCN(X)
          PRINT *,Q,X,F                     IF(F*FL .LT. 0.D0) THEN
    1 CONTINUE                                  XR=X
      STOP                                      FR=F
      END                                   ELSE
                                              XL=X
      FUNCTION FCN(X)                         FL=F
      COMMON /SLOPE/ P                      ENDIF
      REAL*8 FCN,X,P                  1 CONTINUE
      FCN=DSIN(X)-P*X                   RETURN
      RETURN                           END
      END
```

The version of BISECT listed here is just the one we had in §6.4, with no added parameter, and FCN once again has only the single parameter X. The value of p set by the main program in its variable Q is stored at a shared memory location named SLOPE, and is therefore available in FCN as its variable P. Here are some observations about the program.

1⟹ The variable name appearing in the COMMON statement in the main program is local to that routine, and has nothing to do with the variable name appearing in the COMMON statement in FCN. But Q in the main program and P in the function both refer to the same storage location in memory, so the variables must share the same *value*.

2⟹ Just as each actual parameter that is passed to a subprogram should have the same type as the corresponding dummy parameter, variables that refer to the same storage location in COMMON should be of the same type. It wouldn't make sense for P in our example to be, say, REAL*4 while Q is REAL*8.

3⟹ The names of COMMON blocks, such as SLOPE in our example, follow the same rules as the names of SUBROUTINE subprograms. In a COMMON statement, the block name must be enclosed by slashes, as in /SLOPE/. Separate compilation ensures that the names of variables used in different routines have nothing to do with one another (whether or not they appear in COMMON statements), but the name of a COMMON block is known throughout the program and must be the same wherever the COMMON block is used. COMMON block names resemble the names of subprograms in that they are preserved by the compilation process and used by the loader in linking together the program. Because of this the names of different COMMON blocks must be different from one another and from the names of any subprograms used in the program, including system and library routines.

4⟹ By using COMMON storage to pass the value of p from the main program to FCN we avoided the need to modify BISECT at all, and now BISECT knows nothing about the memory region named SLOPE or its contents (Q in the main, P in FCN). This is as it should be, because BISECT itself has no *reason* to know about p. As we shall see in §12.2.2, hiding data from the parts of a program that don't need it is an important principle of good program design.

5⟹ FORTRAN provides COMMON storage so that it can be used to pass data around library and general-purpose routines, as illustrated by this example.

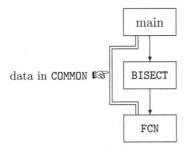

With only two exceptions (described in §11) *this is the only way that COMMON storage should be used.* In particular, COMMON should *not* be used in place of a parameter list for passing variables between two routines when one invokes the other directly (also see §13.8).

8.3 Alignment

The example of §8.2 used COMMON to share a single value between the main program and FCN. A COMMON block can contain more than one variable, and then it is necessary to worry about the order of the variables and possibly about their placement in memory.

8.3.1 Alignment by Order

Just as the actual parameters that are passed to a subprogram correspond to the dummy parameters according to order rather than according to name, variables listed in a COMMON block correspond by order rather than by name. In the code below, A is aligned with B because they are both names for the first doubleword of DATA, and C is aligned with D because they both refer to the second doubleword.

```
        SUBROUTINE STUV(H)              FUNCTION WXYZ(G)
        COMMON /DATA/ A,C              COMMON /DATA/ B,D
        REAL*8 A,C                     REAL*8 B,D
```

If function WXYZ needs to access only the first value, it is permissible for its COMMON block DATA to be **short**, like this.

```
                                C       this makes B and A the same
        SUBROUTINE STUV(H)              FUNCTION WXYZ(G)
        COMMON /DATA/ A,C              COMMON /DATA/ B
        REAL*8 A,C                     REAL*8 B
```

The variable B still aligns with A because they both refer to the doubleword at the beginning of DATA. However, if function WXYZ needs only the *second* value, which it names D, it would still be necessary for its COMMON statement to list both B and D in order to preserve the alignment of D with C. Then one would say that B is present only to **pad** the COMMON block. Writing this

```
                                C       this makes D and A the same
        SUBROUTINE STUV(H)              FUNCTION WXYZ(G)
        COMMON /DATA/ A,C              COMMON /DATA/ D
        REAL*8 A,C                     REAL*8 D
```

would align D with A rather than C, because A and D are now both names for the first doubleword of DATA.

If several routines access data from the same COMMON block, it is sometimes possible to hide data from a routine that does not need it by arranging the variables so the value that is unneeded by that routine comes at the end of the block. Then that routine can use a short block to avoid seeing the unwanted data. Again assuming that WXYZ needs only the value that STUV puts in C, we could rearrange DATA like this.

```
C                                      this makes D and C the same
        SUBROUTINE STUV(H)              FUNCTION WXYZ(G)
        COMMON /DATA/ C,A              COMMON /DATA/ D
        REAL*8 C,A                     REAL*8 D
```

Now WXYZ can use a short block to share only the value it needs.

8.3.2 Alignment in Memory

Variables in a COMMON block, in addition to being aligned with the corresponding variables in other routines where the block appears, are also aligned *on boundaries in memory*. If a COMMON block contains variables of different types, memory alignment can affect the speed with which the data are accessed. A COMMON block always starts on a doubleword boundary, and in most computer architectures the processor can load from and store to memory most efficiently if the variables in the block are aligned on boundaries corresponding to their lengths.

In the memory diagram below, doubleword boundaries are shown as solid vertical lines and labeled with their addresses; word boundaries that are not also doubleword boundaries are dashed.

```
COMMON /RIGHT/ X,I          COMMON /WRONG/ J,Y
REAL*8 X                    INTEGER*4 J
INTEGER*4 I                 REAL*8 Y
```

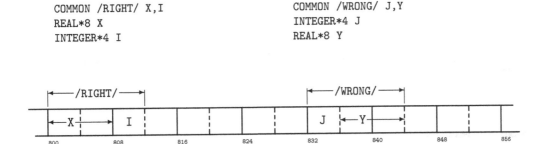

The variables X and Y are REAL*8, so operations that move doubleword-aligned doublewords will be used to access or replace their values. Because X is itself doubleword aligned, one operation can load or store its value. Y is aligned on an odd word boundary, so two memory operations (and perhaps additional logic to dissect the doublewords and reassemble the halves of Y) are required for each load or store. Most UNIX™ compilers issue a warning message about awkward alignments like the one in /WRONG/.

Additional ways in which using COMMON storage can affect program efficiency are discussed in §15.2.10.

8.4   Formal Parameters and COMMON

Variables appearing in a subprogram's parameter list, whether they are actual or dummy parameters, are also referred to as the routine's **formal parameters**, to distinguish them from quantities that are communicated with the routine by means of COMMON. Because formal parameters are passed by reference, it wouldn't make sense for a dummy parameter to also be in COMMON like this.

```
C     this is an error
      SUBROUTINE SUB(X)
      COMMON /BK1/ X
      :
```

The COMMON statement asserts that X is located in memory at the address of /BK1/, but what gets passed into SUB for the dummy parameter X will be the address of the actual parameter in the calling routine. Because of separate compilation, there is no way the compiler can ensure in compiling SUB that these two addresses will be the same. Indeed, SUB might be called several times with *different* actual parameters, and there is no way that they could all be at the same address in /BK1/.

For similar reasons, a variable can't be in more than one COMMON block. A FORTRAN variable is the name of a *unique* location in memory, so it can't name two *different* locations by being in two different COMMON blocks.

In contrast, there is nothing logically wrong with passing a variable that is in COMMON as the *actual* parameter to a subprogram, like this.

```
C     this is legal
      COMMON /BK2/ Y
      CALL SUB(Y)
      :
```

Here the compiler can just pass for the formal parameter the address that it knows Y has in /BK2/.

8.5   Arrays in COMMON

The examples we have considered so far all involved scalars, but arrays can also be in COMMON. In the code below, the matrix RTS is read by the main program and shared via /PRES/ with the function SF.

```
C     main program                    FUNCTION SF(W)
      COMMON /PRES/ RTS               REAL*8 SF,W
      REAL*8 RTS(14,23)               COMMON /PRES/ RTS
      READ *,RTS                      REAL*8 RTS(14,23)
      :                               :
```

Adjustable and assumed-size dimensions are *not allowed* on arrays in COMMON, so both array dimensions on RTS must be integer literals or PARAMETER constants everywhere the COMMON block appears. However, it is permissible to use a short block to ignore unused array elements that come at the right (high-address) end of a COMMON block. For example, SF could instead use the array declaration shown below.

```
C     main program                    FUNCTION SF(W)
      COMMON /PRES/ RTS               REAL*8 SF,W
      REAL*8 RTS(14,23)               COMMON /PRES/ RTS
      READ *,RTS              C        ignore last 3 columns
      :                               REAL*8 RTS(14,20)
```

Because RTS is stored according to column-major order, these dimensions have the effect of hiding its last 3 columns from SF.

When passing arrays in COMMON, just as when passing arrays as formal parameters, it is essential to use the exact leading dimension or dimensions; only the trailing dimension can differ from one routine to another. The largest size declared for an array in COMMON determines the actual size of the array and the actual length of the COMMON block. Some loaders issue a warning message if different occurrences of a COMMON block have different lengths, or if the first occurrence encountered in loading is not the longest.

8.6   BLOCK DATA

Ever since §4.5 we have been accustomed to using compile-time initialization to specify the value that a variable is to be given when the program's executable is loaded into memory. For example, writing

```
INTEGER*4 I/3/
```

sets I to the value 3 before execution begins. There are many circumstances in which it would be convenient to initialize variables in COMMON this way, but the code below illustrates why that would not make sense.

```
      SUBROUTINE SUBA                      SUBROUTINE SUBB
      COMMON /VALUE/ I                     COMMON /VALUE/ I
C     this is illegal                 C    this is illegal
      INTEGER*4 I/3/                       INTEGER*4 I/4/
```

If both of these routines are part of the same program, to which value will I be set? To avoid such an ambiguity, FORTRAN prohibits code like that above and permits the initialization of data in COMMON only with a BLOCK DATA subprogram. This is the third kind of FORTRAN subprogram originally mentioned in §6.1. The following example initializes the COMMON variable I to the value 2.

```
      BLOCK DATA
      COMMON /VALUE/ I
C     here the initialization is allowed
      INTEGER*4 I/2/
      END
```

Here are some observations about this BLOCK DATA subprogram.

1⇨   A BLOCK DATA subprogram must begin with those words, and like all subprograms it must end with an END. In between there are *no executable statements,* only COMMON statements, variable declarations, and possibly PARAMETER statements and comments.

2⇨   The compiler translates a BLOCK DATA into object code that contains the data initializations but no machine instructions. The data initializations are used by the loader, when it links together the executable, to put the given initial values into the memory locations named by the variables. BLOCK DATA can only be used to initialize variables that are in COMMON.

3⇨   A BLOCK DATA subprogram is used only at compile time; it is never called or otherwise invoked by your program at run time. It has no RETURN.

4⇨   Using more than one BLOCK DATA in a program would make it again possible to have the kind of ambiguity we sought to prevent, so most UNIX™ loaders consider that an error. Having at most one BLOCK DATA means that *all* compile-time initializations of variables in COMMON must be performed there. The single BLOCK DATA in a program must therefore include COMMON statements for all of the blocks containing variables that are to be initialized.

5⇨   Many loaders use the information provided by the BLOCK DATA subprogram, if one is present, to lay out *all* of the COMMON storage for the program, so in BLOCK DATA *each block should include all of the variables* that appear in it anywhere in the program. Short blocks cannot be used in BLOCK DATA, even if only some of the variables need to be initialized. Because of separate compilation, the compiler cannot warn you about variables you forget to mention in BLOCK DATA, and your loader might or might not mention length discrepancies between COMMON blocks appearing in BLOCK DATA and elsewhere in the program. Hand-checking is therefore necessary to guard against the omission of COMMON variables from BLOCK DATA.

8.7   Omissions

The only language features concerning COMMON that I have not considered a part of Classical FORTRAN, and that I have therefore omitted from this chapter, are *blank COMMON* and *dimensioning arrays in COMMON statements*. Many bad programming practices have grown up over the years involving the use of COMMON storage, and I have also refrained from discussing them here. These topics are taken up in §13.8.

8.8   Exercises

8.8.1   Explain why it is undesirable to pass a parameter from one routine to another by sending it through an intervening routine that does not otherwise use the parameter.

8.8.2   What is COMMON storage for? How does data in COMMON get from one routine to another?

8.8.3   Does a COMMON block name carry a value? Can it be declared as an array? Explain why a COMMON block name must be different from the names of subprograms used in the program. What are the rules for naming a BLOCK DATA subprogram?

8.8.4   What output is printed by the following program? Why?

```
      COMMON /DATA/ A                    SUBROUTINE SUB1(F,K)
      EXTERNAL G                         EXTERNAL F
      A=2.5                              IF(2*(K/2) .EQ. K) THEN
      DO 1 I=1,3                            PRINT *,F(K)
         CALL SUB1(G,I)                  ELSE
    1 CONTINUE                              PRINT *,'odd'
      STOP                               ENDIF
      END                                RETURN
C                                        END
      FUNCTION G(L)
      COMMON /DATA/ B
      G=B*FLOAT(L)
      RETURN
      END
```

8.8.5   What output is printed by the following program? Rewrite it to eliminate the COMMON block, but don't eliminate subroutine PRT.

```
COMMON /ABC/ X              SUBROUTINE PRT
REAL*8 X(3)                 COMMON /ABC/ A,B,C
X(1)=1.D0                   REAL*8 A,B,C
X(2)=2.D0                   PRINT *,A,B,C
X(3)=3.D0                   RETURN
CALL PRT                    END
STOP
END
```

8.8.6   What output is printed by the following program? Why?

```
COMMON /BAD/ X              SUBROUTINE SUB
REAL*8 X                    COMMON /BAD/ Y
X=1.D0                      PRINT *,Y
CALL SUB                    RETURN
STOP                        END
END
```

Rewrite the program to eliminate the COMMON block, without eliminating subroutine SUB, and to print 1.0 for Y.

8.8.7   In the following program, (a) revise the layout of /LIST/ to hide as much data as possible from routines that don't need it; (b) eliminate /LIST/.

```
C    main program               SUBROUTINE S2
     COMMON /LIST/ A,B,I,J       COMMON /LIST/ A,B,I,J
     REAL*8 A,B                  REAL*8 A,B
     :                           :
     [use A, B, I, and J]        [use only A]
     CALL S1                     :
     CALL S2                     END
     CALL S3
     :
     END

     SUBROUTINE S1               SUBROUTINE S3
     COMMON /LIST/ A,B,I,J       COMMON /LIST/ A,B,I,J
     REAL*8 A,B                  REAL*8 A,B
     :                           :
     [use only A and I]          [use only I, J, and B]
     :                           :
     END                         END
```

8.8.8   In the code below, the main and FUZZY share a COMMON block named BIG. (a) On what memory boundaries are Z, SWITCH(1), and A aligned? (b) How should PAD be dimensioned to align L with SWITCH(3)? (c) Does it matter that PAD differs in type from Z and SWITCH? Explain.

```
C     main program                    SUBROUTINE FUZZY
      COMMON /BIG/ Z,SWITCH,A         COMMON /BIG/ PAD,L
      COMPLEX*16 Z                    INTEGER*4 PAD(?)
      LOGICAL*4 SWITCH(5)             LOGICAL*4 L
      :                               :
```

8.8.9   In which of the following COMMON blocks is the real variable doubleword aligned? Why do awkward alignments elicit a warning from most FORTRAN compilers?

```
      REAL*8 A,B,C
      INTEGER*4 I,J,K,L,M,N
      COMMON /BLK1/ I,J,A
      COMMON /BLK2/ B,K,L
      COMMON /BLK3/ M,C,N
```

8.8.10   The FORTRAN compiler automatically aligns variables that are *not* in COMMON on memory boundaries appropriate to their lengths, but it is the programmer's responsibility to ensure that variables in COMMON are properly aligned in memory. Explain why the compiler cannot relieve the programmer of that task by automatically aligning variables in COMMON.

8.8.11   What is printed by the following program? Does the value of N in /NCOM/ change when N gets incremented in SUBX, or not until SUBX returns to the main program?

```
      COMMON /NCOM/ N                 SUBROUTINE SUBX(N)
      N=0                             N=N+1
      CALL SUBX(N)                    CALL SUBY
      STOP                            RETURN
      END                             END
C
      SUBROUTINE SUBY
      COMMON /NCOM/ N
      PRINT *,N
      RETURN
      END
```

8.8.12   Subroutine NUTSO receives X as a formal parameter and then must communicate its value to other routines in the COMMON block COMX. Why is the code illegal as written? Revise it to accomplish the objective using legal FORTRAN.

```
      SUBROUTINE NUTSO(X)
      REAL*8 X
C     this is illegal
      COMMON /COMX/ X
      :
```

8.8.13 A routine contains the COMMON statements listed on the left below (and no others). Which of the EQUIVALENCE statements shown on the right could it also contain? Why?

```
COMMON /AC/ A,C              EQUIVALENCE(A,C)
COMMON /BD/ B,D              EQUIVALENCE(A,B)
                             EQUIVALENCE(A,X)
```

8.8.14 Why can't a variable be in two different COMMON blocks, like this?

```
C     this is illegal
      COMMON /ONE/ I
      COMMON /TWO/ I
      :
```

8.8.15 The COMMON block /COM/ is used to communicate between the three routines whose beginnings are listed below. Revise this code so that Y(2) and Y(3) are not visible in SC. Inside SC, refer to Y(1) by the name Z.

```
      SUBROUTINE SA                        SUBROUTINE SC
      COMMON /COM/ Y,W                     COMMON /COM/ Y,W
      REAL*8 Y(3),W                        REAL*8 Y(3)
      :                                    :
      [use Y(1), Y(2), Y(3), and W]        [use Y(1) and W]

      SUBROUTINE SB
      COMMON /COM/ Y,W
      REAL*8 Y(3),W
      :
      [use Y(1), Y(2), Y(3), and W]
```

8.8.16 The FORTRAN compiler reports errors for a program containing the following code segment.

```
      PARAMETER(WPHP=746.0)
      COMMON /CONST/ WPHP
      :
```

(a) Explain why this code doesn't make sense. (b) How can the variable WPHP be initialized at compile time?

8.8.17 Does your compiler accept the following code?

```
      COMMON /EQIV/ I
      COMMON /EQIV/ J
      I=1
      PRINT *,J
      STOP
      END
```

If so, what does the program print? Does this sort of coding seem like a good idea?

8.8.18 A program contains the following COMMON block.

```
COMMON /NGC3/ SW3,N,MI,ME,XH,XL
LOGICAL*4 SW3(5)
REAL*8 XH(50),XL(50)
```

It is desired to set the variables to the following values before execution of the program begins: all elements of SW3 to true, N to 3, MI to 2, ME to 0, XH(1) to 1, XH(2) to 2, XH(3) to 3, and the remaining elements of XH and all of XL to 0. (a) Write a BLOCK DATA subprogram to provide the appropriate compile-time initializations. (b) How is the BLOCK DATA invoked from within the program with which it is used? Explain.

8.8.19 Let $h(a)$ be the smallest positive value of x for which $\sin(x) = ax$. Use BISECT to find $h(a)$ for 11 equally-spaced values of a in the range $[0, \frac{1}{2}]$, and print a table showing the a and corresponding $h(a)$ values. Hint: use starting values of XL=1.D0 and XR=3.2D0 to ensure that the desired root is in the initial interval for all values of $a \in [0, \frac{1}{2}]$.

8.8.20 In Exercise 6.8.20 you wrote a subroutine MYRAND(ISEED) that uses the mixed congruential algorithm to replace ISEED by the next number in a pseudorandom sequence. Now suppose that MYRAND is to be used in several different subprograms of a large program to return successive values from the pseudorandom sequence. In such a situation it will probably be inconvenient to pass ISEED around among the various routines in which MYRAND is invoked, so instead of having MYRAND use its input value of ISEED to calculate the new value we would prefer to have ISEED be only an *output* from the routine. That means that MYRAND will have to remember, from one call to the next, the value that ISEED last had. This is easily accomplished if we are content to always use the same starting seed, like this.

```
SUBROUTINE MYRAND(ISEED)
INTEGER*4 N/123457/,A/843314861/,B/453816693/
INTEGER*4 PLUS/Z'7FFFFFFF'/
ISEED=A*N+B
ISEED=IAND(ISEED,PLUS)
N=ISEED
RETURN
END
```

(a) Explain in your own words how this approach makes it unnecessary for a routine that invokes MYRAND to know what the previously-generated number was, and how this is advantageous in practice. (b) In many applications it is desirable to change the random number seed from one run of the program to another. Modify the version of MYRAND listed above to make it possible to set the initial value of N from a main program that does not call MYRAND.

8.8.21 Exercise 7.4.23 asks you to use the NAG library routine D02BAF to solve an initial value problem. (a) Modify the code you wrote for that problem in such a way that the constant a can be adjusted within the main program. (b) If you have access to the NAG library, use the new version of your program to find and print out, in a single run, $y(10)$ for *both* $a = 2$ and $a = 3$.

8.8.22 Exercise 7.4.21 asks if it would be possible to use the BISECT subroutine to solve the equation $f(x) = y$ for x when the name of the subprogram that calculates f is to be passed as an EXTERNAL symbol. This is impossible, because there is no way to get the subprogram name into the function $g(x) = f(x) - y$ that BISECT would invoke to solve $f(x) = y$. Now suppose we are willing to require that the name of the function returning $f(x)$ be F. Write a FUNCTION subprogram that has the calling sequence X=FINV(A,B,Y) and returns the value of x, where $x \in [a, b]$, at which $f(x) = y$, and which calls BISECT to get the answer by solving $g(x) = 0$.

8.8.23 Many problems in engineering and science involve matching the predictions of some theoretical model for a physical system to observations made on the real system. Typically the model contains several constant parameters x_j, $j = 1, \ldots, n$, and for any assumed values of these parameters we can calculate the system response that is predicted by the model. The **parameter estimation** problem is to find the parameter values that make the model's predictions $\hat{y}_i$ agree as closely as possible with some observations y_i, $i = 1, \ldots, L$ made on the actual system. To measure the error in the model we might use

$$z = \sum_{i=1}^{L} (\hat{y}_i - y_i)^2.$$

Because the predictions $\hat{y}_i$ depend on the parameter values x_j used in the model, z is a function of the x_j. The parameter estimation can then be solved by finding the x_j that minimize z. It might be possible to find the best values of the x_j by calling a library subprogram for optimization, as in the program below.

```
REAL*8 X(3)                    FUNCTION Z(X)
EXTERNAL Z                     REAL*8 Z,X(3),YHAT(100)
CALL OPT(Z,X)                  CALL MODEL(X,YHAT)
PRINT *,X                      :
STOP                           [code to compute Z]
END                            :
                               RETURN
                               END
```

In this example $n = 3$ and $L = 100$. The main program calls a library routine named OPT to minimize the error, and OPT in turn invokes Z many times to find the error for different trial parameter vectors X. Each time Z is invoked, it uses the MODEL routine to compute the model response YHAT corresponding to the parameter values that are currently in X, and then it must compute the error function given above.

Revise the program to read the measured values y_i from the keyboard just once, and to use that data in Z for computing the error.

9

Input and Output

Computer programs communicate with the world by receiving inputs and delivering outputs through hardware such as your workstation keyboard and display and the disk drives that store your files. FORTRAN programs do these input and output (**I/O**) operations by reading from and writing to **logical I/O units**. The actual transfers of data are performed by a set of subprograms that are part of FORTRAN, called the **I/O library**. When the FORTRAN compiler translates your source program into machine instructions, it inserts calls to library routines that execute any I/O statements you have used. The I/O library routines associate the logical I/O units mentioned in your source program with **logical I/O devices** such as file names (and in UNIX™ with device names in **/dev**). These logical devices are in turn attached by the operating system to the appropriate physical I/O devices.

So far our programs have done input and output only by using statements such as these.

```
READ *, A,B
PRINT *,'A=',A,'B=',B
```

READ * reads from the logical I/O unit named **standard-in**, which is normally attached to the keyboard, and PRINT * writes to the logical I/O unit named **standard-out**, which is normally attached to the display. (Standard-in and standard-out can be redirected at run time on the UNIX™ command line that invokes the program, as explained in §9.4.)

Another important attribute of the READ * statement is that the values it reads can be in a wide variety of formats. For example, suppose a program contains the statements

```
REAL*4 C
READ *,C
```

and the value of C that is to be input from the keyboard is 37. Typing any one of the following input text strings results in the variable getting that value.

```
37.0
   37,
+37
3.7E+01
```

Because of the variations that are permitted in the format of the values that are entered, READ * is said to do **free-format** input. Programs that receive input from the keyboard *should* read it using free format, so that the user can enter the data in any reasonable way. In the case of PRINT *, we leave it up to the FORTRAN I/O library to decide the precise format to use in writing out our results, and this is referred to as free-format output. Much of the output that typical programs produce doesn't need to be in any particular format.

Sometimes, however, it is desirable to insist that the data be read or written in some particular fixed format, or in binary form rather than as characters, and it is often necessary to read input data from a unit other than standard-in or to write output data to a unit other than standard-out. In this chapter we will take up some of the ways that FORTRAN provides for doing those things.

9.1   READ and WRITE

FORTRAN provides a more general form of the READ statement, and a WRITE statement that is a generalization of PRINT. These statements permit the specification of a logical unit and a data format to be used in the I/O operation, and have the forms

```
READ(unit,format) list
WRITE(unit,format) list
```

where unit specifies the logical I/O unit to use, format specifies the format of the data, and list is a list of variable names (or for WRITE, expressions). If "*" is given for unit, READ reads from standard-in and WRITE writes to standard-out; if "*" is given for format, free format is used. Thus READ(*,*) A is the same as READ *,A and WRITE(*,*) A is equivalent to PRINT *,A.

If unit is not "*" it is an integer constant or variable specifying a **logical unit number** in the range 0–99, where 5 corresponds to standard-in, 6 corresponds to standard-out, and 0 corresponds to **standard-error**. Like standard-out, standard-error is normally attached to the display. It is explained in §9.4 how numbered logical I/O units can be attached within your program to files and other logical devices.

If format is not "*" it is the statement number of a FORMAT statement (in the same routine) that specifies the fixed format of the data.

9.1.1   FORMAT Statements

As an illustration of fixed format, consider the following program.

```
      REAL*8 X/1.23D0/,Y/53.D0/
      J=37
      WRITE(6,901) J,X,Y
  901 FORMAT(1X,I3/'X=',T7,F5.2/D8.2)
      STOP
      END
```

The WRITE statement specifies unit 6, which corresponds to standard-out, and gives 901 as the number of the FORMAT statement to use in transmitting the values of variables J, X, and Y. The FORMAT statement itself might look rather mysterious, but it is easy to understand once you know the meanings of the various **field specifications** that it contains. It says to skip 1 space, print an integer in 3 spaces, skip to the next line, print the string X=, tab to column 7, print a real number using a total of 5 spaces with 2 digits following the decimal point, skip to the next line, and print a real number in fraction-exponent form in a total of 8 spaces with 2 digits following the decimal point. Thus the output produced looks like this.

```
   37
X=    1.23
0.53D+02
```

By providing a FORMAT statement, it is possible to specify exactly how your output will appear on the screen or printed page rather than letting the FORTRAN I/O library decide where to put the characters. The table on the next page summarizes the FORMAT field specifications we need for now.

field specification	meaning
nX	skip n spaces
Iw	print an integer right-justified in w columns
F$w.d$	print a real in w columns, d digits after decimal
D$w.d$	same as F but use fraction-exponent form
L1	print a logical value as T or F
Zh	print a hexadecimal value having h hexits
Tn	tab to column n
'string'	print the text **string**
/	skip to the next line

The total field width w must be big enough to include a minus sign if the number is negative. For F and D fields w must also count the decimal point, and for a D field it must include 4 spaces for the exponent "D±␣␣" (or 5 or 6 spaces if the power of ten will have 3 or 4 digits). If a field is too narrow for the value, the FORTRAN I/O library will print w asterisks instead; writing −123 with an I3 format yields ∗∗∗, and writing 75000.00 with an F5.2 format yields ∗∗∗∗∗. An I11 field will print any INTEGER∗4, and a D24.17 field will print any REAL∗8 to the full precision of its machine representation.

A field specification can be repeated by prepending to it an integer **repetition factor**, and parentheses can be used to group field specifications for repetition. For example, 5I2 specifies five I2 fields, and 3(1X,I2) specifies three repetitions of the pattern 1X,I2.

Usually a FORMAT statement contains an I, F, D, L, or Z field specification corresponding to each scalar variable in list. If more field specifications are given than there are variables, the unused ones on the right are ignored. If more values are to be transmitted than there are field specifications, the FORTRAN I/O library skips to the next output line, goes back to the left parenthesis nearest the right end of the FORMAT statement, and re-uses field specifications starting there. Integers should be transmitted using an I field specification and reals should use F or D. Complex numbers each need *two* field specifications, one for the real part and one for the imaginary part.

If the variable list contains the unsubscripted name of an array, *all* the elements in the array are transmitted, as discussed in §9.3. If the I/O operation is formatted, successive array elements match up one-for-one with successive field specifications in the FORMAT statement. It is also possible for the list of a READ or WRITE to be empty. The READ below just skips over a line of input, and the WRITE prints out Here's some text. An apostrophe inside a quoted string must be doubled.

```
      READ(5,*)
      WRITE(6,902)
  902 FORMAT('Here''s some text.')
```

Each execution of a READ statement reads one or more lines or **records**, and each execution of a WRITE statement writes one or more records, so it is necessary to do, with the FORMAT statement, all of the processing that is required for each execution of a READ or WRITE. This means that it is not possible using WRITE to build up a record piece by piece for later output, or to READ part of a record now and go back later for some other part. READ reads the variables in list and then moves on to the next record. (It *is* possible to build and reread records in FORTRAN, as described in §10.6.1, but not by using just READ and WRITE.)

Several READ or WRITE statements can use the same FORMAT statement. Although FORMAT statements have statement numbers just like branch targets, they are not executable and control cannot be transferred to them. A FORMAT statement can be located anywhere in the source text of the routine where it is used, but placing it immediately after the READ or WRITE that first uses it usually makes the code easier to understand, because it helps to explain what the I/O statement is doing. To prevent the statement numbers of FORMAT statements from being confused with those that identify branch targets and DO terminators, it is important to choose FORMAT statement numbers that are easily recognized. In this book, branch targets are numbered $1, 2, \ldots$, while the numbers $901, 902, \ldots$ are used for FORMAT statements.

When reading records that are known to have a particular fixed format (such as from a logical I/O unit that is attached to a file as described in §9.4) either a free-format READ or a formatted READ can be used. For example, if unit 1 is attached to a file that contains lines all formatted as shown on the left

```
    1  3.712  447289              READ(1,909) I,A,N
  147 -8.411   98766          909 FORMAT(I3,1X,F6.3,I8)
    :    :       :
```

we could read them by repeatedly executing the READ statement on the right. Fixed-format READs should *not* be used when reading from the keyboard, and even when reading from a file they can be tricky (see §13.9.5).

9.1.2 Cursor Control

Interactive programs often prompt for and then read input from the keyboard, as in the following code segment.

```
      WRITE(6,903)
  903 FORMAT('enter value of Z:')
      READ(5,*) Z
```

Unfortunately, after prompting the user this program moves the typing cursor down to the next line on the screen, so the conversation between the program and the user looks like this.

```
enter value of Z:
17.43
```

Here the program has typed the first line and the user the second. Most UNIX™ FORTRAN implementations provide the following way of keeping the typing cursor on the same line as the prompt.

```
      WRITE(6,904)
  904 FORMAT('enter value of Z: ',$)
      READ(5,*) Z
```

Now the conversation between the program and the user looks like this.

```
enter value of Z: 17.43
```

9.1.3 End-of-File and Error Conditions

Often in reading input from a file or the keyboard it is not known beforehand how many records will be found, only that some process is to be performed on each record however many there are. In such cases it is necessary for the program to be able to detect when the end of the file is reached, or when the interactive user sends a ^D (control-D, described in §0.5.5) to mark the end of input from the keyboard. Both of these conditions are referred to as **end-of-file** or **EOF**. FORTRAN provides an optional clause in the READ statement to transfer control upon reaching EOF, as illustrated in this example.

```
      MSUM=0
      I=0
    1 I=I+1
      READ(5,*,END=2) M
      MSUM=MSUM+M
      GO TO 1
    2 ...
```

Successive executions of the READ statement put the input values in M, through the last input record. Then the READ statement gets executed one more time, and finds the end of the file. When that happens control transfers to the statement number 2 given in the END= clause, and M is left unchanged. When control reaches statement 2, I contains the number of times the READ statement was executed, including the one that encountered the EOF, so I-1 records were found.

It is also possible to intercept I/O errors. A read error can happen when, for instance, the program expects a number as input but the user types letters instead. A write error can happen when, for instance, the program tries to expand an output file after the user's disk quota has been reached. Ordinarily the FORTRAN I/O library traps such errors, writes a cryptic message, and stops the program, but in many cases it is preferable to handle these situations within the program instead so that a more informative error message can be generated or some corrective action attempted. To allow for this possibility FORTRAN provides an optional ERR= clause in the READ and WRITE statements to transfer control when an I/O error occurs.

```
      MSUM=0
      I=0
    1 I=I+1
      READ(5,*,END=2,ERR=3) M
      MSUM=MSUM+M
      GO TO 1
C     normal processing continues
    2 ...
C
C     error processing takes place here
    3 ...
```

If this program tries to read something that cannot be interpreted as a number, M is left unchanged and control transfers to the error-handling code segment at statement 3.

9.2 Case Study: Descriptive Statistics

To illustrate some of the ideas about I/O introduced so far, suppose we have some data from a lab experiment and want to find their sample mean μ and sample standard deviation

σ, which are defined like this.

$$\mu = \frac{1}{N}\sum_{i=1}^{N}x_i, \qquad \sigma = \sqrt{\frac{1}{N-1}\sum_{i=1}^{N}(x_i-\mu)^2}$$

The following program prompts for and reads the data values, uses the formulas to calculate μ and σ, and writes out the results.

```
      PARAMETER(IMAX=100)
      REAL*8 X(IMAX),SUM,SSQ,MU,SIGMA
      SUM=0.D0
      N=0
      DO 1 I=1,IMAX
          WRITE(6,901)
901       FORMAT('? ',$)
          READ(5,*,END=2) X(I)
          SUM=SUM+X(I)
          N=N+1
    1 CONTINUE
    2 MU=SUM/DFLOAT(N)
      SSQ=0.D0
      DO 3 I=1,N
          SSQ=SSQ+(X(I)-MU)**2
    3 CONTINUE
      SIGMA=DSQRT(SSQ/DFLOAT(N-1))
      WRITE(6,902) MU,SIGMA
  902 FORMAT(/'mean = ',F7.3/'standard deviation = ',F5.3)
      STOP
      END
```

If the number of data values is small, we might enter them interactively and have a conversation like this with the program.

```
unix[11] a.out
? 3.5
? 4
? 2.9
? ^D
mean =    3.467
standard deviation = 0.551
unix[12]
```

Here are some observations about the code.

1➩ The program permits up to IMAX data values to be input, prompting for and reading them one at a time in the DO 1 loop. It is important for this to be a bounded loop, so that the user cannot inadvertently enter more than IMAX values and overrun the array X.

2➩ If the user sends an end-of-file before entering IMAX values (which is presumably what will happen most of the time) control transfers out of the DO 1 loop to statement 2. If the user enters exactly IMAX values, the program stops prompting and uses the IMAX values that it has read.

3⇨   The READ statement uses free format, so that the values can be entered at the keyboard in any reasonable way without the user having to count columns or include unnecessary decimal points.

4⇨   Because N gets incremented *after* the READ rather than before it, its value at statement 2 is the number of values entered. In the loop, instead of setting N=N+1 we could have set N=I. Which do you think is clearer?

5⇨   The statement numbers of the FORMAT statements, 901 and 902, are chosen so that they cannot be confused with the other statement numbers, which have to do with control flow in the program.

6⇨   The FORMAT statements are placed immediately after their first (and in this case only) uses, as hints to the reader about what the corresponding WRITE statements are doing.

7⇨   The output FORMAT, numbered 902, begins with "/" to move the cursor from where it was left by the final prompt (at the end of the prompt string) down to the beginning of the next line, so that the word **mean** will begin there instead of after the prompt.

8⇨   This program has many limitations and potential problems. Can you identify some of them? This case study is revisited in §9.5, where some improvements are discussed.

9.3   Implied DO Loops

In the READ and WRITE examples that we have considered so far, the variables transmitted were scalars. What if we want to write out a vector V of, say, 5 elements? One obvious way would be like this.

```
      REAL*8 V(5)/1.D0,2.D0,3.D0,4.D0,5.D0/
      WRITE(6,905) V(1),V(2),V(3),V(4),V(5)
  905 FORMAT(5(1X,F7.1))
```

The FORMAT assumes that each of the numbers will fit in an F7.1 field.

As mentioned in §9.1.1, using the unsubscripted name of an array in the variable list of a READ or WRITE transmits all of the elements, so another way of writing the code segment would be like this.

```
      REAL*8 V(5)/1.D0,2.D0,3.D0,4.D0,5.D0/
      WRITE(6,905) V
  905 FORMAT(5(1X,F7.1))
```

Using the unsubscripted name of an array with more than one dimension transmits the elements in column-major order.

Now suppose that we want to print exactly N elements of V, where N is a variable that can have any value from 1 to 5. Neither of the approaches we used above will work, but we could use a DO loop as in the program at the top of the next page

```
      REAL*8 V(5)/1.D0,2.D0,3.D0,4.D0,5.D0/
      N=3
      DO 1 I=1,N
          WRITE(6,904) V(I)
 904      FORMAT(1X,F7.1)
    1 CONTINUE
```

Unfortunately, because each execution of the WRITE statement begins a new record, this prints the values on separate lines like this.

```
      1.0
      2.0
      3.0
```

To permit a *variable* number of values to be written on a *single* line, FORTRAN provides an **implied** DO construct that can be used as an element of the variable list.

```
      REAL*8 V(5)/1.D0,2.D0,3.D0,4.D0,5.D0/
      N=3
      WRITE(6,903) (V(I),I=1,N)
  903 FORMAT(5(1X,F7.1))
```

Here N is less than 5, so the extra field specifications in the FORMAT statement are just ignored and we get this output.

```
      1.0    2.0    3.0
```

9.4   Unit Assignments

Some simple programs need to use only standard-in, standard-out, and possibly standard-error. Programs conforming to the UNIX™ paradigm of a **filter**, for example, read a single stream of input bytes, write a single stream of output bytes, and report errors on the display. The UNIX™ sort utility is a well-known filter program.

As another example of filtering, suppose we want to read integers one per line from an input file, add 37 to each one, and write the resulting values one per line to an output file. Here is a program for doing that.

```
    3 READ(5,*,END=1,ERR=2) NUMBER
      WRITE(6,901) NUMBER+37
  901    FORMAT(I11)
      GO TO 3
C
    2 WRITE(0,902)
  902 FORMAT('error reading input')
    1 STOP
      END
```

The program reads an integer into NUMBER from standard-in (unit 5), writes NUMBER+37 on standard-out (unit 6), and looks for another input value. When the end of the input is reached, the END=1 clause sends control to the STOP. If an error occurs (as would happen if the input contained something other than integers) the `ERR=2` sends control to statement 2, where the trouble is reported on standard-error (unit 0) before the program stops.

The I/O performed by this program can be represented symbolically by the **unit assignment diagram** below.

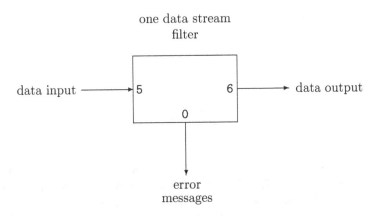

The box corresponds to the program and the arrows to input and output streams. The arrowheads show the direction of information flow, and the numbers are the FORTRAN unit numbers appearing in the `READ` and `WRITE` statements of the program.

If the executable for the program is in the file `a.out`, entering the UNIX™ command

```
unix[13] a.out
```

runs the program with unit 5 attached to the keyboard and units 6 and 0 attached to the display. In UNIX™ a filter program is often used by **redirecting** the input and output data streams so that units 5 and 6 are attached by UNIX™ to files rather than to the keyboard and display. Entering the command

```
unix[14] a.out < input > output
```

causes the program to read input data from the file named `input` and write output data to the file named `output`. This leaves unit 0 attached to the display, so that if an error message is written it will be seen by the interactive user rather than going into the output file.

A filter program provides no way for the user to reply to prompts. Thus, any information that a filter program needs other than the data to be processed, such as option settings, must be provided by means of command-line arguments (described in §14.2.4) or somehow embedded in the input data.

9.4.1 Interactive Programs

To make it possible for the user to reply to prompts from a program, so as to recover interactively from errors and answer questions the program asks, it is necessary to leave a unit attached to the keyboard. One way to do that is by using the unit assignment scheme shown at the top of the next page. Now unit 5 is used for keyboard inputs and a separate unit is used for data read from a file. This extra unit, marked "?" in the drawing, can be any number chosen from the set $\{1,2,3,4,7,\ldots,99\}$. Most FORTRAN implementations allow unit numbers in the range $0,\ldots,99$, but units 0, 5, and 6 already default to standard-error, standard-in, and standard-out, so we are left with the others to choose from. Suppose for example that we pick unit number 1.

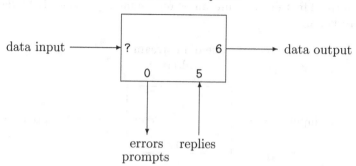

If we just use the new unit number in READ and WRITE statements, the FORTRAN I/O library will associate unit 1 with a UNIX™ file named fort.1 by default. Usually we would prefer to specify the filename, and this can be done within the program by using an OPEN statement. If the file from which we want to read the input data is called data, we could write

```
OPEN(UNIT=1,FILE='data')
```

to attach unit 1 to that file. The CLOSE statement can be used to detach a unit (other than unit 0), like this.

```
CLOSE(UNIT=1)
```

Leaving unit 5 attached to the keyboard and using a different unit for the data input has the disadvantage that it is no longer possible to redirect the data input at run time by using the shell redirection operator <. To preserve this possibility we could retain unit 5 for data input and attach the new unit to the keyboard instead.

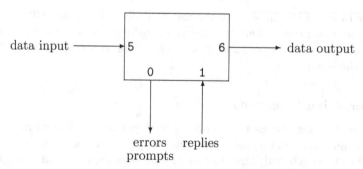

The way UNIX™ treats devices such as the keyboard is similar to the way it treats files, so to accomplish this unit assignment we need only use the right name for the keyboard, /dev/tty, in the FILE= clause of the OPEN statement for unit 1.

Taking this approach we can modify our earlier filter program to allow the increment value to be specified interactively rather than being permanently set to 37. The program

```
      OPEN(UNIT=1,FILE='/dev/tty')
      WRITE(0,901)
  901 FORMAT('increment: ',$)
      READ(1,*) INC
C
    3 READ(5,*,END=1,ERR=2) NUMBER
      WRITE(6,902) NUMBER+INC
  902    FORMAT(I11)
      GO TO 3
C
    2 WRITE(0,903)
  903 FORMAT('error reading input file')
    1 STOP
      END
```

above prompts on unit 0 (the screen) and reads the user's response from unit 1 (the keyboard). Then it works just like the earlier example. Running the program produces an exchange like this.

```
unix[15] a.out < input > output
increment: 53
unix[16]
```

The program reads input data values from unit 5, which shell redirection < has attached to the file **input**, and writes output data values on unit 6, which shell redirection > has attached to the file **output**.

Sometimes an interactive application needs to read several different input streams or write several different output streams. For example, a program might read temperatures, pressures, and volumes from three separate data files and produce two output files, one containing a human-readable table of results and another containing coordinates for a plotting program. If extensive debugging output is to be produced, as is sometimes the case in large legacy codes, that should all be directed to a separate unit that is not also used for data. Then the unit assignment diagram looks like this.

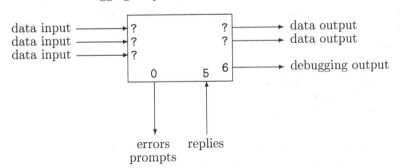

Here we have used unit 6 for the debugging output, so that it can either be read on the screen or redirected to a **log file**. Now it is necessary to select several unit numbers for the data input and data output streams, from the set $\{1,2,3,4,7,\ldots,99\}$. If possible, these numbers should be chosen in a way that is easy to remember. It might be convenient to use odd unit numbers for inputs (just as standard-in is an odd unit number, 5) and even numbers for outputs (like standard-out, unit 6), or it might be that there is some application-specific reason for picking particular unit numbers.

9.4.2   Attaching Files with GETFIL

Sometimes it is desirable to have an interactive program prompt for the name of the file that is to be attached to a logical I/O unit so that the filename can change from run to run, rather than embedding a fixed filename in the code. When we discuss character variables we will see in §10.6.2 that it is straightforward to do this in a naïve way, by reading the filename and using it in an OPEN statement. For a program that does that to be user-friendly, though, it is essential to make some sanity checks before assigning the unit to the file. People make all sorts of mistakes in responding to prompts from a program. What if the file is to be read but it does not exist? In that case, an error message should be written and the prompt repeated. If the file is to be written but it already *does* exist, it would be courteous of the program to ask permission before overwriting it, because the user might have given the name of the wrong file. In some applications the program can suggest a default filename for the user to accept if it is suitable.

Doing all these things carefully is *not* so straightforward, and takes a lot of code. Fortunately, the code is very similar in each case where it is needed, so the action "prompt the user for a filename and attach the file to the given unit" is a natural candidate for a library subroutine. GETFIL, one of the routines listed in §18, performs this function. Here is its calling sequence.

CALL GETFIL(WATFOR,LW,SUGNAM,LS,NUNIT,ACCESS)		
WATFOR	string	what the file will be used for
LW	INTEGER*4	number of characters in WATFOR
SUGNAM	string	suggested filename, if any
LS	INTEGER*4	number of characters in SUGNAM
NUNIT	INTEGER*4	number of unit to be attached
ACCESS	INTEGER*4	1 for read, 2 for write, 3 for both

Suppose a program reads a file of input data and writes a file of coordinates suitable for later input to a separate plotting program, and that the names of the files are to be given by the interactive user. To attach the files, we could code the following calls to GETFIL at the beginning of the program.

```
C     attach the input and output files
      CALL GETFIL('data',4,' ',0,3,1)
      CALL GETFIL('plotter',7,'plotfile',8,9,2)
```

The first call says to prompt for the name of a "data" file and attach it to unit 3. There is no suggested name for this file, and it is to be read. The second call says to prompt for the name of a "plotter" file and attach it to unit 9. The suggested name for this output file is plotfile and it is to be written.

When the program is run, the user might have the exchange with it shown at the top of the next page. Here the program prompts first for the name of a "data" file, to which the user responds mydata. Evidently that file exists, because otherwise GETFIL would

```
unix[17] a.out
Name of data file: mydata
Name of plotter file [plotfile]: ⌐R
The file "plotfile" is to be written, but it exists; ok? y
```

complain. GETFIL attaches `mydata` to unit 3. Then it prompts for the name of a "plotter" file, suggesting the name `plotfile`. The user accepts the suggestion by pressing the return key. GETFIL finds that the file already exists, so it requests confirmation that it may be overwritten and the user replies y. Having received this permission, GETFIL attaches `plotfile` to unit 9. GETFIL has some other handy features that you can find out about by reading the detailed description in §18.3.

9.4.3 Batch Programs

If a program runs for a long time, it might be convenient to run it as a UNIX™ **background process** by starting it with the background command **&**.

```
unix[18] a.out &
```

A program that is run in this way is called a **batch program**. After launching a batch program you can use the workstation window for other tasks or log out and go to lunch while the calculation finishes.

A batch program can't read from the keyboard or write to the screen if the user is not there, so it should read only from files and write only to files. This means that if standard-in, standard-out, and standard-error are used they must be redirected on the command line. In the **bash** shell, this is done in one of the following ways (other shells provide ways of obtaining the same behavior, but might use different syntax).

```
unix[19] a.out < input > output 2> errors &
unix[20] a.out < input 2>&1> output &
```

In the first form, standard-out is directed to the file **output** and standard-error to the file **errors**. In the second form, both standard-out and standard-error are directed to the file **output**. If the program reads user commands through unit 5 in interactive use, the **input** file that is used for a batch run must contain the responses that the user would normally make from the keyboard, so sometimes this file is referred to as a **command file**.

If there are several data input and data output streams, the unit assignment diagram would look like the one below. The data input and data output unit numbers are once again chosen from the set $\{1,2,3,4,7,\ldots,99\}$. Now, however unit 5 is redirected from a command file and units 0 and 6 are redirected to an output file or files.

batch program
multiple data streams

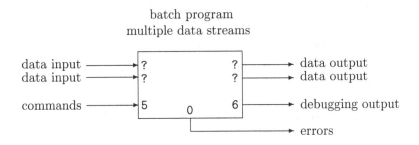

9.5 Descriptive Statistics Revisited

The program of the case study in §9.2 has many limitations and potential problems.

First, it is an interactive program to which the user must enter the data, yet in most cases when a computer is needed to calculate descriptive statistics there will be too much data to type in from the keyboard. Standard-in can be redirected from a data file, but the prompts "? " will still appear on the user's screen, or in the output file if standard-out is redirected.

The next thing we notice upon trying to use the program is that it does not allow mistakes! If the interactive user makes a typo, or if standard-in is redirected from a data file containing a bogus entry, the error stops the program. If there are no data, the program reports a 0/0 NaN for μ and $\sigma = 0$, rather than telling us there is something wrong or (also reasonable) producing no output at all. If N=1 we get $\mu = $ X(1), which is correct, but for σ the program gives a 0/0 NaN rather than 0. Surely the program should handle these "edge" conditions more gracefully.

Finally, a little algebra shows that it is not necessary to save the X values in order to calculate the standard deviation. After all,

$$\sum_{i=1}^{N}(x_i - \mu)^2 = \sum_{i=1}^{N}(x_i{}^2 - 2\mu x_i + \mu^2) = \sum_{i=1}^{N} x_i{}^2 - N\mu^2$$

so if we accumulate $\sum x_i{}^2$ as well as $\sum x_i$ there is no need for X to be a vector. This removes the restriction on how many input values can be read.

A program that incorporates all of these improvements is listed on the next page. Here are some observations about it.

1 ⇨ The new program uses a free loop for reading the input data, because there is no longer an array to protect from overrun and thus no limit on the number of values read.

2 ⇨ The READ loop now accumulates $\sum x_i{}^2$ in SSQ, as well as $\sum x_i$ in SUM and the number of data values in N, and the program uses the rightmost expression above in finding σ.

3 ⇨ If an input value is not a number, the ERR= clause transfers control to statement 2 where an error message is written telling the line number LNUM of the data record that is bad. If the program is being run interactively this line number might not be of much interest, but if the input comes from a file, knowing the line number of a bogus data item will be a big help in fixing the mistake. Notice that N gets incremented only for good data, whereas LNUM must be incremented for each line read, whether or not the datum turned out to be good.

4 ⇨ Rather than stopping, the program ignores bad data and continues reading. This gives an interactive user a chance to re-enter the value, and if the input is redirected from a data file it allows the program to continue checking and perhaps find other errors so that they can all be corrected at once.

5 ⇨ The special cases N=0 and N=1 are now handled separately.

6 ⇨ The mean and standard deviation are stored in ANS(1) and ANS(2) respectively, and ANS is written out using an implied DO loop. This illustrates the use of an implied DO, but it makes the program harder to understand and is therefore *not* an improvement. If we insist on using ANS it would be simpler to write WRITE(6,904) N,ANS rather than using the implied DO.

```
C       improved descriptive statistics program
        REAL*8 X,SUM,SSQ,ANS(2)
C
C       collect the data
        SUM=0.D0
        SSQ=0.D0
        N=0
        LNUM=0
      3 WRITE(0,901)
    901 FORMAT('? ',$)
          LNUM=LNUM+1
          READ(5,*,END=1,ERR=2) X
          N=N+1
          SUM=SUM+X
          SSQ=SSQ+X**2
        GO TO 3
      2 WRITE(6,902) LNUM
    902 FORMAT('bad data at record',I11)
        GO TO 3
C
C       compute and report the statistics
      1 IF(N.EQ.0) THEN
          WRITE(6,903)
    903   FORMAT('no input data')
          STOP
        ENDIF
        IF(N.EQ.1) THEN
          ANS(1)=SUM
          ANS(2)=0.D0
        ELSE
          ANS(1)=SUM/DFLOAT(N)
          ANS(2)=DSQRT((SSQ-DFLOAT(N)*(ANS(1))**2)/DFLOAT(N-1))
        ENDIF
        WRITE(6,904) N,(ANS(J),J=1,2)
    904 FORMAT(/'samples=',I11
      ;         /'mean=',D11.4
      ;         /'standard deviation=',D10.3)
        STOP
        END
```

7⇨ This program reports the number of observations as well as the mean and standard deviation, which helps sanity-check the input. The FORMAT field specifiers for N, ANS(1), and ANS(2) now work no matter what the numbers turn out to be, unlike those in the earlier program.

8⇨ The unit assignment scheme is now as shown at the top of the next page. When the program is run as a batch program, the standard-error (unit 0) output can now be redirected so that it does not appear on the screen or in the output file. The UNIX™ device that acts as a drain or infinite sink for unwanted output is called /dev/null, so to run the program with standard-in redirected we can use this command.

```
unix[21] a.out < input 2> /dev/null
```

Now the program reads its input data from the file **input**, writes its results (and any error messages) to the screen, and sends the unneeded prompts down the drain.

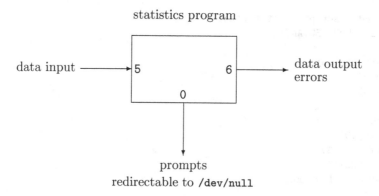

statistics program

data input ──────→ 5   6 ├──────→ data output
                                         errors

0

prompts
redirectable to `/dev/null`

9 ⇨   Standard-out should not be redirected unless standard-in is too, because if the user
is entering values from the keyboard he or she will need to see any **bad data** error messages
that might be produced, rather than having them go into the output file. Exercise 9.10.16
asks how to remove this restriction.

9.6   Positioning In Files

When you open a file by mentioning it in a UNIX™ shell redirection such as

`unix[22] a.out > output`

or by using a FORTRAN `OPEN` statement, or by calling `GETFIL` (which uses `OPEN`), the I/O
operations your program performs all begin at the beginning of the file. An output file that
is attached in any of these ways must start empty or it will be emptied before it is written
to (if you called `GETFIL` that won't happen until you give permission).

If you want standard-out to *append* lines at the bottom of an output file that already has
something in it, you can instead use this shell redirection.

`unix[23] a.out >> output`

Some implementations of FORTRAN provide an extra parameter on the `OPEN` statement
that can be used to achieve this effect from within a program, and for other units besides
standard-out, but other implementations do not. In that case a file can be opened for
append by using a code segment like the one below.

```
C     open the file and read it to the end
      OPEN(UNIT=1,FILE='data')
    2 READ(1,*,END=1)
      GO TO 2
C
C     the end of the file has been reached; now ready to write
    1 ...
```

In a similar way we can read from a file starting at a particular line by skipping lines
down to that one. The program at the top of the next page illustrates this idea.

```
C      open the file and skip to the desired line
       OPEN(UNIT=1,FILE='data')
       LNUM=1
     1 READ(1,*)
       LNUM=LNUM+1
       IF(LNUM.LT.LSTART) GO TO 1
C
C      now positioned at line LSTART; ready to read
```

Occasionally it is necessary to return to the beginning of a file after reading or writing it, so that it can be reread. For this FORTRAN provides the REWIND statement. For example, to return to the beginning of the file attached to unit 1 we could say this.

```
       REWIND(1)
```

It wouldn't make sense to rewind the screen or keyboard, so REWIND is useful only for units that are attached to disk files.

9.7   Case Study: Merging Files

As a further illustration of file I/O, consider the problem of combining two tables of values. Suppose that Sarah and David have each listed the pages in their FORTRAN textbook where they noticed typographical errors. The files **sarah.dat** and **david.dat** contain their lists, in ascending order, but to maximize the author's surprise they want to present him with a single list containing all of the page numbers in order. At first they find only a few mistakes so the lists are easy to combine, like this.

sarah.dat	david.dat	merged list
1	13	1
17	33	13
18	75	17
33		18
42		33
187		33
		42
		75
		187

Later, when the lists get too big to merge by hand, they write the program on the next page to do it for them. Here are some observations about their code.

1⇨   The program begins by OPENing Sarah's file on logical I/O unit 2 and David's file on logical I/O unit 3. Then it uses GETFIL to attach a file in which to write the merged data. When the students compile their program and run the executable they might have the following conversation with it.

```
unix[24] a.out
Name of merged data file [merge.dat]: combined
unix[25]
```

```
C     merge two files of page numbers
C
C     attach the files
      OPEN(UNIT=2,FILE='sarah.dat')
      OPEN(UNIT=3,FILE='david.dat')
      CALL GETFIL('merged data',11,'merge.dat',9,4,2)
C
C     read the first record from each input file
      READ(2,*,END=1) NS
      READ(3,*,END=2) ND
C
C     combine two ordered input files into one ordered output file
    3 IF(NS .LT. ND) THEN
         WRITE(4,901) NS
  901    FORMAT(I4,' S')
         READ(2,*,END=1) NS
      ELSE
         WRITE(4,902) ND
  902    FORMAT(I4,' D')
         READ(3,*,END=2) ND
      ENDIF
      GO TO 3
C
C     reached EOF on sarah.dat first; copy rest of david.dat
    1 WRITE(4,902) ND
      READ(3,*,END=4) ND
      GO TO 1
C
C     reached EOF on david.dat first; copy rest of sarah.dat
    2 WRITE(4,901) NS
      READ(2,*,END=4) NS
      GO TO 2
C
C     reached the end of whichever input file is longer
    4 STOP
      END
```

Here they have overridden the default filename **merge.dat** suggested by the program and used the filename **combined** instead, so **combined** gets attached to logical I/O unit 4.

2⇨ The combined list is to be written in ascending order, so to find out who goes first the program reads the first record from each input file. If Sarah's number NS is lower than David's number ND, it gets written first to the output file. The FORMAT statement numbered 901 also writes the character string ' S' after the page number to show that Sarah discovered that mistake. If David's page number is lower, the ELSE clause writes it first instead, and identifies him as the discoverer. If a mistake was noticed by both Sarah and David, it gets listed twice so that they both get credit for the find.

3⇨ Whenever NS or ND gets written, it is immediately replaced by READing a new value from the appropriate input file. Then the GO TO 3 sends control back to the test and the new value is compared to the number that was larger (or equal) last time.

4⇨ This process continues until the end of one or the other input file is reached, causing a branch to either statement 1 or statement 2. If Sarah's file was shorter, then the rest of the combined list will consist of the remaining entries on David's list; if David's list was shorter, then the rest of the combined list will consist of the remaining entries on Sarah's. When the end of the longer input file is reached, control transfers to statement 4 and the program stops.

9.8 Unformatted I/O

Writing a number out in human-readable form usually takes more characters or bytes of disk storage than are used to represent the number within the computer. For example, to write the integer 12345 takes 5 numerals, which would consume 5 bytes of disk storage if the number were written to a file as characters, even though only 4 bytes of memory (the bytes of an INTEGER*4 variable) are used to represent the number within the machine. Translating numbers from their internal representations to decimal digits and arranging the characters for output according to a FORMAT statement also takes some processing time, and as I mentioned in §4.2, translating real numbers to decimal and back again usually introduces tiny errors.

If a program writes a file that is to be read only by other programs and not by people, it is possible to conserve disk space, save processing time, and preserve the full precision of real values by writing and reading the exact bytes of the data's internal representation. The method that FORTRAN provides for doing this is called **unformatted** I/O. (This is not to be confused with the *free*-format I/O discussed earlier, which converts numbers to and from their decimal forms.) A file that contains unformatted data is sometimes referred to as a **binary** file to distinguish it from one that is human-readable. The FORTRAN READ and WRITE statements can be used to do unformatted I/O simply by omitting the format specification clause. Thus in the program generating the data, an unformatted WRITE statement takes the form

```
WRITE(unit) list
```

and in the program reading the data an unformatted READ statement looks like this.

```
READ(unit) list
```

It is essential for variables in corresponding positions in the WRITE and READ variable lists to be of the same types and dimensions in the two programs.

In many FORTRAN implementations, each record of an unformatted file consists of a 4-byte integer giving the total data length L in bytes, followed by the L bytes of data, but this is not true on all systems. Also, the order of the bytes depends on the endian-ness of the processor (discussed in §4.8). For these reasons, unformatted files written on one computer often *cannot* be read on a computer of a different kind. Another drawback to using unformatted files is that they can't be inspected using conventional editors such as vi and emacs, and this often makes it more difficult to debug the programs that manipulate them. Thus, unformatted I/O should be considered only when disk space, I/O speed, or accuracy in real number transcription is very important.

Unformatted I/O is allowed only on disk files, which must be identified as having the necessary structure by using the FORM= clause of the OPEN statement, as in

```
OPEN(UNIT=1,FILE='data',FORM='UNFORMATTED')
```

9.9   Cautions and Omissions

Programs for engineering and scientific applications typically do lots of numerical calculations and just a little bit of I/O, and FORTRAN's I/O capabilities are adequate to that limited task. Compared to languages that are designed mainly for doing I/O, however, FORTRAN I/O is clumsy and slow. If your application consists mostly of reading and writing files rather than mostly of doing arithmetic, you should seriously consider using a language other than FORTRAN; C and the ancient and venerable COBOL are often superior alternatives for non-numerical data processing.

This chapter presents only a sufficient minimal subset of FORTRAN I/O. The complete details vary somewhat from one implementation of the language to another, and make up a vast and complicated subject; for more information you should consult the manual for your compiler. Some of the many features that I have omitted from Classical FORTRAN or put off discussing until later are listed below.

> *Carriage control; ejecting pages with* `L`; `NAMELIST`; *direct access I/O; expressions as* unit numbers; nesting implied `DO` loops; `ERR=` *in* `OPEN`, *and other* `OPEN` *clauses; the* `FORMAT` field specifications `E`, `Q`, `G`, `A`, *and* `H`; *scale factors for real-number field specifications;* `Iw.z` *field specifications for printing integers with leading zeros; variable expressions in* `FORMAT`s; *literal* `FORMAT` *strings in* `READ` *and* `WRITE`; `READ` *nnn and* `PRINT` *nnn;* *object-time* `FORMAT`s; *in-memory I/O; the* `INQUIRE` *statement; the* `IOSTAT` *clause; the* `IOINIT` *subroutine;* `BACKSPACE`; `ASSIGN`ed `FORMAT` *labels; racing file pointers.*

9.10   Exercises

9.10.1   Explain the difference between free-format, unformatted, and formatted I/O.

9.10.2   After using `PRINT *` and `READ *` for eight chapters, you learned in this one about `WRITE(*,*)` and `READ(*,*)`. (a) How does `PRINT *` differ from `WRITE(*,*)`? How does `READ *` differ from `READ(*,*)`? (b) Why do you suppose I introduced `READ *` and `PRINT *` first?

9.10.3   What output is produced by the following program? Explain why. Can you find any ways to simplify the code?

```
      REAL*8 X(4)/1.D0,2.D0,3.D0,4.D0/
      I=3
      WRITE(6,900) I,X(I)
  900 FORMAT('And the output is'/T1,1X,'X(',I1,')=',F8.1)
      STOP
      END
```

9.10.4   Can a `FORMAT` statement be a branch target? Explain.

9.10.5 What output is produced by the following program? Explain why, and confirm your answer by experiment.

```
      INTEGER*4 K(2,2)/19,186,-4,1237/
      WRITE(6,902) K
  902 FORMAT(I2,1X,(I3,1X))
      STOP
      END
```

9.10.6 The output of a FORTRAN program is to be read in by a spreadsheet program. The spreadsheet program expects its input to be a "comma-separated list," with entries separated by a comma (or a comma and a space or spaces). The data to be written consist of N≤100 numbers each between 0 and 99, which are stored in a 100-element INTEGER*4 vector named LIST. Compose a formatted WRITE statement, and its accompanying FORMAT statement, that will write a suitable output line. The spreadsheet program might not mind if there is a trailing comma at the end of the list, but format the output so there isn't one.

9.10.7 What D format field specification could be used to print a floating-point value in this pattern? ⌞D±⌟⌞ Does your solution work for negative numbers? For what range of values is this field specification suitable?

9.10.8 Write a program to print the REAL*4 representation of the value 3.1 as a hexadecimal number. Does this correspond to the bit pattern given in the example of §4.2?

9.10.9 What is printed by the following program? Explain why.

```
      INTEGER*4 I/Z'01ABCDEF'/
      WRITE(6,901) (I.EQ.2*(I/2))
  901 FORMAT(1X,L1)
      STOP
      END
```

9.10.10 A file named data contains lines of data, each consisting of 26 undelimited digits, as shown below. Write a program segment to read the third line of the file into the variables I, J, K, and L assuming that the numbers are all positive and have, respectively, 5, 6, 7, and 8 digits.

```
15327905432976056708219765
```

9.10.11 The program below assigns a value to PI and then prints it out.

```
      REAL*8 PI
      PI=0.31415926535897932384626643D+01
      WRITE(6,901) PI
  901 FORMAT('0.31415926535897932384626643D+01'/D31.25)
      STOP
      END
```

(a) Explain what the FORMAT statement does. Why is it convenient for this program to print the number appearing on the right side of the assignment statement as characters, above the printout of the numerical value that actually got stored in the variable PI? (b) Run the program. Precisely what does it print? (c) How many correct digits of PI got printed? Explain why this happens. Does it make sense to use a FORMAT specification like D31.25 for a REAL*8 value?

9.10.12 What does this program do? What happens if the input is redirected from an empty file? Revise the program so it prints N=1 in that event.

```
2 READ(5,*,END=1) N
  GO TO 2
1 PRINT *,'N=',N
  STOP
  END
```

9.10.13 What does the following code segment print out? Confirm your answer by experiment, and explain how the code works. How might this idea be useful in a program that runs for a long time?

```
    DO 1 I=1,20
        WRITE(6,901)
901     FORMAT('.',$)
  1 CONTINUE
```

9.10.14 Any logical I/O units that are OPENed by a program but that are not CLOSEd before the program stops are automatically closed by the FORTRAN I/O library before control is returned to the operating system. Furthermore, if a logical I/O unit was OPENed on one file and is subsequently OPENed on another file, the first file is automatically closed before the second is opened. In view of this behavior, why is the CLOSE statement needed at all?

9.10.15 Prove the following identity, which we used in §9.5.

$$\sum_{i=1}^{N}(x_i{}^2 - 2\mu x_i + \mu^2) = \sum_{i=1}^{N}x_i{}^2 - N\mu^2$$

9.10.16 Revise the program of the case study in §9.5 to write its error messages on the display even when standard-out is redirected to a file and standard-error is redirected to /dev/null.

9.10.17 Modify the program of the case study in §9.5 so that it simulates an adding machine. If you enter a set of values followed by a ^D, it should print the sum of those values and prompt for the first value in the next set; if you enter another ^D, the program should stop. How does this program compare to the one you wrote for Exercise 4.10.33?

9.10.18 A program does calculations involving money values in dollars and cents, storing the numbers of dollars and cents in separate INTEGER*4 variables named BUCKS and CENTS. At the end of the calculation the resulting money value is to be printed in the pattern $⎽⎽⎽⎽⎽⎽ Write a code segment to produce this output. What happens if the amount turns out to be greater than $99999.99? What happens if CENTS is greater than 99? What happens if CENTS is less than 10?

9.10.19 Write a SUBROUTINE subprogram to print out M rows of N columns from an array declared INTEGER*4, using as few lines of output as possible but printing no more than 3 values on a line. Label the output in such a way that the user can tell which printed number came from which array element.

9.10.20 In the military and in some technical settings it is customary to measure the time of day on a 24-hour clock. Thus, for example, 00:23 is 12:23 AM, shortly after midnight, and 17:45 is 5:45 PM, around supper time. Write a program to read a 24-hour time in the format just illustrated, read an integer increment in minutes (which could be negative), and print out the 24-hour time corresponding to the given time plus the increment. Here is a typical exchange that a user might have with the program.

```
unix[26] a.out
starting time: 17:45
increment: 20
ending time: 18:05
```

Make sure your program works correctly even when the new time is past midnight and thus into the next (or previous) day.

9.10.21 Write a program that filters an input file to produce an output file as follows. (a) Read a single real value CLIP from the keyboard, or from a command file if the program is running as a batch program. Then read real values of DATA from an input file, one value per line, until the end of the input file is reached. If a DATA value is less than or equal to CLIP, write DATA to an output file, but if DATA is greater than CLIP write CLIP to the output file. If there is an error in reading a DATA value, write a message to the user telling which line of input was wrong and then stop. Explain how your unit assignments work when the program is run interactively, and as a batch program. Where do the error messages go? (b) Modify the program to write the word error in the output file each time an input line is found to be in error, but then continue processing until the end of the input file is encountered.

9.10.22 Write a program that calls GETFIL to attach an input file to unit 3 for reading. The program should read an integer from each line of the file (no matter how many lines the file has) and report the largest value it found. Be sure to do something sensible in the event that a READ error occurs. Test your program using a file named **input** that contains the following data, formatted as shown.

```
14
  -2

5
      287
0
```

You should also test the program in other ways if you think that might be prudent. What happens if the input file is empty? What happens if you run the program like this?

```
unix[27] a.out 3=input
```

9.10.23 The program of §9.7 repeats page numbers that appear on both input lists. Modify the program to print such numbers only once, identifying them with the string "SD" to show that both Sarah and David found the typo.

9.10.24 Write a program to compare two files, each of which consists of an arbitrary number of lines with a single real value on every line. The value on a given line of one file is approximately (but perhaps not exactly) equal to the value on the same line of the other file. A comparison consists of writing out, to a third file named **errors**, the line numbers and differences for all lines in which the absolute difference exceeds an amount called TOL, which the user enters from the keyboard. The names of both files will be specified at the time the program is run. What does your program do if one file is longer than the other?

9.10.25 The program listed below consists of a main and the two subroutines SUB and H.

```fortran
      EXTERNAL H
      COMMON /DATA/ K(3)
      CALL SUB(H)
      WRITE(6,901) (L,K(L),L=2,3)
  901 FORMAT(' result:'/('K(',I2,')=',I5))
      STOP
      END
C
      SUBROUTINE SUB(P)
      EXTERNAL P
      INTEGER*4 M(3,2)/1,2,3,4,5,6/
      CALL P(M,3)
      RETURN
      END
C
      SUBROUTINE H(M,N)
      INTEGER*4 M(N,*)
      COMMON /DATA/ K(3)
      DO 1 I=1,3
         K(I)=M(I,1)+M(I,2)
    1 CONTINUE
      RETURN
      END
```

The boxes below represent the characters of output lines. Fill in the boxes to show exactly what the program prints out (some lines or characters might not be used).

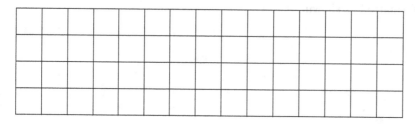

9.10.26 The following code is written as intended (*without* an EXTERNAL declaration in IADROF).

```fortran
      EXTERNAL SUB                    FUNCTION IADROF(SUB)
      WRITE(6,900) IADROF(SUB)        INTEGER*4 SUB
  900 FORMAT(1X,Z8)                   IADROF=SUB
      STOP                            RETURN
      END                            END


                                      SUBROUTINE SUB
                                      RETURN
                                      END
```

What quantity is returned by IADROF, and printed out?

10

Character Variables

Besides doing arithmetic and logical operations, FORTRAN can manipulate letters, numerals, spaces, and punctuation. All sorts of programs for non-numerical processing have been written in FORTRAN by using this capability, including text formatters, compilers, and even operating systems, but there are other languages that are far better for those tasks. The first step in writing a program for any purpose is to pick the right language, and FORTRAN is the obvious choice only for projects that involve numerical calculations.

In engineering and scientific applications, most uses of character variables have to do with I/O. You already know quite a bit about doing I/O in FORTRAN, and many programmers get along fine using only the language features you have already learned. However, character variables can be extremely useful in preprocessing input data, formatting output, and making interactive programs easier to use. It is also possible to draw primitive graphs with programs written in Classical FORTRAN, even on an output device that is not capable of real graphics, by using character variables.

10.1 How Characters Are Stored

FORTRAN stores characters in variables of CHARACTER type, one character per byte. Here are two ways of storing the word Hello.

```
CHARACTER*5 TEXT              CHARACTER*1 TEXT(5)
TEXT='Hello'                  TEXT(1)='H'
                              TEXT(2)='e'
                              TEXT(3)='l'
                              TEXT(4)='l'
                              TEXT(5)='o'
```

In the code on the left, TEXT is a CHARACTER scalar of length 5 bytes. In the code on the right, TEXT is a 5-element array of 1-byte CHARACTER scalars. The CHARACTER*n form of declaration is occasionally necessary, but most of the time we will use a vector of CHARACTER*1 elements so that individual characters can be addressed using array notation. We will often refer to a contiguous sequence of characters (possibly including spaces), or to a contiguous subsequence, as a **string**.

In the examples above, TEXT or its elements are given values by assignment. Compile-time initializations can also be used for strings, like this

```
CHARACTER*5 TEXT/'Hello'/
```

or like this.

```
CHARACTER*1 TEXT(5)/'H','e','l','l','o'/
```

The strings in single quotes, such as 'Hello', 'H', 'e', 'l', and 'o' are **character constants**. Strings that we have used to label printed output, such as 'A=' in the following statements, are also character constants.

```
    PRINT *,'A=',A                     WRITE(6,901) A
                                   901 FORMAT('A=',F7.3)
```

In these examples the character or characters in the string are enclosed by single forward quote marks ('). This is different from the practice in typesetting, where quotations are set off by double quote marks (") or single quote marks that point in different directions (' '). To enclose a single quote by single quotes, the enclosed single quote must be repeated. The declaration

```
    CHARACTER*1 QUOTE/''''/
```

initializes QUOTE to the character constant '.

Instead of using a quoted string, we can give the value of a character constant in a **Hollerith specification** of the form n*Hstring*, where n is the number of characters in *string*. Thus 5HHello defines the character constant Hello and 1H' is a single quote, so earlier we could have written

```
    TEXT=5HHello
```

or

```
    CHARACTER*1 QUOTE/1H'/
```

Hollerith specifications are cryptic compared to quoted strings, and there is always the chance that you could miscount the characters. However, some people find 1H' less confusing than ''''. You might also encounter Hollerith specifications in codes you inherit from others (see §13.9.3).

A third way to state a character constant is by giving the hexadecimal values of the characters. We first encountered hex numbers in §4.6.3, and I mentioned there that they can be used to specify byte codes for characters. Most computers use the **ASCII character code** to define which byte represents which character. The table on the next page shows the ASCII codes for all of the printable characters, and a few codes with other meanings that are sometimes of interest to FORTRAN programmers.

With one hexit we can count up to $F_{16} = 15_{10} = 1111_2$, which serves to specify the values of 4 bits or half a byte (recall from §4.1 that there are 8 bits in a byte). So it takes two hexits to specify a byte, and because a character occupies one byte it takes two hexits to specify a character. Half a byte is also called a **nybble**, so sometimes the first and second hexits in a character's byte code are referred to as the byte code's first nybble and second nybble.

In the table, the first hexit or nybble of each character's byte code is shown at the front of the row in which the character appears and the second is at the top of the column. For example, the letter e has the byte code 65, which we can specify in FORTRAN with the hexadecimal constant Z'65'. So 'e', 1He, and Z'65' are all equivalent ways of representing the letter e. Byte code 20 prints a space, 09 a tab. Among the many ASCII byte codes that do not represent printable characters, only those labeled in the first row of the table are of sufficient interest in FORTRAN programming to merit discussion here. The first, 00, is called the **null** byte and is used in the C programming language to mark the end of a character string. When defining character strings in FORTRAN for use within FORTRAN it second hexit

	0	1	2	3	4	5	6	7	8	9	A	B	C	D	E	F
0	NUL							BEL		TAB	C̸R		PAG			
1																
2	SPC	!	"	#	$	%	&	'	(	)	*	+	,	−	.	/
3	0	1	2	3	4	5	6	7	8	9	:	;	<	=	>	?
4	@	A	B	C	D	E	F	G	H	I	J	K	L	M	N	O
5	P	Q	R	S	T	U	V	W	X	Y	Z	[	\	]	^	_
6	`	a	b	c	d	e	f	g	h	i	j	k	l	m	n	o
7	p	q	r	s	t	u	v	w	x	y	z	{	|	}	~	
8																
9																
A																
B																
C																
D																
E																
F																

first hexit

is *not* necessary to include a null terminator. If you print the 07 byte on standard-out, no character will appear but the workstation will make a sound, if it can. Excessive dinging probably won't endear your program to its users, but on rare occasion the bell might be useful to announce something dramatic. The 0A byte is technically called a **line feed**, but I have marked it C̸R because printing it makes whatever follows begin at the beginning of the next output line. The 0C byte is recognized in UNIX™ (and perhaps elsewhere) as a **page eject**, which you can use to skip to the top of the next printed page. In a file the byte codes 01 through 0F appear as ˆA through ˆO.

Whether a string is declared as a **CHARACTER*n** variable or as a vector of **CHARACTER*1** elements, and however we have specified the values of the characters it contains, the byte codes of the characters occupy adjacent locations in memory. For example, the variable **TEXT** in our first example occupies a piece of memory that looks like this.

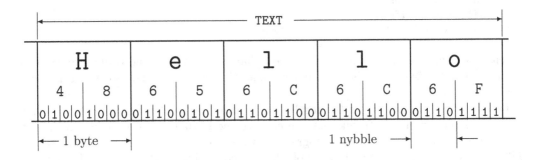

Each byte in this picture is labeled with the character it contains, the character's 2-hexit byte code, and the corresponding bit pattern. Of course, it's the bits that are actually stored in the computer's memory circuits. As mentioned in §4.8, character strings are stored with the first character at the low address in memory regardless of the endian-ness of the processor.

10.2   Writing Out and Reading In CHARACTER Variables

You already know how to write out character *literals* like 'A=', by including them in the list of a PRINT statement or in a FORMAT statement, as was illustrated by one of the examples in the previous section. To read or write the value of a character *variable* requires a new FORMAT field specification, An, which transmits a string of n characters. Using it we can write out a CHARACTER*n variable like this,

```
      CHARACTER*5 TEXT/'Hello'/
      WRITE(6,902) TEXT
  902 FORMAT(A5)
```

or a vector of CHARACTER*1 elements like this.

```
      CHARACTER*1 TEXT(5)/'H','e','l','l','o'/
      WRITE(6,903) TEXT
  903 FORMAT(5A1)
```

In the first example there is one output field that is 5 characters long; in the second there are 5 fields each 1 character long. Both of these code segments produce the same line of output:

```
Hello
```

If an output string has trailing blanks, they are also written. Input is similarly straightforward. We can read an input line into a CHARACTER*n variable like this

```
      CHARACTER*80 LINE
      READ(5,904) LINE
  904 FORMAT(A80)
```

or into a vector of CHARACTER*1 elements like this.

```
      CHARACTER*1 LINE(80)
      READ(5,905) LINE
  905 FORMAT(80A1)
```

In either example, if the input line is shorter than 80 characters the trailing bytes of the variable are set to blanks. If the input line is *longer* than 80 characters, its trailing characters are just ignored.

Often we want to ignore the trailing blanks of an input line but don't know in advance how many there will be. To find out, we can use the LENGTH function listed on the right at the top of the next page. The program shown on its left reads an input line and uses LENGTH to find the index of its last nonblank character. Finding the index of the rightmost nonblank in a string is a basic operation in manipulating character variables, and we will make extensive use of LENGTH from now on. Here are some observations about the function.

1 ⇨   LENGTH treats LINE as a CHARACTER*1 vector, adjustably dimensioned with L elements, because we want to examine the characters individually. The main program also happens to declare LINE as a CHARACTER*1 vector, but because character variables are always stored the same way in memory the program would still work if the main had declared

```
       CHARACTER*1 LINE(80)              FUNCTION LENGTH(LINE,L)
       READ(5,905) LINE                 CHARACTER*1 LINE(L)
   905 FORMAT(80A1)                      DO 1 K=L,1,-1
       LL=LENGTH(LINE,80)                   LENGTH=K
       PRINT *,LL                           IF(LINE(K).NE.' ') RETURN
       STOP                           1 CONTINUE
       END                              LENGTH=0
                                        RETURN
                                        END
```

LINE to be a CHARACTER*80 scalar instead. The number passed to LENGTH for L must be the total length of LINE in bytes, which is 80 in either case.

2⇨ The function compares each character in LINE to the character constant ' ', starting with element L and working back towards the front. As soon as it finds a nonblank character, it returns with the function value set to the index of that character. If the line is all blanks, control instead falls through the bottom of the DO 1 loop and the function returns a length of zero.

3⇨ The IF statement in LENGTH uses the logical operator .NE. to test whether two characters are different. We will likewise use the .EQ. operator to test whether two characters are the same, and the operators .GT., .LT., .GE., and .LE. to compare two characters according to their order in the ASCII code of §10.1.

10.3   Editing Character Strings

Often it is necessary to transform a string by translating certain characters into other characters, deleting or inserting blanks, inserting numerals corresponding to an integer value, or extracting the integer value corresponding to a string of numerals. Here we will consider examples that illustrate character translation and blank removal. A number conversion is discussed in §10.4, and some other editing operations are suggested in the exercises. All of these character manipulations are performed using assignment statements, IF statements, DO loops, and other programming constructs that you are already accustomed to using for numerical calculations. Now the data are characters instead of numbers, and we don't do arithmetic with them.

A familiar character translation is the simple change of case. The routine listed at the top of the next page compares each character in STRING to the lower-case letters in LOWER, and if a match is found the input letter is replaced by the corresponding capital letter from UPPER. These tables obviously could be changed to yield other substitutions.

To remove the leading blanks from a string we can copy the rest of the string to the front and then blank out the vacated positions at the end, as illustrated to the right of the code on the bottom of the next page. The first line shows a starting string with 4 leading blanks and each subsequent line is the string after one more character is copied or overwritten with a blank. The third line is the same as the second because the character that got copied was the blank between a and string.

The first stanza of executable code finds the leftmost nonblank in the string, if there is one. If that's the first character of the string then there are no leading blanks. If there are leading blanks, the DO 3 loop copies the first nonblank to the front of the string, the next character to the second position, and so on. Finally, the DO 4 loop overwrites the vacated trailing positions with blanks.

```
      SUBROUTINE UPSTR(STRING,LS)
C     This routine translates STRING to upper case.
C
      CHARACTER*1 STRING(LS)
      CHARACTER*1 LOWER(26)/'a','b','c','d','e','f','g','h','i',
     ;                      'j','k','l','m','n','o','p','q','r',
     ;                      's','t','u','v','w','x','y','z'/
      CHARACTER*1 UPPER(26)/'A','B','C','D','E','F','G','H','I',
     ;                      'J','K','L','M','N','O','P','Q','R',
     ;                      'S','T','U','V','W','X','Y','Z'/
C
C -----------------------------------------------------------------
C
      IF(LS.LE.0) RETURN
      DO 1 K=1,LS
          DO 2 L=1,26
              IF(STRING(K).NE.LOWER(L)) GO TO 2
              STRING(K)=UPPER(L)
              GO TO 1
2         CONTINUE
1     CONTINUE
      RETURN
      END



      SUBROUTINE SHIFTL(TEXT,L)
C     This routine removes any leading blanks from TEXT.
C
      CHARACTER*1 TEXT(L)
C
C -----------------------------------------------------------------
C
C     find the first nonblank
      IF(L.LE.0) RETURN
      DO 1 K=1,L
          IF(TEXT(K).EQ.' ') GO TO 1
          KNB=K
          GO TO 2
1     CONTINUE
C     the string is all blanks
      RETURN
C
C     is the first nonblank the first character?
2     IF(KNB.EQ.1) RETURN                                        a string
C                                                              a   a string
C     no; copy the string left                                 a   a string
      DO 3 K=KNB,L                                              a s a string
          TEXT(K-KNB+1)=TEXT(K)                                 a sta string
3     CONTINUE                                                  a str string
C                                                               a stristring
C     and blank out the end                                     a strintring
      DO 4 K=L-KNB+2,L                                          a stringring
          TEXT(K)=' '                                           a string ing
4     CONTINUE                                                  a string  ng
      RETURN                                                    a string   g
      END                                                       a string
```

10.4 Object-Time FORMATs

Sometimes it is desirable for a FORMAT to vary depending on the data to be printed. The following program prints the output shown below the listing.

```
      CALL OUT(3)                    SUBROUTINE OUT(N)
      STOP                           WRITE(6,906) N
      END                        906 FORMAT('N=',I9)
                                      RETURN
                                      END
```

```
N=           3
```

The subroutine uses the field specification I9 in case it has to print a large value of N, but when it is used with small values of N the extra spaces make its output hard to read.

We can easily figure out how many decimal digits are needed to print N, especially if we assume that N is positive and has at most 9 digits. Here is a new version of OUT that finds the number of digits k as the smallest integer such that $10^k > N$. For example, if N=237 then the smallest power of 10 that is larger than N is 1000 or 10^3, so k=3 spaces are needed to print the number.

```
      SUBROUTINE OUT(N)
      DO 1 I=1,9
         k=I
         IF(10**k.GT.N) GO TO 2
    1 CONTINUE
    2 WRITE(6,907) N
C     this syntax is illegal
  907 FORMAT('N=',Ik)
      RETURN
      END
```

The variable k is shown in lower case, to suggest that Ik should be interpreted as I1 if k=1, I2 if k=2, and so on. Unfortunately, Classical FORTRAN requires all of the numbers in FORMAT field specifications to be literals like 1 or 2 rather than variables, so this syntax is not permitted. However, Classical FORTRAN does permit a character variable to be given in a READ or WRITE statement in place of a FORMAT statement number, and this makes it possible to change field specifications at run time. A character variable used in that way is called an **object-time** FORMAT.

To use an object-time format in our example, the character string we need is everything that would otherwise appear in the FORMAT statement after the word FORMAT, or ('N=',I), including the parentheses, with the blank space after the I to be filled in according to the value of k. The following compile-time initialization sets FMT to the required string.

```
      CHARACTER*1 FMT(9)/'(',1H',' N',' =',Z'27',',',' I',' ',')'/
```

This object-time format string begins and ends with the enclosing parentheses. The second character, FMT(2), is the quotation mark appearing before the N in ('N=',I), and is specified here by using a Hollerith constant. Next come the N and the =. The closing quote is specified here by giving its byte code, hex 27. The next character, FMT(6), is the comma. Then come the I and a blank space to be filled in depending on the value of k.

To fill in the blank space at FMT(8) we must use the *numeral* that corresponds to the *number* in k. This character is of course quite different from the value of k, as can be seen by examining some bit patterns. If N=237 so that k=3 digits as discussed earlier, the bit pattern in k is the 32-bit binary representation for the integer value 3, shown on the left below.

3=00000000000000000000000000000011   '3'=00110011

The numeral 3, on the other hand, is represented in the ASCII character code by the 8-bit string shown on the right. This is according to the table in §10.1, where the numeral 3 is given the hexadecimal byte code 33, which is 00110011 in binary.

If we store the numerals in a character string like this,

```
CHARACTER*1 NUMERL(10)/'0','1','2','3','4','5','6','7','8','9'/
```

we can insert a numeral into the blank space in FMT using an assignment statement like that shown on the left below.

```
FMT(8)=NUMERL(4)                    WRITE(6,907) N
WRITE(6,FMT) N                  907 FORMAT('N=',I3)
```

NUMERL(4) contains the numeral 3, so that is what the assignment statement inserts into FMT, making it read ('N=',I3). Then WRITE(6,FMT) N does exactly the same thing as the two statements shown on the right. Using these ideas we can now revise the subroutine OUT as follows.

```
      SUBROUTINE OUT(N)
      CHARACTER*1 FMT(9)/'(',1H','N','=',Z'27',',',',I',' ',')'/
      CHARACTER*1 NUMERL(10)/'0','1','2','3','4','5','6','7','8','9'/
      DO 1 I=1,9
          K=I
          IF(10**K.GT.N) GO TO 2
    1 CONTINUE
    2 FMT(8)=NUMERL(K+1)
      WRITE(6,FMT) N
      RETURN
      END
```

This version prints N using exactly the right number of digits, as long as N is positive and fits in 9 digits.

As another example of using object-time formats, consider the problem of prompting the user for some item of input and leaving the cursor hanging at the end of the prompt. As discussed in §9.1.2, that's easy to do with a FORMAT like this.

```
      WRITE(0,908)
  908 FORMAT('enter value of Z: ',$)
```

But what if the prompt string we want to write is stored in a character variable instead of coded directly into the FORMAT statement? For example, suppose we want to write the prompt above with the program at the top of the next page. The number of A1 fields specified by the FORMAT statement, shown as ??, must be replaced by the number of characters in MSG (if it is any more then the space will never be printed, the $ will never be reached in processing the format, and the prompt won't hang).

```
      CHARACTER*17 MSG/'enter value of Z:'/
      CALL PROMPT(MSG,17)
      READ(5,*) Z
      :
      END
C
      SUBROUTINE PROMPT(MSG,LM)
      CHARACTER*1 MSG(LM)
      WRITE(0,909) (MSG(K),K=1,LM)
  909 FORMAT(??A1,' ',$)
      RETURN
      END
```

To solve this problem with an object-time format we can convert LM to numerals for the number of A1 fields, like this.

```
      SUBROUTINE PROMPT(MSG,LM)
C     This routine writes a hanging prompt on unit 0.
C
      CHARACTER*1 MSG(LM)
      INTEGER*4 DIGIT
      CHARACTER*1 FMT(12)/'(',' ',' ','A','1',',',
     ;                    1H',' ',1H',',',',$',')'/
      CHARACTER*1 NUMERL(10)/'0','1','2','3','4',
     ;                       '5','6','7','8','9'/
C
C -----------------------------------------------------------------
C
C     make sure that the number of fields makes sense
      L=MINO(LM,99)
      IF(L.LE.0) RETURN
C
C     convert that number to numerals in the object-time format
      DIGIT=L/10
      FMT(2)=NUMERL(1+DIGIT)
      DIGIT=L-10*DIGIT
      FMT(3)=NUMERL(1+DIGIT)
C
C     write the prompt
      WRITE(0,FMT) (MSG(K),K=1,L)
      RETURN
      END
```

The object-time format template in FMT provides only two spaces for numerals in front of the A1, so this routine begins by assuming there should be no more than 99 fields even if LM is bigger than that. The routine works only for a positive number of fields, so if L is negative or zero it returns without printing anything.

With L guaranteed to be in the range $1, \ldots, 99$, we can easily convert its value to numerals. Integer division truncates, so the tens digit is just L/10. Then the ones digit is L minus ten times the tens digit. For example, $18/10=1$ and $18-10*1=8$. The numeral corresponding to each digit is just NUMERL(1+DIGIT), and these get assigned to FMT(2) and FMT(3). Once the format string is finished, it is used to write the prompt.

The case study of the next section uses PROMPT.

10.5 Case Study: QUERY

Many interactive programs ask yes-or-no questions of their users, and most of them do it in an awkward and unforgiving way. The task is usually performed by some open code like this,

```
      PRINT *,'Want to remove all your files?  Enter 0 for yes, 1 for no.'
      READ(5,910) I
  910 FORMAT(I1)
      IF(I.EQ.0) GO TO 1
      IF(I.EQ.1) GO TO 2
      :
```

and a user interaction might go like this.

```
Want to remove all your files?  Enter 0 for yes, 1 for no.
2
```

What does the program do with this response? At first it might seem that the flow of control must fall through both IF statements, because the response was neither 0 nor 1. However, closer inspection reveals that because of the fixed-format READ and the leading space in the user's reply, the value received for I is actually zero! The hapless user mistyped the response altogether, but it was still taken as "yes."

It would be much better if the user could respond by typing **yes** or **no**, or just **y** or **n**. If the response is something that can't be interpreted as a yes or no, the program should repeat the question rather than mindlessly defaulting to one alternative or the other. Leading blanks in the response shouldn't matter, nor should the case of the letters. All of this could even be done by a FUNCTION subprogram that returned a LOGICAL*4 value of .TRUE. for "yes" or .FALSE. for "no." Using a logical value to represent the answer, rather than an integer, rules out the ambiguity of a third alternative. With such a function named, say, QUERY, we could rewrite the earlier code like this.

```
      LOGICAL*4 QUERY
      IF(QUERY('Want to remove all your files?',30)) GO TO 1
      GO TO 2
      :
```

If QUERY returns .TRUE. the IF succeeds and we GO TO 1; otherwise we GO TO 2. The program's interaction with a fallible human user might now look like this.

```
Want to remove all your files? maybe
What?  Please answer yes or no.
Want to remove all your files? n
```

A question-asking QUERY function having the behavior described above is listed on the next page. Here are some observations about the code.

1 ⇨ The parameters are a string containing the question to be asked, and the number of characters in the string. In the main program above we passed the literal character constant 'Want to remove all your files?' for the string, and its length of 30 characters. In QUERY the string must be treated as an adjustably-dimensioned vector of CHARACTER*1 elements because its length LS is a variable.

```
      FUNCTION QUERY(STRING,LS)
C     This routine asks a yes-or-no question, carefully.
C
      LOGICAL*4 QUERY
      CHARACTER*1 STRING(LS),YORN(80)
      CHARACTER*1 YESNO(3,8)/
     ;              'Y',' ',' ',
     ;              'Y','E','S',
     ;              'Y','E',' ',
     ;              'O','K',' ',
     ;              'T',' ',' ',
     ;              'N',' ',' ',
     ;              'N','O',' ',
     ;              'F',' ',' '/
C
C ----------------------------------------------------------------
C
C     write the question and read the answer
    4 CALL PROMPT(STRING,LS)
      QUERY=.FALSE.
      READ(5,901,END=1) YORN
  901 FORMAT(80A1)
C
C     if the response is too long or too short, complain
      CALL SHIFTL(YORN,80)
      L=LENGTH(YORN,80)
      IF(L.EQ.0 .OR. L.GT.3) GO TO 2
C
C     interpret the response
      CALL UPSTR(YORN,L)
      DO 3 N=1,8
          IF(YORN(1).NE.YESNO(1,N)) GO TO 3
          IF(YORN(2).NE.YESNO(2,N)) GO TO 3
          IF(YORN(3).NE.YESNO(3,N)) GO TO 3
          IF(N.LE.5) QUERY=.TRUE.
          RETURN
    3 CONTINUE
C
C     the response was not a yes or a no; complain and try again
    2 WRITE(0,902)
  902 FORMAT('What?  Please answer yes or no.')
      GO TO 4
C
C     the user sent an end-of-file
    1 WRITE(0,903)
  903 FORMAT('Assuming "no".')
      RETURN
      END
```

2 ⇨   QUERY begins by calling PROMPT (discussed in §10.4) to write out the question and leave the cursor on that line. Then it sets the return value to .FALSE. in case the user responds with an end-of-file, and reads the response YORN as a string of 80 characters. If the user sends an end-of-file, the END= clause of the READ transfers control to statement 1, where an explanation is written before the routine returns .FALSE. as the function value.

3 ⇨ If the READ is successful, the second stanza of executable code uses SHIFTL (from §10.3) to remove any leading blanks from the response and LENGTH (§10.2) to find the length of the result. If the string is blank, or longer than the longest recognizable response of yes, the IF transfers control to statement 2. That stanza explains that the response was not understood and transfers control back to statement 4, where the prompt is repeated.

4 ⇨ If the left-justified response is 1, 2, or 3 characters long, the third stanza of executable code uses UPSTR (§10.3) to translate it to upper case and then compares it, character by character, to the alternatives listed in the columns of the array YESNO. Both upper and lower case response characters translate to upper case, so responses such as Yes, yEs, and YES all match the YES entry in YESNO. There is no harm in requiring YORN(1), YORN(2), and YORN(3) all to match the corresponding characters of an entry in YESNO, because if a listed response has fewer than 3 characters its trailing blanks will match those in YESNO. Storing the allowable responses in YESNO by columns, rather than rows, makes it easy to code the compile-time initializations for the strings.

5 ⇨ The recognized responses include those mentioned earlier and also some other plausible inputs that can safely be taken to mean "yes" or "no." If the YESNO entry that matches YORN is among the first 5, the response is recognized as some variant of "yes" and the routine returns .TRUE.; if the match is after that in YESNO the response is recognized as some variant of "no" and the routine returns .FALSE.. If YORN doesn't match any of the entries in YESNO, the flow of control falls through the bottom of the DO 3 loop to the code stanza beginning with statement 2, and the prompt is repeated as described above.

10.6   CHARACTER Variables in Other Contexts

In addition to the uses we have seen so far, a character variable can also be written to and read from, or used to specify a filename to OPEN, or returned as the value of a FUNCTION subprogram. In all of these contexts it is necessary to use the CHARACTER*n form rather than a vector of CHARACTER*1 elements. This is inconvenient if we also need to manipulate the characters one by one, but as we shall see below that problem can be solved by using EQUIVALENCE (introduced in §4.6.3) to refer to the same string both as a CHARACTER*n scalar and as a CHARACTER*1 vector. In some versions of UNIX™ it is necessary to use the CHARACTER*n form for character variables that are passed as arguments to system routines.

10.6.1   Reading From and Writing To CHARACTER Variables

In the code below, the REAL*8 variable A is written and then reread using an F5.2 format. This rounds the value of A to two decimal places, so that after the READ its value is 1.24 (or, rather, the IEEE floating-point representation nearest 1.24).

```
      REAL*8 A/1.23654D0/
      CHARACTER*5 LINE
      WRITE(LINE,911) A
      READ(LINE,911) A
  911 FORMAT(F5.2)
      :
```

The WRITE translates the numerical value to characters, and the READ translates the characters back to a numerical value. Instead of writing to an output device, the WRITE statement writes into the 5-byte region of memory named by the character variable LINE. The READ, instead of reading from an input device, reads from LINE. A character variable used in this way is sometimes referred to as an **internal file**.

A more important application of internal files is in preprocessing input data. The case study of §9.5 showed how to use the ERR= clause of a READ statement to trap some errors, and how to print a diagnostic message containing the line number of a bogus record that is read from a file. By using character variables it is possible to detect a wider variety of input formatting errors, count the number of data items found on a line, report the column at which a field of bad data begins, or print the offending field even if it cannot be interpreted as data. To illustrate this sort of column-oriented processing, the program below reads a line containing an unknown number of real values separated by blanks.

```
      REAL*8 X(10),V
      CHARACTER*1 TEXT(80)
      CHARACTER*80 LINE
      EQUIVALENCE(TEXT,LINE)
C
C     input a line of characters
      READ(5,912) TEXT
  912 FORMAT(80A1)
      N=0
C
C     shift the text left to the next nonblank token
    3 CALL SHIFTL(TEXT,80)
      L=LENGTH(TEXT,80)
      IF(L.EQ.0) GO TO 1
C
C     read the token as a number
      READ(LINE,*,ERR=2) V
      IF(N.EQ.10) GO TO 1
      N=N+1
      X(N)=V
C
C     blank out the token just read
      K=0
    4 IF(K.EQ.L) GO TO 1
      K=K+1
      IF(TEXT(K).EQ.' ') GO TO 3
      TEXT(K)=' '
      GO TO 4
C
    2 WRITE(0,912) (TEXT(K),K=1,L)
      STOP
    1 PRINT *,N,' values found'
      :
```

Here are some observations about this code.

1➡ The first READ gets an input string of up to 80 characters, presumably containing between 1 and 10 real numbers, from standard-in. N is the number of numbers that have been found in the string so far, zero to begin with. The next stanza removes any leading blanks from the string and finds its length. If the string is all blanks we are done; otherwise it now begins with a nonblank substring or **token**.

2 ⇨   The leftmost numerical value is read from the input string, using free format, into the variable V. This is a context in which the string must be treated as a CHARACTER*n variable, so the READ is from LINE rather than from TEXT. The EQUIVALENCE statement tells the compiler that TEXT and LINE are two different names for the same 80-byte piece of memory, so either of the two names can be used as required by the context.

3 ⇨   If reading from LINE results in an error, as will happen if the token is something other than a number, the ERR= clause of the READ transfers control to statement 2. There the offending field and the remainder of the input string are written to standard-error so the user can see the bad data. If the READ from LINE is successful, the number is counted and its value is copied into X(N).

4 ⇨   The next stanza overwrites the used token with blanks. If the end of the line is reached in doing that, we're done. Otherwise when the end of the token is reached control transfers back to statement 3 where the newly-created leading blanks get shifted out, moving the next token to the front.

Some other uses for internal files are suggested in the exercises.

10.6.2   Using CHARACTER Variables in OPEN

In §9.4.2 I mentioned that by using character variables it is possible to read a filename from the user and then attach the file to a logical I/O unit with OPEN. The example below shows how to do that.

```
      CHARACTER*24 FILNAM
      CALL PROMPT('file name:',10)
      READ(5,913) FILNAM
  913 FORMAT(A24)
      OPEN(UNIT=3,FILE=FILNAM)
      :
```

This program prompts for and reads a filename, arbitrarily limited in length to 24 characters, and then uses OPEN to attach the file to logical I/O unit number 3. In this context the variable FILNAM must be declared as a CHARACTER*24 scalar; if it were instead declared as a vector of CHARACTER*1 elements, OPEN would use only the first element as the file name.

As mentioned in §9.4.2 there are lots of things that can go wrong when attaching a file, so rather than writing open code it's usually preferable to use the GETFIL routine listed in §18.3. But at the heart of GETFIL is an OPEN statement using a character variable for the file name just as in this example.

As we shall see in §14.2.2, a character variable can similarly be used to specify a filename in the FORTRAN INQUIRE statement.

10.6.3   CHARACTER Functions

The final context that we will examine in which the CHARACTER*n form of declaration must be used for a character variable is when a FUNCTION subprogram returns a character value. The program at the top of the next page reads the numerical order of a day in the week and prints out a corresponding abbreviation for the day's name. The function DAY returns in its name the appropriate CHARACTER*3 value, so DAY must be declared that way in the main program rather than as a vector of CHARACTER*1 elements.

Another example involving a character function appears in §14.2.1.

```
      CHARACTER*3 DAY
      READ *,N
      WRITE(6,914) DAY(N)
  914 FORMAT(A3)
      STOP
      END
C
      FUNCTION DAY(N)
      CHARACTER*3 DAY,DAYS(7)/'Sun','Mon','Tue','Wed',
     ;                        'Thu','Fri','Sat'/
      DAY=DAYS(N)
      RETURN
      END
```

10.7 Character Graphics

As R. W. Hamming famously observed, "The purpose of computing is insight, not numbers." Insight is often easiest to get from a picture, so many computing environments include utilities for drawing high-resolution graphs of data and mathematical functions. On UNIX™ systems, commonly available graphics applications include gnuplot [108], xgraph [67], and Data Explorer [14]. MATLAB also includes extensive graphics functionality that you can use to plot data generated by your FORTRAN programs. These and similar products work much better than any substitute you could easily write, and you should use them if you can.

There are situations, however, in which it might be impossible or inconvenient to use a ready-made graphics package. For example, you might be using a machine on which no suitable package happens to be installed, or your program might need to display an intermediate graphical result to guide the user's response to a question that the program asks in the middle of a run. In such circumstances a rough graph made up of typewriter characters might be good enough, or at least better than nothing. This section shows how such a **character graph** can be generated using FORTRAN. Before the development of pixel-addressable displays, graphs were very commonly drawn in this way on electromechanical line printers, so character graphs are sometimes referred to as **line-printer graphs** even when they are drawn on less primitive output devices. The examples of this section are presented as stand-alone programs, but you can easily recast them as subroutines if you must output graphics in the midst of some calculation.

If you need to have the user control your program by, say, clicking a mouse button while pointing to some feature of a graph, then you are doing **interactive computer graphics** and you will need to call subprograms from a **graphics library** rather than using code like that presented here. Several different standard graphics libraries are in widespread use, and their subprograms can be invoked from FORTRAN like other library routines (as discussed in §6.6) but their use is beyond the scope of this text.

10.7.1 X–Y Plots

The most frequently required graphic in numerical computing is a simple plot showing how one variable depends on another. Usually it is most convenient to graph results from a computation *after* the arithmetic is over, using a separate program that reads in the numbers. A one-to-one relationship between two variables can be specified by a table of x and y values like the one on the next page. Each row of the table gives an x value first and then the corresponding value of y. If the table is in a file, or if we are willing to enter the values one line at a time from the keyboard, we can use the program on the following page to obtain the graph on the right below.

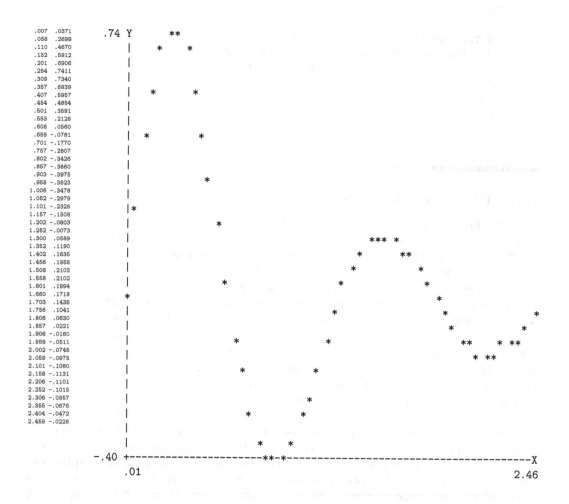

.007	.0371
.058	.2699
.110	.4670
.152	.5912
.201	.6906
.254	.7411
.309	.7340
.357	.6839
.407	.5957
.454	.4854
.501	.3591
.553	.2128
.608	.0560
.659	-.0781
.701	-.1770
.757	-.2807
.802	-.3426
.857	-.3860
.903	-.3975
.958	-.3823
1.006	-.3478
1.052	-.2979
1.101	-.2328
1.157	-.1508
1.202	-.0803
1.252	-.0073
1.300	.0589
1.352	.1190
1.402	.1635
1.456	.1958
1.506	.2103
1.558	.2102
1.601	.1994
1.660	.1718
1.703	.1435
1.756	.1041
1.806	.0630
1.857	.0221
1.906	-.0160
1.959	-.0511
2.002	-.0745
2.059	-.0975
2.101	-.1080
2.158	-.1131
2.206	-.1101
2.252	-.1015
2.306	-.0857
2.355	-.0676
2.404	-.0472
2.459	-.0228

Crude though it is, this graph shows much more clearly than does the table of values that y is a decaying sinusoidal function of x (the formula $y = e^{-x}\sin(5x)$ actually happens to fit the data pretty well). Here are some observations about the program.

1 ⇨   All of the real variables are REAL*4, because only a few significant digits are needed in computing the location of a point to be plotted.

2 ⇨   The first executable stanza of the program (including the loop that ends at statement 1) reads up to 100 lines of input data, each containing the x and y coordinates of a point to be plotted. The variable L counts the data points actually found, of which there happen to be 50 in our example. The limit of 100 on the number of points is fixed by the dimensions given for X and Y. For a curve made up of straight-line segments to appear smooth, even on a high-resolution display the size of a printed page, it is seldom necessary to use more than 200 data points. Of course, with character graphics there isn't much hope of ever getting a curve that looks smooth.

```
      PARAMETER(M=30,N=68)
      CHARACTER*1 GRID(M,N)
      REAL*4 X(100),Y(100)
      REAL*4 XMAX/-1.E10/,XMIN/1.E10/,YMAX/-1.E10/,YMIN/1.E10/
C
C     read the table of values, find extrema, and compute scales
      L=0
      DO 1 K=1,100
          READ(5,*,END=2) X(K),Y(K)
          L=L+1
          XMAX=AMAX1(XMAX,X(K))
          XMIN=AMIN1(XMIN,X(K))
          YMAX=AMAX1(YMAX,Y(K))
          YMIN=AMIN1(YMIN,Y(K))
    1 CONTINUE
    2 DX=(XMAX-XMIN)/FLOAT(N-1)
      DY=(YMAX-YMIN)/FLOAT(M-1)
C
C     on a blank grid, draw X and Y axes
      DO 3 I=1,M
      DO 3 J=1,N
          GRID(I,J)=' '
          IF(J.EQ.1) GRID(I,J)='|'
          IF(I.EQ.1) GRID(I,J)='-'
    3 CONTINUE
      GRID(1,1)='+'
      GRID(1,N)='X'
      GRID(M,1)='Y'
C
C     plot each point as an asterisk
      DO 4 K=1,L
          I=1+IFIX(0.5+(Y(K)-YMIN)/DY)
          J=1+IFIX(0.5+(X(K)-XMIN)/DX)
          GRID(I,J)='*'
    4 CONTINUE
C
C     print the plot from top to bottom
      WRITE(6,901) YMAX,(GRID(M,J),J=1,N)
  901 FORMAT(F4.2,1X,68A1)
      DO 5 I=M-1,2,-1
          WRITE(6,902) (GRID(I,J),J=1,N)
  902     FORMAT(5X,68A1)
    5 CONTINUE
      WRITE(6,901) YMIN,(GRID(1,J),J=1,N)
      WRITE(6,903) XMIN,XMAX
  903 FORMAT(4X,F4.2,61X,F4.2)
      STOP
      END
```

3⇨ After each line is read, the assignment statements for XMAX, XMIN, YMAX, and YMIN update the highest and lowest coordinate values found so far. These variables are initialized at compile time to very high ($+10^{10}$) or very low (-10^{10}) values that are replaced by the first coordinates read in. The built-in functions AMAX1 and AMIN1 return, respectively, the larger and smaller of their arguments, as described in §6.6.1.

4 ⇨ The points we plot will land in the centers of the GRID **pixels**, with the extreme points one-half pixel in from the edges of the grid, so the distance between the highest and lowest value in each direction must correspond to the number of pixels in that direction *minus one*. Thus the scale factors DX and DY are each just the range of the variable divided by *one fewer* than the number of pixels along its axis.

5 ⇨ The loop ending at statement 3 fills in GRID with blanks, overwrites the left column with vertical bars to make the *y*-axis, and overwrites the bottom row with hyphens to make the *x*-axis. Then the intersection of the axes is overwritten with a + sign and each axis is labeled by overwriting its last pixel with the appropriate letter. Assigning some pixels several times is much easier than using more complicated logic to avoid the overwriting.

6 ⇨ The grid used here is M=30 pixels high and N=68 pixels wide, so the pixels are rectangles about two-and-one-quarter times as high as they are wide. I picked the value for M, which fixes the length of the printed Y axis, and then experimented to find a value of N yielding as nearly as possible the same length for the printed X axis. That way, if the data plotted are for a circle the axis scalings will make it look round in the picture. Your display might use a different **aspect ratio**.

7 ⇨ The loop ending at statement 4 again overwrites, with a *, the pixel GRID(I,J) corresponding to the (x, y) coordinates of each point. The calculation of I or J begins by using the scale factor to find the number of pixels the point is from the axis. This will usually turn out to have a fractional part, so I add 0.5 and truncate to round the value off to the nearest integer. Finally, because GRID is indexed from 1 rather than from zero, it is necessary to add 1.

It's easy to verify that these formulas work at the extreme values. For example, suppose Y(K) is YMIN. Then Y(K)-YMIN is zero, IFIX(0.5) is zero (remember from §4.4 that IFIX truncates), and the point gets plotted on the *x*-axis, where I=1. If Y(K) is YMAX, then (YMAX-YMIN)/DY comes out M-1 because of the way DY was found. Adding 1 gives I=M, so the point gets plotted in the top row of GRID.

8 ⇨ The filled-in GRID must be printed starting with its top row (row M), so that when all the lines have scrolled up on the display screen we will see the picture right-side up. The top line of GRID is printed with YMAX to its left, and the bottom line with YMIN to its left, to indicate the scaling of the *y*-axis. To scale the *x*-axis, a line containing XMIN and XMAX is printed last.

9 ⇨ The field specifications used in the FORMAT statements work well for the data of this particular example, and the program could be used as written for other data sets having similar ranges in *x* and *y*. However, to make the program work for *arbitrary* inputs it would be necessary to switch to E-type field specifications or to object-time formats constructed on the fly based on the data. Gracefully labeling tic-marks with values, especially if there are intermediate ones as well as those at the ends of the axes, is the most difficult part of writing a general-purpose graph plotter. Various refinements to this program are proposed in Exercise 10.9.37.

10.7.2   Contour Plots

A function of two variables can sometimes be visualized by looking at a **contour plot** showing the locus of points in the $x - y$ plane where the function takes on a given value. The contour plot on the next page is the locus of points where

$$x^4 + xy + \tfrac{1}{2}y^3 = -0.01$$

```
        FUNCTION F(X,Y)
        REAL*4 A/0.01/
C       add level to plot zero contour
        F=X**4+X*Y+0.5*Y**3 + A
        RETURN
        END
```

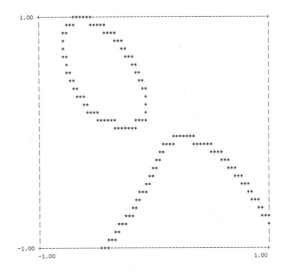

So that I could define both the function and the contour level of $-.01$ in the same routine, which is listed on the left above, I actually plotted the zero contour $f(x, y) = 0$ of the function

$$f(x, y) = x^4 + xy + \tfrac{1}{2}y^3 + 0.01$$

which is of course the same locus mentioned before. One insight we get from this picture comes from the closed contour in the upper left quadrant of the plot, which suggests the presence of a hill or valley whose highest or lowest point is a local maximum or minimum of the function (there actually is a local minimum at $x \approx -.5296$, $y \approx .5942$).

The program that produced this plot is listed on the next page. Here are some observations about it.

1 ⇨ The grid of points is the same size and shape we used for the $x - y$ plot of §10.7.1, so a circular contour would come out round. This time, however, the picture shows a region of the $x - y$ plane. The first stanza of executable code, including the loops that end at statement 1, draws a square around the region.

2 ⇨ This code uses a function subprogram to compute the values of $f(x, y)$, rather than reading data from a file, so the extreme values of x and y are chosen in advance rather than determined from input data. It's possible to contour a function defined by a table of values, but doing that is quite a bit harder than using a function subprogram because the spacing of data points might differ from the spacing of the pixels in the grid. The second stanza of executable code, including the loop that ends with statement 3, calculates the values of $f(x, y)$ at all the pixel corners. The grid has M × N pixels, so there are M+1 × N+1 function values to store in V. This time the extreme values of x and y are in the edges of the picture rather than at the centers of the edge pixels, so in finding DX and DY we divide by the number of pixels along each axis rather than that number minus one.

3 ⇨ If the function value is less than zero at one corner of a pixel and greater than zero at another, we assume it crosses zero somewhere inside and mark the pixel with a * to show that it belongs to the contour.

```
      PARAMETER(M=30,N=68)
      CHARACTER*1 GRID(M,N)
      REAL*4 XMIN/-1.0/,YMIN/-1.0/,XMAX/1.0/,YMAX/1.0/,V(M+1,N+1)
C
C     start with a box enclosing a blank region of the x-y plane
      DO 1 I=1,M
      DO 1 J=1,N
          GRID(I,J)=' '
          IF(I.EQ.1 .OR. I.EQ.M) GRID(I,J)='-'
          IF(J.EQ.1 .OR. J.EQ.N) GRID(I,J)='|'
    1 CONTINUE
      GRID(1,1)='+'
      GRID(1,N)='+'
      GRID(M,1)='+'
      GRID(M,N)='+'
C
C     find function values at the corners of all the pixels
      DX=(XMAX-XMIN)/FLOAT(N)
      DY=(YMAX-YMIN)/FLOAT(M)
      DO 2 I=1,M+1
          Y=YMIN+DY*FLOAT(I-1)
          DO 3 J=1,N+1
              X=XMIN+DX*FLOAT(J-1)
              V(I,J)=F(X,Y)
    3     CONTINUE
    2 CONTINUE
C
C     the contour is the pixels in which function crosses zero
      DO 4 I=1,M
      DO 4 J=1,N
          VMAX=AMAX1(V(I,J),V(I+1,J),V(I,J+1),V(I+1,J+1))
          VMIN=AMIN1(V(I,J),V(I+1,J),V(I,J+1),V(I+1,J+1))
          IF(VMIN.LE.0. .AND. VMAX.GE.0.) GRID(I,J)='*'
    4 CONTINUE
C
C     print the plot
      WRITE(6,901) YMAX,(GRID(M,J),J=1,N)
  901 FORMAT(F5.2,1X,68A1)
      DO 5 I=M-1,2,-1
          WRITE(6,902) (GRID(I,J),J=1,N)
  902     FORMAT(6X,68A1)
    5 CONTINUE
      WRITE(6,901) YMIN,(GRID(1,J),J=1,N)
      WRITE(6,903) XMIN,XMAX
  903 FORMAT(6X,F5.2,57X,F5.2)
      STOP
      END
```

4⇨ Printing the picture works just as in the $x - y$ plotter, but the field specifications in these FORMAT statements are slightly different to make the axis scales look good. Here, as in the $x - y$ plotter, labeling the tick marks nicely is a hard problem to solve in a general way. Some refinements to this program are proposed in Exercise 10.9.39.

10.8   Omissions

In some other languages a single character and a character string differ in type, not just in length. We see a suggestion of this distinction in FORTRAN's CHARACTER*1 vector and CHARACTER*n scalar forms for character variables. I have identified only a subset of FORTRAN-77's character operations as belonging in Classical FORTRAN so that this distinction can be ignored except in the contexts of §10.6. In particular, I have omitted any discussion of hidden-parameter implied lengths for CHARACTER*n variables passed as subprogram arguments. Here are some other topics that might reasonably have been included here.

> The EBCDIC character code; *arithmetic with characters; the colon notation for a substring of a CHARACTER*n variable; storing characters in variables of other types;* graphics libraries such as X and PHIGS.

10.9   Exercises

10.9.1   As explained in §10.1, a character string can be stored as either a CHARACTER*n scalar or a vector of CHARACTER*1 elements. (a) When is it necessary to use the scalar form? (b) When is it necessary to use the vector form? (c) How can the same string be used in both ways in a single routine?

10.9.2   How many bits are in a nybble? How many characters can be stored in a doubleword? What is the meaning of this string of byte codes? Z'0C204F6E650A54776F07'

10.9.3   The ASCII character code is given in §10.1. (a) Write a program that reads in a 2-hexit value and prints out the corresponding ASCII character. (b) Revise the program to print a table of all possible hex codes and the corresponding characters.

10.9.4   State three ways of specifying the single-quote ' as a character constant, and write a program to verify that the three alternatives all yield the correct character. Which method of declaration do you find easiest to understand?

10.9.5   The ASCII byte code for a tab is 09. (a) Suggest a way to confirm this by experiment. (b) Write a program that reads lines from standard-in, translates each tab character into 8 blanks, and writes the transformed lines to standard-out.

10.9.6   What does the 4-byte bit pattern 01010111 01101111 01110010 01100100 mean when it is interpreted as (a) a CHARACTER*4 string; (b) a 4-element vector of CHARACTER*1 elements; (c) an INTEGER*4 number; (d) a REAL*4 number; (e) a 4-byte hexadecimal value?

10.9.7   Write a subroutine BINARY(FW,BITS) that returns in the 32-element CHARACTER*1 array BITS the 32 bits in the fullword value FW. Use your routine to find the bit pattern corresponding to the INTEGER*4 value 1466921572.

10.9.8   The presence of TEXT in this COMMON block introduces a misalignment. How should DATA be rearranged to remove the misalignment?

```
COMMON /DATA/ TEXT,I,X
CHARACTER*5 TEXT
INTEGER*4 I
REAL*8 X
```

10.9.9   Consider the following program.

```
      CHARACTER*4 STRING(2)/'Outp','ut  '/
      WRITE(6,901) STRING
  901 FORMAT(?)
      STOP
      END
```

(a) What format should be used to print STRING? (b) How many bytes get printed? Explain.

10.9.10 This program reads a line of text from the keyboard and writes it back to the screen.

```
      CHARACTER*1 LINE(80)/80*'x'/
      READ(5,901) LINE
      WRITE(6,901) LINE
  901 FORMAT(80A1)
      STOP
      END
```

What does the program print if the user enters the following line of input?

`test`

10.9.11 This program uses the LENGTH function of §10.2.

```
      CHARACTER*32 TEXT/' More   and    more    blanks      '/
      DO 1 L=1,32
          PRINT *,LENGTH(TEXT,L)
    1 CONTINUE
      STOP
      END
```

What does it print, and why?

10.9.12 The LENGTH routine given in §10.2 neglects to check that the input value of L is plausible. (a) If L is negative or zero, what is its meaning as an adjustable dimension for LINE? Revise the declaration so that LINE is correctly dimensioned no matter what value L has. (b) If L is negative or zero, what does the DO loop do? Revise the function so that it returns LENGTH=0 if L is nonpositive, whether the code is compiled using a FORTRAN-66 or a FORTRAN-77 compiler.

10.9.13 The **gematria** of a word is the sum of the numerical values associated with its letters. For example, if a=1, b=2, and so on, the word **cab** has the value 3+1+2=6. (a) Write a FORTRAN program that reads a word of up to 24 lower-case letters and prints out the word's value. (b) Thinking of the value of a word as a percentage, use output from your program to argue that "attitude is everything."

10.9.14 The following list of words is to be sorted: `smith Smith eat! eats XY(1+N)` `xylophone <@> >&< wombat apple`. (a) What is the alphabetical order of these words, according to the ASCII character code? Characters are in alphabetical order when their numerical values are in increasing order. (b) Write a program to read up to 100 words from standard-in, one word per line, and write the list on standard-out one word per line but sorted in alphabetical order. Assume that a word can have up to 24 characters.

10.9.15 Write a program in Classical FORTRAN that copies lines of text from standard-in to standard-out and can thus be used to copy a file. How long will you allow the lines to be, and what will the program do if an input line exceeds that length? Would this task be easier using a programming language that can read or write one byte, rather than one line, at a time?

10.9.16 Write a program that copies records from standard-in to standard-out but omits adjacent repeated lines. How long can the lines be? Read the `man` page for the UNIX™ utility `uniq` and compare its behavior to that of your program.

10.9.17 As explained in §1.1, Classical FORTRAN ignores anything after column 72 of a source statement. (a) Write a FORTRAN program that reads records from standard-in (which will be redirected from an input file), removes anything after column 72, trims any trailing blanks, and writes the resulting output records on standard-out (which will be redirected to an output file). We shall see in §13.1.1 why such a program sometimes comes in handy. (b) Do you suppose FORTRAN is the best language for an application like this? (c) Write a C program to perform the filtering and compare it to the FORTRAN program.

10.9.18 Write a subroutine `READLN(UNIT,LNUM,TEXT,LT,RC)` to read a line of up to `LT` characters into the `CHARACTER` variable `TEXT` from line `LNUM` of the file attached to unit `UNIT`. Use the return code `RC` to signal the outcome of the call. What happens if `LNUM` specifies a line that is not in the file? What if the line in the file is longer than `LT` bytes?

10.9.19 Write a subroutine `GETI4S(PR,LP,IDEF, I,RC)` to prompt for and return the value of an integer `I`. The prompt that is written to standard-error should consist of the string `PR` of length `LP` characters, followed by a space, the default value of `IDEF` in square brackets, a colon, and a space. For example, the call

```
CALL GETI4S('value',5,37, I,RC)
```

should result in the following (hanging) prompt being written.

```
value [37]:
```

If the user enters an integer at the prompt, that value should be returned in `I`, but if the user enters a null line (by simply pressing the ⎍R key) then the default value `IDEF` should be returned for `I`. if the user sends a ^D, the routine should return with the integer return code `RC=1`; if an error occurs it should return with `RC=2`; otherwise it should set `RC=0`. Hint: your FORTRAN I/O library probably will not allow a `READ` of a numerical value to be satisfied by a null response, but a null response *will* satisfy the `READ` of a character variable, and probably sets it to blanks. Read the user's response as a character string, and then extract the integer if it contains one.

10.9.20 Write a subroutine SPACEL(TEXT,L) that replaces any sequence of two or more blanks in TEXT by a single blank, leaving L unchanged. Verify that your code works by using it to remove extra blanks (shown as ⌣) from the top string below, obtaining the bottom string.

⌣More⌣⌣and⌣⌣⌣more⌣⌣⌣⌣blanks⌣⌣⌣⌣⌣
⌣More⌣and⌣more⌣blanks⌣⌣⌣⌣⌣⌣⌣⌣⌣⌣⌣

10.9.21 Write a subroutine FINDST(LINE,LL,STRING,LS, KSTART) to find character string STRING in character string LINE. KSTART should return the index in LINE where STRING begins, or zero if the string is not found, or −1 if the parameters don't make sense. LINE and STRING are CHARACTER*1 vectors of lengths LL and LS respectively.

10.9.22 Exercise 5.8.34 called for a program to compute N! for large N. Revise the program you wrote for that problem so that the result it prints has no leading blanks or zeros in the exponent. For example, it should report 3.3162750924105473E+5735 for 2000!.

10.9.23 The F4.1 format in this program rounds off the value printed to the nearest tenth.

```
      WRITE(6,901) -.049
  901 FORMAT(F4.1)
      STOP
      END
```

(a) Compile and run the program. Rounding off -.049 to the nearest tenth yields zero, but is it printed with a minus sign or not? (b) Write a subroutine having the calling sequence WRITEZ(FMT,X) to print out the REAL*8 value X using the F-type format FMT. If X is exactly zero, print the zero as it is formatted using FMT, without any sign character. If X is actually negative but is small enough that FMT will print it as a zero, prefix the first nonblank character of the output field with a - sign; if X is actually positive but is small enough that FMT will print it as a zero, prefix the first nonblank character of the output field with a + sign. The required behavior is illustrated below; the program on the left should produce the output shown on the right.

```
      REAL*8 Y/-.01D0/,Z/0.D0/,W/.01D0/
      CALL WRITEZ('F4.1',Y)                -.0
      CALL WRITEZ('F4.1',Z)                 .0
      CALL WRITEZ('F4.1',W)                +.0
      STOP
      END
```

10.9.24 In the first example of §10.4 we assumed that the value to be printed, N, was nonnegative and could be printed using 9 digits or fewer. Revise the final version of OUT given there to (a) print values that can have any sign but need a total of 9 or fewer print positions; (b) print any value that can be stored in an INTEGER*4 variable. (c) Can you speed up the loop by avoiding the exponentiation? (d) Can you eliminate the DO loop altogether by using logarithms? Which approach do you think runs faster? (e) Can you eliminate the need for an object-time format by using a free-format PRINT or WRITE statement?

10.9.25 Explain the difference between a number and a numeral.

10.9.26 The PROMPT routine described in §10.4 uses an object-time format to set the number of A1 fields that are to be written out. (a) Write a PROMPT routine that copies the prompt string directly into an object-time format instead of writing out the character variable MSG. (b) Write a PROMPT routine that prints the prompt string using a *fixed* FORMAT, rather than one constructed on the fly. The versions of §10.4 and part (a) insert a blank after the MSG text. Is it possible for this version to do that? If not, how can the prompt be supplied with a trailing blank?

10.9.27 Suppose we want to write out a REAL*8 vector X of length N using a D format and displaying as many significant digits as possible, but with the constraint that the output fit on a single line of less than or equal to 80 characters. Write a subroutine that uses an object-time format to do this.

10.9.28 Write a subroutine BTD(N, STRING,LS,RC) to convert the value in N, which is an INTEGER*4, into numerals in STRING, where STRING is a CHARACTER*1 vector of LS elements. The INTEGER*4 return code RC should be zero if the conversion was successful, 1 if the digits won't fit in a string of the given length, or 2 if LS is nonpositive. Test your routine using both positive and negative values of N.

10.9.29 Write a subroutine DTB(STRING,LS, N,RC) to convert the integer given as numerals in STRING, a CHARACTER*1 vector of length LS, to a numerical value in the INTEGER*4 parameter N. The INTEGER*4 return code RC should be zero if the conversion is successful, 1 if the string contains illegal characters, or 2 if LS is nonpositive or the string contains only blanks.

10.9.30 The first example in §10.6.1 shows how formatted I/O to a character variable can be used to round off a REAL*8 value to two decimal digits. Write a code sequence that performs this operation without doing any I/O.

10.9.31 In §10.6 I claimed that by using an internal file it is possible to detect input data errors that escape the notice of READ, but neither example of that section illustrates how to do so. Consider a case in which fields that look like -123.45 are expected in the input data. A formatted READ using the field specification F7.2 will read this expected pattern but will also cheerfully accept a field such as 6789␣␣ which, having the wrong pattern, might actually be in error. Write a FUNCTION subprogram CHECK(FIELD) that returns the logical value .FALSE. unless the 7-character string FIELD contains a +, -, or blank in column 1; digits in columns 2, 3, 4, 6, and 7; and a decimal point in column 5.

10.9.32 Revise the second example of §10.6 to report the number of the beginning column of any input field that is found to be in error.

10.9.33 The following program uses a WRITE to a character variable.

```
    CHARACTER*11 OUTPUT
    N=123
    WRITE(OUTPUT,901) N
901 FORMAT(I11)
    CALL SHIFTL(OUTPUT,11)
    WRITE(6,902) OUTPUT
902 FORMAT(A11)
    STOP
    END
```

(a) What output does the program write? Explain how it works. (b) Revise the program to edit the OUTPUT string so that this is what gets printed.

1 2 3

Your solution to part (b) should not involve any arithmetic.

10.9.34 The UNIX™ system routine FDATE mentioned in §6.6.2 is discussed further in §14.2.1, which you might find it helpful to read before you attempt this exercise. FDATE returns a CHARACTER*24 value containing the current date and time in the format on the left below.

Sun May 27 14:10:17 2007   Sun 27 May 07 14:10:17

Write SUBROUTINE DATIME(NOW) to return in the 22-byte character variable NOW a date-and-time string in the format on the right. If the number of the day or hour is less than 10, put a leading 0 rather than a blank in the tens place of the number. In calling DATIME, does it matter whether the actual parameter passed for NOW is declared as a CHARACTER*22 scalar or as a vector of 22 CHARACTER*1 elements?

10.9.35 Suppose that an unformatted WRITE statement was used to output records consisting only of INTEGER*4 values, but it is not known *how many* values were in each record. In other words, we know that the data were written by a WRITE statement that looked like this,

```
    WRITE(1) (LINE(I),I=1,N)
```

but we do not know what value N had when the program was run. Write a program to read the unformatted file, recover the integer values, and write them on standard-out in human-readable form. Assume that the unformatted records have the structure described in §9.8, that all the records are the same length, and that N≤10. Hint: read the 4-byte data length from the first record using an A4 format.

10.9.36 The C language provides a macro named assert() for checking whether an assumed condition actually prevails at a given point in a program [74]. For example, before invoking the square root function one might check whether the argument is nonnegative by using assert(), as follows

```
    assert(x>=0);
    y=sqrt(x);
```

In this example, if the logical expression x >= 0 is true the function returns without doing anything, but if it is false the function writes an error message telling what condition was violated, and then stops the program. In the case that assert stops the program, it is said to take a **sideways exit** and never returns to the calling routine. (a) Write a FORTRAN subroutine named ASSERT that simulates the behavior of the C assert() function. One argument should be the logical value to be tested and the other a character string describing the violation to be reported if the test fails. (b) Discuss the limitations of this method for handling error conditions.

10.9.37 Many improvements could be made to the primitive $x - y$ graph-plotting program discussed in §10.7.1. Some of them are described by the parts of this exercise, which are arranged in increasing order of difficulty. (a) Use compile-time initialization to replace the code stanza beginning with the DO 3 loops. (b) If an error occurs in reading a line of input data, report the line number and stop the program. (c) Make the program do something sensible if there is no input data, or if XMAX is equal to XMIN, or if YMAX is equal to YMIN. (d) Permit up to 9 data sets to be given in the input, each separated from the previous one by a blank line. In this case, instead of * use the numeral 1 for points on the first graph, 2 for points on the second, and so on. (e) Remove the restriction on the number of data points by reading the input file once to find the maximum and minimum values for scaling the plot, then rewinding the file and reading it again to plot the points. In this case it doesn't make sense to read the data from the keyboard, so you should use OPEN or the GETFIL routine described in §9.4.2 to attach an input file. (f) Print tick marks along the axes and label them with the corresponding values of X and Y. (g) Pick the scale factors DX and DY so that the tick intervals are a power of ten times 1, 2, 5, 4, 3, or 8, in that order of preference, and each axis is at least 80% filled by the graph.

10.9.38 The $x - y$ graph plotting program of §10.7.1 plots points that it reads from a file. Suppose we want to plot the function $y = e^{-x} \sin(5x)$ for values of x ranging from 0 to 2.45 (a) Write a program that generates an input file containing 50 points, and run the plotting program on that data to make a graph. (b) Revise the plotting program to compute the function values directly, rather than reading them from a file. Which version of the plotting program is more generally useful?

10.9.39 Many improvements could be made to the primitive contour plotting program discussed in §10.7.2. (a) Revise the program to plot up to 9 different contour levels. Instead of * use the numeral 1 for points in the contour at the first level, 2 for points in the contour at the second level, and so on. Is it still possible to define all the details of the problem in the function subprogram, so that the main program does not need to be changed from one problem to another? (b) Revise the function subprogram so that on its first call it reads a data file each of whose lines contains the coordinates x, y, and $f(x, y)$ of a point on the surface to be contoured. Use linear interpolation in this data to approximate $f(x, y)$ at any point (x, y) where the main program might want to know the function value.

10.9.40 Write a program that reads an input file containing one data value on each line, and prints a **histogram** of the data sideways. The example output below shows that there were 3 data values between 0.0 and 1.0, 8 between 1.0 and 2.0, and so on. The range of values covered by each row will depend on the range of the data and the number of rows used. Your program should automatically select the number of rows or **cells** r, based on the number of data values n. To do this it should use **Sturges' rule**, $r = 1 + \lceil \log_2(n) \rceil$, where $\lceil x \rceil$ is the lowest integer not less than x. How does your program handle data values that fall exactly on a cell boundary?

```
0.00 ...
1.00 ........
2.00 .....
3.00 ..
4.00 .
5.00 .
6.00
```

10.9.41 The following program is alleged to generate the first 2500 fractional digits 71828 ... of $e = 2.71828 \ldots$, the base of natural logarithms.

```
      PARAMETER(NA=1000,NAM=NA-1)
      INTEGER*4 A(NA)/0,NAM*1/,B(50)
      DO 1 I=1,50
          DO 2 N=1,50
              M=0
              DO 3 J=NA,2,-1
                  L=A(J)*10+M
                  M=L/J
                  A(J)=L-M*J
3             CONTINUE
              B(N)=M
2         CONTINUE
          IF(I.EQ.1) THEN
              WRITE(6,901) B
901           FORMAT('e=2.',50I1)
          ELSE
              WRITE(6,902) B
902           FORMAT(4X,50I1)
          ENDIF
1     CONTINUE
      STOP
      END
```

(a) With what frequencies do the digits 0-9 appear in the program's output sequence? (b) Plot a histogram showing the distribution of digit frequencies for this data. (c) How would you change the program to print the first 5000 fraction digits?

10.9.42 Character strings are stored with the leftmost character at the low address in memory regardless of the endian-ness of the processor. As explained in §4.8, integers are stored on big-endian machines with their *most* significant byte at the low address in memory but on little-endian machines with their *least* significant byte at the low address in memory. (a) What value is printed for I when the following program is run on a big-endian machine? On a little-endian machine?

```
      CHARACTER*1 BIG(4)/Z'00',Z'00',Z'00',Z'13'/
      EQUIVALENCE(BIG,I)
      PRINT *,I
      STOP
      END
```

(b) Write a program that prints out **big-endian** or **little-endian** according to whether it is run on a machine that uses the corresponding byte ordering. (c) Revise your program to report **neither** if some pattern other than big-endian order or little-endian order is being used to store the bytes of an integer.

11

Memory Management Techniques

Often it is possible to reduce the amount of memory that a program uses or the amount of work it needs to do, just by making thoughtful use of the way in which FORTRAN stores arrays and passes parameters to subprograms. Classical FORTRAN has only one native data structure, the statically-allocated rectangular array, but by using arrays in less obvious ways than those we have so far studied it is also possible to represent more complicated data objects. Certain techniques for performing these memory management tasks are programming clichés, used so often as to be practically standard. This chapter is about some of these commonplace usages.

If you've forgotten how FORTRAN stores and passes arrays, it might be helpful to review §5.3 and §6.2 before reading on.

11.1 Passing Array Columns

The function subprogram listed on the right below returns the sum of the elements in a vector. The program on the left copies the second column of the matrix A into the vector U, and then invokes VSUM to add up the elements.

```
      REAL*8 A(3,2)/1.D0,2.D0,3.D0,          FUNCTION VSUM(V,N)
     ;            4.D0,5.D0,6.D0/            REAL*8 VSUM,V(N)
      REAL*8 U(3),VSUM,SUM                   VSUM=0.D0
      DO 1 I=1,3                             DO 1 J=1,N
          U(I)=A(I,2)                            VSUM=VSUM+V(J)
    1 CONTINUE                             1 CONTINUE
      SUM=VSUM(U,3)                           RETURN
      PRINT *,SUM                             END
      STOP
      END
```

As explained in §6.2, FORTRAN passes parameters to subprograms not by value but by reference, so what VSUM receives for V is actually the *address* of U(1). Based on this starting address and the 8-byte size of each element, the machine code that the compiler generates for VSUM can figure out the memory location where any given element of V is stored, back in the main program where U was originally allocated.

Next consider the simpler main program at the top of the next page, which also passes the second column of A to VSUM. Now when VSUM is invoked what gets passed to it for V is the address of A(1,2). Because FORTRAN stores arrays in column-major order, as described in §5.3, the second column of A is just the three doublewords beginning at that address. To VSUM these three doublewords look just like the vector U that we passed to it from the other main program, so VSUM works just like it did before. Of course, we can pass only an array

```
      REAL*8 A(3,2)/1.D0,2.D0,3.D0,          FUNCTION VSUM(V,N)
    ;            4.D0,5.D0,6.D0/             REAL*8 VSUM,V(N)
      REAL*8 VSUM,SUM                        VSUM=0.D0
C     pass second A column as a vector       DO 1 J=1,N
      SUM=VSUM(A(1,2),3)                          VSUM=VSUM+V(J)
      PRINT *,SUM                          1 CONTINUE
      STOP                                    RETURN
      END                                    END
```

column in this way, not a row, because the method depends on the fact that the elements in a column are stored in adjacent memory locations (but see Exercise 11.9.6).

At first glance this might strike you as a tricky way to pass an array column, and that's why it calls for some explanation. But it is quite transparent once you remember about call by reference and column-major order, and it is used very often in real FORTRAN programs. Copying the column to a vector first, as we did originally, wastes both CPU time and memory for storing U, and the extra DO loop makes the code longer and more complicated. To anyone who understands how to pass an array column as a vector, the code that does so directly is not only more efficient but also easier, rather than more difficult, to understand. However, if someone reading the main program above doesn't know that the first parameter of VSUM should be a vector, it might appear that the single array element A(1,2) is being passed into a dummy parameter that is a scalar. To make this unambiguous to a reader who might not be familiar with the routine you are invoking, it's a good idea to include a comment explaining what you are doing.

11.2   Partitioning Workspace

Classical FORTRAN uses static memory allocation, so the total amount of storage reserved for a program's data is fixed when the code is compiled. In this program, SUB performs some calculation involving the vectors X and Y.

```
      REAL*8 X(5),Y(5)                       SUBROUTINE SUB(X,M,Y,N)
      READ(5,*) M,N                          REAL*8 X(M),Y(N)
      IF(M.GT.5 .OR. N.GT.5) STOP            :
      READ(5,*) (X(I),I=1,M)                 RETURN
      READ(5,*) (Y(J),J=1,N)                 END
      CALL SUB(X,M,Y,N)
      STOP
      END
```

Even though a total of 10 doublewords of memory are reserved for the arrays, neither array can store more than 5 elements. This rules out combinations such as M=6, N=4 or M=1, N=9. If the computer on which we hope to run this program has enough memory, we can of course just increase the size of both arrays in order to accommodate these combinations, but then there will be others that don't work. Because the allocated memory is divided between X and Y in a fixed way, there will always be problems that won't fit even though the total amount of data does not exceed the total space available.

This problem can be solved by a simple generalization of the idea introduced in §11.1. The program below uses a single vector W to store the elements of both X and Y. Now W can be divided between X and Y in any way, as long as the *total* number of elements does not exceed 10. The elements of X are stored in W(1),...,W(M), and Y is W(M+1),...,W(M+N). Because X starts at W(1) and Y starts at W(M+1), the main passes the addresses of those elements to SUB for X and Y. A similar approach could obviously be used for partitioning a fixed workspace among arrays having two or more dimensions, or among scalars.

```
REAL*8 W(10)                      SUBROUTINE SUB(X,M,Y,N)
READ(5,*) M,N                     REAL*8 X(M),Y(N)
IF(M+N .GT. 10) STOP              :
READ(5,*) (W(I),I=1,M)            RETURN
READ(5,*) (W(M+J),J=1,N)          END
CALL SUB(W(1),M,W(M+1),N)
STOP
END
```

Many production codes use a single workspace vector to store the elements of *all* the arrays that can vary in size depending on the problem being solved. When many arrays are stored in a workspace, integer variables are usually introduced to hold their starting indices. Often the lengths of some arrays are related, rather than being independent as in our example, and then more complicated formulas might be needed to compute the starting indices.

If the starting index for an array that is stored in a workspace vector is calculated incorrectly, that can easily result in overflowing one of the constituent arrays into another, or in overflowing the workspace, so great care must be taken to ensure that the starting indices are right.

As we shall see in §17.1.2, Fortran-90 permits arrays to be allocated dynamically, with sizes determined at run time, so that workspace partitioning is not necessary. This shifts the burden of managing workspace from the programmer to the Fortran run-time library and the operating system, and eliminates the possibility that you will make a mistake in computing a starting index. Unfortunately, this benefit is often accompanied by a performance penalty, so in some cases it might be desirable to use workspace partitioning even in Fortran-90, and dynamically allocate only the single workspace vector to accommodate problems of varying total size.

11.3 Sharing Workspace

Often a subprogram uses variables other than those it receives as parameters, and of course the local variables take up space. For example, the subroutine RERANG listed at the top of the next page includes a large local array. RERANG rearranges the elements of T according to the indices listed in INDS. Because any element of the original T might be needed in any iteration of the DO 1 loop, T can't be overwritten until all the switching has been done, and the work vector TEMP is needed to store the result until then. However, TEMP is overwritten in each call of RERANG before it is used, so its values don't need to be saved from one call to the next.

```
      SUBROUTINE RERANG(T,INDS)
      REAL*8 T(10000),TEMP(10000)
      INTEGER*4 INDS(10000)
      DO 1 I=1,10000
          TEMP(I)=T(INDS(I))
    1 CONTINUE
      DO 2 I=1,10000
          T(I)=TEMP(I)
    2 CONTINUE
      RETURN
      END
```

Now suppose that in the same program two other subprograms, shown below, coincidentally happen to include the local temporaries named WRK and LTMP.

```
      FUNCTION GHI(S,Q)
      REAL*16 S,Q(5000),WRK(10000)
      :
      RETURN
      END

      SUBROUTINE JKL(J,K)
      INTEGER*4 J(12),K,LTMP(10000)
      :
      RETURN
      END
```

The total amount of space consumed by the three temporary workspace variables is

$$10000 \times 8 + 10000 \times 16 + 10000 \times 4 = 280000$$

bytes, but only one of the arrays is in use at any given time so only enough space for the largest one, 160000 bytes, is really needed. These three variables *could* share the same storage, and if they did the total amount of memory required by the program would be reduced by 120000 bytes.

To overlap TEMP, WRK, and LTMP in memory, we could allocate a single work vector 160000 bytes long and pass it to each of the three routines as a formal parameter. That would be inconvenient, though, if RERANG, GHI, and JKL aren't all called by the same routine. In that case we would have to allocate the workspace in a higher-level routine, perhaps all the way back up in the main program, and pass it through several layers of subprograms before getting it to the places where it is used.

The other mechanism that FORTRAN provides for variables in different routines to share memory is COMMON. In §8.2, I cautioned against using COMMON for anything besides passing data around a library routine, but I also mentioned that two exceptions to that rule would be discussed in §11, and this is one of them. On the next page RERANG, GHI, and JKL are revised to share their temporary work variables in a COMMON block named /TWORK/. Some programmers, instead of using a labeled COMMON block for shared temporary workspace, use blank COMMON (see §13.8.4) for this one purpose.

When COMMON is used for shared temporary workspace, it does *not* serve to communicate data between routines. In our example the function GHI has no interest at all in TEMP or LTMP, but only wants to borrow the memory they occupy for its own variable WRK. Variables that are placed in shared temporary workspace must really be temporary, because they will probably be overwritten between invocations of the routine in which they occur. If it were

```
      SUBROUTINE RERANG(T,INDS)              FUNCTION GHI(S,Q)
      REAL*8 T(10000),TEMP(10000)           REAL*16 S,Q(5000),WRK(10000)
C     shared temporary workspace            COMMON /TWORK/ WRK
      COMMON /TWORK/ TEMP                    :
      INTEGER*4 INDS(10000)                  RETURN
      DO 1 I=1,10000                         END
          TEMP(I)=T(INDS(I))
    1 CONTINUE                               SUBROUTINE JKL(J,K)
      DO 2 I=1,10000                         INTEGER*4 J(12),K,LTMP(10000)
          T(I)=TEMP(I)                       COMMON /TWORK/ LTMP
    2 CONTINUE                               :
      RETURN                                 RETURN
      END                                    END
```

necessary in our example for LTMP to remain unmolested between calls to JKL, it couldn't
be in /TWORK/.

It doesn't make sense for communicating variables that are aligned in COMMON to be of
different types, so in code where that is done the COMMON block is probably being used for
shared temporary workspace. If you use this technique in writing your own code, you should
include comments to explain what is going on.

As we shall see in §17.1.2, Fortran-90 provides automatic arrays that are allocated when
a subprogram is entered and deallocated upon return. These can be used for temporary
local workspace, though possibly at the cost of increasing run time.

11.4   Sharing Constant Data

Some applications involve large quantities of problem data that can change from one run
of the program to the next but which remain static during each run. For example, a
mechanical design program might use tables of material properties in which the materials
of interest can vary between projects but remain fixed during any one design calculation.
Because such data can change from run to run, they can't be defined once and for all using
PARAMETER constants or compile-time initializations but must be read in, usually from a file.
Because the data might be needed at many different points in the program, independent of
the flow of control used by the algorithm, passing the data through in formal subprogram
parameters might be cumbersome and getting it to where it is needed might require it to go
through routines where it isn't needed. In such a case the least complicated way to share
the data might be in COMMON, and this is the second exception to the general rule of §8.2.

In the example at the top of the next page a subroutine named INPUT is called to read
some data and store it in /DATA/, from which it can then be extracted by any routines that
need it. Here are some observations about the program.

1⟹   PI is fixed forever, so it is defined using a PARAMETER constant rather than being read
in as constant problem data. Different values of X can be used for a given problem, so X is
read from the keyboard rather than from the data file.

2⟹   INPUT must be called before any of the data in TABLE are needed, and because the
data are fixed they are read only once. If necessary an input routine can read more than
one input file, preprocess or consistency-check the data, handle any errors that occur in

```
      REAL*8 PI                          SUBROUTINE CALC(X,Y)
      PARAMETER(PI=3.1415926535897932D0) REAL*8 X,Y
      CALL INPUT                         :
      READ *,X                           CALL LOWR(Z,W)
      CALL CALC(X,Y)                     :
      :                                  RETURN
      STOP                               END
      END


      SUBROUTINE INPUT                   SUBROUTINE LOWR(Z,W)
      COMMON /DATA/ TABLE                COMMON /DATA/ TABLE
      REAL*8 TABLE(127,34)               REAL*8 TABLE(127,34),Z,W
      OPEN(UNIT=3,FILE='data')           :
      READ(3,901) TABLE                  W=Z*TABLE(I,J)
      :                                  :
      RETURN                             RETURN
      END                                END
```

the file opening or reading process, and distribute the data among multiple common blocks rather than a single one as in this example.

3 ⇨   TABLE could have been returned as a subprogram parameter by INPUT, rather than being in /DATA/, but then to get it into LOWR would have required passing it through CALC, which does not itself have any use for the data.

When COMMON is employed in this way, the same data values are used by several routines but are not changed by them during the course of the calculation. In the case of shared workspace, described in §11.3, the quantities in COMMON are changed during the course of the calculation but the values set by one routine are not used by the others. When quantities in COMMON are changed during the calculation *and* the values set by one routine are used by another, that amounts to passing parameters between the routines. For reasons that will be elaborated in §13.8, passing parameters in COMMON is a bad idea except when it is necessary to communicate variables around a library routine.

11.5   Storing a Symmetric Matrix

A matrix is **symmetric** if it is equal to its transpose. Many calculations in linear algebra, like this one, involve symmetric matrices.

$$\mathbf{A}\mathbf{x} = \begin{bmatrix} 2 & -5 & 1 \\ -5 & 3 & 0 \\ 1 & 0 & 8 \end{bmatrix} \begin{bmatrix} 1 \\ 2 \\ 3 \end{bmatrix} = \begin{bmatrix} -5 \\ 1 \\ 25 \end{bmatrix} = \mathbf{y}$$

Matrix-vector multiplication is just a special case of matrix-matrix multiplication, which was discussed in §5.6, so if $\mathbf{A}$ has elements $a_{i,j}$ then the elements of the result vector are

$$y_i = \sum_{j=1}^{3} a_{i,j} x_j, \quad i = 1, 2, 3.$$

This formula works whether **A** is symmetric or not, but because our **A** has $a_{i,j} = a_{j,i}$ it should also be possible to compute each y_i without referring to any elements below the diagonal. The following code does that trick.

```
INTEGER*4 A(3,3)/2,-5,1,-5,3,0,1,0,8/,X(3)/1,2,3/,Y(3)
DO 1 I=1,3
    Y(I)=0
    DO 2 J=1,3
        IF(J.GE.I) Y(I)=Y(I)+A(I,J)*X(J)
        IF(J.LT.I) Y(I)=Y(I)+A(J,I)*X(J)
2       CONTINUE
1 CONTINUE
PRINT *,Y
STOP
END
```

One way of visualizing matrix-vector multiplication is to imagine that we find the i'th row of **y** by laying **x** on its side, superimposing it on the i'th row of **A**, and then adding up the products of the numbers that touch. To avoid using the elements below the diagonal you can now imagine the same process but with **x** bent up into an L shape having its corner touching the diagonal of **A**. The first element of **Ax** gets calculated in the usual way because J is always greater than or equal to I=1. For the second result element, I=2 so the first product we would normally compute, A(2,1)*X(1), uses an element of **A** that is below the diagonal and thus forbidden. But because **A** is symmetric A(1,2)=A(2,1), so we can find the required product by just switching the indices on A, and that is exactly what the code does for the case of J less than I.

Now, since we're not using any elements of **A** below the diagonal, there is no reason to store them! The saving in memory is only 3 words in our example, but for matrices that are large enough to worry about it saves almost half of the space that would be needed to store all the elements.

Storing all the elements is called **full storage mode**. A symmetric matrix is customarily represented in Classical FORTRAN using **symmetric storage mode**, which stores the elements of the upper triangle in a vector using the same order as their column-major order in the matrix [6, §1.2.7]. Here is our example recoded to keep **A** in symmetric storage mode.

```
INTEGER*4 AS(6)/2,-5,3,1,0,8/,X(3)/1,2,3/,Y(3)
DO 1 I=1,3
    Y(I)=0
    DO 2 J=1,3
        IF(J.GE.I) Y(I)=Y(I)+AS( (J-1)*J/2 + I )*X(J)
        IF(J.LT.I) Y(I)=Y(I)+AS( (I-1)*I/2 + J )*X(J)
2       CONTINUE
1 CONTINUE
PRINT *,Y
STOP
END
```

Wherever the previous program referred to A(I,J), this one must refer to the corresponding element in AS. For example, A(2,3) is element 5 of AS. To figure this out from the indices I=2 and J=3 that the element has in **A**, we need only count the elements that come before A(2,3) in the upper triangle. There is one from the first column (the 2), there are two from the second column (the -5 and the 3), and there is the element above A(2,3) in the third column (it's a 1). In general, each element A(I,J) on or above the diagonal will be stored in AS with $1 + 2 + \cdots + (J - 1)$ elements in front of it from the preceding columns of A, and $I - 1$ elements above it from column J. But

$$1 + 2 + \cdots + (J - 1) = (J - 1)J/2$$

so in the code the index in AS is $(J-1)*J/2 + I$. As in the previous program, for elements $A(I,J)$ below the diagonal we just reverse the roles of I and J.

Symmetric storage mode is sometimes indispensable to conserve memory in storing symmetric matrices, and you might encounter codes that use it even when it is not really needed.

11.6   Sparse Matrix Techniques

It might also be possible to conserve memory or avoid unnecessary arithmetic if a matrix is **sparse**, having many zero entries.

11.6.1   Fixed Pattern

In the simplest case, the exact pattern of zeros and nonzeros is fixed and can be taken advantage of in writing special-purpose code. The matrix product indicated below illustrates this idea.

$$\mathbf{AB} = \begin{bmatrix} X & 0 & 0 & 0 \\ 0 & X & 0 & X \\ X & 0 & X & 0 \\ 0 & X & 0 & 0 \end{bmatrix} \begin{bmatrix} 0 & 0 & 0 & X \\ 0 & X & 0 & 0 \\ 0 & 0 & X & 0 \\ X & X & 0 & 0 \end{bmatrix} = \begin{bmatrix} 0 & 0 & 0 & X \\ X & X & 0 & 0 \\ 0 & 0 & X & X \\ 0 & X & 0 & 0 \end{bmatrix} = \mathbf{C}$$

The matrix elements that can be nonzero are marked X, and the matrices **A** and **B** always have the patterns of zero and nonzero elements shown. The actual *values* of the nonzero elements might of course vary from one multiplication to the next. The resulting pattern of zeros and nonzeros in the product matrix **C** contains only six elements that need to be computed. Here is a special-purpose subroutine that does the calculation.

```
      SUBROUTINE ABMUL(A,B, C)
      REAL*8 A(4,4),B(4,4),C(4,4)
      DO 1 I=1,4
      DO 1 J=1,4
          C(I,J)=0.D0
    1 CONTINUE
      C(2,1)=A(2,4)*B(4,1)
      C(2,2)=A(2,2)*B(2,2)+A(2,4)*B(4,2)
      C(4,2)=A(4,2)*B(2,2)
      C(3,3)=A(3,3)*B(3,3)
      C(1,4)=A(1,1)*B(1,4)
      C(3,4)=A(3,1)*B(1,4)
      RETURN
      END
```

The code begins by setting all of C to zero, and then fills in the elements that can be nonzero (of course it might happen, depending on the numbers in A and B, that some of these result elements turn out to be zero too, but we don't avoid computing them). A conventional matrix product code would use 4 multiplications and 3 additions to find each of the 16 elements in the product matrix, or 112 floating-point operations altogether. By avoiding unnecessary calculations, this code uses only 8 floating-point operations. If any of the elements of A or B used in ABMUL were known always to have the value 1, it would be possible to simplify the code further by eliminating unnecessary multiplications.

In this example we have assumed that A, B, and C are stored in full storage mode, but there is really no need to store the zeros at all. For each matrix we could store only the nonzeros in a vector, and just remember what order we put them in. That's probably not worth the trouble for this little example, but a custom-made data structure might be worthwhile for a larger problem in which the matrices have fixed patterns of zero and nonzero elements.

11.6.2 Varying Pattern

In the usual situation where the pattern of zero and nonzero matrix elements is *not* fixed but depends on input data, more sophisticated techniques [51] are required to take advantage of sparseness. These methods all store index vectors as well as the nonzero elements of the matrix represented, so their memory demands can actually be greater than those of full-storage mode if the matrices are not sufficiently sparse. Also, the methods use indirect array indexing, which takes more CPU time than direct indexing, so they can spend longer finding each result than conventional algorithms that operate on matrices in full storage mode. For these reasons, sparse matrix techniques are beneficial only when the matrices are large and very sparse indeed, certainly no more than 10% dense and ideally much sparser than that.

Writing your own code for these methods, rather than using full-storage mode, can increase the complexity and subtlety of your program quite a lot. A few subroutine libraries are available for doing sparse matrix calculations [54] [26] [17], and if possible you should use routines from them rather than writing your own code.

There are several standard schemes for representing a sparse matrix, but the most widely used ones are **IBM format** and **YSMP format**. IBM format, developed at International Business Machines, stores the nonzero elements of a matrix **A** in a vector VA, in the order they are encountered reading from left to right across the rows and from the top row to the bottom row of the matrix (that is, in their row-major order). If **A** has NNZ nonzero elements, then VA must be NNZ elements long to store them. Two integer vectors, IA and JA, are used to record the locations of the nonzero elements in **A**. The index in VA of the first nonzero element in row R of the matrix (or zero if there are none) is stored in IA(R). If **A** has N rows, then IA needs N elements, one for each row. The column index in **A** of the Pth nonzero element is stored in JA(P). That means that JA, like VA, must be NNZ elements long. YSMP format, developed for the Yale Sparse Matrix Package [54], is just the IBM format with the number NNZ+1 stored in IA(N+1). This little addition makes certain calculations much easier to code, so we will use the YSMP format and dimension IA to have N+1 elements. Here is an example to illustrate the scheme.

```
C     represent A using YSMP format
      VA=[1.D0,2.D0,5.D0,7.D0,3.D0,6.D0,8.D0,4.D0]
      IA=[1,2,4,7, 9]
      JA=[1,2,3,1,3,4,3,4]
```

$$
\mathbf{A} = \begin{bmatrix} 1 & 0 & 0 & 0 \\ 0 & 2 & 5 & 0 \\ 7 & 0 & 3 & 6 \\ 0 & 0 & 8 & 4 \end{bmatrix}
$$

It might seem that YSMP format is not the most obvious way to represent a sparse matrix, but it is actually quite ingenious. To see why, we will use it to compute the matrix-vector product at the top of the next page.

$$\begin{bmatrix} 1 & 0 & 0 & 0 \\ 0 & 2 & 5 & 0 \\ 7 & 0 & 3 & 6 \\ 0 & 0 & 8 & 4 \end{bmatrix} \begin{bmatrix} 1 \\ -2 \\ 3 \\ -4 \end{bmatrix} = \begin{bmatrix} 1 \\ 11 \\ -8 \\ 8 \end{bmatrix}$$

Here is some code that does the calculation.

```
      REAL*8 VA(8)/1.D0,2.D0,5.D0,7.D0,3.D0,6.D0,8.D0,4.D0/
      REAL*8 X(4)/1.D0,-2.D0,3.D0,-4.D0/,Y(4)
      INTEGER*4 IA(5)/1,2,4,7,9/,JA(8)/1,2,3,1,3,4,3,4/,R,P
C
      DO 1 R=1,4
         Y(R)=0.D0
         DO 2 P=IA(R),IA(R+1)-1
            Y(R)=Y(R)+VA(P)*X(JA(P))
    2    CONTINUE
    1 CONTINUE
      PRINT *,Y
      STOP
      END
```

To understand how this program works, consider the calculation of, say, Y(3). The result element is first initialized to zero. Then the DO 2 loop runs P from IA(3)=4 up to IA(4)-1=6, so Y(3) will be the sum of three terms. The first term, when P=4, is VA(4)*X(JA(4)), which is VA(4)*X(1) or 7.D0*1.D0. Next, when P=5, the term is VA(5)*X(JA(5)), which is VA(5)*X(3) or 3.D0*3.D0. Finally, when P=6, the term is VA(6)*X(JA(6)), which is VA(6)*X(4). These are just the products we would compute by hand if we were finding Y(3) and skipped the zero in the third row of **A**.

Now suppose that we are finding Y(4), so R=4. To select the two nonzero entries in the last row of **A**, P must run from 7 to 8. The starting value is IA(4)=7, which we determined as the index in VA of the first nonzero in the row, but the ending value of P is IA(5)-1. It is to make this value come out NNZ=8 that the YSMP format calls for setting IA(N+1) to NNZ+1.

The indirect indexing I referred to earlier is evident in the expression X(JA(P)), where the index on X is itself an array element.

In manipulating large matrices that have a lot of zeros it is often worthwhile to use the YSMP format, or some other sparse representation, to conserve memory and save machine time.

11.7   Linked Lists

Consider the simple task of sorting some integers into ascending order. One way to do this would be to read them all into an array, rearrange the elements, and finally write the sorted array back out (this is what you did if you worked Exercise 5.8.21).

Another way is to store the numbers in a list in the order they are read, but also to keep another list telling in what order they should be written. For example, the two-column list at the top of the next page has in its left column some out-of-order values, and in the right column the row index of the next value following each value in ascending order.

node	value	link
1	4	5
2	12	0
3	-1	4
4	2	1
5	5	2
6		
:		

tail points to node 2, head points to node 3.

Starting with the row that contains the lowest value, which is called the **head** of the list, we can follow the next-row numbers or **links** to traverse the list in ascending order. The head of the list is row 3, containing the value -1. Its link is 4, so that is the row containing the next higher value, 2. That row in turn points to row 1, which contains the value 4 and points to row 5. Row 5 contains the value 5 and points to row 2. Row 2 contains the value 12 and has a link of 0 to mark the **tail** of the list. Because the rows or **nodes** in this list are connected by the sequence of links, it is called a **linked list**.

Rows 6 and subsequent in this list are still empty and available for storing more nodes. We can add the next node by storing the new value in the value column of row 6 and then adjusting the next-row numbers to link the new node in the proper order. To see how this process works, suppose the next value to be listed is 3. Traversing the list from the head, we find that the new value belongs between node 4 (which stores the value 2) and node 1 (with a value of 4). To insert the new node we must make node 4 point to it and the new node point to node 1, by changing the links like this.

node	value	link
1	4	5
2	12	0
3	-1	4
4	2	6
5	5	2
6	3	1
:		

tail points to node 2, head points to node 3.

Deleting a node from the list requires only adjusting the links so that in a traversal the deleted node is no longer encountered. For instance, to delete node 5 we search for that row number among the links, finding it in row 1, and replace it with the link, 2, of the node to be deleted. When one or more deleted nodes have accumulated, the list can be rebuilt to move the abandoned space to the end of the array, a process called **garbage collection**.

It can of course happen that an added node belongs before the head of the list, in which case the head designation must change, or that a deleted node is the tail of the list, in which case the zero tail marker must be moved.

The program at the top of the next page reads integers, stores them in a linked list, and then prints them out in ascending order.

The ADDNOD subroutine, listed below the main program, stores VALUE in row N of LIST and then adjusts the links to put the new node in the right order. The routine begins by storing the new value in the value column of row N. If that's the first node in the list, there is nothing more to do so ADDNOD returns. That leaves the first node's link at its initial value of zero, which is correct because a single node is both the head and the tail of the list.

```
      INTEGER*4 LIST(100,2)/200*0/,HEAD/1/,VALUE
      N=0
C
C     build the list
    2 READ(5,*,END=1) VALUE
      N=N+1
      CALL ADDNOD(LIST,N,HEAD,VALUE)
      IF(N.LT.100) GO TO 2
C
C     print the list
    1 IF(N.EQ.0) STOP
      I=HEAD
    3 PRINT *,LIST(I,1)
      I=LIST(I,2)
      IF(I.EQ.0) STOP
      GO TO 3
      END

      SUBROUTINE ADDNOD(LIST,N,HEAD,VALUE)
      INTEGER*4 LIST(100,2),HEAD,VALUE
      LIST(N,1)=VALUE
      IF(N.EQ.1) RETURN
      IF(VALUE.LE.LIST(HEAD,1)) THEN
          LIST(N,2)=HEAD
          HEAD=N
          RETURN
      ENDIF
      I=HEAD
    1 NEXT=LIST(I,2)
      IF(VALUE.LE.LIST(NEXT,1) .OR. NEXT.EQ.0) THEN
          LIST(I,2)=N
          LIST(N,2)=NEXT
          RETURN
      ENDIF
      I=NEXT
      GO TO 1
      END
```

If the node being added is not the first, ADDNOD next compares its value to that of the node at the head of the list. If the new node belongs first, ADDNOD makes the new node's link the row number of the old head and resets HEAD to the number of the new row.

If the node being added doesn't belong before the head of the list, ADDNOD traverses the list, starting with the head, until it finds the first node with a higher value or reaches the tail of the list with NEXT=0. Then it makes the previous node point to the new node, and sets the new node's link to NEXT, which is either the row number of the next node in order or zero to mark the tail of the list.

This is called an **insertion sort**. It's rather complicated and not very efficient for long lists, but it does avoid having to rearrange the values in memory. For some other problems, it is possible using linked lists to construct algorithms that would be difficult to code in any other way [7] [103].

The linked list of this example had one link per node, but in some applications it is necessary for a node to have more than one link. This example involved only adding nodes to the list, but in most applications additional routines are needed for removing nodes and for garbage collection.

11.8 Omissions and Caveats

Here are some topics that would belong in this chapter if they were not beyond the scope of the text or discussed later. Some of them are hinted at in the exercises.

> Passing parts of arrays having more than two dimensions; *memory-access stride;* FORTRAN-*90 dynamic memory allocation;* alignment in memory when partitioning workspace among arrays of different types; *various abuses of* COMMON *storage;* sparse symmetric matrices; sparse matrix storage schemes other than the IBM and YSMP formats; sparse matrix reordering; use of YSMP library routines; algorithms for linked-list node deletion and garbage collection; and multiply-linked lists.

From a linked list one can build stacks, queues, trees, and more exotic data structures, but they are seldom of use in typical engineering and scientific calculations and are therefore beyond the scope of this text. Trees *are* needed in moving-mesh methods for integrating stiff partial differential equations, but if you must write new code to solve that problem you should seriously consider using a language other than Classical FORTRAN.

Each of the techniques presented in this chapter is widely used and sometimes provides the cleanest solution to a programming problem. Several of them, however, are sufficiently unobvious or inviting of error that they should be used only when there is no practical alternative; partitioning workspace, overlapping temporary variables in COMMON, and using sparse matrix techniques are all less desirable than putting more memory in your computer. In §13 we will encounter a large number of other techniques, some of them also used often enough to qualify as clichés, that are so confusing or dangerous they are bad ideas not just some of the time but almost always.

Sound judgement about when to use what approach comes from experience informed by general principles of good program design, and it is those principles that we will take up next, in §12.

11.9 Exercises

11.9.1 How does Classical FORTRAN store an array? How does it pass an array to a subprogram?

11.9.2 According to §8.2, §11.3, and §11.4, what are the three prudent uses of COMMON storage?

11.9.3 Write a subroutine ADDCOL(A,LDA,N, COLSUM) that receives an N × N matrix A and returns in the N-element vector COLSUM the sums of the columns of A. The matrix A is stored in full-storage mode and its leading dimension in the calling routine is LDA. Both A and COLSUM are REAL*8 variables. Hint: Use the function VSUM of §11.1 to add up each column of A.

11.9.4   The following program invokes the LENGTH function of §10.2. Recall that LENGTH returns the index of the last nonblank in a string.

```
      CHARACTER*1 WORDS(5,5)/'t','h','e',' ',' ',
     ;                      's','u','r','l','y',
     ;                      'b','o','n','d','s',
     ;                      'o','f',' ',' ',' ',
     ;                      'e','a','r','t','h'/
      DO 1 K=1,5
          L=LENGTH(WORDS(1,K),5)
          PRINT *,L
    1 CONTINUE
      STOP
      END
```

What gets printed, and why?

11.9.5   Consider the following program.

```
      REAL*8 A(10,10)                    SUBROUTINE SUB(V,N)
      READ *,A                           REAL*8 V(N)
      CALL SUB(A(1,3),10)                :
      :                                  RETURN
      STOP                               END
      END
```

(a) The actual parameter in the CALL is A(1,3), yet the dummy parameter in the subroutine is a vector of length N. How can this possibly make sense? (b) Why might it be a good idea? (c) If the actual parameter is changed to A(3,1), what elements of A get passed for V(1),...,V(10)? Explain.

11.9.6   The technique of §11.1 can be used to pass a matrix *column* as a vector, but not to pass a matrix *row*. (a) Revise the first main program of §11.1 to pass the second row of A by copying it into U first. (b) Explain how the following code works to sum the second row of A without copying it into a vector.

```
      REAL*8 A(3,2)/1.D0,2.D0,3.D0,      FUNCTION VSUMR(V,N,M)
     ;              4.D0,5.D0,6.D0/      REAL*8 VSUMR,V(*)
      REAL*8 VSUMR,SUM                   VSUMR=0.D0
C     pass the second row of A           K=1
      SUM=VSUMR(A(2,1),3,2)              DO 1 J=1,M
      PRINT *, SUM                           VSUMR=VSUMR+V(K)
      STOP                                   K=K+N
      END                            1 CONTINUE
                                        RETURN
                                        END
```

In VSUMR the variable N, for which the main passes the number of rows in A, is called the **stride**. We will encounter the idea of stride again in §15.2.7.

11.9.7   It is desired to compute the **trace** of an $n \times n$ matrix B, $\mathrm{tr}(B) = \sum_{i=1}^{n} B_{i,i}$. Write a code segment illustrating how this can be done by invoking the function VSUMR of Exercise 11.9.6 with the appropriate stride.

11.9.8 What is printed by the following program? Explain why. As part of your explanation, describe the flow of control and the flow of data in the program.

```
BLOCK DATA                        SUBROUTINE SUB(V,L)
COMMON /XXX/ WORD                 CHARACTER*1 V(L)
CHARACTER*9 WORD/'abcdefghi'/     WRITE(6,901) (V(K),K=1,L)
END                           901 FORMAT(A1/T5,A1)
                                  RETURN
COMMON /XXX/ STRING               END
CHARACTER*1 STRING(9)
CALL SUB(STRING(3),4)
STOP
END
```

11.9.9 A partitioned workspace W(1000) is to be used to store the following variables, whose dimensions depend on integers M and N: AS, the symmetric storage mode representation of an N × N matrix; XY, a vector whose length is the larger of N + M and 2 × N × M − N; B, an N × M matrix; X, a vector with N elements; and Y, a vector with M+1 elements. All of the variables are REAL*8. Write a program that reads M and N, checks whether the problem will fit in W, and finds the indices in W where the various constituent arrays should begin.

11.9.10 For problems of size N, a certain calculation uses an N × N REAL*8 matrix A and two N-element REAL*8 vectors X and Y. (a) Assuming that A, X, and Y are to be stored in a 1000-element REAL*8 work array W, write a main program that reads N, checks whether a problem of that size can be solved, computes starting indices in W for A, X, and Y, and calls a subroutine that begins like this.

```
SUBROUTINE CALC(A,X,N,Y)
REAL*8 A(N,N),X(N),Y(N)
   :
```

(b) Is it necessary to pass a leading dimension for the two-dimensional array A, as described in §7.1? Explain. (c) Using the given relationships between the sizes of the arrays, how could they be allocated with fixed dimensions to eliminate the need for a partitioned workspace? When is it advantageous to use a partitioned workspace?

11.9.11 The following program uses a partitioned workspace to store two vectors, I and R, which can vary in size with the input data.

```
REAL*8 W(1000)                    SUBROUTINE GETI(I,NI)
CALL GETI(W(1),NI)                INTEGER*4 I(*)
CALL GETR(W(NI+1),NR)             READ(5,901) NI,(I(J),J=1,NI)
CALL SUBR(W(1))                      :
CALL SUBR(13)
   :                              SUBROUTINE GETR(R,NR)
                                  REAL*8 R(*)
                                  READ(5,902) NR,(R(J),J=1,NR)
                                     :
```

(a) Does the arrangement of I and R in memory waste any space? Explain. (b) Some compilers warn that the parameter passed to SUBR in its second invocation (the INTEGER*4 literal 13) differs in type from the parameter that is passed in the first invocation (W(NI+1), which is declared REAL*8). Is this a problem? Does getting a warning message whenever we compile the code waste our time checking to see whether there is a problem? (c) Rewrite the program to improve its use of partitioned workspace. (d) Further improve the program to reject data sets that will not fit in the allocated workspace.

11.9.12 Why might you decide to store the temporary local variables that appear in several different routines of a program in shared COMMON workspace? Are there any risks associated with doing this?

11.9.13 It is proposed to receive a work vector W as a subprogram parameter and name different parts of it using EQUIVALENCE, like this.

```
SUBROUTINE SUB(W)
REAL*8 W(100),A(50),B(50)
EQUIVALENCE(W( 1),A(1))
EQUIVALENCE(W(51),B(1))
  :
```

(a) Is this permissible? Confirm your answer by experiment. (b) Suggest an alternative way to accomplish the same effect by giving SUB two dummy parameters and passing pieces of W from the calling routine.

11.9.14 Suppose that in the example of §11.3, function GHI invokes subroutine JKL. Under what circumstances would it still be possible for the arrays TEMP, WRK, and LTMP to share temporary workspace in COMMON? Explain your answer.

11.9.15 A program uses a pool of shared temporary workspace in the COMMON block /WS/. One of the routines in the program looks like this before its temporary local variables RTMP and ITMP are placed in /WS/.

```
SUBROUTINE ANOTHR(X,Y,N)
REAL*8 X(N),Y(N),RTMP(5)
INTEGER*4 ITMP(7)
  :
```

(a) How long in bytes must /WS/ be in order to accommodate RTMP and ITMP? What if it is longer, so as to be able to accommodate the temporary local variables of some other routine? (b) Revise ANOTHR to include /WS/ and put RTMP and ITMP in it. Does it matter in what order they appear?

11.9.16 Why is it undesirable to get fixed data into a subprogram by passing it in formal parameters through another routine that does not need the data? Write down all the reasons as you can think of.

11.9.17 Several low-level routines in a program need to use (but not change) a list of integer values, which must arrive presorted into ascending order. The values are to be read, one value per line, from a file named **values**. In the file the values are out of order, and it is unknown ahead of time how many values there will be. Write an INPUT routine that can be called early in the program to make the list of values available to the routines that need it. INPUT should write an informative error message and take appropriate action in the event that the file is missing or can't be read, or an input record contains non-numeric data, or there are more values than INPUT has room for. Use some simple sort (*not* a linked list) to put the values in order. How do the routines that use the data find out how many values are in the table?

11.9.18 If an $n \times n$ matrix is stored in symmetric storage mode, how many elements of storage are saved? Write a FORTRAN program that prints out what fraction of the full storage mode amount is saved for $n \in \{1, 10, 100, 1000\}$.

11.9.19 Revise the first program of §11.5 to avoid referring to any elements of A *above* the diagonal.

11.9.20 How is this matrix represented in symmetric storage mode?

$$\begin{bmatrix} 1 & 4 & -1 & 0 & 6 \\ 4 & 1 & 7 & 8 & -2 \\ -1 & 7 & 2 & 9 & -3 \\ 0 & 8 & 9 & 3 & -4 \\ 6 & -2 & -3 & -4 & 5 \end{bmatrix}$$

How much space does that save?

11.9.21 Explain how to find the transpose of a matrix that is stored in symmetric storage mode.

11.9.22 If $\mathbf{x}$ is an $n \times 1$ vector, the **outer product** $\mathbf{xx}^\top$ is an $n \times n$ matrix. For example,

$$\mathbf{xx}^\top = \begin{bmatrix} 1 \\ 2 \\ 3 \end{bmatrix} \begin{bmatrix} 1 & 2 & 3 \end{bmatrix} = \begin{bmatrix} 1 & 2 & 3 \\ 2 & 4 & 6 \\ 3 & 6 & 9 \end{bmatrix}$$

If $\mathbf{Q}$ is an $n \times n$ matrix, then replacing $\mathbf{Q}$ by $\mathbf{Q} + \mathbf{xx}^\top$ is called a **rank-1 update**. (a) Write a code segment to compute $\mathbf{Q} + \mathbf{xx}^\top$ assuming that $\mathbf{Q}$ is stored in full-storage mode. (b) Write a code segment to compute $\mathbf{Q} + \mathbf{xx}^\top$ assuming that $\mathbf{Q}$ is stored in symmetric storage mode.

11.9.23 A REAL*8 matrix M is stored in symmetric storage mode, but it is to be written out in full, showing all N $\times$ N of its elements. Write a subroutine PRTSYM(M,N) that does this.

11.9.24 Assuming that $\mathbf{A}$ and $\mathbf{B}$ are N $\times$ N matrices stored in symmetric storage mode, write a subroutine to compute the matrix product $\mathbf{AB}$.

11.9.25 It is required to compute many matrix-vector products $\mathbf{y} = \mathbf{Mx}$ of different 4-element vectors $\mathbf{x}$ with different matrices $\mathbf{M}$. Each $\mathbf{M}$ is known to have the structure shown below, where a and b are REAL*8 scalars that vary from one product to the next.

$$M = \begin{bmatrix} 1 & 0 & b & 0 \\ 0 & a & 0 & 0 \\ b & 0 & 1 & -1 \\ 0 & -1 & 0 & a \end{bmatrix}$$

Write a special-purpose subroutine FSTMPY(A,B,X, Y) to compute the result using as few floating-point operations as possible. Avoid multiplications in which one of the numbers is sure to be zero or one, and any other unnecessary arithmetic. How does this approach compare with using the technique described in §11.6.2?

11.9.26 Consider the matrix product indicated below.

$$\mathbf{AB} = \begin{bmatrix} X & 0 & 1 & 0 \\ 1 & X & 0 & X \\ X & 0 & X & 0 \\ 0 & X & 0 & 1 \end{bmatrix} \begin{bmatrix} 1 & 0 & 0 & X \\ 0 & X & 0 & 0 \\ 0 & 0 & X & 1 \\ X & X & 0 & 0 \end{bmatrix} = \begin{bmatrix} X & 0 & X & X \\ X & X & 0 & X \\ X & 0 & X & X \\ X & X & 0 & 0 \end{bmatrix} = \mathbf{C}$$

(a) How many arithmetic operations are needed to compute all of the elements in $\mathbf{C}$ if we ignore the fact that some elements of $\mathbf{A}$ and $\mathbf{B}$ are 0 or 1? (b) How many arithmetic operations are needed to compute just the nonzero elements of $\mathbf{C}$ if we avoid unnecessary calculations? (c) What fraction of the operations in part (a) are avoided by exploiting the fixed pattern of zeros and ones?

11.9.27 Specify vectors VA, IA, and JA to represent this matrix in YSMP format.

$$A = \begin{bmatrix} 0\ 0\ 0\ 0\ 2 \\ 1\ 7\ 0\ 0\ 0 \\ 0\ 0\ 3\ 0\ 0 \\ 0\ 1\ 0\ 0\ 0 \\ 4\ 0\ 0\ 0\ 5 \end{bmatrix}$$

What do we call the order in which the nonzeros are stored in VA?

11.9.28 Write down a matrix for which YSMP format uses more memory than full storage mode.

11.9.29 In §11.6.2 we called the vectors used for representing a sparse matrix in YSMP format VA, IA and JA. If a matrix has N rows and NNZ nonzero elements, the format calls for storing NNZ+1 in IA(N+1). Give an example to show why this turns out to be convenient.

11.9.30 What is indirect array indexing? Why does it usually take longer than direct array indexing?

11.9.31 The example of YSMP sparse matrix format discussed in §11.6 assumed that the matrix **A** did not have a row of all zeros. Modify the code given there so that it still works even if **A** has some rows that are all zeros.

11.9.32 The following main program calls a library routine named LIB, which in turn uses two subprograms whose names SUBA and SUBB are passed in as EXTERNAL symbols.

```
      EXTERNAL SUBA,SUBB
      :
      CALL LIB(SUBA,SUBB)
      :
      STOP
      END
```

Several people in an engineering office use this program, each linking it with a different pair of subprograms SUBA and SUBB to do their own calculations. David's newest application requires his SUBA and SUBB routines both to use a large amount of numerical data read from a file, so he proposes to his officemates that the main program be revised to read the data and place it in COMMON storage before invoking the LIB routine. That way his SUBA and SUBB routines can retrieve the data from COMMON when they need it. Sarah objects that the main program will then be useless for her applications, none of which require any data to be read from a file, so David agrees that some other solution must be found. Nobody has any idea how the LIB routine actually works, so it must be assumed that it invokes SUBA and SUBB more than once and in a sequence that can vary in an unpredictable way from one problem to another. Suggest a way to make sure, without changing the main program, that David's data are read exactly once and are made available in both SUBA and SUBB in time for their first use.

11.9.33 The discussion of linked lists in §11.7 mentions node removal and garbage collection, but doesn't say how to do either. (a) Write a subroutine DELNOD(LIST,N,HEAD,I) that deletes node I from the linked list of §11.7. Set the link of each removed node to -1. (b) Write a routine RELIST(LIST,N,HEAD) to do garbage collection by moving any deleted nodes to the bottom of the list so that they can be used again.

11.9.34 The following linked list contains nodes whose values are letters. Traverse the list and write down the letters in the order you encounter them.

	node	value	link
tail ⇨	1	a	0
	2	a	10
	3	a	9
	4	a	5
	5	b	8
head ⇨	6	C	2
	7	c	1
	8	l	3
	9	n	7
	10	s	4

11.9.35 According to §11.7, sorting with a linked list has the virtue that it avoids having to rearrange the values in memory (only the links are changed). In the example of that section, however, rearranging the values would be no more difficult than rearranging the links. When might it be advantageous not to have to rearrange the values?

11.9.36 Suppose we want to be able to traverse the linked list of §11.7 in either ascending or descending order. To permit this we can add another column of links that go in descending order.

	node	value	up link	down link
	1	4	5	
up tail ⇨	2	12	0	
up head ⇨	3	-1	4	
	4	2	6	
	5	5	2	
	6	3	1	
	:			

(a) Starting with the up tail node, fill in the appropriate down link values. (b) Revise the main program and the ADDNOD routine of §11.7 to print the integers first in ascending order and then in descending order.

12

Design, Documentation, and Coding Style

Writing a program that does exactly what you want the first time you run it is the most fun you can have with a computer. Sadly, many people never really get their programs right no matter how long they work on them. In the early days of programming, when today's legacy codes were being written, this experience was so common that it inspired the poem on the next page, which you should read now.

Much has been discovered about the programming process since those punch card days, and the tools available for writing and debugging programs have improved a great deal. Formal methods have been developed for specifying what a program is supposed to do and for verifying by logic and deduction (as in the poem!) that its source code is correct [38] [83]. The formidable discipline of **software engineering** [3] [61] has revealed rational ways to manage programming projects. New language features have been invented to make some coding errors impossible or less likely. Thanks partly to these advances, the average quality of software, including FORTRAN programs, has gone up dramatically, and the cost of producing it has gone down.

Unfortunately, many programs still turn out wrong, even when they are written in a language intended to prohibit mistakes. In the real world, specifications evolve constantly and the formal methods are hard to apply. Some technical programming projects are big enough to justify the heavy machinery of software engineering, and if you are planning one you should study and use those methods. But most of the special-purpose application programs that engineers and scientists write every day, for themselves or their little work groups, are *not* big or complicated, and these programs are frankly not worth enough to justify a lot of trouble and ceremony in getting them right. No one hires an architect to design a doghouse. For all the reasons outlined in §0.3 we would often like to write these programs in Classical FORTRAN, a language that was not really designed to keep people from making errors. Programs that don't work can be debugged, of course, and I describe how at length in §14.3, but that is much more difficult and time-consuming than getting the code right in the first place, and there is no guarantee that debugging will actually remove all the mistakes from a program.

Both the "What's one little bug?" attitude expressed in the poem, and the notion that a poorly-written mess can somehow be *forced* to work right if only someone stays late at the office, are universal among managers and very common among programmers. People who have to cope with software that is intractably wrong are especially fond of these ideas because of the psychological defense they provide against truths that are just unacceptable. I have had consulting clients tenaciously defend the output from ratty twenty-year-old applications *at the same time* they admitted to being convinced beyond any doubt that the numbers in question were simply numerical noise, the result of applying a complicated algorithm to some random garbage that happened to be in memory where data was expected. Programmers who have been in this kind of denial for a long time about old programs are apt to have similar beliefs about their new programs. Every bug that is discovered must be the last one, and as long as the results are superficially plausible they must be approximately right, even if the code is known to be wrong in fundamental ways. Yet programs are different from physical things, in that a thing made to rough tolerances is still roughly

The Perfect Program
by Lou Ellen Davis

"No program's that perfect,"
they said with a shrug.
"The client is happy.
What's one little bug?"

But he was determined.
The others went home.
He dug out the flowchart,
deserted, alone.

Night passed into morning.
The room was cluttered
with memory dumps, punch cards;
"I'm close," he muttered.

Chain smoking, cold coffee,
logic, deduction.
"I've got it," he cried, "Just
change one instruction!"

Then change two, then three more
as year followed year,
and strangers would comment,
"Is this guy still here?"

He died at the console
of hunger and thirst.
Next day he was buried
face down, nine edge first.

And his wife, through her tears,
at the graveyard gate,
said, "He's not really gone,
he's just working late."

The last bug in sight,
an ant passing by,
saluting his tombstone,
softly whispered "Nice try."

right while a program with even a tiny mistake can be completely wrong! It is extremely difficult to be certain that any program is really correct, and it takes only a little experience to discover that many are not. Even a program that seems to be right and has been used extensively by lots of people can turn out to have been subtly but seriously flawed all along.

Thus, although powerful techniques have been elaborated for ensuring that programs are written correctly, there are serious technical and psychological impediments to the use of those techniques. Few experiences are more annoying than not being able to get your programs to work, so although many years have passed since **The Perfect Program** was written, it is still commonplace to read half-joking slogans such as [161] "Give a man a fish and you feed him for a day; teach a man to fish and you feed him for a lifetime...Give a man an answer, and he's satisfied today; teach him to program, and he will be frustrated for the rest of his life." One of my colleagues [141], with apologies to the psalmist, refers to his struggles with evil code as "walking through the valley of the shadow of death."

Fortunately, there are some simple things we can do to significantly improve the likelihood of getting applications of modest size (thousands or tens of thousands of source lines) right. It is those simple things, rather than proofs of correctness or formal specifications or software engineering, that this chapter is about.

12.1   The Craft of Programming

Computer programming is a variety of creative writing. You will be in distinguished company [9][10] if you therefore think of it as an *art*, but because programs shouldn't be too grand I think of programming as more of a *craft*, as more like telling stories after supper than writing great literature for posterity. Contrary to popular misconception, computer programming is *not* a scientific or engineering enterprise, nor a branch of mathematics or pure logic, though logic is often persuasive in programming just as it is in other forms of writing. The numerical algorithms our programs implement are obviously mathematical, but in programming what we write is just FORTRAN with some comments. A computer program can be regarded as a mathematical object, about which interesting theorems might be proved, but as I mentioned above this formal viewpoint is too abstract to be of much practical use. Some engineering principles can usefully be applied in the design and construction of software, but a program is more than an engineered artifact just as the poem on the facing page is more than an arrangement of ink molecules on paper.

The craft of programming has several objectives, which sometimes conflict with one another. Good code is *reliable*, in that it recovers from errors, handles all cases within its design limits, and surrenders gracefully, rather than crashing, when asked to go beyond them. Good code is *robust*, having design limits wide enough so that it is useful on a large variety of problems. Good code is *easy to use*, which means at least that it is forgiving of human foibles, informative when something goes wrong, and apt to do what the user expects. Good code is *easy to maintain*, so that the inevitable changes and improvements will be possible and can be made without rendering subsequent revisions more difficult. Good numerical code is *accurate*, producing results that are close enough to engineering or scientific reality so that they are useful. Good code is *efficient*, in that it makes responsible use of machine resources and runs fast enough to actually meet the operational need for which it was written. Good code is *portable*, in that it runs on a wide variety of computers. Good code is also ready to use some finite time after it was commissioned, though perhaps not as soon as your manager or client might like. We will touch on many of these topics in this chapter.

But the first and most important motive for studying design, documentation, and coding style is that they are essential for *logical correctness*, and that will be our main focus. All the rest is for nothing if the code is wrong.

To achieve correctness, and the other objectives outlined above, a skillful programmer employs *thoughtful design*, *functional documentation*, *simple coding*, *hand-checking*, *careful testing*, and *performance tuning*. The last of these concerns is addressed in §15, and also motivates §16 and §17.2. Here we will take up each of the other topics in a separate section.

The effective use of any language requires discipline and restraint, and FORTRAN calls for more of both than some less useful languages (but others, such as C, demand even more). The methods I suggest in this chapter are not difficult to apply, but they take time and effort so you might be tempted to ignore them. If so please at least remember that they are here, so that you can return to them after bitter experience has brought repentance.

12.2 Design

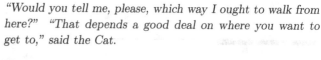

"Would you tell me, please, which way I ought to walk from here?" "That depends a good deal on where you want to get to," said the Cat.

Know what task is to be performed. To paraphrase the Cheshire Cat [133], which way you ought to write your program depends a good deal on what you want it to do. Before you can start designing anything, you need to have a clear idea of its purpose. Just as Alice had many unexpected adventures in Wonderland, your understanding of the requirements will evolve and become more precise throughout the project, especially in the prototyping stage (described later). Thus the objective will change at least slightly from one moment to the next, and perhaps quite a bit over the course of the project. Try to have the current version of the objective plainly in view at all times. Projects involving more than one person call for a written description to which everybody subscribes, and which is kept up to date as the requirements evolve. The difficulty and expense of a project grow faster than the size of the code [3, p88], and quadratically with the number of people who must coordinate their work [3, p18], so don't attempt too much all at once. Always start with something simple and plan from the beginning to introduce enhancements in future versions or project phases.

In command-directed work environments such as a corporate software department, big projects need real software engineering, including detailed formal specifications, experienced professional management, and wide margins for error and surprise [3] [154]. In open-source programming communities such as a voluntary research collaboration, big projects require consensus on the objective, shared values and expectations, flexibility and mutual respect, personal responsibility, wise and charismatic leadership, and excellent communication among the participants [171]. As explained above, all of these considerations relating to big projects are beyond the scope of this book.

Divide and conquer. To perform a complicated task, plan on several little programs each of which does one simple thing and works together with the others in obvious ways. Many engineering and scientific computing projects involve reading several streams of input data, preprocessing it into a form that can be used in calculation, applying numerical algorithms to the preprocessed data, and summarizing the results in various ways. Often, each of these steps is sufficiently complicated to justify a program of its own, as in the example flowcharted on the next page.

In this design there are six separate programs, one in each box, communicating with each other by means of disk files. One of the programs, a plotter, might be a general purpose utility that is already available at the installation where these programs are to be used.

The preprocessor reads the input files (and perhaps also some user commands from the keyboard), sanity-checks the raw data for obvious errors, and massages it into a form that is suitable for consumption by the analysis programs. For example, the preprocessor might

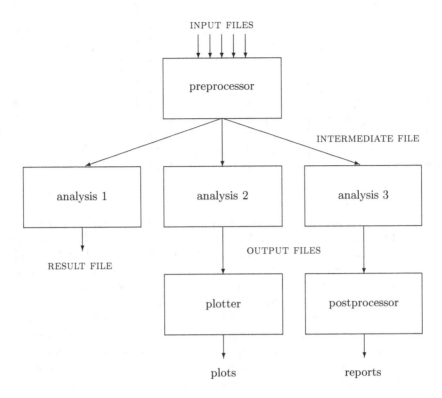

compute electrical properties like inductances and resistances from input data that describe the geometry and materials of a motor. The preprocessed data is written to an intermediate file, possibly in binary form as described in §9.8.

Each of the three analysis programs reads the same intermediate file (and perhaps also some user commands from the keyboard) and performs a different calculation. To continue our hypothetical example, the first might find an electrical impedance in the motor as a function of frequency, the second a transient voltage as a function of time, and the third a temperature rise due to resistive losses. As shown, some of the output files might be further processed to produce plots and reports.

Be deliberate. Good design is intentional, not casual. If you find that you are making a lot of decisions arbitrarily, think about them harder and from different angles until you find a good reason for picking one alternative instead of another. Each design decision should have some rational basis that you can defend when it is challenged, because reality will challenge them all sooner or later.

Plan how you will test the software. It will help to clarify your thinking about the design if you ask yourself, at each stage in the design process, how you are going to test the finished product.

12.2.1 User Interface Design

Help the user solve the problem. Know your audience as well as your subject. Start thinking about each program by imagining how people (or other programs, if they are its clients) will use it. What are their real needs? Where do the input data come from, and

DILBERT by S. Adams, reprinted by permission of United Feature Syndicate, Inc.   © 3/20/94 United Feature Syndicate

what will happen to the output? When you interview prospective users you might find that what they actually want is quite different from what you had assumed they would want (see cartoon). Like the drunk who lost his car keys on the lawn but spent all night searching for them under a streetlight because that is where he could see easily, programmers instinctively value ease of construction over ease of operation. Good programmers acknowledge and guard against this tendency. If you want your work to be loved, or even used, spend some time with the customer before you start. This is necessary even if the customer is *you.*

The user wants a handy tool that is comfortable to manage, not an imperial bureaucracy that tries to manage the user. Your work will be ignored if it is harder or less pleasant to use the program than it would be to perform its function by hand. Users enter data and commands, interpret and respond to prompts and exceptions, and consume results. It must be possible for them to do these things without knowing how the program works inside or becoming experts in the subject. Users make mistakes, overlook warnings, and misinterpret documentation, so your programs need to be simple to use, forgiving of errors, and harmless when they fail. Make each program so obvious to use that its manual is not needed. (You will also make the manual so clear that the program can be learned just by reading about it.)

Now, thinking about the problem from the user's perspective, write a description of how to use the program, and of any files that may be involved. At this stage focus on the task; specify externally-visible functionality, not how the program works inside. You will design the program later. Your written description of how to use the program is the first step towards the external documentation described below. Refine the description as you consider the following more detailed design guidelines.

Strive for conceptual simplicity. In order to use a program, a human must recall and keep in mind a conceptual model of what it does. For example, the UNIX™ sort utility reads a file from standard-in, rearranges the records so they are in order, and writes them to standard-out. A user might occasionally need to look up the options that can be specified for **sort**, or the ordering rules if special characters will be read, but most of the time the simplest conceptual model of what **sort** does is good enough (and it is *never* necessary for the user to know how the program works inside). When you divide your calculation into programs, try to make each appear to the user as conceptually simple as **sort**. Every program should suggest to its user, by what it does and says, a simple conceptual model for its function. Alas, not every function can be performed by a simple filter.

When the function of a program has to be complicated or subtle, and especially when user interaction is required, a much smarter interface might be needed to make it appear to the user that the program conforms to a simple conceptual model. Asking the user a yes-or-no question and getting the user to specify the name of a file are examples of complicated actions that involve a lot of processing if they are to appear simple and natural. Always use routines like QUERY (§10.5) and GETFIL (§9.4.2), so that the user's conceptual model can be "now I answer the question and give the name of the file" rather than "to answer this question I have to remember what the acceptable responses are and whether they need to be capitalized" or "I always need to write down the filename before I run the program, because if I get it wrong all my work will be lost." For similar reasons you should use hanging prompts as described in §9.1.2 and always use free format in reading from the keyboard.

Honor the Principle of Least Astonishment. Try to keep from destroying the user's perception that the program works according to a simple conceptual model. Remember with compassion how confused and upset Alice was when, every time she thought she was beginning to understand something about Wonderland, it turned out that her conceptual model was wrong. *The program should always do the least surprising thing.* Make all of the things it does and says consistent with each other and with its conceptual model, to sustain the appearance (or illusion) of simplicity. It would be hard to keep our simple idea of the **sort** utility in mind if every time we ran the program it blurted out, along with the sorted records, various details about the algorithm and data structures that it used internally to do the sorting, or if it crashed when given an empty input file rather than just not producing any output.

Guard the user from nasty surprises and self-inflicted wounds by requesting confirmation of actions that are seriously irreversible. If confirmation really decreases user convenience, make it possible for the user to set the level of safety provided. Include an "undo" capability whenever that makes sense.

Speak the user's language. Phrase prompts, error messages, and any built-in help in terms the user understands, ideally in the exact words the user would choose. Be specific rather than general, concrete rather than abstract, direct rather than diplomatic (except when suggesting corrections, as mentioned below), and as concise as possible. Specify the units (for example, inches or pounds) in which a numerical response is to be given. Neatness counts; make sure the text fits on the screen without unfortunate linewraps, be consistent in capitalization and indentation, and get the spelling right. Eliminating clutter reduces distraction and thus increases the probability that you will be understood. Focus the user's interest, and anticipate potential misinterpretations. Sacrifice technical precision if that is necessary in order to be understood. Get help from professional writers if possible, and from users themselves, with the language your program speaks.

Don't ask stupid questions. Omit useless features, rather than asking questions about them to which the user's answer is always the same. Don't ask the user to supply values for too many input parameters. If the values of some parameters are irrelevant or can be deduced after others are chosen, arrange the questions in that order and don't ask about anything you don't have to. Pick sensible defaults, and let the user accept or override them easily. One way of doing this is to include the default value in [square brackets] as part of the prompt text, and take a null response (a ^C_R) as an acceptance of the default (the suggested filename parameter to GETFIL is used in this way; see §18.3).

If it is unavoidable that there are many input parameters to set, permit that to be done using a file with a special name (it is customary in the UNIX™ culture to give such files names that start with "." so that they are hidden from the ls command). If the program finds the options file it should say so, perhaps report the parameter values specified there, and prompt only for those inputs that are omitted from the file. If the options file is complicated, consider providing a separate program to prompt the user for the values and write them in a file along with comments to help in manually editing the options later (but a program with too many options usually needs to be subdivided).

Don't ask the user to type too much. If there are only a few legal responses to a question, list them in the text of the prompt or make them into a numbered menu and prompt for the number (but use QUERY, not numbered choices, to ask yes-or-no questions). If you use a menu, consider making one of the choices be to print a more detailed explanation of the question and then ask it again. If the program reads commands, give them meaningful names and allow abbreviations. Use END= to exit from prompt-and-read loops, as in the example of §9.2, rather than asking "do again?" after each pass.

Give meaningful diagnostics when something goes wrong. Expect all input data and user replies to be illegal or inconsistent, sanity-check everything, and give the user as much help as you can to get the inputs right. Trap I/O errors with ERR= and EOFs with END= as described in §9.1.3. Make error messages descriptive, not judgemental. Never blame the user, even when the user is clearly and egregiously at fault. Phrase messages in such a way that the user can figure out how to fix the problem, not in terms of the internal state of the program. If bogus input came from a file, report the filename and the line and column of the offending datum. If possible continue checking input data from files, rather than stopping after the first error is discovered, so that the user can correct several mistakes at once rather than having to rerun the program to find each one. Give the interactive user another chance whenever that is possible, and tactfully suggest corrections if you really can. Don't frustrate the user in an endless loop of failed attempts to correct an error; if repeating the prompt doesn't help, try something different or provide the user some graceful way to exit from the program. If the user keeps giving illegal responses to a prompt, it is usually better to stop than to assume one of the legal choices and continue.

Sometimes the possible error conditions are complicated enough so that long messages are required to report all of the data that might conceivably be of interest, yet in most instances only some of the data about the error are needed. In that case, provide a way for the user to control the verbosity of the error messages. Default the message level to the lowest value, which amounts to assuming the user is skilled, but increase the level automatically if the user gives evidence to the contrary by repeatedly making mistakes.

An error message from a library routine should include the name of the routine.

Give reassurance when nothing goes wrong. When you think you might be lost, there is nothing quite so comforting as a road sign that proves you're not after all. Users are often anxious because they are uncertain of what they are doing, and anxious people make mistakes, so an occasional road sign is a very good thing. Feedback also helps people learn things, including how to use your program, by knowing when they have done something right in addition to finding out from error messages when they have done something wrong. Finally, a little friendly conversation can do wonders for building rapport between user and program, which is the ultimate reward of a good interface. When controllers tried to reawaken the Skylab satellite by a radio signal from the ground, having shut down everything but its standby receiver several years earlier, they were afraid that it wouldn't work. For a few tense moments after sending the wakeup command everybody held their breath, but when the on-board computer replied READY!, wild cheering broke out in the control room. Just then, those users *really* liked that program!

Programs that are too chatty can be distracting, and experienced users typically want less hand-holding than novices, so if you make it possible to get a lot of feedback you should also give the user some way of controlling its verbosity. Often the variable that sets the verbosity of error messages, described earlier, can also be used to control the verbosity of informational messages. As discussed in §14.3.3, debugging output can be an important category of informational messages during the development of a program.

Allow for non-interactive use if it is unavoidable. It is at this early stage that you must anticipate whether the program will run for too long to be conveniently used interactively. Batch processing (often achieved in the UNIX™ environment by backgrounding the job) has a richly-deserved reputation for inconvenience and should be avoided whenever possible, but many engineering and scientific calculations run for so long, even on the most powerful equipment, that waiting for them at the workstation keyboard is out of the question (see §15). Batch programs can't interact with the user, so the whole interface must consist of reading configuration, input data, and command files and writing output data and message files. Sometimes it is desirable to endow a program that is normally interactive with a batch mode so that it can be run in the background when necessary.

Prototype, test, observe, and revise. When you know enough about the external image the finished program will present, write a prototype that simulates the behavior you have in mind but doesn't yet actually do the calculation. Have some users try it out, after explaining to them that the numbers are nonsense for now, and pay attention to the mistakes they make and the complaints they have about how the application looks and feels. Listen to the users, but pay more attention to what they do than to what they say, and decide for yourself how to fix what is wrong. Get the opinions of other programmers whose creations you respect. Revise the prototype and keep testing until everybody is happy.

Read the experts. User interface design involves philosophical and aesthetic issues that are best approached through anecdotes and examples, for which there is inadequate space in this abbreviated summary. If you want to learn more you should read the experts; [41] and [70] are good surveys to start with, and contain references to other sources.

Learn humility. Like all creative artists, programmers are arrogant by nature (and of necessity) yet we succeed only by subordinating our personalities to our inventions. It takes humility to recognize and correct the flaws in one's own work, especially when those flaws themselves stem from overexpression of the self. Just as people who are flashy, petulant, rude, and eccentric annoy their acquaintances, programs with those faults annoy their users. Resist the temptation to scan user inputs for signs of frustration so that you can come back with a snappy rejoinder such as "Your place or mine?" or "Tsk, tsk, you'll never get into medical school talking like that." If the user is frustrated you have failed, so you should be embarrassed and contrite rather than responding like the aggressive smart-aleck you really are.

Programming to show off or act up is childish and unprofessional. As Borenstein [41, p178] sums it up, "The greatest compliment that can be paid to an interface designer is for users to regard the interface as so natural that it never occurs to them that any special skill was required to invent it." This is sometimes referred to as **egoless programming** [105, p56ff.], but I think it is perhaps the ultimate and only desirable *expression* of ego for the programmer, like the Cheshire Cat, to simply disappear.

12.2.2 Program Design

Now that you have perfected a written description of how your program will be used and of the external image that it will present, it is time to work out the internal structure that will achieve that functionality and appearance.

Disentangle the problem from the solution technique. Textbooks, especially older engineering textbooks (e.g., [44, §1-9]), sometimes analyze problems in such a way that the formulation of the mathematical model has embedded in it a custom-made computational algorithm for its solution. For example, a dynamical system might be described by a particular difference equation that is then iterated to approximate the solution, rather than by its exact differential equation which could be solved in a variety of ways. If seeing an algorithm makes it easier to understand the model there is obviously a pedagogical advantage to studying the problem in that way, but it usually provides a bad basis for designing a computer program to do the calculation. Try to extract a precise mathematical definition of the problem to be solved, uncontaminated by hidden assumptions about the numerical approach that will be used to approximate the solution. This makes it much more likely that you will be able to use standard numerical methods for which code is already available. Sometimes restating the equations that describe a physical system in terms of dimensionless parameters helps to reveal the underlying mathematical problem so that it is more obvious how to use standard numerical methods [44, *except* §1-9].

Occasionally it turns out that the entrainment of a problem's formulation in a special-purpose algorithm is *not* for pedagogical convenience but because that algorithm is dramatically superior to any other that has been discovered and is therefore always used (e.g., [63, p413ff.],[47]). Then you must understand how that algorithm exploits the special structure of the problem and plan from the outset to use it rather than a more general approach.

Find appropriate data structures and algorithms. Think of the program as a black box, like one of the boxes in the diagram of §12.2, with inputs and outputs as specified in your written description, and figure out the I/O. Draw a rectangle representing the program with arrows going in and out as in §9.4, and pick unit numbers for all the data streams. In your picture show any files that the program will read or write, and also the user interactions that it will invite.

Then, simultaneously decide how to represent and store the data, and what basic algorithms to use in doing the calculation. This might seem like the first step in a recipe for bear stew, which blithely says "capture one large bear" without giving instructions how to do that, but inventing the basic idea of how to do a calculation is actually the step that engineers and scientists usually find easiest. In fact, this step comes so naturally that novice programmers are likely to mistake it for the *entire* design process. If you have been thinking about *what* the program needs to do you probably have some ideas about *how* to do those things. If you don't, try consulting books on numerical methods [4] [12], algorithm design [9], and data structures [7] [103]. You might need to invent a new algorithm or data structure if nothing published seems suitable. It helps to doodle with flowcharts and to work some simple instances of the calculation by hand, and to discuss the problem with your colleagues (even if it is new to them too). If several cases can occur in the calculation, it might be useful to consider the cases separately. The key is usually finding an appropriate data structure, which then determines the algorithm.

It is at this point that you need to confirm the feasibility of the calculation, by estimating how much memory and processor time it will consume. If the data won't fit in the target machine's memory, or if the algorithms will run for geologic times, you need to come up with a different approach now. Consider using sparse matrix techniques, such as those discussed in §11.6, *only* if there is no other way to make the program fit.

Now is also the time to make a list summarizing the key design decisions you have made so far, such as your choice of algorithms and data structures, the layout of files, I/O unit assignments and formats, dimensions limiting the maximum size of the problems that can be solved, and other important details and assumptions. Arrange the list in order of decreasing likelihood that the decision will have to be changed at some time in the future.

Localize design decisions and data. Next divide the calculation into tasks that are logically separate, replacing the single box that represents the program by a flowchart showing its internal structure. The cleanest structure usually results from decomposing the calculation in such a way that each key design decision affects only one box (or one type of box that is used repeatedly) in the flowchart, so that if any decision is changed later only one part of the program will be affected. This isolation of design decisions is called **information hiding** [94]. The purpose of decomposing the calculation is to control the complexity of the program, and that has not been achieved if changing anything affects everything! Usually, though not always, information hiding is achieved by the same decomposition that minimizes the amount of data the tasks must share, which is called **data hiding**. Many difficulties in programming arise at the interfaces between the parts, so the interfaces must be kept as simple as possible, and that cannot be done if they must share data in complicated ways. It is easier to recognize a decomposition that achieves data hiding than one that localizes design decisions, so start with data hiding and then revise if necessary.

Show on the flowchart where the I/O data streams go into and come out from. Think of each task as being performed by a subprogram, and give the subprograms names. Pick names that do not conflict with the names of other routines that will be visible to the loader, such as FORTRAN built-ins, UNIX™ system routines, and all the members of any libraries you plan to link from.

Use successive refinement. Subdivide the boxes in the flowchart until each subprogram is just small enough to get right. It might be more difficult to localize design decisions and data as the pieces get smaller, but continue trying to do that. It is an indication that the decomposition is correct if some routines are used repeatedly at different places in the detailed flowchart. Because the statements in a code segment can interact with each other not only pairwise but also in more complicated patterns (see §12.4.1), the difficulty of understanding a subprogram, and hence of getting it right, grows in a combinatorial way with the size of the code. Usually, a routine that includes more than a page or two of executable code is too long. On the other hand, if your program consists of numerous tiny routines there will be many interfaces between them, which also make the program harder to understand. The density of errors in software (the number of mistakes per line of code) is a U-shaped function of average subprogram size [68]. It is therefore important to end up with routines that are mostly about one page of code long, though how many lines of FORTRAN will be needed to perform a given task might be hard to guess at this stage in the design process. Ideally, many of the boxes you end up with will be familiar numerical computations, such as matrix multiplication or spline evaluation, that can be performed by standard library routines. Where standard routines can't be made to fit you must plan to write specialized code. Repeatedly subdividing a calculation until the parts are the right size is called **successive refinement** [109] or **top-down design**, or "eating the elephant one bite at a time."

Now work out the details of how data will be shared between the routines, remembering to hide data from routines that don't need it. Be wary of COMMON, except for its one unavoidable use described in §8.2 and possibly for sharing constant problem data as described in §11.4. At this point you might discover that your decomposition of the program is not correct after all and needs to be revised. If you have trouble hiding data from routines that don't need it, or if the same data will have to be read in twice, or if a design decision that might change affects many routines, or if there are going to be big stretches of **replicate code**, code segments that are almost identical, then the structure of the program is wrong. Another important test is that if the structure of the program is too complicated to explain to your dog, it is wrong. Go back to the step of dividing the program into logically separate tasks and try again. Every problem has one or more simple answers that turn out to be wrong, but nothing very complicated has ever turned out to be right (contrast Ptolemy to Copernicus, or our federal tax code to the Declaration of Independence). Simplicity is the seal of truth. Getting the decomposition and the interfaces between the parts correct now will save endless agony later.

Write library routines bottom-up. Once you've got the decomposition right, identify all the tasks that can be performed by general-purpose library subprograms, and write any that you don't already have. By contrast to the top-down design paradigm, this sort of digression is called **bottom-up design**. It's important to write these routines now, provided you're sure you'll use them, because their calling sequences should be dictated by the need for them to be general-purpose rather than by the idiosyncrasies of the larger application in which you plan to first use them. Wring as many reusable library routines out of each project as you possibly can. A professional programmer's mission in life is to avoid ever having to write the same code twice.

Improve the prototype. Next it is time to dig out the user-interface prototype and try to replace its innards with the rough outlines of the program design. The result doesn't need to be perfect this time either, but it should prove your theory about how the pieces will fit together and how the data will flow between them. Omit details from the calculations, but make sure you know what data is needed where and that the data structures you envision will really work. Of course, if they don't you must go back to an earlier step and iterate through the design process again until they do.

Fix the whole mistake. You might discover, in the design stage or later, that you have overlooked some important complication or made a serious mistake. When that happens, you will be tempted to patch up the trouble by making the smallest possible change to what you have already done. As you get farther along in the project it will become harder and harder to make significant revisions, just as it gets harder to trowel a new sidewalk slab as the concrete sets. But compromising the design will only lead to additional problems later on. Even if you find the mistake late in the project and fixing it cleanly will entail a major redesign, it is usually cheapest in the long run to accept the misfortune gracefully and start over.

12.3   Documentation

At this point you might be eager to begin coding, but we're not ready for that yet. Continuing the successive refinement of the design, we must first write, or at least start, the documentation for the program and some or all of its constituent routines. As we shall see, *documentation is the bridge between design and implementation.*

12.3.1   External Documentation

All programs that other people will run, and many that only you will run, need written instructions. This is the only documentation that users of the program will ordinarily see, or should need to see. In the UNIX™ culture it is traditional to supply this documentation in the form of UNIX™ manual pages, also called **man pages**. A **man** page is a file whose contents can be displayed on your workstation screen or printed on paper by using the **man** command. A detailed description of how to prepare, install, and use **man** pages is given in §14.6. If a program is just for you and your immediate work group, you will probably want to write a **man** page for it. If the program is to be used by clients who are not programmers, it is likely that they will prefer some other form of printed manual.

Start with the description you wrote, back at the beginning of the design process, of how to use the program. The style and level of detail in the manual will depend on the audience and the application. However, it should be possible for someone who knows about the subject, but is not necessarily an expert, to learn enough about the program to be able to use it just by reading the manual. For example, if the program predicts the diffusion of chemicals through a membrane, someone who knows the basics about diffusion through membranes should be able to figure out how to use the program just by reading the manual, without attending live training or experimenting with the program, and without knowing how the program works inside. To verify that this is true you should get prospective users to review drafts of the documentation and then ask them questions to see if they learned how to use the program. This might reveal not only flaws in the manual, but also that you have misunderstood something about how the program should behave, in which case you must return to the design stage and fix it before going on. It is essential to write and test at least a good draft of the documentation *before writing the program* to make sure the design is right.

The subprograms that make up the program are of no interest to your client, the end user of the application. They *are* of interest to you, though, and to programmers who might need to repair or modify the program later, and to others who might want to use the routines in a different application. Because programmers are the audience for these routines, any documentation you write for them should be **man** pages. Routines that are peculiar to the application usually do not need **man** pages, because anyone repairing the code will be looking at it and (sadly) nobody will be using the special-purpose routines elsewhere. But any general-purpose library routines that you write for this project should be documented meticulously so that you, and others, can easily use them in future applications.

Because you will ideally be investing most of your documentation labor in writing **man** pages for general-purpose library subprograms, the exposition of this section uses such a routine as an example, but the same basic ideas apply to documenting application-specific subprograms and the program itself.

The example we consider is the **BISECT** subroutine we studied in §6, §7, and §8. A **man** page for **BISECT** is reproduced on the next two pages. The two images are meant to be printed on, or photocopied onto, the two sides of a single sheet of paper. The two-page length is terse enough to read quickly, and having both pages on one printed sheet means there are no attached sheets to come loose and get lost. On rare occasions a **man** page really has to be longer than one sheet, but if that happens with a subprogram you should suspect that the routine needs to be simplified somehow.

The **man** page begins with the NAME and use of the routine. We have chosen a name having not more than six characters, in keeping with a policy outlined in §12.4.2 below. For reasons explained in §14.6, the sentence telling what the routine is used for must fit on the same line. Next comes a SYNOPSIS of how to invoke the routine, with a table listing its parameters and giving the size, type, and meaning of each. The space between **TOL** and **X** in the calling sequence indicates that the first four parameters must be given values before the routine is called, while the last three are outputs. Skipping the next three sections for a moment, we come to LINKAGE. This section gives a UNIX™ command for compiling a program that uses **BISECT**, as described in §14.5. The REFERENCES section lists a book that is cited as a source of additional information about the algorithm the routine implements. The EXAMPLE section won't fit on the first page, so a pointer is provided to the back of the

NAME

    BISECT – Find a zero of a scalar function of one variable.

SYNOPSIS

    CALL BISECT(FCN,XL,XR,TOL, X,F,RC)

FCN	is the EXTERNAL name of a REAL*8 function subprogram (see below)
XL	is the REAL*8 left end of an interval containing a zero
XR	is the REAL*8 right end of an interval containing a zero
TOL(2)	is a REAL*8 vector of convergence tolerances on X and F
X	is the REAL*8 root returned
F	is the REAL*8 function value at X
RC	is the INTEGER*4 return code; 0 => ok, 1 => failure, 2 => no root

DESCRIPTION

    XL and XR, the endpoints of an interval containing the zero that is sought, must be given on input. The routine assumes that the function has a unique zero in the interval, and uses interval-halving [1] to find a value of X near where it occurs. XL and XR are updated during the bisection process, and on return contain the endpoints of an interval that brackets the zero. The routine calls the user-supplied function subprogram FCN(X) to obtain values of the function at points in the interval [XL,XR]. Convergence is judged to have occurred if, simultaneously, the interval width is less than TOL(1) and the function value is less than TOL(2).

DIAGNOSTICS

    If the function has the same algebraic sign on both ends of the current interval at any point in the bisection process, BISECT writes the message 'No root on interval in BISECT' and returns with RC=2. If 100 bisections are performed without the convergence criteria being satisfied, BISECT writes the message 'No convergence in 100 iterations in BISECT' and returns with RC=1 and the best answer found so far in X.

BUGS

    The bisection algorithm can fail if the function has more than one zero in the interval that is given on input. If the starting interval is very large the limit of 100 bisections might not be sufficient to permit convergence, even though the function does have exactly one zero in the interval. It is often impossible to obtain a function value of precisely zero, so TOL(2)=0.D0 should be avoided.

LINKAGE

    f77   source.f   –L/usr/david/lib   –lmisc

REFERENCES

    [1] Burden, Richard L. and Faires, J. Douglas
        Numerical Analysis
        Prindle, Weber, and Schmidt, 1993 (page 23)

EXAMPLE

    See other side.

EXAMPLE

```
        REAL*8 FCN,XL/0.7D0/,XR/0.9D0/,TOL(2)/2*1.D-10/,X,F
        EXTERNAL FCN
        CALL  BISECT(FCN,XL,XR,TOL,X,F,RC)
        WRITE(6,901) X,F
   901  FORMAT('F(',1PD22.15,')=',1PD22.15)
        STOP
        END

        FUNCTION FCN(X)
        REAL*8 FCN,X
        FCN=DEXP(4.D0*X)+(X–4.D0)**3
        RETURN
        END
```

This example produced the following output:

```
    F( 8.585204196526320D–01)=–5.188027785152372D–11
```

sheet (this is far better than continuing the example itself across the page break). Looking there we find a brief but complete program that invokes BISECT, along with the output that it should produce. We have yet to actually code BISECT, of course, so at this stage we can't actually run the example program. However, we *can* solve the example problem in some other way (such as by hand, or by using another program) and present the output that the example program *will* produce when it works correctly. Later we will use this example and its expected output to test the routine after it is written. These sections and the information in the margins of the **man** page are discussed more completely in §14.6.3, and the page template given there suggests other sections that might be appropriate depending on the nature of the routine being documented.

Now let us return to the DESCRIPTION, DIAGNOSTICS, and BUGS sections, which together provide just the minimal information that a user might need about the internal workings of the routine in order to decide whether it is appropriate and to use it correctly. The DESCRIPTION tells what algorithm is used and the assumptions that implies, warns that **XL** and **XR** are updated during the solution process (which means they can't be given as literals in the **CALL**), specifies the convergence test (stricter than the one in the flowchart of Ex 3.8.21), and gives the calling sequence for the user-supplied function **FCN(X)**. The DIAGNOSTICS section tells what error messages the routine might output, and the corresponding return codes **RC**. The BUGS section tells how the routine can fail and states the limitation that **TOL(2)** can't be set to zero. All of this information obviously affects the code we must write to implement the routine, but it is still part of the routine's *external* image. The **man** page tells *what* the routine does and how to use it, from the vantage point of the **CALL**. Only the most general information is given about *how* the routine achieves this external functionality, and the implementation is entirely hidden except for those details needed to understand whether and how to use the routine. The bisection algorithm is so well known that in this example it is enough merely to mention its name. If the algorithm implemented by the routine were less well known and was not described in a reference we could cite, the **man** page description might need to go into more detail, but even then it should tell only what is necessary to decide whether and how to invoke the routine.

12.3.2 Internal Documentation

Once a preliminary version of the routine's external documentation is complete, telling *what* it does, we can begin to describe precisely *how*.

The description takes the form of an ordered list or outline of the steps the routine must perform in order to validate its inputs, perform the algorithm it implements, and return the result. Just write down the steps on a piece of paper, or in a file. You might need one or two levels of indenting to show the logical hierarchy of the steps. For BISECT we come up with this:

```
SUBROUTINE BISECT(FCN,XL,XR,TOL, X,F,RC)
make sure the tolerances are nonnegative
find the function values at the endpoints
do a limited number of iterations
  find the midpoint of the current interval
  evaluate the function there
  check for convergence
  find what side the root is on
  revise the endpoint that changes
set the return code and return
```

Making this list of steps is the hardest part of the design process, because it requires us to switch from one level of abstraction to another as we mentally jump from the outside world of the `man` page, through the `CALL` statement, into the routine. To make the list, you will probably need to refer to your design notes as well as to the external documentation, and perhaps also to a book or research paper describing the inner workings of the algorithm. Occasionally it is helpful to begin with key sentences copied out of the DESCRIPTION section of the `man` page, especially if it was necessary to describe the algorithm in some detail there. Occasionally it is helpful, especially for novice programmers, to make a flowchart before listing the steps, but most routines should be simple enough that a flowchart would be superfluous. It's all right to be long-winded in your first draft of the list, but in your final version each step must fit on a single line. Make the steps simple imperative statements like those in the example above.

Now we must transcribe the list of steps, along with any indentations it might have, into a file (if you didn't compose it in a file to begin with), put a `C` in column 1 of each line, and separate the lines with blank comments (empty except for the `C` in column 1). These preliminary comments are the scaffolding on which we will now hang the code. Each comment will begin a **code stanza**, and each stanza will be separated from the comment heading the next one by a single blank comment. As we fill in the code it might be necessary to slightly revise the preliminary comments so that each agrees precisely with the FORTRAN statements in its stanza.

As we construct the code and revise the stanza comments, we write additional comments that form a **preamble** [72], to produce the code listed at the tops of the next two pages. The listing is printed with line numbers, which the narrative description refers to in boxes . Some principles of good coding are discussed in §12.4, but for now we are concerned only with the internal documentation of the routine and its typographical layout.

As mentioned earlier, the executable statements of a routine usually should not be longer than one page. From this example we can see that the preamble for a routine of that length accounts for roughly another page.

The first thing we notice about this listing is that it looks nothing like the code segments given so far in this book (except for the first example in §1). In §6, §7, and §8, `BISECT` was listed with no comments at all! In the chapters after this one I will return to the practice of using comments only sparingly. This is not really a case of "do as I say and not as I do," because the code segments in this book are everywhere surrounded by explanatory text that really constitutes their internal documentation. A routine that needs to live beyond the shelter of a textbook explaining it must instead carry its explanatory text inside.

The listing begins with the preamble 1-34 , everything above the horizontal line. Every preamble must include an attribution of authorship 2 , the `SUBROUTINE` or `FUNCTION` statement 4 that begins the code (unless the routine is a main program), a terse description of what the routine does 5-7 , a table of variables 15-30 , the variable declarations 32-33 with any compile-time initializations, any `COMMON` blocks that might be needed, and perhaps additional comments such as the table of return code values 9-13 in our example. If the routine does I/O to files it should include a table listing the units used and their purposes.

In some work environments it is appropriate to include a copyright notice in the preamble to each routine. Except when the year is required in a copyright notice, it is a bad idea to include the date of last revision anywhere in the source text for a routine. You are sure to sometimes forget to revise it when you change the code, and the last change time of the file is already available from the operating system (see §14.4.2).

By placing the two pages of a listing one above the other on a desktop we can easily take in the whole source code at once, without having to turn pages. Code that is short enough to be seen all at once, like this example, is said to exhibit **locality** [105, p229], and is much easier to follow, and to get right, than code that lacks locality.

```
 1  C
 2  Code by David A. Scientist
 3  C
 4          SUBROUTINE BISECT(FCN,XL,XR,TOL, X,F,RC)
 5  C     This routine finds the value of X between XL and XR
 6  C     where the function FCN is zero, and returns in F the
 7  C     value of the function at that point.
 8  C
 9  C     RC value  meaning
10  C     --------  -------
11  C     0         all went well
12  C     1         failure to converge in 100 bisections
13  C     2         no root in the interval
14  C
15  C     variable  meaning
16  C     --------  -------
17  C     DABS      Fortran function for |REAL*8|
18  C     DMAX1     Fortran function gives larger of REAL*8s
19  C     F         function value at current solution X
20  C     FCN       routine computes value of function
21  C     FL        function value at XL
22  C     FR        function value at XR
23  C     FTOL      F tolerance used
24  C     I         index on the iterations
25  C     RC        return code; see table above
26  C     TOL       tolerance vector (X,F)
27  C     X         midpoint of [XL,XR]
28  C     XL        left endpoint of interval containing root
29  C     XR        right endpoint of interval containing root
30  C     XTOL      X tolerance used
31  C
32          REAL*8 FCN,XL,X,XR,FL,F,FR,TOL(2),XTOL,FTOL
33          INTEGER*4 RC
34  C
35  C ------------------------------------------------------------------
36  C
37  C     set convergence tolerances
38          XTOL=DMAX1(0.D0,TOL(1))
39          FTOL=DMAX1(0.D0,TOL(2))
```

The variable list is the most important single part of the internal documentation, because it determines whether someone other than the author (such as the author six weeks from now) will be able to figure out how the routine works. If you know what the variables stand for, you might be able to understand the code even without the stanza comments, but if you don't know what the variables stand for, no amount of stanza commenting will make the function of the routine clear. Construct the variable list as you introduce variables while you are writing the code. When you introduce a new variable, interrupt your writing of the code and define the variable in the list before you continue. That way you will have the meaning of each variable precisely in mind as you use it. Every symbol used in the routine should be on the list, including not only the routine's arguments and main variables, but also DO loop counters, intermediate and "temporary" variables, the names of functions and subroutines that are invoked by the routine, and variables that are not used at all but appear only as padding in COMMON statements. Keep the list alphabetical, so that you can

```
40   C
41   C        assume a root will be found
42            RC=0
43   C
44   C        find the function values at the endpoints
45            FL=FCN(XL)
46            FR=FCN(XR)
47   C
48   C        permit only 100 bisections
49            DO 1 I=1,100
50   C            bisect the interval
51                X=.5D0*(XL+XR)
52   C
53   C            evaluate the function at the new point
54                F=FCN(X)
55   C
56   C            check for convergence
57                IF(DABS(XR-XL).LE.XTOL .AND. DABS(F).LE.FTOL) RETURN
58   C
59   C            decide which side the root is on and update the endpoints
60                IF(F*FL .LT. 0.D0) GO TO 2
61                IF(F*FR .LT. 0.D0) GO TO 3
62   C
63   C            there is no root in the interval
64                WRITE(0,901)
65   901          FORMAT('No root on interval in BISECT')
66                RC=2
67                RETURN
68   C
69   C            the root is in the left half
70   2            XR=X
71                FR=F
72                GO TO 1
73   C
74   C            the root is in the right half
75   3            XL=X
76                FL=F
77   1 CONTINUE
78   C
79   C        convergence was not attained in 100 iterations
80            WRITE(0,902)
81   902 FORMAT('No convergence in 100 iterations in BISECT')
82            RC=1
83            RETURN
84            END
```

look up meanings later on and so that you will not be able to inadvertently use the same variable to mean two different things. (Two variables should also not refer to the same thing, but alphabetical order can't help you prevent that.) Even variables whose names seem clearly descriptive must be defined in the variable list.

Each entry in the variable list should fit on a single line, so that you can read them quickly and adjust the order easily to keep it alphabetical. The meanings that you give for the variables should be phrased in terms of the underlying application problem rather than in terms of the code itself. Never leave a description blank until later. Instead of

temporary variable describe what the variable temporarily represents, or tell where it is used in the calculation. Instead of **loop counter** say **index on the trusses** if it is trusses that are being counted, or some similarly informative description. Instead of **data** say what sort of data it is. If a variable represents some physical quantity, state the units in which it is measured. You are writing these descriptions for your own benefit, both now and later, not just because I told you to, so make them useful! It is not unusual for an experienced programmer to spend as much time picking meaningful variable names and describing them precisely in the variable list as on writing the executable statements of the routine.

Often it is useful to arrange the variable type statements, constants, **COMMON** block declarations, and other non-executable material that follows the variable list into related stanzas and comment them just like executable code. This example is simple enough so that is not necessary, but some routines have more, and more mysterious, declarations that call for descriptive comments.

Below the dividing line $\boxed{35}$ are the stanzas of executable statements. Recall from §1.1 that in Classical FORTRAN no line of code can extend beyond column 72, so it is convenient to make the dividing line between the preamble and the executable statements the right length to serve as a visual guide to the lengths of the code lines. Over the space of a page or two the eye might wander by a few columns, so to be safe I make the dividing line end in column 68, and keep all the other lines from extending beyond it. Each code stanza (e.g., $\boxed{38\text{-}39}$) should be glued to the comment $\boxed{37}$ that describes it, so there is no ambiguity about that relationship; too much white space in a listing is just as bad as too little. I will say more about stanza comments below in §12.4.6, because they are tied intimately to the code and often require minor revisions as the code is filled in.

The potential for confusion and the **cognitive load** or subconscious mental work of understanding a listing, whether it is on paper or on the workstation screen, are reduced if the text of the comments looks different from that of the FORTRAN statements. Some FORTRAN programming environments permit the use of special fonts for this purpose, but in most settings we are stuck with only differences in alphabetical case, and this suggests either making the comments lower case (or mixed case) and the code upper case, or making the comments upper case and the code lower case (or mixed case). FORTRAN ignores the case of letters used in statements (except in literal text strings), so there is nothing to be gained by using mixed case in FORTRAN statements, and there is a possibility that doing so might introduce confusion. The following statements are interpreted by the compiler as identical,

```
I=i+K+l+1
I=I+K+L+1
```

but in reading the first one it is necessary to carry the extra cognitive load of remembering that case doesn't matter. Mixed case is meaningless to the compiler, which reads the code, but it is meaning*ful* to human beings, who read the comments. One of the ways this is true is that if the comments are mixed case then variable names that need to be mentioned in comments can be made self-quoting by putting them in upper case, which saves columns on the line. Because of these considerations, the choice of case is not just a matter of taste. Use **mixed case** for the comments and put the code all in **UPPER CASE**. The small added work of getting the case right will be repaid many times by the improved clarity of the listing.

Many professional programmers keep a file containing the empty outline of a subprogram, including the preamble with the headings for a variable list, the dividing line, and a **RETURN END** sequence, which they copy to begin each new routine they write.

Novice programmers always believe that it is best to write the comments *after* the code is finished, and finally the `man` page. After all, then you know what it is you are describing with the documentation. I overhear students working outside my office door in the college computing center say to each other "I finished the program, now all I have to do is put in the comments." They sometimes refer to this process as "decorating the code," and that is, alas, an accurate description, because comments written after the fact are merely decorative, not functional. Programs that were commented at the end of the coding rather than at the beginning often don't work, because by choosing that order the programmer unwittingly made the coding much harder than it needed to be. Functional external documentation not only helps people learn how to use the program, it plays a pivotal role in the design process. Functional internal documentation not only helps people understand the code after it is finished, it helps you figure out what to code. Always write the external documentation first and then the comments, *before* you write the code, so that you know from the description what it is you are supposed to be coding.

12.4   Coding Style

Once you have written the stanza comments and started the preamble, you are ready to begin filling in the code. In the process it will be necessary to introduce variables, describe them in the variable list, declare them as to type and size, give them initial values if necessary, figure out the logic within the code stanzas, and possibly refine the stanza comments and add more comments to reflect the precise details of the implementation.

Novice programmers often mistake coding for programming, so coding is often what they are given to do by their elders, who conspire with management, by a wink and a nod, to keep the more exciting design work for themselves. During the design and initial documentation stages one occasionally gets to contemplate sweeping vistas of artistic creativity, whereas coding consists entirely of gritty little details. After a day of fretting over minutiae of logic and indexing and declarations and syntax it can begin to feel as though you are being gradually gnawed to death by an army of chipmunks. Yet *the code is the only thing that animates the design,* so getting it right is essential to a successful project. The most elegant plans in the world are all just so much daydreaming until they are well and faithfully executed, and that is a task for sage and seasoned artisans (perhaps assisted by eager young apprentices) rather than scut work for the newest or most gullible kid on the team. If you are a new programmer working without a kindly mentor (or if your mentor has been programming for thirty years but still writes code nobody can read) it will be worthwhile to study the suggestions in this section.

Write and test code in small pieces. Some programmers begin the coding process with a working (though empty) routine that consists only of the comments that came from the documentation process and a `STOP END` sequence, or for a subprogram the `SUBROUTINE` or `FUNCTION` statement, declarations of the arguments, the comments, and a `RETURN END` sequence. It might then be possible to construct the code a little at a time, pausing after each piece to confirm that the fragment written so far compiles and runs. Writing and testing code in small pieces makes mistakes easier to find. If you use this approach in coding a filter of the sort described in §9.4, you might find it helpful to start with a program that just copies lines from standard-in to standard-out (see Exercise 10.9.15). Before you test each completed routine you'll want to hand-check it, as described in §12.5.

Start with pseudocode. If you are unsure of FORTRAN syntax or you want to defer some of the details until after you work out the rough outlines of the code, you might find it helpful to make up your own pidgin FORTRAN or **pseudocode** for the first version. When engineers and scientists write pseudocode it typically turns out to be a mixture of English, FORTRAN, and mathematics. Once you have figured out how to code a stanza, translate the pseudocode into FORTRAN.

Edit, edit, edit. Just as revision and rewriting can greatly improve written English, editing your FORTRAN source code (including the comments) can make it clearer, simpler, and more robust. Repeatedly rubbing your nose in the code will also turn up errors that you missed before. As in proofing English, it helps to clean your palate by waiting a few days between readings.

We often think of a computer program as something that "tells the machine what to do," but it is really a communication between *people* (such as yourself today and yourself tomorrow) explaining how a problem is solved, written in such a way that the compiler can eavesdrop on the conversation and translate it into machine language. Imagine as you code that you have a human audience, and try not to embarrass yourself in public.

Read other people's code. You should read other people's programs whenever you get the chance, but only *after* reading this section. Mostly other people's code will teach you what *not* to do, but occasionally you will discover a master worthy of serious study. You should also get other programmers whom you respect to read *your* code, provided they are willing to be brutally honest in telling you what they think. In some organizations one or more formal **code inspections** [56] [61, §6.4.1] [43] are required in the software production process.

Read the experts. There is room here for only a brief discussion of coding style. For a more complete exposition, with longer examples, you should study [8]. There are also other books on programming style, and you should read them too when you run across them, but beware that most of them will contain a mixture of good and bad advice. Be critical in reading anything about style (including this section), and take only the advice for which convincing reasons are offered or obvious. If it's been a while since you took a course in English composition, it might also be helpful to review [179].

12.4.1   Cognitive Complexity

Earlier I mentioned, in connection with the division of an application into programs and the division of a program into routines, the importance of making the pieces small enough to get right. The same advice applies to the code segments within a routine. To see why it is difficult to get a long sequence of related statements correct, consider the brief code segment below

```
      N=9
      DO 1 I=1,N
          DO 2 J=I,N
              X(J)=Y(J,N-I+1)
   2          CONTINUE
   1 CONTINUE
```

Each of these statements can be understood only in context. To understand what the CONTINUE statements are about we need to think of the corresponding DO statements at the same time. To understand the assignment into X(J), we need to also have the N=9 and both DO statements in mind, along with the declarations that were given earlier in the program for the arrays X and Y. Thus, the statements must be considered not only individually, but also in pairs, three at a time, and so on. In general, all possible patterns of interaction must be considered, and in a code having n lines there are $2^n - 1$ of them (see Exercise 12.8.28). This worst-case **cognitive complexity** is a measure of how difficult it might be to understand an isolated code segment and therefore of how difficult it is to get that segment right. Human beings can reason about only a limited number of things at one time, and if there are $2^n - 1$ interactions to worry about simultaneously then n can't be very big without overflowing our capacity. The semantics of FORTRAN often permit us to examine and reject some of the potential interactions very quickly, because there are far fewer legal programs than there are sequences of legal statements, but the difficulty of understanding even a program that is known to be semantically correct still increases exponentially with the length of the code.

Write independent code segments that are not too long. To keep the cognitive complexity low enough to permit human understanding, it is essential for the routines that make up a program to be as independent from one another as possible, with few connections through shared data. That is why I said earlier that the division of a program into routines should usually minimize the amount of data the routines must share. In a similar way it is essential to structure each routine in short code segments (each consisting of one or a few stanzas) that are as independent from one another as possible, with few connections through either shared data or control-flow logic. This is another application of the locality principle we encountered in our discussion of why the listing of a routine ideally should fit on two pages. The code excerpts below perform the same computation.

```
IF(A.GT.B) THEN                     IF(A.GT.B) X=Y
   X=Y                              IF(A.LE.B .AND. C.GT.D) X=Z
ELSE                                IF(A.LE.B .AND. C.LE.D
   IF(C.GT.D) THEN                  ;         .AND. A.GT.C) X=W
      X=Z
   ELSE
      IF(A.GT.C) X=W
   ENDIF
ENDIF
```

The code on the right has three logically independent statements while the code on the left can only be understood whole. The nine statements on the left are not too many to comprehend all at once, but if some set of connected statements is too large you will not be able to see the forest for the trees.

12.4.2 Names

To the FORTRAN compiler, as explained in §1, names mean nothing; they are simply replaced by memory addresses unless they identify subprograms or COMMON blocks. In linking an executable, the loader replaces even those external symbols by addresses in memory. To the machine, a rose by any name whatever has no smell at all, so what's in a name?

Use meaningful names. To people, names are filled with meaning, and they are indispensable to all our processes of reasoning and memory. As the novelist Ursula Le Guin observed, [158, p46], "magic consists in this, the true naming of a thing." The names you use in your code will mean *something* to everyone who reads them, so if they do not convey your thoughts they will surely *mis*convey them. It is therefore very important to name things as truly as you can. In writing Classical FORTRAN code the things we must name are variables, PARAMETER constants, functions, subroutines, and COMMON blocks. The rules given here apply to all of them.

Select names according to context. Names should describe the purposes of routines, the contents of COMMON blocks, and the meanings of variables and PARAMETER constants in terms appropriate to the places where they are used. Subprogram arguments are visible outside the subprogram, so their names, and the name of the subprogram itself, should be chosen based on the external image the routine presents. Likewise, COMMON blocks and the variables they contain are visible in more than one routine and therefore should have names that make sense in all of them.

Variables and PARAMETER constants that appear only *inside* a routine should be named according to their local meaning. If you can easily use the same name for local variables that have the same meaning in the different application-specific routines of your program, do so. But remember that components written at other times or by other people, such as library subprograms, probably use local variables that don't match yours. Because of separate compilation, the compiler must assume that a local variable in one routine has nothing to do with a local variable having the same name in another, whether or not they mean the same thing to you.

Use non-local variable names consistently. If an application-specific subprogram (one that is not a library routine) is always invoked with the same argument names, use those names inside the subprogram as well. Use the same variable names in all the occurrences of a COMMON block. Avoid **replicate data**, the use of more than one variable name to refer to the same quantity (except when it is necessary to interpret the same data in different ways using EQUIVALENCE, as in §10.2). Don't use a variable name to mean more than one thing. For example, if you use I as an index on the rows of a matrix in one part of a routine, don't use it as an index on the columns in another. Filling in the variable list as you go along will protect you from inadvertently using the same symbol to mean different things.

Use Classical FORTRAN names. Pick names that have one to six characters, the first a letter and the others letters and numbers, all upper case. Some compilers allow names to be longer or to include other characters, but as explained in §13.2 there are good reasons for avoiding those extensions.

Follow the default naming rules if you can. If you can find descriptive names that conform to the default conventions for INTEGER*4 and REAL*4 variables, as described in §4, use them. Using an integer named A for a loop counter, or a real variable named N to hold an approximation of π, violates the principle of least astonishment. But if a name with the wrong default type really is ideal, use an explicit type statement to give it the right type. If you run out of default integers for loop counters, follow the mathematical custom of resorting next to the letters P, Q, R, S, and T.

Use names that are the right length. We use symbols in mathematics because that is usually clearer than using words; more is gained from terseness than is lost by having to remember what the variables mean. FORTRAN is mainly for translating formulas, so the most natural variable names are often those that are or describe mathematical symbols, such as X or DELTA. A FORTRAN program is not quite the same as an algebra problem worked by hand, so it is not always obvious whether the code will be easiest to understand if the mathematical symbols are carried over directly or given longer or different names to describe their roles in the problem. The best place to describe a variable is in the variable list of the routine's preamble, not in the variable's name. On the other hand, there are times when the code might be made clearer by using a longer name. For example, ω might be rendered in FORTRAN as W, but will be easier to recognize as OMEGA. If ω represents frequency in the original application, a still better choice might be FREQ, even though it no longer paraphrases the mathematics.

Short names, especially one-character names, can be annoying because they yield a lot of false hits when scanned for using a text editor or a UNIX™ utility such as grep. Long names use up columns, making it more likely that continuation lines will be required.

Taking all of these considerations into account, the best policy is usually to transliterate mathematics as exactly as possible and to give other variables names that are *just long enough* to be descriptive.

Choose variable names that won't be confused. It is easy to get carried away with some system for manufacturing variable names and wind up with identifiers that are hard to tell apart. For example, it takes a lot of effort to understand the code on the left below, whereas the names used on the right are hard to mistake for one another.

```
NN=N**2              NSQ=N**2
NNN=N**3             NCUBE=N**3
NNMNNN=NN-NNN        K=NSQ-NCUBE
NNMNM=NNN-N-1        L=NCUBE-N-1
```

Similar cautions apply to *characters* that are easily confused, such as O with 0, I with 1, S with 5, and Z with 2. Often it is best to avoid mixing characters from these pairs so as to avoid coming up with names like the baffling but perfectly legal O0 (oh-zero, better pronounced "uh-oh!").

Avoid certain names. Make sure that the names of variables, PARAMETER constants, and your subprograms are all different from each other and from the names of FORTRAN built-in functions and UNIX™ system routines. Never call one of your subprograms or COMMON blocks TIME or ERROR. Don't use for a name any FORTRAN keyword, such as THEN. Even if the compiler seems not to be confused by a program that contains a keyword, a variable, and a COMMON block all having the same name, you (and any unfortunates who fall heir to your code) doubtless will be. Don't use variable names starting with DOI or DO followed by a numeral.

12.4.3 Branching Logic

As discussed in §0.2, people noticed early in the history of FORTRAN that the use of GO TO statements can lead to **spaghetti code** that is very hard to understand. The reason for this is that the flow of control can potentially reach a branch target from more than one branch origin, and the branch origins can be located anywhere relative to the target. This enlarges the scope of potentially related statements and thereby increases the cognitive complexity of the code.

Use GO TO statements sparingly. To make it less likely that you will end up with spaghetti code, avoid GO TO statements whenever some other construct can be used instead without making the code harder to understand. Some computer scientists condemn explicit branching altogether, in favor of *implicit* branching such as that embodied in the

DO-CONTINUE and IF-THEN constructs. However, there are instances (such as branching out of the range of a loop, first mentioned in §5.4) when a GO TO yields the simplest and clearest code. Furthermore, explicit branching is unavoidable if we use END= or ERR= in I/O statements as described in §9.1.3. On a more philosophical level, there are many programming contexts where *an explicit style is preferable to one in which the mechanism of action is concealed.* So it is best to treat GO TO in FORTRAN like "ain't" in English; it is effective only if used infrequently, but sometimes it is the best choice.

Use simple and obvious control structures. Good writing is simple. The well-structured code on the right below does the same calculation as the spaghetti code on the left.

```
      :                                     :
      I=1                           C       make A the identity if X < Y
 17 IF(X.LT.Y) GO TO 12                    IF(X.LT.Y) THEN
      J=I                                  DO 1 I=1,N
      GO TO 38                                 DO 2 J=1,N
 12 J=1                                           IF(I.NE.J) A(I,J)=0.DO
 16 IF(J.EQ.I) GO TO 52                           IF(I.EQ.J) A(I,J)=1.DO
      GO TO 38                         2       CONTINUE
 52 A(I,J)=1.DO                        1 CONTINUE
      GO TO 14                             ENDIF
 38 CONTINUE                        C
      A(I,J)=0.DO                    C       otherwise zero out the diagonal
 14 IF(X.GE.Y) GO TO 22                    IF(X.GE.Y) THEN
      J=J+1                                DO 3 I=1,N
      IF(J.LE.N) GO TO 16                      A(I,I)=0.DO
 22 I=I+1                             3 CONTINUE
      IF(I.LT.N+1) GO TO 17              ENDIF
      :                                     :
```

On the right the basic loops are rewritten as DO loops, making the code much easier to understand.

Keep DO-CONTINUE and IF-THEN constructs short. Ideally it should be possible to see the whole thing at one glance. Keeping your routines no longer than two pages helps make this likely.

Avoid unnecessary branching. If you must use a control structure more complicated than you can write clearly using the IF-THEN and DO-CONTINUE constructs, try to minimize the total number of branch origins and targets. Don't branch around branches, as is done in the three statements beginning with number 16 on the left in the example above. If possible replace conditional branches by logical IF statements, as also illustrated in the example. Sometimes branching can be reduced by turning a relational test around. Sometimes a relational test can be simplified by transforming a logical expression using DeMorgan's theorem.

Minimize the number of long branches up. The normal flow of control in FORTRAN code is from top to bottom, so it is less mental work to follow branches down (skipping something) than branches up (forming a loop to repeat something). It's all right to have very short branches up, where the origin and destination of the branch are separated by no more than three or four lines of text, but limit the number of long branches up to one per routine. The branches down should also be short if possible, so that the origin and destination are both visible at a glance.

Number branch targets in the order they are mentioned in the normal flow of control, as illustrated in the BISECT listing given earlier and in all the routines of §18. That way, a statement number that is out of order when you read from top to bottom in the statement number field indicates a branch back. A target that is branched to from outside of its code stanza should begin the stanza. There should be no more than about 10 statement numbers in a routine, exclusive of FORMAT statements. Don't use statement numbers that are not referred to in the program. More advice about statement numbers is given in §12.4.5 below.

12.4.4 Exposition

Writing clear and graceful code depends largely on things we have already discussed: keeping the segments small and independent, calling things by the right names, and making the flow of control easy to understand. But even after you have done those things, many smaller and more local decisions remain to be made about how you will express yourself in FORTRAN. This section outlines some general principles of exposition in coding.

Strive for simplicity of expression. Say just what you mean; save subtlety for conversations with your tax auditor. In coding, explicit and obvious is always better than hidden or amazing. As Piet Hein rhymed it, "There is one art, no more, no less: to do all things with artlessness."

On the left below is some amazing code, slightly revised from the famous introductory example of [8].

```
      DO 1 I=1,N                          DO 1 I=1,N
      DO 1 J=1,N                          DO 1 J=1,N
          X(I,J)=DFLOAT( (I/J)*(J/I) )        X(I,J)=0.D0
    1 CONTINUE                               IF(J.EQ.I) X(I,J)=1.D0
                                       1 CONTINUE
```

Recalling that integer division truncates, we eventually realize that either (I/J) or (J/I) will be 0 if I is different from J, and both fractions will be 1 if I and J are the same. Thus the code on the left puts zeros in the off-diagonal elements of X and ones on the diagonal. The code on the right does the same thing but without the little puzzle. Which is easier to read? Resist the temptation to put something clever or amusing in your code, such as the puzzle method of making an identity matrix, or an unexpected form of some algebraic expression, or a page of statements using only divisions and no multiplications, or line indentations that draw a little picture, or a hidden joke or scrap of graffiti. It is better to have a program that is dull and works than one that is wrong because somebody tried to make it fun to read.

Never write code that you yourself do not understand. Coding should not be a random search through the space of all plausible program variations until you happen to stumble across one that works. Worry about correctness first, before all the other desirable attributes of a program.

Break up complicated expressions; use the rule of thumb that [105, p29] "The mind cannot cope with more than five levels of parentheses." Use parentheses and rearrange expressions, as in the examples at the top of the next page, to remove ambiguities and to save the reader from having to remember the operator precedence rules.

```
Z=A**I**J                          Z=A**(I**J)
Y=F/G/H                            Y=F/(G*H)
W=P/Q*R                            W=(P/Q)*R
```

Compare values to each other, rather than their difference to zero.

```
IF(X-Y .LE. 0.D0) THEN            IF(X.LE.Y) THEN
```

Don't code for special cases unless they really are special; if possible make the same code path work for all cases.

Use lowly subprograms. Back in the design process you identified the major application-specific routines of your program and the general-purpose library subprograms it would obviously need. Now, during the coding process, some additional, smaller opportunities to use subprograms will probably come up as you notice instances of replicate code. If you find that you're doing very similar things in different segments of open code, consider replacing those code segments by invocations of one subprogram. If you can use an extant library routine for this, or write a new one, do that; never write specialized code when you can easily use or write something general. Otherwise, write a special little routine just for this application. Whenever you further decompose a program by introducing a lowly subprogram, remember to hide design decisions and data as recommended in §12.2.2.

Use appropriate data structures. Back in the design process you identified the major data structures of your program or of this routine, but some decisions about local data structures might come up during coding. Try to find the right data structure to make the computation easy. Use data arrays to permit repetitive calculations to be done in a loop. If possible use integer arrays to hold whole-number values. Because FORTRAN stores arrays in column-major order as described in §5.3, working down the columns of a two-dimensional array is often easier than working across the rows.

Use appropriate data types. Don't mix data types in an expression, or use the assignment operator to implicitly convert data types. Use the built-in routines of §4.4 and §4.6.1 to make type conversions explicit.

```
REAL*8 A,B                         REAL*8 A,B
:                                  :
A=B/(I-1)                          A=B/DFLOAT(I-1)
```

Type floating-point constants by using the appropriate exponential form.

```
REAL*8 C,D                         REAL*8 C,D
PARAMETER(D=9.1)                   PARAMETER(D=9.1D0)
:                                  :
C=1.                               C=1.D0
```

Initialize each variable before use, even if its initial value is zero; don't rely on UNIX™ to do it (see also §15.2.2). Use PARAMETER constants for things that *never* change, like π, and to set array dimensions as in §5.5. Use a value in slashes after the type statement to initialize things that need to be set at compile time, but that are later changed. Use executable code to initialize things that are used repeatedly and need to be reinitialized each time.

Don't increment or count with floating-point values, or compare them for exact equality. Floating point values are binary fractions of finite length, not real numbers in the mathematical sense, and floating-point arithmetic is almost always inexact. In comparing a floating-point variable to a tolerance, remember to use the absolute value of the variable if the variable can have either sign.

Some programmers declare all variables, while others declare only those variables that are not properly typed by the default naming rules. Pick the policy you prefer and stick with it. If you declare all variables, use the `IMPLICIT NONE` statement (see §13.4.4) so that the compiler will inform you of any you miss. `IMPLICIT NONE` checks declarations, not initializations.

Leave calculations to the machine. Computers are faster and more accurate than humans at doing arithmetic and counting things.

    FRAC=0.6470858D0   FRAC=11.D0/17.D0

The code on the right not only yields a more accurate value than the code on the left (especially since the decimal given contains a typographical error) but also gives the reader a hint about where the value came from.

Count input data, rather than making the user supply the number of items to be read.

Make the I/O idiotproof. In §12.2.1 I recommended using library subprograms such as `GETFIL` and `QUERY`, and outlined some general principles for designing a program's I/O. Some of those ideas must also be kept in mind when coding, along with a few lower-level issues that we have not discussed before.

Prompt and use free format for input from the keyboard, and either read one item per line or show in the prompt the order of the data items that are to be input. Lay out input data files so that they are easy to prepare and proofread. Report all the errors you can find in the input data, in such a way as to permit the user to easily find and fix the mistakes, and recover somehow if that is possible and does not violate the principle of least astonishment. Even if you do not find any errors, echo critical input data so the user can verify it is correct.

Count input data rather than reading the number of items first. Read data into an array using a `DO` loop to make it impossible to exceed the array dimensions; if control flow exits the loop through the bottom, check for more data and report that not all of it would fit.

Make output to the screen self-explanatory. Write as much of the output as possible, to both files and the screen, immediately after it has been calculated. That way, if the program fails you will have some idea where. This also makes some results available early, so that they can be used while the program is still running. Use output formats for floating-point numbers that match the precision printed to the precision calculated; if a number is computed to within ±10%, don't print 16 decimal places (see Exercise 12.8.39). `REAL*8` values are *never* more precise than 17 significant digits.

Code defensively. Never trust input data, whether you read it or receive it as a subprogram argument or in `COMMON`. Sanity-check scalar inputs for validity (such as correct signs and values in legal range) and plausibility (values having the right order of magnitude), and report errors. Guard against data that could cause array dimensions to be exceeded and use a compiler flag, as described in §14.1.2, to make the program stop if that happens. Whenever you code a division, ask yourself if the denominator can be zero. Whenever you invoke a mathematical function, such as square root, ask yourself whether the argument can be out of range.

Avoid extensions. Many compilers offer extensions, such as long names, free-format source form, or `INTEGER*8` variables. Some extensions are so popular they become universal, and this process drives the evolution of standard FORTRAN (see §17). Some of the features this book includes in Classical FORTRAN began as extensions to FORTRAN-66 (see §0.2). But many extensions are *not* universal, having been wickedly contrived by the vendor to addict your code forever to his compiler! If you want your programs to work on systems other than the one you write them on (such as the one your office will be switching to next week), you must never use anything you recognize as an extension. Good code is portable. Use only standard, or de facto standard, language features.

Isolate system dependencies. Occasionally, especially in interacting with the operating system (see §14.2), it is necessary to write code that clearly will *not* work on other systems. Try to isolate this code in one or a few routines that can easily be replaced with new system-dependent versions when the program is moved to a different machine or operating system.

12.4.5   Typography

Even a simple calculation can be made to appear complex by arranging its code and comments in a way that obscures its logical structure. Source text should be carefully formatted to minimize the cognitive load on the reader and to make later revisions easy. I suggest that for now you imitate the style described here and illustrated throughout the book; later you can make adjustments, if necessary, to better suit your temperament and taste.

Be consistent. Some people regard coding as a Constitutionally-protected form of self-expression, and deride any attempt at consistency as "Fascist programming." They also spend a lot of time making repetitive changes one by one, not being able to find things with the editor, and misreading statements that are written in unexpected ways. Was it `Y = DSQRT ( X + 2.0D+00 )` that you wrote a minute ago, or `Y =DSQRT(X+2.D0 )`, or some other variant? Consistency might be the hobgoblin of little minds, but in coding that is exactly the sort of mind that comes in handy. Adopt policies that you believe in and stick to them in your coding unless you find reason to make an exception. That way you, and other people who have to work with your code, will know what to expect rather than having to mentally syntax-check every line before figuring out what it means. Giving up some freedom to vary the appearance of what we write is a fair exchange for the ability to read the text without needless effort, and always doing things the same way makes it easy to use UNIX™ power tools, such as the stream editor **sed**, for manipulating the code. There remains ample freedom of expression within even rather strict typographical conventions to say what you want in the *content* of what you write. And there are other parts of your life, which don't involve programming, in which you are relaxed, carefree, and spontaneous all the time, right?

Some professional programming shops publish typographical conventions for their writers to follow, and enforce them by means of code inspections.

Avoid clutter. The fewer stray pixels there are in the listing, the easier it is to extract the meaning of the text. Remove extra parentheses that don't make the code easier to understand.

```
W=FCN( (A+(X(I)**2)) )          W=FCN(A + X(I)**2)
V=-(3.D0-(X-W))                 V=X-W-3.D0
```

Eliminate unnecessary continuation lines that don't make the code easier to understand.

```
ALPHA=PI+H*(Q-                    ALPHA=PI+H*(Q-V*DSQRT(W))
; V*DSQRT(W))
```

It is permissible to have as many type declaration statements as you need, so it is never necessary to continue one. Eliminate unnecessary temporary variables, especially extra variables that represent the same thing. Keep the comments as terse as possible without unacceptable loss of precision, like newspaper headlines. Each stanza should have a comment that fits on one line. The description of what the routine does should fit on a few lines. In each routine there should be exactly one comment that is a line across the full width of the page, namely the line that separates the preamble from the executable statements. Don't draw extra lines subdividing the executable code; if the parts are really so separate, they probably belong in different routines. Don't use stars, all capital letters, and similar devices for extra emphasis in comments; if you feel compelled to shout about the code, it isn't clear enough and needs to be rewritten.

Indent to show structure. Indent the bodies of loops, whether they are DO loops or constructed using explicit branching statements, and indent the inside loops of a nest farther. Indent the contents of IF-THEN blocks to reveal the logical structure of the construct, and in a nest indent the inside blocks farther. Whenever you indent code, also indent the attached comment to keep it aligned with the code it describes.

Use consecutive statement numbers. As mentioned above in §12.4.3, branch targets and DO loops should be numbered in the order they are mentioned in the normal flow of control. Make their statement numbers 1, 2, 3, etc., *without* any gaps in between. Many authors advocate leaving room for more statement numbers to be inserted later, but that is an invitation to disaster. Whenever you make any change to a routine, you should consider its effects throughout that routine rather than confining your attention only to the code in the immediate vicinity of the change. Renumbering the statements will afford you the opportunity to look over the whole routine with the change in place. If the routine is too long for that to be convenient, then it is too long altogether and needs to be broken up. If the branching logic is too complicated for renumbering to be convenient, or uses too many statement numbers, then it is just too complicated and needs to be simplified. There shouldn't be more than about 10 statement numbers, not counting FORMATs, in a routine, so renumbering the statements shouldn't be a big deal.

FORMAT statements should also be numbered in the order that they are encountered, but their numbers should be chosen from a sequence that is easily seen to be different from the sequence of numbers used to identify branch targets and DO terminators. In this book I have given FORMAT statements 3-digit numbers beginning with the numeral 9. Remember to put FORMAT statements after their first use, as recommended in §9.1.1, so that they can provide extra hints about what the code is doing.

Right-justify statement numbers in the statement number field, to keep them from being lost among the column-1 Cs of comments, and so that the statement numbers and the leftmost lines of code delimit an easily-seen slot where any continuation characters must go.

Use the right amount and placement of white space. Within columns 7–72, blanks are significant to FORTRAN only in character literals. Thus, the tiny typographical error in the code on the left at the top of the next page (a period where a comma was intended) makes it read to many compilers like the code on the right. The floating-point variable

```
        DO 1 I=1.20                            DO1I=1.20
            X(I)=0.D0                            X(I)=0.D0
      1 CONTINUE                             1 CONTINUE
```

DO1I is given the value 1.20, the array element X(I) (whatever I might be) is set to zero, and the statement 1 CONTINUE does nothing.

To people, though, blanks are delimiters that help us understand the text. Decide where the white space will go in your code and always use it in the same way (see "Be consistent." above). Some programmers set off each operator with blanks, as on the left below.

```
        X = 1.D0                               X=1.D0
        CALL SUB ( X )                         CALL SUB(X)
```

while others find the more compact style on the right easier to read.

Use blank characters to make white space, not tab characters. The default tab reach in most UNIX™ editors is 8 characters, which starts FORTRAN statements too far to the right. It can also be annoying to edit text that is full of tabs. Use blank comments (with a C in column 1), rather than entirely blank or null lines, for vertical spacing.

Keep continued statements readable. Remember that any statement text after column 72 will be ignored by the compiler. If a statement is too long to fit, consider doing the calculation with more than one statement as in the examples below.

```
C       this statement ends in column 82
        ANS=3.71D0*DCOS( (SIGMA**2+1.D0)-DSQRT(OMEGA**2-1.D0) )-HEIGHT/(SIGMA*OMEGA)
C
C       these statements do the same calculation
        ANS=3.71D0*DCOS( (SIGMA**2+1.D0)-DSQRT(OMEGA**2-1.D0) )
        ANS=ANS-HEIGHT/(SIGMA*OMEGA)
```

If that isn't convenient, break the long statement at a delimiter (a comma, or an operator) and continue it on the next line. Break a long text string into two shorter text strings and put the second one on the continued line, rather than running the first line up to column 72 and resuming the text in column 7 of the continuation line.

```
        WRITE(6,900)
C       this statement ends in column 80
  900 FORMAT(' iteration  phase  time              function      X(1)        X(2)')
C
C       these statements print the same heading
        WRITE(6,900)
  900 FORMAT(' iteration  phase  time          function',
      ;               '      X(1)        X(2)')
```

For a continuation character use ";" or some other symbol with no other meaning to FORTRAN. When you continue a line that has symmetry or repetition in it, make the result readable by indenting to reveal the symmetry or repetition as in the example at the top of the next page.

```
C     this line ends in column 78
      Y(I)=Y(I-1)*ALFA*DEXP(XA(I)/(F*GAMMA))+Y(I-2)*DEXP(XB(I)/(G*GAMMA))*BETA
C
C     here it is continued
      Y(I)=Y(I-1)*ALFA*DEXP(XA(I)/(F*GAMMA))+
    ;      Y(I-2)*BETA*DEXP(XB(I)/(G*GAMMA))
```

Format new code by hand. Many legacy codes were written long before the principles of good programming style were discovered, and often they are unformatted or poorly formatted and therefore difficult to read (see §13.1). When people began to understand that well-formatted code is easier to work with, a cottage industry sprang up to write "pretty printer" programs that read ratty source text and write out an equivalent program with loops indented and the branch targets and DO terminators renumbered. These programs are fine for making a first pass at cleaning up old programs, but using one on code you have just written is like hiring somebody else to dance with your sweetheart. New code should be written clearly to begin with, not thoughtlessly hacked out and then mechanically cleaned up with a source reformatter.

12.4.6   Refining the Comments

As you fill in the code, you will probably discover that some of the stanza comments must be adjusted slightly, and that additional comments are needed.

Make the comments agree with the code. In the beginning the comments are to help you write the code, but in the end they must accurately describe it. Thus, after the code is written [105], "The... idea of a comment is to prepare the mind of the reader for a proper interpretation of the instruction or statement to which it is appended."

Keep the comments phrased in terms of the application. You began with comments describing the calculation in terms of the problem; don't change them now to be in terms of the code. The comment on the left below tells nothing.

```
C     increment L              C     consider the next inductor
      L=L+1                           L=L+1
```

Often it is obvious *what* a code stanza is doing; then the comment should tell something about *why* this step is being performed.

Comment the declarations. After the code is written it often becomes obvious that comments are needed to explain array dimensions, PARAMETER constants, and compile-time initializations. Add them now.

Don't over-comment. Outside the preamble there should be one comment heading each stanza, plus perhaps a few others within stanzas where they are really needed to explain what is going on. Any comments added during the course of coding must contribute important new information. The best internal documentation is code so clear and well-structured that it is self-explanatory. If you find yourself writing lengthy comments, the code itself probably needs to be clarified.

12.5   Hand-Checking

At the moment you finish coding a routine, it is hard to believe there could be anything wrong with it. You were careful, and you probably tested parts or all of it as you wrote. Unfortunately, it is very easy to make mistakes in the countless little details of coding, and neither the compiler nor your testing is sure to find them all. For example, the following sort of error will not be noticed by the compiler (because of separate compilation) and might produce wrong results rather than a run-time error even if you used the compiler flag to check for subscripts out of range.

```
      REAL*8 A(2)
      CALL SUB1(A)
      :
      STOP
      END
      SUBROUTINE SUB1(A)
      REAL*8 A(*)
      A(3)=9.D0
      :
```

Mistakes like this can sometimes be discovered through an arduous process of debugging, but it is far easier to find them by systematically hand-checking the code. Patience and thoroughness now will greatly reduce the time it takes to perfect the routine when you start testing, and will improve the quality of the code by identifying errors that would not be revealed by testing. Hand-checking involves the following four steps.

1. Make a listing. To perform the hand-checking process you must have a listing of the source code *on paper.* You will need to check things off on the listing, and you will probably want to mark revisions, write yourself notes, draw arrows, and make other marks near and on the code. These things you cannot do on the workstation screen.

2. Review the logic. Hand-simulate the control flow and processing. Pay special attention to extreme cases such as the first and last iterations of a loop, to find off-by-one errors such as counting wrong or using .GT. where .GE. was needed. At every test, make sure you branch the right way on equality. Verify that all loops are certain to end. Be careful about bottom exits from DO loops that normally exit sideways, and be suspicious if a bottom exit and a side exit go to the same place. Whenever a DO loop is designed to *never* exit normally, ask if that can *ever* happen and what that would mean. Beware of DO limits out of order; DO 1 I=5,3 yields zero passes. Remember never to use a DO index outside the range of the loop, and never to branch into the range of a loop. Verify that all possible exceptions are handled, such as end-of-file conditions and division by zero. Verify that no array subscripts can go out of bounds. Beware of truncation in integer division, and make sure there will be no fixed-point overflows. Verify that all uses of floating-point values do not depend on their being exact, and make sure there will be no floating-point overflows. Verify that the arguments of built-in functions are in range. Check for parameter mismatches at subprogram boundaries and in COMMON. Make sure the code handles special cases and "does nothing" gracefully.

If the code to which a comment refers is correct, the comment should make the code easier to understand, and that's good. But if the code is wrong, a correct comment can lead you to miss the mistake. So in hand-checking, covering up the comments can make it easier to spot a mistake [105, p164]. After checking the code, check the comments to make sure they really wound up agreeing with the code. As you review the logic be alert for typographical errors, such as statements that extend past column 72 and character substitutions of ! for 1, I for 1, O for 0, and . for ,. Also check for statements inadvertently made into comments, and for comments lacking a C in column 1.

3. Make sure every symbol is in the variable list. Reread the code and check off each occurrence of a variable, user-written routine, built-in function, PARAMETER constant, DO index, and variable in COMMON. Each time you check one off, verify that its name is listed and defined in the variable list. Make sure the list is alphabetical. Check for any misspelled variable names that might be revealed by the listing process. Make sure none of the names in the list conflict with those of FORTRAN keywords or built-in functions, UNIX™ system routines, or COMMON blocks.

4. For each symbol in the list, answer The Three Questions. Most errors in FORTRAN programs turn out to be in the data structures, not in the logic. Most errors in the data structures will be revealed by answering the questions boxed below, which you should *memorize*.

Does it have the right type?
Does it have the right size?
How does it get a value?

The Three Questions

By the right *type* I mean scalar data type, such as REAL*8. If a variable doesn't follow the default naming convention, or if you have decided to declare them all, it needs to be declared somewhere in the preamble. FORTRAN knows the types of its built-in functions so you don't need to declare them (but make sure you use the right member of each family, such as DSQRT for a REAL*8 argument). The names of SUBROUTINE subprograms and COMMON blocks don't have types. If a subprogram name is passed as an argument to, or received from, another routine, it needs to be declared EXTERNAL; otherwise it should not be. If the routine you are checking is a FUNCTION subprogram, its name needs to be declared inside the routine if it doesn't follow the default naming convention.

By the right *size* I mean mathematical rank; is it a scalar, a 10 × 12 array, or what? If you used an adjustably-dimensioned array, make sure that both the array and its adjustable dimensions are passed as arguments to the subprogram, and that you handled the leading dimension properly (see §7.1).

There are many ways for a variable to get a value: it can be passed in as an argument of the subprogram, or read in, or set by an assignment statement, or initialized to a value between slashes at compile time, or it can be a DO index. PARAMETER constants are set in the PARAMETER statement, and a function name gets its value from the function. One way or another, all of these symbols must get values before they are used. The names of SUBROUTINE subprograms and COMMON blocks don't have values. If the routine you are checking is a FUNCTION subprogram, its name must be given a value somewhere in the routine.

12.6   Testing, Revision, and Maintenance

If you've written, hand-checked, and tested your code in small pieces, as recommended in §12.4, you've already tried each routine at least informally. When you're ready to put the parts together, it's time to test them, and the whole program, in a more deliberate way. Testing can help you find coding errors and it can expose run-time departures from our idealized expectations about floating-point arithmetic, such as numbers going out of range. It can also reveal hidden assumptions that were made in the design process but turn out to be untrue (sometimes just planning a test procedure can serve this purpose, which is why I recommended doing that in §12.2). If you find something wrong it will be necessary to revise the code or even, occasionally, to return to the design stage and try again. Sometimes it won't be obvious what is wrong, and then it might be necessary to do some actual debugging as described in §14.3. Here, though, we assume that any malfunctions you notice will be easy to diagnose and correct, and that the primary focus of testing is **code validation** rather than debugging.

12.6.1   Testing

In rare instances it is possible to exhaustively test all possible paths of control flow in a routine and to use all possible sequences of input data values. Then, if we have done the testing correctly, we have verified that the program does what the testing assumed it should.

Unfortunately most codes contain conditionals and loops in which statements are executed different numbers of times depending on intermediate results, so exercising (or even enumerating) all possible paths of control flow might be impractical. Unless the inputs to a routine can take on only a modest number of discrete values it is also impractical to test all possible combinations of data. When there are too many code paths or too many input values, testing must be selective rather than exhaustive, and while selective testing can show that a code is *wrong* it can never prove that the code is *right*. It is always possible that errors remain undiscovered in the paths that were not exercised, or only appear for input data values that were not used. If you find bugs and fix them, so that the program gets closer and closer to being right, selective testing is less and less likely to reveal that anything else is wrong even if bugs still remain.

Testing can find only **hard bugs**, errors that affect the outputs of the code. Coding errors that do not affect the outputs, such as statements that initialize the same variable twice without its being used in between, are called **soft bugs** and can be found only by hand-checking.

Test routines separately, then in combination. First validate the library subprograms you wrote, then the application-specific subprograms starting from the lowliest and working your way up, and finally the whole program. Until you get to the testing of the whole program you will need simple driver programs to invoke the pieces you are testing. Test each new library routine using the EXAMPLE program from its **man** page.

Compare test outputs to known right answers. If possible, figure out what results the routine should produce for the inputs you use, by hand calculation or using another program. Rerun each test to make sure the correct results are repeatable and do not, for example, depend on an uninitialized variable miraculously having a value of zero.

Cover as many code paths as possible. As explained above it will usually not be possible to cover all code paths, but try to pick input values that will exercise every executable statement in the source text. Verify at least that you have not accidentally chosen input values all of which exercise only a small part of the code.

Test edge conditions. Choose some test data to demonstrate that the routine does what it should at its design limits and at any special or distinguished values the inputs can take on. For example, a routine that calculates the numerical value of a scalar function might be tested where the function value is supposed to be zero, if those points are known.

Use some randomly-generated input data. Data combinations you never thought of might elicit unexpected behavior.

Repeat earlier tests after every change. Don't stop after fixing the first bug you find. If you discover an error on the tenth experiment, go back and rerun the first nine after fixing the code; this is called **regression testing**. Code validation is an iterative process, unless no errors are found.

If a function has an inverse, test both together. Sometimes a calculation can be verified by performing the inverse operation to recover the original data. For example, one way to check the factors of a matrix is to multiply them together and verify that the product is the original matrix. Using an inverse function written by somebody else decreases the likelihood of the two routines making errors that cancel in the checking.

Read the experts. Software testing is a big field. More information about testing, and citations to additional references, can be found in [61, §6.3].

Get real users to test the final version. Ask the same members of the target audience who tried the user-interface prototype early in the design process to now rate the finished product. Revise the program, if necessary, so that *in their judgement* it meets the final design requirements. If they want to *change* the design requirements one last time on the basis of what they see now, suggest deferring those changes to the next version of the program.

In some organizations a formal **acceptance test** is required before a program is considered done, and in that case it is important to have agreement on the final design requirements before acceptance testing begins.

12.6.2 Revision and Maintenance

During the testing process, as you discover errors you revise the code and test again, until eventually you discover no more errors. You don't need to wonder whether or when to make these development revisions; they are needed right away to get the program working. Once the program seems right and you (or your managers) decide that it is done, you will **release** it for use. This might sound overly dramatic, especially if the only user will be you, but release is an important moment in the life cycle of a program. If the program is a success, its first release will be just the beginning of a long and productive life. Users will probably find little flaws and think of improvements, perhaps leading to a long sequence of revisions. But at first release, the application passes from the development stage to the maintenance stage, and the rules about revision suddenly change.

Software maintenance is a deliberate process through which a program and its documentation get revised after release because bugs have been discovered or the requirements have changed since the code was "finished." After release, people are using the program and don't want to be blindsided by unannounced changes, especially if those changes introduce new bugs (for several examples of bug introduction, see [147]). Also, after release you probably don't want to interrupt whatever you are doing and get back into the finished application just to make some minor adjustment.

Accumulate changes for the next version. Instead of updating the finished application every time someone thinks of a change to make, keep good records of the bugs that people discover and of the suggestions that people have for improving the program. Wait until a serious problem turns up, or until enough little change requests have accumulated to be worthwhile, and then make all of the revisions at once to create a new version of the program. Not all of the ideas in your notes will turn out to be good ones, so be selective in which you adopt.

Number the versions. The original release is version 1. Subsequent versions might be numbered simply $2, 3, 4, \ldots$, or $1.1, 1.2, \ldots, 2, 2.1, \ldots$ to indicate changes of different sizes; you decide. Once you get beyond the first release, the version number should be in the preamble of the source code for the main routine and should be written out by the program as part of its standard output. Always keep the previous version of the source code around for a while (or forever) in case the new one has bugs. Many organizations have elaborate policies about revision control and use sophisticated software tools to keep track of changes.

Some programmers include a revision history in the preamble comments of each routine, but this information is seldom of much use to anybody who doesn't already know the story, and those who *do* know the story don't need to read about it. The saga might be interesting to the managers for fixing blame when something goes wrong, but don't expect it to be of any use to you for fixing a problem. If your boss wants the history of the business written down, try to keep it somewhere outside of the code.

If you revise code that someone *else* wrote, modify the preamble of each affected routine to credit the original author and to say that it was revised by you. That way, people will know whom to ask about the code (if you still happen to be around) and the original author won't get blamed for any mistakes you introduce. If there are several previous authors, add your name to the list, like the last endorser of a check, to show that the most recent improvements are yours.

Do regression testing. Run the test suite again after every revision, to verify that the changes didn't introduce new bugs.

Patch if you must, rewrite when you can. Little changes are easy, and if we designed the program right larger ones will be possible for a long while. But eventually, the accretion of change upon change will result in some part or all of the program no longer having the right structure, and then it is time to throw the part or the whole away and start over. Unfortunately, you probably won't get to rewrite the program when that is what is really needed. The old saying that "there is never enough time to do it right, but there is always enough time to do it over" might be true generally, but in programming it seems there is almost never time to do *anything* over. Managers are congenitally incapable of approving rewrites. To get the work done even though it is forbidden, rewrite little bits and pieces whenever you get the chance or contrive to hide the job inside a new project that doesn't obviously have anything to do with the old code.

12.7 Conclusion and Omissions

I began this chapter by explaining how it would *not* be about formal methods or software engineering, but then went on (and on!) to outline a rather elaborate *in*formal procedure for designing and writing programs. Is all of this really necessary? That depends somewhat on the software and its audience, but every programming project really should give at least passing attention to each of the major points I have mentioned. Fortunately, the process described here, like whistling, is much harder to explain than it is to do. With practice you will be able to follow all of the recommendations much more quickly than you could get a working program in any other way.

On the other hand, programming should be fun, and if toeing the line too strictly makes it misery then the rules have defeated their only purpose. If doing everything in this chapter is too hard, start with a few of the recommendations that seem to you like good ideas and add more when you need them. In the end you must find your own stride as a programmer. But if it is too hard to do *anything* in this chapter, you're not trying hard enough.

Software development is a vast subject, and even though this chapter is very long we had room to consider only the high points. Among the relevant topics omitted are the following.

Formal proofs of correctness; software specifications; software standards, such as `MIL-STD-2167`; software engineering tools and environments; revision control and configuration management, including tools such as `RCS` and `SCCS`; software metrics; object-oriented design; graphical user interfaces; software project estimation and management; validation of software for safety-critical applications [33]; ethics and social responsibility in computer programming.

12.8 Exercises

12.8.1 (historical research) Explain the meaning of the phrase "face down, nine edge first" appearing in the poem.

12.8.2 List as many attributes as you can of well-written programs. Explain the difference between "robust" and "reliable," as those terms are defined in §12.2. What attribute does that section identify as *most* important?

12.8.3 Explain the following ideas, which are mentioned at various points throughout the chapter. (a) the Principle of Least Astonishment; (b) egoless programming; (c) data hiding; (d) successive refinement, or top down design; (e) bottom-up design; (f) replicate code; (g) locality; (h) pseudocode; (i) software maintenance; (j) regression testing.

12.8.4 Explain the difference between programming and coding.

12.8.5 Explain the difference between open code, which is described in the introduction to §6, and open-source code, which is described in §12.2.

12.8.6 In what order should these program development steps be performed? Coding, external documentation, hand-checking, testing and revision, internal documentation, user interface design, maintenance, program design.

12.8.7 In the introduction to this chapter I claimed that while a physical thing made to rough tolerances is still roughly right, a program containing a tiny mistake can be completely wrong. (a) Give an example to show that this claim is true. (b) Does *every* error in a program necessarily make it completely wrong? If not, give an example of an error that has no effect, or only a small one, on the behavior of a program.

12.8.8   The following telephone conversation, or one like it, takes place every day between the user of some program and the program's author or technical support representative.

EXPERT: "What message do you see on the screen?"
NOVICE: "It says 'press enter when ready'."
EXPERT: "Okay, so what's the problem?"
NOVICE: "How do I know if it's ready?"

Suggest a change in the message that might help to eliminate future calls on this topic.

12.8.9   In §12.2.1, the UNIX™ `sort` utility is used as an example of an application with a conceptually simple user interface, but this is strictly true only when `sort` is used in the most basic possible way. Read the `man` page for `sort` and evaluate the command-line parameters according to the user interface design criteria of the section.

12.8.10   Evaluate the UNIX™ `rm` command by the user interface design criteria given in §12.2.1

12.8.11   Improve the following code segment.

```
      :
C     get the number of iterations
      PRINT *,'enter KMAX:'
      READ(5,901) KMAX
  901 FORMAT(I6)
      :
```

12.8.12   Write and test a code segment that prompts for and reads N, an INTEGER*4 number, defaulting the variable's value to 7 if the user enters a C_R.

12.8.13   Write a code segment that displays a menu of four choices and prompts for and reads the user's choice. Guard against bogus responses.

12.8.14   A certain program reads an input file of records, each containing the 8-digit part number of an electronic component in a system that is to be simulated, along with information about how it is connected to other components. Using the part number, the simulation program looks up the electrical characteristics of the component in a database containing information on approximately 1000 different components. Because of data entry mistakes it sometimes happens that the part number in an input record does not match that of any component in the database. (a) What information should the program report to help its user find and fix the mistake? (b) Describe a way that the program could in some cases suggest a correct part number.

12.8.15   How must an interactive program be changed to run as a batch (UNIX™ background) job?

12.8.16   A program solves a dense symmetric system of linear algebraic equations involving 2000 variables. Find a lower bound on the amount of memory needed by the program if REAL*8 values are used.

12.8.17   How big should a subprogram be? How long should a subprogram's `man` page be?

12.8.18   The number of floating-point operations in a calculation varies with the problem size n according to the formula $(n^3 + 3n^2 - n)/3$, and a problem having $n = 1000$ runs for 10 seconds of CPU time. If the arithmetic accounts for most of the running time, about how long will the program run for a problem having $n = 50000$?

12.8.19 The subprogram listed below is complete except for its preamble.

```
C
C
C
      FUNCTION STRAB(STRING,LS,TEMPLT,LT)
C
C
C
C
C
C
C
C
C
C
C
C

C
C ------------------------------------------------------------------
C
C     a string that is empty or too long can't abbreviate template
      IF(O.LT.LS .AND. LS.LE.LT) GO TO 1
      STRAB=.FALSE.
      RETURN
C
C     compare the string to the template, ignoring case
    1 DO 2 K=1,LS
          IF(UPCASE(STRING(K)).EQ.UPCASE(TEMPLT(K))) GO TO 2
          STRAB=.FALSE.
          RETURN
    2 CONTINUE
      STRAB=.TRUE.
      RETURN
      END
```

It returns the logical value .TRUE. if STRING abbreviates TEMPLT. For example, if TEMPLT is the word **banana** and STRING is **b** or **bana** then STRAB returns the value .TRUE.. STRAB uses the function UPCASE, which returns as its value the upper-case letter corresponding to its argument. (a) Construct a preamble for this routine, in the style of §12.3.2. (b) Assuming that you got the preamble of STRAB right, what does the following program print?

```
      CHARACTER*1 TEMPLT(6)/'b','a','n','a','n','a'/
      CHARACTER*1 STRNGS(4,3)/
     ;            'b','a','n','a','n','a','b','a','n','a','n','a'/
      LOGICAL*4 STRAB
      DO 1 K=1,3
          PRINT *,STRAB(STRNGS(1,K),4,TEMPLT,6)
    1 CONTINUE
      STOP
      END
```

12.8.20 When a library subprogram detects a mistake in its input data or a failure of the algorithm it implements, the routine can write a diagnostic message on standard-error, or it can set one of its parameters to let the caller know that something went wrong, or it can do both. Some library subprograms, such as those in the NAG library [26], write a diagnostic message only if their return-code parameter has a certain value on input, and then change its value for return to the caller. This lets the programmer control whether or not a message will be written. Revise the `BISECT` routine listed in §12.3.2 so that if it is called with `RC=-1` it refrains from writing diagnostic messages.

12.8.21 List the sections that should be included in every `man` page.

12.8.22 Explain how to begin the internal documentation for a routine. What should be in the preamble of the source code?

12.8.23 Recall that in addition to `SUBROUTINE` and `FUNCTION` subprograms, Classical FORTRAN also has `BLOCK DATA` subprograms. What should the internal documentation look like for a `BLOCK DATA` subprogram? Is there anything below the preamble?

12.8.24 Some programmers declare all variables, but others declare only those variables that do not have the correct type according to the default naming rules. Give arguments for and against each policy.

12.8.25 How many legal FORTRAN variable names with no more than 6 characters can be made using only the letters `A-Z` and the numerals `0-9`?

12.8.26 In this book I follow and advocate the policy of using **UPPER CASE** for FORTRAN statements and **Mixed Case** for comments, but other authors recommend different policies. Critique each of the following policies by explaining its advantages (if any) and disadvantages (if any). (a) Statements in upper case, comments in lower case (the policy advocated by this book):

```
C     use Stirling's formula
      RFACT=DSQRT(2.D0*PI)*DEXP(-R)*R**(R+0.5D0)
```

(b) Everything in upper case (the style that was obligatory in the early days of FORTRAN when lower-case letters either were not allowed or could not even be typed):

```
C     USE STIRLING'S FORMULA
      RFACT=DSQRT(2.D0*PI)*DEXP(-R)*R**(R+0.5D0)
```

(c) Everything in lower case (a style adopted by lazy typists the moment it became possible, also used by programmers who are embarrassed to be writing in FORTRAN and want their code to look more like C):

```
c     use stirling's formula
      rfact=dsqrt(2.d0*pi)*dexp(-r)*r**(r+0.5d0)
```

(d) Everything in lower case except for array variables denoting matrices, imitative of a convention often used in typesetting mathematics:

```
c     solve the linear system
      call solve(A,b,n, x)
```

(e) Upper case for nonexecutable compiler keywords such as `SUBROUTINE` and for `PARAMETER` constants, but lower case for other statement text:

```
PARAMETER(PI=3.14)
print *,PI
```

This policy is suggested by an important reference book in numerical computing [12, p3] whose listings typically do not include any actual FORTRAN comment lines.

(f) Upper case for all FORTRAN keywords, lower case for variables, mixed case for comments:

```
C     use Stirling's formula
      rfact=DSQRT(2.d0*pi)*DEXP(-r)*r**(r+0.5d0)
```

(g) Mixed case for variable names and comments, lower case elsewhere:

```
C     use Stirling's formula
      RFact=dsqrt(2.d0*Pi)*dexp(-R)*R**(R+0.5d0)
```

(h) Inconsistent use of capitalization (this is, sadly, the actual state of many programs, and is especially common in legacy codes):

```
c     USE stirling's Formula
      RFACT=Dsqrt(2.D0*pi)*DEXP(-R)*r**(r+0.5d0)
```

12.8.27 Programmers who are unskilled typists often find it difficult to use upper case. Write a filter program that reads (from standard-in) FORTRAN source text in which the statements and comments are typed in mixed case and writes (to standard-out) the same text with the statements and comments translated to the appropriate case for some capitalization policy of your choice (other than "use mixed case for both code and comments"). If you have no preference for a policy, follow the one advocated by this book. Be sure to leave the text of any quoted strings unchanged.

12.8.28 In §12.4 it is claimed that the number of potential logical interactions between the statements of a program having n lines is $2^n - 1$. (a) Prove this result. (b) If a program is increased in length by a factor of x, how is the number of potential logical interactions between its statements increased?

12.8.29 The variable K may take one of two values, stored in the variables I1 and I2. (a) What is printed by the following code segment? (b) Revise the loop body to accomplish the effect in a way that is easier to understand.

```
      code giving values to I1 and I2
      :
      I3=I1+I2
      K=I1
      DO 1 L=1,5
         K=I3-K
         PRINT *,K
    1 CONTINUE
```

12.8.30 Improve the names in the following code segment.

```
PARAMETER(SEVEN=6.D0)
   :
A$$$=ENDIF(N)
I=FACTORIAL(J)
I1=I+1
I1I=(I+1)*I
I11I=I1I*+I1
I1I1=I1+I1I
```

12.8.31 Simplify and disambiguate the following code segments.

```
      IF(I.NE.0) I=((I+1)/I)*(I/(I+1))
C
      A=B*C/D*E/F**G**F/E*D/C*B
C
      IF(X.GT.0.D0) THEN
         RT=DSQRT(X)
      ELSE
         IF(X.LT.0.D0) THEN
            RT=DSQRT(-X)
         ELSE
            RT=0.D0
         ENDIF
      ENDIF
```

12.8.32 Unscramble the following code segment.

```
      :
      GO TO 37
52    I=1
  11  J=I
      D=A(J,J)
      IF(D.GT.0.D0) GO TO 8
      PTR=PTR+A(I,I)
      I=J+1
      GO TO 83
37    PTR=PTR-PTR
      GO TO 52
   8 I=I+1
83    IF(I.LE.N) GO TO 11
      :
```

12.8.33 Many textbook authors condemn explicit branching altogether and insist that code should be completely free of statement numbers that are branch targets. Use a `DO` loop and the `IF-THEN` construct to rewrite the program at the top of the next page so that it does not use `GO TO`. Is the resulting code shorter, or longer, than the version given above? Which version do you think is easier to understand? Does using a bounded loop rather than a free one introduce any special problems?

```
      K=0
      M=0
   1  M=M+1
      N=M
      IF(N-3*(N/3).NE.1) GO TO 1
      N=2*(N/3)
      IF(N-3*(N/3).NE.1) GO TO 1
      N=2*(N/3)
      IF(N-3*(N/3).NE.1) GO TO 1
      N=2*(N/3)
      IF(N-3*(N/3).NE.0) GO TO 1
      PRINT *,M
      K=K+1
      IF(K.EQ.2) STOP
      GO TO 1
      END
```

12.8.34 Write a lowly subprogram to simplify the following replicate code.

```
A=(X(1)+X(2)+X(3))/(Y(1)+Y(2)+Y(3))
B=(Y(1)+Y(2)+Y(3))*(W(1)+W(2)+W(3))
C=(W(1)+W(2)+W(3))/(Z(1)+Z(2)+Z(3))
D=(Z(1)+Z(2)+Z(3))*(X(1)+X(2)+X(3))
```

12.8.35 In §12.6.2 it is recommended to keep a program's version number in the preamble of the main routine, and also to write it out. Suggest a simple way to ensure that the number in the preamble always agrees with the one that is printed.

12.8.36 Improve the following code segment:

```
   1  P=Z
   2  Q=P
   3  IF(Q.GT.EPS) THEN
   4  P=EPS
   5  ENDIF
   6  Z=P
   7  N=10
   8  DO 10 I=1,N
   9  X(I)=Z
  10  CONTINUE
```

12.8.37 Improve the following subprogram:

```
      FUNCTION SINC(X)
      REAL*8 SINC,X
      SINC=DSIN(X)/X
      RETURN
      END
```

12.8.38 What output is printed by the program at the top of the next page? Explain why, and confirm your answer by experiment. Does this suggest any pitfalls in the way FORTRAN treats blanks?

```
      I=0
      DO 10 I=1.10
          PRINT *,I
   10 CONTINUE
      STOP
      END
```

12.8.39 What output format should be used to print a floating-point value that is calculated precise to $\pm 10\%$?

12.8.40 Explain the steps in hand-checking the source code of a routine. What are The Three Questions to ask about each symbol in the variable list?

12.8.41 Write a program to test the DSQRT routine and use it to validate the function on your computer.

13

Archaic, Unusual, and Dangerous Usages

> "The trouble with people is not that they don't know
> but that they know so much that ain't so." [131]

How many different Classical FORTRAN programs can we write with 7 characters or fewer, not counting blanks? Using the language elements I have covered so far, this is the only one.

```
    STOP
    END
```

If we let the source text get longer, the number of character combinations that are syntactically legal and semantically meaningful programs increases very quickly. The total grows even faster if we include the FORTRAN statements that I have intentionally omitted until now (listed in the **Omissions** Section of each chapter). For source lengths typical of real applications, the number of possible programs in Classical FORTRAN is unimaginably huge, though it is dwarfed by the number of legal PL1, C, or Ada programs or, as we shall see in §17.1, by the number of legal Fortran-90 programs. Of course, only a tiny fraction of the possible programs in any language do something useful, and only a tiny fraction of those have the desirable attributes listed in §12.1.

In the early days of programming, the teaching of FORTRAN consisted mainly of reciting the manufacturer's compiler manual, after which the student was on his or her own to be creative in using the statements, operators, variable types, and logical constructs of the language. The resulting haphazard approach to coding led over the years to the creation of some pretty bizarre programs, many of which are unfortunately still with us and in constant, buggy use. To this day one occasionally hears of a contest to write the strangest possible legal FORTRAN program, and the results are astonishing, and very funny, to behold [170]. Sadly, many people with more modern training also use FORTRAN in foolish ways unwittingly, even when they are writing new applications that are supposed to be dead serious. Tomorrow's nightmare programs are taking shape even as you read these words.

In this book, I have tried very hard to select a minimal adequate subset of FORTRAN and to illustrate only the safest and most civilized ways of using it. By doing this I have revealed to you only a tiny sheltered garden in the vast wilderness of legal coding. As explained in §0.2, FORTRAN grew wild for a long time and wound up full of bad ideas and idiotic features. Nobody should think of using these things, so I haven't taught them to you. Some readers may find this paternalistic attitude offensive, and if so I apologize. But it was for your own good.

If you've gotten this far you are now grown up (though perhaps not yet mature) as a FORTRAN programmer, so you are entitled to make your own personal variations on the style I suggested in §12.4, and you might decide to use some language features that I have found it prudent to avoid. But please be careful. The power of the Dark Side is seductive, and the penalty for yielding to it is nasty, incorrect, incomprehensible code that you will curse, and for which people will curse you, possibly for decades to come. Beauty may be only skin deep, but ugly, as they say, goes to the bone.

So that you will recognize some of the many things *not* to do, and so that you will be prepared to deal with the legacy codes and other junk programs you will probably encounter, we must now discuss, in a candid and adult way, some of the unpleasant things that lurk out there beyond the safety of the garden wall. Thus if §12 can be regarded as a collection of positive commandments, this chapter contains a lot of negative ones.

This is also the logical place for me to describe some other usages that are not especially treacherous but are just peculiar or old-fashioned. To distinguish the merely odd or somewhat risky from the truly toxic, I will mark the latter with a ☠ skull-and-crossbones symbol.

Sections 1-10 of this chapter each address topics in the subject of the corresponding chapter of the book. Thus, for example, since §1 is an introduction to the source form of FORTRAN programs, §13.1 discusses archaic, unusual, and dangerous usages related to the arrangement of source text.

13.1 Source Form

The FORTRAN-77 standard permits some variation in the layout of source code, and many compilers provide extensions that permit even more. Older FORTRAN-66 programs often have other typographical idiosyncrasies.

13.1.1 Sequence Numbers

Before the invention of timesharing, the usual way to input programs and data to a computer was on punch cards. These came 2000 to a box, and to read in an application of modest size often required handling several boxes. It was not uncommon for the programmer or the operator of the card reader to drop some or all of the cards on the floor, which usually put them out of order. The only insurance against this disaster was to punch a **sequence number** in columns 73-80 of each card, so that if they got scrambled they could (albeit at some inconvenience) be put back in order using a mechanical card sorter.

A program that is stored in a disk file is not at risk of having its statements rearranged in this way so there is no longer a need for sequence numbers, but many legacy codes still carry them. This wastes a lot of disk space, for storing not only the sequence numbers but also the blanks that separate them from the ends of the statements. Sequence numbers also make it inconvenient to edit the text of the statements. Deleting a character from a statement moves the leftmost character of its sequence number into column 72, where it is visible to the compiler and either constitutes a syntax error or changes the meaning of the code.

Whenever you are confronted with a program that has sequence numbers, use an editor or a program like the one described in Exercise 10.9.17 to remove them and the trailing blanks that result from their removal.

13.1.2 Dead Code

Another category of vestigial source text is FORTRAN statements that can never be executed. This **dead code** comes in two varieties, statements that are branched around and statements that have been turned into comments.

☠ Code that is unconditionally branched around, so that it can never be reached, is usually the result of someone deciding it is wrong but not being absolutely sure, or intending to someday return and fix it. Never preserve work in progress this way. Unreachable code makes the text needlessly bigger, which compromises the locality of the parts of the code that are alive. If a reader doesn't realize the code segment is dead, it also increases the cognitive complexity of the routine it infests, and if it contains errors the reader might waste time trying to understand and fix them when they are actually irrelevant to the program. The place for unreachable statements that might someday be of interest is in a separate file, perhaps referred to by a single comment where the corrected code would go. The compiler can sometimes detect unreachable statements and issue a warning about them, but not always; see §13.11.

Code that is "commented out" by a C in column 1 might really be of no current interest, in which case it should be treated just like code that is unconditionally branched around. Often, though, PRINT statements that are commented out are meant to be used occasionally for debugging. Such statements should be made conditional on the value of a DEBUG variable or made into debug comments, as described in §14.3.3. Code segments that are periodically commented or uncommented to change the behavior of a routine are fruitful sources of bugs due to errors made in that process.

13.1.3   Free-Form Source ☠

Many compilers permit departures from the fixed source form described in §1, including statements that begin to the left of column 7 or extend beyond column 72, continuation lines denoted differently from the way we have studied, and even case-sensitive names (so that, for example, Abc is something different from aBc). There is little to be gained in clarity or ease of coding from using these extensions, and they have some serious drawbacks.

As discussed in §12.4.4, using *any* extension makes your code less portable. Compilers differ in the free source form they allow, so a program written for one system might not compile on another. Also, some utilities for manipulating source code expect it to have the fixed source form.

Perhaps even more important, as discussed in §12.4.5 typographical consistency makes it much easier for humans to manipulate and read the source text of a program. It is of course possible in using free source form to depart from the fixed source form in a consistent way, in effect creating an alternative fixed form. Unfortunately such a new personal "standard" will not be enforced by the compiler, so adhering to it will take extra attention in coding, and because it differs from the conventional fixed form it will place an added cognitive load on the reader.

Making names case-sensitive violates the advice in §12.4.2 to pick names that won't easily be confused.

Thus, much as it might appeal to our philosophical conviction that liberty and choice are always preferable to limits and rules, freedom in the source form of FORTRAN programs is far better contemplated than exercised. By all means be daring and different in your *ideas,* which is after all where freedom matters most, but stick to the fixed source form for expressing them in code.

13.1.4   INCLUDE Files ☠

In some applications, several routines need to contain the same line or lines of source text. For example, each routine might use the statements at the top of the next page to access and dimension the array A, which is in COMMON storage. Such repeating text segments are replicate code (see §12.2.2) and introduce the risk that some of the copies might be

```
C       there are at most 37 rivets in an assembly
        COMMON /SNOT/ A
        REAL*8 A(37)
```

overlooked in making a change that should affect them all. This sort of error might be made less likely by moving the code that is to be replicated into a separate file, and somehow copying that file back into the source text at all the appropriate places before compilation. Then there would be only one file to edit, and the new version would automatically be replicated to all the places where it is needed.

The file containing the master version of the code to be replicated is called an **include file**, and in a UNIX™ environment there are two different ways to get it copied into the source text of a program. The first way is to use #include **directives** that are expanded by the C preprocessor program cpp, which is briefly discussed in §14.3.3. The second way is to use the FORTRAN INCLUDE statement, which is recognized by most modern compilers. Thus, if we move the code segment above into a file named, say, setmaxrv.f, we can replace each of its occurrences in the program by this statement.

```
        INCLUDE 'setmaxrv.f'
```

Now, before compiling the program, f77 will replace each INCLUDE by the contents of the file it names. An INCLUDE file can contain any text at all, including not only COMMON statements and type declarations but also PARAMETER statements, executable code, and even other INCLUDE statements.

The trouble with INCLUDEs is that they destroy the locality of the source text (see §12.3.2) and thereby make it much more difficult to understand. Unless we happen to know the contents of setmaxrv.f, and keep them in mind, it is hard to guess what effects it will have in a routine that INCLUDEs it. This kind of ignorance seldom turns out to be bliss. One obvious danger is that we might give some local variable a name that happens to be used in the hidden COMMON block. Legacy codes and other nightmare programs, especially those that make extensive use of COMMON storage, often have many different include files, so to understand a single routine it might be necessary to simultaneously keep in mind not one but several foreign code segments, possibly much longer than the one in our little example. As mentioned in §12.4.3, an important principle of clear exposition in FORTRAN programming is to be explicit rather than using constructs in which the mechanism of action is concealed, and there is no more opaque way of concealing code than to put it in another file altogether! Of course the inner workings of a subprogram are also concealed by putting its source in another place, but its effects, unlike those of INCLUDEd code, are (or at least should be) clearly defined and delimited by a visible calling sequence. Often it is desirable when using COMMON to hide information (see §12.2.2) by using short blocks (see §8.3.1) in some routines, and this is not possible if the COMMON block is brought into all of them by using INCLUDE.

Thus, unfortunately, at the same time INCLUDE files make it less likely that you will err by missing some piece of a global change, they greatly increase the odds that you will make the *wrong* change because you misunderstand the code. INCLUDE files make it easier to maintain a program that doesn't work anyhow because no one can figure it out. It is much better to avoid replicate code, by finding the right information-hiding structure for the program, than it is to automate the replications with INCLUDE. If replicate code is really unavoidable and you must make global changes, it is better to edit by hand (if this is too difficult, the program is too big) or with UNIX™ tools such as the **changeall** shell script described in §18.6 (if this is unreliable, the code is not typographically consistent).

Readers familiar with the C programming language might protest that there is nothing to fear from `INCLUDE` files because every C program uses some. In C it is indeed essential to use `#include` directives to define certain parts of the language, such as the routines used for I/O, but that is not true of FORTRAN. All of FORTRAN is known to the compiler, so the only use for `INCLUDE` in a FORTRAN program is the one described in this section, and it is never unavoidable.

13.1.5 The `PROGRAM` Statement

We are used to giving names to `SUBROUTINE` and `FUNCTION` *sub*programs, but until now our programs have all been referred to by the compiler (and occasionally by us) as `MAIN`. This is really just a default, which can be overridden by using the `PROGRAM` statement as shown below.

```
PROGRAM HELLO
PRINT *,'Hello, world!'
STOP
END
```

Now the compiler, during its internal deliberations, will refer to the main program as `HELLO` rather than as `MAIN` (we might glimpse fleeting evidence of this in the compiler's messages about how the translation is going).

Of course, the name given in the `PROGRAM` statement does not necessarily have anything to do with the name of the UNIX™ file in which the source text of the program is stored, and `f77` still uses `a.out` for the executable (unless we specify another name as described in §14.1). So the name given in a `PROGRAM` statement turns out not to actually be used in any of the places where we need to refer to the program, unless we manually give the source and executable files related names (such as `hello.f` and `hello` for the above example). We might as well have named the program in a comment near the beginning of the code, rather than with `PROGRAM`. Having a name in the listing might help a reader recall what program this is, but it also introduces the risk of forgetting to change the file names if the program name gets changed later, or forgetting to change the program name if the file names change.

If the `PROGRAM` name agrees with the file names it really doesn't add much, and if it disagrees it introduces some unnecessary confusion, so it is probably safest to leave it out and use the name of the source file to identify the code.

13.1.6 No `STOP` Statement

Recall from §1.1 that the FORTRAN statements `STOP` and `END` play quite different roles. `STOP` can appear any number of times in a program, and is executed as an unconditional transfer of control back to the operating system. `END`, in contrast, merely denotes the end of the source text for the current routine, so it is *not* executable and must appear exactly once, as the last statement, in every main program or subprogram. Often `END` is immediately preceded by `STOP` in a main program or by `RETURN` in a subprogram, but any other unconditional transfer of control is also permissible. The example at the top of the next page is legal (if silly) and stops in a way that is not unusual.

When the executable statement preceding `END` in a main program is *not* an unconditional transfer of control, many compilers assume that `STOP` was intended and generate a branch back to the operating system. Because of this automatic correction of an apparent mistake,

```
       I=10
     1 IF(I.EQ.0) STOP
       I=I/2
       PRINT *,I
       GO TO 1
       END
```

STOP can actually be omitted when STOP END is intended, as in the example on the left below. This saves a tiny amount of typing, but it makes the program quite a bit harder to read.

```
       I=10                               I=10
     1 IF(I.GT.0) THEN                   1 IF(I.GT.0) THEN
         I=I/2                               I=I/2
         PRINT *,I                           PRINT *,I
         GO TO 1                             GO TO 1
       ENDIF                               ENDIF
       END                                STOP
                                          END
```

To understand the flow of control, we must figure out how the program stops and mentally fill in the missing STOP statement. It is better to save the reader this effort by coding an explicit STOP as in the program on the right. Relying on the compiler to generate the transfer of control violates the principle that explicit is best.

In some environments a termination message is produced when the executable for a FORTRAN program is run, and that message might be different depending on whether the transfer of control back to the operating system was coded explicitly with STOP or generated automatically by the compiler. Some older compilers flag a missing STOP as an error.

13.1.7   Star and Blank Comments

We have always denoted comments by coding a C in column 1, but in FORTRAN-77 it is also permissible to use c or * for the comment character, and to use an entirely blank line in place of a blank comment.

Mixing the various forms in the same program is a violation of the principle, stated in §12.4.5, that it is usually best to be typographically consistent. Using one style throughout makes the code both easier to edit using UNIX™ power tools and easier for humans to read. The asterisk * already has enough meanings in FORTRAN programs without giving it yet another as the comment character, and there are still FORTRAN-66 compilers out there that don't accept * or c.

13.1.8   Other Continuation Characters

We have always used a ; in column 6 as the continuation character, but it is actually permissible to use any nonblank character *except the numeral zero, which is ignored.* In the days of punch cards, people often serialized multi-line statements by putting a 0 in column 6 of the first card, 1 in column 6 of the first continuation card, 2 in column 6 of the second continuation card, and so forth, as an aid to keeping the cards in the right order when they were handled for keypunching revisions. Other popular choices in more modern code are +, -, and *.

The trouble with continuation characters that have some other meaning in FORTRAN is that they can make the code harder to read, as in the example below

```
X=Y**2*Z+W                          X=Y**2*Z+W
**2.5                               ;*2.5
```

Is that `X=Y**2*Z+W**2.5` on the left, or `X=Y**2*Z+W*2.5`? It would be better to avoid the continuation altogether, of course, but at least the code on the right is less likely to be misunderstood.

It is also remotely possible for a continuation character that winds up in the wrong column to change the meaning of the code rather than causing a compilation error, or to result in a misleading error message that sends you on a wild goose chase. In this example, the line runs up to column 72 and is then continued with a `C` in column 6.

```
      REAL*8 XLONGA(10),THICK,WALLT/39.D0/,W/37.D0/
      :
      XLONGA(ILONGA+2*JLONGA)=XLONGA(ILONGA+3*JLONGA)+3721.54D0*THICK+W
      CALLT
```

If the continuation line is accidentally typed one column to the right, we get the code below, in which the assignment statement ends by adding in `W`, rather than `WALLT`, and the next line is interpreted by the compiler as `CALL T`.

```
      REAL*8 XLONGA(10),THICK,WALLT/39.D0/,W/37.D0/
      :
      XLONGA(ILONGA+2*JLONGA)=XLONGA(ILONGA+3*JLONGA)+3721.54D0*THICK+W
      CALLT
```

Similarly obscure mixups can result from a numeral that should have been a continuation character winding up in column 5 where it appears to be a statement number. The use of a semicolon for continuation seems natural to me because of its role in English; there, it marks the continuation of a sentence. However, as we shall see in 17.1, the semicolon is used in Fortran-90 to separate *different* statements that are typed on the same line, so it might confuse a Fortran-90 programmer who saw it used for continuation, and a Fortran-90 compiler that found it in the wrong column could conceivably generate unintended code rather than flagging a compilation error. If you are writing for people or compilers that might interpret a semicolon as a statement separator, or if you don't like the semicolon for some artistic reason, pick a different continuation character that has no meaning in your context. It might be tempting to favor the ampersand `&` because it can denote continuation in Fortran-90 (though in a different way, not discussed in this book). Unfortunately, ampersand was also used in FORTRAN-66 for alternate returns and for addition, so it is recognized by some old compilers. Another typographically suggestive choice would be `>`, but that has been appropriated by Fortran-90 as a synonym for `.GT.` (another usage that is not discussed in this book). The at-sign `@` means nothing in any version of FORTRAN (thus far) so it would be a safe choice.

13.2   Expressions and Assignment Statements

The main pitfalls to be avoided in composing expressions and assignment statements are ambiguity and needless complexity.

13.2.1   Precedence Dependencies ☠

There are many ways to code formulas that are acceptable to FORTRAN and confusing to human readers, but the worst source of ambiguity is writing an expression in such a way that a reader must remember the rules of operator precedence in order to find its value. On the left below the order of operations is clear to the compiler, but perhaps not to most humans. Is Y set to $(-x)^2$, or to $-(x^2)$?

        Y=-X**2   Y=-(X**2)

The actual meaning taken by the compiler is that shown in the code on the right. Always use just enough parentheses to disambiguate expressions that involve multiple operators. Extra parentheses have no effect on the size or execution speed of the compiled program.

13.2.2   Long Names ☠

In §12.4.2 I recommended giving variables, PARAMETER constants, functions, subroutines, and COMMON blocks names no longer than 6 characters and made up of only letters and numerals. Within those constraints, I suggested transliterating mathematics as exactly as possible and giving other variables names that are just long enough to be descriptive.

It makes sense to transcribe formulas into FORTRAN pretty much as we have written them in algebra, using symbols. Most engineers and scientists write

$$A = \tfrac{1}{2}bh$$

for the area of a triangle, so it is natural to code the calculation that way.

        A=0.5D0*B*H

If the context threatens some confusion about the meanings of A, B, and H we might instead use

        AREA=0.5D0*BASE*HEIGHT

But coding

        AREA_OF_TRIANGLE=0.5D0*BASE_OF_TRIANGLE*PERPENDCULAR_HEIGHT

makes the formula harder, not easier, to recognize. So the most important reason to avoid long names is to keep your formulas readable.

But there are other reasons for using Classical FORTRAN names, reasons that also apply to things other than variables. Long names are hard to type, easy to misspell, and hard to check (like PERPENDICULAR in the example above). They make statements longer, which increases the likelihood that continuation will be required. They also don't fit the format of the variable list for the standard preamble described in §12.3.2.

Many FORTRAN compilers that accept long names do not recognize differences beyond a certain number of characters, so it is easy to be misled into thinking variables are different when the compiler actually considers them to be the same. Some FORTRAN compilers won't accept names longer than 6 characters, or names containing the underscore _ character. Mapping names that are too long down to 6 characters usually cannot be done just by truncation, and doing it with a program that keeps different names unique yields contracted names that are unpronounceable and meaningless, so making a program with long names into one with short names can be as hard as putting toothpaste back in the tube. If you use Classical FORTRAN names, your programs can be compiled everywhere.

Most FORTRAN compilers permit the $ character in names, but that symbol has a special meaning to the UNIX™ shell and to UNIX™ utilities such as `vi`, `sed`, and `grep`, which you will need to use for manipulating your source-code files. Some other applications for manipulating FORTRAN source text, such as pretty-printers, expect Classical FORTRAN names.

13.3 Conditionals and Transfer of Control

To redirect the flow of control from its normal top-to-bottom sequence, we have used the logical `IF` statement, the `IF-THEN` construct, and occasionally the unconditional `GO TO`. FORTRAN also provides some other branching statements that are used often enough to deserve mention here.

13.3.1 ELSE IF

When we have nested `IF-THEN` constructs we have always done so by putting one inside another, as shown on the left. A few lines can be saved by using the equivalent construct shown on the right

```
IF(x) THEN                        IF(x) THEN
   statements a                      statements a
ELSE                              ELSE IF(y) THEN
   IF(y) THEN                        statements b
      statements b                ELSE
   ELSE                              statements c
      statements c                ENDIF
   ENDIF
ENDIF
```

A sequence of `ELSE IFs` can be used to handle multiple cases without the need for a deep nest of `IF-THEN-ELSE-ENDIF` constructs. Placing `IF(y) THEN` after `ELSE` is an exception to the simple rule, stated in §3.3, that `ELSE` must stand alone, so if you use `ELSE IF` you need to remember that no other `ELSE` clause can be used in this way (see Exercise 3.8.13).

13.3.2 The Computed GO TO

Classical FORTRAN also provides a multi-way branch or case statement, called the **computed** `GO TO`. It transfers control to the nth statement number in a list, where n is the value of an integer expression, as illustrated by the example at the top of the next page.

```
C     if N is 1 or 5, go to 9
C     if N is 2 or 3, go to 14
C     if N is 4, go to 2
C
      GO TO(9,14,14,2,9), N
C
C     if N is anything else, fall through to the next statement
```

On rare occasions a computed GO TO can clarify the logic of a code segment, but usually it is better to handle cases with repeated IF-THEN constructs.

13.3.3   The Arithmetic IF ☠

The standard way to test and branch in FORTRAN-II was the **arithmetic** IF statement, so many old programs are full of them. Here are two code segments to show how it works.

```
      IF(X-0.001D0) 1,2,3             C     print 10 values
C     here if X-.001 is negative            N=0
    1 X=0.D0                          37 N=N+1
      GO TO 4                             PRINT *,N
C     here if X-.001 is zero             IF(N-10) 37,58,58
    2 X=Y                             C
      GO TO 4                          58 ...
C     here if X-.001 is positive
    3 X=X-.001D0
C
    4 ...
```

The expression in parentheses must evaluate to a number, but the value can be of any real or integer data type.

Arithmetic IF statements impose a high cognitive load, because the reader must keep in mind the order of the branch targets and figure out what has to be true for the expression to come out negative, zero, or positive. Thus in the example on the right above we must make the mental deduction that N-10 $\geq$ 0 implies N $\geq$ 10 in order to understand the IF. Arithmetic IFs also lead to many statement numbers and thus often to branching that is hard to follow, as discussed in §12.4.3. The surest way to end up with spaghetti code is by starting with arithmetic IFs. Never use or tolerate them.

13.3.4   The Assigned GO TO ☠

The assigned GO TO is another ancient control structure that sometimes turns up in legacy codes. The program on the left below illustrates how it works.

```
      ASSIGN 2 to N                       N=-1
      GO TO N                             ASSIGN 2 TO N
    1 PRINT *,'at 1'                      PRINT *,N
      STOP                                GO TO N
    2 PRINT *,'at 2'                    1 PRINT *,'at 1'
      STOP                                STOP
      END                              2 PRINT *,'at 2'
                                         STOP
                                         END
```

When this program is run it prints **at 2**. The integer appearing in the ASSIGN must be a statement number in the routine where the ASSIGN is used. It is permissible to use multiple ASSIGN statements in a single routine, so that the statement number associated with the branch-target symbol (N in our example) changes during the course of program execution. This possibility imposes an extremely high cognitive load on the reader because at each transfer of control the branch target depends on the history of the flow of control up until then. Your compiler (I used **g77**) might contribute further confusion by distinguishing between the branch-target symbol and an integer variable of the same name, as shown on the right above. When that code is run it produces the output shown below.

```
-1
at 2
```

The integer variable N retains its value of −1 even after the ASSIGN has set the branch-target symbol N to the statement number 2. The surest way to lose your mind is by trying to figure out code that uses assigned GO TO statements. Never use or tolerate them.

13.3.5   Free Loops

In §3 and §4 we made loops by initializing a counter, incrementing the counter, testing it against a limit, and explicitly branching back. That is called a **free loop**, because the number of iterations it performs is limited only by the hand-wrought logic that does the incrementing, testing, and branching. The right-hand example in §13.3.3 is a free loop of that sort. Other free loops have no index at all, and test something else to terminate, as in this example.

```
1 Z=Z-EPS
  CALL VANTZ(Z)
  IF(DABS(Z).GT.EPS) GO TO 1
```

This one might do what the programmer expected if EPS is positive, but if some unforeseen development makes EPS negative, the loop will never end. That's the trouble with free loops.

As soon as we learned about DO loops in §5, we stopped coding free loops except in a few special circumstances, such as a loop of READs that is terminated by an END= exit as discussed in §9.1.3. Even in the bisection routine that has served as an example throughout the book, we made sure that the algorithm could not go on forever by coding the loop with a DO.

DO loops are **bounded**, in that the number of iterations is strictly finite as determined by the starting value, increment, and limit. Of course, in keeping with the Rules of DO Loops stated in §5.4 we must refrain from modifying those values within the loop, but that is easy to remember because the iteration control mechanism is built into the DO-CONTINUE construct rather than being custom-made by us.

Never use a free loop when you can use a DO loop instead. If you must use a free loop, try to wrap it in a DO loop (as we did in BISECT) so that it cannot run away. Control loops by counting, whenever possible, rather than by testing for a unique "flag" data value. If you must terminate a loop based on a flag, be careful to select a value that is sure to be unique, rather than choosing a "magic number" arbitrarily.

When you code a free loop of READs always provide an END= exit rather than expecting the user to interrupt the program with ^C (see §0.5.5) when the calculation is finished, even though that is explicitly condoned in at least one other programming text [74, p52].

13.4 Scalar Data Types

Most bugs in FORTRAN programs turn out to be in the data structures rather than in
the logic (I will have more to say about this in §14.3.3). That is why the hand-checking
process outlined in §12.5 devotes so much attention to ensuring that variables and constants
are described, declared, defined, and used correctly. In this section we take up several
troublesome coding practices and language features relating to the declaration and use of
scalar variables and numerical constants.

13.4.1 Mixed Mode

We have always written expressions so that each operator's operands have the same scalar
data type. For example, in an expression such as A+B we made sure that A and B were
both of the same type, such as REAL*8. If necessary, we used built-in FORTRAN functions
to explicitly convert between integer and real types and between reals of different lengths.
It is actually permissible to leave many of these conversions up to the compiler, by writing
mixed-mode expressions in which an operator such as + or = has operands of *different*
types. The example below illustrates several such **implicit type conversions**.

```
REAL*4 X,Y,A
REAL*8 Z
A=4
X=2/3*A
Y=2*A/3
Z=3.1415926535897932
```

Implicit type conversions might seem like a good idea, because the resulting code is
obviously simpler than it would be if we worried about doing the conversions explicitly, and
we can figure out the results as long as we know what the compiler will do. Unfortunately,
a human reader's cognitive load is usually increased more by having to remember the rules
for implicit type conversions than it is reduced by making the code typographically simpler.
In the code above, do X and Y turn out to be the same? Because both expressions involve
A, a REAL*4 constant set to 4.0, and both get assigned to REAL*4 variables, it would seem
reasonable for the compiler to float the 2 and the 3 in each case before doing the arithmetic.
Or does it do the integer division 2/3 first in computing X, so that the result is zero? In
computing Y, does it float the 3 and do a real division, or fix the 2*4.0 to 8 and do an
integer division? The rules are probably in your compiler manual somewhere, but it is hard
to be sure what will happen until you look them up or run an experiment. In keeping
with the principle that explicit is best, you should never rely on implicit type conversions
even if you think you know how the compiler will do them. The spectacular failure of the
first Ariane-5 rocket in 1996 was traced to a type conversion error in the Ada program
controlling its guidance system.

Some compilers ignore significant digits after the seventh or eighth in real values that are
given without a D exponent, because those digits can't be represented in a REAL*4 constant.
This would result in Z above being assigned the value 3.141593 or 3.1415927, with zeros
or random garbage in its less-significant fraction bits, even though, as a REAL*8 variable, it
could contain the full-precision value (see Exercise §4.10.14). Always use a D exponent in
writing REAL*8 literals, including 0.D0 and 1.D0, to make it clear to the compiler (and to
the reader) that they have that type.

Many compilers recognize real constants written like 3D0, without a decimal point, but for consistency with the general rule that real constants have a decimal point you should always include one, as in 3.D0 . Writing 3.0D0 might seem even clearer, but insisting on a 0 between the . and the D for every whole number would make many lines of code longer, increasing the likelihood that continuation is required. Use the .D0 form instead.

13.4.2 Generic Functions ☣

Implicit type conversions are normally not allowed in invocations of FORTRAN built-in functions. For example, the argument you pass to DSQRT must be REAL*8, and if you supply some other type instead the compiler will object. It might seem that if a REAL*4 quantity were passed, the function could just use those bits for the most significant part of the REAL*8 dummy variable and set its less significant bits to zero or at random, so that the value would be approximately right although not fully precise. This is in fact roughly what happened years ago when REAL*4 and REAL*8 scalar subprogram parameters were mixed up on computers using the IBM S/390 floating-point number representation, so some old codes contain type mismatches that were benign when the mistakes were originally made. Unfortunately, as described in §4, the bit patterns for REAL*4 and REAL*8 values in the IEEE floating-point representation that is now standard are different from one another (and from the bit patterns for integers) in ways that make type conversions by padding or truncation impossible. Old codes that used to work might now fail because of this, and function invocations must pass arguments of the right type even if you're not fussy about their precision (which you should be).

Yet it is inconvenient, and at first glance confusing, to have to use different names for the same mathematical operation depending on the type of the argument. Isn't the compiler smart enough to figure out whether SQRT or DSQRT or CDSQRT is required?

Many modern compilers will in fact try to match built-in functions to the argument types you give, provided you use the version of the function name that the compiler recognizes as **generic**. Some older compilers [16, p154] require that you also code a GENERIC statement before the first executable statement of the routine that invokes functions by their generic names. In the example below, X is REAL*8 so the first invocation of the sine routine should actually be DSIN.

```
GENERIC
REAL*8 X/3.D0/,Y        REAL*8 X/3.D0/,Y
REAL*4 Z/5./,W          REAL*4 Z/5./,W
Y=SIN(X)                Y=DSIN(X)
W=SIN(Z)                W=SIN(Z)
PRINT *,Y,W             PRINT *,Y,W
STOP                    STOP
END                     END
```

Even though the version on the left asks for SIN, the GENERIC makes the compiler use DSIN just as in the code on the right. The use of SIN to mean both SIN and DSIN is an example of **function overloading**, just as using +, -, *, and / for all types of arithmetic operands is an example of operator overloading. Function overloading plays an important role in the programming style used by the C++ language, but it has no place in Classical FORTRAN.

The use of generic function names can result in a typographical simplification of the code, which is beneficial, but because it involves a sort of implicit type conversion (of the function name) it suffers from the same drawbacks as the use of mixed mode in expressions and assignments. There are some circumstances in which it is not obvious what the compiler will do, and letting it decide is a violation of the principle that explicit is best. In Classical

FORTRAN the parameters you pass to a SUBROUTINE, or to a FUNCTION of your own, *must* match the types of the corresponding dummy arguments, so making the FORTRAN built-in functions behave differently introduces an inconsistency that must be remembered. To avoid these problems, always use the correct function name.

13.4.3 IMPLICIT ☠

According to the default naming conventions described in §2.2, integer variables start with I, J, K, L, M, or N, and real variables start with the other letters. In §4 we learned how to override these defaults with explicit type declarations, *but we did not forget the defaults*. Although some programmers explicitly declare the type of every variable, I have in this book declared only those variables that do not conform to the rules. It is possible in FORTRAN-77 to *change* the default naming conventions by making an IMPLICIT type declaration as in the example on the left below.

```
IMPLICIT REAL*8 (A-H,O-Z)          REAL*8 X
I=7                                I=7
X=DFLOAT(I)                        X=DFLOAT(I)
PRINT *,X                          PRINT *,X
STOP                               STOP
END                                END
```

The IMPLICIT statement declares that all variables beginning with the letters A-H and O-Z are to be regarded as REAL*8 (rather than REAL*4). This is more convenient than having to declare each variable that departs from the traditional defaults, but for that very reason it is, at least in the attitude it betrays, bad. It amounts to asking the compiler to look after the details of variable typing for you because you don't consider them important enough to be deserving of your attention. As discussed in §12.5, the most painless way to get programs right is to rub your nose in the code by meticulous hand-checking. IMPLICIT precludes an important part of that process by eliminating some (though usually not all) explicit type declarations.

Changing the default naming conventions violates the Principle of Least Astonishment, and requires the reader to remember what the new convention is (it might be more complicated than the simple exchange of REAL*4 for REAL*8 illustrated above). If there is a typo in the IMPLICIT statement its effects (such as unintended loss of precision) might be both subtle and widespread, making the mistake both serious and hard to find. IMPLICIT obviously violates the principle that *explicit* is best.

13.4.4 IMPLICIT NONE

There is, however, one use of IMPLICIT that is potentially beneficial, and that is to entirely *remove* the default naming conventions. This asks the compiler to require that each variable be explicitly typed, as in the example at the top of the next page. Omitting the declaration of I now constitutes an error that the compiler would flag. If you have adopted the policy that you will explicitly declare all variables, using IMPLICIT NONE will make sure that you don't overlook any.

Inserting IMPLICIT NONE temporarily, just to make the compiler report the names of all the variables you didn't declare, can be helpful in checking, and especially in finding misspelled names, even if you don't normally use it.

```
IMPLICIT NONE
INTEGER*4 I
REAL*8 X
I=7
X=DFLOAT(I)
PRINT *,X
STOP
END
```

IMPLICIT NONE obviously celebrates the principle that "explicit is best," and for that reason some people use it all the time, but it has some drawbacks. The most serious problem is that it often clutters the preamble with superfluous declarations, as illustrated by the following example.

```
IMPLICIT NONE
INTEGER*4 I,J,R,L1,L2,M,K1,L3,N        INTEGER*4 R
REAL*4 T,S,K,U,A,TT,F1,F3              REAL*4 K
  :                                      :
L1=M*R                                 L1=M*R
K=T+A                                  K=T+A
L2=L1+I                                L2=L1+I
T=S/U                                  T=S/U
  :                                      :
```

The code on the right makes it obvious that R and K are the only variables *not* conforming to the default naming rules, and these few exceptions are easy to remember as you read the code. If every variable is declared, as on the left, you will need to search for each one among the declarations in order to confirm its type. Unless you have a very good memory, you will in fact have to search for each variable's declaration over and over, *each time* you want to know its type. In a real program the missing code represented by the vertical dots could of course involve many more variables than conjectured in this example, and in that case the declarations required by IMPLICIT NONE would have to be much longer even if all of the additional variables followed the default naming conventions. In cases like this IMPLICIT NONE increases the cognitive load on the reader, making the code more difficult to understand and therefore harder, rather than easier, to get correct. If you decide to type every variable, you should at least segregate the declarations into "necessary" and "pro forma" categories, to keep the ones that actually matter easy to find.

IMPLICIT NONE can also engender a false sense of security by tempting the programmer to think that if the compiler reports no undeclared variables nothing is wrong. Lots of things can be wrong even if every variable has the correct type, so you will need to hand-check the code anyhow, and that is also the best way to make sure that you have declared everything.

13.4.5   Other Data Types

In this book I have used or mentioned variables and constants having only a few scalar data types: INTEGER*4, REAL*4, REAL*8, REAL*16, COMPLEX*8, COMPLEX*16, COMPLEX*32, LOGICAL*4, and CHARACTER*n. A few other types are standard in FORTRAN-77, and they should be used only with caution. Some compilers recognize additional *non*standard types, which should *never* be used.

Of the standard types that I have not mentioned before, the most common is INTEGER*2. Many legacy codes use 2-byte integers to conserve memory, and in rare instances that might still be a useful strategy, but it has two serious drawbacks. First, a 2-byte integer can count up to only 32767. It is easy to mistake an `INTEGER*2` for an `INTEGER*4` and inadvertently overflow the value. Second, most memory architectures need extra clock cycles to fetch a quantity that is not aligned on a word boundary, and an `INTEGER*2` has only a 50-50 chance of being word-aligned, so using them can make a program run slower.

☃ Some compilers recognize nonstandard types such as `INTEGER*8` and `BYTE`, but which are supported varies from one compiler to another. If you want your program to be portable, avoid using them.

13.4.6   Other Forms of Type Declaration

Our type declarations have always specified the length of the variable in bytes, and have sometimes included compile-time initializations, as in the statements on the right below.

```
INTEGER Y                       INTEGER*4 Y
REAL I                          REAL*4 I
DOUBLE PRECISION X              REAL*8 X/1.D0/
DATA X/1.D0/
```

In most environments, the older-style declarations on the left are equivalent to those on the right, because the default lengths for `REAL` ("single precision") and `DOUBLE PRECISION` variables are respectively 4 and 8 bytes on any machine that implements the IEEE floating-point standard. The default size of an `INTEGER` is 4 bytes except on some personal computers. But omitting the length is a violation of the principle that explicit is best, and `DOUBLE PRECISION` hardly seems an apt description for the type of variable that we use for essentially all floating-point calculations. (It would make more sense to instead refer to `REAL*4` quantities as *half* precision.) Avoid `DOUBLE PRECISION`, and give the length in all your type declarations.

The `DATA` statement predates the ability to specify compile-time initializations in type statements, and can still be used, but it should be avoided if possible. It is easier to grasp the properties of a variable when they are all specified in one place. Unfortunately, some FORTRAN compilers for personal computers do not permit the use of compile-time initializations like the one on the right above, and require that `DATA` be used instead.

The compiler or your own hand-checking might turn up variables that are declared but never actually used; if so, for the sake of clarity, remove the superfluous declarations.

13.4.7   Abuses of EQUIVALENCE

Recall from §4.6.3 that `EQUIVALENCE` associates more than one name with the same storage location. We use it routinely to refer to the same character variable both as one long unit and as an array of letters. There are some other rare occasions on which `EQUIVALENCE` is useful for overlaying variables in memory, but it is not needed in typical numerical calculations.

In antiquity `EQUIVALENCE` was sometimes a last resort to conserve memory, by using the same storage location for several different variables that were not needed simultaneously. That was risky, and storage is now cheap enough so that overlaying to save space is seldom worth the trouble.

☃ Now it is more common to find `EQUIVALENCE` abused to equate variables that used to be different. Using more than one name for the same thing makes code harder to understand. Instead, revise the code to eliminate all but one of the variable names that now mean the same thing.

13.5 Arrays and DO Loops

Some of the Rules of DO Loops given in §5.4 are enforced by the compiler, but others are not. In this section we take up the most important problems that result from breaking those rules, and discuss some oddities relating to the use of subscripted variables.

13.5.1 The DIMENSION Statement

We have always dimensioned arrays in their type statements, as on the right below.

```
REAL*8 A                        REAL*8 A(10,20)
DIMENSION A(10,20)
```

It is possible to use instead a separate DIMENSION statement, as shown on the left. As I mentioned in §13.4.6, it's usually better to state all of a variable's attributes in one place. If an array's type declaration and dimensioning are separated by intervening statements, as might happen if DIMENSION is used, it's hard to tell by looking at the type statement that A is an array, and hard to know when reading the DIMENSION statement that A is REAL*8.

13.5.2 Abuses of DO Loops ☠

One of the Rules of DO Loops actually has a dangerous exception that I refrained from mentioning in §5.4. There is a situation when a branch is permitted into the range of the loop, and that is if the flow of control got outside the loop by a branch from inside. In other words, it is permissible to have a sort of *cul de sac* of code hanging out of the loop, with branches from the range of the loop to it and back, as illustrated on the left below.

```
      DO 5 J=1,1000             DO 5 J=1,1000
         GO TO 6                   K=J*2
7        PRINT *,K                 PRINT *,K
5 CONTINUE                   5 CONTINUE
      GO TO 8                  8 ...
6 K=J*2
      GO TO 7
8 ...
```

The index keeps its value during the excursion, so the loop works as usual even though some of its logical innards are geographically elsewhere. Using this feature obviously leads to a complicated flow of control and to branching logic that is harder to follow than if the whole loop were between the DO and CONTINUE as on the right. Never branch out of a loop and then back in.

Many legacy codes violate one of the other Rules of DO Loops by using the index outside the logical body of the loop, as on the left at the top of the next page. In that example there is no branch back into the range of the loop, so the GO TO 2 takes the flow of control out of the range and the index need *not* remain defined. The variable I will have *some* value outside but, because the index is no longer needed by the loop, what the value will be depends on the compiler. So that you can be certain what your code will do without having to conduct experiments, and so that it will run the same way everywhere, use the index only inside the loop. Copy it to another variable before branching out, as illustrated

```
      DO 1 I=1,10                          Y=0.D0
          IF(X(I).GT.0.D0) GO TO 2         DO 1 I=1,10
    1 CONTINUE                                 IF(X(I).GT.0.D0) THEN
      Y=0.D0                                       Y=X(I)
      GO TO 3                                       GO TO 3
    2 Y=X(I)                                    ENDIF
    3 ...                                 1 CONTINUE
                                          3 ...
```

in §5.4, or recode the calculation so the value is not needed outside of the loop, as on the right above.

13.5.3 Abuses of CONTINUE ☠

We have always used CONTINUE to terminate a DO loop, and we have never used it for anything else. Actually, it is permissible for CONTINUE to appear anywhere in a FORTRAN program, and it is permissible to end a DO loop with any executable statement *except* a branch statement or another DO. These variations are illustrated on the left below.

```
      IF(M.LE.0) GO TO 2                   IF(M.LE.0) GO TO 2
      DO 1 L=1,M                           DO 1 L=1,M
      CONTINUE                                 K=L+9
      K=L+9                                    PRINT *,K
    1 PRINT *,K                          1 CONTINUE
      PRINT *,'done with loop'             PRINT *,'done with loop'
    2 CONTINUE                           2 X=1.D0
      X=1.D0
```

The last statement in the loop is the one that prints K, and the CONTINUE embedded in the loop does nothing. The code on the right achieves the same behavior using the coding style you have learned.

The second CONTINUE in the code on the left carries a branch target, and this is typical in legacy codes. In the punch card days many programmers used CONTINUE statements for *all* branch targets, so statement numbers could be moved by simply rearranging cards rather than repunching them.

Ending DO loops with something other than CONTINUE makes them harder to recognize, and it diminishes the visual effectiveness of indenting to show the structure of the loop. It also requires the programmer to remember the exceptions so as to avoid ending a loop with one of the forbidden statements mentioned above (what were they?). Using CONTINUE to carry branch targets makes the reader search for matching DO statements that turn out not to be there. All of this makes the code harder to read. Use CONTINUE to end every DO loop and for nothing else.

Some compilers recognize a DO-ENDDO construct in which a statement number is optional, as shown below.

```
      SUM=0.D0
      DO 1 I=1,M
          IF(X(I).EQ.0.D0) GO TO 1
          DO J=1,N
              SUM=SUM+A(I,J)
          ENDDO
    1 ENDDO
```

Each DO has a matching ENDDO, in the same way that the IF and ENDIF match in an IF-THEN construct. In the example above, the inner DO and ENDDO are not connected by a statement number, but the outer pair are so as to provide a branch target for the test. Eliminating statement numbers that are not needed reduces clutter, and that is good, but it also makes the syntax of the DO-ENDDO construct vary depending on the context in which it is used, and that is bad. Thus it is not clear that this is a dramatic improvement over the DO-CONTINUE construct. DO-ENDDO is not recognized by all compilers.

13.5.4 DO WHILE ☠

It is often natural to think of an iterative process as continuing while some logical condition remains true, so some FORTRAN compilers recognize a DO WHILE syntax that makes it possible to express the loop control directly in terms of the logical condition. In the example below, the iterations of the loop continue until it is no longer true that I-J > 4.

```
I=10
J=5
DO WHILE(I-J .GT. 4)
    I=I-1
    J=J+1
ENDDO
```

What are the values of I and J after this loop? To begin with, I-J is 5, which is greater than 4, so we execute the statement I=I-1, which leaves I equal to 9. Now I-J is 4, which is no longer greater than 4. If the loop really continues only until the condition is no longer satisfied, as its name suggests, it should end now with I=9 and J=5, and that is exactly what most beginning programmers assume it will do. This behavior would imply the operation of a hidden dæmon that checks the logical condition after each statement in the loop. Experienced programmers usually find that implausible and assume, correctly, that the test is actually performed only at the top of the loop. Thus in our example the statement J=J+1 does get executed, the logical condition is tested a second time only at the top of the loop, I-J is then equal to 3, and the loop ends with I=9 and J=6.

DO WHILE actually keeps DOing for a little while *after* the logical condition is no longer satisfied. This might seem innocuous, but if it misleads even rookies it is a bad idea. The technical meaning that we give to ordinary words must often be more precise or limiting than the plain meaning of those words, but it should not be *contradictory* to the plain meaning, and DO WHILE is. Use it at peril of being misled by your subconscious interpretation of the English, however well your conscious mind understands the true meaning of the FORTRAN. And never ever use DO WHILE (as is, alas, often deliberately done) in teaching innocents to program.

13.6 Subprograms

☠ The most egregious blunder in using subprograms is to define them by a typographical, rather than a functional, decomposition of the program. In the dark ages of programming, people would write vast stretches of open code before it occurred to them that using subroutines might make things easier. The next step was to lay out a listing of the program on a long table and draw a line across it every thousand statements or so, like slicing a salami.

Each piece could then be separated from the rest by sticking a SUBROUTINE statement to its head and a RETURN END sequence on its tail. All the variables had to go in COMMON, and the COMMON had to be included in each routine, and a main program had to be provided to call the pieces in the right order. If there were branches back across module boundaries, extra logic was needed, often involving added flag variables, to get the flow of control right. The hardest part of this process was picking names for the subroutines, since they were manufactured in an arbitrary way. Sometimes people used names like SUB01, SUB02, and so on.

If you studied §12.2.2, you should be losing your lunch right about now. Fortunately, we have learned quite a lot about structuring programs over the years. Unfortunately, FORTRAN contains some language features that, at least when they are used indiscriminately, encourage the salami-slicing approach to program decomposition. In this section we will consider some of these, along with other coding practices that can lead to disaster in the use of subprograms.

13.6.1   Alternate RETURNs ☠

Our subprograms have always RETURNed to the same place, namely the next executable statement after the CALL that invoked the subroutine or the next machine instruction in the expression that invoked the function. It is actually possible to arrange for control to be transferred somewhere else upon return to the calling routine, as illustrated in the example below.

```
      :
C     statement-number arguments are denoted by * or &
      CALL SUB(I,*12,&5)
      PRINT *,'zero'
      GO TO 9
   12 PRINT *,'even'
      GO TO 9
    5 PRINT *,'odd'
      GO TO 9
      :
C
      SUBROUTINE SUB(I,*,*)
      IF(I.EQ.0) RETURN
      IF(MOD(I,2).EQ.0) RETURN 1
      IF(MOD(I,2).EQ.1) RETURN 2
      END
```

Here SUB tests whether I is zero, even, or odd. In the first case it executes a normal RETURN, which transfers control to the statement PRINT *,'zero' in the calling program. If I is evenly divisible by 2 then I mod 2 is zero and SUB takes a RETURN 1. This transfers control back through the first * in SUB's dummy argument list and thence to statement 12 in the calling program. So that the compiler will know that the second parameter in the CALL to SUB is a statement number, it is prefixed with a *. If I is odd, SUB takes a RETURN 2, which transfers control to statement 5 in the calling program. That statement number is prefixed in the CALL by the older marker for statement-number parameters, &, which is still recognized by some compilers.

An alternate return is like a `GO TO` statement that crosses a subprogram boundary, so all of the caveats mentioned in §12.4.3 apply with added weight. Instead of alternate returns, use a return code parameter like this.

```
      :
      CALL SUB(I,KODE)
      IF(KODE.EQ.0) PRINT *,'zero'
      IF(KODE.EQ.1) PRINT *,'even'
      IF(KODE.EQ.2) PRINT *,'odd'
      GO TO 9
      :
C
      SUBROUTINE SUB(I,KODE)
      IF(I.EQ.0) KODE=0
      IF(MOD(I,2).EQ.0) KODE=1
      IF(MOD(I,2).EQ.1) KODE=2
      RETURN
      END
```

In this version `KODE` is set in `SUB` and tested in the main, and no alternate returns are needed.

13.6.2 ENTRY

Normally the entry point for a program is the beginning of the routine named `MAIN`, and the entry point for a subprogram is its `SUBROUTINE` or `FUNCTION` statement. The `ENTRY` statement is used to define an alternate entry point to a subprogram, as in the code on the left below.

```
      CALL INIT
      DO 1 I=1,10                    DO 1 I=1,10
          CALL CALC(I)                   CALL CALC(I)
    1 CONTINUE                   1 CONTINUE
      STOP                           STOP
      END                            END
C                          C
      SUBROUTINE INIT                SUBROUTINE CALC(I)
      REAL*8 PI,X                    REAL*8 PI/3.1415926535897932D0/
      PI=4.D0*DATAN(1.D0)            X=PI*DFLOAT(I)
      RETURN                         PRINT *,X
      ENTRY CALC(I)                  RETURN
      X=PI*DFLOAT(I)                 END
      PRINT *,X
      RETURN
      END
```

The call to `INIT` enters at the `SUBROUTINE` statement, computes `PI` using the formula $\pi = 4\arctan(1)$, and returns, leaving the value defined and ready for use anywhere in the subroutine. Each call to `CALC` enters the subroutine at the `ENTRY` statement and uses the value of `PI` found earlier. This avoids having to calculate `PI` on each call to `CALC`. The simpler solution shown on the right is easier to understand.

It is only on very rare occasions (such as in a routine for computing values of functions that are closely related like `SIN` and `COS`) that the use of `ENTRY` might clarify the code.

13.6.3   Abuses of Subprogram Arguments ☠

What value of N is printed by the following program?

```
N=1                          FUNCTION K(N)
N=N+1+K(N)                   N=N+1
PRINT *,N                    K=N+1
STOP                         RETURN
END                          END
```

The function K(N), in addition to returning a value, also has the **side effect** of changing N. By the rules of operator precedence, K(N) is evaluated first in the calculation of the right-hand side N+1+K(N), and the function returns a value K(1)=3. But what value of N is then used in finishing the right-hand side calculation N+1+3? It might be 1 or 2, so that after the assignment N is either 1+1+3=5 or 2+1+3=6. Using a FUNCTION subprogram in this way is technically in violation of the FORTRAN standard, but because of separate compilation the compiler can't recognize or report the infraction, and which answer we get is implementation-dependent. This main program can be rewritten so that the calculation is unambiguous, but it would be far less tricky if K(N) did not change the value of its argument.

In the example above, K(N) always increments N by 1. This side effect is troublesome only because N is used elsewhere in the expression where K(N) appears. It is also possible for side effects to make the return value from a FUNCTION subprogram depend on the history of its invocations as well as on the value of its argument, as in this example.

```
M=1                          FUNCTION L(N,M)
PRINT *,L(1,M),L(2,M)        M=M+1
M=1                          L=N*M
PRINT *,L(2,M),L(1,M)        RETURN
STOP                         END
END
```

The first PRINT prints 2 6, but the second prints 4 3. This **context effect** clearly violates the Principle of Least Astonishment, because our experience with functions in mathematics leads us to expect that the values of L(1,M) and L(2,M) should not depend on the order in which they are calculated.

Avoid side effects in writing FUNCTION subprograms, so that they behave like mathematical functions.

Because a SUBROUTINE does not return a value in its name, it can return results only by changing the values of its arguments. As discussed in §6.2, subprogram parameters are passed by address. Great care must therefore be taken to avoid passing a literal value for a parameter that will change. Below, OOPS is passed a literal but changes the value of its dummy argument.

```
CALL OOPS(7)                 SUBROUTINE OOPS(NR)
   J=I+7                     NR=5
   :                         RETURN
                             END
```

A literal like the INTEGER*4 constant 7 is typically stored by the compiler in a memory location and then used like a variable whose value is assumed not to change. Some FORTRAN environments permit a subroutine like OOPS to change the contents of the memory location containing a constant, but others do not (see Exercise 13.13.27). If OOPS changes the memory location containing 7 in our example, the assignment J=I+7 will really be computing J=I+5.

To guard against the possibility of altering a literal, some programmers adopt the policy of *never* passing a literal as a subprogram argument.

A related problem can result from passing the same actual parameter for two dummy parameters, when one or both of the dummy parameters is changed by the subprogram. Passing a single actual parameter effectively equivalences the two dummy arguments, which in some cases leads to unexpected behavior of the kind discussed in §6.2.

In other cases nothing bad happens so, although it is risky, passing the same actual parameter for two dummy parameters is not *always* an error even if one of the dummy parameters gets changed (see for example the INTINS and STRINS routines of §18.2, in which the input string and output string can be the same actual parameter and the input length and output length can be the same actual parameter, or see Exercise 6.8.9). And it is of course always safe, and often appropriate, to pass the same actual parameter for several dummy parameters if they do *not* change.

13.6.4   Call by Value

As explained in §6.2, modern FORTRAN compilers pass subprogram parameters by reference. The subprogram manipulates the contents of memory locations corresponding to the actual parameters, back in the routine where they were originally allocated. Some old compilers [16] passed arrays by reference but passed scalar subprogram parameters **by value**. Instead of using the storage location named by the actual parameter, a subprogram made a local copy of the value, changed it if necessary, and replaced the value in the calling routine only upon return. To override this default behavior and insist that a scalar parameter be passed by reference instead, these compilers recognized the syntax

```
CALL OLDSUB(/I/)
```

in which surrounding a parameter by slashes meant "transmit this by reference." Old codes using this syntax can be updated for most modern compilers by simply omitting the slashes. On the other hand, old code in which scalar subprogram arguments are written *without* slashes might depend on the value in the caller not being replaced until the subprogram returns.

13.6.5   Functions Without Arguments

All of our FUNCTION subprograms have had at least one argument, but it is actually permissible for the argument list to be empty as in the following example.

```
REAL*8 PI
PRINT *, PI()
STOP
END
FUNCTION PI()
REAL*8 PI
PI=4.D0*DATAN(1.D0)
RETURN
END
```

To distinguish a function having no arguments from an ordinary variable, the former must be written with an empty set of parentheses () as shown.

Functions without arguments are typically used to return a constant, as in this example (in which case they can easily be replaced by PARAMETER constants), or to return a value that is based on information passed to the function in COMMON, or they are UNIX™ system routines such as the IARGC function mentioned in §14.2.4. (Readers familiar with the C programming language, in which UNIX™ is written, will recall that C has *only* function subprograms.)

A FUNCTION subprogram with no arguments might clarify the coding in some rare instances, but it is another departure from our expectation that FORTRAN functions will be like mathematical functions. In calculus class we learn that a mathematical function expresses a relationship between a dependent variable and one or more independent ones, so, at least in the kind of applied mathematics that engineers and scientists commonly use, it doesn't make sense to talk about a mathematical function with no arguments. Empty parentheses () are an unusual occurrence in FORTRAN source text, so it is also easy to mistake them for the letter O or the numeral 0, especially on a paper listing.

13.6.6   Statement Functions

When the same calculation must be performed in several different places, our usual approach has been to write a FUNCTION or SUBROUTINE subprogram. A subprogram is compiled separately from the routines that invoke it, so it can be used anywhere and its object code can be stored separately in a .o file or library as described in §14.5.

FORTRAN also provides a way to define a brief calculation as a **statement function** that is strictly local to the routine in which it is used.

```
      REAL*8 A,F,X,Y, G,H,P
      F(X,Y)=DSQRT(A*DSIN(X)+(1.D0-A)*DCOS(Y))
C
C -----------------------------------------------------------------
C
      A=0.9D0
      G=F(2.5D0,0.1D0)
      H=F(2.5D0,G)
      P=F(F(H,0.1D0),G)
      :
```

Here F(X,Y) is a statement function that tells how to compute F using the dummy arguments X and Y and the regular variable A. The definition itself is not executed, and it must appear before the first executable statement, but it must also follow the declarations of any variables it uses. That means that in commented code it belongs in the preamble just above the line (see §12.3.2).

A statement function's definition must consist of only a single statement, it can be invoked only within the routine where it is defined, and its name cannot be passed as an EXTERNAL argument to a subprogram. These restrictions severely limit the applicability of statement functions, and even when a calculation can be expressed in one it might be worthwhile to write it as a subprogram instead so that it can be used in other places as well. Thus, statement functions are useful only rarely, for calculations that are simple enough to fit in one statement and so specialized as to be of little interest outside of a single routine.

13.6.7   Archaic Names for Built-In Functions

In very old programs you might discover references to functions named ATANF, ABSF, COSF, EXPF, LOGF, SINF, or SQRTF. These were the built-in elementary mathematical functions of FORTRAN-II, and correspond to the modern REAL*4 built-in functions having the same names without the trailing F.

13.7 Adjustable Dimensions and EXTERNAL

The major pitfalls in the use of adjustable dimensions are discussed at length in §7.1, and the consequences of omitting an EXTERNAL declaration are explained later in §14.3.2, so it remains to point out here only some oddities you might encounter in other people's code.

13.7.1 Arrays Dimensioned (1)

In a subprogram, the dimension of a vector parameter (or the trailing dimension of an array parameter having more than one dimension) can be given as an integer constant, or as an integer variable that also appears in the parameter list of the subprogram, or as *. We use * for the adjustable dimension when it is inconvenient or impossible to pass the actual dimension as a parameter, and think of it as implying that we mean to respect the dimension that was given where the array was originally declared. The code on the right below uses such an adjustable dimension.

```
      REAL*8 X(100),Y,SUM                    REAL*8 X(100),Y,SUM
      :                                      :
      Y=SUM(X,N)                             Y=SUM(X,N)
      :                                      :
C                              C
      FUNCTION SUM(X,N)                      FUNCTION SUM(X,N)
      REAL*8 SUM,X(1)                        REAL*8 SUM,X(*)
      SUM=0.D0                               SUM=0.D0
      IF(N.LE.0) RETURN                      IF(N.LE.0) RETURN
      DO 1 J=1,N                             DO 1 J=1,N
          SUM=SUM+X(J)                           SUM=SUM+X(J)
    1 CONTINUE                             1 CONTINUE
      RETURN                                 RETURN
      END                                    END
```

Apparently N can be zero or even negative in this example, so it wouldn't make much sense to adjustably dimension the vector X(N). It might be a good idea to pass the 100 in a third parameter to SUM and use it as the adjustable dimension (that would also allow us to verify that N does not exceed it) but here we have simply used a *. FORTRAN-66 did not recognize the * syntax, but it didn't check for subscript overflows either, so any positive constant dimension could be used just to show the compiler that a variable was an array. It became the custom in those cases to use 1 in the same way that we use * today, so many legacy codes have arrays adjustably dimensioned (1) as in the code on the left above.

It is a great inconvenience to have adjustable dimensions of 1, because if we use the compiler flag that generates checks for array subscript overflow, as discussed in §14.1.2, it will treat the 1 as an actual limit and report an error every time it is exceeded. Also, some old programs use adjustable dimensions of 1 even in cases where the actual size of an array is passed as an argument and could have been used instead, which would have helped to make the code understandable. Whenever you run into an adjustable dimension of 1, change it to the actual array size, if that is available as a parameter, or to * if the actual size is not passed.

13.7.2   Overuse of EXTERNAL

If the name of one subprogram is passed as an argument to another, the passed name must be declared EXTERNAL. We saw this in our study of BISECT, where we passed as a parameter the name of the function whose zero was to be found. This let us use BISECT to find the zeros of several different functions, each defined by its own FUNCTION subprogram.

Some programmers (not having read §7.2) make the mistake of declaring *all* subprogram names EXTERNAL, including those that are *not* passed to other subprograms as arguments. The documentation for at least one major commercial scientific subroutine library [26] contains hundreds of example programs in which this is done. (The examples given in that and other library manuals have for generations provided naïve programmers with the seed crystals of their eventual nightmare codes.) Declaring as EXTERNAL names that aren't is harmless to the program, but it is confusing to a programmer who understands what EXTERNAL means. Seeing several names given that attribute raises the expectation that they will indeed be passed as parameters and so makes it harder to understand a program in which it turns out that they are not.

13.8   COMMON

Just as the use of a GO TO statement can on rare occasions simplify a program's control flow, so the use of COMMON storage can occasionally simplify a program's data structures and contribute to data hiding. But abuses of COMMON storage do to the organization of a program's data what abuses of the GO TO statement do to the organization of a program's branching logic, and that makes COMMON the single most common source of errors in FORTRAN programs. This section describes some egregious practices to avoid, and also introduces the harmless but new idea of unnamed COMMON.

13.8.1   Indiscriminate Use of COMMON ☠

As discussed in §8.2, COMMON is unavoidable when data must be sent *around* a library or multi-use subprogram, from the routine that calls it to a routine that it calls. There are also a few situations in which COMMON could be avoided but proves useful in simplifying the organization of data, such as when a table of constants that changes from run to run, but not within a run, must be made accessible to many routines independent of the flow of control, as discussed in §11.4. But programmers are constantly tempted to use COMMON in other circumstances as well, as a way of getting data where it is needed in a program that has somehow come to have the wrong structure for passing the data in formal parameters. Many legacy codes make no pretense of having a logical structure like that described in §12.2.2, and pass *all* subprogram parameters in COMMON blocks. There are several reasons for resisting this temptation, even if doing so means rethinking and rewriting the program to get the structure right.

Passing any parameters at all in COMMON discourages subprogram reuse, because it fixes which variables (i.e., what locations in memory) those parameters are. In the example shown at the top of the next page, SUB is needed twice, and before each invocation its parameters must be copied to the variables in /PARS/.

```
C     passing parameters in COMMON
      COMMON /PARS/ I,J,K                      SUBROUTINE SUB
      :                                        COMMON /PARS/ I,J,K
      I=M(1)                                   K=I+J
      J=M(2)                                   RETURN
      CALL SUB                                 END
      PRINT *,K
      I=N(1)
      J=N(2)
      CALL SUB
      PRINT *,K
      STOP
      END
```

If there are lots of parameters in COMMON, copying them in and out is a big nuisance, so the further temptation arises to instead copy the *subprogram* and send the correct data to each clone in a separate COMMON block, as shown below. The routine SUB2 is replicate code, because its logical content and function are identical to those of SUB1. The program is longer and harder to understand, and when a bug is found in SUB1 somebody must remember that it also needs to be fixed in SUB2. As mentioned in §12.2.2, replicate code should be avoided if at all possible. If it occurs to you that the replication might be minimized by using an INCLUDE file for the parts of SUB1 and SUB2 that are the same, then your journey to the Dark Side is complete! As the cartoon character Pogo might exclaim, "We have met the enemy, and they is us!"

```
C     cloning to avoid copying data
      COMMON /PARS1/ M,K1                      SUBROUTINE SUB1
      COMMON /PARS2/ N,K2                      COMMON /PARS1/ L,K
      :                                        K=L(1)+L(2)
      CALL SUB1                                RETURN
      PRINT *,K1                               END
      CALL SUB2                    C
      PRINT *,K2                               SUBROUTINE SUB2
      STOP                                     COMMON /PARS2/ L,K
      END                                      K=L(1)+L(2)
                                               RETURN
                                               END
```

In the simpler COMMON-free code shown below, the subroutine has formal parameters that can be given different values on the different calls.

```
C     passing formal parameters    C     this subroutine is reused
      :                                        SUBROUTINE SUB(L,K)
      :                                        INTEGER*4 L(2)
      CALL SUB(M,K)                            K=L(1)+L(2)
      PRINT *,K                                RETURN
      CALL SUB(N,K)                            END
      PRINT *,K
      STOP
      END
```

The pitfalls hinted at above are only the beginning of the trouble with COMMON. Most programs have lots of subprograms, each needing access to a different subset of data values, and some values are needed by more than one of the subprograms. For example, SUBX might need A and B, but SUBY might need A and C. If we use one COMMON block to share data with SUBX and another to share data with SUBY, there is a problem because A can be in only one of the COMMON blocks, so copying is again needed. On the other hand, if we put all three variables in one COMMON block, then each subprogram receives data that it otherwise would not need to know about, which is a violation of the data-hiding principle. The only way to be sure of avoiding this is to put each variable in its own COMMON block, but that usually results in an unmanageable number of them. In programs that use COMMON to pass subprogram parameters, it often turns out that even though there are a great many COMMON blocks, most of them are needed in most of the routines. In the worst case, every variable is present everywhere and the main advantages of modularity are lost.

Finally, the use of COMMON introduces the possibility of wonderfully obscure errors due to inadvertent misalignments and type mismatches, none of which, thanks to separate compilation, are detectable by the compiler. (The alignment of variables in COMMON is discussed in §8.3.) Of course, these considerations again suggest using INCLUDE files to automate the copying of the COMMON block definitions.

All of this is *madness*. COMMON blocks and INCLUDE files are the warts and toenails of FORTRAN programming. If you find it necessary to use COMMON for anything except sending data around a library routine, as discussed in §8.2, you should suspect that there is something wrong with the way the program has been decomposed into subprograms.

13.8.2   Extending COMMON by EQUIVALENCE ☠

Consider the code segment on the left below, in which EQUIVALENCE is used to make Y(1) occupy the same memory location as X(2).

```
C     main program                    C     subprogram
      COMMON /LONG/ X                        COMMON /LONG/ Z
      REAL*8 X(3),Y(3)                       REAL*8 Z(4)
      EQUIVALENCE(Y(1),X(2))                 :
      :
```

This has the effect of extending the COMMON block to a length of 4 doublewords, because Y(3) now hangs out in memory beyond the end of X [87, p115]. The subprogram on the right above can now access all four values $Z(1) \equiv X(1)$, $Z(2) \equiv X(2) \equiv Y(1)$, $Z(3) \equiv X(3) \equiv Y(2)$, and $Z(4) \equiv Y(3)$. It is not allowed to extend a COMMON block *backward*, toward lower addresses, so trying to align Y(2) with X(1) would elicit a compilation error.

Extending COMMON by EQUIVALENCE was a standard trick in the early days of FORTRAN, so you might encounter it in legacy codes, but it obviously has the potential to be needlessly confusing so you should never use it yourself.

13.8.3   References Past the End of an Array ☠

Another technique that takes advantage of the contiguity of data items in COMMON is illustrated by this example.

```
      COMMON /ZERO/ W,A,B,C,D
      REAL*8 W(1),A,B,C,D
      DO 1 I=1,5
         W(I)=0.D0
    1 CONTINUE
      :
```

Here W(2) is just the address of A, and so on, so the effect of the DO loop is to initialize all of the variables in the COMMON block to zero. This will be a mystery to anybody who doesn't know the trick. It will also stop the program if you use the compiler option for subscript checking, which means you *can't* use it to find genuine subscript errors. Never refer to elements beyond the dimensioned size of an array.

13.8.4 Blank COMMON

Each FORTRAN program can contain one COMMON block that is unnamed, and which is thus referred to as **blank COMMON**. The syntax simply omits the usual slash-enclosed name, like this:

```
COMMON E,F
```

Blank COMMON is like any other COMMON block except that variables in blank COMMON *cannot* be initialized using a BLOCK DATA subprogram. It is only because of this peculiarity, and because it really isn't needed, that I have not mentioned blank COMMON until now. Blank COMMON is often used, and you might well encounter it in other people's code.

13.8.5 Arrays Dimensioned in COMMON Statements

We have always dimensioned arrays in type statements, but if an array appears in a COMMON statement it is permissible to dimension it there instead. The code segment on the right below is equivalent to that on the left.

```
COMMON /ARY/ S                    COMMON /ARY/ S(350)
REAL*8 S(350)                     REAL*8 S
```

An array can be dimensioned only once in a routine, so dimensioning S in the COMMON statement on the right means it cannot also be dimensioned in the REAL*8 declaration there.

Dimensioning an array in a COMMON statement might on rare occasions make some code easier to understand, but it is usually better to dimension arrays in their type statements. That puts the type and dimension information in one place, and it's where we are accustomed to finding the dimensions of arrays that are *not* in COMMON.

13.9 Input and Output

As mentioned in §9.9, FORTRAN I/O is a big subject and I have presented only enough of it so that you can write your own programs. In reading other people's code you might run across a wide variety of unfamiliar features. There is not enough room here to describe them all, but a few are (or were) used often enough to merit discussion.

13.9.1 Carriage Control

Once upon a time, computers wrote their output on electromechanical printers. The machines could position the fan-fold paper under their print hammers according to commands encoded in the first character of each line printed. The table on the next page lists all the

character	meaning
+	overprint the previous line
blank	single space
0	double space
−	triple space
6	skip to top of next sixth page
4	skip to top of next quarter page
2	skip to top of next half page
1	skip to logical top (physical line 3) of next page
:	skip to physical top of next page
8	skip to logical bottom of this page (leave 2 physical lines)
<	skip to physical bottom of this page
9	print across page boundaries

possible codes. If, for example, the printer found a 1 in column 1 it would eject enough paper to skip to the top of the next page before printing the rest of the line. Anything in column 1 that wasn't recognized as **carriage control** got printed as text, and text that looked like carriage control moved the paper instead of getting printed.

This example skips a line (because of the 0 printed in column 1 of the first line), prints K and F, then goes to the next line (single spacing because of the blank the 1X puts in column 1 of the second line) and prints X.

```
      WRITE(6,901) K,F
  901 FORMAT('0AT ITERATION',I3,' FORCE=',F7.1)
      WRITE(6,902) X
  902 FORMAT(1X,'DISPLACEMENT=',D12.6)
```

Carriage control cannot be used with laser printers and other modern output devices, nor in printing to your workstation screen. When you find carriage control in an old program, either expand it with a filter program to simulate the behavior of a line printer, such as by using the -f option of the UNIX™ lpr command (also see Exercise 13.13.38), or rewrite the FORMAT statements to produce the spacing you want on your workstation display or laser-printed page. In the example, a / would give double spacing, and the 1X could be removed.

13.9.2   Scale Factors

It is conventional in many fields of engineering and science to express very large or very small numbers using **scientific notation**, as for example the speed of light in vacuum $c = 2.99792458 \times 10^8$ m/sec. To write out a floating-point value as a fraction times a power of 10 we have used the FORMAT field specification D, which would print c as .299792458D+09 instead. FORTRAN makes it possible to move the decimal point s places by prepending a **scale factor** sP to the field specification. For example, to print c in scientific notation we could code

```
      REAL*8 C/2.99792458D+08/
      WRITE(6,901) C
  901 FORMAT('c=',1PD14.8,' m/sec')
      STOP
      END
```

which yields this output.

```
c=2.99792458D+08 m/sec
```

When a scale factor is used to move the decimal point in a D field, the exponent is adjusted to keep the value unchanged.

▓ A scale factor can also be used with the F field specification, but then there is no exponent to adjust so moving the decimal point *changes the value printed* as shown by the program on the left below.

```
      REAL*8 C/2.99792458D+08/              REAL*8 C/2.99792458D+08/
      WRITE(6,901) C                   C    print 100c to change units
C     print 100c to change units            WRITE(6,901) 100.D0*C
  901 FORMAT('c=',2PF12.0,' cm/sec')     901 FORMAT('c=',F12.0,' cm/sec')
      STOP                                   STOP
      END                                    END
```

Both of these programs yield this output.

```
c=29979245800. cm/sec
```

Occasionally the change in order of magnitude of the printed number is a desirable effect, as it is here where we use it to convert from meters per second to centimeters per second. This sort of scaling is implicit, however, which violates the rule that explicit is best, and many a programmer has been led on a merry chase looking everywhere else for a missing or extra power of ten in the output. In this example it is better to calculate $100c$ explicitly, as on the right above. Either kind of scaling calls for a comment to explain what is happening.

▓ Some FORTRAN-66 compilers [16, p65] treat scale factors as **sticky;** once the program's flow of control encounters an I/O statement that uses a scale factor, that scale factor remains in effect until another one is encountered. If the scale factor is sticky this program prints the output shown below.

```
      REAL*8 X/1.D0/,Y/2.D0/,Z/3.D0/
      WRITE(6,901) X,Y,Z
  901 FORMAT(F4.1,1X,1PD8.1,1X,F4.1)
      STOP
      END
```

```
 1.0 2.0D+00 30.0
```

A sticky scale factor can mysteriously scale fields that are located far away in the source code from the original application of the scale factor, in different FORMAT statements. If you are using a compiler that does this, you should code a 0P scale factor wherever you want a scale factor of zero (that is, no scaling). The output from a legacy code that was written to depend on a sticky scale factor can change when the program is ported to a compiler that applies scaling only to the field where it is specified.

13.9.3   Hollerith Strings in FORMATs

In §10.1 we used Hollerith constants for defining single characters, as in

```
CHARACTER*1 EXX
EXX=1Hx
```

which sets EXX to the bit pattern representing the lower-case letter x. Character strings enclosed in single quotes did not become part of FORTRAN until FORTRAN-77, so many legacy codes put output labels in FORMAT statements by using Hollerith constants, as on the left below.

```
    WRITE(6,901) I,J,X(I,J)              WRITE(6,901) I,J,X(I,J)
901 FORMAT(2HX(,I2,1H,,I2,2H)=,F5.1)  901 FORMAT('X(',I2,',',I2,')=',F5.1)
```

The constant 2HX(has the character-string value X(because the 2 in front of the H indicates that the value is the 2 characters following the H. The need to count characters introduces the possibility that you will count them wrong, as in 3HX(,I2 which makes the comma part of the string. Whenever you run into character literals specified by Hollerith constants in a FORMAT specification, change them to quoted strings as on the right above (except for the single-quote character, which must be doubled or handled as described in §10.1).

13.9.4   Printing Leading Zeros

When an In field specification is used to print an integer having fewer than n characters, the FORTRAN I/O library prints leading blanks before the first digit (or before the sign, if the value is negative). Occasionally it is desirable to print leading *zeros* instead of blanks, so many modern FORTRAN implementations provide an I$n.m$ field specification for doing that. In this form, n is the total field width and m is the number of columns that must be made nonblank, if necessary by printing leading zeros. The following program produces the output shown below the listing.

```
    DO 1 I=1,5
        WRITE(6,901) 13**I
901     FORMAT(I7.5)
  1 CONTINUE
    STOP
    END
```

```
 00013
 00169
 02197
 28561
371293
```

13.9.5   Formatted READs

As explained in the introduction to §9, the free-format READ statement should always be used for input from the keyboard. For input from files in which the data are known to have a particular layout, it is sometimes preferable to use a fixed-format READ so that the I/O library can catch some (though not all) departures from the expected layout. The errors can then be trapped using the `ERR=` clause of the `READ` statement. For data not delimited by blanks or commas (as in Exercise 9.10.10), a fixed-format `READ` is the only choice.

In reading integer data with a fixed format, *trailing blanks are interpreted as zeros*. Thus, for example, an I4 field containing the data ⌴10⌴ is read as the value 100. In reading floating-point data with fixed format there are some other wrinkles that I did not mention in §9. Similar considerations apply to both F and D field specifications, but I will illustrate using an F since that is more commonly used in reading input from files.

A specification like F5.2 says the data will occupy 5 columns with 2 digits following the decimal point, like these numbers:

```
12.54
-8.21
+1.43
```

✎ Actually, if the decimal point is to be regarded as in the column implied by the field specification, it may be *omitted*. Thus when the following numbers are read using an F5.2 field specification, they are interpreted exactly like the numbers with decimal points given above.

```
1254
-821
 143
```

This feature was originally meant to save space on punch cards, so that more data could be squeezed into 80 columns, but having input records of limited length is seldom a problem with disk files. Leaving out the decimal points makes an input file much more difficult for humans to compose and check, because to interpret the data you need to know what field specification is being used to read them.

If a decimal point is given, it actually need not be in the column implied by the field specification. A decimal point in some other place overrides the field specification, so F5.2 will also read numbers like these:

```
125.4
.0083
-10.1
```

Discovering input values in a format different from the one in the field specification can be confusing, especially if you are trying to match up input values with the field specifications that read them. If you need this sort of flexibility, use free format instead.

13.9.6 Direct-Access I/O

FORTRAN file I/O is normally **sequential**, progressing from the first record to the second, then the third, and so on. In §9.6 we saw how to position to a given line by starting at the beginning and sequentially skipping lines.

In many implementations of FORTRAN it is possible to directly access a particular line of a file, by its number. This is also referred to as **random access**. In the example at the top of the next page we open a direct access file, write 5 records into it, and then read the 3rd record.

```
     OPEN(UNIT=2,FILE='fyle',
   ;      ACCESS='DIRECT',RECL=10,FORM='FORMATTED')
     DO 1 I=1,5
         WRITE(2,900,REC=I) I**2
900      FORMAT(I10)
   1 CONTINUE
     READ(2,900,REC=3) J
     PRINT *,'line 3 contains ',J
     STOP
     END
```

The program produces the output shown below.

```
line 3 contains     9
```

The OPEN statement now needs to specify that the file is for direct access, has records 10 bytes long to match the output format I10, and will contain formatted data. (Direct access can also be used with unformatted I/O.) The READ and WRITE statements must contain a REC= clause telling what record is to be written or read, even if the record happens to be next in sequence.

Some legacy programs use an old syntax [16, p71-78] in which the I/O statements of the example program above would be WRITE(2'I,900) I**2 and READ(2'3,900) J, and the file is described in a DEFINE FILE statement rather than in an OPEN. Update such codes to use the modern syntax.

Direct access is useful only for files having a maximum line length that is known before the file is OPENed. If any of the lines have fewer bytes than RECL, they are padded to full length, and this is wasteful of disk space. In many UNIX™ FORTRAN implementations, the I/O library does direct-access I/O by skipping lines rather than directly addressing the disk locations for the desired record, so using direct-access might not save any processing time.

13.9.7   NAMELIST ☠

In §12.2.1 we considered the problem of supplying a program with some input parameters that control its behavior. I recommended *against* designs that require the user to specify too many such options, and suggested reading them from a file if it is unavoidable that there will be a large number of them. When the options file is complicated, getting the values in the right places and in the right formats by hand is tedious and error-prone, so I advocated using a separate program to prompt the user for the values, read them from the keyboard using free format, and write the options file.

Another approach is to make the options file easier to compose manually, by allowing the user to *label* the values with the names of the variables they are to be read into. The NAMELIST feature makes this possible. The code on the left at the top of the next page reads H, I, and J using the list of names in VARS, and then reads K with an ordinary READ, from the file options listed on the right.

The NAMELIST values are given in the data file in the form of assignment statements, in any order, on one or more lines between the &VARS and &END. As shown in the example, each line of NAMELIST input must begin in column 2 of the file (or to the right). Starting any NAMELIST input line in column 1, or mentioning a variable that is not actually in the list (as could result from misspelling a name) results in an I/O error; omitting a variable from the data just (dangerously) leaves it undefined after execution of the READ statement. This example is straightforward, but the precise rules for NAMELIST input data are extremely

```
      REAL*8 H                          &VARS
      NAMELIST /VARS/ H,I,J             J=9 H=2.37D0 I=0
      OPEN(UNIT=3,FILE='options')       &END
      READ(3,VARS)                      123456789
      READ(3,901) K
  901 FORMAT(I9)
      :
```

complicated, so if your program uses this feature for anything elaborate be sure to consult the compiler manual. If you are using a Fortran-90 compiler you might need to specify an option for it to recognize the f77 NAMELIST data syntax illustrated above.

In addition to being tricky to use in any but the simplest ways, NAMELIST has the serious drawback of requiring the program's user, or at least the person who prepares the input file, to know and remember the internal names of the variables. This should never be necessary, and is especially onerous if the executable program is to be supplied to the user without source code.

13.10 Character Variables

Except in a few special situations, we have always stored text strings as CHARACTER*1 vectors and manipulated them one character at a time. There are other ways to handle character variables in FORTRAN that you will almost certainly encounter.

13.10.1 Characters in Variables of Other Types ☠

Until FORTRAN-77 there was no CHARACTER data type, so text had to be stored in variables of other types as in this example. The output of the program is shown below the listing.

```
      INTEGER*4 MSG(3)/'A me','ssag','e   '/
      WRITE(6,901) MSG
  901 FORMAT(3A4)
      STOP
      END
```

```
A message⎵⎵⎵
```

Because each character is internally just a pattern of 8 bits, characters can be stored in any sort of variable, one character per byte. This example uses each element of an INTEGER*4 vector to store 4 characters, but other popular choices in FORTRAN-66 programs were REAL*8 and COMPLEX*16 variables. Storing characters 4 or 8 or 16 at a time obviously makes it difficult to manipulate them individually, and if the string being stored is not a multiple of 4 or 8 or 16 characters some space is wasted for trailing blanks as in the example. To avoid these problems some programs used LOGICAL*1 vectors, which store 1 character per element just like a CHARACTER*1 vector. (This is about the only sensible use that LOGICAL*1 variables ever had.)

Using a variable that is not of type CHARACTER to hold character data is a violation of the Principle of Least Astonishment and makes the code harder to understand. Revise the program to use CHARACTER*1 vectors.

13.10.2   Arithmetic With Characters ☠

As discussed in §10.1, the bit patterns that most modern computers use to represent characters are specified by the ASCII character code. The order of the characters, or **collating sequence**, places letters that are adjacent in the alphabet next to each other in binary value. Thus, for example, a is represented by the bit pattern 01100001, b by 01100010, and so on. Similarly, A is represented by 01000001, B by 01000010, and so on.

It is possible to translate one character into another by doing arithmetic with these one-byte binary values. The approach is widely used in the C programming language, where it is easy to convert between variables of character and integer types, and it occasionally turns up in FORTRAN programs too. FORTRAN syntax does not permit the use of arithmetic operators directly with character operands, or the assignment of a character value to an integer variable, so it is necessary to use the subterfuge illustrated below.

```
FUNCTION UPPER(C)
CHARACTER*1 UPPER,C,ZZZC(4)
EQUIVALENCE(I,ZZZC(1))
I=0
ZZZC(4)=C
I=I-32
UPPER=ZZZC(4)
RETURN
END
```

This function receives a lower-case letter in C and returns the corresponding upper-case letter in the function value. Because of the EQUIVALENCE statement, the 4-byte integer I occupies the same memory locations as the 4-element character array ZZZC (meaning "zero-zero-zero-character"). Setting I=0 makes all the bytes of ZZZC zero. Then assigning ZZZC(4)=C puts the bit pattern of the given character into the least significant byte of I (this assumes the processor is big-endian). Now we can use ordinary integer arithmetic on I to subtract the difference in value between a lower-case letter and the corresponding upper-case letter. This leaves the character code for the upper-case letter in ZZZC(4), which is copied into the function name for return.

The difference in value between any lower-case letter and the corresponding upper-case letter can be found by subtracting the binary value of A from that of a, as follows:

$$01100001_2 - 01000001_2 = 00100000_2 = 2^5 = 32$$

Translations based on character arithmetic can run faster than the table lookups we used in §10.3. However, in typical FORTRAN applications, where text manipulation accounts for only a tiny proportion of the machine time used, this advantage is far outweighed by the drawbacks of character arithmetic.

The most serious drawback is that the whole approach is arcane and unobvious. To understand how a code like our example works, many readers would need a long explanation like the one provided above. Using EQUIVALENCE to get a byte value into an integer for manipulation is a trick far removed from the straightforward numerical computing that most FORTRAN programmers do. To see where the 32 came from we had to know the exact character codes for a lower case letter and the corresponding upper case letter, and do some binary arithmetic.

To work with arbitrary input values, our UPPER function should really be improved to return unchanged any character that is not a lower-case letter. To be portable to a computer using different character codes (such as the EBCDIC codes), in which the difference in value between a lower-case letter and the corresponding upper-case letter might not be 32, the routine would have to compute the numerical value of 'a'-'A'. These improvements would add several more lines of obscure code.

It is far simpler, and much less error-prone, to do character translations by table lookup as discussed in §10.3. Save character arithmetic, if you must use it at all, for your C programs, where it can at least be done more gracefully.

13.10.3 Substrings, Concatenation, and Character Built-Ins

When a character string is stored in the CHARACTER*n form rather than as a vector of CHARACTER*1 elements, some additional notation is required to allow the manipulation of substrings. The code segments below each replace x.y by 5.2 in FMT.

```
CHARACTER*4 FMT/'Fx.y'/          CHARACTER*1 FMT(4)/'F','x','.','y'/
FMT(2:4)='5.2'                   FMT(2)='5'
                                 FMT(4)='2'
```

The code on the left uses **substring notation** while that on the right uses the familiar array element notation. The integers denoting the first and last character in a substring are not restricted to being literal constants as shown in this example, but can be any integer expressions.

There is also a **concatenation operator** that combines character strings. In the code on the left below, LOOK is concatenated with either OUT or UP to form MSG, producing the result strings shown on the right.

```
CHARACTER*8 MSG
CHARACTER*5 LOOK/'look '/
CHARACTER*4 OUT/'out!'/
CHARACTER*2 UP/'up'/
IF(OK) THEN
    MSG=LOOK // UP                       look up⌴
ELSE
    MSG=LOOK // OUT                      look out
ENDIF
```

If the concatenation is shorter than the target string, as in the example when OK is .TRUE., the result is padded with blanks on the right. If the concatenation is longer than the target string, as in the ELSE case above, the result is truncated to the target length.

Finally, FORTRAN-77 includes some built-in functions that have character arguments or results. The program below produces the output shown to its right.

```
    CHARACTER*12 LONG/'wxy     zz '/
    WRITE(6,901) CHAR(65)                   A
901 FORMAT(A1)
    WRITE(6,902) ICHAR('A')                 65
    WRITE(6,902) LEN(LONG)                  12
    WRITE(6,902) INDEX(LONG,'z')            10
902 FORMAT(I2)
    STOP
    END
```

CHAR returns the character having a given position in the collating sequence. Here we asked for the character whose numerical value is $65_{10} = 01000001_2$, which I claimed above is A.

ICHAR returns the numerical value of a character's bit pattern. If numerals are adjacent in the collating sequence, CHAR(ICHAR('0')+I) gives the digit corresponding to the integer I, and ICHAR(DIGIT)-ICHAR('0') gives the integer corresponding to the numeral DIGIT. If we were ever going to use character arithmetic, these functions would be useful in contexts such as the UPPER routine of §13.10.2.

The LEN function returns the total length of its argument string, *not* the position of the last nonblank. INDEX returns the position in a string of the first occurrence of a given substring, or zero if the substring is not found. These functions are useful only with strings stored in CHARACTER*n form.

Using CHARACTER*n variables can result in code that is shorter than that required to do the same operations using CHARACTER*1 vectors, and it permits searches using INDEX. But it introduces the need for the substring notation and the concatenation operator, which add to the syntax the programmer needs to remember. CHAR and ICHAR permit terse conversions from integer to numeral and back, but at some expense to clarity. In the unlikely event that your compiler does not permit the use of EQUIVALENCE to overlay a CHARACTER*n variable on a CHARACTER*1 vector, there might be situations in which you are forced to use substrings.

13.11   Case Study: A Legacy Code

To illustrate some of the usages discussed in this chapter, we now examine a subroutine that resembles many encountered in typical legacy codes and in badly-written contemporary programs. This example (perhaps *parody* would be a more accurate description) was made up using bits and pieces from actual applications, but all the details have been changed to spare the original authors the embarrassment of being identified by their doggerel.

There are unfortunately two respects in which this example is *not* representative of real programs. First, although the code is a little long by the criteria of §12.2.2, it is far too short to represent an average routine from a legacy program. Bad programs often have subroutines that are thousands of lines long. Second, I made this example considerably less obscure than most legacy routines are, so that the reader will have some chance of unraveling it in Exercise 13.13.46.

You should study the source code next, and try to understand it, before reading the observations that follow the listing. As you do this, try to imagine that this is not just an example, but that you have been asked by your boss to investigate and correct a bug in the FORTRAN.

13.11.1   Source Listing

```
//FORT.SYSIN DD *
      SUBROUTINE AGHRWE                                          AGH00010
** WARNING ** WARNIG ** DO NOT USE WITH -12 VERSION!!!!!!       AGH00020
      INCLUDE (INC1)                                            AGH00030
      INCLUDE(INC3)                                             AGH00040
      INCLUDE(INC4NEW)                                          AGH00050
C ================================================================= AGH00060
C THIS IS THE AGHRWE MODULE.  IT USED TO WORK FOR -12 UNTIL WE HAD TO AGH00070
C CHANGE THE WAY CPI WAS HANDLED, WHICH USED TO BE THE OTHER WAY.  AGH00080
C PLEASE DO NOT SCREW AROUND WITH IT UNLESS YOU ARE DESPERATE!  G.B. AGH00090
C ================================================================= AGH00100
```

```
          COMMON/BARF/C(KKMAX)                                       AGH00110
          DIMENSION TEMP(100)                                        AGH00120
          EQUIVALENCE (N2,NGG),(K,L,C)                               AGH00130
C         MIKE K.'S OLD EXTENTION IS THE "MAGIC NUMBER"              AGH00140
          DATA MAGIC/6558/                                           AGH00150
C         MLL WILL BE CALCULATED                                     AGH00160
          I=1                                                        AGH00170
1527      IF(CPI(I).EQ.0.0) GO TO 1528                               AGH00180
          MLL=CPI(I)                                                 AGH00190
          GO TO 20                                                   AGH00200
1528      I=I+1                                                      AGH00210
          GO TO 1527                                                 AGH00220
20        J=I+1                                                      AGH00230
35        IF(CPI(J).EQ.0.0) GO TO 30                                 AGH00240
          IF(CPI(J).LT.MLL) MLL=CPI(J)                               AGH00250
30        J=J+1                                                      AGH00260
          IF(J.GT.KK) GO TO 10032                                    AGH00270
          GO TO 35                                                   AGH00280
10032     GO TO 921                                                  AGH00290
10033     CONTINUE                                                   AGH00300
*             quick fix GMB 8/19/84                                  AGH00310
              iopt=iopt+1                                            AGH00320
c             Rod Serling strikes again! MK 6/12/87                  AGH00330
          GOTO(58,57,4),IOPT                                         AGH00340
          iopt=iopt-1                                                AGH00350
 57       DO 3 L=1,N-1                                               AGH00360
          DO 3 M=L+1,N                                               AGH00370
          IF(A(M)-A(L)) 12,3,4                                       AGH00380
12        TEMP(L)=A(L)                                               AGH00390
          A(L)=A(M)                                                  AGH00400
          A(M)=TEMP(L)                                               AGH00410
C         DO NOT REMOVE THE FOLLOWING CARD!!  IGNORE COMPILER WARNING AGH00420
4         CONTINUE                                                   AGH00430
3         CONTINUE                                                   AGH00440
          GO TO 58                                                   AGH00450
C         I=2                                                        AGH00460
*         abandon all hope, ye who enter here                       AGH00470
149       J=MOD(I+1,2)                                               AGH00480
          K=I+J/2-1                                                  AGH00490
          C(K)=TEMP(J+NG*I)                                          AGH00500
          IF(K-J) 147,247,347                                        AGH00510
 147      K=K-1                                                      AGH00520
C         I=I+J                                                      AGH00530
          GO TO 149                                                  AGH00540
247       K=K+1                                                      AGH00550
          IF(C(K).EQ.MAGIC)THEN                                      AGH00560
          WRITE(0,23)                                                AGH00570
          STOP                                                       AGH00580
          ENDIF                                                      AGH00590
C         I=I+1                                                      AGH00600
          GO TO 149                                                  AGH00610
347       K=I                                                        AGH00620
          I=0                                                        AGH00630
```

```
      GO TO 149                                              AGH00640
58    iopt=iopt-1                                            AGH00650
      DO 5 L=1,N                                             AGH00660
5     A(L+1)=A(L+1)+A(L)                                     AGH00670
      GO TO 999                                              AGH00680
921   NGG=NG                                                 AGH00690
      DO 16 J=1,NG                                           AGH00700
      DO 16 I=1,N2                                           AGH00710
      WORK(I+(J-1)*NG)=0.                                    AGH00720
      K=0                                                    AGH00730
 28   K=K+1                                                  AGH00740
      WORK(I+(J-1)*NG)=WORK(I+(J-1)*NG)+G(I,K)               AGH00750
     **B(K,J)                                                AGH00760
C     WRITE(6,109) (I+(J-1)*NG),WORK(I+(J-1)*NG)             AGH00770
      IF(K.LT.NG) GO TO 28                                   AGH00780
  16 CONTINUE                                                AGH00790
      DO 8 J=1,N2                                            AGH00800
      DO 8 I=1,NG                                            AGH00810
      GBG(I,J)=0                                             AGH00820
      DO 8 K=1,NG                                            AGH00830
      GBG(I,J)=GBG(I,J)+WORK(I+(K-1)*NG)*G(K,J)              AGH00840
   8 CONTINUE                                                AGH00850
      GO TO 10033                                            AGH00860
 999 RETURN                                                  AGH00870
 109 FORMAT(5HWORK(,I2,2H)=,1PE13.6)                         AGH00880
  23 FORMAT('Arrrgh!')                                       AGH00890
      END                                                    AGH00900
```

13.11.2   Observations

1⇨   The first thing we notice is that the top line does not appear to be a FORTRAN statement at all. It is in fact some job control language from an IBM batch operating system called System/360 OS, under which many legacy codes were developed. Detritus like this is commonly found in files containing old programs, and must be removed with an editor before the program can be compiled in UNIX™.

2⇨   The next glaring abnormality is the sequence numbers in columns 73-80 of the FORTRAN statements. These "numbers" actually consist of the letters AGH, which are taken from the routine name, followed by a 5-digit integer that serializes the statements. The standard program that wrote these sequence numbers used an increment of 10 so that extra cards inserted between the statements of the program could be sequence-numbered too, without being out of order or requiring old cards to be repunched to make room between the numbers. You should remove sequence numbers as described in §13.1.1, but here we will use their numerical values, in ⎣ boxes ⎦, to identify the statements we are discussing.

3⇨   It is hard to imagine what the routine name AGHRWE means, though perhaps it did mean something to the author. There is no description of what this code does, but right away ⎣20⎦ we find a warning (partly misspelled) about something it does *not* do. Unfortunately, only the cognoscenti will have any idea what the "dash twelve version" might be, or why this routine can't be used there. Whatever this routine is for, it seems in any event not to be a general-purpose subprogram. (Though it is not obvious, the routine in fact performs several unrelated special-purpose calculations, which is typical in poorly-structured programs.)

4⇨ There are no formal parameters, so it must be that this routine communicates with the outside world entirely by means of COMMON. We can see 110 the block named (alarmingly) /BARF/, but it contains only the array C (dimensioned there) whereas the first segment of executable code 160-220 has to do with finding MLL, so it is likely that other COMMON blocks are brought in by the three INCLUDEs 30-50 . As mentioned in §13.1.4, an included file can contain almost anything, but from the placement of these INCLUDES among the declarations we can guess that they do not contain any executable statements. Just what they *do* contain is a mystery unless we look at them.

5⇨ Only the people who participated in the change mentioned by G.B. might find his comments 60-100 about it meaningful, and they would probably remember the details just as well without this reminder. Of course, both he and they are probably now retired or working somewhere else. We do learn that the change affecting the –12 version had to do with the CPI array, but it's not clear what "the other way" was to handle it, and this is the last we hear about the matter. The imprecation not to change the code "unless you are desperate" suggests that perhaps G.B. got this routine to work only with difficulty and worried that the slightest change might break it. Perhaps it was he who made the "quick fix" in 1984 310 .

6⇨ The impression of fragility is reinforced several times by comments about Rod Serling (the host of a science fiction program popular in the 1960's) 330 , about the need to ignore a compiler warning rather than correcting the code 420 , and about the difficulty of understanding some part of the code 470 . One of the FORMAT statements 890 also suggests that somebody was once frustrated while debugging the routine. (All of these things were *not* invented for this example, but were borrowed verbatim from production codes now in use.) The compiler warning is about the branch from 340 to 4, which is into the range of the DO 3 loop.

7⇨ Aside from the useless history and dire warnings, and some code that is commented out (e.g., 460) we find few actual comments. At first glance it is not clear whether MLL WILL BE CALCULATED 160 threatens something that will happen soon or much later, but then we notice 190 a value being assigned to MLL, so it must mean now. But why did we need the comment, if all it does is echo the code? Most of the comments are in upper case, just like the code, so it is hard to find the ones that aren't set off by being not indented. Some of the comments (e.g., 20) start with a * in column 1, others with C or c.

8⇨ A DATA statement 150 is used to set the value of MAGIC to a telephone extension (the word is misspelled in the comment), which is used later 550 as a flag to mark the end of a list of values in C. (This is also borrowed from a production code now in use.) Adopting a "magic" number as a flag can obviously fail if actual data happens to take on that value.

9⇨ The local work array TEMP (which doesn't really need to be an array at all) is declared using DIMENSION, but it is not explicitly typed. It appears to be REAL*4, but one of the INCLUDE files might contain a type statement for it so we can't be sure. It is similarly impossible to tell whether MLL is an integer or is declared real in one of the INCLUDE files; if it is an integer, it is involved in implicit type conversions 190 250 and a mixed-mode comparison 250 , unless CPI is declared integer in one of the INCLUDE files. If GBG is real it receives a mixed-mode assignment 820 . Elsewhere (e.g., 720) all the real literals are shown as single precision (without a D suffix), so it is possible that all of the floating-point variables in this routine are REAL*4. Many legacy codes used short reals to save space, back in the days when a big computer had 64K bytes of memory. If, on the other hand, one of the INCLUDE files contains an IMPLICIT REAL*8 (A-H,O-Z) then all of the reals are actually double precision and the literals are written wrong. Without looking inside the INCLUDE files it is impossible to know.

10 ⇨ The EQUIVALENCE statement 130 contains two parenthesized lists. The first list, (N2,NGG), seems straightforward, but the second, (K,L,C), makes the INTEGER*4 scalars K and L occupy the same storage with the first word of the (apparently) REAL*4 array C, which is furthermore in COMMON and might thus have a value assigned upon entry. It is always worrisome to find numerical variables of different types assigned to the same storage location, though it is not clear at first glance whether a problem actually results here.

11 ⇨ There are several arithmetic IF statements in the routine (e.g., 380) and a computed GO TO 340 . Evidently GMB found it necessary to temporarily adjust IOPT in order to make the computed GO TO work right.

12 ⇨ There are several DO loops in the routine (e.g., 350-430) but they are hard to see because the loop bodies are not indented. It is also hard to recognize them because some (e.g., 660-670) do not end with CONTINUE, and because CONTINUE is sometimes used as a branch target rather than to terminate a DO (e.g., 300). There is also an unindented IF-THEN construct 550-580 .

13 ⇨ The statement numbers are out of order, randomly justified in the statement number field, and in some cases quite long. There are two rather long branches back 640 860 and some branching around branches 270 . The branching logic could be simplified by moving some code segments. Although it is not flagged by the compiler (or obvious to the reader), the code segment starting at 460 is unreachable.

14 ⇨ The FORMAT statements are collected at the end of the routine rather than being placed where they might help to clarify what is happening, and have numbers that are not noticeably different from those of branch targets. One of them uses H field specifications and a floating-point scale factor.

15 ⇨ The statement that begins at 750 is continued on the next line, but the continuation character is * so it appears at first glance that B(K,J) is an exponent.

16 ⇨ Although it is not obvious until near the end of the listing 790 , most of the statements begin in column 8, not in column 7 as we have grown accustomed to expect. Some programmers start in column 8 "just to be sure" of not accidentally starting *before* column 7, but this makes it hard to right-justify the statement numbers or to see that continuation characters are in the correct column.

13.11.3 Cleaning Up the Mess

How does code get to be a tangled mess, and what can be done about it then? Many engineers and scientists, or the organizations they work for, depend for their livelihood on the correctness of big applications that have somehow fallen from grace, so these are questions of great practical and economic importance!

Some programs are made bad on purpose, because of the ignorance or indifference of the programmers who work on them (not having studied §12), or because of intentional vandalism by employees seeking revenge or job security (see cartoon), or because of limitations imposed by the available hardware or by the software development environment, or because of shortsighted policy decisions by managers. Many legacy codes went bad this way in their youth decades ago, when heroic measures (such as memory overlays) were essential in order to shoehorn useful calculations into computers that were little more than laboratory curiosities, and drove design "compromises" that we would now consider "just giving up." For past sins may we all be forgiven, if only we do not repeat them.

But most programs go bad by evolution. The boss says "I need you to make this little change for me. While I wait." and starts drumming her fingers on your doorjamb. This is not the time to redesign the program, change hundreds of lines of code, debug, and regression test the result. The thing that is required can be done in a trice by sending this number over there in an added COMMON block. Voilà! A brand new wart has just been grown on this code. Tomorrow there will be another, and then another and another, each so trifling that it cannot by itself justify the effort that would be needed to do the job in a clean and sanity-preserving way. Eventually the code is an intractable mass of slag, and people are calling in sick to avoid working on it.

The best (and by far the cheapest) way to deal with the mess is to keep it from happening in the first place, by following the good programming practices outlined in §12 both at the outset and during code maintenance. Don't do the awful things that are decried in *this* chapter. Resist whenever you can the management lust for a "quick fix," by arguing the merits of the case, making up reasons why patching is technically impossible, lying about how long it will take to do, and if necessary rewriting in secret as suggested in §12.6.2.

If you are inescapably confronted with a full-grown mess and you really can't throw it away and start over (nor change jobs) the outlook is less promising but not entirely bleak. Here is some advice about how to proceed.

Never promise to fix the bug. Junk codes are terminal patients, and agreeing to fix what is wrong or to make the change that is wanted is like guaranteeing to cure a fatal illness. Without ruling out the chance of a miracle, all you can promise is that you will treat the symptoms and try conventional therapies that have sometimes helped in other cases. Clarifying the code might well turn up an error or make it obvious how to change its function (that's why you're going to the trouble) but it also might not.

Work only on the code that gets executed. Most old programs, and many new ones, are filled with code that is either dead or might as well be. Start by adding a PRINT statement to the front of each routine so you can trace the flow of control and find out which parts of the program are actually involved in producing the behavior you want to fix or change.

Make sure you do no harm. The ancient physician Hippocrates counseled his students to use only therapies that will leave the illness no worse than it was at the beginning. To make sure you are not introducing new bugs, make only a few changes at one time and then test to confirm that the program still does correctly whatever it did correctly before you began.

DILBERT by S. Adams, reprinted by permission of United Feature Syndicate, Inc.   © 6/10/94 United Feature Syndicate

Clean up the source you work on. Remove sequence numbers and dead code. Make DO loops end with CONTINUE statements, and remove CONTINUE statements that were used only as branch targets. Fix the indenting, statement numbers, and continuation markers. Translate any comments that might be present to mixed case, and translate lower-case code to upper case. Replace arithmetic IF statements and computed GO TO statements with simpler equivalent logic. Make any other superficial changes that seem appropriate to tidy up the code and put it in a familiar, legible form. Add a variable list to the routine so you can record the meanings of variables as you figure them out. As you learn about the data structures and logic, add comments to describe them.

Do incremental untangling. There is less to many code segments than meets the eye. If you can identify a code segment that is performing some self-contained operation, it might be possible to replace it by a simpler sequence that is easier to understand and more likely to be correct. In our case study, the first functional block is seen to be $\boxed{\text{160-280}}$, which is excerpted below.

```
C     MLL WILL BE CALCULATED
      I=1
1527  IF(CPI(I).EQ.0.0) GO TO 1528
      MLL=CPI(I)
      GO TO 20
1528  I=I+1
      GO TO 1527
20    J=I+1
35    IF(CPI(J).EQ.0.0) GO TO 30
      IF(CPI(J).LT.MLL) MLL=CPI(J)
30    J=J+1
      IF(J.GT.KK) GO TO 10032
      GO TO 35
```

A little pondering reveals that the effect of this calculation is to give MLL the smallest nonzero value found among the array elements CPI(1),...,CPI(KK). Understanding that this is the intent of the code segment makes it easy to rewrite as shown below.

```
C     set MLL to the smallest nonzero entry in CPI
      MLL=0.0
      DO 1 I=1,KK
          IF(CPI(I).NE.0.0 .AND. MLL.EQ.0.0) MLL=CPI(I)
          IF(CPI(I).NE.0.0 .AND. CPI(I).LT.MLL) MLL=CPI(I)
    1 CONTINUE
```

Ideally one would like to phrase comments in terms of the application problem rather than in terms of the FORTRAN variables, and in our example that would be possible if the meaning of CPI or MLL could be discovered by examining other routines from the program.

Often it is possible to greatly simplify a routine by rewriting all of its free loops as DO loops.

Write any new code in a clear style. Don't imitate the bad style of a legacy program in order to make your new or replacement code blend in. Follow the principles outlined in §12.4, and hope that piece by piece you will eventually get to replace all of the old stuff with code that is easier to read. Of course, there might be things about the program, such as the global organization of its data structures, that you can't find a way to change piecemeal.

Debug if you must. If cleaning up the code does not reveal what is wrong, use the debugging techniques outlined in §14.3. These are much easier to apply to code that has been laundered than to a mess like the one listed in our case study.

13.12 Conclusion and Omissions

Some readers of this chapter will doubtless have begun in the hopeful expectation that I would validate their habits and idiosyncrasies, or that I would at least endorse some familiar articles of faith, only discovering to their horror that I have instead condemned various language features and coding practices that they cherish and use all the time. My friends are unanimous in their approval of the INCLUDE statement, for example, even though the longer I think about it the worse it seems to me. There, and in the many other places where my own experience has compelled me to reject the conventional wisdom or to take a position that might be different from yours, I have tried to explain why in an objective and logical way. But even the most carefully reasoned arguments about style depend on the weights assigned to competing objectives, and your opinions about what is most important for success might be different from mine. If you were thinking to yourself a few minutes ago that either you are a terrible failure or I am not the fine fellow you originally believed, let me hasten to concede that many successful programmers use statements and coding practices that would lead me to ruin, and which I have therefore dismissed here as ☠ toxic. I would be remiss in my responsibility as your author if I denied you the insights of my long experience and considered judgement. But the final and overriding lesson of this chapter is that you should seriously ponder the issues discussed here and decide about them for yourself, in a rational and dispassionate way, rather than passively accepting dogmatic expert pronouncements from anybody, including me.

Even in this chapter, the cobwebby attic of the book, I haven't mentioned every possible FORTRAN oddity you might discover. The leftovers are all the items mentioned in the **Omissions** Sections of the previous chapters in vertical, rather than *slanting*, type. None of those things are difficult to understand, but most are unusual enough that you might never run into them. If you do encounter something I haven't discussed, consult your compiler vendor's language manual; even ancient features are probably still in there.

13.13 Exercises

13.13.1 As discussed in §1, there are 47 nonblank characters that can be used in FORTRAN source statements, ignoring the text in character strings. (a) How many different patterns of exactly N nonblank characters can be formed using the 47 in the FORTRAN character set? (b) How many different patterns of from 1 to N nonblank characters can be formed?

13.13.2 The introduction to this chapter shows the only Classical FORTRAN program that can be written with 7 characters or less, not counting blanks. (a) How many typographically different programs can be written using exactly 10 characters? (b) Exactly 11?

13.13.3   List the desirable program attributes mentioned in §12.1.

13.13.4   What does the 💀 skull-and-crossbones mean in this chapter? What section of this chapter concerns topics in the subject of Chapter 5?

13.13.5   The source code displayed in §13.11 includes sequence numbers. (a) How many bytes of disk space are needed to store the text? (b) How many bytes are needed if the sequence numbers are removed?

13.13.6   Most FORTRAN compilers are incapable of detecting every instance of unreachable code. Construct an example in which a code segment cannot be reached, but that fact can be determined only by analyzing the logic, not just the syntax, of the program.

13.13.7   In §12.2.2, information hiding and data hiding are described as hallmarks of good program design. Yet §13.1.4 recommends *against* the use of INCLUDE files, which hide design decisions and data. How can the two chapters be consistent? If information hiding and data hiding are different from the kind of concealment that INCLUDE files provide, explain how.

13.13.8   Rewrite the program below to eliminate the INCLUDEs.

```
      INCLUDE 'stuff.f'          C       this is file "stuff.f"
      STOP                               REAL*8 Y,T
      END                                Y=0.D0
                                         DO 1 I=1,100
C     this is file "body.f"                  INCLUDE 'body.f'
      T=0.1D0*DFLOAT(I)          1 CONTINUE
      Y=Y+DSQRT(T)*0.1D0
      PRINT *,T,Y
```

13.13.9   Explain the difference between STOP and END. Revise the following programs to include the missing STOP statements.

```
C     part (a)                  C     part (b)
    1 M=0                             M=0
    2 READ(5,*,END=1) I               N=1
      IF(I.EQ.0) THEN           1 N=N+M
         PRINT *,M              2 N=N+M/2
      ELSE                            PRINT *,N
         M=M+I                        M=M+1
         GO TO 2                      GO TO(1,2), N
      ENDIF                           END
      END
```

13.13.10 Rewrite the following program in the style of §12.2.2.

```
      OPROGRAM
      1MAIN
      READ *,X,Y_COORDINATE
      Z=X**-2+Y_COORDINATE
**-2 ;

      PRINT *,Z
C     STOP
      END
```

13.13.11 Rewrite the following code segment to eliminate the arithmetic IF and computed

GO TO statements, and to delete any unreachable code.

```
 5 IF(X) 27,38,14
 2 PRINT *,X
27 IF(X-1.D0) 18,19,19
   GO TO 2
14 GO TO(27,38,19), L
   PRINT *,L
19 STOP
38 X=X-1.D0
   GO TO 5
18 ...
```

13.13.12 The built-in function DABS returns the absolute value of a REAL*8 argument. In the program on the left, F should be typed REAL*8 but the declaration has been forgotten so the compiler stops with an error message. Even after reading the error message, the programmer can't find the mistake. However, he discovers by trial and error that changing the program as shown on the right makes it compile without error, and the executable seems to run correctly.

```
READ *,F                              READ *,F
IF(DABS(F).LT.1.D0) F=F+1.D0          IF(DABS(F+0.D0).LT.1.D0) F=F+1.D0
PRINT *,F                             PRINT *,F
STOP                                  STOP
END                                   END
```

Explain why some compilers might accept F+0.D0 as an argument of DABS. Is the output of the resulting executable always the same as it would have been if F had been declared REAL*8?

13.13.13 Rewrite the following code segment to eliminate the arithmetic IF and computed GO TO statements, and to delete any unreachable code. Add a comment to describe what the code segment does.

```
   I=1
   J=2
11 IF(Y(I)-Y(J)) 1,2,3
 3 GO TO (5,2),METH
   GO TO 8
 1 GO TO(2,5), METH
   GO TO 8
 5 TEMP=Y(I)
   Y(I)=Y(J)
   Y(J)=TEMP
 2 IF(J-N) 6,7,8
 6 J=J+1
   GO TO 11
 7 IF(I-N+1) 9,10,8
 9 I=I+1
   J=I+1
   GO TO 11
 8 PRINT *,'impossible'
   STOP
10 ...
```

13.13.14 In the code below, does the compiler invoke SQRT or DSQRT? (SQRT is the generic name, so if your compiler does not recognize GENERIC but does recognize generic names, you can remove the GENERIC for testing and get the intended result.) Will the output that is printed be anything like $\sqrt{2}$? Recode the program so that it unambiguously prints DSQRT(2.D0).

```
GENERIC
REAL*4 U,V
REAL*8 Z,W
EQUIVALENCE (U,Z),(V,W)
Z=2.D0
V=SQRT(U)
PRINT *,W
STOP
END
```

13.13.15 If this is the only type declaration in a routine, what are the types of the variables? How is it possible to remove all default variable typings?

```
IMPLICIT INTEGER*4 (A-F,N-S,W)
```

13.13.16 The example of §13.4.1 contains the following statements:

```
A=4
X=2/3*A
Y=2*A/3
```

(a) Write a program to execute these statements and print out the results. (b) Recode the statements to make the results unambiguous.

13.13.17 Explain why an INTEGER*2 variable can't be used to store positive values larger than 32767. What is the most negative value it can store?

13.13.18 Rewrite the following declarations in the style of §4.

```
COMPLEX Z
DOUBLE PRECISION X
DIMENSION X(5)
DATA X/1.D0,2.D0,3.D0,4.D0,5.D0/,Z/(2.,3.)/
```

13.13.19 Some alleged FORTRAN compilers require arrays to be dimensioned using the DIMENSION statement rather than in a type statement, and some require compile-time initializations to be given in DATA rather than in a type statement. Is it desirable for different attributes of a variable to be specified in separate FORTRAN statements? Explain.

13.13.20 Recode the DO WHILE of §13.5.4 (a) as a free loop; (b) as a DO loop.

13.13.21 Improve the following program. What does it do?

```
      DIMENSION X(20),Y(10)
      EQUIVALENCE(X,Y),(I,J)
      DATA Y/10*0.0/
      READ *,(X(I),J=10,20)
      YLIM=1.D0
      DO 1 I=1,20
          IF(Y(I)-YLIM) 3,2,2
    3 CONTINUE
    1 X(J)=YLIM
      STOP
    2 PRINT *,I
      GO TO 1
      END
```

13.13.22 Is it better to decompose a long program into subprograms by making a typographical division or a logical one? Explain.

13.13.23 Comment on the following often-heard advice. "To avoid run-time errors, always code DSQRT(DABS(X)) in preference to DSQRT(X)."

13.13.24 What gets printed when this program is run, and why? Revise the code to correctly accomplish the initialization that was apparently desired.

```
      COMMON /BLK/ I(3),J,K
      DO 1 J=1,5
          I(J)=0
    1 CONTINUE
      PRINT *,I,J,K
      STOP
      END
```

13.13.25 What is the flow of control in this program? What gets printed?

```
      CALL FIRST(*1)              SUBROUTINE FIRST(*)
      CALL LAST(*2)              RETURN
      STOP                     1 RETURN 1
    1 PRINT *,'first'            ENTRY LAST(*)
      STOP                       GO TO 1
    2 PRINT *,'last'             END
      STOP
      END
```

13.13.26 The FUNCTION subprogram listed below returns in F the value of the function $f(x) = x^3 - 2x - 5$ and includes an ENTRY that returns in FP the derivative $f'(x) = 3x^2 - 2$.

```
      FUNCTION F(X)
      REAL*8 F,FP,X
      F=X**3 - 2.D0*X - 5.D0
      RETURN
      ENTRY FP(X)
      FP=3.D0*X**2 - 2.D0
      RETURN
      END
```

(a) Confirm that $f(x) = 0$ has one real root, at $x \approx 2.0945514815423266$. (b) Write a program that uses **Newton's method** to approximate the solution of $f(x) = 0$. Starting from an initial guess x_0, Newton's method computes successive approximations to a root using the formula

$$x_{k+1} = x_k - \frac{f(x_k)}{f'(x_k)}.$$

For what values of x_0 does the algorithm converge to the root? (c) Based on its use in this example, can you think of any advantages to using ENTRY? Explain.

13.13.27 Write a program to investigate what happens in your computer system when a subroutine tries to change the value of a parameter for which a literal value is passed in the CALL statement. Does the value get changed in the calling program? Is any error message produced?

13.13.28 Consider the first example in §13.6, which is reproduced below.

```
N=1
N=N+1+K(N)
PRINT *,N
STOP
END
FUNCTION K(N)
N=N+1
K=N+1
RETURN
END
```

(a) Run this program on your computer to find out what value of N is printed. (b) Recode the main program so that the result is no longer implementation dependent even though the function has a side effect. (c) Recode the function so that it no longer has a side effect, and adjust the main program to produce the same output as before.

13.13.29 Consider the following program, in which FCN has a context effect.

```
COMMON /DATA/ Q              FUNCTION FCN(X)
REAL*8 Q,FCN                 COMMON /DATA/ Q
Q=1.D0                       REAL*8 FCN,X,Q
PRINT *, FCN(2.D0)+FCN(3.D0) Q=2.D0*Q
STOP                         FCN=Q*X
END                          RETURN
                             END
```

(a) What is printed? (b) What is printed if the PRINT statement is changed to PRINT *, FCN(3.D0)+FCN(2.D0)? (c) Are context effects generally desirable in a FUNCTION subprogram? Explain.

13.13.30 Consider the program listed at the top of the next page. (a) Predict what will be printed for J, and explain why. (b) Run this program on your computer to confirm your prediction. (c) Recode the subroutine so that it does not have side effects (i.e., so that it changes only its output parameter J).

```
      I=1
      CALL SHNOOK(I,I, J)
      PRINT *,J
      STOP
      END
      SUBROUTINE SHNOOK(L,M, J)
      L=L+1
      M=M+1
      J=L+M
      RETURN
      END
```

13.13.31 Rewrite the following code so that FCN has a formal parameter. Fix any other problems you notice.

```
      COMMON P                    FUNCTION FCN()
      EXTERNAL FCN                COMMON P
      P=3.                        F(X)=P**X
      F=FCN(X)                    FCN=F(P)
      PRINT *,F                   RETURN
      STOP                        END
      END
```

13.13.32 Rewrite the first version of the EXCH subprogram given in §6.2 so that it performs the expected exchange even when the same actual parameter is passed for both dummy parameters of the subroutine. Use the main program given in that example to print 2 1 after each call, proving that your version of EXCH works.

13.13.33 What values are assigned to G, H, and P in the example of §13.6.6?

13.13.34 In debugging a program that someone else wrote, you suspect that an array dimension might be exceeded, so you use a compiler option to enable array bounds checking. Now when you run the executable, it stops right away with an error message about a subscript out of range, but the error occurs far from the code that you suspected of being wrong. The routine where the subscript is out of range begins as shown below.

```
      SUBROUTINE OLD(ZY)
      REAL*8 ZY(1)
      DO 1 I=1,10
          ZY(I)=2.34D0*ZY(I)
    1 CONTINUE
      :
```

(a) Why is the array dimensioned ZY(1)? How did this code *ever* work? (b) Revise the statements shown to eliminate the spurious error message, so that the run-time array bounds checking can find the error you were actually looking for.

13.13.35 The first three programs in §13.9.2 print C using different scale factors. (a) Modify the first example to print the value as 2997.92458D+05. (b) Determine by experiment whether negative scale factors s also work.

13.13.36 What output is printed by this program? Rewrite SETEM to eliminate the COMMON and EQUIVALENCE.

```
COMMON /XXY/ ALPHA,BETA,GAMMA          SUBROUTINE SETEM
CALL SETEM                             COMMON /XXY/ X
PRINT *,ALPHA,BETA,GAMMA               REAL*4 Y(4)
STOP                                   EQUIVALENCE(X,Y)
END                                    DO 1 I=1,4
                                              Y(I)=DFLOAT(I)
                                    1 CONTINUE
                                      RETURN
                                      END
```

13.13.37 Consider the following subprogram.

```
SUBROUTINE MPY324
COMMON A(3,2),B(2,4),C(3,4)
REAL*8 A,B,C
DO 1 I=1,3
DO 1 J=1,4
    C(I,J)=0.D0
    DO 2 K=1,2
        C(I,J)=C(I,J)+A(I,K)*B(K,J)
2       CONTINUE
1 CONTINUE
RETURN
END
```

(a) Write a main program to invoke MPY324 twice, first to find $D = E \times F$ and then to find $G = H \times Q$, where the arrays D, E, F, and G, H, Q have respectively the same dimensions as the COMMON variables C, A, and B. (b) Rewrite the routine so that it can be used to find the product C of *any* conformable matrices A and B, and so that it passes its arguments as formal parameters rather than in COMMON. What does your main program look like now?

13.13.38 In §13.9.1 I suggested using a filter to expand carriage control. (a) Write a program that reads lines of text from standard-in, simulates any actions that might be specified by carriage control characters in the input, and writes the result to standard-out. If the output is going to a file or to a laser printer, rather than to a line printer, some carriage control actions must be interpreted differently (e.g., overprinting) or do not make sense at all (e.g., printing across the page boundary). (b) At least one PC FORTRAN environment just blanks the first character of each output line it prints, so that characters in column 1 are lost. How would your program have to be changed to work in such an environment?

13.13.39 What output is printed by this program? Explain why.

```
REAL*8 PI/3.1415926535897932D0/
WRITE(6,901) PI,PI
901 FORMAT(1PD12.6,2H<>,F8.5)
I=-12345
WRITE(6,902) I
902 FORMAT(I9.9)
STOP
END
```

Suggest a general way of printing either positive or negative integers with leading zeros, so that −12345 would appear in a 9-column field as −00012345 and 12345 would appear as +00012345.

13.13.40 If a.out contains the executable for the following program and the user enters the input shown on the right, what is the output?

```
      READ(5,901) I                      unix[28] a.out
  901 FORMAT(I10)                        1
      WRITE(6,901) I
      STOP
      END
```

13.13.41 (a) What is the main drawback of direct-access I/O? (b) What is the main drawback of NAMELIST?

13.13.42 What is printed by this program?

```
      CHARACTER*9 A/'dangerous'/
      CHARACTER*6 B/'maniac'/
      PRINT *,B(1:3)//A(2:2)//A(4:6)
      STOP
      END
```

13.13.43 What is printed by the following program if it is run on a machine that uses the ASCII character codes?

```
      DO 1 K=65,90
          WRITE(6,901) K
  901     FORMAT(A4)
    1 CONTINUE
      STOP
      END
```

Comment on the clarity of this approach. Rewrite the program to achieve the same result using character variables.

13.13.44 As §13.10.3 explains, the built-in function INDEX(STRING,WORD) returns the character position in STRING where WORD first begins, or zero if WORD is not in STRING. Unfortunately, INDEX can only be used if STRING and WORD are stored in the CHARACTER*n form. Write a function named INDX(STRING,LS,WORD,LW) that does the same thing when STRING(LS) and WORD(LW) are stored as CHARACTER*1 vectors.

13.13.45 List the suggestions given in §13.11.3 for cleaning up junk code.

13.13.46 Suppose the legacy routine of §13.11.1 uses these INCLUDE files.

```
C     this is the file INC1
      PARAMETER(KKMAX=10)
      COMMON /BLK1/ IOPT,IDUM,CPI(KKMAX),KK

C     this is the file INC3
      COMMON /BLK2/ MLL,N,NG,A(100),G(20,20),B(20,20),GBG(20,20)
      REAL*4 MLL

C     this is the file INC4NEW
      COMMON /BLK3/ WORK(KKMAX**2)
```

Rewrite AGHRWE to conform as closely as possible to the principles of good programming style outlined in §12.2.2.

14

UNIX™ *Issues*

The FORTRAN syntax introduced so far is largely platform-independent, and the goal of further enhancing portability motivated some of the recommendations in §12 and §13 about program design and the choice of language features and coding practices. However, there have been many occasions on which we encountered the UNIX™ operating system in passing and several on which we could not avoid studying some aspect in more detail. The discussions of program compilation and execution in §1, of system routines in §6.6.2, of hanging prompts in §9.1.2, of unit assignments in §9.4, and of **man** pages in §12.3.1 all assumed that we develop and run our programs under UNIX™, and in a few cases it was convenient also to assume that we use the **bash** interactive shell. We will meet up with UNIX™ later when we consider performance measurement in §15.1, the **GETFIL** routine of §18.3, the **TIMER** routines of §18.5, and the **changeall** shell script of §18.6. It is UNIX™ that runs our programs for us, and most programs also rely on additional operating system services for interacting with the human user, doing I/O to files, finding out what time it is, and other functions that depend on the world outside of FORTRAN. The program development process also depends in many ways on the compiler, debugger, and other tools provided with the operating system.

In this chapter we take up several operating system issues that are often important to a FORTRAN programmer working in a UNIX™ environment, and that are touched on only briefly or not at all elsewhere in the book: compiler options, obtaining system services from within a program, debugging, automatic compilation, object-code libraries, and writing custom manual pages. In some places the discussion assumes the Linux implementation of UNIX™, or refers specifically to the **g77** compiler that is a standard part of Linux.

14.1 Using the Compiler

As discussed in §1.2, your FORTRAN source program cannot be directly executed by a computer but must first be translated into machine instructions and then linked with routines from the system I/O and elementary function libraries. Both of these operations are performed by the compiler, which reads a FORTRAN source file and produces an executable program as its output. In most UNIX™ environments the name of the compiler program is **f77**, or **f77** is an alias for the actual name of the compiler (such as **g77**). Then, if your source code is in the file **prog.f** you can compile it by issuing the UNIX™ command

```
unix[29] f77 prog.f
```

In §1.3 I said that the name of the source file should end in ".f". It can also end in ".F" if you are using the C preprocessor **cpp**, a possibility mentioned briefly in §14.3.3. If the filename does not end in .f or .F, UNIX™ compilers write a misleading error message such as **bad magic number** or **file format not recognized** and stop.

If the compiler finds errors in the source program, it will write messages to the display (standard-error) describing, perhaps cryptically, what it thinks is wrong. The phrasing and format of error messages vary widely among compilers, and some compilers notice mistakes that others overlook. If there are many errors, the report might scroll off the top of your screen. To read it one page at a time using the UNIX™ `more` program, you can enter this command.

```
unix[30] f77 prog.f 2>&1 | more
```

If no errors are detected, the compiler will produce an executable file named `a.out`, which you can then execute by entering

```
unix[31] a.out
```

If the current directory is not listed in your UNIX™ `PATH` environment variable, you might need to tell the shell that the executable is in the current directory, like this.

```
unix[32] ./a.out
```

In some environments (e.g., `cygwin`) the executable might be named `a.exe` instead of `a.out`.

Often it is desirable to modify the behavior of the compiler by specifying **command line options**. Some FORTRAN-77 compilers assume that variables local to subprograms are *not* to be saved across subprogram implementations, whereas we have always assumed that they will be, so you might find it necessary to specify a compiler option that requires local variables to be saved. For g77 the appropriate option is `-fno-automatic`. Some compilers assume compile-time initializations will *not* be specified as hexadecimal values, whereas we have frequently done that, so you might find it necessary to specify a compiler option that permits the use of hex initializations. For g77 the appropriate option is `-ftypeless-boz`. To use both of these g77 options you can enter

```
unix[33] g77 -fno-automatic -ftypeless-boz prog.f
```

Your compiler probably offers many options, which you can find out about by reading the compiler's `man` page or paper manual. In the following sections we consider some other options that are often useful and that are common to many UNIX™ FORTRAN compilers.

14.1.1 Naming the Executable File

It often happens that one needs to have several executable programs in a single directory, and the files obviously must have different names. The `-o` option causes `f77` to write the executable program in a file of a given name rather than using the default name `a.out`. Thus, for example, we can cause the compiler to put the executable program in the file `prog` by entering this command.

```
unix[34] f77 -o prog prog.f
```

This is equivalent to letting the output filename default to `a.out` and then renaming the file with the UNIX™ `mv` command like this.

```
unix[35] f77 prog.f
unix[36] mv a.out prog
```

14.1.2 Checking Array Subscripts

The `-C` option (or the `-fbounds-check` option of g77) makes the compiler insert into the object program extra machine instructions that compare each array subscript value to the range specified in the dimensions for the array. This can reveal many common programming errors. To see how it works, consider the file `wrong.f` listed below.

```
      COMMON /BUGGY/ MAT,INT
      INTEGER*4 MAT(10)
      INT=0
      DO 1 J=1,11
          MAT(J)=J
    1 CONTINUE
      PRINT *,INT
      STOP
      END
```

Compiling this program without subscript checking yields the following behavior, in which the value of INT mysteriously changes from 0 to 11.

```
unix[37] f77 wrong.f
unix[38] a.out
   11
```

Because MAT and INT are adjacent in memory, storing a value in MAT(11), beyond the dimensioned size of the array, actually changes the value of INT. In the early days of computing some programs were intentionally written to work like this, but as discussed in §13.8.3 this is a confusing and dangerous way to code. This example puts MAT and INT adjacent in COMMON to ensure they are adjacent in memory, so that the result of the subscript error is obvious, but subscript errors can of course also occur in programs that do not use COMMON.

To catch the mistake, we can use the -C compiler option as shown below (here with a Sun Microsystems compiler).

```
unix[39] f77 -C wrong.f
unix[40] a.out
Subscript out of range on file wrong.f, line 4, procedure MAIN.
Attempt to access the 11-th element of variable mat.
Abort
```

The phrasing and format of error messages vary among UNIX™ systems. Subscript checking takes CPU time, so if execution speed is important this option should not be used for production runs of a program that is believed to be correct. However, many errors in FORTRAN programs result from runaway subscripts, so if -C or -fbounds-check is available it should *always* be used for debugging, and also for production runs when CPU time is not a consideration.

14.1.3   Other Compiler Options

The -g option tells the compiler to prepare the executable for debugging with dbx, which is discussed in detail in §14.3.

The -O option tells the compiler to **optimize** the program, if possible, by rearranging the machine code in various ways that can result in increased execution speed. In many compilers the code movements that take place in this process make the symbolic debugging information included by the -g option incorrect, so -O cancels -g; other compilers permit the options to be used together. Optimization increases compilation time, but usually reduces the resulting executable's running time. The -p option tells the compiler to insert code for gathering statistical information about the CPU time that is consumed by different parts of your program when it runs, and these data can later be used to construct an **execution profile** that identifies program segments that might benefit from optimization. Both compiler optimization and execution profiling are discussed further in §15.

The -c option tells the compiler to translate a subprogram's source code into machine instructions, but to refrain from linking the result together with any other routines from your program or with routines from the FORTRAN I/O and elementary function libraries. The -c option is used when the pieces of a program are to be compiled separately and linked together later, by another run of f77 that might serve only that purpose. How this is done, and why it is often preferable to compiling and linking all the pieces of a program at once, is explained in §14.4.

14.1.4 Summary

This table summarizes the f77 compiler options discussed above, and lists the sections where they are discussed more fully.

option	effect	§
-fno-automatic	(g77 only) save local variables	14.1
-ftypeless-boz	(g77 only) allow hex initializations	14.1
-C	(-fbounds-check in g77) check array subscripts	14.1.2
-c	make a .o file, not an executable	14.4
-g	generate symbols for debugging with dbx	14.3
-O	optimize for minimum running time	15.2
-o prog	put executable in file prog	14.1.1
-p	link for profiling with prof	15.1.2

Other options might be important to you because of peculiarities of your compiler, so you should read the documentation for each compiler you use to familiarize yourself with its features.

14.2 Operating System Services

User programs ultimately depend on the operating system for date and time information, for the management of I/O units and files, and for communication with the command shell. These services can be obtained and controlled by invoking UNIX™ system routines. The routines that can be directly invoked from FORTRAN programs are listed in the **man** page that should be displayed when you enter

```
unix[41] man 3f intro
```

The 3f clause in this command tells **man** to look up the page in chapter 3F of the UNIX™ manual, which concerns system routines that can be invoked from FORTRAN. You can also use the **man** command to get additional information about each routine individually. Here we will discuss only the most commonly needed ones.

For your programs to be easily portable to other operating systems, and between different versions of UNIX™, it is important for any system calls you use to be isolated in one or a few subprograms (as I mentioned in §12.4.4) and to be carefully commented. Then if you move to a different system, or give your code to someone who uses a different system, it will be as simple as possible to modify the system calls or replace them with equivalents for the new environment.

14.2.1   Current Date and Time

The current date and time are returned in a character string by the FDATE subroutine and in integer arrays by IDATE and ITIME. Here is a program that illustrates their use.

```
      CHARACTER*24 STRING
      INTEGER*4 HMS(3),DMY(3)
      CALL FDATE(STRING)
      WRITE(6,901) STRING
  901 FORMAT(A24)
      CALL ITIME(HMS)
      CALL IDATE(DMY)
      WRITE(6,902) HMS,DMY
  902 FORMAT(I2,':',I2,':',I2,1X,I2,1X,I2,1X,I4)
      STOP
      END
```

When I ran the program it produced the following output:

```
unix[42] a.out
Sun May 26 14:10:17 1996
14:10:17 26  5 1996
```

There are also UNIX™ system routines for measuring CPU time, and for measuring the time of day with finer resolution than one second; these routines are discussed in §15.1.3 and §18.5 respectively.

14.2.2   I/O Units and Files

The FORTRAN INQUIRE statement can be used to find the name of a file that is attached to a given logical unit, or whether a logical unit has been OPENed, or whether a file exists, or various other facts about I/O units and files. This program illustrates the use of INQUIRE.

```
      LOGICAL*4 OK
      CHARACTER*5 FN
      INQUIRE(FILE='input',EXIST=OK)
      IF(OK) THEN
         OPEN(UNIT=1,FILE='input')
         INQUIRE(UNIT=1,NAME=FN)
         WRITE(6,901) FN
  901    FORMAT(A5)
      ELSE
         WRITE(6,902)
  902    FORMAT('"input" does not exist')
      ENDIF
      STOP
      END
```

The first INQUIRE asks whether the file **input** exists, and sets the logical variable OK accordingly. If the file is there, the program attaches it to unit 1 and then uses INQUIRE again to get the name of the file attached to unit 1. So if **input** exists, the program just writes

input, and if the file does not exist it writes the message saying that. The first parameter in an INQUIRE statement must be either FILE= or UNIT=. Consult your compiler manual to find out what keywords are supported on your system in addition to EXIST and NAME.

Some information about files that is not available via INQUIRE can be obtained from the UNIX™ functions STAT and FSTAT. These routines return the same data about the file, and differ only in that STAT uses the filename and FSTAT uses the logical unit number. The table below gives their calling sequences.

RC= STAT(FILNAM, INFO)		
RC=FSTAT(UNITNO, INFO)		
FILNAM	string	the name of the file
UNITNO	INTEGER*4	the number of the unit
RC	INTEGER*4	return code; $0 \Rightarrow$ success
INFO(13)	INTEGER*4	return values

Most of the return values are of little interest in typical engineering and scientific applications, but there are a few that are occasionally useful: INFO(8) contains the file size in bytes, INFO(10) contains the time of the last change to the file's contents, and INFO(12) contains the block size of the file system where the file is located (see §15.2.8). For more information about the return values, see [84] or the **man** page for STAT. The program below illustrates the use of STAT and FSTAT.

```
      INTEGER*4 STAT,FSTAT,INFO(13),RC
      RC=STAT('fyle',INFO)
      WRITE(6,901) INFO(8)
  901 FORMAT('"fyle" size =',I11,' bytes')
      OPEN(UNIT=1,FILE='input')
      RC=FSTAT(1,INFO)
      WRITE(6,902) INFO(8)
  902 FORMAT('"input" size =',I11,' bytes')
      STOP
      END
```

In their function values STAT and FSTAT return an integer that is zero on success and nonzero on failure, here received in RC and ignored. The invocation of STAT gets information about a file named **fyle**, of which we write out only the file size. After attaching a file named **input** to unit 1 with the OPEN statement, we invoke FSTAT and pass it that unit number. Of the information that is returned about **input**, we again write out only the file size.

Getting disk I/O underway is time-consuming, so UNIX™ stores the output from your program in memory until enough bytes have accumulated to make an I/O event worthwhile, or until the run is over. This **output buffering** can frustrate attempts to monitor the progress of a program by watching an output file (e.g., with the **more** command). To flush an I/O buffer so that the output is written right away, we can call the UNIX™ system routine FLUSH(NUNIT) after each WRITE and pass it the number NUNIT of the logical I/O unit whose buffer is to be flushed.

Often it is desirable to attach a file to a FORTRAN logical I/O unit from outside a program, rather than using an OPEN statement or the GETFIL subroutine inside the program. If the unit in question is 0, 5, or 6, we can use shell redirection to attach the file, as described in §9.4; for other unit numbers, we can use the UNIX™ **ln** command. Suppose for example that we need to attach unit 7 to a file named **unit7file**. In the program we can let the unit's file assignment default (see §9.4.1) to `fort.7`, and before running the executable, at a UNIX™ prompt or in a shell script, we can issue a link command like this:

```
unix[43] ln -s unit7file fort.7
```

This makes a **symbolic link** from the actual file `unit7file` to the name `fort.7`. If the name of the actual file is available in a shell variable, say `VAR`, (as might happen in a shell script) we can use `ln` like this:

```
unix[44] ln -s $VAR fort.7
```

Sometimes it is desirable to remove a file from within a program, and that can be done by calling the UNIX™ system routine `UNLINK`. Here a temporary or **scratch file** named `/tmp/junk` is removed.

```
      CALL UNLINK('/tmp/junk')
      STOP
      END
```

14.2.3 Shell Variables

It is possible to find out the value of a shell variable (also called an **environment variable**) from inside a FORTRAN program, by calling the UNIX™ system routine `GETENV` as in this program.

```
      CHARACTER*24 SHLVAR
      CALL GETENV('VAR',SHLVAR)
      OPEN(UNIT=7,FILE=SHLVAR)
      WRITE(7,902)
  902 FORMAT('Here is a line of output.')
      STOP
      END
```

If this source code is in a file `tryenv.f`, we might have the following exchange with UNIX™.

```
unix[45] f77 tryenv.f
unix[46] export VAR=unit7file
unix[47] a.out
unix[48] more unit7file
Here is a line of output.
```

After compiling the program we set the shell variable `VAR` to the filename `unit7file`. When we run `a.out`, the program calls `GETENV` to put the value of `VAR` in the character variable `SHLVAR`, attaches the file to unit 7, and writes a line of output there. When the program stops we use the UNIX™ `more` command to verify that the output was written in the file. This is another way to make a file assignment based on a name in a shell variable. Of course shell variables can contain text other than file names, and there are many other situations in which it might be useful for a program to know the value of a shell variable.

If a shell variable read by `GETENV` contains a text string longer than the dimensioned size of the character variable that is to receive it, FORTRAN will receive only as many characters as will fit. Thus, in the example above if `VAR` had contained a filename longer than 24 characters only the first 24 characters would have wound up in `SHLVAR`.

14.2.4   Command Line Arguments

It is also possible to pass command line arguments into a FORTRAN program. The UNIX™ system function IARGC returns the number of arguments given on the command line, and the subroutine GETARG returns the text of any single argument, as shown by the example below. Functions with no arguments, such as IARGC, are discussed briefly in §13.6.5.

```
      CHARACTER*24 TEXT
      NARGS=IARGC()
      DO 1 N=1,NARGS
          CALL GETARG(N,TEXT)
          WRITE(6,900) N,TEXT
  900     FORMAT('Argument ',I1,' is: ',A24)
    1 CONTINUE
      STOP
      END
```

If this source code is in **tryarg.f**, we might have the following exchange with UNIX™.

```
unix[49] f77 tryarg.f
unix[50] a.out first second
Argument 1 is: first
Argument 2 is: second
```

When we run **a.out**, we supply two command line arguments. IARGC returns the value 2, so the DO loop retrieves NARGS=2 arguments with GETARG and writes them out. If we gave an argument longer than TEXT, we would get only the first 24 characters. Both IARGC and GETARG are used in the GETFIL routine of §18.3.

14.2.5   Issuing UNIX™ Commands

Occasionally it is useful to have a completely general way of issuing shell commands from inside a program, and that can be done using the SYSTEM subroutine. Here is an example in which the UNIX™ **grep** utility is used to search for a character string in all files in the current directory having a .txt suffix.

```
      INTEGER*4 RC,SYSTEM
      RC=SYSTEM('grep banana *.txt')
      IF(RC.EQ.0) PRINT *,'found!'
      STOP
      END
```

The SYSTEM routine returns the exit code of the UNIX™ command that it executed, so in this case a return code of zero means that **grep** found the string. Running the program in a directory that has a .txt file containing the word "banana" yields output like this on the display:

```
unix[51] a.out
Time flies like an arrow, but fruit flies like a banana.
 found!
```

The first line of output is from **grep**, which echoes the text in which it found the target word. The second line of output is from the FORTRAN program, reporting that the **grep** was successful. Unfortunately there is no elegant way for a program to capture the *output* from a UNIX™ command that it issues via SYSTEM. However, often (and in this case) one could (inelegantly) redirect the UNIX™ command's output to a file and then read the file from inside the program.

14.2.6 Setting a Return Code

Normally a FORTRAN program sets a nonzero return code only in the event of an error that is detected by the operating system, such as an integer divide by zero. If your program will be running in a shell script, it might be convenient to have it set a nonzero return code in other circumstances as well. To do this you can call the UNIX™ system subroutine EXIT rather than using the FORTRAN STOP statement. CALL EXIT(0) corresponds to STOP, but if the argument is an integer in the range [1,255] that becomes the return code of the FORTRAN program. The example below sets a return code of 1.

```
CALL EXIT(1)
END
```

The shell stores the value in a parameter named ?, which can be tested in a script or displayed using echo.

```
unix[52] a.out
unix[53] echo $?
1
```

It is possible to do many other useful things by invoking UNIX™ system routines, so you should consult the intro manual page mentioned at the beginning of this section whenever you need to communicate with the operating system from inside your FORTRAN programs. Remember that, as explained in §10.6, it is necessary under some versions of UNIX™ to use the CHARACTER*n form for character variables that are passed as arguments to system routines.

14.3 Debugging and dbx

Debugging is sometimes unavoidable as a last resort of even good programmers, but it is the *first* resort only of incompetent ones. It is costly of time and effort, likely to produce collateral damage, and a humiliating admission of failure to get things right by other means. Nothing could make debugging pleasant or easy, or less work than writing correct code in the first place, but the hints in this section might help.

14.3.1 Compile-Time Errors

Syntax mistakes (such as misplaced commas) and certain locutions that don't make sense in context (such as variable declarations among executable statements) elicit error messages, also called **diagnostics**, from f77 and prevent translation of the source code into machine language. The only cure for these **compile-time errors** is to read the messages, study the offending lines of code, review the relevant sections of this book or the compiler manual, and correct the source text.

The compiler itself is unfortunately seldom much help with this, because it can't anticipate your intentions and it has nothing like a real understanding of FORTRAN. At some tasks (see §15.2) the compiler is truly an idiot savant, but it is still an IDIOT. Code translation might look like magic, but it is more akin to text processing. The compiler can refer only to the symbols you use, not to the ideas that you were hoping they would embody, so the best messages it can manage are often obtuse and confusing. They *do* contain the line number where the trouble was discovered, and some compilers even give the column, and these hints are often very helpful. On the other hand, it is common for a single error to confuse the compiler sufficiently that it produces pages of additional complaints that turn out to be groundless once the original mistake is corrected. Fix the errors you understand and recompile to see if the others go away.

Compile-time errors vary in severity. Fatal blunders result in an "error" message, whereas things that are probably harmless, like declaring a variable that is never used, elicit only a "warning" message. Sometimes a warning message can't be avoided, such as when a COMMON block has different lengths in different routines. This is often appropriate in order to hide information from routines that do not need it, and then it is *not* an error. Of course, you might have made a mistake that resulted in COMMON blocks of different lengths, so you should check to make sure that everything is correct, but then ignore that warning.

Most compilers provide an option for turning off the warning messages, but don't do that. Fix all the warnings you can fix without doing violence to the code. It's nice to get a **clean compile**, one that produces no diagnostics of any severity, but only if you can keep the compiler happy without breaking the rules of good programming.

It might be some consolation to beginning coders that only beginning coders make a lot of compile-time errors, or find them difficult to identify and fix. The hand-checking called for in §12.5 should virtually eliminate compile-time errors.

14.3.2   Run-Time Errors

The *hard* problems, which occasionally beset even experienced programmers, are **run-time errors**. Of these there are two kinds, those that are detected by the FORTRAN run-time environment or the operating system and those that merely make the output wrong. The ones that are detected are called **exceptions** and the others are euphemistically referred to as **bugs**. Run-time errors result from flaws in the underlying algorithm, mistakes in the data structures or logic of the program, or numerical difficulties such as roundoff errors and overflows. None of these things can be anticipated by the compiler.

Exceptions are usually easier to find than bugs, because they result in error messages. In addition to telling *that* something went wrong, the messages sometimes tell *what* went wrong, though usually not *where* in the source code.

I/O Errors The most elementary exception is reaching the end of an input file, which the following program is bound to do eventually.

```
      LOGICAL*4 MORE/.TRUE./
      OPEN(UNIT=1,FILE='junk')
    1 READ(1,*)
      IF(MORE) GO TO 1
      PRINT *,'Here I am.'
      STOP
      END
```

This code gives a clean compile, but when the executable is run it stops with an error message before reaching the PRINT statement.

```
unix[54] a.out
list read: [-1] end of file
logical unit 1, named 'junk'
lately: reading sequential list external IO
part of last format: ext list io
part of last data: third^J|
Abort
unix[55]
```

The error number [-1] is the standard UNIX™ return code denoting EOF. The file junk used in this example had three lines, containing respectively the words "first", "second", and "third", so the last data read was the word "third"; the suffix ^J| marks the end of the input.

Other I/O errors can result from exceeding your disk quota, from file system and network failures, and from mistakes in programming. The code below tries to open a logical I/O unit numbered -1. The unit number -1 is illegal so, as shown below the listing, when the program is run it produces an error message and stops before reaching the PRINT statement.

```
OPEN(UNIT=-1,FILE='junk')
PRINT *,'Here I am.'
STOP
END
```

```
unix[56] a.out
open: [1001] illegal unit number
unix[57]
```

This error number [1001] is peculiar to the f77 compiler that I used, and identifies the error as having come from the FORTRAN run-time system (in this case the open routine in the I/O library). The manufacturer's manual for the compiler [32] offers the terse additional explanation "It is illegal to close logical unit 0. Negative unit numbers are not allowed. The upper limit is $2^{31} - 1$." Breaking any of those rules elicits the same message. Your compiler manual probably contains a list of all the error messages that can come from its run-time system, with their possible causes.

Recall from §9 that the READ statement takes an optional END= clause, and that the READ, WRITE, and OPEN statements all take an optional ERR= clause. These transfer control to a given statement when an EOF or I/O error occurs. If you use END= and ERR= to handle these exceptions within your program, you will be able to tell what statement is at fault and in some cases you might be able to take corrective action rather than stopping the program.

Floating point arithmetic errors. Meaningful messages are also generated for floating-point errors such as the ones in this program.

```
REAL*8 Z1,Z2,X,Y
Z1=0.D0
Z2=0.D0
X=1.D0/Z1
PRINT *, X
Y=Z1/Z2
PRINT *, Y
STOP
END
```

The divisions by zero do *not* interrupt the program. In IEEE floating-point arithmetic [19] [27] they are **fixed up** by assigning to X and Y special bit patterns representing, respectively, $+\infty$ and NaN or "not a number" (see §4.7). Only after the program stops normally do we get the error message.

```
unix[58] a.out
  Infinity
  NaN
Note: the following IEEE floating-point arithmetic exceptions
occurred and were never cleared; see ieee_flags(3M):
 Division by Zero;  Invalid Operand;
unix[59]
```

Our PRINT statements output the words Infinity for X and NaN for Y, rather than numbers. If you find Infinity or NaN printed where you expected a number in your output, it must be that somewhere in the calculation an illegal floating-point operation was fixed-up to that value. The error message refers us to a **man** page that describes IEEE floating-point arithmetic, and then it lists the two exceptions. Section 3M of the UNIX™ manual is about math functions. Other IEEE floating-point errors generate similar messages. In addition to genuine exceptions for *division by zero*, *invalid operand* (such as asking for 0.D0/0.D0 or the square root of a negative number), and *exponent overflow* (a result too large to represent), IEEE floating-point implementations also report *underflows* (results rounded to zero because they were too small to represent) and *inexact* results (those differing from their infinitely-precise values). Underflows and inexact results might be of concern from the standpoint of numerical analysis (though they are usually benign), but they can safely be ignored if what you are trying to get right is the logic of the code. The other errors must be found and, except in the unlikely event that the standard fixup is what you want, corrected.

Integer arithmetic errors. Unfortunately, there are also exceptions for which the error message is not much help.

```
    I=0
    J=1/I
    PRINT *,'Here I am.'
    STOP
    END
```

Unlike an IEEE floating-point divide by zero, this **integer divide check** stops the program with a diagnostic that does not tell what went wrong.

```
unix[60] a.out
Abort
unix[61]
```

But now you know that an integer division by zero is one thing to check for.

Memory access errors. A **segmentation fault** results from an attempt by the program to access memory not belonging to it. The program at the top of the next page assigns values to storage locations outside the dimensioned size of the array M, eventually addressing a memory location it is not allowed to change.

```
      INTEGER*4 M(2)
      I=0
    1 I=I+1
        M(I)=I
      IF(I.GE.1) GO TO 1
      STOP
      END
```

```
unix[62] a.out
*** TERMINATING
*** Received signal 11 (SIGSEGV)
Segmentation fault
unix[63]
```

Recall that many subscript problems can be identified by using the -C or -fbounds-check compiler option, as explained in §14.1.2.

Trying to access data in a way that conflicts with the alignment of the data in memory causes a bus error.

```
      COMMON /X/ C
      CHARACTER*1 C(5)
      CALL SUB(C(2))
      STOP
      END
      SUBROUTINE SUB(I)
      PRINT *,I
      RETURN
      END
```

COMMON blocks begin on doubleword boundaries, so C(2) is the second byte of a doubleword and hence *not* fullword aligned. Yet SUB tries to access it as though it were an integer, which *must* be fullword aligned.

```
unix [64] a.out
*** TERMINATING a.out
*** Received signal 10 (SIGBUS)
Bus error
unix [65]
```

The bus error message, like the segmentation fault message, gives no indication what might be wrong with the source code, or where. This example put C in COMMON to ensure that it would be doubleword aligned, but the compiler might have aligned C on a doubleword boundary even if we did not require it. Thus, alignment errors can also occur in programs that do not use COMMON.

Forgetting to declare as EXTERNAL a subprogram name that is passed as an argument to another routine also produces an error message that might be difficult to interpret, as illustrated by this program.

```
      CALL SUB(NAME)
      STOP
      END
      SUBROUTINE SUB(NAME)
      CALL NAME
      RETURN
      END
```

NAME is a subprogram name and should thus be declared EXTERNAL in both routines so that it can be passed as an argument to SUB. Failing to do that results in NAME containing garbage rather than the address of a subroutine, and what is at that garbage address turns out not to be a machine instruction, so we get the error message shown below.

```
unix[66] a.out
*** TERMINATING a.out
*** Received signal 4 (SIGILL)
Illegal instruction
unix[67]
```

A similar problem can occur when you forget to dimension an array in a routine where it is referred to with a subscript. The compiler naturally assumes this is a reference to a FUNCTION subprogram (remember that even if you dimensioned the array somewhere else, separate compilation prevents the compiler from remembering that). Depending on the circumstances, the error will be recognized either at link time or at run time, but in both cases the error message gives little indication of what is really wrong. The following examples, which we assume are in the files `baffle1.f`, and `baffle2.f`, illustrate what happens.

```
INTEGER*4 IX(3)/1,2,3/             INTEGER*4 IX(3)/1,2,3/
CALL SUB(IX,2)                     CALL SUB(IX,2)
STOP                               STOP
END                               END
SUBROUTINE SUB(IX,J)               SUBROUTINE SUB(IX,J)
INTEGER*4 IX(3)                    PRINT *,IX(J)
PRINT *,IY(J)                      RETURN
RETURN                             END
END
```

```
unix[68] f77 baffle1.f             unix[70] f77 baffle2.f
baffle1.f:                         baffle2.f:
 MAIN:                              MAIN:
        sub:                              sub:
ld: Undefined symbol               unix[71] a.out
 _iy_                              *** TERMINATING a.out
unix[69]                          *** Received signal 4 (SIGILL)
                                   Illegal instruction
                                   unix[72]
```

On the left, a typographical error in SUB has resulted in a reference to IY(J) where IX(J) was intended. Linking of the executable fails because ld thinks it is missing the code for a FUNCTION subprogram named IY.

On the right, IX(J) is spelled correctly in SUB but its declaration as an array has been forgotten. The compiler assumes that IX is a subprogram name (even though it is not declared EXTERNAL) so the executable links successfully. However, when the program runs, what gets passed to SUB is *not* the address of an EXTERNAL routine named IX but the address of some data that does not consist of machine instructions.

Hidden Subprogram Name Conflicts. All FORTRAN compilers recognize built-in function names other than those tabulated in §6.6.1 for Classical FORTRAN, and all UNIX™ implementations have system routines other than the ones listed in §6.6.2. Libraries such as those mentioned in §6.6.3 typically contain hundreds of subprograms of which you typically use only a few at a time, and those few probably invoke subsidiary routines whose names you don't know and cannot easily find out. If you unwittingly give one of your routines a name that the loader finds somewhere else instead, your program might invoke the wrong routine with unpredictable consequences. (This can happen to programs written in any language.) Name conflicts are rare, but if you suspect you might have one you should code PRINT statements in your subprograms to confirm that they are indeed being entered in the expected sequence.

Summary. This table summarizes the run-time errors discussed above.

message or symptom	probable cause and diagnostic action
EOF	reading too far in a file; use END=
I/O error	cause usually given in message; use ERR=
IEEE error	impossible floating-point operation (fixed up)
unexplained Abort	integer divide check
segmentation fault	runaway array subscript; use f77 -C or g77 -fbounds-check
bus error	data misaligned in COMMON or subprogram linkage
illegal instruction	routine name passed but not declared EXTERNAL
missing routine	array not dimensioned
bizarre behavior	right name, wrong routine; print entry messages

The handling of IEEE floating-point errors is specified by the standard [19] so it is similar from one version of UNIX™ to another and from one FORTRAN compiler to another, but the reporting of other exceptions varies significantly between manufacturers. It might be worthwhile to experiment with your system to see how it handles different exceptions, so that you can guess the cause when run-time error messages appear unexpectedly.

14.3.3 Debugging with Output Statements

Even when a useful diagnostic is generated, it might not be obvious what caused a run-time error or where in the source code it happened. If the error message is inscrutable, or if the program gives incorrect output *without* causing any error messages, it is often hard to know even where to start looking for the mistake. In these situations we need a systematic way to learn more about what is wrong.

The traditional and still the most often-used way of finding run-time errors is to pepper the code with PRINT or WRITE statements, to track the flow of control and report values of the key variables that determine the evolution of the calculation. Usually, watching where the program goes and what it does makes the problem obvious. We will study this approach using the program at the top of the next page, which looks harmless but contains a bug. Can you find the mistake by inspection, before we begin debugging?

This program reads 16 values into the array A and then calls SUB for each column, passing A and the column and row indices of the diagonal element in the column. The subroutine finds the largest entry in column K by initializing CMAX(K) to the diagonal value and then examining the elements of the column from the diagonal up to the top, replacing CMAX(K) with any larger values that it finds. This algorithm is not particularly efficient, because it compares the diagonal element to itself in checking each column, but it does have the virtue of simplicity. The DO loop in the subroutine is a little unusual because it counts down, but otherwise the code is straightforward.

The run-time error this program exhibits is that it never terminates. The code compiles and links without error, and the executable runs without generating any exceptions, but no output is ever produced and the program continues running until it is interrupted. Recall

```
      REAL*8 A(4,4),CMAX(4)
      READ *, A
C     find maximum entry in each column on or above diagonal
      DO 1 I=1,4
          CALL SUB(A,I,I, CMAX)
    1 CONTINUE
      WRITE(6,901) CMAX
  901 FORMAT('maxima: ',4F10.2)
      STOP
      END
C

      SUBROUTINE SUB(A,K,J, CMAX)
      REAL*8 A(4,4),CMAX(4)
      CMAX(K)=A(J,K)
      DO 1 J=K,1,-1
          CMAX(K)=DMAX1(CMAX(K),A(J,K))
    1 CONTINUE
      RETURN
      END
```

from §0.5.5 that we can stop a program that is running interactively in UNIX™ by typing ^C.

Is it just that this calculation *ought* to take a long time, or is the program waiting for us to enter something more from the keyboard, or is it stuck in an endless loop? With no output or error messages, it is hard to tell (though the UNIX™ ps command might reveal whether the executable is actually consuming processor time). This ambiguous situation is very common in debugging, especially if the program is one that might plausibly run for a long while.

But given the trivial calculation this program is supposed to do, it should be done in a flash. To investigate why it is not, we insert some output statements as shown at the top of the next page.

Adding debugging PRINT and WRITE statements disturbs the source code, so care must be taken to avoid introducing another error (that would be the "collateral damage" referred to earlier). In the implied DO we use an index of L, which is not used elsewhere in the program. Later, when the code is working, we will want to remove the debugging statements, so we indent them in a way that makes them easy to find. To make it even more obvious that the added FORMAT statement is just for debugging, we give it a number outside the usual sequence.

Running the revised program yields the output shown below. The pattern of subroutine entry and exit announcements repeats for as long as we like, filling the screen until we send a ^C.

```
start of program
     1.00      3.00     12.00      5.00
    83.00      4.00     95.00     11.00
     2.00     51.00     10.00      6.00
    78.00      6.00     11.00     10.00
entering SUB, K=  1 J=  1
exiting SUB, K=  0 J=  0
entering SUB, K=  1 J=  1
exiting SUB, K=  0 J=  0
  :
```

```
      REAL*8 A(4,4),CMAX(4)
       PRINT *,'start of program'
      READ *, A
      WRITE(6,999) (A(L,1),A(L,2),A(L,3),A(L,4),L=1,4)
  999 FORMAT(4F10.2)
C     find maximum entry in each column on or above diagonal
      DO 1 I=1,4
          CALL SUB(A,I,I,CMAX)
    1 CONTINUE
      WRITE(6,901) CMAX
  901 FORMAT('maxima: ',4F10.2)
      STOP
      END
C
      SUBROUTINE SUB(A,K,J,CMAX)
      REAL*8 A(4,4),CMAX(4)
       PRINT *,'entering SUB, K=',K,' J=',J
      CMAX(K)=A(J,K)
      DO 1 J=K,1,-1
          CMAX(K)=DMAX1(CMAX(K),A(J,K))
    1 CONTINUE
       PRINT *,'exiting SUB, K=',K,' J=',J
      RETURN
      END
```

From the output we can see that the program does actually start, read the data, and enter the loop of calls to SUB. Control actually does get transferred to SUB, which actually does return. So it is the DO loop in the main program that is endless. The only way that a DO loop can be endless is if something is interfering with its indexing mechanism.

Examining the values of K and J on entering and exiting SUB reveals the problem. The loop in the subroutine uses J for an index. The value of a DO index can be anything outside of the loop, and in this case it turns out to be zero. But J in the subroutine corresponds to I in the main program, and that is *its* loop index. So the subroutine keeps setting the main's loop index back to zero, which means that loop never ends. We can remove the bug by passing a copy of I, rather than I itself, as the third parameter to SUB. The revised code is shown on the next page, and its output is shown below. Now the program terminates, and from the debugging output shown below it is clear that the subroutine is no longer changing the main's DO index.

```
 start of program
       1.00        3.00       12.00        5.00
      83.00        4.00       95.00       11.00
       2.00       51.00       10.00        6.00
      78.00        6.00       11.00       10.00
 entering SUB, K=  1 J=  1
 exiting SUB, K=  1 J=  0
 entering SUB, K=  2 J=  2
 exiting SUB, K=  2 J=  0
 entering SUB, K=  3 J=  3
 exiting SUB, K=  3 J=  0
 entering SUB, K=  4 J=  4
 exiting SUB, K=  4 J=  0
 maxima:        1.00        4.00       95.00       11.00
```

```
      REAL*8 A(4,4),CMAX(4)
       PRINT *,'start of program'
      READ *, A
       WRITE(6,999) (A(L,1),A(L,2),A(L,3),A(L,4),L=1,4)
  999 FORMAT(4F10.2)
C     find maximum entry in each column on or above diagonal
      DO 1 I=1,4
          J=I
          CALL SUB(A,I,J,CMAX)
    1 CONTINUE
      WRITE(6,901) CMAX
  901 FORMAT('maxima: ',4F10.2)
      STOP
      END
C
      SUBROUTINE SUB(A,K,J,CMAX)
      REAL*8 A(4,4),CMAX(4)
       PRINT *,'entering SUB, K=',K,' J=',J
      CMAX(K)=A(J,K)
      DO 1 J=K,1,-1
          CMAX(K)=DMAX1(CMAX(K),A(J,K))
    1 CONTINUE
       PRINT *,'exiting SUB, K=',K,' J=',J
      RETURN
      END
```

The reported maxima are indeed the largest elements on or above the diagonal of the matrix, so it seems that nothing else is wrong with the code, and we could now remove the debugging statements.

Notice that the bug we found was not really in the logic of the program, although it did affect the DO loop in the main. The mistake was in passing a variable that should not be modified to a subroutine that unexpectedly modified it. Most bugs in FORTRAN programs turn out to be in the storage, passing, or protection of data, rather than in flow-of-control logic. People are much better at reasoning than they are at keeping data correctly organized. Errors in type declarations, array dimensions, subscript values, subprogram parameters, and the alignment of variables in COMMON are much more frequent than incorrectly coded tests or wrong branch targets.

This example was contrived to have a single mistake, but real programs, especially if they are long and complicated, might harbor many bugs at the same time. There are nightmare legacy codes that are veritable roach hotels. In trying to deal with seriously wrong programs, it is prudent to bear in mind the famous slogan that "The bug you find is never the one you are looking for." Sometimes just when you think you've killed the last bug, and removed all the debugging output statements, another symptom turns up and you have to put them all back in. To avoid this annoyance it is sometimes worth the trouble to permanently build debugging code into a program, possibly directing its output to a special file just for debugging messages (see §9.4.1).

If you use permanent debugging code, you might want to provide an easy way to turn it off and on by using a LOGICAL variable. Thus, in the preceding example we might permanently revise the subroutine as shown at the top of the next page. With DEBUG initialized to .FALSE., the PRINT statements are turned off. If more trouble crops up we need only change DEBUG to .TRUE. and recompile SUB, avoiding the more extensive editing that would be required if we removed the PRINT statements altogether and later want them back.

```
      SUBROUTINE SUB(A,K,J,CMAX)
      REAL*8 A(4,4),CMAX(4)
      LOGICAL*4 DEBUG/.FALSE./
      IF(DEBUG) PRINT *,'entering SUB, K=',K,' J=',J
      CMAX(K)=A(J,K)
      DO 1 J=K,1,-1
          CMAX(K)=DMAX1(CMAX(K),A(J,K))
    1 CONTINUE
      IF(DEBUG) PRINT *,'exiting SUB, K=',K,' J=',J
      RETURN
      END
```

"Commenting out" debugging statements by inserting a C in column 1, and removing the C's when the statements are to be put back into the program, involves editing that is very easy to get wrong, so in §13.1.2 I recommended against it. The IF statements that are typically needed to control debugging output in the manner outlined above use a negligible amount of CPU time and confer the great convenience and relative safety of being able to control all the debugging statements in a routine by changing one constant in its preamble.

A natural generalization of the DEBUG flag idea is to permanently build into the program a **message level variable** that provides several steps of control over the verbosity of output, as discussed in §12.2.1. Output that might normally be used to track the progress of a calculation and examine intermediate results can also be very useful in finding the cause when something goes wrong.

Some compilers permit the use of **debug comments**, which have a D rather than a C in column 1 and are either ignored or compiled depending on an f77 command-line parameter. D comments permit debugging statements to be turned on and off without *any* modification of the FORTRAN source, but at the cost of making the program less portable and possibly harder to understand. Another approach to switching debugging code on and off uses the UNIX™ C preprocessor program cpp. If the FORTRAN source code is in a file whose name ends in .F rather than .f, then f77 filters it through cpp before compilation, and preprocessor directives can be used to include or exclude code segments based on the value of a preprocessor variable. This method has the drawback of cluttering the source code with cpp directives, but might be appropriate if the preprocessor is already being used for other reasons (such as the regrettable one of expanding C-style #include directives). For more information on cpp, see its man page.

14.3.4 Vanishing Bugs

You might sometimes be frustrated in debugging your code because adding PRINT statements as suggested in §14.3.3 mysteriously causes the bug to disappear or the symptoms to change. As first suggested in Exercise 5.8.36, this is often due to an array subscript going out of bounds.

In UNIX™ systems an executable is constructed and loaded into memory in such a way that its machine instructions or **program text**, its data (including array storage), and its subprogram parameter **stack** are located in three separate places or **memory segments**. The operating system keeps the machine instructions from being changed by your program, but they can be read and the data and stack segments can be changed.

If your program refers to an element outside the dimensioned size of an array, it will get the wrong data or possibly interpret a piece of its own machine code or of the parameter stack as data. Remember that memory contains only binary 1's and 0's, which might represent numbers or characters or addresses or machine instructions. If the program *changes* an array element outside the dimensioned size, it will change the wrong data, or UNIX™ will interrupt the program with a memory-access exception (if it tried to change the program text), or it will corrupt the parameter stack. The stack contains, among other things, return addresses for subprogram invocations. If the runaway subscript changes an address, there can be a **wild branch** when a subprogram tries to return. If the branch is to outside the memory assigned to your program, UNIX™ will again interrupt it. If a wild branch is into your data or stack segment, the binary numbers there might be interpreted as machine instructions (at least for a few instructions) and in that case almost anything can happen.

Adding a statement, such as PRINT, alters the size and layout of the text segment, so the runaway subscript now causes something different to be erroneously used or modified by the program, and the symptoms change or disappear. Programs written in any compiled language, not just FORTRAN, can exhibit this behavior.

Whenever a bug changes or seems to go away when you make some apparently unrelated revision to the FORTRAN source, you should suspect that an array subscript is going outside its dimensioned bounds or that an array is typed differently in different subprograms where it is used. Hand-check the code to look for such errors, and use a compiler option as described in §14.1.2 to check for subscripts out of range. If the mistake still eludes you try using dbx, as described in the next section, instead of adding PRINT statements.

14.3.5   The dbx Debugger

There are several drawbacks to using output statements for debugging. It is impossible to guess ahead of time everything you might need to know, so it usually turns out that you have not printed the one clue that will explain what is broken. Usually it is necessary to repeatedly revise the code and try again as you follow the trail of the bug. Printing everything in sight makes it more likely that you will get the evidence you need, but exhaustive debugging output uses up lots of disk space and examining it takes lots of your time. Whether you proceed sequentially or exhaustively, it takes work to code the PRINT statements, and there is a chance that in the process of putting them in and taking them out you will introduce additional bugs.

It would be safer and more convenient to be able to step through a program, follow the flow of control, and inspect variable values interactively. Happily, UNIX™ provides the dbx utility for doing exactly those things. Even though dbx is quite primitive and works best on C programs, it is very useful for debugging FORTRAN. Here I will describe only the most basic things about how to use it; for more information see [84], the man page for dbx, and any supplementary documentation that your UNIX™ system manufacturer might provide for their version of dbx. Linux systems come with a debugger called gdb, which resembles dbx sufficiently that most of what I have to say in this section applies to it as well. An excellent manual [102] is available on-line for gdb, and you can consult it for details about the things that do *not* work the same in dbx and gdb.

In order for dbx to know what storage locations in memory correspond to the variables in a FORTRAN source program, a **symbol table** must be included in the program's executable file. Ordinarily, as discussed in §6.1, the compiler replaces your variable names by memory addresses in the process of translating the source code into machine instructions, so the names are forgotten. The -g option tells f77 to generate a symbol table in which the names are saved. This slightly increases the size of the executable file, and in many compilers it cancels the -O option (see §14.1.3), so you might not want to use -g unless you are actually planning to use dbx.

To demonstrate dbx, we will use it to debug the program at the top of the next page, which we will assume is in the file pgm.f. Below the listing is a conversation we might have with UNIX™ and dbx in the process of discovering and investigating the problem.

```
        N=0
        DO 1 I=1,100
            J=1+I/2
            K=1+J/(J-I+2)
            L=1+K/(J-K+3)
            M=(I*J)/(K*L)
            N=N+M
    1   CONTINUE
        WRITE(6,901) N
  901   FORMAT('N=',I10)
        STOP
        END
```

```
unix[73] f77 pgm.f
 MAIN:
unix[74] a.out
Abort
unix[75] f77 -o pgm -g pgm.f
 MAIN:
unix[76] dbx pgm
Reading symbolic information for pgm
(dbx.bin) run
Running: pgm
signal ABRT (abort) in kill at 0xef763178
kill+8: bgeu    noerr
Current function is MAIN
      4               K=1+J/(J-I+2)
(dbx.bin) print J
j = 3
(dbx.bin) print I
i = 5
(dbx.bin) print (J-I+2)
j-i+2 = 0
(dbx.bin) quit
unix[77]
```

Not expecting any trouble, we first try compiling and running the program in the usual way, and get the **Abort** diagnostic. Based on the examples discussed in §14.3.2, this message suggests the possibility of an integer divide check. There are several divisions in the program, and the error message says nothing about which one might be responsible.

To investigate we recompile the program using the **-g** flag, and put the executable in a file named **pgm** rather than letting it default to **a.out**. To compose informative responses to our questions, **dbx** needs to correlate the program's source text with the symbol table that **-g** put in the executable file. For **dbx** to find the **.f** file without our having to tell it where to look, the executable **pgm** *must* have the same name as the front part of the source file name **pgm.f**.

When the compilation using **-g** is finished, we invoke **dbx** on the executable. We are informed that **dbx** is reading the symbol table, and then it presents the prompt (**dbx.bin**). Some implementations might report that additional symbol tables are also being read for FORTRAN library routines the program uses, and the prompt varies from one version of **dbx** to another.

Next we give the **dbx** command **run**, to execute the program. Once again we get an **abort** message, this time including some technical details about the interrupt. But now **dbx** also tells the routine in which the exception occurred, and prints the line number (in `pgm.f`) and text of the offending FORTRAN source statement

Our next step is to examine the variables involved in that source statement by using the `dbx print` command. As shown, we can get the values of variables or of simple expressions. The division turns out to be 3/0 when `J=3` and `I=5`, so we have found the cause and circumstances of the exception. Finally we `quit dbx` and return to the UNIX™ command prompt. Figuring out what to do about the integer divide check is of course up to the programmer.

We used only the `run`, `print`, and `quit` commands of `dbx`, but there are many others as well. The table below summarizes the ones that are most often useful in debugging FORTRAN programs.

command	action
run	execute the program from the beginning
stop	stop `in` a given routine or `at` a given statement
catch	stop where a given UNIX™ signal occurs
step	execute the next FORTRAN statement
next	execute the next FORTRAN statement in this routine
cont	continue execution from this point
where	tell where the program stopped
dump	print all variables in the current routine (not in `gdb`)
print	print a given variable in the current routine
help	tell about all the `dbx` commands
quit	exit `dbx` and return to UNIX™

The `stop` command sets **breakpoints** at which execution of the program is suspended and control is returned to the interactive user. The `catch` command causes the same thing to happen when a given UNIX™ signal occurs. Because the default handling of an IEEE floating-point error is to apply the standard fixup and continue, `dbx` might ignore those exceptions unless you tell it to `catch fpe`. It might also be necessary to use an `f77` option to get the executable to generate a `SIGFPE` signal when an IEEE exception occurs, rather than taking the fixup and going on; consult your compiler manual.

The `step` and `next` commands do the same thing unless the statement to be executed invokes a user-written `FUNCTION` or `SUBROUTINE` subprogram. In that case, `step` steps into the subprogram but `next` executes the whole invocation and stops at the following statement in the current routine. The `cont` command releases the program to continue execution from the current place, until the next breakpoint or the end of the program.

The `where` command prints the source statement that will be executed next when a `step`, `next`, or `cont` command is given. When `dbx` suspends execution at a breakpoint, it tells where it stopped without being asked.

The `dump` and `print` commands write out the values of variables. If the routine you are stopped in has a large number of variables, `print` might be more convenient to use than `dump`. In referring to arrays, some versions of `dbx` use the C syntax of square brackets and consider arrays having more than one dimension to be stored in row major order. In that case, to print for example `M(2,3)` we must tell `dbx` to `print m[3][2]`. Other versions of `dbx` recognize that the executable belongs to a FORTRAN program and know how to interpret FORTRAN-style array syntax. Make sure you find out which way your version of `dbx` works before you use it to print the values of array elements.

The `help` command prints prototypes and terse summaries of all the commands, and descriptions of some special symbols that `dbx` uses. If your debugging needs are modest, you might find that you can learn as much as you need by just using `help` and trying things.

14.4 Automatic Compilation with make

Suppose an application consists of a main program and 29 subroutines, or 30 routines in all, and that each one takes 10 seconds to compile. That means it takes $30 \times 10/60 = 5$ minutes to compile them all. Doing this once is no big deal. You could get a cup of coffee while you wait for f77 to finish.

Now suppose the application is almost perfect, but you are still modifying a few of the routines to fix bugs or get the output formats just right. You make 10 little changes, each edit taking only a minute, but after each one you rebuild the program to verify that the change did what you expected. How long does this take? The actual code revisions require only $10 \times 1 = 10$ minutes, but the compiles take $10 \times 5 = 50$ minutes, so altogether the work takes an hour! I made up the numbers, but something like this has happened to anyone who ever developed a big program. It gets to be pretty annoying to spend 50 minutes out of every hour, or even 10 minutes out of every hour, waiting for the compiler, especially if you don't drink coffee.

14.4.1 Incremental Recompilation

It would be much faster to recompile only the pieces you changed, and then link their object codes with those of the other routines to make a new executable. The link step is fast compared to compiling everything, so we neglected it in estimating the total time above. If linking takes 30 seconds and if each change affects only one routine, the work would take a total of $10 \times (1 + [10 + 30]/60) = 16\frac{2}{3}$ minutes instead of an hour. The ability to recompile only the routines you changed makes separate compilation one of FORTRAN's most endearing features.

To use this approach of recompiling only what needs it, we must keep the source code for each routine in a separate .f file, have the compiler generate an unlinked object or .o file for each routine, save all the .o files from one time to the next, and use the compiler to link them together when we need to make a new executable.

All of this turns out to be easiest to manage if we keep the files in a separate directory devoted to the application. To illustrate how we might set up such a directory suppose the following program, consisting of a main and three subroutines, is in the file myprog.f.

```
CALL SUB1
CALL SUB2
CALL SUB3
STOP
END
SUBROUTINE SUB1
WRITE(6,*) 'This is subroutine 1.'
RETURN
END
SUBROUTINE SUB2
WRITE(6,*) 'This is surboutine 2.'
RETURN
END
SUBROUTINE SUB3
WRITE(6,*) 'This is subruotine 3.'
RETURN
END
```

First we use the UNIX™ command `mkdir` to create a subdirectory named `myprog`, and we move the source file to it. Then we use `cd` to change to that directory so we can work there.

```
unix[78] mkdir myprog
unix[79] mv myprog.f myprog
unix[80] cd myprog
```

Next we need to separate the routines into different .f files. The UNIX™ utility program `fsplit` reads several FORTRAN routines from a single file and writes each to its own .f file. The version I use puts our (unnamed) main program in `main000.f`, so we move it to `main.f`. The `fsplit` program leaves the original file containing all four routines, but we don't need that once it has been successfully split up, so we remove it.

```
unix[81] fsplit myprog.f
main000.f
sub1.f
sub2.f
sub3.f
unix[82] mv main000.f main.f
unix[83] rm myprog.f
```

Now it is necessary to make a .o file from each of the .f's, by using the -c compiler option mentioned in §14.1.3.

```
unix[84] f77 -c main.f sub1.f sub2.f sub3.f
 MAIN:
sub1.f:
        sub1:
sub2.f:
        sub2:
sub3.f:
        sub3:
unix[85] ls
main.f  main.o  sub1.f  sub1.o  sub2.f  sub2.o  sub3.f  sub3.o
```

Each .f file is separately compiled to create a corresponding .o file. Then we use the UNIX™ command `ls` to list the files in the subdirectory, just to show that the .o's were created. The object files take up some disk space, but to save recompilations we will have to keep them around. Finally, we link the .o files to make an executable:

```
unix[86] f77 -o prog main.o sub1.o sub2.o sub3.o
unix[87] ls
main.f  prog    sub1.o  sub2.o  sub3.o
main.o  sub1.f  sub2.f  sub3.f
```

The file `prog` contains the executable, and running it turns up a mistake.

```
unix[88] prog
 This is subroutine 1.
 This is surboutine 2.
 This is subruotine 3.
```

In SUB2, the word "subroutine" is misspelled, so we fix it by editing the source text, here using the `vi` editor. Then we recompile only the routine that changed, and relink.

```
unix[89] vi sub2.f
unix[90] f77 -c sub2.f
sub2.f:
        sub2:
unix[91] f77 -o prog main.o sub1.o sub2.o sub3.o
unix[92] prog
 This is subroutine 1.
 This is subroutine 2.
 This is subruotine 3.
```

14.4.2   Deciding Which Routines to Recompile

The only pitfall in this approach is that in a big application where we are doing a lot of development work, we might forget just which of the many `.f` files we have changed since last relinking the executable. To be sure we are recompiling everything that needs to be, we could check the times the files were last changed, as reported by the `ls -l` command (which rounds off, for display, more precise times returned to it by the `STAT` routine).

```
unix[93] ls -l
    1 -rw-------  1 sarah        69 Jun 16 10:40 main.f
    1 -rw-------  1 sarah       544 Jun 16 10:41 main.o
  160 -rwx------  1 sarah    163840 Jun 16 10:49 prog*
    1 -rw-------  1 sarah        86 Jun 16 10:40 sub1.f
    1 -rw-------  1 sarah       504 Jun 16 10:41 sub1.o
    1 -rw-------  1 sarah        86 Jun 16 10:47 sub2.f
    1 -rw-------  1 sarah       504 Jun 16 10:48 sub2.o
    1 -rw-------  1 sarah        86 Jun 16 10:40 sub3.f
    1 -rw-------  1 sarah       504 Jun 16 10:41 sub3.o
```

Here we can see that the executable `prog` was written at `10:49`, after all of the `.o` files, and that each `.o` file was written after its corresponding `.f` file, so it must be that everything is up to date. If we saw a `.f` file that had been changed after its `.o` was created, we would know that it needed recompiling.

The process of comparing the last change times of the files comprising an application, and then doing whatever is necessary to bring the files up to date, is automated by a UNIX™ utility called `make`. To use `make` for managing an application we compose a **makefile** containing a description of what pieces go into the executable and how they should be put together. A makefile for the application we have been studying is shown at the top of the next page. The first line in each stanza begins with a filename called a **target**, followed by a colon and then a list of **dependencies**. Here the target `prog`, the executable file, depends on all of the `.o` files. The second line in each stanza *begins with a tab character* and then gives a **rule** for bringing the target up to date if it is found to be older than one of the things it depends upon. Thus if, for example, `sub2.o` is found to be older than `sub2.f`, the command in that stanza tells `make` how to recompile the source file. That recompilation changes the last change time of the file `sub2.o`, of course, so now `make` discovers that `prog` is out of date. The command in `prog`'s stanza tells how to relink the executable, so that is done next. Finally everything is up to date again, so `make` is finished.

If more than one command is needed to bring some target up to date, they can all be listed after the dependency line in the stanza for that target. Each command line must begin with a tab, not spaces. If you use spaces instead of a tab, `make` will issue an error

```
prog: main.o sub1.o sub2.o sub3.o
        f77 -o prog main.o sub1.o sub2.o sub3.o

main.o: main.f
        f77 -c main.f

sub1.o: sub1.f
        f77 -c sub1.f

sub2.o: sub2.f
        f77 -c sub2.f

sub3.o: sub3.f
        f77 -c sub3.f
```

message complaining about an unexpected end of line. A dependency line or a command line can be continued by putting a backslash "\" at the end, but if there are any blank spaces after the backslash make will also give the unexpected end of line error.

The makefile described above can actually be simplified quite a bit by using a **default compilation rule**. This replaces the four stanzas for the .o files with a single rule that tells make what to do whenever it finds a .o file that is out of date. Here is the revised makefile.

```
.f.o:
        f77 -c $*.f

prog: main.o sub1.o sub2.o sub3.o
        f77 -o prog main.o sub1.o sub2.o sub3.o
```

The default compilation rule has a "target" of .f.o and a "rule" (preceded by a tab as usual) of f77 -c $*.f Together these say that whenever it is necessary to make a .o file from a .f file, make should issue the UNIX™ command f77 -c *routine*.f where *routine* is the name of the routine whose .o file was found to be out of date. The strange syntax of the default compilation rule might make it seem arcane and undesirable, but if there are many .o files this little bit of magic is preferable to the tedious and error-prone task of making each of them an explicit target. (And if you learn more about make the locution $*.f will turn out not to be so strange after all.)

For make to find our instructions without our having to tell it where to look, the makefile must be called Makefile or makefile. There is some advantage to using the name Makefile, as it will then be listed in the output from ls commands ahead of the files comprising the application, which typically all begin with lower-case letters. Suppose we put the simplified text shown above in Makefile, and use it to maintain myprog.

```
unix[94] ls
Makefile  main.o    sub1.f    sub2.f    sub3.f
main.f    prog      sub1.o    sub2.o    sub3.o
unix[95] make
'prog' is up to date.
unix[96] prog
 This is subroutine 1.
 This is subroutine 2.
 This is subruotine 3.
```

Issuing the UNIX™ command make causes make to read Makefile and check whether the target `prog` is up to date. We left it that way, so `make` just reports that nothing needs to be done. When we run `prog` we notice another error, this time in SUB3's spelling of "subroutine". Now that we have a makefile, we can fix the error and rebuild the application very easily.

```
unix[97] vi sub3.f
unix[98] make
f77 -c sub3.f
sub3.f:
       sub3:
f77 -o prog main.o sub1.o sub2.o sub3.o
unix[99] prog
 This is subroutine 1.
 This is subroutine 2.
 This is subroutine 3.
```

Usually, the last change times tell `make` to do exactly what we want. Occasionally, though, it is useful to be able to get `make` to recompile some or all of an application, or to relink the executable, even though the last change times do not reveal that to be necessary. The UNIX™ `touch` command lets us manually reset the last change time for one or more files, so that `make` finds a target out of date and rebuilds it. For example, we could force `make` to replace the code for SUB1 as follows.

```
unix[100] touch sub1.f
unix[101] make
f77 -c sub1.f
sub1.f:
       sub1:
f77 -o prog main.o sub1.o sub2.o sub3.o
```

The power and convenience of `make` are difficult to appreciate from the foregoing toy example, but it is so useful in managing real UNIX™ applications as to be practically indispensable. You will save yourself countless hours and endless grief if you put each of your programming projects in its own directory and write a makefile for it. The `make` utility can do many more things than I have outlined here, and we shall see some of them in the following sections. For a more thorough and systematic exposition of `make`, see [92].

14.5 Libraries

A **subprogram library** is a collection of object modules that can be linked into user programs as needed. Several libraries are described in §6.6, and in §12.2.2 I recommended writing your own. One way to keep such a library would be in the form of separate `.o` files that the user would mention by name in the `f77` command that links each program. This would permit code reuse, but it would be inconvenient to have to remember what library routines each program invokes, or to have to build that information into every program's makefile. Each library routine that is used might invoke other library routines, which would also have to be included. Of course, one could link *all* of the routines into each program, but that would increase linking time and bloat every executable with large amounts of unused code.

To circumvent these problems, UNIX™ provides a way to build a **random access archive** file for storing the object modules of a library. When the .o files have been combined in an archive file, the loader can copy out just the object modules that are needed, based on what the program invokes rather than on a list supplied by the user. If any of the library routines invoke other library routines, they can also be copied out, automatically, without the user having to know anything about the internals of the library routines.

14.5.1   Using Libraries

Consider the following program, in the file findhyp.f, which invokes a FUNCTION subprogram to compute a complex hyperbolic tangent.

```
      COMPLEX*16 Z/(0.5D0,0.5D0)/,CDTANH,RESULT
      RESULT=CDTANH(Z)
      WRITE(6,901) RESULT
  901 FORMAT(F17.16' + ',F17.16,'i')
      STOP
      END
```

The function CDTANH is not built into FORTRAN, so the compiler cannot automatically include it from the FORTRAN elementary function library. Suppose that CDTANH is in an archive file named /lib/libmisc.a, along with a lot of other object modules. Archive files have a suffix of .a, just as the suffix .f denotes a FORTRAN source file. To compile the program and link in CDTANH from that library, we would use the following f77 command.

```
unix[102] f77 findhyp.f -L/lib -lmisc
hyper.f:
 MAIN:
unix[103] a.out
.5640831412674984 + .40389645553160256i
```

The option -L/lib tells f77 the name of the UNIX™ directory containing the archive file, and the option -lmisc tells f77 that the archive file itself is named libmisc.a. Notice that it is not necessary to tell f77 what routines to get from the library; it knows that CDTANH is needed because that function is invoked in the main program, and if CDTANH uses other library routines it will link them in too. If the findhyp application is managed with a makefile, the same library reference can be used there.

```
.f.o:
        f77 -c $*.f

findhyp: findhyp.o
        f77 -o findhyp findhyp.o -L/lib -lmisc
```

The library enters only the link step, not the default compilation rule. If we were worried that changes to the library might render the application's executable out of date, we could include the archive file /lib/libmisc.a along with findhyp.o as a dependency for findhyp.

14.5.2   Building Libraries

Suppose you have a collection of .f files, each containing the source code for a single subprogram, and you want to build your own library out of them. This is a very *good* thing to suppose, because if you have been following the advice in §12.2.2 you have (or you will shortly have) just such a collection, and you were probably wondering how to make it as easy as possible to use. Where should you put what, and how do you hook up the pieces?

It is traditional in the UNIX™ culture to put source code in a subdirectory named src and libraries (i.e., archive files) in a subdirectory named lib, beneath one's home directory. Thus if your UNIX™ login name is, say, sarah, you might put the .f files in ~sarah/src and build an archive file containing their object modules in ~sarah/lib. The building is almost always done by a makefile in the src directory, something like this.

```
# This makefile maintains Sarah's library.
.f.o:
        f77 -c $*.f
LIBDIR = ${HOME}/lib

${LIBDIR}/libmisc.a:                    \
   matmpy.o spline.o rombrg.o bisect.o \
   rkf.o euler.o
        ar ruv ${LIBDIR}/libmisc.a      \
   matmpy.o spline.o rombrg.o bisect.o \
   rkf.o euler.o
        ranlib ${LIBDIR}/libmisc.a
```

This makefile begins with an explanatory comment, denoted by the #. Then we find the familiar default compilation rule for making a .o file from a .f file whenever that is necessary. Next comes the definition of a **macro** named LIBDIR, which contains the fully-qualified name of the lib directory. It is defined using the shell variable HOME, which contains the path to Sarah's home directory. Writing ${HOME} evaluates the shell variable to yield the character string that HOME contains. It is necessary to use HOME in the makefile because make does not know how to evaluate the shell construct ~sarah.

Finally we find the stanza that actually builds and maintains the library. The target is the archive file, whose full name is ${LIBDIR}/libmisc.a, and its dependencies are the .o files listed on the following two lines. The continuation characters "\" glue the first three lines of this stanza together into one long line. The rule for making libmisc.a consists of two UNIX™ commands, **ar** and **ranlib**. The **ar** program, with options ruv, replaces in the archive file any of the listed .o files that have changed since the archive file was last updated. The **ranlib** program adds or updates a table of contents at the beginning of the archive file, so that the .o files it contains can be copied out at random.

The steps that are automated in this makefile could of course be done simply by entering the UNIX™ commands interactively, but the **ar** command in particular will get pretty unwieldy if the library grows to contain hundreds of object modules. It is much safer, in addition to being more convenient, to record the details in the makefile instead of trying to manage the library by hand.

With the makefile in place we can build the archive by cd'ing to the src directory and entering the **make** command. The first time we do this all of the .o files will be missing, so the default compilation rule will cause them to be created. Then **ar** will put them in the archive file and **ranlib** will build the archive's table of contents. Thereafter the src directory will contain not only the .f files and Makefile but also the .o files, and the lib directory will contain the libmisc.a archive. If Sarah changes one of her .f files all she has to do is **make** again to have it compiled, to replace the .o file in the archive, and to update the archive's table of contents. For more information about **ar** and **ranlib**, see their **man** pages.

If a library is to be public, the final step in building it is to permit the archive file so that it can be linked from by other users. In traditional UNIX™ environments that is done by using the `chmod` command; if instead your environment uses a distributed file system such as AFS, consult the user documentation for that system. In order for other people to use your library routines it is necessary for them to be able to read the archive file, but they do not need to be able to read the `.f` files in your `src` directory.

14.6   Writing Custom Manual Pages

In §12.3.1, I advocated writing your own `man` pages as the external documentation for your library subprograms. The standard UNIX™ description of how to do that consists of the manual page you get by entering

```
unix[104] man 7 man
```

This `man` page specifies conventions for the layout of manual pages, and describes a set of text processing macros for composing them. Unfortunately, this does not constitute enough information to actually get anyone started writing `man` pages, and the conventional page layout has some shortcomings for documenting FORTRAN subprograms. This section describes in detail one method of setting up custom manual pages, and suggests a more appropriate page layout.

14.6.1   How the `man` Command Works

The `man` command searches a list of directories for a file containing the page you request, and invokes a text processing program named `troff` [93] to display the file on your screen. To make it possible to display custom manual pages, it is strictly necessary only to write input files for the pages and to tell `man` where to find them. Unfortunately, this minimal approach is not very satisfactory, for several reasons.

The first problem is that including FORTRAN source and math symbols in `man` pages requires the use of two preprocessors, named `tbl` and `eqn`, for preparing the input files. It is very important, as I mentioned in §12.3.1, that the `man` page for a library routine include an example program showing how to use the routine, and because many of the routines you will document are for engineering and scientific applications you will often need to include formulas with Greek letters, subscripts, superscripts, and special symbols.

The minimal approach also requires `man` to reformat a page each time it is to be displayed, and does not permit our custom pages to be searched for by purpose rather than by name. By using additional programs to postprocess the input files, we can arrange for `man` to use preformatted pages for display, which makes them appear much faster, and for it to be able to tell us what routine is appropriate for a given purpose.

To do this preprocessing and postprocessing by hand is tedious and error prone, so it is much more convenient to organize the files in a special way and to manage their processing with a makefile.

14.6.2   Your `man` Directory

Just as it is traditional in the UNIX™ culture to use a `src` directory and a `lib` directory as mentioned in §14.5.2, it is also customary to keep `man` pages in a directory named `man` beneath your home directory. In order for the `man` command to find the pages describing your library routines, your `man` directory *must* contain a `man3` subdirectory. The "3" in the name of any **man** subdirectory indicates that the pages belong in section 3 of the UNIX™ manual, which contains documentation for subprograms. (If you write custom **man** pages that belong in some other section of the manual, such as section 1 for application programs, you will need another subdirectory for those.) In addition to the required **man3** subdirectory, it is convenient to include some other files and subdirectories. All of these files and directories are summarized in the table below.

contents of the **man** directory	
man3	page definition directory
.p files	original page definition files
.3 files	pure-**troff** page definition files
Makefile	makefile for maintaining the **man** pages
cat3	displayable pages directory
.3 files	**man** pages typeset for screen display
whatis	the database used by the **man -k** command
template	blank template for a page definition file
test	test program directory
.f files	programs from **man** page **EXAMPLE** sections

The **man** page for each of your library subprograms is defined by a separate **original page definition file** in the man3 directory. If the page is for a subprogram named *routine*, then *routine*.p is the name of this file. Each original page definition file contains the text for the page along with **troff**, **tbl**, and **eqn** typesetting directives that describe how it is to be formatted. The makefile invokes the UNIX™ **eqn** and **tbl** programs to translate those directives into **troff** directives, yielding a **pure-troff page definition file** whose name is *routine*.3, the "3" once again indicating the manual section where the page belongs. These steps are the preprocessing described earlier.

Then the makefile uses the UNIX™ **catman** program to produce a typeset version of the page in the **cat3** directory. When we use the **man** command to show a page on the workstation display screen, it is this **cat3** file that gets copied. (We can also use the **man** command to print a page on paper, and in that case it invokes **troff** to typeset the **man3** file for the appropriate output device, rather than just copying the **cat3** file). In addition to making the displayable version of a page, the **catman** program also constructs the **whatis** database. This file contains the one-line subprogram description from each of your **man** pages, and is searched by the **man -k** command. If you don't remember what routine to use for a given task, you can use **man -k** to search the descriptions for a text string. For example, if you want a routine that inverts matrices you might enter

```
unix[105] man -k inver
```

to search the subprogram description lines for the text string "inver" (as in "invert" or "inverse" or "inversion"). At many UNIX™ installations **man -k** is aliased to the command name **apropos**. Making the **cat3** file and the **whatis** database constitutes the postprocessing described earlier.

Thus each of our custom pages will have two files (with suffixes .p and .3) in the man3 directory, and one file (with suffix .3) in the **cat3** directory.

The **template** file contains a **troff** page template, discussed in §14.6.3, which you can copy to the **man3** directory and fill in whenever you need to define a new page. The **troff** template specifies the page layout, so that your **man** pages will come out looking like **man** pages, but has blank spaces or dummy entries where the actual text of the page belongs.

Finally, the **test** directory provides a place for FORTRAN source files to contain the sample programs that we will include in the **EXAMPLE** section of each **man** page we write.

14.6.3   The Page Template

The text processing language that **man** pages use is **troff** [93]. Unlike a *word* processor, which formats a document on your screen as you compose it, *text* processors such as **troff** require **formatting directives** to be embedded in the text. The file containing both text and directives is then processed to produce the formatted document as output. The **troff** command language is adequate for typesetting much more complicated documents than **man** pages, so learning all of it would be a lot of work. Fortunately, it is only necessary to learn a little in order to be able to write simple **man** pages. Many of the **troff** directives we use for writing **man** pages are the macros that are described in the **man 7 man** page mentioned earlier.

For typesetting tabular material and mathematical symbols, additional directives are needed that are not part of **troff**, although they look very much like **troff**. The directives for setting tables are preprocessed by the **tbl** program into **troff** directives, and those for setting mathematics are preprocessed by the **eqn** program into **troff** directives. Then **troff** itself can be used to produce the finished document. In what follows we will not distinguish between **tbl** and **troff** directives.

The directives that are most often needed are those used in the **template** file, which is shown at the top of the next page. The table below summarizes the directives used in the page template.

directive	meaning
.B	switch to bold text
.ds	define a string
.SH	subheading
.TH	begin a new page with given title, section, and date
.TS	start a table, using the description on the next line
.TE	end the table
.br	break to the next line
.in	change indentation
.sp	skip a line

Each directive starts a new line in the file. The first directive signals the beginning of a **man** page and specifies the name of the routine, the manual section where the page belongs, and (in double quote marks) the date the page was last revised. We have specified manual section 3F, but section 3M might be more appropriate if the routine performs a mathematical calculation.

The **.ds** directive redefines a string having the coded name]W, which contains the text that will be printed at the left end of the **man** page footer. Normally this indicates the UNIX™ system release number, but since this template is for custom pages it is more appropriate for it to contain something else.

The **.SH** directives define the sections of the page. It is unusual that all of the sections are appropriate; the ones that don't apply to the routine being documented will be removed later when we fill in the text. Some of these sections were discussed in §12.3.1, where we considered an example **man** page in the discussion of external documentation.

The **NAME** section gives the name of the routine and a one-line description. The dash is escaped by a backslash so **troff** will print it long enough to see. This is the line that **catman** will copy into the **whatis** database.

The **SYNOPSIS** section gives the routine's calling sequence, in boldface type. We will remove either the **CALL** statement or the function reference, depending on whether the subprogram being documented is a **FUNCTION** subprogram or a **SUBROUTINE**. Then there is

```
.TH routine 3F "dd Mmm yy"
.ds ]W footer
.SH NAME
routine \- One line description.

.SH SYNOPSIS
.B CALL routine(arguments)
.B RESULT=routine(arguments)
.br
.TS
l l.
parameter <tab> is...
.TE

.SH WARNING

.SH DESCRIPTION

.SH "SEE ALSO"

.SH DIAGNOSTICS

.SH NOTES

.SH BUGS

.SH LINKAGE

.SH EXAMPLE
.TS
r1 c1 l.
<tab> <tab> statement
     1<tab> numbered statement
<tab>;<tab> continued statement
.TE
.in -0.5i
.sp
This example produced the following output:
.sp
.in +0.5i
output produced
.br

.SH REFERENCES
[1] reference
```

a table for describing the parameters. The columns of the table must be separated by a tab character.

The WARNING section is for describing dangerous or unexpected effects of using the routine; hopefully this won't be necessary very often. DESCRIPTION gives a narrative explanation of what the routine does. SEE ALSO lists related routines in which the reader might be interested, and possibly also other library routines that are called by this one. DIAGNOSTICS tells what error messages can issue from the routine, and what gives rise to each. NOTES is for material that is not essential for understanding what the routine does or how it works, but which might be useful for reference.

BUGS describes known deficiencies and design limitations of the routine that cannot be fixed or are not worth fixing. For example, a root-finding routine might be incapable of finding complex roots. This is not really a bug in the sense that we defined the word in §14.3 (the routines that you put in your library should be free of errors). But BUGS is the traditional name for this section in UNIX™ man pages, so it is probably best to stick with it even though according to our lexicon it is a misnomer.

LINKAGE tells how to link this routine into a FORTRAN program. The ideal text for this section is an f77 command giving the -L and -l clauses needed to get to the library containing this routine.

Next we come to the EXAMPLE, often the most important section for someone who is trying to write code that invokes the routine. This is another table, which is designed to represent FORTRAN source code. The three columns of the table are for the statement number if any, a continuation character if one is needed, and the statement text. We will fill in the table with a complete program that invokes the subprogram being documented and produces output to illustrate how it works. The program's output is reproduced verbatim at the end of the section. It is this example program that we will copy into a .f file in the test directory, where it will be available for testing the routine to verify that it actually does produce the output given in the man page.

Finally there is a section for REFERENCES. Sometimes a routine implements an algorithm from a journal article or book, and in that case it is appropriate to give the literature citation so that an interested reader can find out more.

It might be appropriate for you to add or delete section definitions in making your own template file. For example, depending on who will be reading your pages it could make sense to include an AUTHOR section where you can claim responsibility for the man page and the routine it describes.

14.6.4   A Typical Page Definition

To use the page template, we must copy it to the man3 directory and fill in the text. Suppose our friend Sarah plans to write a new routine named GRADCD, which will approximate a gradient vector by finite differencing. Following the advice given in §12.3.1, she decides to compose the man page first, and begins to do so as follows:

```
unix[106] cd man/man3
unix[107] cp ../template gradcd.p
unix[108] vi gradcd.p
```

In UNIX™ ".." is shorthand for the parent directory, in this case man (that's where the template file is). Now she uses an editor to fill in the details about GRADCD and to delete any template sections that are inappropriate for that routine, producing the result shown below and on the next page.

```
.TH GRADCD 3F "25 Jul 95"
.ds ]W Sarah's library
.SH NAME
GRADCD \- Approximate a gradient vector by central differencing.

.SH SYNOPSIS
.B CALL\h'+0.2m' GRADCD(X,N,I,G)
.br
.EQ
delim $$
.EN
```

```
.TS
1 1.
X(N)    is the REAL*8 point at which the gradient vector is wanted
N       is the INTEGER*4 number of variables
I       is the INTEGER*4 number of the function whose gradient is wanted
G(N)    is the REAL*8 gradient vector approximation returned
.TE
```

```
.SH DESCRIPTION
```
For each variable J=1...N, this routine uses the REAL*8 function subprogram
FCN(X,N,I) to find the values of function $f \; sub \; I$ at the points
X+$delta \; e \; sub \; J$ and X-$delta \; e \; sub \; J$, where $e \; sub \; J$ is the J'th
unit vector and $delta = 6.93176495678764213$ times 10 sup -6$ for IEEE
REAL*8 values according to the advice given in [1]. Then the routine
uses the central difference formula to approximate the J'th partial
derivative G(J) as
```
.EQ
{partial f sub I} over {partial X sub J}~~approx~~
{f sub I (X + {delta e sub J})~-~
 f sub I (X - {delta e sub J})}
 over {2 delta}
.EN
```

```
.SH LINKAGE
f77 source.f \-L/usr/sarah/lib \-lmisc
```

```
.SH REFERENCES
```
[1] Conte, A. and deBoor, Carl, Elementary Numerical Analysis: an
algorithmic approach,
\h'+2.1m'McGraw-Hill Book Company, 1972 (page 282).

```
.SH EXAMPLE
.TS
r1 c1 1.
                REAL*8 X(2)/1.D0,2.D0/,G(2)
                CALL\h'+0.3m' GRADCD(X,2,1,G)
                WRITE(6,901) G
901             FORMAT('G=',2(1X,1PD22.15))
                STOP
                END
                FUNCTION FCN(X,N,I)
                REAL*8 FCN,X(N)
                FCN=X(1)**2+X(2)**3+X(1)*X(2)
                RETURN
                END
.TE
.in -0.5i
.sp
```
This example should produce close to the following output:
```
.sp
.in +0.5i
G=  4.000000000000000D+00   1.300000000000000D+01
```

The spaces separating entries in each row of a table are actually tabs, and the dashes in the f77 command are escaped with backslashes so they will be printed long. The tie character "~" specifies a blank space. A \h'*nm*' code inserts *n* em's of horizontal space.

In addition to troff and tbl directives from the page template, this file also uses the eqn directives .EQ and .EN to specify the typesetting of mathematical formulas. In their first invocation they bracket the declaration of the $ character as a delimiter for in-line mathematical text, so that Greek letters, subscripts, and superscripts can be used in the DESCRIPTION section. In their second invocation, .EQ and .EN bracket a displayed formula that follows the DESCRIPTION. For more information about eqn and tbl directives, see their man pages and the printed documentation supplied by your UNIX™ vendor. The typeset man page that results from the above definition is reproduced in §14.6.7.

Having finished the man page, Sarah will next copy the example program to a file named, say, gradcdtest.f in her man/test directory and replace the tabs with blanks. Then she can write the GRADCD routine itself and use the program to test it. Finally, she must revise the man page to replace the output that the program *should* produce with the output that it actually *does* produce, which will probably be slightly different from the ideal results on account of roundoff errors.

14.6.5   Processing the Page Definition

Having composed some original page definition files, we need to expand any tbl and eqn directives they might contain, typeset versions for display, and put the one-line descriptions in the whatis database. These operations are all performed by the makefile, man/man3/Makefile. Assuming that Sarah has written a man page for each of the routines in her subroutine library, which was used as an example in §14.5.2, her Makefile might look like this.

```
.SUFFIXES: .p .3
.p.3:
        rm -f $*.3
        tbl < $*.p | eqn > $*.3

${HOME}/man/whatis:                        \
   matmpy.3 spline.3 rombrg.3 bisect.3 \
   rkf.3 euler.3 gradcd.3
        catman -M ${HOME}/man 3
        sort -u < ${HOME}/man/whatis > /tmp/whatis
        cp /tmp/whatis ${HOME}/man/whatis
```

This makefile uses familiar features and introduces new ones. The default compilation rule tells how to make a file with a .3 suffix from one with a .p suffix. These suffixes, unlike the .f, .o, and .a we used earlier, are unfamiliar to make and therefore must be declared using the .SUFFIXES line.

The default compilation rule says that whenever a .p file is found to be more recent than the corresponding .3 file, two UNIX™ commands are to be performed. First, the old .3 file is removed (the -f option says not to complain if there wasn't one). Then we invoke the tbl program, redirecting its input from the .p file and sending its output through a UNIX™ **pipe** to the input of the eqn program, whose output in turn is written to a new .3 file. This step turns any tbl and eqn directives that might be in the .p file into troff directives in the .3 file. If Sarah changes one of the .p files and then issues a make command, the corresponding .3 file will automatically be updated.

The next stanza has all of the `.3` files as its dependencies, so updating one of them will cause this rule to fire and update the **whatis** database. That file is in the **man** directory, whereas the makefile is in **man/man3**, so we need to give the path to it. This stanza's rule consists of three UNIX™ commands. The first runs **catman**, which replaces the appropriate **cat3** file and rebuilds the **whatis** directory. Unfortunately, in building the **whatis** file, **catman** extracts anything that looks like a NAME entry from *every* file in the **man3** directory, including both the `.p`'s and the `.3`'s, so **whatis** winds up containing two copies of each description line. We therefore use the UNIX™ **sort -u** utility to delete the duplicates, writing its output to the scratch file **/tmp/whatis**. The final UNIX™ command replaces **whatis** by the version without the duplicates.

This makefile is analogous to the one we used in §14.5.2. It resides in the directory with the `.p` and `.3` files, just as the previous one was located with the `.f` and `.o` files of a library. It contains a default compilation rule for making `.3` files from `.p` files, just as the other had a rule for making `.o` files from `.f` files. And just as the other makefile updated an archive file, this one updates the **whatis** database.

14.6.6 How **man** Finds Your Custom Pages

The **man** command finds out where to look for pages to display by examining a shell variable named MANPATH, which contains a colon-separated list of **man** directories to be searched in the order they are listed. For **man** to find your pages, it is necessary to modify this variable as follows:

```
export MANPATH=$HOME/man:$MANPATH
```

This redefines MANPATH to be the fully-qualified name of your **man** directory, followed by the original list. Now, when you ask for a page **man** will look in your directory first and then wherever it looked before.

If you want other people to be able to use your **man** pages, you will need to permit your **man**, **man3**, and **cat3** directories so that they can read the contents, and they will need to put your pages in their **man** path.

14.6.7 Printing **man** Pages

The next page shows (at $\frac{3}{4}$ size) what the GRADCD **man** page, whose `.p` file was discussed in §14.6.4, looks like when it is printed on paper.

The **cat3** version of a **man** page can be printed on paper by just piping **man**'s output to **lpr**, like this.

```
unix[109] man gradcd | lpr
```

Unfortunately, this prints just what you see on your workstation screen, rather than formatting the output to take advantage of the fancy fonts and high resolution of your laser printer. This is apt to be disappointing, especially if the page includes mathematical formulas.

To print pages that look like they were printed rather than displayed, it is necessary to invoke **troff** to typeset the **man3** file for the output device you are using. This is done by using the `-t` option of the **man** command. When this option is used, **man** looks in the shell variable TROFF to find out what version of **troff** to use, and in TCAT to find out where to send the output. Thus, to get the printed version, Sarah had to enter UNIX™ commands like those shown below the man page image.

The appropriate settings for TROFF and TCAT are installation specific, so you will need to consult your friendly UNIX™ system administrator for the values to use.

NAME

　　GRADCD – Approximate a gradient vector by central differencing.

SYNOPSIS

　　CALL GRADCD(X,N,I,G)

　　X(N)　is the REAL∗8 point at which the gradient vector is wanted

　　N　　is the INTEGER∗4 number of variables

　　I　　is the INTEGER∗4 number of the function whose gradient is wanted

　　G(N)　is the REAL∗8 gradient vector approximation returned

DESCRIPTION

　　For each variable J=1...N, this routine uses the REAL∗8 function subprogram FCN(X,N,I) to find the values of function f_I at the points $X+\delta e_J$ and $X-\delta e_J$, where e_J is the J'th unit vector and $\delta=6.93176495678764213\times10^{-6}$ for IEEE REAL∗8 values according to the advice given in [1]. Then the routine uses the central difference formula to approximate the J'th partial derivative G(J) as

$$\frac{\partial f_I}{\partial X_J} \approx \frac{f_I(X+\delta e_J) - f_I(X-\delta e_J)}{2\delta}$$

LINKAGE

　　f77 source.f –L/usr/sarah/lib –lmisc

REFERENCES

　　[1]　Conte, A. and deBoor, Carl, Elementary Numerical Analysis: an algorithmic approach, McGraw-Hill Book Company, 1972 (page 282).

EXAMPLE

```
      REAL*8 X(2)/1.D0,2.D0/,G(2)
      CALL GRADCD(X,2,1,G)
      WRITE(6,901) G
901   FORMAT('G=',2(1X,1PD22.15))
      STOP
      END
      FUNCTION FCN(X,N,I)
      REAL*8 FCN,X(N)
      FCN=X(1)**2+X(2)**3+X(1)*X(2)
      RETURN
      END
```

This example should produce close to the following output:

　　G= 4.000000000000000D+00　1.300000000000000D+01

```
unix[110] export TROFF=ptroff
unix[111] export TCAT="lpr -Pprinter"
unix[112] man -t gradcd
```

14.7 Omissions

UNIX™ is a sophisticated operating system, and many of its capabilities can be used by FORTRAN programs and in constructing FORTRAN programs and their documentation. UNIX™ environments vary from vendor to vendor, from time to time, and from one computing installation to another. Because of these factors, it has been possible in this chapter to touch on only a few of the UNIX™ issues that might conceivably be of concern to a FORTRAN programmer. I have tried to tailor the topics and the depth of coverage to the immediate practical needs of *most* users, by neglecting many details and by omitting altogether subjects that are important only occasionally or only to *some* users. With experience and specialization you will probably outgrow this chapter; then you must resort to the UNIX™ manual, other books, the support personnel at your computing facility, your colleagues, and the resources of the World Wide Web. Here are some things I left out:

Many `f77` options; most `INQUIRE` keywords; some useful system subroutines; decoding `STAT` time values; variations between vendors in run-time error messages; error messages due to exceeding UNIX™ limits on CPU time, memory, and disk space; most of `cpp`; many `dbx` commands; using `dbx` on `core` files; much of `make`, and all of `imake`; source revision control systems; the FORTRAN mode of `emacs`; most contents of the UNIX™ manual; most of `troff`, `tbl`, and `eqn`; `xman`; calling subprograms written in other languages; dynamically-linked libraries and run-time linking of subprograms; program interrupt exits.

14.8 Exercises

14.8.1 Explain the following UNIX™ commands:
(a) `f77 -O -o O o.f`
(b) `g77 -fbounds-check -c -g g.f`

14.8.2 Write a program to check the existence of a file named `bye`. If the file is found, the program should report its size in bytes and then remove it.

14.8.3 A shell variable named `SECRET` contains a secret word. Write a program that takes one command line argument, compares it to the secret word, and sets a return code equal to the number of characters in which the argument and the secret word differ.

14.8.4 Write a FORTRAN program that simulates the UNIX™ `echo` command. If you don't know what `echo` does, how can you find out?

14.8.5 Write a program that changes the name of its own executable file, if necessary, to either `AM` or `PM` depending on whether the program is run before or after noon. Compile the program in such a way that its executable starts in `AM`, and test it several times both before and after noon. The program should avoid moving the executable if it already has the appropriate name.

14.8.6 Are compiler warnings about variables that are declared but never used always harmless? Explain.

14.8.7   Explain the difference between diagnostic messages, which your program or a library subprogram might write to tell why it failed, and run-time errors of the kind discussed in §14.3.2. Which sort of problem is easier to understand and correct? Can code ever be written to generate a diagnostic where a run-time error would otherwise result? If so, give an example to illustrate how.

14.8.8   Run the example programs of §14.3.2 on your system to find out what error messages they elicit.

14.8.9   Fix the errors in the following code to get a clean compile and an executable that works correctly.

```
Code with 12 misteaks or so
C
C     REAL*8, A(2)\I.DO,Z.DO,3.DO,4.DO,5.DO,6.DO,7.DO,8.DO,9.DO,10.DO\
      PRINT * A(1),A(2)
   ;         A(3)
      STOP
      END
```

14.8.10   Suggest a way of guarding against integer divide checks.

14.8.11   Explain the difference between a `segmentation fault` and a `bus error`.

14.8.12   On your computer does this program compile? Link? Run? Explain what happens and why.

```
      EX=0.
      CALL SUBX(EX)
      STOP
      END
      SUBROUTINE SUBX(EX)
      CALL EX
      RETURN
      END
```

14.8.13   What run-time error does your system report when a FORTRAN subroutine calls itself recursively? To find out, write a program in which `SUBA` calls `SUBB` and `SUBB` calls `SUBA`.

14.8.14   (a) Give three possible reasons for a program to run for longer than you expected. (b) Suppose you code `WRITE` statements every so often throughout the program, but output is written only after you interrupt the run with ˆC. What could explain this?

14.8.15   Check whether your FORTRAN compiler supports D comments, and find out how to use them.

14.8.16   Use dbx or gdb to debug the example program of §14.3.3.

14.8.17 Does the following program link successfully? If so, what output does it produce? Explain.

```
INTEGER*4 MOD(3,2)/1,2,3,4,5,6/
CALL SUB(MOD)
STOP
END
SUBROUTINE SUB(MOD)
PRINT *,MOD(3,2)
RETURN
END
```

14.8.18 (a) Why would anyone want to use `make`? (b) How does `make` decide whether to perform the rule associated with a target? (c) How can `make` be forced to update a target?

14.8.19 Suppose that `/usr/jones/lib/libgraphics.a` is the fully-qualified name of a certain archive file, and that your program `draw.f` calls one of its subroutines. Write an `f77` command to compile and link `draw.f`.

14.8.20 What two UNIX™ programs are used to build a random-access archive file, and what do they do?

14.8.21 (a) What text processing language is used for writing UNIX™ `man` pages? (b) How can FORTRAN listings and mathematical formulas be included in a `man` page?

14.8.22 (a) What does `catman` do? (b) Where is Katmandu?

14.8.23 Sarah has written a `man` page for her GRADCD routine, but David gets the error message `No manual entry for GRADCD.` when he tries to read it. What could account for this response?

14.8.24 Explain the difference between `man -k` and `man -t`.

15

Measuring and Maximizing Serial Execution Speed

The most common programmer's lament is that an application does not do what it should, either because it contains errors or because it works as designed but the user now wants something else. We spent §12 elaborating a style that helps in getting programs right, §13 condemning practices that often lead to programs being wrong, and §14.3 studying how to debug programs after they are written. Correctness does come first!

But the *second* most common complaint about computer programs for technical applications is surely that they take too long to run. Engineering and scientific computations are very often **numerically intensive**, in that the number of floating-point arithmetic operations they require is vast even for modest problem sizes and grows very quickly as the problem size increases. The most notorious example of such a calculation is integrating the partial differential equations of fluid flow, but many other problems of great practical importance are also numerically intensive.

Waiting for numerically intensive programs to run limits the number of design alternatives that an engineer can consider, or the number of experimental data sets that a scientist can analyze, and determines in countless other settings the speed at which people can do their work. In real-time applications, such as securities trading, nuclear reactor control, or landing a supersonic fighter jet on the pitching deck of an aircraft carrier, finishing the calculation a little late is probably more than just inconvenient.

So once a computer program is correct, speed is often important too. On rare occasions, extraordinary measures are justified to achieve the highest possible speed because delivering the answer before a deadline arrives is literally a matter of life and death.

This chapter is about making programs run faster.

What can be done to make a program run faster? The most naïve way of speeding up a calculation is to *use a faster computer*. For many years the rapid evolution of microprocessors ensured that each new generation would be faster than the previous one, and maybe you can still buy a faster machine than the one you have. Unfortunately, physical laws now seem to be limiting how fast a processor can be made to go, and economics will probably always dictate that most people do not have access to the fastest possible hardware.

If a single computer isn't fast enough, we might try somehow to *use several computers at once*. Some calculations can be broken up into parts and each of the parts performed by separate circuits, all at the same time. In §16 and §17.2 I will discuss several different approaches that can be used for doing more than one part of a calculation simultaneously.

Given that we must use a particular single computer, the most effective way of speeding up a program is usually to *improve the algorithm*. A surprising number of programs use linear search where they could use binary search, or an antique algorithm instead of a much faster one that was discovered just recently. Often the key to improving an algorithm is finding a more appropriate data structure for storing the information that defines the problem, and often it turns out that the time used by an algorithm can be reduced by using more memory. The design and analysis of algorithms and data structures is beyond the scope of this book, but there are excellent references on the subject; see, for example, [2] [1]. Always investigate recent work on the problem you need to solve and use the best available method. In many application areas, a good way to get a fast implementation of the best known algorithm is to *use high-quality library subprograms* such as those found in LAPACK [37] and some commercial libraries.

As we learned in §14.1.3, most UNIX™ FORTRAN compilers have a -O option that we can invoke to *make the compiler try harder* to generate efficient machine code. Using compiler optimization increases compile time and makes the program more difficult to debug, so this is something you won't want to do until the code is right, but then it is always worth a try. If after doing this we're still not satisfied with the quality of the machine code the compiler produces, we could *hand-code the algorithm in the assembly language of the processor* we plan to use. This is sometimes worth the trouble, because most applications can be speeded up by 20% or so by using assembly language, and some can be speeded up by much more, but this definitely falls in the category of "extraordinary measures" mentioned above. Assembly language programming can be a true joy, but switching languages would make the program no longer FORTRAN so that technique is, alas, also outside the scope of this text.

Finally, the first thing that occurs to most programmers, and the last thing anyone should actually attempt, is to somehow *tune the source code* so that the program runs faster. This process has the potential to introduce bugs and to make the program harder to understand, and the things that people first think to try can actually slow the program down. However, if done carefully and in an informed way, code tuning can sometimes avoid unnecessary calculations or make it possible for the compiler to generate more efficient machine code. It is this approach to maximizing serial execution speed that will occupy us in §15.2.

How fast a computation will run depends not only on the computer's architecture, the algorithms, data structures, and coding that are used, and how the compiler translates the source program into machine instructions, but also on subtle and complex interactions *between* these factors. The net effect of any change is therefore hard to predict with certainty, and must be confirmed by experiment. So before we take up code tuning, which has the objective of *reducing* the CPU time used by a program, we must first consider ways of *measuring* CPU time in a UNIX™ environment.

15.1   Measuring Serial Execution Speed

Suppose we make some change to a program in an attempt to speed it up. How do we know whether the change had that effect? The simplest way is to measure the running time of each version with a wristwatch, or with the clock on your workstation screen. If the time drops from one hour to one minute, manual observations are all you need! If the times you are measuring differ by only seconds, though, manual timing requires close attention and good reflexes. It also measures the time of day, or **wallclock time**, rather than the CPU time that the processor uses, so the value will vary from one measurement to another according to the load on the computer. Another drawback is that measurements of total running time tell nothing about how it is distributed among the different parts of a program.

To mitigate these problems, UNIX™ provides some standard tools and system subprograms for measuring execution time.

15.1.1   The UNIX™ time Command

The simplest of the UNIX™ timing tools is the **time** command, which runs your program for you and then reports how long it took. For example, to time an executable file named a.out we might have the following exchange with the operating system.

```
unix[113] time a.out
 17.6 real       15.9 user       0.6 sys
```

The output from **time** says the program took 17.6 seconds of "real" or wallclock time. Of this, 15.9 seconds was CPU time devoted to executing the machine instructions in a.out and 0.6 seconds was CPU time that the operating system used for things it needed to do in order to run the program, such as loading the machine code into memory. Although the resolution of the measurements made by **time** is rather coarse, it probably does better than we could with a stopwatch. It is also convenient that **time** segregates user-state from system-state CPU time, because most of the changes we might try will affect the user-state time. System-state time includes paging and is therefore, like the wallclock time, affected by system load as well as by code changes we make.

15.1.2   Statistical Profiling with prof

Typical FORTRAN programs spend more than 50% of their running time in less than 4% of the code [77]. The part of the code that uses most of the time is the best place to look for opportunities to improve the algorithm or the program, or to rephrase the FORTRAN so it is easier for the compiler to translate it into efficient machine code. For a large application it might be impractical to refine more than a small part of the code, so in that case we certainly need to know which part is the worst bottleneck.

Finding out where a program spends its time is called **profiling**. The standard facility that UNIX™ provides for profiling consists of the -p compiler option and a utility program called **prof**. The -p option causes the compiler to insert profiling code into the executable program. When the executable is run, this extra code generates an interrupt at regular intervals and counts the occasions that the flow of control is found to be within each of the program's subprograms at the moment of an interrupt. At the end of the profiling run, this **histogram data** is written to a file named mon.out, in the current directory. Then the **prof** program can be used to read the mon.out file and display a table on standard-out. This kind of profiling is statistical in nature because, instead of making direct measurements of time intervals, it uses periodic observations of where the flow of control is to estimate the proportion of the total CPU time that is spent in each routine. This is how we would profile a program whose FORTRAN source code is in the file **prog.f**.

```
unix[114] f77 -p prog.f
unix[115] a.out
unix[116] prof a.out | more
 %time  cumsecs  #call  ms/call  name
  97.6    2.81       1  2810.00  _sub_
   1.4    2.85   20000     0.00  _sqrt
   0.6    2.87       1    17.00  _MAIN_
   0.3    2.88                   mcount
   0.0    2.88      64     0.00  .rem
   0.0    2.88       2     0.00  .udiv
   0.0    2.88       3     0.00  .umul
    :       :        :       :    :
```

The table contains an entry for each subprogram in the executable, including the FORTRAN main and subprograms, elementary function library routines, I/O library routines, and UNIX™ system routines, arranged in decreasing order of CPU time consumption. Only the first few entries of the table are shown here. Each line shows the percentage of the total CPU time that the routine used, the cumulative time used by that routine and all the ones above it in the table, the number of calls that were made to the routine, how long each call took in milliseconds, and the internal name given to the routine by the compiler. The name "_sub_" in this example is manufactured by the compiler to correspond to the subroutine name SUB in the FORTRAN source program, and "_MAIN_" corresponds to the unnamed main program; all the other routines were inserted by the compiler.

The mcount routine is the added code that makes the profiling measurements, so it must be ignored in assessing the distribution of CPU time among the permanent parts of the program. Profiling writes a mon.out file (which can grow to a large size) and consumes CPU time (in this case 0.3% of the total, but sometimes much more), so you should use the -p compiler option *only* when you really want to produce a profile.

From this profile we can see that most of the work is done in SUB, and some of that consists of calls to a square root function (actually DSQRT). To speed up this program we might try to make improvements in SUB and if possible reduce the number of DSQRT references used.

15.1.3   System Subprograms for Measuring CPU Time

In addition to time and prof, UNIX™ also provides system subroutines for measuring CPU time. Of these the most useful is ETIME, which has the following calling sequence.

TOTAL=ETIME(TARRAY)		
TOTAL	REAL*4	total (user+system) CPU time since program start
TARRAY(1)	REAL*4	user-state CPU time since program start
TARRAY(2)	REAL*4	system-state CPU time since program start

To use ETIME, we call it like this:

```
      REAL*4 TSTART(2),TSTOP(2)
      TOTAL=ETIME(TSTART)
      [code segment to be timed]
      TOTAL=ETIME(TSTOP)
      WRITE(6,901) TSTOP(1)-TSTART(1)
  901 FORMAT('User-state CPU time = ',F6.2,' seconds')
      STOP
      END
```

In most versions of UNIX™ the resolution of ETIME is 0.01 seconds, so if the [code segment to be timed] runs for longer than that there will be a difference between TSTART and TSTOP. Many engineering and scientific applications for UNIX™ use an approach like this to report the CPU time they use.

Some UNIX™ implementations provide a routine named MCLOCK instead of or in addition to ETIME. MCLOCK is a function with no arguments and returns an INTEGER*4 value that is the sum of user-state and system-state CPU times used by the program since it started, in hundredths of a second. The example at the top of the next page shows how to use MCLOCK. Functions with no arguments are discussed briefly in §13.6.5. Notice that MCLOCK does not report user-state and system-state time separately.

```
      INTEGER*4 TSTART,TSTOP
      TSTART=MCLOCK()
        [code segment to be timed]
      TSTOP=MCLOCK()
      WRITE(6,901) FLOAT(TSTOP-TSTART)/100.
  901 FORMAT('Total CPU time = ',F6.2,' seconds')
      STOP
      END
```

15.1.4   Direct Profiling with TIMER

The statistical profiling described in §15.1.2 is a useful technique for identifying where a program spends most of a run, but for making absolute measurements of the CPU time consumed by particular code segments it is imprecise and hard to use. The prof utility records *total* CPU time, including system overhead as well as the time your program uses, and it reports by routines whereas we would often prefer an accounting based on some other division of the code. On short runs (where timings might still be of interest even if the code does not need speeding up) prof collects too few observations for the statistics to be meaningful.

It would be much more convenient to directly measure the user-state CPU time consumed by different parts of a program. Unfortunately, as we have seen in §15.1.3, the resolution of the CPU timer in most versions of UNIX™ is only 0.01 second. In that interval a typical scientific workstation can execute tens of millions of machine instructions, and the code paths we typically want to time are much shorter than that. Other operating systems have provided CPU timer resolutions as fine as a single clock cycle [99, p503-506], and it has been proposed to dramatically improve the CPU timer resolution supported by the Mach kernel of UNIX™ [39], but for the moment it looks like we users of most ordinary UNIX™ machines are stuck with CPU time measurements that are much too coarse for direct profiling (also see Exercise 18.8.22).

Sometimes it is possible to estimate the CPU time that a short code segment uses by writing a program that just executes that code segment repeatedly in a loop. Then the loop can be timed, the time for an empty loop subtracted, and the result divided by the number of iterations in the loop. This approach is impractical for a complicated application, because it requires writing a special program for each code segment that is to be timed. Also, the machine code produced by the compiler for the test program, even if no compiler optimization is used, might differ significantly from that produced for the code segment when it is embedded in the application, so the timings will differ. Finally, it is often difficult to faithfully simulate in the test program the data that are input to the code segment when it is embedded in the application.

It so happens that UNIX™ *does* supply a timer having a resolution of 1 microsecond (even less on some hardware), but it measures the time of day rather than CPU time. The wall-clock time used by a program is usually much greater than the CPU time, because in a multiprocessing environment like UNIX™ your program shares the processor with root processes and other users' programs, and even while it is running it has to wait for system services like I/O. The ratio of the wallclock time that an application takes to the CPU time that it uses is called the **expansion factor**. You can estimate the expansion factor of a program from the output of the UNIX™ time command by dividing the **real** time by the **user** time. Of course this is only an average over the whole run of the program, because the load on the machine varies during the run, but the idea of measuring an expansion factor suggests a strategy for estimating CPU time with more resolution than the UNIX™ CPU timer has (see also [60]).

Suppose that we accumulate wallclock time in **timing bins** corresponding to the code paths we want to study, until enough CPU time has elapsed so that we can measure it reliably using the timer with 0.01-second resolution. If we wait for half a second of CPU time, that will be 50 counts of the CPU timer, so its measurement will be precise to within 1 part in 50 or ±1%. Then we can estimate the average expansion factor for that interval of CPU time, and divide each timing bin's wallclock time by the expansion factor to get estimates of the CPU time that should be attributed to each bin. This process is repeated every half-CPU-second for the entire run of the program, using a fresh estimate of the expansion factor for each half-CPU-second interval.

The TIMER subroutine, described and listed in §18.5.1 and §18.5.2, implements this strategy. TIMER provides timing bins for different segments of the code under study, plus a bin for the overhead of making the timing measurements, plus a bin for everything else. In its model of the timing process, CPU time is thought of as continuously flowing and the function of TIMER is merely to control into which bin the time is flowing. To use TIMER, it is necessary to **instrument** the program under study by inserting subroutine calls at the beginning of the code and at those points where it is desired to switch bins.

In instrumenting a program for timing measurements it is usual that calls to TIMER are needed in subprograms other than the main routine, yet we would usually like to retrieve the measurements in the main so that we can write them out. This is the situation, described in §8.2, where information must be shared between two routines (the main and TIMER) but one does not directly invoke the other and the information is not needed by the intermediary routines, so the obvious solution is to store the measurements in COMMON.

Here is the calling sequence for TIMER, showing both the formal parameters that must be passed to TIMER at every call and the COMMON block /EXPT/ (from EXPerimenT) in which the timing measurements are stored.

COMMON /EXPT/ TIMING,NONALG,NBIN,TOPBIN,NTMEAS,TOH,BINCPU(2,22)		
CALL TIMER(TCC,STA)		
BINCPU	INTEGER*4	timing bin CPU times in [sec,μsec] format
NBIN	INTEGER*4	bin where time is now being accumulated
NONALG	INTEGER*4	bin where non-algorithm time is accumulated
NTMEAS	INTEGER*4	number of timing measurements made so far
STA	INTEGER*4	station number of the CALL TIMER statement
TCC	INTEGER*4	$-1 \Rightarrow$ reset, $0 \Rightarrow$ update, $> 0 \Rightarrow$ change to bin TCC
TIMING	LOGICAL*4	.TRUE. $\Rightarrow$ timing is enabled
TOH	INTEGER*4	per-call TIMER overhead correction
TOPBIN	INTEGER*4	highest bin number used so far

The formal parameters that need to be specified at each call to TIMER are the **timer control code** TCC and the **station number** STA. The timer control code tells whether to initialize the timing process (the first call to TIMER must have TCC $= -1$), or redirect time into new bin number TCC (> 0), or update the measurements without changing the bin (TCC $= 0$). The station number is an integer chosen by the programmer to distinguish the CALL TIMER statements in the program from one another, so that any error message TIMER writes can identify the offending CALL. The example on the next page shows a simple use of TIMER.

The program begins by setting TIMING=.TRUE., to indicate that timing measurements are to be made. Measuring CPU time takes additional CPU time, and in many situations it is not worthwhile to time every run. If TIMING is false, then TIMER just returns without making any measurements.

```
      COMMON /EXPT/ TIMING,NONALG,NBIN,TOPBIN,NTMEAS,TOH,BINCPU
      LOGICAL*4 TIMING
      INTEGER*4 TOPBIN,TOH,BINCPU(2,22)
      TIMING=.TRUE.
      CALL TIMER(-1,1)
      CALL TIMER( 1,2)
        [first code segment to be timed]
      CALL TIMER( 2,3)
        [second code segment to be timed]
      CALL TIMER(NONALG,4)
        [print results from second code segment]
      CALL TIMER( 0,5)
      DO 1 K=1,2
          WRITE(6,901) K,1.D+06*DFLOAT(BINCPU(1,K))+DFLOAT(BINCPU(2,K))
  901     FORMAT('segment ',I1,' CPU time =',1PD13.6,' microseconds')
    1 CONTINUE
      STOP
      END
```

Next the program calls TIMER with TCC $= -1$ to initialize the timing process. This sets NONALG, which is the number of the bin that TIMER uses for NONALGorithm or "other" time, it sets the current timing bin NBIN to NONALG, and it initializes BINCPU to zeros. As CPU time elapses, BINCPU(1,K) and BINCPU(2,K) will respectively accumulate the seconds and microseconds of CPU time for bin number K. Bins $0, \ldots, 20$ are for the code segments being timed, NONALG is 21, and bin 22 accumulates the time used in making the timing measurements.

The pair of integers BINCPU(1,K) and BINCPU(2,K) that specify the [sec,μsec] time in each bin is called a **two-part value**. Some subprograms for manipulating two-part values are listed and described in §18.4, but in the WRITE statement of this example we deal with the two parts explicitly.

The second call to TIMER switches the timing bin from NONALG (where it was left by the initialization call) to bin 1, and the first code segment is performed. Then TIMER is called to switch the timing to bin 2, and the second code segment is performed. Before the results of the calculations are printed, TIMER is called again to switch to bin NONALG. Finally, TIMER is called with TCC $= 0$ to update the values in BINCPU, and the times recorded for the two code segments are written out.

The values in BINCPU get updated periodically as CPU time accumulates, but to make sure that the values are up to the moment it is necessary to make a call with TCC $= 0$. The CPU time that the example program writes out for code segment K is the real number corresponding to the two-part value [BINCPU(1,K),BINCPU(2,K)] that contains the seconds and microseconds accumulated in bin K.

In our example we used only bins 1 and 2 besides NONALG (and TIMER itself used bin 22 to record the time it used) but in most real profiling situations one would use more timing bins. We picked STA parameter values that just number the TIMER calls in the order they appear in the source program.

Because TIMER needs user-state CPU times for its algorithm, it calls ETIME and cannot be used in UNIX™ implementations where only MCLOCK is available. Precisely how TIMER works internally, and the roles of the other variables in the COMMON block /EXPT/, are discussed in §18.5.2. In typical applications TIMER consumes large amounts of CPU time internally in order to measure the CPU time used by an instrumented code. This can be avoided if your program is the *only* task executing on your computer and if your processor provides a way for application programs to read its hardware cycle counter. In that case there is no need to estimate expansion factors, and the CPU time consumed by your program can be measured directly with great precision and little overhead. A version of TIMER that uses this approach and which has the same calling sequence described above is discussed in §18.5.4.

15.1.5 Operation Counting

There are many difficulties in using CPU time to determine the amount of computational work in a program. Time must be *measured*, so it is subject to experimental errors. The measurement process is complicated if done carefully, and depends on operating system services of limited precision. Computers differ widely in speed [48] and FORTRAN compilers differ in competence, so it is hard to compare running times measured on different machines.

To circumvent these problems it is sometimes desirable to instead determine the amount of computational work in a program by *counting* something. This avoids the measurement problems and yields a result that would seem to depend only on the program, not on the environment in which it is executed. The most obvious things to count are elementary arithmetic and logical operations, such as additions, subtractions, multiplications, divisions, and comparisons. Some applications include higher-level operations that can be counted, such as iterations, exchanges, pivots, function evaluations, or subproblems. In §15.1.2 we saw that the prof utility reports counts of subprogram invocations, and there are software tools [50] for counting other things, such as tcov which counts executions of individual source code statements. All of these counts can be useful in some circumstances, and you should use them if you think they will help you to understand and improve the performance of your programs.

One of the biggest advantages to counting is that the number of operations performed by an algorithm can sometimes be determined by mathematical analysis without running, or perhaps even writing, any code. A major area of computer science is the study of **computational complexity**, in which algorithms are analyzed and compared by finding formulas that tell how much work they do as a function of their inputs. Studies of computational complexity have yielded important insights into the behavior of some algorithms, and have led to the development of improved algorithms. The algorithm having the lowest theoretical complexity is often the one that will use the least CPU time in practice, and algorithms having exponential complexity, in which the amount of work grows combinatorially with the size of the input, often turn out to be intractable in practice.

Unfortunately, operation counting and complexity analysis are usually of little use either in tuning programs or in predicting the actual performance of complicated algorithms. Often it is not clear what to count, because implementation decisions by the programmer or the compiler can yield very different programs for doing the same calculation. For example, an algorithm that requires floating-point arithmetic might be implemented with bit manipulations that accomplish the same results without actually using any floating-point instructions at all. Some processors can overlap operations, so that a multiply followed by an add takes the same time as a single instruction, but only in certain circumstances. Integer arithmetic can sometimes be substituted for floating-point or conversely. Counting more than one thing yields a vector of values, rather than a single quantity of computational work, and it is usually not obvious how to combine the counts into a single number for use in comparing programs. Complexity analysis is difficult for simple algorithms and impossible for complicated ones; often the only useful results that can be obtained are asymptotic, true only in the limit of large problems, whereas most real applications involve problems of intermediate size.

Thus, while operation counting is useful in some settings, we are usually driven to use CPU time measurements, annoying though they are to make, for performance tuning and for comparing real programs.

15.2   Tuning FORTRAN Source Code

If a skillful programmer works hard at the craft, what should result is source code that is correct, robust, easy to use, easy to maintain, and breathtaking in its eloquence and simplicity. Programmers are human, and the language, as we have seen, has limitations of its own, but we are entitled to expect that a well-written program is at least close to a local optimum in the design space of possible solutions to the problem at hand.

Code tuning is the process of hacking this near-perfect creation so that it will run faster.

Clear and simple code is always the best place to start in seeking high performance because code that is obvious to us is the most likely to be obvious to the optimizing compiler too, but usually there is then some tweaking that can make it run faster still. Thus, *in tuning code we take a conscious decision to deliberately make the program harder to understand, and we usually take a significant chance of accidentally making it wrong, in order to make it faster.* This is a tradeoff not to be taken lightly. In the improbable event that some improvement to efficiency leaves your artistic creation aesthetically undamaged, then try it. Otherwise you should carefully weigh the cost to clarity, and the risk to correctness, against the actual improvement in performance. When you decide that you *must* make changes that decrease the clarity of the source program, try hard to use additional comments to make it clear again.

Many optimizations depend intimately on the processor, memory architecture, and compiler. Some compilers are exceedingly clever, and clumsy attempts to help them out just get in their way. Always read the compiler manual, with special attention to the options and the vendor's advice about optimization. If preprocessors are available, learn all about them too.

Profile the program, and work on the parts that are using the time. It does not matter how fast a code segment runs if it never gets executed. Within the parts of the program that are using the time, optimize the most likely code paths. If some particular condition or data value happens more often than others, try to take advantage of that fact.

Any particular change can make a program run faster or slower, depending on many factors only some of which are evident to the programmer. Try one thing at a time and measure the change in execution speed before going on to the next thing you think might help. The changes that are suggested below often decrease execution time, but code tuning is a tedious, empirical business in which there are many surprises and no guarantees!

I have tried to make this exposition thorough, but if you plan to spend a noticeable amount of your professional life squeezing microseconds out of FORTRAN programs, you might consider making a hobby of the voluminous folklore on the subject. Read the experts [2] [100] [28], [13], experiment constantly, and, with salt shaker always at the ready, skim the newsgroup `comp.lang.fortran` once in a while in search of new ideas about efficiency.

15.2.1   Algorithm Implementation Details

Earlier, I begged off discussing the design of algorithms and data structures, even though they have a profound influence on performance, because that is a vast subject beyond the scope of this book. Here we assume that the algorithm has already been decided upon, and focus instead on programming it in FORTRAN. Often, though, even after an algorithm is quite precisely specified, many small details of its implementation remain to be worked out in the coding, and the choices that the programmer makes about those details can also have a big influence on performance. This section presents some general principles that often lead to faster programs.

Optimize for normal function, not for error conditions. If an error will stop the program anyhow, there is little need to worry about handling it efficiently, especially if doing so would slow down the code when everything is working correctly.

For example, consider the problem of factoring a matrix that is expected to be diagonally dominant and hence nonsingular. One could check for the diagonal dominance in advance and stop the program if it is not confirmed. If the only real requirement is for the matrix to be nonsingular, though, it is much faster to just attempt the factorization and stop if it fails. In that case some work would have been wasted on a matrix that could not be factored, but in the usual case where it can be we save the work of checking beforehand.

Select the method based on the data. Sometimes a calculation can be performed in several different ways that yield identical results but take different running times depending on the data.

For example, a sophisticated sorting algorithm will be the fastest if there are lots of items to sort, but a simple insertion sort has less overhead and is therefore best if there are fewer than about twenty [10, p379ff.] [12, p321]. To select the best method when such a choice is to be made, we can write code like this:

```
      IF(N.GT.20) THEN
          CALL FANCY(X,N)
      ELSE
          CALL PLAIN(X,N)
      ENDIF
```

Use closed-form results instead of iterative processes. Suppose one step of some algorithm requires the calculation of

$$\sum_{i=2}^{n} \frac{1}{i^2 - 1}$$

for several different values of n. We could code the calculation like this:

```
      SUM=0.D0
      DO 1 I=2,N
          SUM=SUM+1.D0/DFLOAT(I**2-1)
    1 CONTINUE
```

However, it is easy to find, from a symbolic math package or published tables, that the series has the closed-form sum computed by this code segment:

```
C     find sum{1/(i^2-1),i=2...n} = 3/4 - 1/(2n) - 1/(2n+2)
      SUM=0.75D0-1.D0/DFLOAT(2*N)-1.D0/DFLOAT(2*N+2)
```

Except for very small values of n, the formula requires less arithmetic than the DO loop. In a similar way, it usually takes less computation to evaluate the formula for a closed-form integral than it does to find the value with a numerical integration routine. Of course, if a sum or integral really has no closed form, then the iterative calculation can't be avoided.

Small systems of linear algebraic equations can often easily be solved in general and the formulas for the variables evaluated for different coefficients or right-hand sides, rather than using numerical Gaussian elimination for each case. For example, we could solve the system

$$ax + 2y - z = 0$$
$$x + 2y \quad\;\; = b$$
$$3y + z = 4$$

for several values of a and b by calling linear algebra subroutines to factor the coefficient matrix and do forward- and back-substitutions, or we could just solve analytically for x, y, and z and evaluate them using these formulas.

```
X=(8.D0-5.D0*B)/(2.D0*A-5.D0)
Y=(A*B-4.D0)/(2.D0*A-5.D0)
Z=(-3.D0*A*B-8.D0+8.D0*A)/(2.D0*A-5.D0)
```

Other opportunities to use closed-form results might present themselves in the course of your programming if you remember to look for them.

Store precomputed values. Sometimes a small number of values are needed over and over, and can be stored rather than calculated repeatedly.

In some introductory programming courses, especially those using languages that support recursion [74, p205], an obligatory early project is to write a program for finding $n! = 1 \times 2 \times 3 \times \cdots \times n$ by integer multiplication (in contrast see Exercise 5.8.34). The factorial function grows so quickly, though, that the largest value we can store in an INTEGER*4 variable is $12! = 479001600$. If there are only a dozen values, we might as well compute them once and for all and save them like this:

```
      INTEGER*4 FACTS(12)/1,2,6,24,120,720,5040,40320,362880,
     ;                     3628800,39916800,479001600/
```

A more practical example is in defining mathematical constants like π and e. We can easily find π by using a formula from trigonometry such as $\pi = \cos^{-1}(-1)$. Here it is in FORTRAN.

```
      PI=DACOS(-1.D0)
```

Unfortunately, this requires an elementary function evaluation each time PI is calculated, which might be repeatedly and in several different routines of a program. It saves computing time to set the value once and for all, in each routine where it is needed, using a compile-time initialization.

```
      REAL*8 PI/3.1415926535897932D0/
```

This is also clearer, and on machines whose floating-point arithmetic complies with the IEEE standard it is equally portable. It is better still to make an unchanging value like π a PARAMETER constant, as discussed in §4.5.

A table can sometimes be used to eliminate tests from a loop, as in the following example.

```
      DO 1 I=1,1000
          IF(L(I).EQ.1 .OR. L(I).EQ.4) A(I)=1.5D0
          IF(L(I).EQ.2 .OR. L(I).EQ.3) A(I)=2.7D0
    1 CONTINUE
```

It might be faster to code the calculation like this:

```
      REAL*8 TABLE(4)/1.5D0,2.7D0,2.7D0,1.5D0/
      :
      DO 1 I=1,1000
          A(I)=TABLE(L(I))
    1 CONTINUE
```

Other opportunities to save time by storing precomputed results might present themselves in the course of your programming if you remember to look for them.

Start searching where you found it last time. In many situations where it is necessary to search an ordered table, the value with which the table is to be entered changes only a little from one search to the next. In that case it makes sense to first check the cell where the previous value was found, and perhaps the adjacent cells, before looking elsewhere in the table.

Similarly, there are occasions when it is necessary to solve a sequence of nonlinear algebraic equations or minimize a sequence of functions in which each problem differs from the previous one only by some data values being slightly changed. In that case it is usually better to start each search for the solution or minimum from the preceding result rather than from an arbitrary starting point.

Consider using approximations. Sometimes an accurate but expensive result can be replaced by one that is less accurate but faster to compute.

The most obvious application of this idea is in setting tolerances. If some step in your algorithm requires a numerical solution of a nonlinear equation, or a function minimization, or a quadrature, or some other infinitely-convergent iterative process, you can probably make it stop early if you are willing to accept a less precise result. When a sub-algorithm result is used in a larger iterative solution process, it might be possible to start with rather imprecise values early on and only gradually tighten the sub-algorithm tolerances as the solution of the larger problem is approached [89].

If a complicated function of one (or two) variables must be evaluated many times for arguments over a known range, it might be faster to compute the value at a smaller number of points, fit the data with a cubic (or bicubic) spline, and use the spline to approximate the function at the many argument values where it is needed. The spline's coefficient table should be searched using bisection, or by some still faster method if you can devise one. The spline-evaluation routines of some otherwise excellent commercial scientific subroutine libraries use linear search instead, so beware of using them. The comments above about starting a table search in the right place apply especially to searching the coefficient table for a spline.

If your algorithm already uses a cubic spline, consider reducing the number of cells in the spline's coefficient table to speed up the searching of the table at the expense of some accuracy in the approximation. Some time can also be saved by using a quadratic spline instead of a cubic spline, or even a piecewise linear or piecewise constant approximation, depending on how much error can be tolerated.

It is also sometimes possible to approximate expensive functions by simple formulas. Consider the problem of finding the hypotenuse h of a right triangle whose sides are a and b. Using the Pythagorean theorem we can calculate the exact value from $h = \sqrt{a^2 + b^2}$, but this requires two multiplications, one addition, and an invocation of the square-root function. Notice that the hypotenuse can't be longer than the sum of the sides, nor shorter than the longer side, so $\max(a, b) \leq h \leq a + b$. The average of these extreme values,

$$\hat{h} = \tfrac{1}{2}[a + b + \max(a, b)].$$

provides a crude estimate of h that might be good enough in some situations (see Exercise

15.4.10), and which can be coded in this simple way.

```
IF(A.GE.B) THEN
    HHAT=A+0.5*B
ELSE
    HHAT=B+0.5*A
ENDIF
```

Taylor series approximations can also be useful provided the function value is to be found only for arguments in a limited range. For example,

$$e^x \approx 1 + x + \tfrac{1}{2}x^2 + \tfrac{1}{6}x^3$$

is not a bad approximation for $x \in [0, 1]$ (see Exercise 15.4.11), and is probably faster than using DEXP.

In some cases, introducing approximations such as those described here clearly amounts to changing the basic algorithm, and cannot be regarded as a mere implementation detail. The process of tuning code for efficiency often suggests refinements to the algorithm, and then it is hard to draw a clear line between the algorithm and its implementation.

15.2.2 Variable Typing and Initialization

Experiment with real types. Depending on the processor, REAL*8 arithmetic can be faster, slower, or the same speed as REAL*4 arithmetic, but REAL*16 operations invariably take much longer. Using more precision increases the amount of memory occupied by an array, which can affect cache and paging activity (see §15.2.7). Some processors have an option to do floating-point arithmetic faster by not being strictly compliant with the IEEE standard. The results are usually *more* accurate than those prescribed by the standard, so if your application does not need to produce answers that are bit-for-bit identical across processors, you should consider using this option. Floating-point calculations might be either faster than the corresponding integer operations or slower, depending on the processor and the operation.

Type other variables to be fullwords. Because of the way in which most processors access data in memory, you should prefer INTEGER*4 (the default) to INTEGER*2 and LOGICAL*4 to LOGICAL*1 variables.

Avoid EQUIVALENCE statements. They make it harder for the compiler to determine that the handling of the variables involved can be optimized.

Avoid type conversions. Conversions from one scalar data type to another, whether explicit or implicit, require a significant amount of processing (also see §15.2.3).

Do not use critical variables for certain purposes. Variables that are used in I/O statements, in subprogram argument lists, and in COMMON usually cannot be handled in ways that speed execution. Scalar variables that are manipulated extensively by your program, especially DO indices, should not be used in any of these ways.

Initialize scalars and small arrays at compile time. Assignment statements and arithmetic take time during the execution of the program, but data initializations are done when the program is loaded into memory and brief ones often do not take any extra loading time. The code on the left wastes execution time on initializations, but the code on the right does not.

```
I=3                              INTEGER*4 I/3/,J/4/,K/12/
J=4                              REAL*8 Z/0.D0/
K=I*J
Z=0.D0
```

Most UNIX™ systems set most variables to zero at load time if no compile-time initializations are given for them, but it is risky to bet the correctness of your program on this operating-system quirk. Even if it works on your system, it will make your program non-portable to other systems, including the one you might be using a month from now. Initialize variables that should start at zero along with those that have other initial values.

Initialize large arrays at run time. Data initializations that enlarge the executable make loading the code into memory take longer, and the increase in loading time can outweigh the time saved in execution.

15.2.3   Arithmetic Expressions

This section discusses the coding of arithmetic expressions *except* for exponentiation, which is sufficiently involved to merit a section of its own, §15.2.4. Some of the optimizations described here fall in a general category called **strength reduction** [28], in which division is replaced by multiplication or multiplication is replaced by addition. Some modern processors can overlap floating-point multiplications and additions in certain circumstances, and the simple transformations suggested here might prevent that from happening, so when that kind of strength reduction is used it is especially important to confirm an actual decrease in running time.

Exploit algebraic identities. Calculations that are algebraically equivalent can use different amounts of computer time. The statements on the right below probably take less time than those on the left, but give results that are identical except for roundoff and exceptions.

```
X=DLOG(A)+DLOG(B)-DLOG(C)              X=DLOG(A*B/C)
Y=DLOG(F**7)                           Y=7.D0*DLOG(F)
W=(DSIN(Z))**2+3.D0*Z+(DCOS(Z))**2     W=3.D0*Z+1.D0
```

Change division to multiplication where possible. On most computers a REAL*8 divide takes between 7 and 19 times as long as a REAL*8 multiply, depending on the processor and the operands, so the code on the right runs faster than that on the left.

```
X=A/B/C/D                         X=A/(B*C*D)
Y=Z/5.D0                          Y=0.2D0*Z
                                  VINV=1.D0/V
W1=G1/V                           W1=VINV*G1
W2=G2/V                           W2=VINV*G2
W3=G3/V                           W3=VINV*G3
```

Change subtraction to addition where convenient. On most processors an isolated REAL*8 subtract and an isolated REAL*8 add take exactly the same amount of time. However, because addition is commutative $(a + b = b + a)$, casting an expression with additions rather than subtractions makes it easier for the compiler to optimize the calculation. The effect of this change on the machine code that is generated will depend on the compiler and the context in which the statement appears.

Minimize the number of type conversions. Conversions between real and integer and between REAL*4 and REAL*8 require several instructions on most processors. In particular, floating an integer is usually more expensive than adding two REAL*8 values, so the code on the right runs faster than that on the left.

```
                              X=1.D0
      DO 1 K=1,1000           DO 1 K=1,1000
          A(K)=DFLOAT(K)          A(K)=X
          B(K)=K                  B(K)=X
    1 CONTINUE                    X=X+1.D0
                            1 CONTINUE
```

In the code on the left above, a type conversion is performed whether explicitly indicated by the use of DFLOAT or merely implied by the assignment into B(K), so there is nothing to be gained, and some clarity to be lost, by omitting the DFLOAT. If mixed-mode arithmetic is unavoidable, group the integer and floating-point calculations separately to minimize type conversions.

```
      Y=DFLOAT(I)+DFLOAT(J)          Y=DFLOAT(I+J)
```

These code segments give the same result as long as there is no overflow in the calculation of I+J.

Factor expressions. Often algebraic simplification can reduce the amount of arithmetic needed to calculate an expression. The code on the right uses two fewer multiplications than that on the left.

```
      Y=X*A+B*X+X*C                  Y=(A+B+C)*X
```

The value of this transformation, like many other optimizations, depends on the context in which the statement appears. If the products X*A, B*X, and X*C were recently calculated, they might still be available in the machine program (even if they are not assigned to variables by the FORTRAN source) and could simply be added to find Y. Measure the effect of each change on the running time of your program.

Make recurring subexpressions obvious to the compiler. If a subexpression is used in several places the compiler can generate code to calculate it only once, provided it can *recognize* the subexpression as the same in each place. Because of the operator precedence rules described in §2.5, your compiler might recognize recurring subexpressions only if they appear at the left end of the calculation or are grouped inside parentheses, and if they are typographically identical in each occurrence.

```
      X=A*B*DSQRT(C)*D*Y             X=B*Y*DSQRT(C)*A*D
      Z=DSQRT(C)*Y*B*G              Z=B*Y*DSQRT(C)*G
      W=(H**2)*B*Y*Q*DSQRT(C)       W=(H**2)*(B*Y*DSQRT(C))*Q
```

Here the code on the right renders the subexpression B*Y*DSQRT(C) recognizable to the compiler.

Do not introduce intermediate variables. When you recognize a recurring subexpression it might be tempting to eliminate it by assigning it to a variable, as in the code on the left.

```
TEMP=B*Y*DSQRT(C)
X=TEMP*A*D                      X=B*Y*DSQRT(C)*A*D
Z=TEMP*G                        Z=B*Y*DSQRT(C)*G
W=(H**2)*TEMP*Q                 W=(H**2)*(B*Y*DSQRT(C))*Q
```

This can actually impede the compiler's optimization of the code. Putting the subexpression value in a variable causes many compilers to store the value in memory, whereas in the code on the right the compiler need not do so. Also, as explained in [100], having found TEMP defined, the compiler has to worry about it. Is it used later? What pattern of assignment and reference does it possess? It is better to make subexpressions obvious to the compiler and let it deal with them. You might have other good reasons for defining intermediate variables, but don't do it in an attempt to improve performance, unless you intend to turn off the compiler's optimization altogether.

Make constants obvious to the compiler. It is easier for the compiler to optimize code in which it can recognize that constant values are in fact unchanging. If a variable is in COMMON or a subprogram parameter list, the compiler must assume that its value changes at each subprogram invocation.

```
COMMON /CONST/ VAL
VAL=1.23D0                      REAL*8 VAL/1.23D0/
:                               :
CALL SUBA                       CALL SUBA
A=VAL*B                         A=VAL*B
```

In the code on the left above, the compiler must assume that VAL is changed by SUBA and retrieve the (possibly new) value from /CONST/ before using it. In the code on the right, it is clear that the value does not change.

```
                                Q=Z
CALL SUBB(Z)                    CALL SUBB(Q)
A=Z*B                           A=Z*B
```

In the code on the left above, Z might be changed by SUBB, but on the right it is undisturbed.

Replace MAX and MIN functions with IF. If there is less than an even chance that the condition is true, the code on the right might be faster than the code on the left.

```
A=DMIN1(A,S)                    IF(A.GT.S) A=S
```

Both statements generate a test, but if the test fails there is no assignment in the code on the right.

15.2.4 Exponentiation

Use integers for whole-number exponents. To raise to a *real* power, as in X**Y, FORTRAN uses logarithms, like this:

$$x^y = e^{y \ln x}$$

Approximating the log and exponential functions takes a lot of arithmetic, so the library subprogram that performs this calculation uses a lot of CPU time. The method also fails when $x \leq 0$, even if y is a whole number (so that x^y has a value), because $\ln(x)$ is undefined for $x \leq 0$.

To raise to an *integer* power, as in X**N, FORTRAN uses a sequence of squarings and multiplications, like this:

$$x^5 = (x^2)^2 \times x$$

Most library subprograms for doing this use a heuristic called the right-to-left binary method [9, §4.6.3] to select the sequence of squarings and multiplications in a way that minimizes the total number of multiplications required. This algorithm uses much less arithmetic than the method based on logarithms, and works just as well for zero and negative values of x as for positive ones. For zero powers the routine returns 1, and for negative powers it just raises the number to the positive power and divides the result into 1.

$$x^{-5} = \frac{1}{x^5} = \frac{1}{(x^2)^2 \times x}$$

Some library routines for raising to a real power test for the power being a whole number and use the integer-power method in that case, but yours might not. Thus, the code on the right might be both more robust and much faster than that on the left, and it will never be slower.

```
Y=X**3.D0                          Y=X**3
```

X*X is no faster than X2** Any competent compiler, even with optimization turned off, has the brains to implement squaring as a multiplication rather than invoking the library routine for raising to a power. There is no advantage to obscuring the meaning of your code by writing X*X when what you mean is X**2, except that it saves typing one character. But remember to make the exponent an integer!

Inline exponentiations whose integer power is fixed. The linkage overhead of invoking a library routine that raises to an integer power can be avoided by coding the sequence of squarings and multiplications it would do.

```
B=A**7                             T1=A*A
                                   T2=T1*T1
                                   T1=T1*T2
                                   B=T1*A
```

Some compilers might generate in-line machine instructions for the statement on the left but others will not, so, especially if the calculation appears in a loop that is performed many times, it might be worthwhile to code it as on the right. To apply this technique when the power is a variable rather than a fixed number would require inlining the whole routine for raising to an integer power, which is almost certainly not worth the trouble.

Use DSQRT(X) in preference to X**0.5D0 The exponentiation generates a call to the
FORTRAN library routine for raising to real powers, which as we have seen must resort
to logarithms to handle arbitrary powers and is then very slow. In contrast, the DSQRT
reference generates a call to a different FORTRAN library routine for square root, which uses
a very fast algorithm tailor-made for that job (perhaps even implemented in hardware).
Some library routines for raising to a real power test for the power being one-half and use
DSQRT in that case, but yours might not. Thus the code on the right might be faster than
that on the left, and it will never be slower.

```
Y=X**0.5D0                          Y=DSQRT(X)
Z=X**(-0.5D0)                       Z=1.D0/DSQRT(X)
W=X**1.5D0                          W=X*DSQRT(X)
```

Avoid raising to a power that is the index of a loop. A formula for the sum of an
alternating series is often written with a term like $(-1)^n$ as a concise way of describing the
alternation of signs. For example,

$$y = -1 + \frac{1}{4} - \frac{1}{9} + \frac{1}{16} - \cdots = \sum_{n=1}^{\infty} \frac{(-1)^n}{n^2}$$

We might approximate this sum using the loop on the left below, but that would use 1000
calls to the routine for raising to an integer power, just to make the signs alternate. The
code on the right accomplishes the same calculation with much less work.

```
                                    Y=0.D0
       Y=0.D0                       S=-1.D0
       DO 1 N=1,1000                DO 1 N=1,1000
           Y=Y+((-1.D0)**N)/DFLOAT(N**2)    Y=Y+S/DFLOAT(N**2)
     1 CONTINUE                         S=-S
                                      1 CONTINUE
```

It would be even faster to eliminate the sign variable S by computing two terms on each
pass, as on the left below. To eliminate the type conversion we could introduce a real
variable R to track N as on the right.

```
                                    R=1.D0
       Y=0.D0                       Y=0.D0
       DO 1 N=1,1000,2              DO 1 N=1,1000,2
           Y=Y-1.D0/DFLOAT(N**2)        Y=Y-1.D0/R**2
           Y=Y+1.D0/DFLOAT((N+1)**2)    R=R+1.D0
     1 CONTINUE                         Y=Y+1.D0/R**2
                                        R=R+1.D0
                                      1 CONTINUE
```

Some loops involve raising quantities other than -1 to successive powers, and these calculations can also be simplified. The code on the left below makes 1000 calls to the integer

power routine; that on the right makes none.

```
                               R=1.DO
                               XN=X
        Y=0.DO                 Y=0.DO
        DO 1 N=1,1000          DO 1 N=1,1000
            Y=Y+(X**N)/DFLOAT(N**2)    Y=Y+XN/R**2
      1 CONTINUE                   XN=XN*X
                                   R=R+1.DO
                             1 CONTINUE
```

Use Horner's rule to evaluate polynomials. This is an important special case of the factoring idea discussed in §15.2.3. These expressions for W and Z yield equal results, except for roundoff, but the factored form uses multiplications instead of the routine for raising to an integer power, and it involves fewer intermediate results so it is easier for the compiler to optimize.

```
W=A*X**5 + B*X**4 + C*X**3 + D*X**2 + E*X + F
Z=(((((A*X+B)*X+C)*X+D)*X+E)*X+F
```

15.2.5   Conditionals

Exploit logical implications. Tests can sometimes be replaced by logically equivalent tests that are faster. The statements on the right below probably take less time than the corresponding ones on the left.

```
IF(DSQRT(X).LT.DSQRT(Y)) GO TO 1     IF(X.LT.Y) GO TO 1
IF(X**2 .GT. 0.DO) GO TO 2           IF(X.NE.0.DO) GO TO 2
IF(.NOT.A .AND. .NOT.B) GO TO 3      IF(.NOT.(A.OR.B)) GO TO 3
```

Order tests to minimize the expected amount of work they require. Logical tests should be arranged so that inexpensive and often-successful tests precede those that are expensive and rarely successful. This applies to both the ordering of conditions in an IF statement and the ordering of a series of IF statements. If an early test is definitive, the later ones can be avoided. Thus, if expression L1 is more likely to be true than expression L2, order the conditions in IF statements like this:

```
IF(L2 .AND. L1) ...
IF(L1 .OR.  L2) ...
```

Expression L2 being .FALSE. resolves the first test without requiring the evaluation of L1, whereas expression L1 being true resolves the second without requiring the evaluation of L2.

Avoid forcing the evaluation of logical conditions. When several logical relations must be tested, try to put all of the .AND. relations in one statement and all of the .OR. relations in another. This may permit the compiler to generate code that evaluates the conditions, and possibly resolves the test, one condition at a time in the order they are specified. If .AND. and .OR. conditions are mixed, or if .NOT. operators or parentheses are used, then the whole logical expression may have to be evaluated before the result can be determined.

The statement on the left below uses parentheses that might force the evaluation of the whole expression, but that on the right permits the conditions to be examined one at a time with the possibility that the outcome can be determined without testing `C.GT.D`

```
IF((A.GT.B).OR.(C.GT.D)) GO TO 1        IF( A.GT.B .OR. C.GT.D ) GO TO 1
```

Eliminate intermediate logical variables. In the code on the left, OK must be stored and considered by the compiler in its optimization of the program. The code on the right probably runs faster.

```
OK=X.LT.Y
IF(OK) THEN                             IF(X.LT.Y) THEN
   A=B                                     A=B
ELSE                                    ELSE
   B=C                                     B=C
ENDIF                                   ENDIF
```

Rewrite GO TO constructs as IF-THEN constructs. The code on the right is more easily optimized than that on the left.

```
  IF(A.GT.1.DO) GO TO 1                 IF(A.GT.1.DO) THEN
  A=A+1.7DO                                A=A-2.43DO
  GO TO 2                               ELSE
1 A=A-2.43DO                               A=A+1.7DO
2 ...                                   ENDIF
```

Rewrite paired IF statements as IF-THEN constructs. The code on the right is more easily optimized than that on the left.

```
                                        IF(B.GT.0.DO) THEN
                                           G=2.DO+A
  IF(B.GT.0.DO) G=2.DO+A                ELSE
  IF(B.LE.0.DO) G=1.DO-A                   G=1.DO-A
                                        ENDIF
```

Consider rewriting a cascade of IF statements as a computed GO TO. The FORTRAN on the right might yield faster machine code than that on the left.

```
  IF(I.EQ.1) GO TO 5                    GO TO(5,8,7,7,9), I
  IF(I.EQ.2) GO TO 8
  IF(I.EQ.3) GO TO 7
  IF(I.EQ.4) GO TO 7
  IF(I.EQ.5) GO TO 9
```

Some compilers generate a branch table for the computed GO TO, which is faster than the sequence of tests. In that case, the order of the alternatives does not affect the speed of execution.

15.2.6 Loops and Indices

The cumulative delay from lots of inefficient code segments can be noticeable even if each is executed only once, but to really waste CPU time in style requires a loop. Most of the tuning ideas outlined so far can be applied to code in loops, but there are also some considerations that are peculiar to loops.

Use DO loops in preference to free loops. In addition to the reasons discussed in §5.2 and §13.3.5 for using DO loops rather than free loops, they are also much more easily recognized by your optimizing compiler. In §16.1 we will see that this is also true of vectorizing compilers.

Protect the DO loop index variable. As explained in §15.2.2, the index should be typed INTEGER*4 and should not be EQUIVALENCEd, or be a subroutine argument, or be in COMMON.

Unroll short loops. The overhead of initializing a loop counter, testing, and branching can be avoided by explicitly coding the operations performed by the body of the loop for the successive values of the index. The code on the right below runs faster than that on the left.

```
      SUM=0.DO
      DO 1 I=1,5
          SUM=SUM+X(I)                SUM=X(1)+X(2)+X(3)+X(4)+X(5)
    1 CONTINUE
```

In some cases, such as the example above, unrolling a loop can also make the code easier to understand. Loop unrolling is most easily used when the number of passes is fixed, but can also be used when the number of passes can take on only a few values. The code on the right below unrolls the loop for both possible values of N.

```
      SUM=0.DO
      N=5                           N=5
      IF(K.LT.37) N=3               IF(K.LT.37) N=3
      DO 1 I=1,N                    IF(N.EQ.3) THEN
          SUM=SUM+X(I)                  SUM=X(1)+X(2)+X(3)
    1 CONTINUE                      ELSE
                                        SUM=X(1)+X(2)+X(3)+X(4)+X(5)
                                    ENDIF
```

If N is not needed later, we can simplify this code sequence further, as on the left and right below.

```
                                  SUM=X(1)+X(2)+X(3)
                                  IF(K.GE.37) SUM=SUM+X(4)+X(5)
      IF(K.LT.37) THEN
          SUM=X(1)+X(2)+X(3)
      ELSE
          SUM=X(1)+X(2)+X(3)+X(4)+X(5)
      ENDIF
```

Avoid tests based on the loop index. Often it is possible to avoid testing in a loop by some simple rearrangement. The code on the right below runs faster than that on the left.

```
      DO 1 I=1,100                  DO 1 I=1,100
      DO 1 J=1,100                      DO 2 J=1,100
          A(I,J)=0.DO                       A(I,J)=0.DO
          IF(I.EQ.J) A(I,J)=1.DO     2      CONTINUE
    1 CONTINUE                           A(I,I)=1.DO
                                    1 CONTINUE
```

Here is another example of the same idea, in which the code on the right again runs faster than that on the left.

```
    DO 1 I=1,100                         DO 1 I=1,50
        IF(I.LE.50) X(I)=1.D0                X(I)=1.D0
        IF(I.GT.50) X(I)=2.D0                X(I+50)=2.D0
  1 CONTINUE                           1 CONTINUE
```

Move out operations that do not depend on the loop index. Naïve coding sometimes leaves constant factors in a loop, as in the examples on the left. The code on the right runs faster.

```
                                     A=F*DSQRT(DEXP(G))
    DO 1 I=1,1000                    DO 1 I=1,1000
        X(I)=F*DSQRT(DEXP(G))*X(I)        X(I)=A*X(I)
  1 CONTINUE                        1 CONTINUE

    Y=0.D0                           Y=0.D0
    DO 2 J=1,N                       DO 2 J=1,N
        Y=Y+B*Z(J)                       Y=Y+Z(J)
  2 CONTINUE                        2 CONTINUE
                                     Y=B*Y
```

The optimizing compiler might perform these code motions for us, provided the constant factors can be recognized. As explained in §15.2.3 constant factors should be placed at the left end of the expressions where they occur or should be grouped in parentheses. Thus, for example, we should code `F*DSQRT(DEXP(G))*X(I)` as shown, rather than `X(I)*F*DSQRT(DEXP(G))`.

Tests that do not depend on the index should also be moved out of the loop. The code on the right runs faster than the code on the left.

```
    DO 1 I=1,100                     DO 1 I=1,100
    DO 1 J=1,100                         IF(A(I).LT.0.D0) B(I)=H
        IF(A(I).LT.0.D0) B(I)=H          DO 2 J=1,100
        X=X+A(J)*B(I)                        X=X+A(J)*B(I)
  1 CONTINUE                        2     CONTINUE
                                    1 CONTINUE
```

The optimization of subscript calculations should usually be left up to the compiler, as discussed below.

Use strength reduction in loops. In §15.2.4 we saw an example of replacing exponentiation by multiplication in a loop. Division should always be factored out of a loop, by changing it to multiplication as explained in §15.2.3. The code on the right runs faster than that on the left.

```
                                     ZINV=1.D0/Z
    DO 1 I=1,1000                    DO 1 I=1,1000
        X(I)=Y(I)/Z                      X(I)=ZINV*Y(I)
  1 CONTINUE                        1 CONTINUE
```

It might also be possible to replace multiplication by addition. The code on the right runs faster than that on the left.

```
                                         X=3.D0
    DO 1 I=1,1000                        DO 1 I=1,1000
        Y(I)=3.D0*DFLOAT(I)                  Y(I)=X
  1 CONTINUE                                 X=X+3.D0
                                       1 CONTINUE
```

Fuse loops having the same index range. The overhead of one loop is avoided by fusing the two loops on the left below into the one on the right.

```
    Z=0.D0
    DO 1 I=1,100                         Z=0.D0
        Z=Z+A(I)*B(I)                    DO 1 I=1,100
  1 CONTINUE                                 Z=Z+A(I)*B(I)
    DO 2 J=1,100                             Y(I)=A(I)+C(I)
        Y(J)=A(J)+C(J)                 1 CONTINUE
  2 CONTINUE
```

In this example the loop fusion is especially advantageous because both calculations refer to the elements of A, each of which must now be loaded from memory only once for each value of I. For loops to be candidates for fusion it is of course necessary for them not to have **data dependencies** that would make the results different when the loops are fused. The loops below cannot be fused, because Z cannot be used in the second loop until it is found by the first.

```
    Z=0.D0
    DO 1 I=1,1000
        Z=Z+X(I)
  1 CONTINUE
    DO 2 J=1,1000
        Y(J)=Z+C(J)
  2 CONTINUE
```

Use scalars rather than arrays as accumulators. If a scalar variable is used to accumulate a sum, the compiler can probably avoid many references to memory. The code on the right runs faster than that on the left.

```
    DO 1 I=1,100                         DO 1 I=1,100
        X(I)=0.D0                            SUM=0.D0
        DO 2 J=1,100                         DO 2 J=1,100
            X(I)=X(I)+A(J,I)                     SUM=SUM+A(J,I)
  2     CONTINUE                         2     CONTINUE
  1 CONTINUE                                 X(I)=SUM
                                       1 CONTINUE
```

Do not change arrays into vectors for subscripting. The compiler is better at managing subscript calculations than you are. The code on the right below runs faster than that on the left.

```
    REAL*8 A(100),B(100)                 REAL*8 A(10,10),B(10,10)
    :                                    :
    DO 1 I=1,10                          DO 1 I=1,10
        A(I+10*(J-1))=B(I+10*(J-1))          A(I,J)=B(I,J)
  1 CONTINUE                            1 CONTINUE
```

Do not introduce temporary variables for subscripting. Unnecessary temporaries, especially when they involve the DO index, spread out the subscripting calculations and make them more difficult for the compiler to optimize. The code on the right is more easily optimized than that on the left.

```
    DO 1 I=1,10
        K=I+1
        DO 2 J=1,10                     DO 1 I=1,10
            L=2*J+1                     DO 1 J=1,10
            A(J,K)=B(K,L)                   A(J,I+1)=B(I+1,2*J+1)
2       CONTINUE                    1 CONTINUE
1   CONTINUE
```

Write subscript expressions consistently, such as I+1 in the example above, so that the compiler can recognize them as the same quantity in all the places where they appear. Subscript expressions that are used more than once are recurring subexpressions as described earlier in §15.2.3.

Avoid negative subscript offsets. Some processors have indexed machine language instructions through which it is possible to reference array elements with a fixed positive address offset. This avoids some integer arithmetic in the calculation of array element addresses. Negative subscript offsets, and positive subscript offsets that are too large, might prevent your optimizing compiler from being able to use indexed machine instructions, so the code on the right might run faster than that on the left.

```
    DO 1 I=2,11                     DO 1 I=1,10
        A(I)=B(I-1)+B(I+1)              A(I+1)=B(I)+B(I+2)
1   CONTINUE                    1 CONTINUE
```

Use arrays with the same shape and element length. If all of the arrays participating in a calculation have the same shape and element length, an address offset computed for one can be used for the others.

```
    REAL*8 A(10,10),B(4,10)         REAL*8 A(10,10),B(10,10)
    :                               :
    DO 1 I=1,10                     DO 1 I=1,10
        A(2,I)=B(2,I)                   A(2,I)=B(2,I)
1   CONTINUE                    1 CONTINUE
```

Consider dimensioning arrays larger than they need to be in order to make them the same size as the others you are using. On the right six rows of B are wasted, but the code runs faster than that on the left because in the machine code one offset instead of two must be maintained for addressing into the arrays.

The addressing simplicity of using arrays that have the same dimensions is lost if the elements are of different lengths. Consider typing arrays so that the elements are longer than they need to be, if that allows you to make them the same length as the elements of other arrays you are using. The code on the right runs faster than that on the left.

```
    LOGICAL*1 S(10)                 LOGICAL*4 S(10)
    INTEGER*4 NUMS(10)              INTEGER*4 NUMS(10)
    :                               :
    DO 1 I=1,10                     DO 1 I=1,10
        IF(S(I)) NUMS(I)=I              IF(S(I)) NUMS(I)=I
1   CONTINUE                    1 CONTINUE
```

The use of LOGICAL*4 in preference to LOGICAL*1 variables is in keeping with a recommendation from §15.2.2.

Make the loop lower bound and increment both 1 if possible. This process, called **normalizing** the loop, might make it easier for the compiler to optimize the loop [28, p143].

15.2.7 Memory Reference Patterns and Stride

Consider the two code segments shown below, which compute the same result vector Y.

```
REAL*8 A(30,100),X(100),Y(100)        REAL*8 A(100,30),X(100),Y(100)
   :                                     :
DO 1 J=1,100                          DO 1 J=1,100
      Y(J)=A(1,J)*X(J)                      Y(J)=A(J,1)*X(J)
 1 CONTINUE                            1 CONTINUE
```

The only difference between them is that on the left the loop steps from column to column along the first row of A, while on the right the loop steps from row to row down the first column of A.

These calculations might seem to be essentially the same, but the one on the right almost surely runs much faster than the one on the left. To see why, it is necessary to consider how the elements of A are stored in memory. Recall from §5.3 that memory is linear, and that the elements of an array are laid out in **column-major order**. This means that the elements of A are stored in the order A(1,1), A(2,1), ..., A(30,100). This arrangement, and the process of accessing a row of A, are shown schematically as follows.

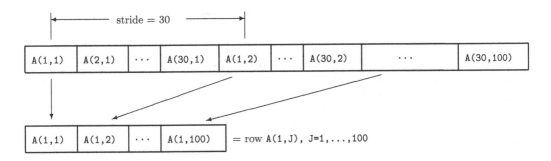

The distance between the storage locations that contain the successive elements of row A(1,J), 30 doublewords, is called the **stride** of the loop on the left. In the loop on the right, the elements of A are stored in the order A(1,1), A(2,1), ..., A(100,30) and accessed like this:

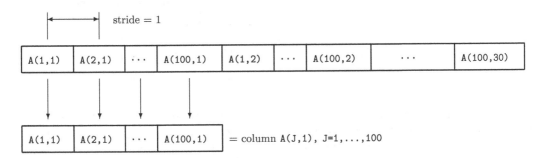

Working down a column of A, the loop loads the successive values that it needs from storage locations that are immediately adjacent, so its stride is 1. Data that are accessed at stride 1 are said to have good **locality of reference** and are likely to be much more quickly accessed than data that are scattered through memory with large stride or irregularly. This is because of the hardware storage hierarchy that is used in typical computers.

It is the CPU that does the processing, so for data to be manipulated they must reach the CPU from wherever they are stored. The diagram below shows the various places that data can come from, and how long it takes the first byte to ascend each level.

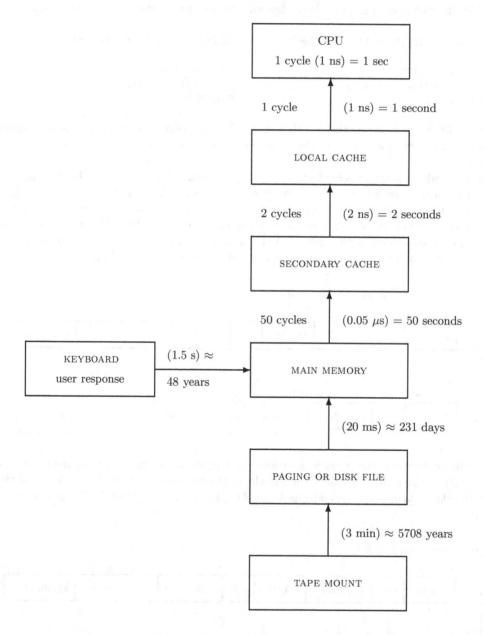

We assume that the processor's internal clock has a cycle time of 1 ns, or 1×10^{-9} seconds. A RISC processor executes one machine instruction every clock cycle, so such a machine would execute $1/(1 \times 10^{-9}) = 1000$ million instructions per second, or 1000 MIPs.

Nobody can imagine how brief a nanosecond really is, because everything in our sensory experience takes many orders of magnitude longer than that. Therefore, as an aid to your intuitive grasp of the access times listed in the diagram, suppose that a processor clock cycle takes 1 second instead of 1 ns. Then we can figure out what the other times would be on that more-human scale. The actual access times and the scaled times are both shown on the diagram, with the actual times in parentheses. As computing evolves, the names in some of the boxes change and all of the hardware-related times decrease, but there will always be faster and slower parts of the storage hierarchy.

The closest storage to the CPU is its local or **L1 cache**. This is a very small memory that has very high speed and is therefore very expensive per byte compared to slower-speed storage. When the CPU requires a piece of data that is not already in the cache, the hardware and operating system arrange for a contiguous piece of memory containing it to be loaded into the cache. This is called a **cache flush**; finding the data already in the cache when the CPU needs it is called a **cache hit**. A flush of the local cache is unfortunate, but it takes only 2 cycles, or 2 seconds of scaled time, provided the data sought are in the secondary or **L2 cache**. If A(1,1) is in the local cache, then A(2,1), the adjacent storage location, probably is too, but A(1,30) is far enough away that it might not fit and a cache flush will be necessary to get it. The secondary cache feeds the local cache and works the same way except that it is larger and takes much longer to flush.

Long arrays probably don't fit in the secondary cache, so they must be kept in main storage, which is much bigger. Main storage is random-access semiconductor memory like the caches, but it is much slower and therefore less expensive per byte. To flush the secondary cache and get something from main memory [29] takes several dozen cycles; let's say 50 to keep the numbers round. That's almost a minute of scaled time.

A large program might not fit in main storage either, and in that case parts of it, measured in units called **pages**, are stored temporarily in a disk file. Needing a byte that happens to be paged out causes an operating system event called a **page fault**, and servicing one of those [29] takes 20 milliseconds or more, some 231 *days* of scaled time.

Now we can see why locality of reference is so important to performance! Real programs always generate cache activity, and most also page, because they don't fit in the fastest parts of the memory hierarchy. But cache misses and page faults that are not really essential must be avoided to achieve high performance. Above all, 𝕿𝖍𝖔𝖚 𝕾𝖍𝖆𝖑𝖙 𝕹𝖔𝖙 𝕻𝖆𝖌𝖊. In our example, accessing the elements of A at stride 1 by going down a column ensures that the data will be made available to the CPU with the least possible exercise of the memory hierarchy.

With this preamble, we are now ready to give some guidelines for code tuning to manage memory reference patterns.

Process array elements in the order they are stored in memory. Reorder loops to use stride 1 memory reference patterns. The code on the right in the example above runs faster than that on the left. In addressing the elements of an array that has two (or more) dimensions, the leftmost subscript (or subscripts) should vary most rapidly so that access is down columns rather than across rows. If you cannot achieve stride 1, reorder loops to minimize the stride.

Preserve stride 1 in reordering loops to remove overhead. Sometimes it is possible to rearrange a nest of loops so as to reduce the total amount of loop initialization overhead, as in the example at the top of the next page.

The nest on the left requires 1 initialization of the K loop, 200 initializations of the J loop, and for each pass of the J loop 40 initializations of the I loop, for a total of $1 + 200 + 200 \times 40 = 8201$. The nest on the right computes the same result but uses only $1 + 2 + 2 \times 40 = 83$ loop initializations. Unfortunately, it changes stride 1 references to G

```
      REAL*8 G(2,40,200)                REAL*8 G(2,40,200)
      :                                 :
      DO 1 K=1,200                      DO 1 I=1,2
      DO 1 J=1,40                       DO 1 J=1,40
      DO 1 I=1,2                        DO 1 K=1,200
          G(I,J,K)=A(I)+B(J)+C(K)           G(I,J,K)=A(I)+B(J)+C(K)
    1 CONTINUE                        1 CONTINUE
```

into stride 8000 references, which will hurt performance far more than removing the loop initializations will help it. To keep the nest at stride 1, we reorder G as shown below. Now the nest once again accesses G at stride 1.

```
                  REAL*8 G(200,40,2)
                  :
                  DO 1 I=1,2
                  DO 1 J=1,40
                  DO 1 K=1,200
                      G(K,J,I)=A(I)+B(J)+C(K)
                1 CONTINUE
```

Look up the cache specifications for your computer. The sizes and architectures of the caches affect the optimization of memory reference patterns when data are used more than once or at strides greater than 1. Some processors have an L3 cache.

Keep the executable small to minimize paging. The smaller the executable program, the less cache and paging activity it will generate. Unfortunately, the objective of having a small machine program conflicts with several of the other things we often think to try in code tuning. To keep the program small we should initialize arrays at run time rather than at compile time, avoid using computed GO TO statements having many labels (because the resulting branch table takes up space), and refrain from unrolling loops or inlining subprograms. One of the reasons it is important to time the program after making each tuning change is that many factors have multiple effects, some of which tend to decrease execution time while the others tend to increase it. On the other hand, you can almost always make a memory-bound program run faster by increasing the real memory in your computer, or by killing other tasks that compete for the available memory.

15.2.8   I/O Considerations

As mentioned in §9.9, FORTRAN is the wrong language for applications that do large amounts of I/O on non-numeric data. However, some applications for which FORTRAN obviously *is* the appropriate language involve large amounts of I/O on *numerical* data, and that can have a big effect on execution time. A glance back at the storage hierarchy diagram in §15.2.7 reveals that disk I/O, user interactions, and tape mounts all take an eternity compared to the CPU cycle time.

Eliminate unnecessary I/O. Some snarled-up legacy codes write data to a file from one routine and read it back into another, because someone thought that was more convenient than passing the data between the routines in parameters or COMMON storage. Go to the trouble of figuring out the mess enough to avoid this. There is seldom any reason for a program to write a disk file for itself to read later.

   If you need to access some input data repeatedly, read it into memory rather than rereading a file.

Put switches on extensive diagnostic output and optional results, and turn them on only as needed. If the program you are working on writes a file that nobody has used since 1962, it is now probably safe to stop having it do that.

Minimize the number of I/O statement executions. Often this means writing the longest possible records so that there are as few as possible of them. This is sometimes referred to as using a large **data set blocking**. Each READ, WRITE, or PRINT generates an invocation of a FORTRAN I/O library routine. The code on the right generates fewer, so it runs faster.

```
    WRITE(1,900) U
    WRITE(1,900) V
    WRITE(1,900) W
    WRITE(1,900) X
    WRITE(1,900) Y
    WRITE(1,900) Z                      WRITE(1,900) U,V,W,X,Y,Z
900 FORMAT(1PD23.16)                900 FORMAT(1PD23.16)
```

Recall that when the FORMAT statement is exhausted before the list of variables, the I/O library returns to the rightmost left parenthesis and starts over, so the two code segments above produce identical output.

Minimize the number of file system blocks transmitted. Use a data set blocking that is a multiple of the file's block size. In a UNIX™ environment the blocksize is returned by the UNIX™ system routine STAT (see §14.2.2).

Minimize the number of variables transmitted. In many FORTRAN I/O library implementations, a lower-level routine is invoked to transmit each variable. The code on the right below transmits one variable, that on the left 300. Use array operands if possible, rather than individual array elements.

```
    REAL*8 B(300)                       REAL*8 B(300)
    :                                   :
    WRITE(1,901) (B(K),K=1,300)         WRITE(1,901) B
901 FORMAT(F9.2)                    901 FORMAT(F9.2)
```

Keep FORMAT statements simple. Many FORTRAN I/O libraries use a lower-level routine to interpret each FORMAT field specification, or token, each time it is used. The code on the right has fewer tokens to be parsed, so it runs faster than the code on the left. Note that (I4,I5) yields the same spacing as (I4,1X,I4), provided each number fits in an I4 field.

```
    WRITE(1,902) I,J                    WRITE(1,902) I,J
902 FORMAT(I4,1X,I4)                902 FORMAT(I4,I5)
    WRITE(2,903) K,L,M                  WRITE(2,903) K,L,M
903 FORMAT(I5,I5,I5)                903 FORMAT(3I5)
```

Avoid object-time FORMATs. The text of an object-time FORMAT cannot be compiled into the machine instructions but must be loaded from the program's data memory each time it is to be interpreted. For the same reason you should **Specify constant strings in the FORMAT statement, not in variables.** The code on the right runs faster than that on the left.

```
     CHARACTER*5 HDG/'Title'/
     WRITE(6,904) HDG                        WRITE(6,905)
 904 FORMAT(A5)                          905 FORMAT('Title')
```

Use unformatted I/O. All the overhead associated with format conversions can be avoided by writing the data as bytes, as described in §9.8. If the data are to be read by another program rather than by humans, there is no reason to waste time in converting numbers from internal form to numerals and back. In debugging a program that uses an unformatted file, it is helpful to write a companion viewing program that reads the unformatted file and translates it to something humans can understand.

Avoid unnecessary file-positioning operations. Rewinding or skipping records takes time. Organize the I/O so that the bytes of a file are accessed in the order they are stored.

15.2.9   Subprograms

As we first discussed in §6, and as we have seen over and over since then, SUBROUTINE and FUNCTION subprograms are so indispensable that their artful use is the very essence of computer programming. The way in which subprograms are used can have a big effect on execution speed.

Avoid unnecessary subprogram invocations. In §15.2.3 we saw some examples of rewriting arithmetic expressions in such a way as to use fewer elementary function calls. It might also be possible to avoid needlessly repeating function calls by storing some results. The code on the left uses $50 \times 50 \times 2 = 5000$ calls to DSQRT, while that on the right uses only $50 \times 2 = 100$ calls.

```
     DO 1 I=1,50                          DO 1 I=1,50
     DO 1 J=1,50                              ASRT(I)=DSQRT(A(I))
         X(I)=X(I)+DSQRT(A(I))                BSRT(I)=DSQRT(B(I))
 ;                +DSQRT(B(J))         1 CONTINUE
   1 CONTINUE                               DO 2 I=1,50
                                            DO 2 J=1,50
                                                X(J)=ASRT(I)+BSRT(J)
                                          2 CONTINUE
```

Inline subprogram invocations. The linkage overhead of a subprogram invocation can be avoided by expanding the source code of the subprogram at the point where it would be invoked. This also permits the operations that were formerly in the subprogram to be optimized along with those in the calling routine. In §15.2.4 we saw an instance of inlining, when we imitated the statements that would be performed by the built-in function for raising to an integer power. The program on the left at the top of the next page uses 1000 invocations of the function F, but that on the right uses none.

Some compilers can automatically inline designated procedures, making it unnecessary to risk obscuring the logical structure of the program by actually changing the source code. By inlining subprograms, even if we do it with the compiler rather than by hand, we give up many of the advantages of separate compilation discussed in §6.1.

```
      REAL*8 X(1000),Y(1000),F              REAL*8 X(1000),Y(1000)
      :                                      :
      DO 1 I=1,1000                          DO 1 I=1,1000
          X(I)=F(Y(I))                           X(I)=1.D0-DEXP(DSQRT(Y(I)))
    1 CONTINUE                            1 CONTINUE
      STOP                                   STOP
      END                                    END
      FUNCTION F(Z)
      REAL*8 F,Z
      F=1.D0-DEXP(DSQRT(Z))
      RETURN
      END
```

Use highly-optimized subprograms. It is sometimes tempting to write a special-purpose subprogram rather than using a general-purpose routine that is already available as a built-in function or in a public library. For example, if we need to raise a lot of numbers to the 7th power, we might try writing a function based on the code we inlined in §15.2.4, rather than using the ** operator to get the built-in function for raising to an arbitrary integer power. Our special-purpose code might be faster, because it could avoid some steps that are required in the general-purpose built-in function, but it might turn out to be slower just because the built-in function is more highly optimized (such as by being coded in assembler language).

Keep subprograms from being either very long or very quick. The effectiveness of an optimizing compiler depends on its not running out of space in the internal data structures that it uses to represent your source code. Small routines are therefore much more strongly optimized than very large ones. In some architectures, another factor that affects the strength of optimization is that code addressing within a routine is easier if the routine does not exceed a certain size.

On the other hand, if a subprogram does very little calculation then the linkage overhead of invoking it is a significant fraction of the total time it uses. A tiny subprogram that is called many times will waste a lot of time in its entry and exit sequences.

Avoid using arrays with more than one adjustable dimension. If an array dimension *other than the trailing one* is adjustable, additional addressing calculations must be performed in the entry sequence to a subprogram.

Other suggestions strongly recommended against. It is a devoutly-held article of faith among old-time FORTRAN programmers that passing subprogram arguments in COMMON is faster than passing them as explicit parameters. Depending on the hardware architecture, operating system, and compiler, it can indeed be true that this saves a few machine instructions and makes more sparing use of certain scarce processor resources. So, like eating snails, passing parameters in COMMON is something you should try once, if you really must, just to get it out of your system. But putting a variable in COMMON, as we have seen in §15.2.2, probably interferes with the compiler's optimization of code segments involving that variable. And using COMMON in anything but the one circumstance for which it was designed is, as we have seen in §13.8, so fraught with trouble that this tactic, even if it does improve run time, is a bad bargain in the tradeoff between speed and sanity.

Another dubious scheme for saving time is to avoid some subprogram entry overhead, and possibly also variable initializations that you have coded at the beginning of a subprogram, by using an alternate entry below that code. This use of ENTRY was discussed, and recommended against, in §13.6.2. If you want to avoid repeating initializations, use a flag to identify the first invocation as described in §6.5.

15.2.10 COMMON

Avoid using COMMON. As mentioned in §15.2.2 and reiterated in §15.2.9, variables that are in COMMON prevent certain kinds of compiler optimizations on the code segments in which they are used. So in addition to making your program harder to understand, harder to get right, and harder to maintain, COMMON can also make it slower.

As discussed in §15.2.2, do not put critical variables in COMMON. Redefine constants like π, rather than putting them in COMMON. Do not use COMMON for sharing workspace, as described in §11.3, unless there is no other way to make the program fit in memory. Use COMMON only for getting data from one routine to another when, as described in §8.2, the second routine is called not by the first but by an intermediary routine that does not itself need the data.

Avoid using multiple COMMON **blocks.** Depending on the architecture of the processor and memory, addressing variables in multiple COMMON blocks can tie up certain scarce processor resources and interfere with the compiler's ability to optimize the code. The code on the right probably runs faster than that on the left.

```
      COMMON /B1/ X
      COMMON /B2/ Y
      COMMON /B3/ Z                     COMMON /B/ X,Y,Z
      Y=Y+X/Z                           Y=Y+X/Z
```

Arrange variables in COMMON so as to minimize the number of COMMON blocks referenced within each routine. (Remember that a variable can be in only *one* COMMON block.) In doing this try to follow the principle of information hiding discussed in §12.2.2 (also see Exercise 8.8.7).

Align COMMON **data on appropriate memory boundaries.** As discussed in §8.3.2, REAL*8 variables should be doubleword-aligned rather than on odd word boundaries, 4-byte variables should be word-aligned rather than on odd halfword boundaries, and so on. Usually this means putting the variables in decreasing order of element length. The code on the left has an alignment error, but that on the right does not.

```
      COMMON /WRONG/ I,X          COMMON /RIGHT/ X,I
      INTEGER*4 I                 REAL*8 X
      REAL*8 X                    INTEGER*4 I
```

Order COMMON **data by increasing array size.** Addressing calculations are often simplified by keeping the offsets of variables from the beginnings of their COMMON blocks as small as possible. Therefore, scalars should be placed before arrays and arrays should be ordered so that those with the fewest bytes come first. It is probably faster to address the variables in the COMMON block on the right.

```
      COMMON /BAD/ A,B,C          COMMON /GOOD/ C,B,A
      REAL*8 A(1000),B(10),C      REAL*8 C,B(10),A(1000)
```

In /BAD/, the offsets to A, B, and C are respectively 0, 8000, and 8080 bytes, but the offsets in /GOOD/ are 0 bytes to C, 8 bytes to B, and 88 bytes to A.

Make local copies of often-used COMMON variables. The work of copying a variable from COMMON (and back to it again, if necessary) might be more than offset by the improvement that using a local variable permits in the compiler's optimization of code segments containing the variable.

15.2.11 Summary

The code-tuning recommendations of this section are collected below for convenient reference.

Optimize for normal function.
Select the method based on the data.
Use closed-form results.
Store precomputed values.
Start searching where you found it last time.
Consider using approximations.
Type real variables REAL*8.
Type other variables to be fullwords.
Avoid EQUIVALENCE statements.
Avoid type conversions.
Do not use critical variables for certain purposes.
Initialize scalars and small arrays at compile time.
Initialize large arrays at run time.
Exploit algebraic identities.
Change division to multiplication where possible.
Change subtraction to addition where convenient.
Minimize the number of type conversions.
Factor expressions.
Make recurring subexpressions obvious to compiler.
Do not introduce intermediate variables.
Make constants obvious to the compiler.
Replace MAX and MIN with IF.
Use integers for whole-number exponents.
X*X is no faster than X**2.
Inline exponentiations whose integer power is fixed.
Use DSQRT(X) in preference to X**0.5D0.
Avoid raising to a power that is the index of a loop.
Use Horner's rule to evaluate polynomials.
Exploit logical implications.
Order tests to minimize the work they require.
Avoid forcing the evaluation of logical conditions.
Eliminate intermediate logical variables.
Rewrite GO TO as IF-THEN.
Rewrite paired IFs as IF-THEN.
Rewrite IF cascade as computed GO TO?
Use DO loops in preference to free loops.

Protect the DO loop index variable.
Unroll short loops.
Avoid tests based on the loop index.
Move out operations independent of the loop index.
Use strength reduction in loops.
Fuse loops having the same index range.
Use scalars, not arrays, as accumulators.
Do not change arrays to vectors for subscripting.
Do not use temporary variables for subscripting.
Avoid negative subscript offsets.
Use arrays with the same shape and element length.
Make loop start and increment 1 if possible.
Process array elements in the order they are stored.
Reorder loops to reduce overhead.
Look up the cache specifications for your computer.
Keep the executable small to minimize paging.
Eliminate unnecessary I/O.
Minimize I/O statement executions.
Minimize file system blocks transmitted.
Minimize variables transmitted.
Keep FORMAT statements simple.
Avoid object-time FORMATs.
Use unformatted I/O.
Avoid unnecessary file-positioning operations.
Avoid unnecessary subprogram invocations.
Inline subprogram invocations.
Use highly-optimized subprograms.
Keep subprograms from being too long or too quick.
Avoid making multiple array dimensions adjustable.
Use COMMON only for its one intended purpose.
Skip initialization code rather than using ENTRY.
Avoid using COMMON.
Avoid using multiple COMMON blocks.
Align COMMON data on memory boundaries.
Order COMMON data by increasing array size.
Make local copies of often-used COMMON variables.

15.3 Omissions

The design and analysis of algorithms and data structures; architectural details of processors and memories, including the impact of L3 and deeper cache; how optimizing compilers work; the UNIX™ utilities gprof, lprof, tcov, and pixie; the UNIX™ dtime and *gettimeofday* routines; preprocessors, such as VAST and KAP; *vector and parallel processing;* benchmarks; self-tuning software.

15.4 Exercises

15.4.1 List some ways that a program's execution time can be reduced *without* tuning the source code.

15.4.2 Find the expansion factor of the **time** example in §15.1.1.

15.4.3 Explain why profiling is useful in code tuning.

15.4.4 Modify the **ETIME** example program in §15.1.3 to report total (user + system) CPU time instead of user-state CPU time.

15.4.5 What is the largest time value that can be stored in an **INTEGER*4** as microseconds? What is the largest time value that can be stored in a two-part value as [sec,μsec]? What is the precision with which the largest [sec,μsec] two-part time value could be represented as a **REAL*8**?

15.4.6 Measure on your computer how long it takes to add, subtract, multiply, divide, and find the square root of (a) **REAL*8** numbers; (b) **REAL*4** numbers.

15.4.7 How many comparisons are performed by this code segment?

```
      DO 1 I=1,N-1
      DO 1 J=I+1,N
          IF(A(I).LE.A(J)) GO TO 1
          TEMP=A(I)
          A(I)=A(J)
          A(J)=TEMP
    1 CONTINUE
```

How many exchanges are made of A(I) for A(J)? Is the number of exchanges a good measure of the amount of work in this code segment?

15.4.8 Using (a) **ETIME** and (b) **TIMER**, time the code of §4.5 as presented there and after revision to compute the sine value by invoking **DSIN**. How much faster is the version that uses **DSIN**? (c) How do the measurements from **ETIME** and **TIMER** compare?

15.4.9 Show that the formulas given for x, y, and z in §15.2.1 satisfy the linear system.

15.4.10 Show that the approximation $\sqrt{a^2 + b^2} \approx \frac{1}{2}[a + b + \max(a, b)]$ is always an *over*-estimate and has a maximum error of about 12% when $a = \frac{1}{2}b$ or $b = \frac{1}{2}a$. Plot a graph of the relative error $E = (\text{approximate-exact})/(\text{exact})$ as a function of $r = a/b$, for $r \in [0, 3]$.

15.4.11 The approximation $e^x \approx 1 + x + \frac{1}{2}x^2 + \frac{1}{6}x^3$ is suggested in §15.2.1. (a) How would you code the formula in FORTRAN? (b) Find the maximum error of the approximation over $x \in [0, 1]$. (c) Find values for a, b, c, and d so as to minimize the total error

$$\int_0^1 (f(x) - e^x)^2 dx$$

of the approximation $e^x \approx f(x) = a + bx + cx^2 + dx^3$. Do these values come out the same as the Taylor series coefficients?

15.4.12 Consider the numerical approximation of a derivative by the **central difference** formula

$$f'(x) \approx \frac{f(x + \Delta) - f(x - \Delta)}{2\Delta}.$$

For what functions $f(x)$ does this approximation yield the exact value? Write down a function that has a closed-form derivative, and for which the approximation takes *more* work than evaluating the formula. Can you find a function that has a closed-form derivative, but for which the approximation takes *less* work than evaluating the formula?

15.4.13 In Section §15.2.1 we saw that the largest factorial that can be stored in an `INTEGER*4` is 12! = 479001600. What is the largest factorial that can be stored in a `REAL*8`? Would it make sense to table them and look up the ones you need, rather than computing them on the fly?

15.4.14 Using a hand calculator to find logs and exponentials, compute this quantity.

$$3.72^6 = e^{6\ln 3.72}$$

Using a hand calculator to do the multiplications, compute this quantity.

$$3.72^6 = 3.72 \times 3.72 \times 3.72 \times 3.72 \times 3.72 \times 3.72$$

Now try $(-3.72)^6$ both ways. Write a FORTRAN program to compute 3.72^6 and $(-3.72)^6$ by using the `**` operator.

15.4.15 Write a FORTRAN program to test whether `X**0.5D0` takes longer than `DSQRT(X)` on your computer.

15.4.16 Write a code segment that uses Horner's rule to evaluate this sum.

$$y = \sum_{i=1}^{N} a_i x^i$$

15.4.17 It is proposed to replace the code on the left below with that on the right, on grounds of efficiency. The code on the right uses fewer loop iterations and does one fewer addition. Does it always work? Explain.

```
      NUM=0                        NUM=LIST(1)
      DO 1 I=1,K                   DO 1 I=2,K
          NUM=NUM+LIST(I)              NUM=NUM+LIST(I)
    1 CONTINUE                   1 CONTINUE
```

15.4.18 Use strength reduction to rewrite the following loop so that it runs faster.

```
      DO 1 K=1,100
          INDEX(K)=K*(K-1)/2
    1 CONTINUE
```

15.4.19 At what stride are the elements of B accessed? Rewrite the nest to be stride 1. What happens to the number of loop initializations? Unroll the inner loop of your stride-1 nest.

```
      REAL*8 B(5,7),S
      :
      S=0.D0
      DO 1 J=1,5
          DO 2 I=1,7
              S=S+B(J,I)
    2     CONTINUE
    1 CONTINUE
```

15.4.20 One of the examples in §15.2.6 contains a nest having stride greater than 1. Find the example and rewrite it so that it has stride 1.

15.4.21 Rewrite the following code segment so that it runs faster.

```
      REAL*8 A(300,200)
      :
      DO 1 J=1,200
      DO 1 I=1,300
          WRITE(3) A(I,J)
    1 CONTINUE
```

16

Vector and Parallel Processing

In §15 I mentioned several ways to reduce the wall-clock running time of a numerically-intensive program, including improving the algorithm, using compiler optimization, and tuning the FORTRAN source code. Another approach that can sometimes be used, along with those methods or by itself, is to divide the problem into pieces and do them all at the same time, using separate electronic circuits for each piece of the calculation. At first glance this might seem like a hare-brained scheme, but two different ways have in fact been devised to make concurrent processing practical for a wide variety of technical computing problems [96].

The first of these is **vector processing**, which performs the same elementary operation on all the numbers in a vector in a way that makes the calculations appear logically to have occurred all at the same time. Because a **S**ingle **I**nstruction is applied to **M**ultiple items of **D**ata, vector processing belongs to a general category known as **SIMD** computing.

The first vector processors were physically separate from the computers with which they were used. They were known formally as **array processors**, but were often referred to as **stunt boxes** because of the amazing speed with which they endowed their scalar hosts. Add-on array processors have been marketed for personal computers and are also used in some special-purpose hardware configurations for applications such as seismic data processing. The drawback to this approach is that the array processor usually must communicate with its host computer over I/O channels, which are very slow compared to the logic paths within either processor. To achieve higher speed, general-purpose vector computers integrate vector circuits into their CPUs and provide machine instructions to invoke them.

Vector processing can yield a large increase in speed for a modest increase in cost, but it has not proved to be of much use outside of engineering and scientific applications, so the market for vector computers is relatively tiny and the price of the machines is correspondingly high. As a result, the technology has been mostly confined to large and extremely expensive **vector supercomputers**. These magnificent machines are used in the design of nuclear weapons, aircraft, automobiles, and pharmaceutical molecules. Unfortunately, because of their cost they are found mostly in the research laboratories of the federal government, large corporations, and a few technical universities.

Some savants have predicted [122] that cheaper approaches to high performance computing will eventually make vector supercomputers extinct even at the elite institutions that can afford them. As I write this, however, new vector machines continue to be announced [119] and planned for the future [112], so the age of the vector supercomputers does not seem to be drawing to a close just yet. There is a big investment in vectorized production codes, and somebody considers them important enough to justify the supercomputers they now run on, so even after there is a better alternative the demand for these machines will continue for as long as it takes to rewrite or replace those applications. Vector processing is much easier to use than the other kinds of concurrent processing now available, and its basic idea is very appealing for its elegance and simplicity, so the technology might well survive indefinitely in some other form even if the big iron does someday vanish. At least one PC has been marketed with a CPU that supports vector processing [57]. We will take up vector processing in §16.1.

The parallelism in vector processing is said to be **fine-grained**, because the computational tasks that are done simultaneously (or at least apparently at the same time) are a single arithmetic or logical operation on each of the vector elements. The idea of **parallel processing** is to divide a calculation into much bigger pieces and use a separate computer to perform each piece. Because each piece of the calculation is performed by a separate processor there is no requirement that the parallel calculations be the same, so parallel processing is referred to as Multiple Instruction, Multiple Data, or **MIMD**, computing. Of course, parallel processing can also be used for SIMD computations; then the parallel calculations just happen all to be the same. In this sense SIMD is a subset of MIMD.

Some supercomputers consist of multiple vector processors that can be used in parallel. However, the popular appeal of parallel processing lies at the other end of the hardware spectrum with inexpensive and relatively slow commodity microprocessors (or personal computers) connected together in such a way that they can be used at the same time on the different parts of a calculation. It is not strictly necessary for the processors that take part in a parallel computation to be near each other physically, and some newsworthy problems (such as factoring large integers) have been solved using workstations distributed around the world and communicating with each other only by email. The SETI@home project uses a screen-saver program and the World Wide Web to distribute calculations involved in the search for signals from alien civilizations (see `http://setiathome.ssl.berkeley.edu/`). Some use has also been made of **workstation clusters** located in the same building or college campus and communicating across a local area network by UNIX™ socket connections, which are much faster than email or Web transactions. For reasonable performance on some problems, though, it is necessary for the processors to be able to share data even more quickly, so **parallel computers** usually package the processors together in one box and connect them using either **shared memory** or a high-speed internal network called a **switch**. The architectural model in which the processors communicate by **message passing** across a network or switch is now believed to work better than shared memory, and is much more widely used, so that is the approach that we will consider in §16.2.

In §15.2.9 I mentioned that some serial programs can be speeded up by replacing custom code by calls to optimized library subprograms. Vectorized and parallelized library subprograms are also available at some computing installations, and using them can be a relatively painless way to speed up a program. Because the details of the vector or parallel processing used by these routines are mostly hidden inside of them, they can be used without having to learn very much about the technology.

It is seldom worth taking the trouble to vectorize or parallelize a code if it doesn't run for a long time. In this chapter we assume as usual that the programs under discussion will be run interactively by someone sitting at a keyboard and display. However, many numerically-intensive computations run for so long, even on vector or parallel machines, that it would not be convenient to wait for them. Thus, most production vector and parallel computing installations provide for long runs to be made in the background or **batch** rather than interactively. In the case of parallel computing, where a single user's program might monopolize most of the available processors, a **batch queuing system** such as DQS [52] or LoadLeveler [22] is usually necessary to schedule the parallel batch jobs and keep them from interfering with each other. Although this issue is not further mentioned in this book, you should anticipate that in order to actually use vector or parallel processing you will need to learn about the batch queuing system at your computing installation.

16.1 Vector Processing

To begin our study of vector processing we must delve just a little into the machine instructions that the compiler generates from FORTRAN source code.

Consider the task of computing $z_j = x_j y_j$ for $j = 1, \ldots, 100$. Here is a FORTRAN program that does the job.

```
REAL*8 X(100),Y(100),Z(100)
:
[give values to X and Y]
DO 1 J=1,100
      Z(J)=X(J)*Y(J)
1 CONTINUE
[use the results]
:
STOP
END
```

As discussed in §1.2, a program like this can't be executed directly but must first be compiled.

16.1.1 Scalar Machine Instructions

Compiling a program translates the source code into machine instructions chosen from the **instruction set** of the processor on which the program is to be run, and it is only the machine instructions that can actually be executed. Every type of processor has a particular instruction set, but, especially when it comes to scalar arithmetic and branching logic, they all include instructions that do the same basic things. For illustration, we will suppose that the FORTRAN source code shown above gets translated into the machine instructions listed below for some hypothetical scalar processor.

```
         [entry code]
         [give values to X and Y]
         :
         L    R0,1              J=1
         L    R1,addr[X(1)]     address of X(1) in R1
         L    R2,addr[Y(1)]     address of Y(1) in R2
         L    R3,addr[Z(1)]     address of Z(1) in R3
LOOP LF  FR0,R1                 FR0=X(J)
         MF   FR0,R2            FR0=FR0*Y(J)
         STF  FR0,R3            Z(J)=FR0
         A    R0,1              J=J+1
         A    R1,8              increment pointer into X
         A    R2,8              increment pointer into Y
         A    R3,8              increment pointer into Z
         C    R0,100            compare J to 100
         BC   LOOP,LE           branch to LOOP on less or equal
         :
         [use the results]
         [exit code]
```

The symbols in the first complete column of the listing are the names or **mnemonics** of machine instructions, one per line. The next column lists the **operands** of the machine instructions. The word LOOP in the margin of the LF instruction is a **branch target**. The listing shows only the part of the machine-language program that corresponds to the DO loop in our FORTRAN source; I have omitted the code for [give values to X and Y] and [use the results]. The complete machine-language program would also allocate memory for X, Y, and Z, and would include some [entry code] to receive control from the operating system and [exit code] to return it at the STOP.

The instruction mnemonics, operands, and branch target represent the entire output of the compiler for this part of the program. The last column in the listing, which consists of explanatory comments, was written not by the compiler but by me, after I figured out what the machine instructions do in terms of the FORTRAN source program.

Our hypothetical processor has **integer registers**, with names like R0 and R1, and **floating-point registers**, with names like FR0 and FR1. A register is a circuit, separate from the memory of the machine, where a value can be stored temporarily for use as an operand of a machine instruction. Many of the machine instructions use and change the values in registers, and some of them also use or change values in memory.

The machine program segment begins by putting the value 1 into integer register R0. This counter tells the value of J for which the multiplication will next be performed. Next R1, R2, and R3 are initialized with the addresses in memory of the three vectors that enter into the calculation. The instructions beginning with LF and ending with BC are a loop that gets executed repeatedly until R0 is no longer less than or equal to 100. The LF puts the value pointed to by R1, namely X(J), in floating-point register FR0. The MF multiplies that value by the value in memory at the address in R2, namely Y(J), and leaves the product in FR0. The STF then stores the product from FR0 into the memory location pointed to by R3, namely Z(J). The next instruction A R0,1 increments R0, which represents J. The remaining A instructions increment the addresses of X(J), Y(J), and Z(J) by 8 bytes (one doubleword) each, so that they now point to the next elements in the vectors. The C instruction compares R0 with 100 and sets a hardware flag that is examined by the following BC or branch-on-condition instruction. The BC causes a branch back to LOOP if the flag set by the compare instruction says that R0 was less than or equal to 100.

These instructions are executed one at a time, from top to bottom except for following the branch. The machine program does things in smaller steps than FORTRAN and therefore includes more instructions than there are statements in the source code, but the correspondence between the two is straightforward. Each pass through the loop consists of floating-point instructions to load, multiply, and store, and some integer instructions for indexing and addressing calculations.

16.1.2   Vector Machine Instructions

What if it were possible in the machine language program above to do all of the floating-point loads at once, then all of the multiplies, and finally all of the stores, rather than needing to loop through the 100 elements of the vectors one at a time? That could result in a big speedup! The idea of vector processing is to do precisely that, by using extra circuits for arithmetic, added **vector registers** to hold the intermediate results, and added **vector machine instructions**. A **vectorizing compiler** can then be used to translate an ordinary FORTRAN program into machine language that uses the vector machine instructions.

On a vector computer, the machine code for our FORTRAN program might be as shown on the next page. The VSET sets the length of the vectors to be processed. The other instructions having mnemonics that begin with V resemble the corresponding floating-point instructions but operate on whole vectors at once. The VLF loads all 100 values X(1),

```
[entry code]
[give values to X and Y]
    :
    L      R1,addr[X(1)]    address of X(1) in R1
    L      R2,addr[Y(1)]    address of Y(1) in R2
    L      R3,addr[Z(1)]    address of Z(1) in R3
    L      R4,100           number of elements to process
    VSET   R4               process R4 elements
    VLF    VR0,R1           VR0=X
    VMF    VR0,R2           VR0(J)=X(J)*Y(J),J=1...100
    VSTF   VR0,R3           Z=VR0
    :
[use the results]
[exit code]
```

$X(2), \ldots, X(100)$ into vector register VR0. The VMF multiplies each element in VR0 by the corresponding element of Y in memory, and leaves the products in VR0. Then the VSTF stores the result in $Z(1), Z(2), \ldots, Z(100)$.

In this example the vectors are 100 elements long, and we have assumed that the circuits of our hypothetical processor can manipulate vectors of that size. Typical vector processors have vector registers that are 128 or 256 or 512 doublewords long. If the vectors to be processed are longer than the vector register length, or **section size**, the vectors must be broken into pieces that will fit. Thus, if the section size is 256 and we increase the size of the vectors in our example to 1000, we get the machine code below.

```
[entry code]
[give values to X and Y]
        :
        L     R0,1             J=1
        L     R1,addr[X(1)]    address of X(1) in R1
        L     R2,addr[Y(1)]    address of Y(1) in R2
        L     R3,addr[Z(1)]    address of Z(1) in R3
        L     R4,1000          total number of elements
LOOP  VSET    R4               process n=min(R4,256) elements
        VLF   VR0,R1           VR0=X(J)...X(J+n-1)
        VMF   VR0,R2           VR0=X(J)*Y(J)...X(J+n-1)*Y(J+n-1)
        VSTF  VR0,R3           Z(J)...Z(J+n-1)=VR0
        A     R0,256           J=J+256
        A     R1,2048          address of X(J+256) in R1
        A     R2,2048          address of Y(J+256) in R2
        A     R3,2048          address of Z(J+256) in R3
        S     R4,256           number of elements left to do
        C     R4,0             compare that number to zero
        BC    LOOP,GT          branch to LOOP if any are left
        :
[use the results]
[exit code]
```

Now we see that VSET actually uses, for the number n of elements to process, the smaller of its operand (R4 here) and the section size. When there were 100 elements, that is the number that VSET used. Here, the first time VSET is executed it sets the number of elements to process at 256. Then the load-multiply-store sequence works just as before on that section of 256 elements. Next J gets incremented by the section size and the pointers into

X, Y, and Z get incremented by 256 doublewords or 2048 bytes. The S instruction subtracts the section size from the number of elements left to be processed, and the C checks whether any remain. At the end of the first pass, there are $1000 - 256 = 744$ elements left to do, so the BC sends us back to LOOP.

The instructions beginning with VSET and ending with BC are called a **section loop**, because one section of elements is processed in each pass through the loop. When three passes have been completed, there remain $1000 - 3(256) = 232$ elements to process. VSET sets that number for the final pass, and at the bottom of the loop the S makes R4 negative so the loop ends.

The vector machine code including a section loop is similar to the scalar machine code we started with, but instead of doing 1000 passes through the scalar loop for vectors of length 1000, now we do 4 passes through the loop of vector instructions. The integer instructions that are needed to manage the section loop are fast compared to the floating-point instructions, so even with the section loop we might expect a big speedup from using vector instructions.

16.1.3 Pipelining

Do we actually get a speedup by doing a few executions of a vector machine instruction rather than many of the corresponding scalar instruction? That depends on how long the instructions take. Vector processors usually have microcoded complex instruction set (CISC) architectures, in which machine instructions do not all take the same number of cycles. In a typical vector processor, each integer machine instruction takes one or two cycles, each floating-point instruction takes three or four cycles, and each vector instruction takes something like $24 + n$ cycles, where n is the number of elements in the result vector. Using these values we can figure out whether a particular calculation is speeded up by using vector instructions.

But wait just a minute. Earlier, I said that the idea of vector processing is to do an elementary arithmetic operation on *all* the elements of a vector *at the same time*. If that is what happens, how can the time for a vector instruction depend on the number of elements? The answer to this seeming contradiction is that vector instructions *do* process all the elements of a section *in one machine instruction,* but that single instruction actually does not perform all of the calculations at the same instant. To do that would be possible in principle, but much too expensive even for the government bomb designers. If the section size is 256 it would require replicating all of the arithmetic circuits 256 times, and that is just too much hardware. At the level of assembly- or machine-language programming it is useful to think of vector instructions as atomic operations that *apparently* process all the elements of a section at once, but inside they actually work by **pipelining**.

To understand the idea of pipelining, we must look inside a floating-point arithmetic operation such as the MF machine instruction of our hypothetical scalar processor. What steps are required to multiply two floating-point numbers? In finding the product

$$(3.0 \times 10^5) * (6.0 \times 10^{-7}) = 18.0 \times 10^{-2} = 1.8 \times 10^{-1}$$

in scientific notation, we must add the exponents (call this the "A" step), multiply the fractions (the "M" step), and normalize the result so that the number before the power of 10 is between 1 and 10 (the "N" step). In computer arithmetic there might be an additional formatting ("F") step required between the A and M steps [178, p322] on account of the way in which floating-point numbers are stored. Finding one product then involves the four steps AFMN, each performed by a different electronic circuit or **functional unit**.

Once the A step is done for a particular product, the A unit is idle and could get started on the A step for the next pair of numbers. Then, by the time the A step is done for that pair, the F unit will be finished with A's previous result and can start on this one. Meanwhile, the A unit is idle again and could start on a third product. And so on. Overlapping the steps like this, so that all of the functional units are always busy like workers on an assembly line, is pipelining, and the cascade of functional units is called a **pipeline** or **pipe**. Pipelined execution of the VMF vector machine instruction in our example is illustrated in the diagram below.

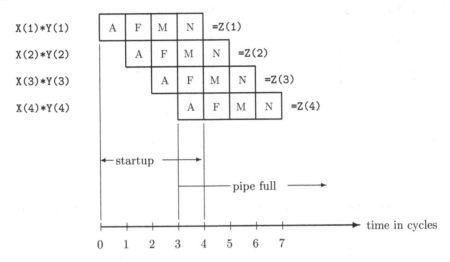

Each step takes one clock cycle, the time between transitions of the CPU clock. The first result, Z(1), comes out of this pipeline at clock transition 4, so the **startup time** of the pipe is 4 cycles. After the startup time, one result is produced each clock cycle. At clock transition 3, all of the functional units N, M, F, and A are busy for the first time, and they will remain busy for as long as the operands keep coming, through the A step of X(1000)*Y(1000). While all of the units are busy, the pipe is said to be **full**.

In a vector computer, each vector machine instruction is pipelined to produce one result per clock cycle after the startup time. Earlier I said that a vector instruction typically takes about $24 + n$ cycles, which means the startup time is 24 cycles rather than the 4 we found in our simplified analysis of pipelining. In a vector processor an elementary arithmetic operation like floating-point multiply is broken down into more steps than the four we described above, and additional circuit operations are required to move the operands where they are needed.

Some vector computers can pipeline *between* as well as within vector machine instructions, so that in our example the VMF could get started as soon as the VLF had loaded X(1), and so on. This is called **chaining**. However, most vector machines execute one vector instruction at a time, with pipelining only *within* the vector instructions, so that is what we will assume.

Now that we know how a vector instruction gets executed, we can figure out how much of a speedup to expect from vectorizing our simple example, assuming the vectors have N elements. The scalar and vector machine code are listed at the top of the next page, along with the numbers of cycles that we assume the instructions take: 1 for integer instructions, 4 for scalar floating-point instructions, and $24 + n$ for vector instructions.

Remember that n is either the section size, which we assumed above is 256, or the number of elements that are left over after dividing N into sections. In the section-loop machine code discussed earlier, the integer register R0 was included and incremented to clarify the explanation, but it was never actually used so it is omitted from this listing.

```
        [entry code]                                [entry code]
        [give values to X and Y]                    [give values to X and Y]
        :                                           :
        L     R0,1           1                      L     R1,addr[X]   1
        L     R1,addr[X]     1                       L     R2,addr[Y]   1
        L     R2,addr[Y]     1                       L     R3,addr[Z]   1
        L     R3,addr[Z]     1                       L     R4,1000      1
LOOP  LF      FR0,R1         4          LOOP  VSET   R4               24+n
        MF    FR0,R2         4                  VLF  VR0,R1           24+n
        STF   FR0,R3         4                  VMF  VR0,R2           24+n
        A     R0,1           1                  VSTF VR0,R3           24+n
        A     R1,8           1                  A    R1,2048           1
        A     R2,8           1                  A    R2,2048           1
        A     R3,8           1                  A    R3,2048           1
        C     R0,100         1                  S    R4,256            1
        BC    LOOP,LE        1                  C    R4,0              1
        :                                       BC   LOOP,GT           1
        :                                       :
        [use the results]                       [use the results]
        [exit code]                             [exit code]
```

For N vector elements there are N passes through the scalar loop, so the scalar times add up like this.

$$T_s = 4 \times 1 + N(3 \times 4 + 6 \times 1) = 4 + 18N$$

The vector code makes $\lfloor N/256 \rfloor$ passes through the section loop with $n = 256$, plus a final pass with $n = N \bmod 256$, where $\lfloor q \rfloor$ means the largest integer less than or equal to q, also called the **floor** of q, and $N \bmod 256$ is the remainder of the integer division $N/256$. Thus the times for the vector version add up like this.

$$T_v = 4 + \lfloor N/256 \rfloor (4(24 + 256) + 6) + 4(24 + (N \bmod 256)) + 6$$

The vectorized version is faster when $T_v < T_s$, which turns out to be when $N > \lceil 51/7 \rceil = 8$. The notation $\lceil q \rceil$ means the smallest integer greater than or equal to q, also called the **ceiling** of q. The ratio of scalar to vector run time, $\eta = T_s/T_v$, is only 1.07 for $N = 8$, but rises to $\eta = 4.09$ for large values of N. Many vectorizable code paths yield smaller η values than these, but some yield asymptotic values as large as $\eta = 7$ on machines having a section size of 256.

These results are encouraging, because they suggest that we can benefit from vector processing with vectors of even modest length, and speed up our calculations by a factor of up to at least 4, and maybe 7, if the vectors are long enough. Vectorizing compilers conduct the sort of analysis outlined above in deciding whether to generate scalar or vector machine instructions for a code path, given the known or assumed lengths of the vectors.

16.1.4 Amdahl's Law

There is, alas, another factor affecting the speedup achievable with vector processing: all the parts of your code that can't be vectorized. Every program does some I/O, and most also do some other calculations that are inherently sequential, in addition to the parts that are vectorizable. Suppose that when the program is compiled to produce scalar machine code its wall-clock running time is T_s seconds, and that of this work the fraction p can be vectorized, where $0 \leq p \leq 1$. That means the **vectorizable part** accounts for pT_s seconds of the running time, and the **scalar part** makes up the remaining $T_s(1 - p)$ seconds, as shown in the top part of the figure below.

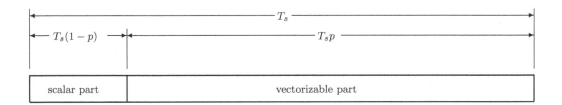

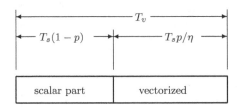

In the diagram, the lengths of the bars represent wall-clock time. When the program is compiled to generate vector machine code, the vectorizable part of the code is reduced in running time to $T_s p/\eta$, where η is the ratio of scalar to vector running time for the vectorizable code paths, as we found in the previous section. The scalar part of the program is unaffected, and still runs in time $T_s(1 - p)$.

The total running time of the vectorized program is the sum of those times.

$$T_v = T_s(1 - p) + T_s p/\eta$$

The **speedup** due to vectorization is then defined as

$$S = \frac{T_s}{T_v} = \frac{T_s}{T_s(1 - p) + T_s p/\eta} = \frac{1}{(1 - p) + p/\eta}$$

which is independent of T_s. The final formula is called **Amdahl's law**. It shows that the speedup depends on the vectorizable fraction p and the ratio η of the execution time of the vector machine instructions to that of the scalar instructions they replaced. If the application is 100% vectorizable, so that $p = 1$, Amdahl's law predicts $S = \eta$. If none of the application can be vectorized, $p = 0$ and $S = 1$. If changing from scalar machine instructions to vector ones for the vectorizable part yields the same running times for those code paths (as happened approximately in the previous section for $N = 8$), so that $\eta = 1$, then $S = 1$ no matter how much of the program can be vectorized. If $\eta < 1$, so that the vector instructions run slower than the corresponding scalar instructions (which happens if the vectors are too short), $S < 1$ and there is a slowdown instead of a speedup.

To get a better feel for the performance that can be expected with applications that are not at the extreme values of p or η, it is helpful to look at some **speedup graphs**. The graph on the next page plots S as a function of p for various values of η.

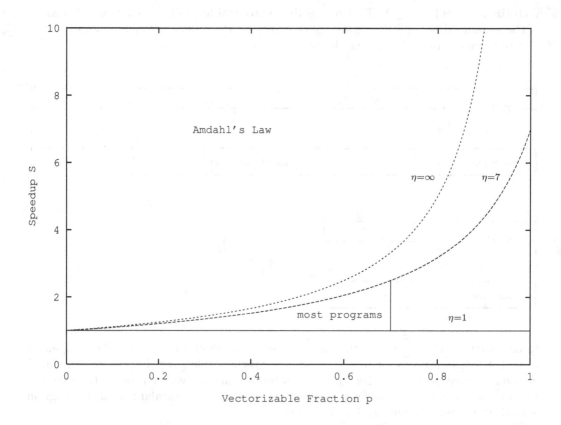

Experience shows that few applications are more than about 70% vectorizable, so $p < 0.7$ in practice. As mentioned above, the typical vector computer we have been discussing achieves a ratio of vector to scalar execution speeds of no more than $\eta = 7$. Most real applications thus fall on the graph in the region between the curves for $\eta = 1$ and $\eta = 7$ and between $p = 0$ and $p = 0.7$, so the speedups we expect to get most of the time are between 1 and 3.

16.1.5   Vector Compilers and Performance Tuning

We have seen that vector processing can decrease the running time of some programs. By using a vectorizing compiler we can translate a FORTRAN source program into vector machine instructions, and if the vectors are long enough those code paths will run faster than they would if scalar machine instructions were used. The amount of speedup we realize by doing this depends on how much of the program can be vectorized, which in turn depends on the *algorithm*, and upon how effectively the compiler can identify and translate the code paths that are candidates for vectorization, which depends on the *coding*. The interaction of these factors is summarized in the following table, the entries of which are values of the speedup S that is obtained for typical applications.

	coding		
algorithm	untuned FORTRAN	tuned FORTRAN	assembly language
not vectorizable	0.9	1.0	1.2
some vectorization	1.4	2.0	2.5
highly vectorizable	1.6	3.0	7.0

The $S = 0.9$ entry is because an algorithm that really has no vector content can actually be slowed down if the compiler translates it into vector machine instructions anyhow. The $S = 1.2$ comes from the observation, mentioned in the introduction to §15, that almost any application can be speeded up by 20% or so just by hand-coding it in assembly language. The **tuned** FORTRAN referred to in the table is source code written in such a way that the compiler can figure out how to translate the loops into vector instructions.

What makes an algorithm vectorizable? The same calculations must be performed on multiple data items, so that the algorithm can be implemented in FORTRAN using arrays to hold the data. Because of Amdahl's law, these array calculations must account for a large part of the program's running time. The calculations must also be free of **data dependencies** that make it impossible for them to be done concurrently. For example, a compiler cannot easily vectorize the calculation

$$x_i = f(x_{i-1}), \quad i = 2, \ldots, n$$

because x_i can't be found until *after* x_{i-1} is. Finally, the vectors must be long enough so that the overhead of section looping and instruction startup does not exceed the time saved by getting one result per cycle when the pipe is full. The design of vectorizable algorithms was an active area of research in computer science for a long time, and good ones are known for many common tasks in numerical analysis [49][97].

Assuming the algorithm is vectorizable, code tuning consists of avoiding **vectorization inhibitors** and using compiler directives. Different compilers have different weaknesses, but here are some common things that inhibit many compilers from vectorizing a loop.

loops other than DO loops   Only DO loops over the elements of array data get vectorized.

logical dependencies preventing the interchange of loops in a nest. An example of this would be an outer DO variable modifying a parameter of an inner DO loop. In a nest of DO loops, the compiler tries to pick the best one to vectorize.

certain branches including branches out of a loop, around an inner loop, or backwards within a loop.

subprogram invocations   Sometimes this inhibitor can be removed by expanding the subprogram contents inside the loop, or by moving the loop to be vectorized inside the subprogram.

certain I/O statements   Which vectorize and which do not will depend on the compiler.

relational expressions whose results must be stored. For example, the statement L=A.GE.B generates machine code to store L.

data of certain types, or that is misaligned in memory   Some data types that might inhibit vectorization are CHARACTER and LOGICAL*1.

RETURN or STOP in the loop.

Vectorization might also be inhibited by the use of certain other FORTRAN statements that I have relegated to §13.

Often in making decisions about what loops to vectorize, the compiler needs information that it cannot deduce from the FORTRAN source code. For example, if the number of vector elements N gets a value only when the program is run, the compiler might make the wrong decision about whether to vectorize a loop such as this

```
    DO 1 J=1,N
        Z(J)=X(J)*Y(J)
  1 CONTINUE
```

Special comments called **compiler directives** can be used to provide the compiler with information about vector lengths, tell it to vectorize or not vectorize a particular loop (ignoring its analysis of whether vectorization would be faster), tell it to ignore a potential data dependence, and so on. What directives are available and how to code them depend on the compiler.

Competent vectorizing compilers generate a **vectorization report** that shows, on a listing of the FORTRAN source code, which loops were vectorized and what prevented the others from being vectorized. The vectorization report is very useful in the code tuning process.

16.1.6   Case Study: Tuning Code for Vectorization

Suppose we want to tune this code segment for compiler vectorization.

```
    J=1
  1 OK=X(J).LT.Y(J)
    Z(J)=0.D0
    IF(.NOT.OK) GO TO 2
    Z(J)=X(J)+Y(J)
  2 J=J+1
    IF(J.LE.1000) GO TO 1
```

The compiler's vectorization report indicates that it did not recognize the GO TO 1 loop. Recalling that only DO loops are eligible for vectorization, we rewrite the free loop as a DO loop.

```
    DO 1 J=1,1000
        OK=X(J).LT.Y(J)
        Z(J)=0.D0
        IF(.NOT.OK) GO TO 1
        Z(J)=X(J)+Y(J)
  1 CONTINUE
```

Now the compiler finds the DO loop and tries to vectorize it, but fails due to another of the inhibitors listed above. (Which one?) Revising the program further yields a vectorizable version.

```
    DO 1 J=1,1000
        Z(J)=0.D0
        IF(X(J).LT.Y(J)) Z(J)=X(J)+Y(J)
  1 CONTINUE
```

Here are some observations about this example.

1 ⇨   The vectorization inhibitor removed in the final rewriting was a relational expression whose result (OK) needed to be stored. Remember that vectorization inhibitors vary from one compiler to another.

2⟹ Often, as in this example, the simpler the program is, the easier it is for the compiler to vectorize. This is another reason to strive for simplicity of coding, as advocated in §12.4.

3⟹ Often, as in this example, it takes several revisions, guided by vectorization reports, to tune a program.

4⟹ After persuading the compiler to vectorize a program, it is prudent to compare the actual running times of the vector and scalar executables to determine whether vectorization was worthwhile.

If you are serious about using vector processing, you will find it indispensable to study the user's guide for the vectorizing compiler of the computer you plan to use.

16.2 Parallel Processing

Suppose that we need to compute the number

$$\varphi = \left[\max_{i=1,\ldots,m} \{\cos(x_i)\} \right] \bigg/ \sum_{j=1}^{n} e^{y_j}$$

where x is a vector of $m = 10$ elements and y is a vector of $n = 20$ elements. A serial program for doing this calculation is shown below.

```
      REAL*8 X(10),Y(20),NUMER,DENOM,PHI
      OPEN(UNIT=1,FILE='data')
      READ(1,*) X
      READ(1,*) Y
C
      NUMER=-2.D0
      DO 1 I=1,10
          NUMER=DMAX1(NUMER,DCOS(X(I)))
    1 CONTINUE
C
      DENOM=0.D0
      DO 2 J=1,20
          DENOM=DENOM+DEXP(Y(J))
    2 CONTINUE
C
      PHI=NUMER/DENOM
      PRINT *,'PHI=',PHI
      STOP
      END
```

The program reads the vector X from the first line of the file **data** and the vector Y from its second line. The next stanza computes the numerator in the formula for φ. The cosine function is never less than -1, so initializing NUMER to -2 ensures that the loop ending at statement 1 will replace it by the largest $\cos(x_i)$. The third stanza accumulates the sum in the denominator of the formula for φ. Finally, φ is calculated and printed out.

16.2.1   Problem Decomposition

Because the calculations of NUMER and DENOM do not depend on each other, they could be performed simultaneously if we used two computers, and overlapping the calculations might decrease the wall-clock running time needed to find φ. Dividing the work up in that way is called **functional decomposition** of the problem. In this example, functional decomposition leads to an MIMD computation, in which the parallel processes perform *different* calculations on different data.

In other problems, such as calculating area, volume, or physical quantities throughout a given region of space, it is more natural to think of dividing up the work according to the locations of the different area or volume elements in the mathematical model. That kind of division is called **domain decomposition**, and often leads to an SIMD computation in which the parallel processes perform the *same* calculations on different data. The case study of §16.2.4 illustrates the use of domain decomposition to calculate an integral as the area under a curve.

In keeping with our functional decomposition of the φ calculation, imagine the above serial code broken into two programs, a **master program** running on computer "0" and a **worker program** running on computer "1." The master program reads in the data and sends Y to the worker program. Then, while the master program calculates NUMER, the worker program receives Y, uses it to find DENOM, and sends DENOM back to the master. Finally, the master receives DENOM, uses it along with NUMER to calculate PHI, and writes out the result. Some practical implementations of parallel processing permit exactly this kind of programming, in which the master program and the worker program are different from each other.

We could also achieve this behavior by running an instance of the *same* program on each computer. All we need to do is build some logic into the program so that if it is running on computer "0" it behaves like the master and if it is running on computer "1" it behaves like the worker. For our example such a parallel program would appear as shown at the top of the next page Now, as long as we can tell somehow from inside the program which computer it is running on, we can run the program on both computers and get the appropriate behavior in each place. This approach, called the **S**ingle **P**rogram, **M**ultiple **D**ata or **SPMD programming model**, is the one that is almost always used for parallel programs.

16.2.2   Message Passing

The SPMD program on the next page is rather vague about how Y and DENOM get sent between the master program and the worker program. In a message passing environment of the kind that we have assumed, the actions described on the program listing in [square brackets] are performed by subprograms from a **message passing library**. Precisely how these subprograms work varies from one library to another and from one computer manufacturer's implementation to another, but typically the message passing code in each copy of the program communicates with a UNIX™ background process, or **dæmon**, running on its computer. The dæmons then use some network protocol to exchange the messages with each other. The details of this process are usually not important to the programmer except for the influence they have on performance, which is discussed in §16.2.5.

There are several different message passing libraries in common use, including some that run only on certain computers. For a parallel program to be portable from one kind of machine to another, which is desirable in the scientific research community where people often share their codes, it is necessary to choose a message passing library that is available on all of the machines where the program might be run. The library that is most widely

```
      REAL*8 X(10),Y(20),NUMER,DENOM,PHI
      IF(this instance is the master) THEN
         OPEN(UNIT=1,FILE='data')
         READ(1,*) X
         READ(1,*) Y
C
         [send Y to the worker]
C
         NUMER=-2.D0
         DO 1 I=1,10
            NUMER=DMAX1(NUMER,DCOS(X(I)))
    1    CONTINUE
C
         [receive DENOM from worker]
C
         PHI=NUMER/DENOM
         PRINT *,'PHI=',PHI
      ELSE this instance is the worker
C
         [receive Y from the master]
C
         DENOM=0.D0
         DO 2 J=1,20
            DENOM=DENOM+DEXP(Y(J))
    2    CONTINUE
C
         [send DENOM to the master]
C
      ENDIF
      STOP
      END
```

available is the Message Passing Interface Library, **MPI**, so that is the one we will study. MPI is available in public-domain implementations as well as in vendor-specific proprietary implementations. MPI [101] [65] gets its name from a published standard [25] that defines the calling sequences and behavior of the routines in the library. The standard was developed in 1992-1994 to permit computer vendors and others to easily implement a library, in the hope that implementations would eventually be made for all parallel computers. The MPI standard was very widely accepted, and since its promulgation several implementations have been written.

An MPI program must be run under the control of a **parallel run-time system** that allocates processors to the job. In some environments this action is performed by extensions to the UNIX™ operating system, in others by the batch queuing system or some other monitor program.

16.2.3   Case Study: Functional Decomposition

The code on the next page is our SPMD program completed with MPI calls to do the communication. To transform the code of §16.2.1 into an MPI program requires a few things besides replacing the actions listed in [square brackets] with calls to message passing subprograms. Here are the details.

```
C     get the definitions of the MPI symbols
      INCLUDE 'mpif.h'
C
      INTEGER*4 RC,STAT(MPI_STATUS_SIZE)
      REAL*8 X(10),Y(20),NUMER,DENOM,PHI
C
C -----------------------------------------------------------------
C
      CALL MPI_INIT(RC)
      CALL MPI_COMM_RANK(MPI_COMM_WORLD,MYID,RC)
      IF(MYID.EQ.0) THEN
C     master instance
C       read the data
        OPEN(UNIT=1,FILE='data')
        READ(1,*) X
        READ(1,*) Y
C
C       send y to the worker instance
        CALL MPI_SEND(Y,20,MPI_DOUBLE_PRECISION,1,1,
     ;                   MPI_COMM_WORLD,RC)
C       compute the numerator
        NUMER=-2.D0
        DO 1 I=1,10
            NUMER=DMAX1(NUMER,DCOS(X(I)))
    1   CONTINUE
C
C       receive the denominator from the worker instance
        CALL MPI_RECV(DENOM,1,MPI_DOUBLE_PRECISION,1,2,
     ;                   MPI_COMM_WORLD,STAT,RC)
C       compute and report the result
        PHI=NUMER/DENOM
        PRINT *,'PHI=',PHI
      ELSE
C     worker instance
C       receive y from the master instance
        CALL MPI_RECV(Y,20,MPI_DOUBLE_PRECISION,0,1,
     ;                   MPI_COMM_WORLD,STAT,RC)
C       compute the denominator
        DENOM=0.D0
        DO 2 J=1,20
            DENOM=DENOM+DEXP(Y(J))
    2   CONTINUE
C
C       send the denominator back to the master instance
        CALL MPI_SEND(DENOM,1,MPI_DOUBLE_PRECISION,0,2,
     ;                   MPI_COMM_WORLD,RC)
      ENDIF
      CALL MPI_FINALIZE(RC)
      STOP
      END
```

1 ⇨ The INCLUDE statement tells the compiler to copy the named file into the program at that point, before translating the source into machine code. The included file, mpif.h, comes with MPI, and your system administrator will have arranged for f77 to find it. *Every* routine that calls MPI subprograms must start with this INCLUDE statement.

2 ⇨ In §13.1.4 I recommended *against* using INCLUDE, on the grounds that it violates the "explicit is best" rule of programming style. Here, sure enough, it is responsible for the mysterious appearance of the symbols MPI_STATUS_SIZE, MPI_DOUBLE_PRECISION, MPI_COMM_WORLD, and many others that are not needed in this simple program. It also secretly introduces PARAMETER statements that give constant values to some of the symbols it defines (so that they are not variables and cannot be changed), and a COMMON block (named /MPIPRIV/) by means of which MPI dynamically sets the values of other symbols. Even as we recoil in horror and revulsion at this obscure magic, we are compelled to use it because that is the way MPI is made. The only alternative would be to copy the (130-line) file mpif.h into the source code ourselves. That would make what it does visible, but would introduce far more confusion than it would eliminate.

3 ⇨ While we are on the subject of programming style, notice that the names MPI uses for its subprograms and variables contain underscores (_) and are often longer than 6 characters. This unfortunate departure from the policy outlined in §12.4.2 is also beyond our control, so MPI can only be used with a FORTRAN compiler that accepts long names. When using MPI's names it is of course essential to *spell them correctly*. Misspelling MPI_COMM_WORLD as MPI_COM_WORLD, for example, will elicit no error message from the compiler (the misspelling is simply an undefined variable) but will lead to disaster when the program is run.

4 ⇨ This program uses these five most basic MPI subprograms.

MPI_INIT	initialize MPI
MPI_COMM_RANK	find out which process this one is
MPI_SEND	send a message
MPI_RECV	receive a message
MPI_FINALIZE	terminate MPI

5 ⇨ The program begins by calling MPI_INIT, which sets things up so the message passing subprograms used later can pass messages between the processes. MPI_INIT must be called exactly once by each instance of the program, before any other MPI routines are used. When the program is finished using MPI, it calls MPI_FINALIZE to terminate the MPI environment and abandon the message-passing connections that MPI_INIT set up. MPI_FINALIZE must also be called exactly once by each instance of the program.

6 ⇨ After initializing MPI, the program finds out which instance it is (which processor it is running on) by calling MPI_COMM_RANK. This routine uses MPI_COMM_WORLD, which is one of the symbols defined by the INCLUDE and which describes the communication context and the processes that make up the parallel program. Based on this information, MPI_COMM_RANK returns in MYID the integer **process ID**. The process IDs that MPI assigns are consecutive integers starting with 0, so for our example they are 0 and 1. We have chosen arbitrarily to regard process 0 as the master instance of the program and process 1 as the worker. MPI's process IDs are not to be confused with UNIX™ PIDs, which are different numbers.

7 ⇨ The IF-THEN-ELSE-ENDIF distinguishes between the master instance (MYID=0) and the worker instance (MYID=1). The master and worker programs work exactly as described earlier in §16.2.1.

8 ⇨ The parameters of MPI_SEND and MPI_RECV are summarized in the table on the next page.

CALL MPI_SEND(DATA,COUNT,TYPE,DEST,TAG,COMM, RC)		
CALL MPI_RECV(DATA,COUNT,TYPE,ORIG,TAG,COMM, STAT,RC)		
DATA	specified by TYPE	the data to be sent
COUNT	INTEGER*4	number of scalars in DATA
TYPE	INTEGER*4	code telling the scalar type of DATA
DEST	INTEGER*4	ID of process where DATA is to be sent
ORIG	INTEGER*4	ID of process where DATA originated
TAG	INTEGER*4	code telling what kind of data this is
COMM	MPI_COMM_WORLD	MPI communicator
STAT	INTEGER*4 array	source, tag, and count of message
RC	INTEGER*4	return code, 0 if all went well

The TAG parameter provides a way to distinguish between messages sent from the same process. In the example, we arbitrarily gave the Y message a tag of 1 and the DENOM message a tag of 2. Thus, in the master instance, the MPI_SEND call specifies that 20 elements of the REAL*8 vector Y are to be sent to processor 1 with tag 1. In the worker instance, the MPI_RECV call specifies that the message is coming from processor 0 and has tag 1. Similarly, the single REAL*8 value DENOM is sent from process 1 to process 0 with tag 2.

9 ⇨   When MPI_RECV is called, if the message that is expected has not yet arrived execution is suspended inside MPI_RECV and the process waits until the message does arrive. This is called **blocking**.

10 ⇨   Every MPI subprogram returns an error code as its last argument, referred to in our program as RC, having a value equal to the constant MPI_SUCCESS if the call succeeded. We have ignored this parameter to improve the readability of our example program, but in a real program it would be prudent to check each return code and write an error message if a subprogram invocation fails.

16.2.4   Case Study: Domain Decomposition

Next consider the problem of approximating a definite integral by the **rectangle rule**, according to this formula.

$$\int_a^b f(x)\,dx \approx \sum_{i=1}^k hf(a + [i - \tfrac{1}{2}]h), \quad h = \frac{b-a}{k}$$

As you might recall from your calculus course, the rectangle rule approximates the area under a curve by summing the areas of adjacent rectangles each of width h and having its height equal to the value of the function at the center of the rectangle. (The graph in §17.2.6 illustrates the construction for one particular $f(x)$.) This is not a very accurate method of numerical integration, but it is useful as an example of the domain decomposition approach mentioned earlier.

We could divide the calculation between two processors by having the master sum the areas of the odd-numbered rectangles while the worker sums the areas of the even-numbered ones. Then the master process could add together the two results to find the whole area. To divide the calculation between a larger number of processors, say n of them, we could have processor 0 do rectangles $1, n+1, 2n+1, \ldots$, processor 1 do rectangles $2, n+2, 2n+2, \ldots$, and so on up to processor $n-1$ which would do rectangles $n, 2n, 3n, \ldots$. Then the master process could add together all of the partial sums to find the whole area. If we have enough processors to set $n = k$, this scheme has each processor do one rectangle, but there is no way we can use more than k processors. A program that implements this algorithm is shown on the next page.

```fortran
      INCLUDE 'mpif.h'
      INTEGER*4 RC,STAT(MPI_STATUS_SIZE),K/2000/
      REAL*8 AB(2),H,SUM,X,F,VAL,ANS
C
C     ----------------------------------------------------------------
C
      CALL MPI_INIT(RC)
      CALL MPI_COMM_SIZE(MPI_COMM_WORLD,N,RC)
      CALL MPI_COMM_RANK(MPI_COMM_WORLD,MYID,RC)
C
C     get the limits
      IF(MYID.EQ.0) THEN
         WRITE(6,901)
  901    FORMAT('limits of integration: ',$)
         READ(5,*) AB(1),AB(2)
      ENDIF
C
C     send or receive the limits
      CALL MPI_BCAST(AB,2,MPI_DOUBLE_PRECISION,0,
     ;                MPI_COMM_WORLD,RC)
C
C     add up the rectangles assigned to this process
      H=(AB(2)-AB(1))/DFLOAT(K)
      SUM=0.D0
      DO 1 I=MYID+1,K,N
         X=AB(1)+(DFLOAT(I)-0.5D0)*H
         SUM=SUM+F(X)
    1 CONTINUE
      VAL=H*SUM
C
C     all but the master send their results back
      IF(MYID.NE.0) THEN
         CALL MPI_SEND(VAL,1,MPI_DOUBLE_PRECISION,0,1,
     ;                MPI_COMM_WORLD,RC)
         GO TO 2
      ENDIF
C
C     master adds up the partial sums and writes the answer
      IF(MYID.EQ.0) THEN
         ANS=VAL
         DO 3 L=1,N-1
            CALL MPI_RECV(VAL,1,MPI_DOUBLE_PRECISION,L,1,
     ;                   MPI_COMM_WORLD,STAT,RC)
            ANS=ANS+VAL
    3    CONTINUE
         WRITE(6,*) ANS
      ENDIF
    2 CALL MPI_FINALIZE(RC)
      STOP
      END
```

Here are some observations about the program.

1⇨   To use this program we need to supply a FUNCTION subprogram F(X) that returns the REAL*8 value of the integrand function $f(x)$ at any given x between a and b. We use $k = 2000$ rectangles, but how many are actually needed for any given level of accuracy in the integral approximation depends on what function $f(x)$ is.

2⇨   Notice the INCLUDE, and the MPI_INIT and MPI_FINALIZE calls, which are needed in every MPI program.

3⇨   In addition to the five MPI subprograms introduced in the earlier case study, this program also uses two more:

MPI_COMM_SIZE	find out how many processes there are
MPI_BCAST	broadcast a value to all processes

Together these seven MPI routines make up a minimal set that are just sufficient for writing a wide variety of parallel programs.

4⇨   Because we have decomposed this problem into an arbitrary number of pieces, we use MPI_COMM_SIZE to find N, the number of processors actually assigned by the run-time system. That wasn't necessary in §16.2.3 because the functional decomposition we used there required exactly two processors.

5⇨   The master process prompts for and reads the limits of integration, and broadcasts them. Each process then adds up the areas of the rectangles for which it is responsible, in the loop ending at statement 1. Notice that the increment of the DO statement is N, the number of processors being used, in order to obtain the assignment of rectangles to processes described above.

6⇨   MPI_BCAST has the following calling sequence.

CALL MPI_BCAST(DATA,COUNT,TYPE,ORIG,COMM, RC)		
DATA	specified by TYPE	the data to be sent and received
COUNT	INTEGER*4	number of scalars in DATA
TYPE	INTEGER*4	code telling the scalar type of DATA
ORIG	INTEGER*4	ID of process where DATA originates
COMM	MPI_COMM_WORLD	MPI communicator
RC	INTEGER*4	return code

Each of the processes makes exactly the same call to MPI_BCAST. In the process for which MYID matches ORIG, the call to MPI_BCAST sends the data, and in all of the other processes the call to MPI_BCAST receives the data.

7⇨   Each worker process uses MPI_SEND to return its partial sum to the master. These messages all have the same tag, which we have arbitrarily chosen to be 1. In the loop ending at statement 3, the master uses MPI_RECV to receive all these messages, and accumulates the partial sums starting with the one found by the master process. Then it writes the answer.

The preceding case studies illustrate only the most basic capabilities of MPI. The functional and domain decomposition techniques that they use can be applied to the solution of many real problems, but worthwhile implementation refinements are possible by using MPI subprograms and features that I do not have room to describe here. For example, it is possible to use a single MPI subprogram invocation to accumulate all of the partial sums in the case study of this section, rather than an MPI_SEND in the workers and a loop of MPI_RECV calls in the master. If you are serious about parallel programming with MPI, you will find [64] both indispensable and a pleasure to read.

TIGER by Bud Blake, reprinted by permission of King Features Syndicate, Inc.   © 7/20/85 King Features Syndicate

16.2.5   Amdahl's Law Revisited

The master and worker processes of a parallel program run on different processors, so they execute simultaneously. If the computational work is divided evenly between them, we might expect the wall-clock running time T_2 of the calculation using 2 processors to be about half of the **serial** running time T_1, the time a single program would take to compute the result. The ratio of these times is the **speedup** S that is obtained by using parallel processing. In general we might expect the speedup achieved by a parallel computation using n processors,

$$S_n = T_1/T_n,$$

to be about n. Unfortunately this ideal speedup is never observed in practice, for several reasons.

First, no calculation is completely parallelizable; there are always pieces that must be done in order. In each of our case studies, the master process read some input data at the beginning, and computed and printed out the answer at the end. This work is inherently serial. In real applications both the preparation of the data and the post-processing of the results are typically more elaborate, and often little or none of that work can be done in parallel. For many applications (see cartoon) no effective parallel algorithm is known at all. Indeed, the discovery and development of parallel algorithms is an important area of ongoing research in computer science [58].

Second, it takes some time to send the data that are shared between the various processes that make up a parallel program. This time depends on the capacity and congestion of the hardware communication paths over which the messages must travel, on the speed of the software protocols that are used to manage the message-passing process, and on the length of the messages. Suppose that in a certain parallel computer the average time MPI takes to send a message of b bytes from one processor to another and back again is the same as the time it takes one of the compute nodes to perform about

$$m = 20000 + 2b$$

floating-point operations. Thus, because $b > 0$, every round-trip message takes *at least* 20000 floating-point operation times.

The influence of these effects on the speedup achievable by parallel processing is shown by the bar graphs at the top of the next page. The lengths of the bars represent wall-clock running time for a program that takes T_1 seconds on one processor. The top graph illustrates that if the **parallelizable part** of the calculation accounts for a fraction p of the serial running time, or $T_1 p$ seconds, then the part of the calculation that cannot be parallelized, the **serial part**, must use $T_1(1-p)$ seconds. Parallelizing the program yields the situation illustrated in the bottom bar graph, in which the parallelizable part has been

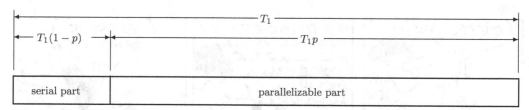

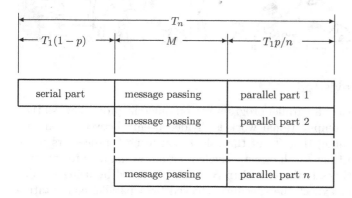

divided into n parallel processes that are assumed each to take the same time of $T_1 p/n$ wall-clock seconds. The serial part still runs for $T_1(1-p)$ seconds, and the message passing associated with each parallel process is assumed to take M seconds. The parallel processes and their associated message-passing activities are shown below one another because they occur simultaneously, during the same wall-clock time. The **parallel running time** for the program is then the following sum.

$$T_n = T_1(1-p) + M + T_1 p/n$$

The diagram gives a highly idealized and somewhat optimistic picture of what happens when a program is parallelized. When a real calculation is divided into parallel parts they seldom turn out all to run in exactly the same time, so a more realistic picture would show "parallel part" boxes of different lengths, some of them longer than $T_1 p/n$. An important consideration in the design and implementation of parallel algorithms is **load balancing** between the processors (but the random preoccupation of processors with operating system housekeeping tasks can cause variations in the run times of the parallel parts even when the load is perfectly balanced [104]). Similarly, the message passing usually cannot be neatly partitioned among the parallel processes in the way the diagram suggests. Although the communications hardware might permit any number of messages to be in transit simultaneously, messages can interfere with one another and we have not modeled this congestion effect. There might also be an ordering inherent in the communications process, so that perfect parallelism in message passing is not possible. A more realistic picture would thus show "message passing" boxes also of varying lengths, some of them longer than the average value of M that we have assumed. Nevertheless, this simple model approximates reality well enough so that the predictions we make from it about actual parallel programs turn out to be at least qualitatively correct.

Using our earlier definition of speedup as the ratio of serial to parallel wall-clock execution time, we calculate it as follows.

$$S_n = \frac{T_1}{T_n} = \frac{T_1}{T_1(1-p) + M + T_1 p/n} = \frac{1}{(1-p) + M/T_1 + p/n}$$

Thus, the speedup depends on p, the fraction of the application that is parallelizable, on n, the number of processors used, and on the *ratio* of the message passing overhead associated with each parallel process to the serial running time. We will denote this **communicate/compute ratio** by $r = M/T_1$ so that the speedup is given by this formula.

$$S_n = \frac{1}{(1 - p) + r + p/n}$$

It is easy to see that our analysis makes sense for extreme values of p, n, and r. If there is no message-passing overhead then $r = 0$ and we get

$$S_{n,r=0} = \frac{1}{(1 - p) + p/n}$$

which is independent of T_1. This is just Amdahl's law, which we encountered earlier in §16.1.4. If, also, the application is 100% parallelizable then $p = 1$ and we get the ideal speedup of $S_n = n$. If the application cannot be parallelized at all then $p = 0$ (and no messages get passed so we still have $r = 0$) yielding a speedup of $S_n = 1$.

If r is very large, the speedup S_n will be small no matter what p and n are, and can easily be less than 1. Physically this means that the time spent passing messages to coordinate the parallel processes turns out to be more than the time saved by overlapping the calculations, so there is a net slowdown instead of a net speedup from parallelizing. To get a speedup of $S_n > 1$ it is necessary to have

$$r < r_{max} = p(1 - 1/n)$$

and the smaller r is relative to r_{max} the better the speedup will be. This means making the communicate/compute ratio r as small as possible, the parallel fraction p as large as possible, and using as many processors as are available. Applications for which $r \ll r_{max}$ are said to be "embarrassingly parallel" and show near-ideal speedups. An example would be n instances of the same program all running in parallel, each processing a different set of input data and writing a different set of output data so that very little or no inter-process communication is required.

To get a better feel for the performance that can be expected with applications that are *not* at the extreme values of p or r, it is helpful to look at some speedup graphs. Experience suggests that $p < 0.7$ for most applications, so we now set $p = 0.7$ and plot, at the top of the next page, S_n versus r for several values of n.

From inspection of the graph, an application that is 70% parallelizable has a maximum possible speedup of only $S_\infty = 3\frac{1}{3}$ even if an infinite number of processors could be used. For $n = 2$ processors, the number we used in the case study of §16.2.3, the maximum speedup is $S_2 \approx 1.5$. For $n = 16$ processors, the maximum speedup is $S_{16} \approx 2.9$. These values are respectively less than 2 and 16 (the numbers of processors) just on account of Amdahl's law. No matter how fast we make the parallelizable part of the calculation run, the serial part still takes the same time, and this limits the speedup that can be achieved.

Taking message-passing overhead into account, the speedup drops below $S = 1$ if the communicate/compute ratio is greater than about $r = \frac{1}{3}$ for $n = 2$ processors or $r = \frac{2}{3}$ for $n = 16$. Recalling that $r = M/T_1$, this means that to achieve any speedup at all it is necessary for the message-passing overhead to be less than $\frac{1}{3}$ of the serial running time for 2 processors and less than $\frac{2}{3}$ of the serial running time for 16.

Using the foregoing analysis, it is possible to predict the speedup that is likely to be obtained for a particular application. For example, suppose that a calculation is 70% parallelizable, so that $p = 0.7$, that the work is evenly divided between $n = 16$ processes,

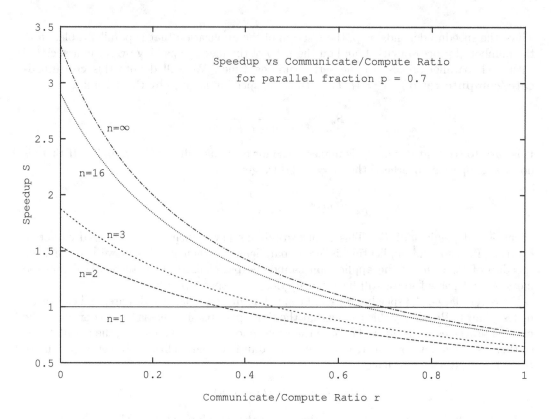

and that during a run the processes exchange 1600 round-trip messages of 200 Kbytes each. Using the assumption we made above that the round-trip time for a message is $m = 20000 + 2b$ floating-point operation times, we find that the total wall-clock time used for message passing is

$$M = 1600m = 1600[20000 + 2(204800)] \approx 6.87 \times 10^8$$

floating-point operation times. Now suppose that each compute node performs 500 million floating-point operations per second, or 500 **megaflops**, and that the serial running time of the application on one of the nodes is 10 seconds. Then $T_1 = 10(500 \times 10^6) = 5 \times 10^9$ floating-point operation times, $r = M/T_1 \approx 0.137$, and the running time with $n = 16$ processors is about

$$\begin{aligned}
T_{16} &= T_1(1 - p) + M + T_1 p/n \\
&= (5 \times 10^9)(1 - 0.7) + 6.87 \times 10^8 + (5 \times 10^9)(0.7/16) \\
&\approx 2.41 \times 10^9
\end{aligned}$$

floating-point operation times. From this we can predict the speedup.

$$S = T_1/T_{16} \approx (5 \times 10^9)/(2.41 \times 10^9) \approx 2.08$$

The results of this section show what is necessary for an application to benefit from parallel processing. First, the problem must contain a large amount of natural concurrency and the algorithm that is used to solve it must effectively exploit that concurrency, so that the parallelizable fraction p is close to one. Second, the algorithm must use only a small amount of message passing relative to the compute time of each parallel process, so that the communicate/compute ratio r is close to zero. Finally, the number n of processors that can be used must be large enough to yield a speedup that justifies the effort required to parallelize the application. These factors are related, because the amount of message passing required by a parallel algorithm often depends on the number of processors used.

16.2.6 Deadlocks and Races

In addition to higher speed, parallel programming also makes possible certain logic errors that can't happen in a serial program. Consider the SPMD example below, in which a master process and a single worker process are supposed to exchange messages.

```
      INCLUDE 'mpif.h'
      INTEGER*4 RC,STAT(MPI_STATUS_SIZE)
      REAL*8 X,Y
      CALL MPI_INIT(RC)
      CALL MPI_COMM_RANK(MPI_COMM_WORLD,MYID,RC)
      IF(MYID.EQ.0) THEN
C        master sends X to worker and receives Y back
         X=2.D0
         CALL MPI_SEND(X,1,MPI_DOUBLE_PRECISION,1,1,
     ;                  MPI_COMM_WORLD,RC)
         CALL MPI_RECV(Y,1,MPI_DOUBLE_PRECISION,1,1,
     ;                  MPI_COMM_WORLD,STAT,RC)
         PRINT *,Y
      ELSE
C        worker receives X and sends Y back to master
         CALL MPI_RECV(X,1,MPI_DOUBLE_PRECISION,0,2,
     ;                  MPI_COMM_WORLD,STAT,RC)
         Y=DSQRT(X)
         CALL MPI_SEND(Y,1,MPI_DOUBLE_PRECISION,0,1,
     ;                  MPI_COMM_WORLD,RC)
      ENDIF
      CALL MPI_FINALIZE(RC)
      STOP
      END
```

This program contains a little mistake involving the message tags. The master sends X to the worker in a message with tag 1, and then blocks in its MPI_RECV waiting for Y to come back. Meanwhile, the worker waits for a message from the master having tag 2. And it waits, and waits, until the human running the program decides that something is wrong and interrupts it. This is called a **deadlock**.

The deadlock is easy to spot in this simple example, because no process *ever* sends a message with tag 2 that could satisfy the worker's receive. In more complicated programs, especially when more than two processes are involved in the deadlock, the effect can be more subtle. Even if there is a correct send to match up with every receive, they might not be in the right order. In that case the general pattern is that a process waits to receive message A before it sends message B, but the other process that should be sending message A to the first one can't do that until it receives message B.

A deadlock will also occur if a message gets sent but never received. MPI expects the sends and receives to match perfectly, so that there are neither unsatisfied receives nor orphaned messages when MPI_TERMINATE is called. If a program's pattern of sends and receives is conditional on the data of the problem being solved, a deadlock might occur for certain inputs and not for others. The only way to guard against deadlocks is to keep the communications pattern of the program simple enough so that you can think it through and verify that all the messages eventually get received.

Another problem that is unique to parallel programming arises from ambiguity about the *order* in which messages are received. To see how this can affect a parallel program, consider the example below.

```
      INCLUDE 'mpif.h'
      INTEGER*4 RC,STAT(MPI_STATUS_SIZE)
      CALL MPI_INIT(RC)
      CALL MPI_COMM_SIZE(MPI_COMM_WORLD,N,RC)
      CALL MPI_COMM_RANK(MPI_COMM_WORLD,MYID,RC)
      IF(MYID.EQ.0) THEN
C        master prints process IDs in order received
         DO 1 L=1,N-1
            CALL MPI_RECV(I,1,MPI_INTEGER,MPI_ANY_SOURCE,1,
     ;                        MPI_COMM_WORLD,STAT,RC)
            PRINT *,I
    1    CONTINUE
      ELSE
C        each worker sends its process ID to the master
         CALL MPI_SEND(MYID,1,MPI_INTEGER,0,1,
     ;                    MPI_COMM_WORLD,RC)
      ENDIF
      CALL MPI_FINALIZE(RC)
      STOP
      END
```

This program can run on any number of processors greater than 1. Each worker process simply sends its MPI process ID to the master, which prints them out. The type code MPI_INTEGER is used to show that the process IDs being sent and received are of type INTEGER*4, and the message-origin parameter in the MPI_RECV call is MPI_ANY_SOURCE to indicate that a message from any of the processes is acceptable. The symbols MPI_INTEGER and MPI_ANY_SOURCE are, like the other MPI_ symbols we have encountered before, defined in the mpif.h INCLUDE file.

In what order do the process IDs get printed? Our performance analysis of §16.2.5 above used an *average* message transit time, and in most parallel programming we can think of each message as taking exactly that time. In a case like this, however, it is obvious that the messages must arrive in some order, rather than simultaneously. The *actual* time that it takes for any particular message to go from one processor to another can differ from the average because of other network traffic and little variations in the physical behavior of the electronic components that carry the signal, so the order in which the messages arrive will be random, or at least unpredictable. This is called a **race**.

Races should be avoided, just as deadlocks are, by carefully checking the logic of the program. In the rare instances when we *want* a program to behave in a way that is apparently nondeterministic, it is better to generate pseudorandom numbers intentionally and use them to achieve the effect, rather than depending on physical phenomena outside the control of the program.

16.3   Omissions

In this brief introduction to vector and parallel processing I have intentionally omitted the following topics that are also pertinent to the subject.

> The effect of memory reference patterns on vectorization and the performance of vectorized code; vectorization-enhancing preprocessors such as VAST; PVM; most of MPI; other message-passing environments such as Linda; shared-memory parallel environments such as OpenMP; threads; VLIW architectures; custom configurable computers such as Teramac [69]; dataflow programming and Occam; functional programming languages such as Sisal; parallel program development tools, which include remarkable debuggers and execution analyzers; vector and parallel benchmarks; and batch queuing systems, except for the mention of DQS and LoadLeveler.

16.4   Exercises

16.4.1   If the number of elements in a vector calculation is known at compile time, it might be possible for a clever compiler (or for a human writing assembler language) to generate vector machine code without section loops. Modify the machine code of §16.1.2 to eliminate the section loop while still processing vectors of 1000 elements. How does this change affect η for the code path? How does it affect the size of the machine-language program?

16.4.2   Modify the scalar machine code of §16.1.1 and the vector machine code of §16.1.2 to compute $z_j = x_j y_j^2$. How does this affect η?

16.4.3   Execution of a pipelined vector instruction begins at the zeroth clock transition, and the pipe first becomes full at the 11th clock transition. What is the startup time of the pipe in clock cycles? How long does it take to deliver a result consisting of n vector elements?

16.4.4   The timing analysis of §16.1.3 claims that $T_v < T_s$ when $N > 8$. Can you find this result, the smallest value of N such that $T_v < T_s$, analytically? Write a FORTRAN program to perform the calculation.

16.4.5   What is the largest speedup S that can be obtained by using vector processing on a program that is 90% vectorizable?

16.4.6   Is the recurrence $x_1 = 1$, $x_2 = 1$, $x_i = x_{i-1} + x_{i-2}$, which generates the Fibonacci sequence $1, 1, 2, 3, 5, 8, 13, \ldots$, vectorizable? Explain.

16.4.7   The following program was not vectorized by a certain compiler, even though the processor has a vector instruction for finding $\sum x_i y_i$. Rewrite the code so that it is likely to be vectorizable.

```
      REAL*8 X(1000),Y(1000),SUM              SUBROUTINE SUB(Z,W,SUM)
      [give values to X and Y]                REAL*8 Z,W,SUM
      SUM=0.D0                                SUM=SUM+Z*W
      DO 1 I=1,1000                           RETURN
          CALL SUB(X(I),Y(I),SUM)             END
    1 CONTINUE
      [use SUM]
      STOP
      END
```

16.4.8   Are vectorizable algorithms known for a wide variety of computing problems that are important in engineering and science? What about parallel algorithms? Which approach to concurrent computing is usually easier to use? Which has the potential to give the largest speedup?

16.4.9   Explain the difference between SIMD, MIMD, and SPMD. Can an SPMD program implement an MIMD calculation?

16.4.10   The MPI symbols MPI_ANY_SOURCE, MPI_SUCCESS, MPI_DOUBLE_PRECISION, and MPI_INTEGER have integer values. (a) Where are these values set? Are they variables, or PARAMETER constants? (b) Write a program that prints out the values, and run it on a machine where MPI is installed.

16.4.11   Could x and y be read in parallel in the case study of §16.2.3? If so, would it speed up the program? Explain.

16.4.12   Consider the problem of computing the dot product of two 100-element vectors x and y as follows.

$$x^\top y = \sum_{j=1}^{50} x_j y_j + \sum_{j=51}^{100} x_j y_j$$

Write an SPMD program that uses 2 processors to find the indicated partial sums in parallel and then adds them together. Is this a functional decomposition of the problem, or a domain decomposition?

16.4.13   Is there a way to use MPI to parallelize the solution to Exercise 5.8.33? If there is, outline an approach you think would work. If there is not, explain why not.

16.4.14   Write an MPI program to find

$$\min_{i=1,\ldots,m} \{f_i(x)\}$$

where the $f_i(x)$ are defined by a FUNCTION subprogram having the calling sequence FCN(X,I).

16.4.15   Revise the program of §16.2.4 to approximate

$$\int_0^1 f(x)dx, \quad f(x) = \begin{cases} x^2 - 1, & 0 \le x \le \frac{1}{2} \\ e^x \sin(x), & \frac{1}{2} < x \le 1 \end{cases}$$

Does your revised program use domain decomposition, or functional decomposition, or both?

16.4.16   Consider the program of 16.2.3. (a) Find the number of floating-point operations used and the number and lengths of the messages that are passed. (b) If the program is run on a parallel computer having the message-passing times assumed in 16.2.5, what speedup do we expect to achieve by using parallel processing with $n = 10$ processors? Given this amount of message-passing activity, what would the serial running time T_1 of the calculation need to be in order for $S_{10} > 1$? (c) Repeat the analysis assuming the round-trip time for a message of b bytes is instead given by $m = 10 + 3b$ floating-point operation times. This machine has much lower latency than the one we first assumed. If you find that the performance is not dramatically improved, explain why.

17

Modern Fortran and HPF

> "I never wanted to be
> A FORTRAN programmer before...
> But seeing 8X from X3J3,
> I never want to even more!" [126]

The quotation refers to the draft of a new FORTRAN language standard produced by the X3J3 committee of the American National Standards Institute. Originally the standard was to be released in 1988 and called FORTRAN-88 (after FORTRAN-66 and FORTRAN-77) but factional warfare in the committee repeatedly delayed completion of its work so the language came to be referred to as FORTRAN-8X, with the X to be filled in when agreement was finally reached. In the end that was 1991, but the language [121] was called **Fortran-90** (and no longer spelled like the acronym that it is). Subsequent revisions of the standard have described Fortran-95 and Fortran-2000 (the latter colloquially known as Fortran-03, its standard having been published in November of 2004). Additional "requirements" are being considered for Fortran-08 as I write this, which suggests an ongoing process [164] in which a new version of the language is produced every five years or so. In §0.2 I began referring to Fortran-90 and all of its successors as Modern Fortran, to distinguish them from the Classical FORTRAN discussed elsewhere in this book.

The 8X committee's modest goals were to introduce array operations, standardize some common programming practices not anticipated in the FORTRAN-77 document, and add a few new features such as dynamic memory allocation. The unfortunate product of these good intentions is an enormous hodgepodge in which the charming simplicity of Classical FORTRAN is hard to recognize. Fortran-90 has 85 statements, compared to 46 in FORTRAN-77, 32 in the C programming language, and 32 in Classical FORTRAN (see [76, p7-10] [55, §A] [74, §2.4] and Exercise 0.10.12). Fortran-90 introduces 75 new built-in functions, free-form source code, user-defined data types, operator overloading, pointers, recursion, new ways of specifying subprograms, new ways of declaring the attributes of variables, and numerous smaller features. FORTRAN has always evolved with the addition of new capabilities, as discussed in §0.2, but never before on such a vast industrial scale! Each subsequent version of Modern Fortran has further enlarged and altered the language. As in the past it will probably turn out that many of the new ideas in Fortran-90 and its successors are bad ideas, that some find only limited application in numerical computing, and that some are easier to use by programming in other languages. To embrace all of the added features it would be prudent to think of Modern Fortran as a completely new (and periodically changing) language that is related to Classical FORTRAN more and more distantly as time goes by.

Just as we considered only a subset of FORTRAN-77 in earlier chapters, we will here ignore the most recent developments in Modern Fortran and consider only a small subset of the functionality that was added at the Fortran-90 revision of the standard (for a complete exposition of Fortran-90 see [98] or [76]). Except for a few gotchas, this will allow us to view Fortran-90 as just an extension of Classical FORTRAN. Several vendors market Modern Fortran compilers, and the free compilers `g95` and `gfortran` also support the features of Fortran-90 discussed here.

Although Fortran-90 introduces array operations that cry out for vector or parallel implementation, the language provides no way for the programmer to specify whether multiple circuits are to be used or how the calculations are to be assigned to them. To make it possible to request parallel execution, a collaboration of academic, government, and industry researchers wrote a standard [18] in 1994 for **H**igh **P**erformance **F**ortran. **HPF** consists of Fortran-90 plus compiler directives, a few new statements, and many new built-in functions. HPF directives, like the vectorization directives described in §16.1.5, are special comments added to a serial program.

HPF supports **data parallel** programming, which is a variety of the domain decomposition model described in §16.2.4. Some prominent researchers advocated [136] that the data-parallel approach and HPF be regarded as the standard paradigm and used for all parallel processing, but this view was challenged by others [184] who favored explicit message passing with MPI. Certain problems seem to require functional decomposition and thus apparently do not fit the data parallel model. In a survey [80] of typical applications for which HPF *is* appropriate, parallelizing with HPF took about half as much development time as parallelizing with MPI but yielded only about half the speedup. In practice implementations of HPF generate calls to message passing routines, so MPI is present even though it is hidden from the programmer. For these reasons and others [75] HPF has not achieved the wide acceptance that its designers expected. However, some parallel programs can be written much more easily with HPF than with MPI, a commercial HPF compiler [30] is available, and the language is used extensively in at least one important research community: the NEC Earth Simulator [113], a large supercomputer used for studying global climate models, is programmed in HPF. The data-parallel programming model on which HPF is based is, like vector processing, a good enough idea that it will probably continue to play a role in high-performance computing even if HPF itself is someday abandoned. To introduce the ideas of data-parallel programming I will give in §17.2 only a brief overview of the version of HPF-1 described in [18].

17.1   Fortran-90

Programs written in the Classical FORTRAN that has been our subject up until now should work unchanged in Fortran-90, with four exceptions.

First, Fortran-90 compilers are not required to recognize the Hollerith constants mentioned in §10 (though most still do). To be compliant with the standard your program should use the other methods described in §10.1 for declaring character constants.

Second, Fortran-90 provides a new way to do hanging prompts, using what it calls **nonadvancing input**. In Classical FORTRAN, we keep the cursor on the same line as a prompt by using the locution shown on the left below and described in §9.1.2.

```
C     Classical Fortran              C     Fortran-90
      WRITE(6,901)                          WRITE(6,901,ADVANCE='NO')
  901 FORMAT('enter Z:',$)             901 FORMAT('enter Z:')
      READ(5,*) Z                            READ(5,*) Z
```

In Fortran-90 the standard way is with the `ADVANCE='NO'` clause shown on the right (though most compilers still accept the earlier syntax).

Third, and much more significant, a `SAVE` statement is needed to guarantee that a local variable in a subprogram keeps its value from one invocation to the next. `SAVE` is a FORTRAN-77 statement that I have refrained from mentioning until now because its effect is precisely the default behavior of almost all pre–Fortran-90 compilers, even though that

```
C     Classical Fortran              C     Fortran-90
      SUBROUTINE ADDON(X)                  SUBROUTINE ADDON(X)
C                                          SAVE
      REAL*8 X,S                           REAL*8 X,S
      LOGICAL*4 FIRST/.TRUE./              LOGICAL*4 FIRST/.TRUE./
      IF(FIRST) THEN                       IF(FIRST) THEN
         S=X                                  S=X
         FIRST=.FALSE.                        FIRST=.FALSE.
      ELSE                                 ELSE
         X=S+X                                X=S+X
         S=X                                  S=X
      ENDIF                                ENDIF
      RETURN                               RETURN
      END                                  END
```

does not conform to the FORTRAN-77 standard. In the code on the left above the value of S is automatically remembered from one call to the next. To get this behavior in Fortran-90, it is necessary to add a **SAVE** statement as in the code on the right. Using **SAVE** as shown causes *all* local variables to be remembered, as in Classical FORTRAN. Variables that are initialized at compile time, such as **FIRST**, are remembered from call to call even if **SAVE** is not specified.

Finally, programs written in Classical FORTRAN might unwittingly use names that are the same as those of new Fortran-90 built-in functions [76, §11] [98, §C]. Before compiling a Classical FORTRAN program with a Fortran-90 compiler, it is necessary to check for conflicts and if necessary rename any offending subprograms and **COMMON** blocks.

17.1.1 Array Operations

The added features of Fortran-90 that are most immediately useful in numerical computing are array expressions and assignment statements, matrix arithmetic functions, and a syntax for specifying array sections.

Array expressions and assignment statements. If A, B, and C are M × N arrays, the code segment on the left can be replaced in Fortran-90 by the single array assignment on the right.

```
C     Classical Fortran              C     Fortran-90
      DO 1 I=1,M                            A=B*C
      DO 1 J=1,N
         A(I,J)=B(I,J)*C(I,J)
    1 CONTINUE
```

Similarly, +, -, and /, when written with array operands, denote the addition, subtraction, and division of corresponding elements. Each element of A**B is the corresponding element of A raised to the power that is the corresponding element of B, A**3 is the array whose elements are the cubes of the corresponding elements of A, and -A is the array whose elements are the negatives of the elements of A. In an array assignment all right-hand side elements are evaluated before the left-hand side is replaced.

If an operand in an array expression is a scalar, it is treated as though it were an array of the correct size with each element equal to the scalar value. Thus, for example, A=A+7.D0 adds 7.D0 to every element in the array A, and the expression 1.D0/A evaluates to an array whose elements are the reciprocals of the corresponding elements in A.

Matrix arithmetic functions. Fortran-90 also provides several functions for matrix arithmetic, of which the most important are these. Each returns a result of the same type as the argument or arguments it is passed.

function	result
T=TRANSPOSE(A)	$t_{i,j} = a_{j,i}$
P=MATMUL(B,C)	$p_{i,j} = \sum_k b_{i,k} c_{k,j}$
S=SUM(A)	$s = \sum_{i,j,\dots} [a_{i,j,\dots}]$
U=MAXVAL(A)	$u = \max_{i,j,\dots} [a_{i,j,\dots}]$
V=MINVAL(A)	$v = \min_{i,j,\dots} [a_{i,j,\dots}]$
XTY=DOT_PRODUCT(X,Y)	$x^\top y = \sum_j x_j y_j$

The elementary functions from Classical FORTRAN, such as DSQRT and DEXP, are interpreted in Fortran-90 array expressions as applying to every element in the array argument, and return an array result. Thus, for example, the code segment on the left below can be replaced by the single array assignment on the right.

```
C     Classical Fortran              C     Fortran-90
      DO 1 I=1,M                            R=DSIN(A)
      DO 1 J=1,N
            R(I,J)=DSIN(A(I,J))
    1 CONTINUE
```

Array-valued functions. Recall from §6.3 that in Classical FORTRAN a FUNCTION subprogram can return only a scalar value. In Fortran-90 the TRANSPOSE and MATMUL built-ins, and the elementary functions when they have array arguments, return an array as the function value. User-written Fortran-90 functions can also be array-valued, as in this example.

```
      REAL*8 A(2,2)/2.D0,3.D0,5.D0,8.D0/
      REAL*8 B(2,2)
      INTERFACE
         FUNCTION DESQ(A)                   FUNCTION DESQ(A)
         REAL*8 DESQ(2,2),A(2,2)            REAL*8 DESQ(2,2),A(2,2)
         END                                DESQ=A
      END INTERFACE                         DESQ(1,1)=DESQ(1,1)**2
      B=DESQ(A)                             DESQ(2,2)=DESQ(2,2)**2
      WRITE(6,901) B                        RETURN
  901 FORMAT(1X,F4.1,1X,F4.1)               END
      STOP
      END
```

Within DESQ, the function name is declared to be a 2×2 REAL*8 array, so that is what is returned as the value of the function. The value of DESQ is just its argument array A with the diagonal elements squared. If the code is in the file prog.f and we compile it with a Fortran-90 compiler named f90, a terminal session might look like this:

```
unix[117] f90 prog.f
unix[118] a.out
  4.0  3.0
  5.0 64.0
```

In the main program, it is necessary to declare the function name DESQ to be REAL*8, just as we would type the name of any user-written scalar function returning a REAL*8 value. Now, however, we must also specify the dimensions of the array value that DESQ returns. At first it might seem that we could do that by just adding the appropriate declaration to the type statements for the main program:

```
C     wrong; this makes DESQ look like an array, not a function
      REAL*8 A(2,2)/2.D0,3.D0,5.D0,8.D0/,B(2,2),DESQ(2,2)
      B=DESQ(A)
      WRITE(6,901) B
  901 FORMAT((1X,F4.1,1X,F4.1))
      STOP
      END
```

But this causes the compiler to report a syntax error, because separate compilation prevents it from knowing that DESQ is a function subprogram and not an ordinary array. Because we dimensioned it as an array, the compiler expects us to address its elements with two integer subscripts, yet we have written DESQ(A). To remove the ambiguity about what we mean, it is necessary to use the INTERFACE **block** shown in the listing.

Passing arrays to subprograms. In order for Fortran-90 array operations to work in a subprogram, it is necessary for the compiler to know what the actual dimensions of the arrays will be at run time. In the example above this was no problem, because the array dimensions were fixed at 2×2 everywhere. It is also permissible to use adjustable dimensions, but only if all of the dimensions are passed; if any of them are specified in the subprogram as *, then array operations cannot be used on that array.

```
      REAL*8 A(2,2)/2.D0,3.D0,5.D0,8.D0/        SUBROUTINE APST(A,N, T)
      REAL*8 T                                  REAL*8 A(N,N),T
      CALL APST(A,2, T)                         A=(A+1.D0)**2
      PRINT *,T                                 T=SUM(A)
      STOP                                      RETURN
      END                                       END
```

In this example A is adjustably dimensioned in the subroutine as A(N,N). Writing A(N,*) instead, as we might do in Classical FORTRAN, elicits compilation errors for the statements using array operations.

We have made APST a subroutine, so it returns no value in its name and therefore does not require an INTERFACE block to dimension a returned value. However, if we provide an INTERFACE block the compiler can figure out the dimensions of A without our having to pass them.

```
      REAL*8 A(2,2)/2.D0,3.D0,5.D0,8.D0/
      REAL*8 T
      INTERFACE
        SUBROUTINE APST(A, T)                   SUBROUTINE APST(A, T)
        REAL*8 A(:,:),T                         REAL*8 A(:,:),T
        END                                     A=(A+1.D0)**2
      END INTERFACE                             T=SUM(A)
      CALL APST(A, T)                           RETURN
      PRINT *,T                                 END
      STOP
      END
```

A subprogram argument array whose dimensions are specified using the notation (:,:) is called an **assumed shape array**. The array A in our example must be declared to have an assumed shape in both the INTERFACE block and the subroutine.

Array Sections. A **section** of an array is another rectangular array, of the same scalar data type, whose elements are selected from the original array. The elements to be selected can be specified by giving the subscript range in each dimension of the original array. For example, if an array is declared INTEGER*4 M(5,3) then the whole array is M or M(:,:) or M(1:5,1:3) and

M(3,2)   is the single element in row 3, column 2
M(2:3,1:2)   is the submatrix in rows 2 and 3, columns 1 and 2
M(4,:)   is the entire fourth row

Some array sections are illustrated below.

$$M = \begin{bmatrix} 1 & 6 & 11 \\ 2 & 7 & 12 \\ 3 & 8 & 13 \\ 4 & 9 & 14 \\ 5 & 10 & 15 \end{bmatrix} \quad M(:,2) = \begin{bmatrix} 6 \\ 7 \\ 8 \\ 9 \\ 10 \end{bmatrix} \quad M(4,:) = \begin{bmatrix} 4 & 9 & 14 \end{bmatrix} \quad M(2:3,1:2) = \begin{bmatrix} 2 & 7 \\ 3 & 8 \end{bmatrix}$$

It is also possible to skip elements by specifying the spacing of those to be selected, as in this example.

$$M(1:4:3,1:3:2) = \begin{bmatrix} 1 & 11 \\ 4 & 14 \end{bmatrix}$$

The selected elements are in rows 1 through 4 with a spacing of 3, which means just rows 1 and 1+3=4, and in columns 1 through 3 with a spacing of 2, which means just columns 1 and 3. An even more general method of selection is to supply integer vectors specifying the rows and columns containing the elements desired. If we declare INTEGER*4 ROWS(3)/4,2,1/, COLS(2)/2,3/ then we get

$$M(\text{ROWS}, \text{COLS}) = \begin{bmatrix} 9 & 14 \\ 7 & 12 \\ 6 & 11 \end{bmatrix}$$

Array sections can be used in array assignment statements, provided no element in the left-hand side array gets replaced more than once.

In Classical FORTRAN we are accustomed to thinking of a two-dimensional array as a vector whenever it is convenient to do so, because as explained in §5.3 that is how the elements are actually stored, in column-major order. Thus, for example, we can use EQUIVALENCE to force a vector to occupy the same memory locations as a matrix, and refer to the elements using either name.

```
INTEGER*4 VEC(9)/1,2,3,4,5,6,7,8,9/,MAT(3,3)
EQUIVALENCE(VEC(1),MAT(1,1))
PRINT *,MAT(1,1),MAT(1,2),MAT(1,3)
PRINT *,MAT(2,1),MAT(2,2),MAT(2,3)
PRINT *,MAT(3,1),MAT(3,2),MAT(3,3)
STOP
END
```

This code initializes VEC, but because MAT occupies the same memory locations we can also refer to the data as a two-dimensional array. The program produces the following output.

```
1 4 7
2 5 8
3 6 9
```

Fortran-90 stores arrays the same way Classical FORTRAN does, so we can still overlay variables using EQUIVALENCE.

```
INTEGER*4 VEC(9),MAT(3,3)/1,2,3,4,5,6,7,8,9/
EQUIVALENCE(VEC(1),MAT(1,1))
PRINT *,VEC(1:9:4)
STOP
END
```

This code initializes MAT, but uses array section notation to print out the diagonal elements by specifying a spacing of 4 in VEC.

```
1 5 9
```

Fortran-90 also provides a built-in PACK function for explicitly converting an array of more than one dimension into a vector. The program below prints the diagonal of MAT. The second argument of PACK, set to .TRUE. in the example, is a logical expression called the **mask**. For information about the use of masks in PACK, see [76, p93].

```
INTEGER*4 VEC(9),MAT(3,3)/1,2,3,4,5,6,7,8,9/
VEC=PACK(MAT,.TRUE.)
PRINT *,VEC(1:9:4)
STOP
END
```

17.1.2 Dynamic Memory Allocation

A serious limitation of Classical FORTRAN is that it uses static memory allocation. All of the storage that a program will use is reserved at the time the executable is loaded, *before* the program begins to run. This means that array sizes are fixed at compilation, and cannot be set on the fly according to the size of the problem being solved, so it is necessary to use dimensions big enough for the largest problem contemplated. It is possible to share a fixed allocation of storage among several different arrays that can vary in size depending on the problem, but this requires a sophisticated memory management strategy such as the one discussed in §11.2. Fortran-90 supports **allocatable arrays** that can be sized at run time.

Static allocation also means many subprograms that are to be used for problems of varying size, such as library routines, must be passed workspace arrays as arguments even though the calling routine would not otherwise need to know about the workspace, and this is a violation of the data hiding principle discussed in §12.2.2. In Fortran-90 this embarrassment can be avoided by using **automatic arrays**.

Allocatable Arrays. Consider the program at the top of the next page, in which the subroutine SUB finds out how many elements A is to have before allocating and using the array. In order for an array to be allocatable it must be declared that way, before it is typed, using the ALLOCATABLE statement. Because the size of A is not known until run time, the ALLOCATABLE statement gives it the dimension (:). An array having 2 dimensions would

```
      REAL*8 DOT(2)                    SUBROUTINE SUB(DOT)
      CALL SUB(DOT)                    ALLOCATABLE A(:)
      PRINT *,DOT                      REAL*8 DOT(2),A
      STOP                             READ *,N
      END                             ALLOCATE(A(N))
                                       READ *,A
                                       DOT(1)=0.D0
                                       DO 1 I=1,N
                                            DOT(1)=DOT(1)+A(I)**2
                                     1 CONTINUE
                                       DOT(2)=DSQRT(DOT(1))
                                       DEALLOCATE(A)
                                       RETURN
                                       END
```

be dimensioned (:,:), and so on. Thus, while the *size* in each dimension can be specified at run time, the *number* of dimensions or **rank** of the array is fixed at compilation by the number of colons appearing in its declaration.

When we are finished with A, we release the storage that was assigned to it by using the DEALLOCATE statement. This is good programming practice because it makes clear what we mean, but this program would still work the same way if we had omitted the DEALLOCATE. That is because a dynamically-allocated array automatically becomes deallocated when the flow of control leaves the array's **scope of definition**, which consists of the routine in which the array is allocated and any subprograms to which the array is passed as an argument. In our example, the scope of A is just the subroutine SUB. The scope of DOT is the whole program, so if we had dynamically allocated DOT in the main, rather than giving it fixed dimensions as we did, it would remain allocated throughout the call to SUB and back in the main after the subroutine returned, until the STOP statement was executed.

The automatic deallocation of an array when the flow of control leaves the array's scope of definition is prevented by inserting a SAVE statement in the routine where it is allocated. Thus if we used SAVE in the SUB subroutine of our example, but wanted A to be deallocated upon return, we would *have* to DEALLOCATE the array explicitly as shown. On the other hand, if we wanted A to remain allocated upon return we would have to both omit the DEALLOCATE statement and include a SAVE.

It is an error to try to allocate the same array more than once. If an array is SAVEd across invocations of the subprogram where it is dynamically allocated, or if input data determine when an array gets allocated, we might need a way to test whether an ALLOCATE statement should be skipped because the allocation has already been performed. For making this test, Fortran-90 provides the built-in function ALLOCATED, which returns the LOGICAL*4 value .TRUE. if the given array is already present. The following example allocates the array M when I=1, but when I=2 and I=3 the test fails so the ALLOCATE statement is not repeated.

```
      ALLOCATABLE M(:)
      DO 1 I=1,3
           PRINT *,I,ALLOCATED(M)
           IF(.NOT.ALLOCATED(M)) ALLOCATE(M(12))
    1 CONTINUE
      STOP
      END

  1 F
  2 T
  3 T
```

Like Classical FORTRAN, Fortran-90 makes a static allocation of memory for COMMON storage, so it wouldn't make sense to put a dynamically allocated array in COMMON. It is also impossible to dynamically allocate the array that will be the value returned by an array-valued function.

Automatic Arrays. Now consider the following example, in which the subroutine SWAP uses array assignments to interchange X with Y. This requires a work array V, which must be the same length as X and Y. In Classical FORTRAN we would be obliged to dimension V in the main program and pass it as an argument to SWAP. In Fortran-90 we could explicitly allocate V using the statements we have just discussed, or we can simply dimension it in the subroutine as shown below.

```
REAL*8 X(2)/1.D0,2.D0/          SUBROUTINE SWAP(X,Y,N)
REAL*8 Y(2)/3.D0,4.D0/          REAL*8 X(N),Y(N),V(N)
CALL SWAP(X,Y,2)                V=X
CALL SWAP(X,Y,2)                X=Y
PRINT *,X                       Y=V
STOP                            RETURN
END                            END
```

The work vector V is automatically allocated with N elements the first time SWAP is entered. Whether V is deallocated when SWAP returns is implementation dependent, so you shouldn't rely on an automatic array being saved across invocations (even if you include a SAVE statement in the subprogram) or on its being reinitialized every time the subprogram is entered. It's not possible to use the ALLOCATED function to find out whether an automatic array is allocated, and it's not necessary to worry about trying to allocate it more than once. Like an allocatable array, and for the same reason, an automatic array cannot be in COMMON. The g77 compiler (unlike most FORTRAN-77 compilers) supports automatic arrays.

17.1.3 Other New Features

This section describes some improvements in Fortran-90 that are less dramatic than its array operations and dynamic memory allocation but are also of interest in programming engineering and scientific calculations.

Floating-point arithmetic functions. In §4.2 we studied the IEEE standard representation for floating-point numbers. In that scheme [19] a REAL*8 number is stored in 64 bits, where the first bit denotes the sign s, the next 11 bits are the binary value of the biased exponent p, and the last 52 bits are the binary fraction f, representing the value

$$r = (-1)^s \times 2^t \times (1 + f) = (-1)^s \times 2^{t+1} \times (1 + f)/2$$

where $t = p - 1023$. In Fortran-90 it is possible to find out various minutiæ about floating-point numbers, including the values of t and f in the IEEE representation of a given number, by using the built-in functions summarized in the table at the top of the next page (also see [76, p224-231]).

function	returns
HUGE(X)	largest value of same real or integer type as X
TINY(R)	smallest value of same real type as R
EPSILON(R)	difference between 1 and next real of same type as R
EXPONENT(R)	$t + 1$ for real R
FRACTION(R)	$(1 + f)/2$ for real R
FLOOR(R)	highest whole number not greater than real R
CEILING(R)	lowest whole number not less than real R
NEAREST(R,U)	real value nearest R in direction U

The program below and its output illustrate how these functions work.

```
    PRINT *,HUGE(1.D0),HUGE(1)
    PRINT *,TINY(1.D0)
    PRINT *,EPSILON(1.D0)
    PRINT *,EXPONENT(37.5D0)
    PRINT *,FRACTION(37.5D0)
    PRINT *,FLOOR(37.5D0)
    PRINT *,CEILING(37.5D0)
    PRINT *,37.5D0,NEAREST(37.5D0,+1.D0)
    STOP
    END
```

```
0.179769313486231571E+309  2147483647
0.222507385850720138E-307
0.220446049250031308E-15
6
0.585937500000000000
37
38
37.5000000000000000  37.5000000000000071
```

HUGE gives the largest representable value for variables and constants having the same real or integer type as the argument supplied, so this program prints out the largest REAL*8 and the largest INTEGER*4. TINY gives the smallest positive normalized floating-point value for the type of its argument (recall that smaller values can be represented by unnormalized numbers, and see the table in §4.7). EPSILON returns the spacing between real numbers at 1.D0 on the number line. Each of these functions uses only the type, not the value, of its argument.

In terms of the IEEE floating-point representation of an argument value, EXPONENT and FRACTION return $t + 1$ and $(1 + f)/2$. In our example, 37.5 is positive so the sign bit s is zero, $t + 1 = 6$, and $(1 + f)/2 = 0.5859375$, representing $(-1)^0 \times 2^6 \times 0.5859375$ or 37.5 exactly.

The FLOOR and CEILING functions return, in our example, the next whole number less than or equal to 37.5 and the next whole number greater than or equal to 37.5 . The last line of output prints the argument passed to NEAREST (namely 37.5) and the next higher representable floating-point value. From this result it is clear that the number 37.5000000000000030, for example, is not exactly representable as a REAL*8. The NEAREST function uses only the sign of its second argument, not its value (which can't be zero) so we could have gotten the value just below 37.5 by passing -1.D0 for U.

Most programmers can imagine uses for FLOOR and CEILING, and EPSILON might be of interest to numerical analysts because the value it returns is just slightly less than *twice*

machine epsilon [5, §2.2]. Machine epsilon is the number ϵ such that $1 + \epsilon$ is indistinguishable from 1 in floating-point arithmetic (also see Exercise 4.10.26). Applications for some of the other functions are suggested in the exercises of this chapter.

Binary constants and FORMAT specifications. In §4.6.3 we saw how to use decimal and hexadecimal values to set the bit pattern contained by a variable. Often it is more convenient to think of a bit pattern as a binary number, so Fortran-90 provides ways to specify and print binary values directly.

```
      INTEGER*4 I/1758173168/,J/Z'68CB97F0'/
      INTEGER*4 K/B'01101000110010111001011111110000'/
      WRITE(6,901) I,J,K
  901 FORMAT(B32/B32/B32.32)
      STOP
      END
```

The three initializations use decimal, hexadecimal, and binary constants to set I, J, and K all to the same numerical value, and the B field descriptor prints out the value as a bit string.

```
 1101000110010111001011111110000
 1101000110010111001011111110000
01101000110010111001011111110000
```

The B32 says to print a binary value in 32 columns, and (as with the I field specification) leading zeros are suppressed. To print leading zeros we can use B32.32, or in general to print a binary value in w columns with at least m nonblank characters we can use a B$w.m$ field specification.

Typographical conventions. Of the Fortran-90 extensions to the permissible form of source programs, the most useful are end-of-line comments, multiple statements on a line, and double-quotes as delimiters for character constants. These features are illustrated in the example below.

```
!     an exclamation point now marks the start of a comment
C     it can be used in column 1 just like C
C
      REAL*8 A ! but it can also be used after a statement
C
C     a line can have multiple statements separated by semicolons
      A=1.D0; I=0; J=1
C
C     character strings can be delimited by double quotes
      WRITE(6,901)
  901 FORMAT("Here is a string with a ' single quote in it."/
     ;        'Here is a string with a " double quote in it.')
      STOP
      END
```

17.1.4   Case Study: Matrix Multiplication

To further illustrate some of the new features described earlier, let us reconsider the matrix multiplication problem first introduced in §5.6. Recall that if **A** is $m \times n$ and **B** is $n \times p$, the matrix product $\mathbf{C} = \mathbf{AB}$ is $m \times p$ and has elements

$$c_{i,j} = \sum_{k=1}^{n} a_{i,k} b_{k,j} \quad j = 1, \ldots, p, \ i = 1, \ldots, m.$$

Using the formula we find, for example, the following matrix product in which $m = 2$, $n = 3$, and $p = 4$.

$$AB = \begin{bmatrix} 1 & 3 & 5 \\ 2 & 4 & 0 \end{bmatrix} \begin{bmatrix} 6 & 2 & 4 & 8 \\ 1 & 7 & 0 & 9 \\ 0 & 3 & 5 & 1 \end{bmatrix} = \begin{bmatrix} 9 & 38 & 29 & 40 \\ 16 & 32 & 8 & 52 \end{bmatrix} = C$$

The program below computes this result using Classical FORTRAN,

```
C       Classical Fortran
        REAL*8 A(2,3)/1.D0,2.D0,
        ;             3.D0,4.D0,
        ;             5.D0,0.D0/
        REAL*8 B(3,4)/6.D0,1.D0,0.D0,
        ;             2.D0,7.D0,3.D0,
        ;             4.D0,0.D0,5.D0,
        ;             8.D0,9.D0,1.D0/
        REAL*8 C(2,4)
        DO 1 J=1,4
        DO 1 I=1,2
            C(I,J)=0.D0
            DO 2 K=1,3
                C(I,J)=C(I,J)+A(I,K)*B(K,J)
    2       CONTINUE
    1 CONTINUE
C
        DO 3 I=1,2
            WRITE(6,901) (C(I,J),J=1,4)
  901       FORMAT(4(1X,F3.0))
    3 CONTINUE
        STOP
        END
```

and produces the following output:

```
  9. 38. 29. 40.
 16. 32.  8. 52.
```

Inspecting the loop that ends at 2, we notice that the index K runs across the I'th row of A and down the J'th column of B. In Fortran-90, these vector sections are just A(I,:) and B(:,J), and A(I,:)*B(:,J) yields a vector whose elements are the three products computed in the K loop. We can use the built-in function SUM to add up the products, yielding the simpler and more obvious program shown at the top of the next page

```
C       Fortran-90
        REAL*8 A(2,3)/1.D0,2.D0,
      ;              3.D0,4.D0,
      ;              5.D0,0.D0/
        REAL*8 B(3,4)/6.D0,1.D0,0.D0,
      ;              2.D0,7.D0,3.D0,
      ;              4.D0,0.D0,5.D0,
      ;              8.D0,9.D0,1.D0/
        REAL*8 C(2,4)
        DO 1 J=1,4
        DO 1 I=1,2
            C(I,J)=SUM(A(I,:)*B(:,J))
    1 CONTINUE
C
        DO 3 I=1,2
            WRITE(6,901) (C(I,J),J=1,4)
  901       FORMAT(4(1X,F3.0))
    3 CONTINUE
        STOP
        END
```

Of course, the whole matrix multiplication can also be performed by one invocation of the Fortran-90 built-in function MATMUL, as follows:

```
C       better Fortran-90
        REAL*8 A(2,3)/1.D0,2.D0,
      ;              3.D0,4.D0,
      ;              5.D0,0.D0/
        REAL*8 B(3,4)/6.D0,1.D0,0.D0,
      ;              2.D0,7.D0,3.D0,
      ;              4.D0,0.D0,5.D0,
      ;              8.D0,9.D0,1.D0/
        REAL*8 C(2,4)
        C=MATMUL(A,B)
C
        DO 3 I=1,2
            WRITE(6,901) (C(I,J),J=1,4)
  901       FORMAT(4(1X,F3.0))
    3 CONTINUE
        STOP
        END
```

In §17.2 we will study several ways of coding this calculation in HPF so that the arithmetic operations are performed in parallel.

17.1.5 Omissions

We have treated Fortran-90 as an extension of Classical FORTRAN, except for the few gotchas mentioned at the beginning of §17.1, but you should keep in mind that there is much more to the language than I have described here. Some of the reckless coding practices that I condemned in §13 are rendered obsolete by Fortran-90 while others are, regrettably, endorsed on the grounds that they are widely used. I have omitted those "features" that clearly violate the principles of good coding outlined in §12.4. Some other new features, at least as implemented by current compilers, don't really solve the problems that seem to have motivated their introduction, so they are left out too. Finally, I have omitted many parts of Fortran-90 from this introduction simply because they are neither essential to our discussion of HPF nor natural extensions of Classical FORTRAN. For example, some of the most interesting features of Fortran-90 are derived data types and modules [90, §13]. These can be used for object-oriented programming [46], which is emblematic of the C++ language but remote from Classical FORTRAN.

Here is a list of the new statements and concepts that are in Fortran-90 but not covered here:

> Free source form; alternate symbols for relational operators; a new syntax for compile-time initializations; `RECURSIVE` subprograms, and `RESULT`; keywords in a subprogram argument list; optional subprogram parameters, and `PRESENT`; `INTENT`; `%REF()` and `%VAL()`; naming `IF` constructs and `DO` loops; `DO WHILE` and `DO` forever loops, `CYCLE`, and `EXIT`; `SELECT CASE`; `WHERE`, `ELSEWHERE`, `ALL`, `ANY`, and the use of masks; array re-shaping and shifting; functions returning the attributes of an array; the `MAXLOC` and `MINLOC` functions; zero-sized array dimensions; modules; pointers and targets; user-defined data types; user-defined generic subprograms; overloaded operators, including assignment; new clauses in I/O statements for manipulating files; list-directed I/O of character strings; octal and engineering `FORMAT` field specifications; functions returning properties of the floating-point arithmetic model; `KIND` and related statements for specifying scalar data types; attribute-list type declarations; new character-manipulation functions; built-in functions for date, time, and pseudorandom numbers.

17.2   High Performance Fortran

Classical FORTRAN assumes that the elements of an array are stored in contiguous locations of a single memory according to column-major order, and that statements are executed one at a time on a single processor. These assumptions yield a model of computation that has been very successful because of its conceptual simplicity, but which does not directly permit the exploitation of distributed-memory parallel computers. It is true, as we saw in §16, that with obvious extensions to this model we can use vector processing to do the same arithmetic operation on several pieces of data at once, or we can do MIMD parallel processing by explicit message-passing. But vector processing assumes the data are all in the same memory, and hand-coding calls to MPI subroutines for message-passing is tedious and error-prone. It would be far more convenient for the programmer if the compiler were somehow able automatically to distribute both data and calculations across multiple processors, but there is no way in Classical FORTRAN to specify that that should be done. Fortran-90 array assignment statements and array-valued functions express concurrency, but Fortran-90 provides no way of specifying how a parallel calculation and its data should be divided among processors.

High Performance Fortran (HPF) adds to Fortran-90 some more ways of expressing concurrency and a convenient mechanism for specifying the distribution of data, and hence calculations, to multiple processors. On a message-passing parallel computer, an HPF compiler can automatically translate an HPF source program into an executable that calls MPI routines to parallelize the calculation.

17.2.1   Data Parallel Programming

In the case study of §17.1.4 we considered several ways of computing the matrix product

$$AB = \begin{bmatrix} 1 & 3 & 5 \\ 2 & 4 & 0 \end{bmatrix} \begin{bmatrix} 6 & 2 & 4 & 8 \\ 1 & 7 & 0 & 9 \\ 0 & 3 & 5 & 1 \end{bmatrix} = \begin{bmatrix} 9 & 38 & 29 & 40 \\ 16 & 32 & 8 & 52 \end{bmatrix} = C$$

starting with the Classical FORTRAN code segment shown below.

```
      REAL*8 A(2,3),B(3,4),C(2,4)
      :
      DO 1 J=1,4
      DO 1 I=1,2
          C(I,J)=0.D0
          DO 2 K=1,3
              C(I,J)=C(I,J)+A(I,K)*B(K,J)
    2     CONTINUE
    1 CONTINUE
      :
```

Now suppose we can use a computer that has eight processors rather than just one. How could the work of this calculation be divided among the processors? The simplest approach would assign a different processor to find each of the result elements C(I,J). For example, if the processors are numbered $1, \ldots, 8$ then C(I,J) could be found by processor I+2*(J-1). Even easier, if we think of the processors as themselves arranged in a 2×4 array then C(I,J) can be found by processor (I,J). Each parallel processor would do this part of the calculation for its particular I and J.

```
          C(I,J)=0.D0
          DO 2 K=1,3
              C(I,J)=C(I,J)+A(I,K)*B(K,J)
    2     CONTINUE
```

To compute its result, processor (I,J) uses only the I'th row of A and the J'th column of B. This decomposition of the problem has several notable features.

operation-level parallelism   The same instruction sequence is executed by multiple processors at the same time on different data items. Each result element is computed using the same formula.

single thread of control   One program (our original code segment) defines all of the operations in the calculation, and we can think of them as taking place sequentially even though the C(I,J)s will actually be found in parallel.

single logical memory   One set of variables (the arrays A, B, and C of our program) hold all the data used in the calculation, and we can think of them just as we would in a serial program even though each parallel processor will actually use only part of the data.

intermittent synchronization   Synchronization of the parallel processes is necessary only at certain points in the calculation. In our example this is after the 1 loop is complete, when the individual results C(I,J) come together into a complete matrix C for use in the next part of the program. While each processor is doing its piece of the problem it does not need to coordinate with the other processors or to know what they are doing.

Decomposing a problem in this way is called **data parallel programming**. It always consists of *finding an array whose elements can be assigned in parallel and dividing that work, along with the data it requires, among the processors*. We can do this automatically, or almost automatically, by using HPF.

17.2.2   Parallelization by HPF

Rewriting the matrix multiplication to accomplish the data parallel decomposition suggested in §17.2.1 yields the HPF code below.

```
      REAL*8 A(2,3),B(3,4),C(2,4)
CHPF$ PROCESSORS PROCS(2,4)
CHPF$ DISTRIBUTE C(BLOCK,BLOCK) ONTO PROCS
CHPF$ ALIGN A(I,*) WITH C(I,*)
CHPF$ ALIGN B(*,J) WITH C(*,J)
      :
CHPF$ INDEPENDENT,NEW(I)
      DO 1 J=1,4
CHPF$ INDEPENDENT,NEW(K)
      DO 1 I=1,2
          C(I,J)=0.D0
          DO 2 K=1,3
              C(I,J)=C(I,J)+A(I,K)*B(K,J)
    2     CONTINUE
    1 CONTINUE
```

This is just the serial code segment with some special comments added. Here are some observations about the HPF code.

1 ⇨   The comments beginning CHPF$ are interpreted by the HPF compiler as **parallelization directives**, but they are of course ignored by non-HPF compilers.

2 ⇨   PROCESSORS PROCS(2,4) tells HPF that there are 8 processors and we will think of them as being in a 2×4 array. The mapping of these abstract processors to physical processors will be performed by the computer's parallel run-time system and cannot be specified in the HPF source program. The name PROCS follows the rules for naming subroutines, and must not conflict with the name of a subprogram or COMMON block in your program or with a variable or PARAMETER constant in the routine where it appears.

3 ⇨   DISTRIBUTE C(BLOCK,BLOCK) ONTO PROCS tells HPF to compute C(I,J) on the processor PROCS(I,J). Later I will have more to say about what a BLOCK distribution is.

4 ⇨   ALIGN tells HPF what data are needed on the same processor. To compute C(I,J) we need the I'th row of A and the J'th column of B on processor PROCS(I,J). The ALIGN directives tell HPF to distribute only those pieces of A and B. Thus, for example, processor PROCS(2,1) gets sent only

$$A(2,*) = \begin{bmatrix} 2 & 4 & 0 \end{bmatrix} \quad \text{and} \quad B(*,1) = \begin{bmatrix} 6 \\ 1 \\ 0 \end{bmatrix}$$

and sends back only C(2,1).

5⇨   An array that is DISTRIBUTEd, or ALIGNed with something that is DISTRIBUTEd, has each element assigned to exactly one processor; arrays that are not get copied whole to all of the processors. Each processor computes all of the result array elements assigned to it, so if any array is present on more than one processor those calculations are repeated. In our example C is distributed, so each result element C(I,J) is present on only one processor and is therefore computed exactly once.

6⇨   INDEPENDENT tells HPF that the iterations of the DO loop can be done at the same time on different processors. The calculation for each value of the loop index must not depend on a result obtained for any other value of the loop index. Thus, the innermost loop DO 2 is *not* independent and cannot be divided among different processors; to find C(I,J) for K=2 we need the value from K=1, so the iterations can't be done simultaneously. When correctly used, INDEPENDENT does not change the results computed by the DO to which it applies.

7⇨   If something prevents the iterations of a loop from being partitioned among the processors, the whole loop is run on each processor. There is no warning about this from the compiler, and the results are correct, but the calculation does not run any faster that it would on a single processor.

8⇨   NEW says a variable is local to each iteration of the loop and can vary within the iterations independently. For example, the I variable on each processor where J=1 can take the values 1, 2, and 3 at different instants from those at which the values are taken by the I variable on the J=2 processors, because they are really different variables even though they share the name I in the source. This restriction on the scope of I allows the J=1 and J=2 calculations to be done simultaneously. Similarly, declaring K as NEW allows the I loop iterations to be done at the same time. Without the NEW(I) directive, the J loop would not be independent, and without the NEW(K) the I loop would not be independent. It isn't necessary to declare J as NEW, because it already gets a different value in each process, but any scalar assigned *within* a loop and not declared NEW gets copied to all of the processors.

9⇨   HPF automatically arranges for only the first processor, PROCS(1,1) in this example, to do all of the program's I/O.

As this example illustrates, the basic idea of HPF is to run a calculation on several processors in parallel by using INDEPENDENT and NEW to tell the compiler what work can be divided, then using DISTRIBUTE to say what result values are to be computed by which process, and finally using ALIGN to send only the needed data to each processor.

17.2.3   Distributing Data

In the example above we used 8 processors to find 8 result elements, computing C(I,J) on processor PROCS(I,J). This is shown schematically below, where each result element in the array C is marked with the coordinates (I,J) of the processor assigned to compute it.

```
PROCESSORS PROCS(2,4)
DISTRIBUTE C(BLOCK,BLOCK) ONTO PROCS
```
$$\begin{bmatrix} (1,1) & (1,2) & (1,3) & (1,4) \\ (2,1) & (2,2) & (2,3) & (2,4) \end{bmatrix}$$

If there are fewer processors than result values to compute, then some or all of the processors must find more than one result, in a pattern that depends on the distribution of the data. Suppose for example that there are only 4 processors and we think of them in a 2×2 array. Then the result elements are distributed among the processors like this.

```
PROCESSORS PROCS(2,2)
DISTRIBUTE C(BLOCK,BLOCK) ONTO PROCS
```
$$\begin{bmatrix} (1,1)\ (1,1)\ (1,2)\ (1,2) \\ (2,1)\ (2,1)\ (2,2)\ (2,2) \end{bmatrix}$$

From this example we can see that the BLOCK distribution divides the result elements into contiguous blocks for delegation to processors. It is also possible to specify that the delegation be the same across rows, so that whole columns are distributed, or across columns so that whole rows are distributed.

```
PROCESSORS PROCS(2)
DISTRIBUTE C(*,BLOCK) ONTO PROCS
```
$$\begin{bmatrix} (1)\ (1)\ (2)\ (2) \\ (1)\ (1)\ (2)\ (2) \end{bmatrix}$$

```
PROCESSORS PROCS(2)
DISTRIBUTE C(BLOCK,*) ONTO PROCS
```
$$\begin{bmatrix} (1)\ (1)\ (1)\ (1) \\ (2)\ (2)\ (2)\ (2) \end{bmatrix}$$

A CYCLIC distribution delegates consecutive rows or columns to consecutive processors, as in the example below.

```
PROCESSORS PROCS(3)
DISTRIBUTE C(*,CYCLIC) ONTO PROCS
```
$$\begin{bmatrix} (1)\ (2)\ (3)\ (1) \\ (1)\ (2)\ (3)\ (1) \end{bmatrix}$$

In larger examples various patterns of delegation can be obtained by using combinations of *, BLOCK, and CYCLIC distribution.

The PROCESSORS directive and the ONTO clause of the DISTRIBUTE directive are optional. If the processor layout is specified, as in the examples above, its rank must be equal to the number of dimensions that are not distributed * in arrays that are distributed onto it [81, p107 #8]. If the processor layout is *not* specified, HPF distributes the result elements onto whatever processors it is given to use by the parallel run-time system. Thus our example could have been coded as shown below.

```
      REAL*8 A(2,3),B(3,4),C(2,4)
CHPF$ DISTRIBUTE C(BLOCK,BLOCK)
CHPF$ ALIGN A(I,*) WITH C(I,*)
CHPF$ ALIGN B(*,J) WITH C(*,J)
      :
CHPF$ INDEPENDENT,NEW(I)
      DO 1 J=1,4
CHPF$ INDEPENDENT,NEW(K)
      DO 1 I=1,2
          C(I,J)=0.D0
          DO 2 K=1,3
              C(I,J)=C(I,J)+A(I,K)*B(K,J)
    2     CONTINUE
    1 CONTINUE
```

Now the delegation of result elements to processors will depend on the number of processors made available when the program is run.

The speedup that can be obtained by using parallel processing depends on how much message passing the calculation requires (see §16.2.5). Using DISTRIBUTE C(*,BLOCK) above we send both rows of A and 2 columns of B to each processor, 24 elements altogether, but using DISTRIBUTE C(BLOCK,*) we send one row of A and all 4 columns of B to each processor, 30 elements. In more complicated calculations the amount of communication required can depend more strongly on the distribution of result elements to processors, and then it is important to use DISTRIBUTE directives that minimize the message passing. Try BLOCK when nearest-neighbor communication is required, CYCLIC otherwise, and experiment to find the distribution that gives the best performance for your problem.

The volume of communication required for a given distribution of data might also depend on whether the information can be **broadcast** to all of the processors or must be sent in individual messages. As mentioned in §17.2.2⟿5, any arrays that are not DISTRIBUTEd, or ALIGNed with something that is DISTRIBUTEd, get copied whole to all of the processors. If your parallel computer can use broadcasting, it might reduce message traffic to broadcast read-only data (variables that are not changed in the calculation) by allowing HPF to replicate them on all the processors, rather than distributing them piecemeal.

17.2.4 Expressing Concurrency

In the example of §17.2.2, the hint that allowed HPF to recognize that the array elements C(I,J) could be computed concurrently was that the assignment statement is inside a DO loop that is **independent**. For a loop to be independent it must be free of both data dependencies and control dependencies.

A **data dependence** exists when the right-hand side of an assignment statement for one iteration of a loop involves the left-hand side from some other iteration, as in the code on the left below.

```
          X(1)=1.D0                    C      no data dependence
C     data dependence                  CHPF$ INDEPENDENT
      DO 1 I=2,N                             DO 1 I=1,N
          X(I)=X(I-1)+1.D0                        X(I)=DFLOAT(I)
    1 CONTINUE                            1 CONTINUE
```

Here each element of X depends on the previous one, so the results must be found in order rather than simultaneously. In this case it is possible to rewrite the calculation as on the right, but often, as in the example below, there is no obvious way to remove a data dependence.

```
      F(1)=1.D0
      F(2)=1.D0
      DO 2 J=3,N
          F(J)=F(J-1)+F(J-2)
    2 CONTINUE
```

According to the definition given above, it is also a data dependence for more than one iteration of a loop to assign into the same left-hand side.

```
C     data dependence                 C      no data dependence
      DO 3 K=1,100                            S=Y(100)
          S=Y(K)
    3 CONTINUE
```

The iterations of the loop cannot be performed in parallel, because the value left in S would depend on a race between the processors rather than always being Y(100). In a nest of DO loops, inside indices and other temporary variables must be declared NEW to avoid this sort of data dependence, as mentioned above in §17.2.2. HPF also assumes a data dependence to exist if different iterations of a loop perform I/O operations on the same file. Data dependencies are discussed further in §16.1.5 and in Exercise 16.4.6, and in [50, p154-159].

A **control dependence** exists when the result of one iteration affects the flow of control in another iteration, as in the code on the left below.

```
      K(1)=1                              C     no control dependence
C     control dependence            CHPF$ INDEPENDENT
      DO 3 L=2,M                           DO 3 L=1,M
          IF(K(L-1).GT.0) K(L)=L              K(L)=L
    3 CONTINUE                          3 CONTINUE
```

Here the execution of each assignment is conditional on the result of the previous one, and if the test fails K(L) retains the value (unknown to us) that it had upon entering this code segment. In this case the test will always succeed so we can rewrite the calculation as on the right above, but if the value of K(1) were unknown at compile time, as in the code below, it would not be possible to remove the control dependence.

```
      READ *,K(1)
C     control dependence
      DO 3 L=2,M
          IF(K(L-1).GT.0) K(L)=L
    3 CONTINUE
```

An IF statement in the body of a DO loop introduces a control dependence only if the test depends on something that is computed in a different loop iteration. HPF also considers a control dependence to exist, and refrains from parallelizing a loop, if there is a permanent transfer of control out of the loop, such as a GO TO whose target is outside the loop, or a STOP or RETURN. Control dependencies are discussed further in [81, p193-194] and [50, p159-160].

In some cases it might be possible for your HPF compiler to recognize that a loop is independent and can be parallelized, even if you omit an INDEPENDENT directive. In other cases it is impossible for the compiler to determine whether a loop is independent even though you know that it is or will be at run time. The loops below are independent if it turns out that each K(I) is equal to I, but HPF probably cannot anticipate at compile time whether that will be true when the program is run.

```
C     loops assumed not independent    C     but here we promise they will be
C                                       CHPF$ INDEPENDENT
      DO 4 I=1,N                              DO 4 I=1,N
          A(I)=A(K(I))+1.D0                      A(I)=A(K(I))+1.D0
    4 CONTINUE                            4 CONTINUE
C                                       C
C                                       CHPF$ INDEPENDENT
      DO 5 I=1,N                              DO 5 I=1.N
          A(K(I))=A(I)**2                        A(K(I))=A(I)**2
    5 CONTINUE                            5 CONTINUE
```

Loops that are not independent cannot be correctly parallelized by HPF, so minimizing data and control dependencies is an important consideration in the design of parallel algorithms. If a loop that contains either kind of dependence is asserted to be INDEPENDENT, the HPF compiler might recognize the dependence and ignore the directive, or [80] it might believe the false claim and generate parallel machine code that gives a wrong answer.

Parallel Fortran-90 Built-In Functions. Even though a DO loop that contains a dependence cannot be parallelized by HPF, a parallel algorithm might be known for the calculation it describes. The loop on the left below has a data dependence, so it can't be parallelized as it is written; to perform the assignment for I=2 we need to have previously found the value of TOT for I=1, and so on.

```
        TOT=0.D0
        DO 1 I=1,100
            TOT=TOT+X(I)                    TOT=SUM(X)
    1 CONTINUE
```

Yet there are parallel algorithms for accumulating a sum. We could, for example, first compute the partial sums X(1)+X(2), X(3)+X(4), ... , then add those results in pairs, and so forth until we had the answer (see Exercise 17.4.42). At each stage of this algorithm, finding the partial sums is a parallel (in fact, a data-parallel) calculation. Finding a sum is an example of a **reduction operation**, which are so named because they yield results of lower rank than their inputs. Many reduction operations can be parallelized.

As described in §17.1.1, Fortran-90 provides several new functions for matrix arithmetic, such as SUM and MATMUL, as well as array versions of elementary functions such as DSQRT. HPF uses parallel algorithms in these functions so that, for example, the data-dependent loop on the left above can be replaced by the parallelizable Fortran-90 function invocation on the right.

Parallel Fortran-90 Array Assignments. A Fortran-90 array assignment is a single statement, so it can never contain a control dependence. Because the right-hand side is completely evaluated before the left-hand side is replaced and no left-hand side element is replaced more than once, a legal array assignment can never have a data dependence either. Thus, legal array assignments are always parallelizable by HPF. Whether and how much this speeds up the calculation depends on the need for **synchronization** between the parallel processors. Synchronization is necessary when a data dependence would be introduced if one processor replaced its left-hand sides before some other processor was finished using the old values in computing its right-hand sides.

In assignments where each result element depends on only the *corresponding* elements of the right-hand side arrays, there could never be a data dependence even if some left-hand sides were replaced before all of the right-hand sides were evaluated. HPF can always parallelize such an assignment without synchronizing the processors. For example, it can parallelize this statement involving arrays S, T, and U

```
    S=S+5.D0*T-U
```

without worrying about when the left-hand sides get replaced, because each processor uses only the elements that it replaces.

In fact, if an array assignment would be free of data dependencies if it were coded as a DO loop instead, the array assignment can always be parallelized by HPF without synchronizing the processors. This code assigns MB(1)=MA(3), MB(2)=MA(1), and MB(3)=MA(2).

```
    INTEGER*4 COLS(3)/3,1,2/          INTEGER*4 COLS(3)/3,1,2/
    INTEGER*4 MA(3)/10,20,30/,MB(3)   INTEGER*4 MA(3)/10,20,30/,MB(3)
    MB=MA(COLS)                       DO 1 I=1,3
                                          MB(I)=MA(COLS(I))
                                    1 CONTINUE
```

An element in any given position of the result array is found using an element from a *different* position in the right-hand side array, but because MA and MB are different arrays the left-hand sides can be replaced at any time without changing the result.

Now consider an assignment that is *not* independent if it is written as a DO loop.

```
INTEGER*4 COLS(3)/3,1,2/          INTEGER*4 COLS(3)/3,1,2/
INTEGER*4 MA(3)/10,20,30/         INTEGER*4 MA(3)/10,20,30/
MA=MA(COLS)                       DO 1 I=1,3
                                       MA(I)=MA(COLS(I))
                                1 CONTINUE
```

In the code on the left, the array assignment evaluates the entire right-hand side first and only then replaces the left-hand side, yielding MA=[30,10,20]. On a single processor the DO loop on the right first assigns MA(1)=30, then MA(2)=MA(1)=30, and finally MA(3)=MA(2)=30. If the array assignment code has its result elements distributed by HPF to different processors, each processor will use elements that are about to be replaced by some *other* processor. In such a case there is said to be an **overlap** between the calculations. To preserve the array assignment semantics each processor must wait to replace its left-hand sides until the other processors have finished computing their right-hand sides, and that synchronization delay or **barrier** can reduce the speedup achieved by doing the assignment in parallel.

The FORALL Statement. Fortran-90 array assignments can be used to tell HPF to parallelize a wide variety of calculations, but they lack the flexibility of DO loops. For example, it is not obvious how an array assignment could be used to replace the loop in this code segment.

```
CHPF$ INDEPENDENT
      DO 1 I=1,N
      DO 1 J=1,N
      DO 1 K=1,N
            TEMP(I,J,K)=A(K,J,I)
    1 CONTINUE
      A=TEMP
```

On the other hand, DO loops do not have the semantics of array assignment, so to rearrange A as shown we must introduce some temporary storage and copy the array twice. It would be more natural and convenient if we could express calculations like this one in the form of array assignments, but to do so we need greater freedom than array assignment provides for controlling which result elements get assigned where.

The FORALL statement generalizes the Fortran-90 array assignment, to preserve its semantics while permitting freedom of control similar to that of a DO loop. The code segment above can be replaced by the single statement

```
FORALL(I=1:N,J=1:N,K=1:N) A(I,J,K)=A(K,J,I)
```

which is clearer and more concise and is also parallelizable, and which does not require us to introduce the work array TEMP (though the compiler might do something similar behind the scenes). Anything that can be expressed using a FORALL can be expressed using DO loops, but in situations like this one the FORALL syntax is much simpler. The predicate of a FORALL statement can only be an assignment (possibly involving references to PURE functions as described in §17.2.5 below). Thus, although FORALL is more general than array assignment, it is not as flexible as a DO loop.

In a FORALL, the limits on the indices are separated by a colon rather than the comma we use in a DO loop, so in the example I, J and K all run from 1 to N. It is also possible to specify the stride of a FORALL index, so here we could have written 1:N:1 wherever we wrote 1:N.

Allowing the starting value, limit, or stride of one FORALL subscript to affect another introduces a control dependence. In the first line below, the limit on J is I so the calculation is not data parallel.

```
FORALL(I=1:N,J=1:I        ) G(I,J)=G(I,J)/G(I,I)

FORALL(I=1:N,J=1:N, J.LE.I ) G(I,J)=G(I,J)/G(I,I)
```

The second line removes the control dependence by letting J vary independently of I but performing the assignment only where $J \leq I$. The logical expression J.LE.I is called a **mask**. A FORALL mask expression can involve any variables, not just the FORALL indices.

In a FORALL, unlike in an array assignment, the arrays don't have to be the same size and shape. In these examples the assignments involve arrays that differ in rank.

```
FORALL(I=1:N) D(I)=A(I,I)
```

```
CHPF$ INDEPENDENT
      FORALL(J=1:N) H(INDX(J),INDY(J))=W(J)
```

The calculation described by the second statement is data-parallel only if no element of H gets assigned more than once, which will be true only if no pair of index values (INDX(J),INDY(J)) ever repeats. This probably can't be determined by the compiler even if you know that it will be true at run time, so HPF can't parallelize the FORALL unless we assert that it is INDEPENDENT. Your HPF compiler might recognize some FORALLs as independent even if you do not assert that they are.

If a left hand side element in a FORALL assignment *does* get replaced more than once, the code is actually illegal, but your compiler probably *cannot* detect the error.

In asserting that a nest of DO loops is independent, we must declare the inside indices to be NEW so that their repeated use by the outside loops would not constitute data dependencies. In a FORALL, the scope of each index is limited to the FORALL statement itself, so it is never necessary to declare a FORALL index as NEW.

A FORALL is executed in four stages. First, the **valid set** of index combinations is found from the index starting values, limits, and strides. In the example above involving G, the valid set consists of the N^2 index pairs $(1,1), \ldots, (N,N)$. Then, the mask expression is used to select from the valid set an **active set** of index combinations for which the assignments will be performed. Our mask is J.LE.I so the active set consists of the $\frac{1}{2}N(N+1)$ index pairs on and above the diagonal, $(1,1), (2,1), (2,2), (3,1), (3,2), (3,3), \ldots, (N,N)$. If no mask expression is specified, the active set is equal to the valid set. Next, the right-hand sides for all the result elements in the active set are calculated. Finally, the left-hand sides are replaced by the right-hand sides just computed. The order in which the assignments are made is up to HPF and we can neither predict what it will be nor find out from inside a program what it was.

On a single processor, each stage in the execution of a FORALL must be finished before the following stage can begin. If distributing a FORALL across parallel processors results in overlap between the calculations, synchronization is required to preserve these semantics, just as in the case of array assignment. For example, in this assignment

```
      FORALL(I=1:10) A(I)=A(K(I))
```

there can never be a data dependence and it should not be necessary to tell the compiler so by using an INDEPENDENT directive. However, if the compiler cannot determine whether there will be an overlap when the calculation is distributed, it must assume the worst and synchronize the stages of the FORALL across the processors. But suppose we know that there will be no overlap at run time, because A is distributed in such a way that each processor uses only the elements that it will update, as in the example below.

```
      REAL*8 A(10)
      INTEGER*4 K(10)/2,1,4,3,6,5,8,7,10,9/
CHPF$ PROCESSORS FIVE(5)
CHPF$ DISTRIBUTE A(BLOCK) ONTO FIVE
CHPF$ INDEPENDENT
      FORALL(I=1:10) A(I)=A(K(I))
      :
```

Processor 1 swaps A(1) with A(2), processor 2 swaps A(3) with A(4), and so on, with no overlap between the parallel calculations. If we assert that the FORALL is independent, the compiler will omit the barrier it would otherwise use to synchronize the processors. In practice this can turn out to be an important optimization.

In asserting that a FORALL is independent we promise that there will be *no* interferences between the calculations for the different index values in the valid set. This means that there must be neither data dependencies from assigning a result value more than once, nor overlap between the parallel calculations. If a FORALL that contains either kind of interference is asserted to be INDEPENDENT, the HPF compiler might recognize the interference and ignore the directive, or it might believe the false claim and generate parallel machine code that gives the wrong answer.

HPF Built-In Routines. In addition to parallelizing the Fortran-90 built-in functions, HPF adds some 55 new routines for inquiring about the arrangement of abstract processors and performing various data-parallel computations. NUMBER_OF_PROCESSORS, the most commonly needed inquiry function, is described below in the case study of §17.2.6. Most of the HPF computational routines have complicated inputs and behaviors. To get the flavor of these routines, we will consider one representative example.

Suppose we want to compute a *result* array R each element of which is the corresponding element of a *base* array B plus certain selected elements of a *data* array D. To specify what elements of D get accumulated into the value of R(I,J), we will provide matrices IR and IC corresponding to D and containing the row and column indices of the elements in R to which each element of D contributes. Given this data we can compute R, in parallel, by a single invocation of the HPF function SUM_SCATTER.

To illustrate the calculation with numbers we will use the data shown at the top of the next page, which are from [81, Example 7.3]. To find R(1,1) we start with B(1,1) and add in any elements of D for which the corresponding indices in IR and IC are (1,1). The only elements in D for which the corresponding entry is 1 in both IR and IC are the diagonal elements, so it must be that

$$R(1,1) = B(1,1) + D(1,1) + D(2,2) + D(3,3).$$

$$D = \begin{bmatrix} 1 & 2 & 3 \\ 4 & 5 & 6 \\ 7 & 8 & 9 \end{bmatrix} \quad B = \begin{bmatrix} -1 & -2 & -3 \\ -4 & -5 & -6 \\ -7 & -8 & -9 \end{bmatrix}$$

$$IR = \begin{bmatrix} 1 & 1 & 1 \\ 2 & 1 & 1 \\ 3 & 2 & 1 \end{bmatrix} \quad IC = \begin{bmatrix} 1 & 2 & 3 \\ 1 & 1 & 2 \\ 1 & 1 & 1 \end{bmatrix}$$

$$R = \begin{bmatrix} 14 & 6 & 0 \\ 8 & -5 & -6 \\ 0 & -8 & -9 \end{bmatrix}$$

The other elements of R are determined similarly, yielding the result shown. The single HPF statement on the left below does the calculation.

```
R=SUM_SCATTER(D,B,IC,IR)          DO 1 I=1,3
                                   DO 1 J=1,3
                                      R(I,J)=B(I,J)
                                 1 CONTINUE
                                   DO 2 I=1,3
                                   DO 2 J=1,3
                                      R(IR(I,J),IC(I,J))=
                                 ;    R(IR(I,J),IC(I,J))+D(I,J)
                                 2 CONTINUE
```

The code segment on the right does the example in Classical FORTRAN. SUM_SCATTER can be used with data arrays having more dimensions (in which case additional index arrays must be supplied), and a logical mask argument can be provided to restrict which elements of D participate in the operation. The result, base, and data arrays must have the same type, but that can be any numeric type. Several similar "scatter" routines are built into HPF for other reduction operators, such as PRODUCT. Other HPF routines perform array manipulations that are quite different from "scattering" but are also quite sophisticated. For details about all the routines, see [81, §7].

17.2.5   Using Subprograms

In addition to using the built-in routines mentioned in §17.2.4, you can of course also write your own FUNCTION and SUBROUTINE subprograms in HPF. The compiler parallelizes each subprogram in the same way that it parallelizes a main program, by distributing result array elements, and the calculations that produce them, among the processors.

Array Argument Distribution. It is necessary for each HPF routine that uses an array to know whether and how the array is distributed. Because of separate compilation those facts must be stated in each routine where the array is present. In the routine where an array originates, it can be distributed by including a DISTRIBUTE directive like those we considered in §17.2.3. An array that is received as a formal parameter by a subprogram must also have its distribution described within the subprogram.

The most straightforward way to describe the distribution of a subprogram parameter is to say exactly what it should be.

```
      REAL*8 G(10,10)                      SUBROUTINE SUB(G)
CHPF$ DISTRIBUTE G(BLOCK,BLOCK)            REAL*8 G(10,10)
      CALL SUB(G)                   CHPF$ DISTRIBUTE G(BLOCK,BLOCK)
      :                                    :
```

The directive in the subroutine specifies how G is to be distributed there, without regard to how it is distributed in the main. This is called a **prescriptive distribution**. If a prescriptive distribution disagrees with the one that is used in the calling routine, HPF will **remap** the data upon entry, so that it has the prescribed distribution within the subprogram, and put it back again when the subprogram returns. In our example the directives are the same, so no remapping takes place. Remapping involves processing and communication, so it takes time and should usually be avoided. On the other hand, a remapping might be worthwhile if the new distribution permits a better speedup to be obtained when the code in the subprogram is parallelized.

It is also possible to describe the distribution of a subprogram parameter as **inherited** from the calling routine, so we could have written this.

```
      REAL*8 G(10,10)                      SUBROUTINE SUB(G)
CHPF$ DISTRIBUTE G(BLOCK,BLOCK)            REAL*8 G(10,10)
      CALL SUB(G)                   CHPF$ DISTRIBUTE G *
      :                                    :
```

Now the directive in SUB specifies a **transcriptive distribution**. If the distribution is inherited, the data will never be remapped. However, because the compiler is now ignorant of the distribution, it might generate much less efficient code than for a prescriptive distribution [91].

Array Argument Dimensions. In §17.2.1 we observed that in a data parallel program we can think of the data as stored in a single logical memory that is accessible to all of the processors, even though only parts of the data might actually be needed by each parallel process. This is just how we think of the data in an ordinary serial program, so it would be natural to suppose that HPF lays out array data in storage according to the traditional FORTRAN linear memory model. For example, if the following code segment is compiled using f77, the array H ends up as a contiguous sequence of 15 adjacent doublewords beginning at the address corresponding to H(1,1) and arranged in column-major order. The assumption that arrays are stored like this is pervasive to Classical FORTRAN programming, and many standard coding techniques (including several described in §11) depend on it.

```
      REAL*8 H(3,5)
      DO 1 I=1,3
          DO 2 J=1,5
              H(I,J)=DEXP(DFLOAT(I*J))
  2       CONTINUE
  1 CONTINUE
```

Even if we DISTRIBUTE the array H between 2 processors, as in the code at the top of the next page, it would still be possible in principle for HPF to retain the traditional FORTRAN memory model.

```
      REAL*8 H(3,5)
CHPF$ PROCESSORS SPLIT(2)
CHPF$ DISTRIBUTE H(BLOCK,CYCLIC) ONTO SPLIT
CHPF$ INDEPENDENT,NEW(J)
      DO 1 I=1,3
          DO 2 J=1,5
              H(I,J)=DEXP(DFLOAT(I*J))
    2     CONTINUE
    1 CONTINUE
```

Now one processor does the assignments for columns 1, 3, and 5 of H, while the other does the assignments for columns 2 and 4. If we were writing an MPI program by hand, as described in §16.2.2, we might send individual columns as messages, or we might handle the even columns on processor 0 and copy the odd columns into a message for processor 1, then copy the results back into H after the parallel assignments were made. An HPF compiler obviously could do those things as well.

Unfortunately, sending multiple messages or copying arrays back and forth to rearrange data can be very inefficient. In our example it might be possible to greatly reduce the message passing and the copying of data if we could instead store the even columns together in one place and the odd columns together in another, and somehow keep track of their true order. To be able to do this sort of thing, HPF *abandons sequential storage* and represents distributed arrays internally using more complicated data structures that do *not* conform to the traditional FORTRAN memory model. The precise way in which this is done depends on the distribution and alignment of the data and is compiler-dependent. To store the array elements that end up on a given parallel processor, the dimensions might be permuted so that the undistributed ones (the dimensions that get copied everywhere) vary most rapidly, then dimensions distributed BLOCK, and finally those distributed CYCLIC [79].

HPF's abandonment of sequential storage for arrays has many consequences, some quite subtle and all potentially surprising to the Classical FORTRAN programmer. Array elements that would be adjacent in column-major order, such as consecutive elements of a vector, might not be stored in adjacent memory locations on any of the processors. If the vector X is DISTRIBUTEd, ALIGNing Y(1) with X(1) does *not* ensure that Y(2) and X(2) will be sent to the same processor; to match up all the elements we must explicitly ALIGN Y(I) WITH X(I). Sequential storage can be secured for variables that are *not* DISTRIBUTEd or ALIGNed, but only by listing them in a SEQUENCE directive (illustrated below). Special care is necessary in using COMMON and EQUIVALENCE [81, §4.10].

The non-sequential way in which HPF stores arrays also has serious implications for the passing of array arguments to subprograms. In Classical FORTRAN we are accustomed to regard an actual argument as a pointer to the beginning of the data, which are stored sequentially in column-major order. This is called **sequence association.** In the example below, each call to ADDCOL passes a single column of the matrix S into the dummy argument vector V, and returns the scalar T into the vector element SUMS(I).

```
C     Classical Fortran                    SUBROUTINE ADDCOL(V,T)
      REAL*8 S(10,20),SUMS(20)             REAL*8 V(10),T
      :                                    T=0.D0
      DO 1 I=1,20                          DO 1 J=1,10
          CALL ADDCOL(S(1,I),SUMS(I))          T=T+V(J)
    1 CONTINUE                           1 CONTINUE
      :                                    RETURN
                                          END
```

HPF allows returning the scalar T into the array element SUMS(I), but regards S(1,I) as the scalar value of that single array element rather than as a starting address for the dummy argument vector V. This example can be made acceptable to HPF by declaring that S and V are sequential. However, declaring S and V this way means they cannot be DISTRIBUTEd.

```
C      HPF sequential                            SUBROUTINE ADDCOL(V,T)
       REAL*8 S(10,20),SUMS(20)            CHPF$ SEQUENCE V
CHPF$ SEQUENCE S                                 REAL*8 V(10),T
       :                                         T=0.D0
       DO 1 I=1,20                               DO 1 J=1,10
           CALL ADDCOL(S(1,I),SUMS(I))               T=T+V(J)
     1 CONTINUE                                1 CONTINUE
       :                                         RETURN
                                                 END
```

An alternative that doesn't interfere with distribution is to specify a Fortran-90 array section, as in the code below. If an array or array section that is not sequential is passed as a subprogram argument, the corresponding dummy argument must match it in both size and shape. Adjustable dimensions cannot be used for non-sequential array parameters.

```
C      HPF distributed                           SUBROUTINE ADDCOL(V,T)
       REAL*8 S(10,20),SUMS(20)            CHPF$ DISTRIBUTE V(*)
CHPF$ DISTRIBUTE S(*,BLOCK)                       REAL*8 V(10),T
CHPF$ ALIGN SUMS(I) WITH S(*,I)                   T=0.D0
CHPF$ INDEPENDENT                                 DO 1 J=1,10
       :                                              T=T+V(J)
       DO 1 I=1,20                             1 CONTINUE
           CALL ADDCOL(S(:,I),SUMS(I))           RETURN
     1 CONTINUE                                  END
```

EXTRINSIC Routines. The last example above is a data parallel program, in which result elements are distributed with columns of S to the available processors. ADDCOL is invoked *once for each column,* and runs on the processor to which that column was distributed. HPF also provides a way to specify that the subroutine should be run *once on each processor,* to process all of the columns distributed to that processor. HPF calls such a routine EXTRINSIC.

```
       REAL*8 S(10,20),SUMS(20)                  EXTRINSIC(HPF_LOCAL)
CHPF$ DISTRIBUTE S(*,BLOCK)                   ;  SUBROUTINE ADDCOL(S,SUMS)
CHPF$ ALIGN SUMS(I) WITH S(*,I)                  REAL*8 S(:,:),SUMS(:)
       INTERFACE                                 T=0.D0
         EXTRINSIC(HPF_LOCAL)                    ILO=LBOUND(S,2)
     ;     SUBROUTINE ADDCOL(S,SUMS)             IHI=UBOUND(S,2)
         REAL*8 S(:,:),SUMS(:)                   DO 1 I=ILO,IHI
         DISTRIBUTE S(*,BLOCK)                       SUMS(I)=0.D0
         DISTRIBUTE SUMS(BLOCK)                      DO 2 J=1,10
         END                                             SUMS(I)=SUMS(I)+S(J,I)
       END INTERFACE                          2     CONTINUE
       CALL ADDCOL(S,SUMS)                     1 CONTINUE
       :                                         RETURN
                                                 END
```

The INTERFACE block is needed so HPF will know, when it is compiling the main program, that the subroutine ADDCOL is EXTRINSIC. Now each invocation of ADDCOL receives in S *all* of the columns (and only those columns) distributed to the processor on which it is running. That is why S is declared as an assumed-shape array in the subroutine, and that is why no argument of an EXTRINSIC routine can be declared SEQUENCE. Now ADDCOL uses two Fortran-90 built-in functions that we have not needed previously, LBOUND and UBOUND, to determine the range of columns that are present on this processor. It adds up these columns and returns the sums in the appropriate elements of SUMS, which must also be assumed-shape.

From inside an EXTRINSIC subprogram it is possible to do explicit message passing with MPI, as part of an HPF program, to parallelize pieces of a calculation that are not data-parallel. Also, EXTRINSIC(HPF_SERIAL) can be used to identify a subprogram that should run on a single processor, such as a routine written in a language other than HPF.

PURE Functions. In §17.2.4, I mentioned that although the predicate of a FORALL statement can only be an assignment, the right-hand side of the assignment can invoke FUNCTION subprograms that are PURE. That is HPF's name for a function that only returns a value, having no side effects such as changing other variables (including its arguments) or doing I/O. Elementary functions like DSQRT and HPF built-ins like SUM_SCATTER are PURE, and if you write FUNCTION subprograms of your own that have no side effects you can declare them to be PURE. The example below shows the use of a PURE function. The INTERFACE block tells HPF when it is compiling the main program that R will not have side effects that could prevent parallelization of the FORALL.

```
       REAL*8 X(10),Y(10)              PURE FUNCTION R(Z)
CHPF$ DISTRIBUTE X(BLOCK)              REAL*8 R,Z
CHPF$ ALIGN Y(I) WITH X(I)            R=DSQRT(DEXP(Z))
       INTERFACE                       RETURN
         PURE FUNCTION R(Z)            END
         REAL*8 R,Z
         END
       END INTERFACE
       FORALL(I=1:10) Y(I)=R(X(I))
       :
```

A subprogram invoked within a DO loop must also not have any side effects if the loop is to be independent, but it need not be declared PURE.

17.2.6 Case Study: Integration Again

As mentioned in the introduction to this chapter, data parallel programming is a variety of the domain decomposition model described in §16.2.4. For comparison with the MPI approach, we will now solve the problem of that case study using HPF. Recall that our task was to approximate a definite integral using the rectangle rule.

The interval of integration, from $x = a$ to $x = b$, is divided into k rectangles of equal width $h = (b - a)/k$, each as high as the function value at the midpoint of its base. Thus,

$$\int_a^b f(x)\,dx \approx \sum_{i=1}^k hf(a + [i - \tfrac{1}{2}]h).$$

Here it is helpful to be specific about the function, so we will use this $f(x)$, which is the function shown in the graph on the next page.

$$f(x) = \frac{\sin(x)}{1 + x^2}$$

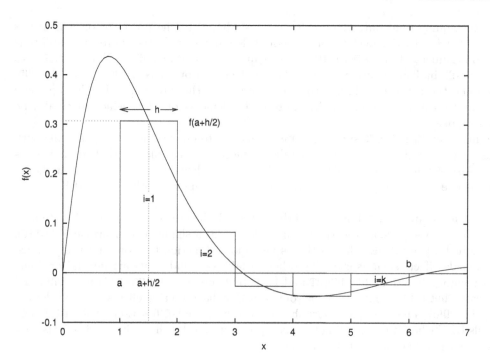

Here is a Classical FORTRAN program that computes the approximation using $k = 2000$ rectangles.

```
      INTEGER*4 K/2000/
      REAL*8 AB(2),H,VAL,X,F
C
C     get the limits
      WRITE(6,901)
  901 FORMAT('limits of integration: ',$)
      READ(5,*) AB(1),AB(2)
C
C     add up the rectangles and write the answer
      H=(AB(2)-AB(1))/DFLOAT(K)
      VAL=0.D0
      DO 1 I=1,K
           X=AB(1)+(DFLOAT(I)-0.5D0)*H
           VAL=VAL+H*F(X)
    1 CONTINUE
      WRITE(6,*) VAL
      STOP
      END
C
      FUNCTION F(X)
      REAL*8 F,X
      F=DSIN(X)/(1.D0+X**2)
      RETURN
      END
```

To do this calculation in a data-parallel fashion we need an array whose elements can be assigned in parallel, so that we can divide that work, along with the data it requires, among the parallel processors. The serial code doesn't contain any such array *so we must introduce one.* If there are n processors we could find n partial sums in parallel and afterwards add them up, exactly as described in §16.2.4. To store these partial sums we will make VAL a vector and add a loop over the processors, as shown in the HPF program below. The code illustrates several of the ideas we have discussed in the preceding sections.

```
       INTEGER*4 K/2000/
       REAL*8 AB(2),H,X,F
       ALLOCATABLE VAL(:)
       REAL*8 VAL
CHPF$ DISTRIBUTE VAL(CYCLIC)
C
C      make space for as many partial sums as there will be
       N=NUMBER_OF_PROCESSORS()
       ALLOCATE(VAL(N))
C
C      get the limits
       WRITE(6,901)
  901 FORMAT('limits of integration: ',$)
       READ(5,*) AB(1),AB(2)
C
C      find a partial sum on each processor
       H=(AB(2)-AB(1))/DFLOAT(K)
CHPF$ INDEPENDENT, NEW(I,X)
       DO 2 L=1,N
C             add up the rectangles
              VAL(L)=0.D0
              DO 1 I=L,K,N
                    X=AB(1)+(DFLOAT(I)-0.5D0)*H
                    VAL(L)=VAL(L)+H*F(X)
    1         CONTINUE
    2 CONTINUE
C
C      add up the partial sums and write the answer
       WRITE(6,*) SUM(VAL)
       STOP
       END
C
       FUNCTION F(X)
       REAL*8 F,X
       F=DSIN(X)/(1.D0+X**2)
       RETURN
       END
```

1➭ This program leaves it up to the interactive user to decide at run time, and specify through the parallel run-time system, how many processors are to be used. It finds out that number from the built-in HPF inquiry function NUMBER_OF_PROCESSORS, which has no parameters. The number of processors is returned in the function name and assigned to N. Using any HPF built-in subprogram means the program cannot be linked using a Fortran-90 compiler, even if you want to run it serially. Fortran-90 ignores HPF directives because they are just comments, but it cannot ignore a subprogram invocation and it knows nothing about the routines that are built into HPF.

2➭ Because we don't know at compile time how many processors there will be, we declare VAL to be ALLOCATABLE and ALLOCATE the right number of elements after finding out N. VAL gets DISTRIBUTEd across the processors, as required by the directive, at the moment it is actually allocated.

3 ⇨   As described in §16.2.4, we will use the first of the n processors to add up rectangles $1, n+1, 2n+1, \ldots$, the second to add up rectangles $2, n+2, 2n+2, \ldots$, and so on. This is a cyclic distribution of the rectangles among the processors, so VAL must be distributed CYCLIC. Just as in the MPI solution, we can't make use of more processors than there are rectangles, so this code assumes that N is less than K=2000.

4 ⇨   After allocating VAL, we get the limits of integration and compute the rectangle width H. Then comes the loop over the N processors, which is to be parallelized by HPF. For each value of L (which is to say on each processor) the body of the DO 2 loop adds up the areas of the rectangles delegated to that processor. The starting value L and increment N of the DO 1 loop yield the cyclic delegation of rectangles to processors described above. This loop is quite similar to the one we used in the program of §16.2.4. It is not obvious how the DO 1 loop could be replaced by a FORALL.

5 ⇨   The inside DO index I and the temporary variable X must be declared NEW so that they can be different on each processor and the DO 2 loop will not have a data dependence.

6 ⇨   To add up the elements of VAL we use the Fortran-90 built-in function SUM, whose work HPF might do in parallel if there are enough elements in VAL to make that worthwhile.

7 ⇨   The function subprogram F(X) does not have any side effects, so it can be used in the DO 1 loop without interfering with its independence. Because it is invoked in a DO rather than a FORALL, it does not need to be declared PURE (even though it is).

17.2.7   Caveats

HPF is theoretically important as an implementation of the data-parallel model and practically useful as a tool for parallelizing certain calculations, but both the model and the language have significant limitations. Some parallelizable calculations are not data-parallel, and although HPF can make programming seem easy for those that are, the inherent difficulty of parallel processing is really just hidden and can manifest itself in covert and baffling ways. Run-time errors result in nonzero return codes from MPI, but because the MPI calls are automatically generated the best diagnostic that HPF can produce might not reveal to the user very much about what went wrong. The object code generated by the HPF compiler is far from the source code you wrote, so debugging with traditional tools like dbx is difficult.

The speedup achieved by an HPF program depends on communication costs and load balancing, exactly as described in §16.2.5 for explicit message passing. The only difference is that now the HPF compiler is generating the MPI calls automatically, according to the data-distribution directives and concurrency expressions in your source program. The message-passing code generated by an HPF compiler is less clever than what you might compose by hand so better performance can usually be achieved, at the cost of doing more work, by using MPI directly.

17.2.8   Omissions

This introduction has touched on only the highest points of HPF, which is vaster and more subtle even than Fortran-90. Among the many topics I have intentionally omitted or glossed over are these: complications that arise in using various of those Fortran-90 features (such as user-defined data types) that I omitted from §17.1; the TEMPLATE, DYNAMIC, REDISTRIBUTE, and REALIGN directives; an optional skipping parameter that can be used in BLOCK and CYCLIC distributions; the FORALL construct (interpreted like a sequence of one-line FORALL statements); descriptive distribution of subprogram parameters; PURE SUBROUTINE subprograms, and technical small print that makes PURE stricter than just having no side effects; the inquiry functions HPF_ALIGNMENT, HPF_TEMPLATE, HPF_DISTRIBUTION, and PROCESSORS_SHAPE; most HPF built-in computational functions, HPF_LIBRARY and HPF_LOCAL_LIBRARY routines, and USE; EXTRINSIC(HPF) (equivalent to omitting EXRINSIC); INHERIT (the same as DISTRIBUTE *); and NOSEQUENCE (the default). To learn about these things, you will have to read another book [81].

17.3   The Future of FORTRAN

Fortran-90 and HPF are both quite distant from Classical FORTRAN, and the more recent flavors of Modern Fortran are more distant still. If the trend persists we can expect that future versions of the language will be even more subtle, abstract, complex, and difficult to learn, use, and be sure of getting right. This evolution is mainly driven *not* by the modest everyday needs of engineers or physical scientists, but by the intellectual curiosity of language theorists, the search by compiler vendors for novel features of value in marketing their products, and the desire of a few bleeding-edge users to solve problems that are a poor fit to the current version whatever it is. Some language developers apparently intend the eventual "obsolescence" and extinction of Classical FORTRAN entirely, through its piecemeal replacement by a quite different language bearing a stolen name. Indeed, a guiding principle in the design of Modern Fortran seems to be that if one really must show one's low breeding and provincial taste by writing programs in FORTRAN at all, one should at least use a version of the language that looks as little like FORTRAN as possible. The ultimate result of these developments might well be a language that is beyond the grasp of casual programmers and can be used only by professional computer scientists.

As I pointed out in §0.4, Classical FORTRAN always lags behind, and remains a subset of, the latest official dialect. In this chapter I have tried to be optimistic that the few parts of Fortran-90 and HPF that strike me as widely useful will find their way into the practice of working engineers and scientists and thus eventually come to be regarded by them as part of the language they know as FORTRAN. But the pace of change is now so fast that the time has clearly come to *treat Classical FORTRAN as a separate language,* as I have done in this book, while Modern Fortran hurtles away along its own path of natural selection to become a different species altogether. Already there are a few subset compilers [114] [146] that depart from the long tradition of upward compatibility and exclude many old features (some of them parts of Classical FORTRAN) while retaining ugly new locutions that will strike most FORTRAN programmers as profoundly alien. The subset languages that remain after these excisions are still immense lumbering beasts, so if a subset compiler is really desirable it would be far easier to build one for Classical FORTRAN. A standardized Classical FORTRAN could omit the features that are condemned ☠ in §13, the parts of Fortran-90 and HPF that are omitted from this chapter, PRINT *, READ *, and the need for CHARACTER*n variables. A Classical FORTRAN compiler could be tiny, fast, clever, and (like g77) free, a sort of mammal among the new dinosaurs. Until that happens there is some risk that as the sauropod that is Modern Fortran grows ever skyward it will collapse of its own weight and take Classical FORTRAN with it.

But dreams both good and bad are, according to tradition [124], only one-sixtieth of prophecy. It is time alone that will tell for sure how academic fashion, market forces, political correctness, historical inertia, and the genuine needs of engineers and scientists conspire to further shape the language of peasants.

17.4   Exercises

17.4.1   The chapter introduction gives a statement census of 32 for Classical FORTRAN.
(a) How many extra statements (not counting new built-in functions) are introduced from
Fortran-90 in §17.1? The new total is what fraction of the full Fortran-90 statement census? (b) How many additional statements are introduced from HPF in §17.2? How many
directives?

17.4.2   What are the things that might keep a Classical FORTRAN program from working
in Fortran-90?

17.4.3   Revise the following program so it is sure to work in Fortran-90.

```
      CHARACTER*1 PRMPT(9)/'k','i','d',1H','s',' ','w','t',':'/
      TOTAL=0.
    2 WRITE(6,901) PRMPT
  901 FORMAT(9A1,$)
      READ(5,*,END=1) WT
      CALL SUM(WT,TOTAL)
      GO TO 2
    1 WRITE(6,902) TOTAL
  902 FORMAT(' '/'total=',F5.0)
      STOP
      END
C
      SUBROUTINE SUM(WT,TOTAL)
      TOTAL=TOTAL+WT
      RETURN
      END
```

17.4.4   The second example in §17.1 shows how a variable local to a subprogram and not
initialized at compile time can become undefined between invocations of the routine if SAVE
is not used. Construct a different example to illustrate the same idea.

17.4.5   What is printed by this Fortran-90 program? Why?

```
      REAL*8 A(2,2)/1.D0,2.D0,3.D0,4.D0/
      A=DSQRT(1.D0+(4.D0-A)*A)
      PRINT *,MAXVAL(A)
      STOP
      END
```

17.4.6   The CALL syntax in the following program is illegal in FORTRAN-77 but legal in
Fortran-90. (a) Why? (b) What does the program print when it is run?

```
      REAL*8 X(2)/1.D0,2.D0/          SUBROUTINE SUB(Y)
      CALL SUB(-X)                    REAL*8 Y(2)
      STOP                            PRINT *,Y(1),Y(2)
      END                             RETURN
                                      END
```

17.4.7 Compute the following matrix product

$$\begin{bmatrix} 1 & -2 \\ 3 & 0 \\ 5 & 1 \end{bmatrix} \begin{bmatrix} 8 & 4 \\ -1 & 0 \end{bmatrix}$$

(a) by hand calculation; (b) by writing a program that invokes the `MATMUL` function. (c) What does `MATMUL` do if its arguments are not **conformable**, i.e., if the number of rows in the right-hand matrix is not equal to the number of columns in the left-hand matrix?

17.4.8 Explain how the array expression `1.D0/A` differs from the matrix inverse $\mathbf{A}^{-1}$, and how the array expression `A*B` differs from the matrix product $\mathbf{AB}$. There is no function built into Fortran-90 for the matrix inverse. Is there a function for matrix multiplication?

17.4.9 Explain why an `INTERFACE` block is needed in a routine that invokes a user-written array-valued function. Describe another situation in which it is necessary to use an `INTERFACE` block in a Fortran-90 program.

17.4.10 Construct an example to show how, by using array sections, it is possible for an array assignment to replace an element in the left-hand side array more than once. Why is this an error? Is it detected by your Fortran-90 compiler? By your HPF compiler?

17.4.11 An N × N matrix A can be raised to the K'th power by successive matrix multiplications of A by itself. Write an array-valued function `MATPOW(A,N,K)` to return $\mathbf{A}^K$, and test your function with a main program that invokes it to compute some result that you can also find by hand.

17.4.12 Write a function `TRACE(A)` that uses array operations (rather than a `DO` loop) to compute the **trace** of the N × N matrix A, $\text{tr}(\mathbf{A}) = \sum_j \mathbf{A}_{j,j}$.

17.4.13 What do A and B contain after these array assignments? Why?

```
INTEGER*4 M(3,3)/1,2,3,4,5,6,7,8,9/,A(3,3),B(3,3)
INTEGER*4 INDX1(3)/3,2,2/,INDX2(3)/3,2,1/
A(INDX2,INDX2)=M(INDX1,INDX1)
B(INDX1,INDX1)=M(INDX2,INDX2)
   :
```

17.4.14 Write a Fortran-90 code segment using array section notation to compute a vector X as the sum of the columns of a matrix A (that is, each element of X is the sum of the elements in the corresponding row of A).

17.4.15 In the following code segment, what are the dimensions and final contents of the arrays (a) A? (b) B? (c) C? (d) D? (e) E?

```
INTEGER*4 MAT(4,4)/1,2,3,4,5,6,7,8,9,10,11,12,13,14,15,16/
[declarations for INTEGER*4 arrays A, B, C, D, E]
   :
A=MAT(1:2,1:2)
B=MAT(3,:)
C=MAT(1:4:3,1:4:3)
D=TRANSPOSE(MAT(:,3))
E=DOT_PRODUCT(MAT(2,:),MAT(:,2))
   :
```

17.4.16 Give two reasons why it is sometimes desirable to use dynamic memory allocation. Can dynamic memory allocation be used to set the rank of an array based on input data that a program reads at run time?

17.4.17 In §17.1.2, the example involving SUB explicitly deallocates the work array A before the subroutine returns. Modify this example so that the main program calls SUB twice but the array A is allocated within DOT only once.

17.4.18 Memory can be dynamically allocated in Fortran-90 by using either allocatable arrays or automatic arrays. (a) Explain the difference between these two array types. (b) Rewrite the §17.1.2 examples that use allocatable arrays to use automatic arrays instead. (c) Rewrite the §17.1.2 example that uses an automatic array to use an allocatable array instead.

17.4.19 In the following program, some arrays are allocated statically and others dynamically. Tell which method of allocation is used and the scope of definition for the arrays (a) A, (b) B, (c) C, (d) D, and (e) E.

```
        ALLOCATABLE A(:),B(:)         SUBROUTINE SUB2(A,N,D)
        REAL*8 A,B,C(5)               SAVE
        ALLOCATE(A(3),B(4))           ALLOCATABLE E(:)
        CALL SUB1(A,3,C)              REAL*8 A(N),D(*),E
        STOP                          ALLOCATE(E(7))
        END                           RETURN
C                                     END
        SUBROUTINE SUB1(A,N,C)
        ALLOCATABLE D(:)
        REAL*8 A(N),C(5),D
        ALLOCATE(D(6))
        CALL SUB2(A,N,D)
        RETURN
        END
```

17.4.20 Exercise 10.9.16 asks for a program that removes adjacent repeated lines, similar in behavior to the UNIX™ utility uniq. Now suppose it is desired to remove duplicate lines even if they are *not* adjacent. One approach would be to sort the input so that all repeated lines are adjacent, without changing the order of the other lines, and then use uniq. Instead, modify the program you wrote for Exercise 10.9.16 so that it can remember all of the unique lines found so far and identify duplicates by comparing them to this list. Use Fortran-90 features to make the program suitable for use when it is not known in advance how many unique lines there will be.

17.4.21 The statement X=Y*Z sets X to the product Y*Z if that number is representable, or to the IEEE representation for $+\infty$ or $-\infty$ upon overflow. (a) Assuming all the variables have type REAL*8, write a code segment that sets X to the product Y*Z if that number is representable, or to +HUGE(X) or −HUGE(X) upon overflow, and counts the number of overflows that it fixes up. (b) IEEE arithmetic denotes $+\infty$ by the binary value $011\cdots11$ and $-\infty$ by $111\cdots11$. Revise your code segment to use these values, rather than +HUGE(X) and −HUGE(X).

17.4.22 Write a Fortran-90 statement to compute the quantity $\lfloor \log_2(x) \rfloor$, where $\lfloor q \rfloor$ means the largest integer less than or equal to q, *without* using an intrinsic function for logarithm.

17.4.23 What does this program print, and why?

```
    WRITE(6,901) 37.5000000000000030D0
901 FORMAT(F19.16)
    STOP
    END
```

17.4.24 Write a program that reads an integer value from the keyboard and writes out the corresponding 32-bit binary value, without doing any arithmetic. Be sure to print any leading zeros that might be in the binary value. Does your program work for negative numbers?

17.4.25 Find the exact `REAL*8` values that bracket the true value of π, and print the values out in binary.

17.4.26 Is the following a legal Fortran-90 program? Is the program easier to read written on one line, or written with one statement per line?

```
    DO 1 I=1,10; PRINT *,I; 1 CONTINUE; STOP; END
```

17.4.27 Is the following statement legal in a Fortran-90 program?

```
    X=(-B+DSQRT(B**2-4.D0*A*C)) ! this is the numerator
;   /(2.D0*A)                   ! this is the denominator
```

Confirm your answer by experiment.

17.4.28 Consider the program below. (a) Identify and explain all the features that are new to Fortran-90. (b) Where is the statement number "1" referred to in the `GO TO`? (c) Suggest an improvement to the typographical layout of the program.

```
      INTEGER*4 SUM/0/ !initialize
!
!     get the next input value
1     READ(5,*,END=2) I; SUM=SUM+I; GO TO 1
!
!     output total
   2 WRITE(6,901) SUM
 901 FORMAT("Sum=",B32.32)
     STOP
     END
```

17.4.29 Write a Fortran-90 program to print the following output:
`This line contains both single ' and double " quotes.`

17.4.30 Rewrite your solutions to the following Exercises in Fortran-90, using the new features described in this chapter. (a) 5.8.20, (b) 7.4.11, (c) 11.9.22.

17.4.31 Recode your solution to Exercise 5.8.33 in Fortran-90. This time, prompt for and read from the user the number N of rows and columns to use and the values of u at which the boundary cells are to be fixed. In your solution use allocatable arrays, nonadvancing input, array assignment, array sections, the `SUM` and `MAXVAL` functions, an end-of-line comment, and a character string delimited by double quotes.

17.4.32 Data parallel programming is the domain decomposition approach on which HPF is based. (a) What attributes characterize data parallel calculations? (b) How can a calculation be decomposed in a data parallel way?

17.4.33 Contrast HPF with MPI. In what circumstances is each to be preferred, and why?

17.4.34 List the HPF directives discussed in §17.2 and briefly describe the function of each.

17.4.35 How does HPF distribute arrays that are not mentioned in an `ALIGN` or `DISTRIBUTE` directive?

17.4.36 Add directives to the code below so that the `DO 1` loop can be parallelized by HPF (a) assuming there are 10 processors; (b) assuming there are 5 processors.

```
      DO 1 L=1,10
          P(L)=1.D0
          DO 2 K=1,10
              TMP=A(K,L)
              P(L)=P(L)*TMP
    2         CONTINUE
    1 CONTINUE
```

17.4.37 With the distribution shown below, what elements of `RSLT` are computed on which processor?

```
      REAL*8 RSLT(6,4)
      PROCESSORS SMALL(3,2)
      DISTRIBUTE RSLT(CYCLIC,BLOCK) ONTO SMALL
```

17.4.38 If B is distributed as shown below, what elements of A must be present on each processor in order to complete the calculation? How should A be distributed? If the calculation is repeated for N different values of A, how many elements of A must be sent to the processors?

```
      REAL*8 A(4,4),B(3,3)
CHPF$ PROCESSORS PROCS(3)
CHPF$ DISTRIBUTE B(CYCLIC,CYCLIC) ONTO PROCS
      [code to give values to A]
CHPF$ INDEPENDENT, NEW(I)
      DO 1 J=1,3
      DO 1 I=1,3
          B(I,J)=A(I,J)+A(I,J+1)+A(I+1,J)+A(I+1,J+1)
    1 CONTINUE
```

If the distribution is changed as shown below, how many elements of A must be sent to the processors?

```
      REAL*8 A(4,4),B(3,3)
CHPF$ PROCESSORS PROCS(3)
CHPF$ DISTRIBUTE B(*,BLOCK) ONTO PROCS
CHPF$ ALIGN A(*,J) WITH B(*,J)
CHPF$ ALIGN A(*,J+1) WITH B(*,J)
      [code to give values to A]
CHPF$ INDEPENDENT, NEW(I)
      DO 1 J=1,3
      DO 1 I=1,3
          B(I,J)=A(I,J)+A(I,J+1)+A(I+1,J)+A(I+1,J+1)
    1 CONTINUE
```

17.4.39 Rewrite this code segment to remove the data dependence.

```
    DO 1 I=1,N-1
        X(I)=DSIN(ALPHA(I))
        X(I+1)=X(I)
  1 CONTINUE
```

17.4.40 Rewrite this code segment to remove the data dependence.

```
    INTEGER*4 K(1000)/1000*0/
    DO 1 I=1,999
        K(I)=K(I)+I
        K(I+1)=K(I)+1
  1 CONTINUE
```

17.4.41 Rewrite this code segment to remove the control dependence.

```
    DO 1 I=1,N
        IF(X(I).GE.0.D0) X(I)=X(I)-1.D0
        IF(DEXP(X(I)).LT.0.D0) X(I+1)=0.D0
  1 CONTINUE
```

17.4.42 A parallel algorithm for computing the sum of N values is described in §17.2.4. (a) How many groups of partial sums are calculated, counting the original list of values as one group and the final result as another? (b) Write a program in Classical FORTRAN to implement the algorithm, and test it on some small sets of values to verify that it works. (c) Can you add directives to translate your Classical FORTRAN program into HPF? If possible run it on the same test cases to verify that it works. (d) Replace your code by a call to the Fortran-90 built-in function SUM and confirm that it returns the same result. Does SUM necessarily use the algorithm suggested in the text?

17.4.43 Can HPF parallelize the following Fortran-90 array assignment?

```
    V(2:10)=V(1:9)
```

If not, explain why not. If so, is synchronization required between the processors?

17.4.44 In HPF, can a Fortran-90 array assignment *always* be rewritten as an INDEPENDENT DO or nest of DOs? If so, explain why. If not, present a counterexample.

17.4.45 (a) Explain how a FORALL construct is different from a DO loop or nest of DO loops. (b) Explain how a FORALL construct is different from a Fortran-90 array assignment.

17.4.46 There are two reasons why we might need to assert that a FORALL is INDEPENDENT. What are they?

17.4.47 In §17.2.4, the following code segment was used to illustrate a control dependence.

```
    READ *,K(1)
C       control dependence
    DO 3 L=2,M
        IF(K(L-1).GT.0) K(L)=L
  3 CONTINUE
```

If K is initially a vector of zeros, the effect of the loop is to assign K(L)=L for all elements after the first if and only if the value read for K(1) is positive. (a) Write HPF code to show how this process can be parallelized after all, using (a) an INDEPENDENT DO loop or (b) a FORALL statement.

17.4.48 Rewrite the following array assignment using a simpler FORALL.

```
A(2:M-1,2:N-1)=A(1:M-2,2:N-1)+A(3:M,2:N-1)
;               +A(2:M-1,1:N-2)+A(2:M-1,3:N)
```

17.4.49 Is the FORALL below independent? Why or why not? What happens if a directive is added to assert that it is INDEPENDENT?

```
FORALL(I=1:N,J=1:N,K=1:N) A(I,J,K)=A(K,J,I)
```

17.4.50 Rewrite the matrix multiplication code of §17.2.2 by (a) replacing the K loop by an invocation of the SUM built-in; (b) using a FORALL that invokes SUM; (c) using the MATMUL built-in.

17.4.51 The Classical FORTRAN shown below, adapted from [66], replaces each inside element of G with the average of its neighbors. Similar operations are used in the iterative solution of partial differential equations.

```
      REAL*8 G(16,16)
      [code to assign values to G]
      DO 1 J=2,15
      DO 1 I=2,15
            GTMP(I,J)=0.25D0*(G(I,J-1)+G(I,J+1)+G(I+1,J)+G(I-1,J)
    1 CONTINUE
      DO 2 J=2,15
      DO 2 I=2,15
            G(I,J)=GTMP(I,J)
    2 CONTINUE
```

Write an HPF code segment to parallelize the calculation using a FORALL.

17.4.52 The built-in HPF function SUM_SCATTER is described in §17.2.4. (a) Starting from the Classical FORTRAN code fragment given in the text, write a Fortran-90 FUNCTION subprogram that returns an array value and simulates the behavior of SUM_SCATTER. (b) Can you describe one practical application in which such a calculation arises?

17.4.53 Explain the difference between prescriptive and transcriptive distribution of subprogram parameters.

17.4.54 Why does HPF abandon the sequential storage model of Classical FORTRAN? Describe some consequences of this design decision.

17.4.55 What makes a function PURE? When does it need to be declared as PURE in an INTERFACE block? Revise this function to make it PURE.

```
FUNCTION SXPA(X,A)
REAL*8 SXPA,X,A
X=X+A
SXPA=DSIN(X)
RETURN
END
```

17.4.56 Why might it be necessary for an EXTRINSIC subprogram to use the LBOUND and UBOUND built-in functions?

17.4.57 Is there a way to use HPF to parallelize the solution to Exercise 5.8.33? If there is, outline an approach you think would work. If there is not, explain why not.

17.4.58 On February 13, 1997 the committee charged with writing a standard for the new language Fortran-2000, known as ISO/IEC JTC1/SC22/WG5, declared the "required content of Fortran-2000" to include the following extensions beyond Fortran-90: allocatable components, asynchronous I/O, derived type I/O, constructors/destructors, floating-point exception handling, inheritance, internationalization, interoperability with C, interval arithmetic, parameterized derived types, polymorphism, and procedure pointers. In addition, the following "minor technical enhancements" were to be considered for inclusion: access to status error messages, allowing PUBLIC entities of PRIVATE type, command line arguments, derived type encapsulation, enhanced complex constants, extending max/min intrisics to character, extended initialization expressions, generic rate_count and system_clock, IEEE I/O rounding inquiry intrinsics, increased statement length, intent for pointer arguments, mixed case syntax elements, named scratch files, passing specific/generic names, PUBLIC and PRIVATE derived type components, renaming defined operators, specifying pointer lower bounds, stream I/O, and a VOLATILE attribute.

(a) From the perspective of an engineer or scientist who uses Classical FORTRAN for some of the routine calculations required by his or her everyday work, which of these new features sound like needed improvements? Do the deliberations of the committee seem to reflect your concerns, or those of most programmers you know? (b) How much of an increase in the complexity of FORTRAN would you personally be willing to endure in exchange for gaining access to the improvements promised in this statement? If you need some of these features, would you be more inclined to use the added functionality of Fortran-2000 (which was eventually released as Fortran-2003) or to learn another language to get them? (c) As mentioned in the introduction to this chapter, new versions of Modern Fortran are now being standardized every five years or so. Assess the likely impact of this policy on compiler cost and availability, compilation speed, correctness of the generated object code, executable size, and execution speed. (d) How is the ongoing development of Modern Fortran likely to affect the portability of programs between computing environments? (e) In your estimation, is there still a role for Classical FORTRAN in computing for engineering and scientific calculations?

18

Some Utility Routines

Earlier I referred to `GETFIL` and `TIMER`, two FORTRAN subroutines that have wide utility and merit careful study but are too complicated to discuss thoroughly in the places where they are first mentioned. This chapter presents those routines in detail, along with several new routines that they invoke.

routine	purpose	§
BTD DTB	number-numeral conversions	18.1
INTINS STRINS	string insertions	18.2
GETFIL	attaching a file	18.3
TPVADD TPVSUB TPVNML TPV2R8 R82TPV TPVSCL	arithmetic on two-part values	18.4
TIMER	measuring CPU time	18.5

`GETFIL`, first described in §9.4.2, prompts an interactive user for the name of a file and then attaches the file to a specified logical I/O unit. It invokes the UNIX™ system routines `IARGC`, `GETARG`, and `UNLINK`, which are discussed in §14.2; the `LENGTH`, `SHIFTL`, `PROMPT`, and `QUERY` routines discussed in §10; and the new character manipulation routines `DTB`, `INTINS`, and `STRINS`. In turn, `INTINS` invokes another new routine, `BTD`.

`TIMER`, first described in §15.1.4, estimates the CPU time used by different parts of a program. It invokes the UNIX™ system routines `ETIME` (discussed in §15.1.3) and `gettimeofday` (indirectly) and four new routines, `TPVADD`, `TPVSUB`, `TPVSCL`, and `TPV2R8`, which in turn invoke `TPVNML` and `R82TPV`. These new routines do arithmetic on two-part values, which are discussed in §18.4. A cycle-counting variant of `TIMER` is presented in §18.5.4.

In addition to being useful for the tasks they perform, the routines of this chapter are instructive as examples of real, live (albeit mainly non-numerical) code. Most of the code segments shown elsewhere in the book are fragmentary, uncommented, and contrived to illustrate particular things about FORTRAN. In contrast, these routines were copied verbatim from a subprogram library that is in daily use, and they are listed here complete and with comments. For convenience in identifying FORTRAN statements, source code line numbers are shown on the listings and are ‖boxed‖ in the running commentary about each routine.

Besides `GETFIL` and `TIMER` I also mentioned earlier, in §13.1.4, a UNIX™ shell script named `changeall` that can be used to make the same text substitution in several files. That script is listed and described in §18.6.

18.1 Number-Numeral Conversions

The discussion of object-time formats in §10.4 included two examples of converting an INTEGER*4 number to its CHARACTER*1 numeral or numerals. This process, and the inverse process of finding the integer value represented by a string of numerals, are carried out in a general way by the routines of this section.

18.1.1 Integer to Numerals

BTD converts the number (or "binary") value of an INTEGER*4 quantity to a character string containing the digits of the number's decimal representation. The beginning of the routine is listed below, and the rest on the next page.

```
 1 C
 2 Code by Michael Kupferschmid
 3 C
 4       SUBROUTINE BTD(N, STRING,LS,RC)
 5 C     This routine converts the integer N into numerals
 6 C     right-justified in STRING (Binary To Decimal).
 7 C
 8 C     variable   meaning
 9 C     --------   -------
10 C     IABS       Fortran function returns |INTEGER*4|
11 C     K          index on the digits in |N|
12 C     KFNB       index of the first nonblank digit in STRING
13 C     LS         the number of characters in STRING
14 C     M          integer part of what's left of |N| at the moment
15 C     N          the integer to be converted
16 C     NUMERL     the digits 0...9
17 C     RC         return code; 0 => ok, 1 => error
18 C     STRING     character string returned
19 C
20 C     formal parameters
21       CHARACTER*1 STRING(LS)
22       INTEGER*4 RC
23 C
24 C     local variable
25       CHARACTER*1 NUMERL(10)/'0','1','2','3','4',
26     ;                        '5','6','7','8','9'/
27 C
28 C ------------------------------------------------------------------
29 C
30 C     if the length of STRING is not positive, something is wrong
31       RC=1
32       IF(LS.LE.0) RETURN
```

The preamble 1-27 follows the layout described in §12.3.2, and declares the same vector of numerals, NUMERL, that we saw in the PROMPT routine of §10.4. The executable code begins 31-32 by making sure that LS is positive, because without a place to put the digits of the number there is no way to make the conversion.

```
33 C
34 C      convert the absolute value of the number
35        M=IABS(N)
36        DO 1 K=LS,1,-1
37            STRING(K)=NUMERL(1+M-10*(M/10))
38            M=M/10
39      1 CONTINUE
40 C      did the digits of the number fit in the spaces allowed?
41        IF(M.NE.0) RETURN
42 C
43 C      blank out any leading zeros
44        DO 2 K=1,LS
45            KFNB=K
46            IF(STRING(K).NE.'0') GO TO 3
47            STRING(K)=' '
48      2 CONTINUE
49 C      the string was all zeros; put the rightmost one back
50          STRING(LS)='0'
51 C
52 C      insert a "-" if the number is negative
53      3 IF(N.LT.0 .AND. KFNB.EQ.1) RETURN
54        IF(N.LT.0) STRING(KFNB-1)='-'
55        RC=0
56        RETURN
57        END
```

The second stanza $\boxed{\text{35-41}}$ finds the digits, working from right to left. In the first iteration of the DO 1 loop $\boxed{\text{36-39}}$ K=LS and M is the absolute value of the number N to be converted, so M-10*(M/10) $\boxed{37}$ is the value of the rightmost digit in the number. For example, if M=851, M/10=85 and M-10*(M/10)=851-10*85=1.

Then 1+M-10*(M/10)=2 is the index in NUMERL of the numeral '1', which gets copied into STRING(LS). Then $\boxed{38}$ M is divided by 10 to chop off the rightmost digit. In our example, we now have M=85. The next iteration of the loop copies $\boxed{37}$ the numeral '5' to STRING(LS-1), and $\boxed{38}$ divides M again to leave M=8. Then an '8' is copied into STRING(LS-2). The next division yields M=0, so zeros are inserted in all the digit positions of STRING farther to the left.

If there aren't enough positions to hold the digits of M, then M will not have been divided down to zero by the time the loop exits $\boxed{41}$ and the routine returns with RC still set $\boxed{31}$ at 1 to flag the error.

If the number fits, the third stanza $\boxed{\text{44-50}}$ blanks out any leading zeros. As soon as a nonzero is found $\boxed{46}$, control transfers to statement 3. If the original number was N=0, then all of the digits will be '0' and we must retain the rightmost one. This is done by replacing the rightmost blanked-out zero $\boxed{50}$. Finally, the last stanza $\boxed{\text{53-56}}$ takes care of the sign character. If the number is negative but its first digit is already occupying the leftmost digit position, then the conversion fails and BTD returns $\boxed{53}$ with RC still set $\boxed{31}$ to 1. Otherwise, either the number is positive or zero and does not need a sign, or it is negative and there is room to insert a minus sign $\boxed{54}$. Only then $\boxed{55}$ is RC set to 0, to indicate success, before the routine $\boxed{56}$ returns.

18.1.2   Numerals to Integer

The inverse of BTD is DTB, listed below and on the next page.

If STRING has nonpositive length $\boxed{34}$ or is all blank $\boxed{42}$, DTB returns with RC set $\boxed{32}$ at 1 to indicate an error, and $\boxed{33}$ N=0. Otherwise the number to convert is assumed to be right-justified in STRING. The third stanza of executable code $\boxed{45\text{-}52}$ determines the sign of the number and stores it as +1 or −1 in the variable SIGN.

If the leftmost nonblank is a minus sign $\boxed{45}$, we make $\boxed{46}$ SIGN negative and $\boxed{47}$ skip over the minus sign. Otherwise the number is positive, so $\boxed{50}$ we set SIGN to +1 and if there is a plus sign $\boxed{51}$ we skip over it. If the string consists only of a sign character, this process leaves KFDGT=LS+1, in which case $\boxed{52}$ we return with RC still set $\boxed{32}$ to 1. Next $\boxed{55\text{-}65}$ the remaining characters are considered from left to right and each is compared $\boxed{58}$ to the digits stored in NUMERL. If for some character no match is found, control falls through the bottom of the DO 5 loop and the routine returns $\boxed{64}$ with RC still set $\boxed{32}$ to 1 and $\boxed{63}$ N=0.

If a digit is found, its positional value is added $\boxed{59}$ to N, which started out as zero $\boxed{33}$. Digit position LS of the input string is the ones' position, position LS-1 is the tens' position, and in general position K is the 10^{LS-K} position. If a digit matches NUMERL(L), its value is L-1, so its positional value in the number is (L-1)*10**(LS-K). The value of the number N is the sum of the positional values of the digits. If STRING contains '8', '5', '1', then LS=3, KFDGT=1, and the digits are found at L=9, L=6, and L=2, so the value of the number is computed like this.

$$N=\ \ 0+(9-1)*10**(3-1)=800$$
$$N=800+(6-1)*10**(3-2)=850$$
$$N=850+(2-1)*10**(3-3)=851$$

When the DO 4 loop is finished, N contains the absolute value of the integer corresponding to the digits in STRING. To complete the conversion, we $\boxed{68}$ multiply by SIGN, set $\boxed{69}$ RC=0 to indicate success, and $\boxed{70}$ return.

```
 1 C
 2 Code by Michael Kupferschmid
 3 C
 4       SUBROUTINE DTB(STRING,LS, N,RC)
 5 C     This routine converts the right-justified numerals in
 6 C     STRING to an integer in N (Decimal To Binary).
 7 C
 8 C     variable   meaning
 9 C     --------   -------
10 C     K          index on the characters of STRING
11 C     KFDGT      index of first digit in STRING
12 C     L          index on the digits in NUMERL
13 C     LS         the number of characters in STRING
14 C     N          the integer returned
15 C     NUMERL     the digits 0...9
16 C     RC         return code; 0 => ok, 1 => error
17 C     SIGN       sign of the number
18 C     STRING     the string of numerals to be converted
19 C
```

```
20 C      formal parameters
21        CHARACTER*1 STRING(LS)
22        INTEGER*4 RC
23 C
24 C      local variables
25        INTEGER*4 SIGN
26        CHARACTER*1 NUMERL(10)/'0','1','2','3','4',
27        ;                     '5','6','7','8','9'/
28 C
29 C -----------------------------------------------------------------
30 C
31 C      if the string is empty, something is wrong
32        RC=1
33        N=0
34        IF(LS.LE.0) RETURN
35 C
36 C      skip leading blanks
37        DO 1 K=1,LS
38            KFDGT=K
39            IF(STRING(K).NE.' ') GO TO 2
40      1 CONTINUE
41 C      the string is all blanks
42        RETURN
43 C
44 C      determine the sign and the index of the first digit
45      2 IF(STRING(KFDGT).EQ.'-') THEN
46          SIGN=-1
47          KFDGT=KFDGT+1
48          GO TO 3
49        ENDIF
50        SIGN=+1
51        IF(STRING(KFDGT).EQ.'+') KFDGT=KFDGT+1
52      3 IF(KFDGT.GT.LS) RETURN
53 C
54 C      examine the digits and construct the value of the number
55        DO 4 K=KFDGT,LS
56 C          add in the positional value of the digit
57            DO 5 L=1,10
58                IF(STRING(K).NE.NUMERL(L)) GO TO 5
59                N=N+(L-1)*10**(LS-K)
60                GO TO 4
61      5      CONTINUE
62 C          the character is not a digit
63            N=0
64            RETURN
65      4 CONTINUE
66 C
67 C      give the value the correct sign
68        N=SIGN*N
69        RC=0
70        RETURN
71        END
```

18.2 String Insertions

Sometimes in constructing a character string it is convenient to begin with a **template**
containing text that does not change from one use to another, and insert the text that
varies into the template or a copy. The varying text is most often the numerals of an
integer, or another string.

18.2.1 Inserting an Integer Into a String

In each of the examples in §10.4, all that was required to finish an object-time format was
to insert the numerals of an integer whose size was known in advance. That would be easy
to do with BTD, now that we have that routine. Often, though, the task of inserting the
numerals of an integer into a string is more complicated because we don't know how many
digits there will be. Then it is necessary to leave space in the template for the largest
possible value, and to remove any extra blanks that remain after the value is inserted. The
INTINS routine, which is listed below and on the next page, uses BTD to translate an integer
to numerals, optionally adjusts the spacing of the string, and finds the length of the result.

```
1 C
2 Code by Michael Kupferschmid
3 C
4         SUBROUTINE INTINS(STRING,LS,INT,LOC,JOB, RESULT,LR)
5 C     This routine inserts the numerals corresponding to the
6 C     integer INT in STRING, starting at location LOC.
7 C
8 C     JOB  spacing
9 C     ---  -------
10 C     0    leave spacing unchanged
11 C     1    leave 1 blank at the beginning of the inserted number
12 C     2    leave no blanks at the beginning of the inserted number
13 C     3    provide leading sign and zeros
14 C
15 C     variable  meaning
16 C     --------  -------
17 C     BTD       routine converts an integer to numerals
18 C     INT       the integer to be inserted
19 C     JOB       what to do about spacing; see table above
20 C     K         index on the characters of RESULT
21 C     KEND      last character to zero out
22 C     LENGTH    function returns index of last nonblank in a string
23 C     LINT      number of character positions for the integer
24 C     LOC       location in STRING where INT is to be inserted
25 C     LR        index of the last nonblank in RESULT
26 C     LS        number of characters in STRING
27 C     MINO      Fortran function returns smaller of INTEGER*4s
28 C     RESULT    result string
29 C     RC        return code from BTD; nonzero => error
30 C     SHIFTL    routine removes leading blanks from a string
31 C     STRING    the character string in which INT is to be inserted
32 C
```

```
33        CHARACTER*1 STRING(LS),RESULT(*)
34        INTEGER*4 RC
35 C
36 C  ----------------------------------------------------------------
37 C
38 C    can't insert into an empty string
39        IF(LS.LE.0) THEN
40           LR=0
41           RETURN
42        ENDIF
43 C
44 C    copy the template into the result
45        DO 1 K=1,LS
46              RESULT(K)=STRING(K)
47      1 CONTINUE
48        LR=LS
49 C
50 C    can't insert outside the string
51        IF(LOC.LE.0 .OR. LOC.GT.LS) RETURN
52 C
53 C    insert the integer, if it will fit
54        LINT=MIN0(11,LS-LOC+1)
55        CALL BTD(INT, RESULT(LOC),LINT,RC)
56 C
57 C    if the integer wouldn't fit, put stars
58        IF(RC.NE.0) THEN
59           DO 2 K=LOC,LOC+LINT-1
60              RESULT(K)='*'
61      2      CONTINUE
62        ENDIF
63 C
64 C    do the requested spacing
65        IF(JOB.EQ.1 .AND. LOC.LT.LS) CALL SHIFTL(RESULT(LOC+1),LS-LOC)
66        IF(JOB.EQ.2 .AND. LOC.LE.LS) CALL SHIFTL(RESULT(LOC),LS-LOC+1)
67        IF(JOB.EQ.3) THEN
68           DO 3 K=LOC+LINT-1,LOC,-1
69              KEND=K
70              IF(RESULT(K).EQ.'-') THEN
71                 RESULT(LOC)='-'
72                 GO TO 4
73              ENDIF
74              IF(RESULT(K).EQ.' ') THEN
75                 RESULT(LOC)='+'
76                 GO TO 4
77              ENDIF
78      3      CONTINUE
79      4      IF(KEND.EQ.LOC) GO TO 5
80           DO 6 K=LOC+1,KEND
81              RESULT(K)='0'
82      6      CONTINUE
83        ENDIF
84      5 LR=LENGTH(RESULT,LS)
85        RETURN
86        END
```

INTINS also handles errors in the number conversion by filling the field with stars, just as the FORTRAN I/O library does when an integer won't fit in an output field.

The first stanza of executable code $\boxed{\text{39-42}}$ returns with the result length LR=0 if the template string length LS is not positive. If LS is positive, the second stanza $\boxed{\text{45-48}}$ copies the template STRING into the output RESULT, so that STRING itself will not be changed (of course, the caller could pass the same variable for both STRING and RESULT if it is not important for the template to be preserved). The third stanza $\boxed{\text{51}}$ returns if the location at which the integer is to be inserted is outside the template.

Then comes $\boxed{\text{54-55}}$ the conversion of the integer INT to numerals, which will be stored starting at location LOC in RESULT. As you might recall from §4.1, the largest positive INTEGER*4 has 10 decimal digits, so 11 spaces are enough for the digits and sign of any possible value that might be in INT. On the other hand, if the field starts at LOC and STRING is a vector of LS characters, then there is room in RESULT for only LS-LOC+1 characters. So LINT, the number of spaces that BTD is permitted to use for the numerals, is taken $\boxed{\text{54}}$ to be the smaller of 11 and the number of spaces that are left. If $\boxed{\text{58}}$ the return code RC from BTD is nonzero, indicating that the number wouldn't fit in the allowed space, then the DO 2 loop $\boxed{\text{59-61}}$ fills the field with stars. Finally, RESULT is adjusted $\boxed{\text{65-83}}$ to format the output string according to the value of JOB, and $\boxed{\text{84}}$ the length LR of RESULT is found before the routine $\boxed{\text{85}}$ returns.

18.2.2   Inserting One String Into Another

The STRINS routine listed below and on the next page can be used to insert one string into another. This process is quite similar to inserting an integer, and the first three stanzas of executable code $\boxed{\text{35-38}}$ $\boxed{\text{41-44}}$ $\boxed{\text{47}}$ are in fact identical to those of INTINS.

```
 1 C
 2 Code by Michael Kupferschmid
 3 C
 4       SUBROUTINE STRINS(STRING,LS,INSERT,LIIN,LOC,JOB, RESULT,LR)
 5 C     This routine inserts one string in another.
 6 C
 7 C     JOB  spacing
 8 C     ---  -------
 9 C      0   leave spacing unchanged
10 C      1   leave one blank at the end of the insert
11 C      2   leave no blanks at the end of the insert
12 C
13 C     variable  meaning
14 C     --------  -------
15 C     INSERT    string to be inserted
16 C     JOB       what to do about spacing; see table above
17 C     K         index on the characters of a string
18 C     L         index in RESULT of rightmost unshifted character
19 C     LENGTH    function returns index of last nonblank in a string
```

```
20 C      LI         number of characters used from INSERT
21 C      LIIN       number of characters provided in INSERT
22 C      LOC        where in STRING to insert INSERT
23 C      LR         index of the last nonblank in RESULT
24 C      LS         number of characters in STRING
25 C      MINO       Fortran function gives smaller of INTEGER*4s
26 C      RESULT     result string
27 C      SHIFTL     routine removes leading blanks from a string
28 C      STRING     template string
29 C
30        CHARACTER*1 STRING(LS),INSERT(LIIN),RESULT(*)
31 C
32 C ------------------------------------------------------------------
33 C
34 C      can't insert if there is no template
35        IF(LS.LE.0) THEN
36           LR=0
37           RETURN
38        ENDIF
39 C
40 C      copy the template into the result
41        DO 1 K=1,LS
42             RESULT(K)=STRING(K)
43      1 CONTINUE
44        LR=LS
45 C
46 C      can't insert outside the template
47        IF(LOC.LE.0 .OR. LOC.GT.LS) RETURN
48 C
49 C      insert as much of the insertion as will fit, starting at LOC
50        LI=MINO(LIIN,LS-LOC+1)
51        IF(LI.LE.0) RETURN
52        DO 2 K=1,LI
53             RESULT(LOC+K-1)=INSERT(K)
54      2 CONTINUE
55 C
56 C      do the requested spacing
57        IF(JOB.NE.1 .AND. JOB.NE.2) GO TO 3
58        L=LOC+LI-(JOB-1)
59        IF(LS.GT.L) CALL SHIFTL(RESULT(L+1),LS-L)
60      3 LR=LENGTH(RESULT,LS)
61        RETURN
62        END
```

The number LI of characters that can be inserted is 50 the smaller of the number provided, LIIN, and the spaces available, LS-LOC+1. The check 47 assures LS-LOC+1 will be at least 1, but a mistake in calling might make LIIN non-positive, so we verify 51 that LI is positive before 52-54 copying the insert into the template copy. If the target field is too small to hold the entire insertion, STRINS inserts as many characters as will fit. The result spacing here 57-59 affects blanks *following* the inserted string, whereas that in INTINS affected blanks *preceding* the inserted integer.

18.3 Attaching a File

Several times now I have recommended using the subroutine GETFIL to attach a UNIX™ file to a FORTRAN logical I/O unit. Recall from §9.4.2 that GETFIL has the following calling sequence.

CALL GETFIL(WATFOR,LW,SUGNAM,LS,NUNIT,ACCESS)		
WATFOR	string	what the file will be used for
LW	INTEGER*4	number of characters in WATFOR
SUGNAM	string	suggested filename, if any
LS	INTEGER*4	number of characters in SUGNAM
NUNIT	INTEGER*4	unit number of logical unit to be attached
ACCESS	INTEGER*4	1 for read, 2 for write, 3 for both

As illustrated there, GETFIL prompts the user for a filename, perhaps suggesting a default, and uses OPEN to attach the file to unit NUNIT. If the user names a file that cannot be attached, or if the file is to be read but contains nothing, GETFIL prompts again; if the file is to be written but already contains something, GETFIL asks permission to empty the file.

Although I did not mention it in §9.4.2, GETFIL also allows units to be assigned on the command line that is used to run the program. For example, if a program whose executable is named bigprog uses GETFIL to attach a file to unit 3, then invoking the program with the UNIX™ command

```
[119] bigprog 3=data5
```

attaches the file data5 to unit 3. This allows bigprog to be run as a batch program, where user interaction is impossible, or inside a UNIX™ shell script that generates the filename. If no command-line unit assignment is found, GETFIL assumes the program is being run interactively and prompts as usual.

The code of GETFIL begins with a long preamble. The CHARACTER*1 vectors PAR $\boxed{63}$ and FILNAM $\boxed{69}$ hold strings that will also appear in contexts where they must be referred to as CHARACTER*n scalars, so EQUIVALENCE statements are used $\boxed{64}$ to overlay PAR on ARG and $\boxed{71}$ to overlay FILNAM on LONGNM. The variables FNPRT $\boxed{68}$, QUEST $\boxed{75\text{-}81}$, EROR1 $\boxed{86\text{-}91}$, and EROR2 $\boxed{92\text{-}97}$ are templates containing the fixed parts of character strings that will be completed later. The dimensions of these strings are chosen so the prompt, the trailing blank that PROMPT adds, the filename response, and the typing cursor _ all fit in a UNIX™ window 80 columns wide. (This choice is arbitrary, but some definite value must be assumed.) To leave room for the added blank and the typing cursor, FNPR $\boxed{69}$ and its template FNPRT $\boxed{68}$ are 78 characters long. A typical prompt from GETFIL looks like this.

```
Name of plotter file [plotfile]: _
```

Here WATFOR contains plotter, having LW=7, and SUGNAM contains plotfile, with LS=8. Now consider an 80-character prompt line having LW=LS=0.

```
Name of file: fffffffffffffffffffffffffffffffffffffffffffffffffffffffffffffffff_
```

This leaves the maximum possible space for the filename, shown here as a string of f's. There are 65 of them, so that is the dimension $\boxed{69}$ of FILNAM. A command-line unit assignment is the filename plus two or three characters, so PAR is dimensioned $\boxed{63}$ for 68 characters.

```
 1 C
 2 Code by Michael Kupferschmid
 3 C
 4        SUBROUTINE GETFIL(WATFOR,LWIN,SUGNAM,LSIN,NUNIT,ACCESS)
 5 C    This routine attaches a file to a given unit.
 6 C
 7 C    ACCESS   operations to be performed
 8 C    ------   --------------------------
 9 C      1      read
10 C      2      write
11 C      3      read and write
12 C
13 C    variable   meaning
14 C    --------   -------
15 C    ACCESS     access required to the file; see above
16 C    ARG        a command-line token as a CHARACTER*68
17 C    DTB        routine converts numerals to an integer
18 C    EROR       error message text written out
19 C    EROR1      "The file ? is to be read, but it does not exist."
20 C    EROR2      "The file ? cannot be opened; IOSTAT=?."
21 C    FILNAM     name of the file to open
22 C    FNPR       filename prompt string written out
23 C    FNPRT      filename prompt string template
24 C    GETARG     system routine gets a given command-line token
25 C    IARGC      system function returns # of command-line tokens
26 C    INTINS     routine inserts an integer in a character string
27 C    IPAR       index on the command-line tokens
28 C    K          index on the characters of a string
29 C    LE         finished length of EROR
30 C    LENGTH     function returns index of last nonblank in a string
31 C    LF         number of characters in FILNAM
32 C    LN         number of characters in a command-line unit number
33 C    LONGNM     FILNAM as a CHARACTER*65
34 C    LP         finished length of FNPR
35 C    LQ         finished length of QUES
36 C    LS         number of characters of SUGNAM actually used
37 C    LSIN       number of characters in SUGNAM
38 C    LW         number of characters of WATFOR actually used
39 C    LWIN       number of characters in WATFOR
40 C    MAXO       Fortran function gives larger of INTEGER*4s
41 C    N          a unit number assigned on the command line
42 C    NPAR       number of tokens appearing on the command line
43 C    NUNIT      unit number to assign
44 C    OK         T => unit is already assigned or file exists
45 C    PAR        a command-line token as a vector of CHARACTER*1s
46 C    PROMPT     routine prompts for input from the terminal
47 C    QUERY      function asks a yes-or-no question
48 C    QUES       question text written out
49 C    QUEST      "The file ? is to be written, but it exists; ok?"
50 C    RC         return code from DTB or OPEN
51 C    SHIFTL     routine removes leading blanks from a string
52 C    STRINS     routine inserts a string in a template
53 C    SUGNAM     suggested or default filename
54 C    UNLINK     system routine destroys a file
55 C    WATFOR     string telling what the file is to be used for
```

```
56 C
57 C      formal parameters
58        CHARACTER*1 WATFOR(LWIN),SUGNAM(LSIN)
59        INTEGER*4 ACCESS
60 C
61 C      prepare to check for command-line unit assignments
62        CHARACTER*68 ARG
63        CHARACTER*1 PAR(68)
64        EQUIVALENCE(ARG,PAR)
65        INTEGER*4 RC
66 C
67 C      prepare to prompt for and read a filename
68        CHARACTER*1 FNPRT(78)/'N','a','m','e',' ','o','f',' ',70*' '/
69        CHARACTER*1 FNPR(78),FILNAM(65)
70        CHARACTER*65 LONGNM
71        EQUIVALENCE(FILNAM,LONGNM)
72 C
73 C      prepare to ask about emptying a file to be written
74        CHARACTER*1 QUES(113)
75        CHARACTER*1 QUEST(113)/'T','h','e',' ','f','i','l','e',' ',
76       ;                        '"', 65*' ','"',' ',
77       ;                        'i','s',' ','t','o',' ','b','e',' ',
78       ;                        'w','r','i','t','t','e','n',',',' ',
79       ;                        'b','u','t',' ','i','t',' ',
80       ;                        'e','x','i','s','t','s',';',' ',
81       ;                        'o','k','?'/
82        LOGICAL*4 OK,QUERY
83 C
84 C      prepare to report errors
85        CHARACTER*1 EROR(114)
86        CHARACTER*1 EROR1(114)/'T','h','e',' ','f','i','l','e',' ',
87       ;                        '"',65*' ','"',' ',
88       ;                        'i','s',' ','t','o',' ','b','e',' ',
89       ;                        'r','e','a','d',',',' ','b','u','t',' ',
90       ;                        'i','t',' ','d','o','e','s',' ',
91       ;                        'n','o','t',' ','e','x','i','s','t','.'/
92        CHARACTER*1 EROR2(114)/'T','h','e',' ','f','i','l','e',' ',
93       ;                        '"',65*' ','"',' ',
94       ;                        'c','a','n','n','o','t',' ','b','e',' ',
95       ;                        'o','p','e','n','e','d',';',' ',
96       ;                        'I','O','S','T','A','T','=',
97       ;                        11*' ','.'/
98 C
99 C ------------------------------------------------------------------
```

The executable statements begin with some sanity checks. As I mentioned in §9, legal FORTRAN logical I/O unit numbers are in the range 0, . . . , 99 and units 0, 5, and 6 should remain permanently assigned in UNIX™ to standard-error, standard-in, and standard-out respectively. If NUNIT is a legal unit number for attaching to a file with OPEN, the test [102-103] in the first stanza transfers control to statement 1. Otherwise, GETFIL writes an error message [104-105] and [106] stops the program. If the unit number is legal, the second stanza uses [109] the INQUIRE statement of §14.2.2 to find out whether the unit is already attached (by an OPEN somewhere else in the program, or by a previous call to GETFIL). If it is, GETFIL just [110] returns.

```
100 C
101 C      check for a sensible unit number
102        IF(NUNIT.GE.0 .AND. NUNIT.LE.99 .AND.
103      ;    NUNIT.NE.0 .AND. NUNIT.NE.5 .AND. NUNIT.NE.6) GO TO 1
104        WRITE(0,991) NUNIT
105    991 FORMAT('In GETFIL, bad unit number',I11,'; stopping.')
106        STOP
107 C
108 C      see if the unit is already attached
109      1 INQUIRE(UNIT=NUNIT,OPENED=OK)
110        IF(OK) RETURN
111 C
112 C      check for a sensible access code
113        IF(ACCESS.EQ.1 .OR. ACCESS.EQ.2 .OR. ACCESS.EQ.3) GO TO 2
114        WRITE(0,992) ACCESS
115    992 FORMAT('In GETFIL, bad access code',I11,'; stopping.')
116        STOP
117 C
118 C      find actual input string lengths
119      2 LW=MAX0(0,LWIN)
120        LW=LENGTH(WATFOR,LW)
121        LS=MAX0(0,LSIN)
122        LS=LENGTH(SUGNAM,LS)
123 C
124 C      decide how the words will fit into the prompt string
125        IF(LW.GT.0 .AND. LS.GT.0 .AND. LW+LS.GT.61) LS=0
126        IF(LW.EQ.0 .AND. LS.GT.0 .AND.      LS.GT.62) LS=0
127        IF(LW.GT.0 .AND. LS.EQ.0 .AND. LW   .GT.63) LW=63
```

If the unit number is legal and the unit is not already attached, the third stanza checks 113-116 that ACCESS has a recognizable value.

The stanza beginning with statement 2 ensures that the values used for LW and LS make sense. If a negative value is passed for LWIN or LSIN by mistake, zero is used instead. The input strings WATFOR and SUGNAM might have trailing blanks, so LENGTH is used to find their true lengths.

Next we construct the prompt, starting with the template 68 in FNPRT. To decide whether WATFOR and SUGNAM will both fit, it is necessary to consider some other pathological examples of 80-character prompt lines.

```
Name of wwwwwwwwwwwwwwwwwwwwwwwwwwwwwwwwwwwwwww file [sssssssssssssssssssss]: _
Name of file [ssssssssssssssssssssssssssssssssssssssssssssssssssssssssssssssss]: _
Name of wwwwwwwwwwwwwwwwwwwwwwwwwwwwwwwwwwwwwwwwwwwwwwwwwwwwwwwwwwwwwwwww file: f_
```

In the first of these lines both a description and a suggested name are given, so a total of 19 characters are used up for the fixed words, spaces, punctuation, and the cursor. That leaves 61 characters that can be divided between WATFOR and SUGNAM. The second line includes only a suggested name, and counting the s's shows that LS can't be more than 62 in this case. In the last line LS=0 so no default name is suggested and a filename response f at least one character long must be given; typing that character leaves the cursor in column 80, as shown. We can count the w's to determine that LW must not exceed 63 in this case.

These limits are enforced by the tests of 125-127. If WATFOR and SUGNAM won't both fit, GETFIL omits the suggested name altogether rather than including only part of it or decreasing the amount of WATFOR that is used.

```
128 C
129 C      construct the prompt string
130 C        what the file is for
131         CALL STRINS(FNPRT,78,WATFOR,LW,9,0, FNPR,LP)
132 C
133 C        the word " file"
134         CALL STRINS(FNPR,78,' file',5,LP+1,0, FNPR,LP)
135 C
136 C        the suggested filename, in square brackets
137         IF(LS.LE.0) GO TO 3
138         CALL STRINS(FNPR,78,' [',2,LP+1,0, FNPR,LP)
139         CALL STRINS(FNPR,78,SUGNAM,LS,LP+1,0, FNPR,LP)
140         CALL STRINS(FNPR,78,']',1,LP+1,0, FNPR,LP)
141 C
142 C        the colon
143      3  CALL STRINS(FNPR,78,':',1,LP+1,0, FNPR,LP)
144 C
```

Then a sequence of STRINS calls is used to insert 131 the text from WATFOR, 134 the word ⌴file, 138 a space and left square bracket ⌴[, 139 the text from SUGNAM, 140 a right square bracket], and 143 the colon :. If there is no suggested filename, 137, that stanza is skipped. Notice that the first STRINS call receives the template FNPRT but returns its result in FNPR; the subsequent calls all operate on that copy.

Next we check for a command-line assignment of unit NUNIT. The UNIX™ system routine IARGC returns 146 the number NPAR of command-line parameters; if 147 there are none we skip this processing.

```
145 C      check for command-line parameters
146         NPAR=IARGC()
147         IF(NPAR.EQ.0) GO TO 4
148 C
149 C      examine each in search of an assignment like "3=fyle"
150         DO 5 IPAR=1,NPAR
151 C          get the text of this command-line parameter
152           CALL GETARG(IPAR,ARG)
153 C
154 C          look for an = in column 2 or 3
155           LN=0
156           IF(PAR(2).EQ.'=') LN=1
157           IF(PAR(3).EQ.'=') LN=2
158           IF(LN.EQ.0) GO TO 5
159 C
160 C          convert the numerals to an integer
161           CALL DTB(PAR,LN, N,RC)
162           IF(RC.NE.0) GO TO 5
163 C
164 C          is this assignment the one we are looking for?
165           IF(N.NE.NUNIT) GO TO 5
166           DO 6 K=1,65
167               FILNAM(K)=PAR(LN+1+K)
168      6      CONTINUE
169           GO TO 7
170      5 CONTINUE
```

The DO 5 loop uses $\boxed{152}$ the UNIX™ system routine GETARG to put the text of each command-line parameter in ARG. As mentioned in §10.6, some versions of UNIX™ require that the CHARACTER*n form be used for string arguments of system routines; ARG is $\boxed{64}$ overlaid on PAR so that we can refer to the characters of ARG as elements of PAR. Unit numbers have either one or two digits, so if PAR is a legal unit assignment its second or third character must be =. If this is true, we try $\boxed{161}$ to convert the numerals of the unit number to an integer. If $\boxed{162}$ the conversion fails, this must not be a unit assignment. If the conversion succeeds, the unit assignment we have found might $\boxed{165}$ be for a unit other than NUNIT, but if it is the one we were looking for the filename it contains is $\boxed{166\text{-}168}$ copied into FILNAM. In that case, we $\boxed{169}$ branch to statement 7 without examining any further command-line parameters.

If there are no command-line parameters, or if the unit assignment is not found among them, control falls through to statement 4.

```
171 C
172 C      prompt for and read the filename to try
173    4 CALL PROMPT(FNPR,LP)
174      READ(5,900,END=9) FILNAM
175  900 FORMAT(65A1)
176      GO TO 10
177 C      end-of-file means the user wants to quit
178    9 STOP
179 C
180 C      check for a null or blank response
181   10 CALL SHIFTL(FILNAM,65)
182      IF(FILNAM(1).NE.' ') GO TO 7
183 C
184 C      zero-length line; use suggested name if one was given
185      IF(LS.EQ.0) GO TO 4
186      DO 11 K=1,LS
187          FILNAM(K)=SUGNAM(K)
188   11 CONTINUE
189 C
190 C      see if the named file already exists
191    7 LF=LENGTH(FILNAM,65)
192      INQUIRE(FILE=LONGNM,EXIST=OK)
193 C
```

The call $\boxed{173}$ to PROMPT writes out the prompt string FNPR that we constructed earlier, and a filename response of up to 65 characters $\boxed{175}$ is read $\boxed{174}$ from standard-in. If the user sends an end-of-file, the END=9 stops the program $\boxed{178}$. If the READ is successful, we $\boxed{181\text{-}182}$ remove any leading blanks from the filename and branch to statement 7 if the result is nonblank.

If the user's response is a string of blanks, or just ^C_R, GETFIL assumes that the suggested filename in SUGNAM is to be used. If $\boxed{185}$ there is no suggested name, then the user's response must have been a mistake so we branch back to statement 4 and repeat the prompt. If LS is not zero, we $\boxed{186\text{-}188}$ copy SUGNAM into FILNAM. Since $\boxed{126}$ LS can be no greater than 62, SUGNAM is sure to fit into FILNAM, which is dimensioned $\boxed{69}$ for 65 characters.

Now we need to check whether it makes sense to attach the file in the way specified by ACCESS. In anticipation that we might need to write an error message including the filename, we $\boxed{191}$ find its length. The INQUIRE statement $\boxed{192}$ sets OK=.TRUE. if the file already exists.

```
194 C      if the file is only to be read, it must exist
195        IF(ACCESS.NE.1 .OR. OK) GO TO 12
196        CALL STRINS(EROR1,114,FILNAM,LF,11,2, EROR,LE)
197        WRITE(0,993) (EROR(K),K=1,LE)
198    993 FORMAT(114A1)
199        GO TO 4
200 C
201 C      if the file is only to be written, maybe it shouldn't exist
202    12 IF(ACCESS.NE.2 .OR. .NOT.OK) GO TO 13
203        CALL STRINS(QUEST,113,FILNAM,LF,11,2, QUES,LQ)
204        IF(.NOT.QUERY(QUES,LQ)) GO TO 4
205        CALL UNLINK(LONGNM)
206 C
```

The next stanza checks $\boxed{195}$ whether the file exists if it is only to be read (ACCESS=1). If it does not exist, STRINS is used $\boxed{196}$ to insert the filename in the message template EROR1, and the resulting error message EROR is written $\boxed{197}$ on standard-error. Assuming the wrong filename was given (either as a command-line parameter or in response to a prompt), we branch back $\boxed{199}$ to statement 4 and repeat the prompt.

The next stanza checks whether, if the file is to be written (ACCESS=2), it does *not* already exist. If it does exist, we $\boxed{203}$ insert the filename in the template QUEST and $\boxed{204}$ use QUERY to ask whether the file can be emptied. Recall from §9.6 that UNIX™ empties an extant file before writing to it. If the reply is no, we assume the wrong filename was given and $\boxed{204}$ branch back to statement 4 to repeat the prompt. If the reply is yes, we $\boxed{205}$ use the UNIX™ system routine UNLINK to remove the file (it will be recreated momentarily).

```
207 C      attach the named file to the specified unit
208    13 OPEN(UNIT=NUNIT,FILE=LONGNM,IOSTAT=RC)
209        IF(RC.EQ.0) RETURN
210 C
211 C      the OPEN failed; report the error number and try again
212        CALL INTINS(EROR2,114,RC,103,2, EROR,LE)
213        CALL STRINS(EROR,114,FILNAM,LF,11,2, EROR,LE)
214        WRITE(0,993) (EROR(K),K=1,LE)
215        GO TO 4
216        END
```

Finally, we are ready $\boxed{208}$ to OPEN the file. If the OPEN succeeds, GETFIL returns $\boxed{209}$. Otherwise, we $\boxed{212}$ use INTINS to insert the return code from OPEN in the message template EROR2, then $\boxed{213}$ insert the filename, write $\boxed{214}$ the error message on standard-error, and $\boxed{215}$ branch back to statement 4 to prompt for another filename.

Compared to the routines listed earlier in this chapter, and according to the rule of thumb given in §12.3.2, GETFIL is about twice as long as a subprogram ideally should be. Rather than one page of preamble and one page of executable code, it has two pages of preamble and two pages of code. It would not be unreasonable to try shortening this routine by moving some of its open code into subprograms, but it is not obvious how to do that using subprograms that would be general-purpose. A subprogram to search command-line parameters for a unit assignment could be called to replace the open code $\boxed{146\text{-}170}$ for doing that, but other pieces of GETFIL would have to be replaced by routines that were dedicated to this one application. Usually it is more convenient to have a library routine like GETFIL be a little long than it is to have it depend on special-purpose subprograms that only it uses (though in §18.5.4 we shall see how that is sometimes unavoidable).

18.4 Arithmetic With Two-Part Values

In some applications it is traditional for a single quantity to be measured using a combination of different units, such as feet and inches or hours and minutes. The TIMER routine of §15.1.4, whose internals we will study in §18.5, uses time measurements that are stored as seconds and microseconds (or, in §18.5.4, seconds and nanoseconds) in order to retain high precision. We will find it convenient to represent such a **two-part value** by a two-element array, and to think of a two-part value as a standard data type that can be used much like the basic data types discussed in §4.

To add or subtract two-part values we operate on the large and small units separately. For example,

```
[2 ft, 9 in] + [1 ft, 6 in] = [3 ft, 15 in]
```

Then, to express the result in a natural way we must **normalize** it so the small units represent less than one of the large units.

```
[3 ft, 15 in] = [4 ft, 3 in]
```

In many settings it is also eventually useful to express a two-part value in terms of the larger unit of measure.

```
[4 ft, 3 in] = 4.25 ft
```

Here are these calculations coded in FORTRAN. The two-part values are stored in arrays A, B, and C.

```
      INTEGER*4 A(2)/2,9/                 INTEGER*4 A(2)/2,9/
      INTEGER*4 B(2)/1,6/                 INTEGER*4 B(2)/1,6/
      INTEGER*4 C(2)                      INTEGER*4 C(2)
C                                         REAL*8 TPV2R8
C     add                           C
      C(1)=A(1)+B(1)                C     add and normalize
      C(2)=A(2)+B(2)                      CALL TPVADD(A,B,12, C)
C                                   C
C     normalize                           PRINT *,C,TPV2R8(C,12)
    1 IF(C(2).GT.12) THEN                 STOP
         C(2)=C(2)-12                     END
         C(1)=C(1)+1
         GO TO 1
      ENDIF
C
      PRINT *,C,DFLOAT(C(1))+DFLOAT(C(2))/12.
      STOP
      END
```

The program on the right invokes the subprograms TPVADD and TPV2R8 to achieve the same result as the open code on the left. These and several related routines are presented next. All of these subprograms use L to represent the number of small units per big unit (12 in/ft, in this example).

18.4.1 Addition and Subtraction

TPVADD is listed below. It begins ⟨20-21⟩ by normalizing the quantities to be added, in case one or both of them is unnormalized and happens to have a small part large enough so that a fixed-point overflow would occur when the two small parts are added together. TPVNML, which is described in §18.4.2, normalizes a two-part value in-place. After the prenormalization, TPVADD sums the big parts ⟨24⟩ and the small parts ⟨25⟩ separately. This process might result in the small part of SUM representing more than one unit of the big part, so TPVNML is used again ⟨28⟩ to normalize SUM.

```
 1 C
 2 Code by Michael Kupferschmid
 3 C
 4       SUBROUTINE TPVADD(A,B,L, SUM)
 5 C     This routine adds the two-part values in A and B to form SUM.
 6 C
 7 C     variable  meaning
 8 C     --------  -------
 9 C     A         the first value
10 C     B         the second value
11 C     L         number of small things in a big one
12 C     SUM       A+B
13 C     TPVNML    routine normalizes a two-part value
14 C
15       INTEGER*4 A(2),B(2),SUM(2)
16 C
17 C ----------------------------------------------------------------
18 C
19 C     normalize to guard against overflow in the smalls
20       CALL TPVNML(A,L)
21       CALL TPVNML(B,L)
22 C
23 C     add the pieces
24       SUM(1)=A(1)+B(1)
25       SUM(2)=A(2)+B(2)
26 C
27 C     normalize the result
28       CALL TPVNML(SUM,L)
29       RETURN
30       END
```

TPVSUB, listed on the next page, looks and works very much like TPVADD. Our earlier example involved positive numbers of feet and inches, but two-part values can be negative or have big and small parts that differ in sign. Thus, for example, TPVSUB might find ⟨24-25⟩ a DIFF of

```
[5 ft, 1 in] - [2 ft, 4 in] = [3 ft, -3 in]
```

which the final call ⟨28⟩ to TPVNML normalizes to [2 ft, 9 in].

```
 1 C
 2 Code by Michael Kupferschmid
 3 C
 4        SUBROUTINE TPVSUB(A,B,L, DIFF)
 5 C     This routine finds DIFF=A-B.
 6 C
 7 C     variable  meaning
 8 C     --------  -------
 9 C     A         the minuend two-part value
10 C     B         the subtrahend two-part value
11 C     DIFF      the difference two-part value A-B
12 C     L         number of small things in a big one
13 C     TPVNML    routine normalizes a two-part value
14 C
15        INTEGER*4 A(2),B(2),DIFF(2)
16 C
17 C -----------------------------------------------------------------
18 C
19 C     normalize to guard against overflow in the smalls
20        CALL TPVNML(A,L)
21        CALL TPVNML(B,L)
22 C
23 C     subtract
24        DIFF(1)=A(1)-B(1)
25        DIFF(2)=A(2)-B(2)
26 C
27 C     normalize the result
28        CALL TPVNML(DIFF,L)
29        RETURN
30        END
```

18.4.2   Normalization

```
1 C
2 Code by Michael Kupferschmid
3 C
4         SUBROUTINE TPVNML(TPV,L)
5 C       This routine normalizes the two-part value TPV.
6 C
7 C       variable  meaning
8 C       --------  -------
9 C       BIGS      number of big things among the smalls
10 C      L         number of small things in a big one
11 C      SMALLS    number of small things moved to the BIGS slot
12 C      TPV       the two-part value to be normalized
13 C
14         INTEGER*4 TPV(2),BIGS,SMALLS
15 C
16 C ----------------------------------------------------------------
17 C
18 C       move L's of SMALLs from the SMALLS slot to the BIGS slot
19         BIGS=TPV(2)/L
20         TPV(1)=TPV(1)+BIGS
21         SMALLS=L*BIGS
22         TPV(2)=TPV(2)-SMALLS
23 C
24 C       make the signs the same
25         IF(TPV(1).GT.0 .AND. TPV(2).LT.0) THEN
26            TPV(1)=TPV(1)-1
27            TPV(2)=TPV(2)+L
28         ENDIF
29         IF(TPV(1).LT.0 .AND. TPV(2).GT.0) THEN
30            TPV(1)=TPV(1)+1
31            TPV(2)=TPV(2)-L
32         ENDIF
33         RETURN
34         END
```

In the open code of the introductory example we normalized a [ft, in] value by repeatedly subtracting 12 inches from the number of inches and adding 1 to the number of feet, until the number of inches remaining was less than 12. TPVNML, listed above, instead uses integer division to figure out how many big units are contained in the small part of the two-part value. Starting with TPV=[3 ft, 15 in] and L=12 in/ft, TPVNML would compute `19` BIGS=15/12, finding that 1 foot's worth of inches, or `21` SMALLS=12*1 inches, need to be moved from the inches part to the feet part. This strategy works no matter what signs the big and small parts of TPV have. For an example involving mixed signs, suppose TPV=[3 ft, -27 in]. Then BIGS=-27/12=-2 and SMALLS=12*(-2)=-24, yielding [1 ft, -3 in]. By considering some examples having other sign patterns it is easy to see that the first stanza of this routine always yields a small part whose absolute value is less than L. A normalized value should have both signs the same, so the routine ends with some code `25-32` to ensure that the small part has the same sign as the big part. Because of the adjustments already made by the first stanza, if the small part differs in sign from the big part, the sign of the small part can always be corrected by moving exactly one big unit one way or the other.

18.4.3 Conversion To and From REAL*8

TPV2R8, listed below, converts a two-part value to a REAL*8 value having the units of the big part (feet, in the examples we have been using).

```
 1 C
 2 Code by Michael Kupferschmid
 3 C
 4       FUNCTION TPV2R8(TPV,L)
 5 C     This routine returns the REAL*8 value corresponding to TPV.
 6 C
 7 C     variable  meaning
 8 C     --------  -------
 9 C     DFLOAT    Fortran function gives REAL*8 for INTEGER*4
10 C     L         number of small things in a big one
11 C     TPV       the two-part value to be converted to REAL*8
12 C
13       REAL*8 TPV2R8
14       INTEGER*4 TPV(2)
15 C
16 C ----------------------------------------------------------------
17 C
18       TPV2R8=DFLOAT(TPV(1)) + DFLOAT(TPV(2))/DFLOAT(L)
19       RETURN
20       END
```

The calculation is done by the single assignment statement $\boxed{18}$, which floats the big part and then adds in the number (a fraction less than one, if TPV is normalized) of big parts in the small part. This routine is so tiny that it might seem easier to just write the formula in-line as open code wherever it is needed. However, making it a function relieves us of having to figure out the formula each time, supplies a routine name that we can describe in the variable list of the routine where it is used, and makes it convenient to form expressions like TPV2R8(X,L)*TPV2R8(Y,L)/TPV2R8(Z,L), which would be long and clumsy written as open code.

R82TPV, listed on the next page, is only slightly more complicated. It begins $\boxed{24}$ by putting the whole-number part of R in TPV(1), the big part of the two-part value. The fractional part of R is then R-DFLOAT(TPV(1)), and to express this in terms of the small units we $\boxed{27}$ multiply by the number of small units per big one.

The resulting number T of small units needed to represent the fractional part of R is probably itself not a whole number, so we must round it up or down to the nearest whole number of small parts. To see how the rounding works, first suppose that R=37.48D0 ft and L=12 in/ft. Then TPV(1)=37 ft, T=12.D0*(37.48D0-37.D0)=5.76 in, and rounding to the nearest inch we should get TPV(2)=6 in. As I mentioned in §4.4, a positive real value can be rounded to the nearest whole number by adding 0.5 and truncating. Because T is positive, the code $\boxed{28}$ does this, finding 5.76+0.5=6.26 and chopping off the fraction. Now suppose that R=-41.83D0 ft. Then TPV(1)=-41 ft, the fractional part is T=12.D0*(-41.83D0-(-41.D0))=-9.96 in, and rounding to the nearest inch we should get TPV(2)=-10 in. Because T is negative, rounding to the nearest whole number is accomplished $\boxed{29}$ by *subtracting* 0.5, to get -9.96-0.5=-10.46, and truncating. The normalization $\boxed{30}$ is necessary because roundoff errors in the floating-point arithmetic can result in TPV(2) being equal to L.

```
 1 C
 2 Code by Michael Kupferschmid
 3 C
 4       SUBROUTINE R82TPV(R,TPV,L)
 5 C     This routine returns the two-part value corresponding to R.
 6 C
 7 C     variable  meaning
 8 C     --------  -------
 9 C     DFLOAT    Fortran function gives REAL*8 for INTEGER*4
10 C     IFIX      Fortran function gives INTEGER*4 for REAL*4
11 C     L         number of small things in a big one
12 C     R         the REAL*8 value to be converted to two-part value
13 C     SNGL      Fortran function gives REAL*4 for REAL*8
14 C     T         fractional part as a REAL*8
15 C     TPV       the result two-part value
16 C     TPVNML    routine normalizes a two-part value
17 C
18       REAL*8 R,T
19       INTEGER*4 TPV(2)
20 C
21 C ------------------------------------------------------------------
22 C
23 C     put the whole-number part of R in TPV(1)
24       TPV(1)=IFIX(SNGL(R))
25 C
26 C     put the fraction in TPV(2)
27       T=DFLOAT(L)*(R-DFLOAT(TPV(1)))
28       IF(T.GE.0.D0) TPV(2)=IFIX(SNGL(T)+0.5)
29       IF(T.LT.0.D0) TPV(2)=IFIX(SNGL(T)-0.5)
30       CALL TPVNML(TPV,L)
31       RETURN
32       END
```

18.4.4 Scaling

The final operation that we will consider is multiplication of a two-part value by a real scalar. TPVSCL, listed below, uses $\boxed{22}$ TPV2R8 to convert TPV to a REAL*8, multiplies by S, and then $\boxed{25}$ uses R82TPV to convert the result T back to a two-part value in TPV.

```
 1 C
 2 Code by Michael Kupferschmid
 3 C
 4       SUBROUTINE TPVSCL(TPV,L,S)
 5 C     This routine scales the two-part value TPV by factor S.
 6 C
 7 C     variable  meaning
 8 C     --------  -------
 9 C     L         number of small things in a big one
10 C     R82TPV    routine converts a REAL*8 to two-part value
11 C     S         the scale factor
12 C     T         the scaled value as a REAL*8
13 C     TPV       the two-part value to be scaled
14 C     TPV2R8    function gives REAL*8 for a two-part value
15 C
16       INTEGER*4 TPV(2)
17       REAL*8 S,T,TPV2R8
18 C
19 C ------------------------------------------------------------------
20 C
21 C     convert TPV to a REAL*8 and scale it
22       T=S*TPV2R8(TPV,L)
23 C
24 C     convert the result back to a two-part value
25       CALL R82TPV(T,TPV,L)
26       RETURN
27       END
```

18.5   Measuring CPU Time

As discussed in §15.1.4, TIMER is a subroutine for measuring CPU time in increments smaller than the 0.01-second resolution of most UNIX™ CPU timers. It does this by accumulating wallclock time increments, measured with 1-μs resolution, and periodically converting them to CPU time increments. To find a CPU time increment, the corresponding wallclock time increment is multiplied by the inverse of an expansion factor. The expansion factor inverse is estimated from CPU time increments greater than 0.5 second, long enough so they can be measured accurately with the UNIX™ CPU timer. The wallclock and corresponding CPU times are accumulated in timing bins, so that separate measurements can be made of different code segments in an instrumented program.

18.5.1 Algorithm

The process is outlined in the flowchart on the next page. Upon entry to the routine we get TE, the time of entry, from the 1-μs time-of-day (TOD) clock, after saving the previous value of TE in TL. TE is the wallclock time at which the flow of control came into TIMER from having been out in the code that is being timed. Immediately before exiting the routine we get TX, the time of exit, from the TOD clock. TX is the wallclock time at which the flow of control goes back out into the code being timed.

After noting TL and TE, we check the timer control code TCC for legal values, and stop with an error report if the value does not make sense in context. For example, remember that the first call to TIMER must be with TCC=-1, to request initialization.

If TCC has a legal value, we next check whether it is -1, and if so initialize the timing process. The number 2 outside the "initialize" box, like similar numbers on the flowchart, is a statement number in the source listing we will consider later. BINTOD is a vector of two-part values, one for each timing bin, in which wallclock time increments will be accumulated. BINCPU is a vector of two-part values, one for each timing bin, in which CPU time will be accumulated. Initialization zeros out the TOD and CPU bin counts, and sets the current timing bin to NONALG, the bin for non-algorithm time.

If TCC is legal but not -1, it must be 0 or the number of a new timing bin to switch to. In either case we must account the wallclock time we just spent out in the code, between the previous exit from TIMER and this entry, TE-TX, to the timing bin that was set during that interval, NBIN. This is accomplished by incrementing the two-part value BINTOD(NBIN). Similarly, the wallclock time we spent inside TIMER during the previous call is TX-TL, so we add that amount to BINTOD(MAXBIN), the bin for timing overhead.

Our strategy now calls for converting the accumulated wallclock times in all of the BINTOD bins to CPU times, using an expansion factor inverse EFINV that we calculate based on more than a half-second's CPU time lapse. So we next get the current CPU time CPU and check whether more than a half-second has elapsed since CPUOLD, the CPU time of the previous CPU count updating. If enough CPU time *has* elapsed to accurately compute a new EFINV, we do so and use EFINV to update all the bins in BINCPU. Having consumed the values in BINTOD, we reset those bins to zero. Finally, we note the wallclock and CPU times TOLD and CPUOLD of this update, to use in the testing and in finding EFINV next time. This way of computing EFINV and updating BINCPU is opportunistic, in the sense that we do it when we get the opportunity because enough CPU time was used out in the code to permit an accurate measurement. Opportunistic calculations of EFINV are desirable, because they are based on CPU time that was used out in the code by the algorithm under test. Once we have updated the CPU counts we can change to the new timing bin given by TCC, unless TCC=0; for update calls we leave the timing bin alone. Then we get TX and return.

If when we check the CPU time not enough has elapsed since the previous update to compute EFINV accurately, then we must ask whether the CPU counts need to be updated anyway. If TCC=0, this is an update call and we must bring the BINCPU values up to the moment whether we like it or not. In that case we execute a **spin loop**, a nonsense calculation that serves only to use up some CPU time in arithmetic, and repeat the test. If CPU-CPUOLD is still not greater than half a second we do it again, and so on, until the test succeeds. Then we can calculate EFINV and update BINCPU in the usual way. Spin looping is undesirable, because it adds to the timing overhead and is composed of operations that might not be representative of the algorithm code segments being timed, but it is unavoidable when the caller demands that we bring the BINCPU values up to the moment right now.

If CPU-CPUOLD is too small for an update but TCC is not zero, there is no need to update the CPU counts. In this (most usual) case, we just reset the timing bin to the new value given in TCC, get TX, and return.

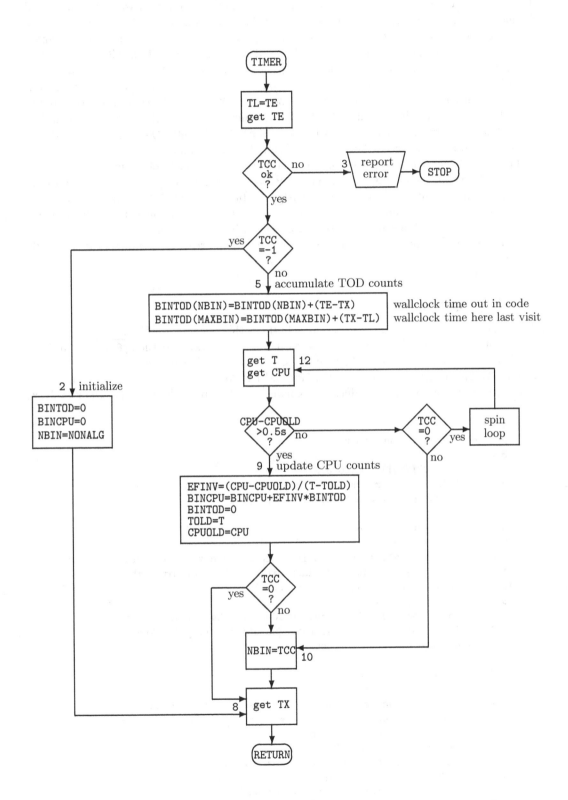

The flowchart describes the basic algorithm of TIMER in the simplest possible way, as an aid to understanding the most important ideas. For clarity it omits many little details and two significant refinements that are needed to get accurate measurements. The first refinement is that time spent out in the code should be used to estimate EFINV only if it is *algorithm* time. Nonalgorithm time typically includes operations, such as I/O, that are not representative of those in the code paths being timed, and can yield an expansion factor very different from that for algorithm code paths. If the time just spent out in the code was attributed to bin NONALG, we ignore it in finding EFINV. This means we have no EFINV to use in translating NONALG time from wallclock to CPU, so we set BINCPU(NONALG)=BINTOD(NONALG) and accumulate wallclock time rather than CPU time for bin NONALG.

The second refinement corrects for the time it takes to enter TIMER and get TE, and for the time between getting TX and arriving back out in the code. Both of these times are timing overhead, but are instead erroneously attributed to bin NBIN. We experimentally determine the average sum TOH of these times and correct its attribution by subtracting it from bin NBIN and adding it to the timing overhead in bin MAXBIN.

CPU timing, and the correction of measurement errors, are discussed further in [82, §3.6].

18.5.2   Implementation

The logic of the FORTRAN follows the flowchart, so this discussion will mostly concern the details of the coding. The preamble begins in the usual way and then $\boxed{8\text{-}16}$ reminds us about the meanings of the formal parameters. An example showing their values in a typical use of TIMER was given in §15.1.4. BINCPU and BINTOD are described in the variable list $\boxed{20\text{-}21}$ as vectors of [sec,μsec] values, as explained in the earlier discussion of the flowchart.

```
 1 C
 2 Code by Michael Kupferschmid
 3 C
 4       SUBROUTINE TIMER(TCC,STA)
 5 C     This routine measures the user-state CPU time used in
 6 C     executing different parts of a program.
 7 C
 8 C     TCC  action taken
 9 C     ---  ------------
10 C     -1   initialize; reset all bin counts and times to zero
11 C      0   update counts and times without changing bin number
12 C     >0   switch timing to bin number TCC
13 C
14 C     The parameter STA is used to identify the origin of the
15 C     TIMER call in the event that TCC has an illegal value
16 C     or some other error occurs.
17 C
18 C     variable  meaning
19 C     --------  -------
20 C     BINCPU    vector of visible [sec,usec] CPU bin counts
21 C     BINTOD    vector of accumulated [sec,usec] TOD bin counts
22 C     CPU       current CPU time
23 C     CPUOLD    previous CPU time
24 C     DBLE      Fortran function gives REAL*8 for REAL*4
25 C     DELTA     a TOD time interval
26 C     DMIN1     Fortran function gives smaller of REAL*8s
27 C     DUMMY     unused; for ETIME
```

```
28 C       EFINV     1/(expansion factor), CPU sec per TOD sec
29 C       ETIME     system routine returns coarse CPU times
30 C       GETIMEOFDAY stub to TOD clock precise to 1 microsecond
31 C       INITMX    parameter sets MAXBIN
32 C       INITOH    parameter sets TOH
33 C       J         index in spin loop
34 C       L         index on the bins
35 C       MAX0      Fortran function gives larger of INTEGER*4s
36 C       MAXBIN    highest permissible bin number
37 C       NBIN      number of bin just receiving time
38 C       NONALG    number of bin for non-algorithm time
39 C       NTMEAS    number of timing measurements made so far
40 C       OLDTCC    previous value of TCC
41 C       RESET     T => reset times used in finding EFINV
42 C       SQRT      Fortran function for square root of a REAL*4
43 C       STA       number designating CALL statement in source
44 C       T         TOD at an expansion factor determination
45 C       TARRAY    [user,system] CPU times returned by ETIME
46 C       TCC       timer control code; see table above
47 C       TE        TOD at entry to this routine
48 C       TIMING    T => timing is enabled
49 C       TL        TOD at previous entry
50 C       TOH       per-call overhead correction
51 C       TOH2      TOH(2)
52 C       TOLD      previous value of T
53 C       TOPBIN    highest bin number used so far
54 C       TPV2R8    routine converts a 2-part value to a REAL*8
55 C       TPVADD    routine adds 2-part values
56 C       TPVSCL    routine scales a 2-part value
57 C       TPVSUB    routine subtracts 2-part values
58 C       TX        TOD at exit from this routine
59 C       X         dummy variable in spin loop
60 C       ZONE      unused; for GETIMEOFDAY
61 C
62 C       formal parameters
63         INTEGER*4 TCC,STA
64 C
65 C       store timing information in common
66         PARAMETER(INITMX=22,INITOH=1)
67         COMMON /EXPT/ TIMING,NONALG,NBIN,TOPBIN,NTMEAS,TOH2,BINCPU,
68       ;               EFINV
69         LOGICAL*4 TIMING
70         INTEGER*4 TOPBIN,TOH2,BINCPU(2,INITMX)
71         REAL*8 EFINV
72 C
73 C       prepare to get CPU and TOD times
74         REAL*4 TARRAY(2)
75         REAL*8 CPU,CPUOLD
76         INTEGER*4 TE(2)/2*0/,TL(2),TX(2)/2*0/
77         INTEGER*4 T(2),TOLD(2),ZONE(2)
78 C
79 C       local variables
80         INTEGER*4 OLDTCC/-2/
81         INTEGER*4 BINTOD(2,INITMX),DELTA(2),TOH(2)
82         REAL*8 TPV2R8
83         LOGICAL*4 RESET
```

The long name ⎡30⎤ GETIMEOFDAY (with one T) belongs to a FORTRAN-callable interface to gettimeofday (with two T's), the UNIX™ system routine mentioned in §15.1.4 that returns time of day to 1-μs resolution. GETIMEOFDAY is listed and described in §18.5.3.

The declarations show that what we mean by a vector of [sec,μsec] values is a matrix with 2 rows and as many columns as there are values. It is the columns of BINCPU ⎡70⎤ and BINTOD ⎡81⎤ that store their two-part values. The number of bins is defined by the PARAMETER constant INITMX ⎡66⎤ so that it can easily be changed. INITOH ⎡66⎤ sets the experimentally-determined correction, here 1 μsec, for the entry and exit sequences of TIMER. Later, during the initialization stanza, TOH2 gets set to INITOH. TOH2 is in /EXPT/ ⎡67⎤ so that it can be reset by a calibration program that calls TIMER to measure the value that TOH2 should have (see exercise 18.8.21). OLDTCC is initialized ⎡80⎤ at compile time to −2 so that we can tell whether this is the first call to TIMER or not in the tests below for legal values of TCC.

```
 84 C
 85 C   ------------------------------------------------------------------
 86 C
 87 C        do nothing unless timing is enabled
 88          IF(.NOT.TIMING) RETURN
 89 C
 90 C        find TOD on entry so calculations here are timed separately
 91          TL(1)=TE(1)
 92          TL(2)=TE(2)
 93          CALL GETIMEOFDAY(TE,ZONE)
 94 C
 95 C        make sure that the first call is to initialize
 96          IF(OLDTCC.GE.-1) GO TO 1
 97          IF(TCC.EQ.-1) GO TO 2
 98          GO TO 3
 99 C
100 C        this is not the first call; is this an update?
101        1 IF(TCC.NE.0) GO TO 4
102          IF(OLDTCC.NE.-1) GO TO 5
103          GO TO 3
104 C
105 C        this is not an update call; if TCC repeats assume it is wrong
106        4 IF(TCC.EQ.OLDTCC) GO TO 3
107 C
108 C        here TCC should be in the range -1,1...MAXBIN
109          IF(TCC.GT.MAXBIN) GO TO 3
110          IF(TCC.GT.-1) GO TO 6
111          IF(TCC.EQ.-1) GO TO 2
112          GO TO 3
```

If timing is not enabled, TIMER returns immediately. Otherwise, we save the previous time of entry TE and get the current value. GETIMEOFDAY returns the wallclock time in the two-part value TE, and the time zone in ZONE (which we ignore). Next ⎡95-117⎤ there is some logic to ensure that TCC has a legal value in the context of the previous call, with possible branches to statements 2, 3, and 5. Statement 2 begins the initialization stanza, statement 3 begins the stanza that handles error reporting, and statement 5 begins the accumulation of TOD counts (see the flowchart). It often happens that mistakes in the instrumentation of a program result in successive calls to TIMER having the same bin number, so if that happens TIMER assumes it is an error ⎡106⎤.

```
113 C
114 C      keep track of the highest bin index used so far
115     6 IF(OLDTCC.GE.NONALG) GO TO 5
116       IF(OLDTCC.GT.TOPBIN) TOPBIN=OLDTCC
117       GO TO 5
118 C
119 C      reset bin counts and times (TCC=-1)
120     2 MAXBIN=INITMX
121       NONALG=MAXBIN-1
122       NBIN=NONALG
123       TOPBIN=0
124       NTMEAS=0
125       TOH2=INITOH
126       DO 7 L=1,MAXBIN
127           BINTOD(1,L)=0
128           BINTOD(2,L)=0
129           BINCPU(1,L)=0
130           BINCPU(2,L)=0
131     7 CONTINUE
132       OLDTCC=-1
133       GO TO 8
134 C
135 C      accumulate wallclock time for bin NBIN (TCC=0,1...MAXBIN)
136     5 CALL TPVSUB(TE,TX,1000000,DELTA)
137       TOH(1)=0
138       TOH(2)=TOH2
139       CALL TPVSUB(DELTA,TOH,1000000,DELTA)
140       DELTA(1)=MAX0(0,DELTA(1))
141       DELTA(2)=MAX0(0,DELTA(2))
142       CALL TPVADD(BINTOD(1,NBIN),DELTA,1000000,BINTOD(1,NBIN))
143       NTMEAS=NTMEAS+1
144 C
```

We keep track 116 of the highest algorithm timing bin number used so far, in TOPBIN. This information is useful in routines that process the values in BINCPU, so it is returned in /EXPT/. Next comes the initialization stanza. We first set MAXBIN, the highest permissible bin number, to INITMX, the column dimension of BINTOD and BINCPU. Bin MAXBIN will store the timing overhead. Then we set NONALG, the bin that will store nonalgorithm time, and start NBIN at that value. So far no algorithm timing bins have been used, so TOPBIN=0, and no timing measurements have yet been made so NTMEAS=0. We copy the correction for the time of a TIMER entry-and-exit into TOH2 and zero the timing bins 126-131. On the next call the previous value of TCC, OLDTCC, will be -1 132. The branch target, statement 8, is to get TX and exit (see the flowchart).

Next we find the wallclock time that was just spent out in the code, TE-TX, and attribute it to bin NBIN. TE and TX are two-part values, so 136 we find the difference DELTA using TPVSUB. Then we form the two-part correction for the time spent entering and exiting TIMER, in TOH 137-138, subtract it from TE-TX 139, and make sure the result is not negative 140-141. (If the time spent out in the code is very short, it might be slightly less than the average value we use for TOH.) Then 142 we add the resulting corrected increment to bin NBIN using TPVADD, and count the timing measurement in NTMEAS. On the next page 146-148, we find the time spent inside TIMER during the previous call, TX-TL, correct it by adding TOH, and add the result to bin MAXBIN.

```
145 C      accumulate wallclock time used making timing measurements
146        CALL TPVSUB(TX,TL,1000000,DELTA)
147        CALL TPVADD(DELTA,TOH,1000000,DELTA)
148        CALL TPVADD(BINTOD(1,MAXBIN),DELTA,1000000,BINTOD(1,MAXBIN))
149 C
150 C      convert wallclock times to CPU times
151 C        NONALG time can't be used in finding EFINV
152        RESET=(NBIN.GE.NONALG)
153 C
154 C      snapshot the wallclock time and the CPU time
155     12 CALL GETIMEOFDAY(T,ZONE)
156        DUMMY=ETIME(TARRAY)
157        CPU=DBLE(TARRAY(1))
158 C
159 C      throw away NONALG time
160 C      this is sure to happen after the initialization call
161        IF(RESET) THEN
162           CPUOLD=CPU
163           TOLD(1)=T(1)
164           TOLD(2)=T(2)
165           RESET=.FALSE.
166        ENDIF
167 C
168 C      has enough CPU time elapsed to measure it reliably?
169        IF(CPU-CPUOLD.GT.0.5D0) GO TO 9
170 C
171 C      no; do we need to update BINCPU anyhow?
172        IF(TCC.NE.0) GO TO 10
173 C
174 C      yes; spin to accumulate enough CPU time to measure
175        X=2.
176        DO 11 J=1,100
177              X=SQRT(3.-X)
178     11 CONTINUE
179        GO TO 12
180 C
181 C      increment the CPU time bins by scaled wallclock amounts
182      9 CALL TPVSUB(T,TOLD,1000000,DELTA)
183        EFINV=(CPU-CPUOLD)/TPV2R8(DELTA,1000000)
184        EFINV=DMIN1(1.D0,EFINV)
185        DO 13 L=1,MAXBIN
186           IF(L.NE.NONALG) CALL TPVSCL(BINTOD(1,L),1000000,EFINV)
187           CALL TPVADD(BINCPU(1,L),BINTOD(1,L),1000000,BINCPU(1,L))
188           BINTOD(1,L)=0
189           BINTOD(2,L)=0
190     13 CONTINUE
191        CPUOLD=CPU
192        TOLD(1)=T(1)
193        TOLD(2)=T(2)
194 C
195 C      if this is an update, leave the bin number alone; else reset it
196        IF(TCC.EQ.0) GO TO 8
197     10 NBIN=TCC
198        OLDTCC=TCC
199 C
```

Now we need to convert the wallclock times we have accumulated in the timing bins into CPU times, if that is possible or required. If the time we just spent out in the code was nonalgorithm time, we can't use it in finding the expansion factor inverse and RESET turns out true $\boxed{152}$. To test whether enough CPU time has accumulated to measure accurately, we find the current CPU time CPU $\boxed{156\text{-}157}$. In case it turns out to be enough, we also get the corresponding wallclock time T $\boxed{155}$. The UNIX™ system subprogram ETIME returns a function value we don't care about (the total CPU time), and the user-state and system-state CPU times we want as REAL*4s in TARRAY. If RESET is true (we were in bin NONALG), we throw away the accumulated CPU time $\boxed{162\text{-}165}$ by setting CPUOLD=CPU and TOLD=T.

At last we are ready to test $\boxed{169}$ whether a half-second of CPU time has elapsed since the previous conversion from TOD values to CPU values. If it has, we take the branch to statement 9. If not, we ask $\boxed{172}$ whether an update is required anyhow because TCC is zero; if not, we skip the update by branching to statement 10. If an update *is* required, we perform the spin loop $\boxed{175\text{-}178}$ and branch back to statement 12 to repeat the process; eventually the CPU test $\boxed{169}$ succeeds and we wind up at statement 9.

The CPU count updating is now straightforward. First $\boxed{182}$ we find the difference DELTA in wallclock times since the previous updating. The expansion factor inverse is then $\boxed{183}$ just the difference in CPU times divided by this difference in wallclock times. CPU-CPUOLD is a REAL*8 value, so we use the function TPV2R8 to convert DELTA to a REAL*8. If the expansion factor is very close to 1 it is possible that measurement errors will make our calculation yield an EFINV that is slightly more than 1, so we rule out that possibility $\boxed{184}$. Then $\boxed{186}$ we convert each TOD bin count to a CPU time, except for bin NONALG. TPVSCL multiplies the two-part value in column L of BINTOD by EFINV, and $\boxed{187}$ TPVADD adds the result to the accumulating CPU counts in BINCPU. Having consumed the values in BINTOD, we set them back to zero $\boxed{188\text{-}189}$. Once the updating is over we $\boxed{191\text{-}193}$ reset CPUOLD and TOLD for use in the next updating.

If $\boxed{196}$ this is not an update call (TCC is not zero) we $\boxed{197}$ switch the timing bin to TCC before going back out into the code, and $\boxed{198}$ save the value in OLDTCC. If this *is* an update call, we skip over the changing of the bin number.

When we have completed the time measurement successfully, we wind up at statement 8, get the time of exit TX, and go back out into the code. If TCC had a value that did not make sense in context, we wind up at statement 3 and write an error message. If the station number STA is nonzero, it is included in the error message $\boxed{207}$ as an aid to debugging.

```
200 C      find the TOD upon returning to the instrumented code
201      8 CALL GETIMEOFDAY(TX,ZONE)
202        RETURN
203 C
204 C      handle errors
205      3 IF(STA.EQ.0) WRITE(0,901)
206    901 FORMAT('A call to TIMER')
207        IF(STA.NE.0) WRITE(0,902) STA
208    902 FORMAT('A call to TIMER at station',I10)
209        WRITE(0,903) TCC,OLDTCC
210    903 FORMAT('gives the illegal control code',I10/
211      ;        'the previous control code was ',I10/)
212        STOP
213        END
```

TIMER, like GETFIL, is a little long. It could perhaps be shortened by moving some segments of its open code into other subprograms, but it is not obvious how to do that in such a way that the new routines would turn out to be useful in any other context. TIMER already depends, regrettably, on the special-purpose routine GETIMEOFDAY discussed in the next section.

18.5.3 Two Stub Routines

As we saw in §6.6, some UNIX™ services are available via system routines that can be invoked from FORTRAN. Unfortunately, the system routines that provide other UNIX™ services must be invoked from the C programming language instead. To use them we can write a brief FORTRAN-callable C routine or **stub** whose only function is to invoke the system routine we really want and return its output in variables that have FORTRAN data types. The UNIX™ routines listed in §6.6 are in fact probably just stubs that someone wrote for us.

The GETIMEOFDAY stub, which is used by the version of TIMER we have discussed so far, is listed below with line numbers for reference. As in the FORTRAN listings we have seen earlier, these line numbers are not part of the source text. This code is for Linux; the #include files might be different in other UNIX™ implementations.

```
 1 /* return [sec,usec] time of day to two-part value */
 2
 3 #include "g2c.h"
 4 #include <asm/timex.h>
 5
 6 int getimeofday_(t, zone)
 7 integer *t, *zone;
 8 {
 9     gettimeofday((struct timeval*) t, (struct timezone*) zone);
10     return 0;
11 }
```

All this stub does is 3,4,6,7 describe how the results should be stored and 9 invoke gettimeofday to return the time t and the zone **zone**. The C structure that is used to store each of these quantities corresponds precisely to a FORTRAN two-part value, so GETIMEOFDAY can be invoked as illustrated above on lines 93 and 155 of the TIMER listing. To compile this routine we must use a C compiler, and to link its object code into a FORTRAN program that uses TIMER we must use a FORTRAN compiler that permits the invocation of C routines compiled with that C compiler. The **gcc** and **g77** compilers, which are native to Linux and **cygwin**, cooperate in this way, so if the FORTRAN program that uses TIMER is in the file **program.f** we can prepare an executable by issuing this sequence of UNIX™ commands.

```
unix[120] gcc -c getimeofday.c
unix[121] g77 program.f timer.f getimeofday.o
```

First **gcc** compiles **getimeofday.c** producing **getimeofday.o**, then **g77** compiles **program.f** and **timer.f** and links all three object modules to produce an executable in **a.out**.

The version of TIMER that we will take up in the next section uses a different stub routine GETCYC to read a Pentium processor's 64-bit cycle counter. To read the cycle counter it is necessary to execute the Pentium machine-language instruction having mnemonic **rdtsc** [21], which is done by the C routine at the top of the next page.

```
1 /* return Pentium processor cycle count to INTEGER*8 */
2
3 #include <asm/timex.h>
4
5 void getcyc_(long t[])
6 {
7     rdtsc(t[0],t[1]);
8 }
```

The C data type used by `rdtsc` corresponds to the FORTRAN data type `INTEGER*8`. In §12.4.4 and §13.4.5 I cautioned against using variables of this type on the grounds that not all FORTRAN compilers support it. However, the g77 compiler *does,* so if we again use gcc and g77 then accepting delivery from `rdtsc` in an `INTEGER*8` is a concession we can reluctantly make. If the program in `program.f` now invokes the `TIMER` routine described in §18.5.4, we can build an executable by issuing this sequence of UNIX™ commands.

```
unix[122] gcc -c getcyc.c
unix[123] g77 program.f timer.f getcyc.o
```

18.5.4   A Cycle-Counting `TIMER`

The `TIMER` routine of §18.5.2 uses a spin loop to accumulate CPU time if the CPU time that has otherwise elapsed since the most recent update call is not enough to be measured reliably by `ETIME`. If updated timing estimates are required frequently the processor can spend most of its cycles in the spin loop rather than executing the code under test, greatly increasing the wall-clock time required to run the program.

The spin-looping can be avoided if it is possible to conduct computational experiments on a machine that is effectively empty and idle except for the code under test. This condition is difficult to achieve even on a computer that is not shared with other users because, as I mentioned in §15.1.4, housekeeping tasks running in the background and other operating-system activities such as paging normally compete with the user program for processor cycles. However, you might be able to minimize this noise by closing applications and extra windows, killing selected background processes, resetting the priority of other processes relative to that of your program, and disconnecting the network. Your UNIX™ system administrator can help you choose and make temporary changes to the configuration of your system, and you can refrain from nonessential mouse and keyboard use while your program is running. If these measures are successful, your program's expansion factor will be close to 1 (so that it need not be measured) and the wallclock time that elapses while your program is running will be a reliable surrogate for the CPU time that it consumes. If you have achieved an empty-and-idle test environment, the wallclock time that your program uses should be almost the same over many repeated runs, possibly spiking up dramatically on just a few of them. Those anomalous observations result from unfortunately-timed paging events and can simply be ignored. To minimize paging you might consider installing more fast memory in your computer.

Some microprocessors count the CPU clock cycles that have elapsed since the machine was last powered on, and allow a user program to read the counter. If your code runs alone, the difference between two cycle counts is a direct measurement of the time it has used.

This section presents a version of `TIMER` that has the same calling sequence as the earlier routine but assumes an empty-and-idle test environment and uses the stub routine `GETCYC`, which was described in §18.5.3, to read the cycle counter of an Intel Pentium processor. The source code begins on the next page.

```
 1 C
 2 Code by Michael Kupferschmid
 3 C
 4       SUBROUTINE TIMER(TCC,STA)
 5 C    This routine measures the CPU time used in executing
 6 C    different parts of a program.
 7 C
 8 C    TCC   action taken
 9 C    ---   ------------
10 C    -1    initialize; reset all bin counts and times to zero
11 C     0    update counts and times without changing bin number
12 C    >0    switch timing to bin number TCC
13 C
14 C    The parameter STA is used to identify the origin of the
15 C    TIMER call in the event that TCC has an illegal value
16 C    or some other error occurs.
17 C
18 C    variable  meaning
19 C    --------  -------
20 C    BINCPU    vector of visible [sec,nsec] CPU bin counts
21 C    BINCYC    vector of processor cycle bin counts
22 C    CPS       number of processor cycles per second
23 C    DELTA     a cycle count interval
24 C    DFLOAT    Fortran function gives REAL*8 for INTEGER*4
25 C    GETCYC    Pentium chip cycle counter, precise to 1 cycle
26 C    GETMHZ    routine gets processor speed
27 C    IFIX      Fortran function gives INTEGER*4 for REAL*4
28 C    INITMX    parameter sets MAXBIN
29 C    INITOH    initial value for TOH in cycles
30 C    L         index on the bins
31 C    MAXBIN    highest permissible bin number
32 C    NBIN      number of bin just receiving time
33 C    NCYC      number of cycles in this bin
34 C    NONALG    number of bin for non-algorithm time
35 C    NSEC      a number of nanoseconds
36 C    NSPCYC    nanoseconds per cycle
37 C    NTMEAS    number of timing measurements made so far
38 C    OLDTCC    previous value of TCC
39 C    SECCYC    number of cycles in SECS seconds, as INTEGER*8
40 C    SECS      a number of seconds
41 C    SNGL      Fortran function gives REAL*4 for REAL*8
42 C    SPEED     processor speed in MHz millions of cycles per second
43 C    STA       number designating CALL statement in source
44 C    TCC       timer control code; see table above
45 C    TE        cycle count at entry to this routine
46 C    TIMING    T => timing is enabled
47 C    TL        cycle count at previous entry
48 C    TOH       overhead correction in cycles
49 C    TOPBIN    highest bin number used so far
50 C    TX        cycle count at exit from this routine
51 C
52 C    formal parameters
53       INTEGER*4 TCC,STA
54 C
```

```
55 C     communicate timing information in common
56       PARAMETER(INITMX=22)
57       COMMON /EXPT/ TIMING,NONALG,NBIN,TOPBIN,NTMEAS,TOH,BINCPU,
58       ;             SPEED
59       REAL*8 SPEED
60       INTEGER*4 TOPBIN,TOH,BINCPU(2,INITMX)
61       LOGICAL*4 TIMING
62 C
63 C     other local variables
64       REAL*8 CPS,NSPCYC
65       INTEGER*8 TE/0/,TL,TX/0/,DELTA
66       INTEGER*8 BINCYC(INITMX),NCYC,SECCYC
67       INTEGER*4 OLDTCC/-2/,INITOH/1000/,SECS,NSEC
68 C
69 C ------------------------------------------------------------------
70 C
```

Many of the variable definitions and declarations are the same as those in the first version of TIMER.

We no longer need to measure an expansion factor so instead of EFINV the COMMON block /EXPT/ 57-58 now returns SPEED, the processor's clock rate. This will be obtained from the helper routine GETMHZ, which is described in §18.5.5. This version of TIMER accumulates cycle counts for the different timing bins in BINCYC 66 . The measured initialization overhead INITOH must now be stated 67 in cycle counts too, here 1000.

As in the other version of TIMER we 72 return immediately if timing is not enabled. Otherwise we 75 remember the time TL of the previous entry and 76 get the time TE of this entry. Here these quantities are measured in cycles. Then 78-100 comes the same logic we used before to check TCC for legal values and to figure out what to do.

```
71 C     do nothing unless timing is enabled
72       IF(.NOT.TIMING) RETURN
73 C
74 C     get cycle count on entry so calculations here timed separately
75       TL=TE
76       CALL GETCYC(TE)
77 C
78 C     make sure that the first call is to initialize
79       IF(OLDTCC.GE.-1) GO TO 1
80       IF(TCC.EQ.-1) GO TO 2
81       GO TO 3
82 C
83 C     this is not the first call; is this an update?
84     1 IF(TCC.NE.0) GO TO 4
85       IF(OLDTCC.NE.-1) GO TO 5
86       GO TO 3
87 C
88 C     this is not an update call; if TCC repeats assume it is wrong
89     4 IF(TCC.EQ.OLDTCC) GO TO 3
90 C
91 C     here TCC should be in the range -1,1...MAXBIN
92       IF(TCC.GT.MAXBIN) GO TO 3
93       IF(TCC.GT.-1) GO TO 6
94       IF(TCC.EQ.-1) GO TO 2
95       GO TO 3
```

```
 96 C
 97 C      keep track of the highest bin index used so far
 98      6 IF(OLDTCC.GE.NONALG) GO TO 5
 99        IF(OLDTCC.GT.TOPBIN) TOPBIN=OLDTCC
100        GO TO 5
101 C
102 C      reset times (TCC=-1)
103      2 MAXBIN=INITMX
104        NONALG=MAXBIN-1
105        NBIN=NONALG
106        TOPBIN=0
107        NTMEAS=0
108        TOH=INITOH
109        CALL GETMHZ(SPEED)
110        WRITE(0,901) SPEED
111    901 FORMAT('TIMER assumes processor speed is ',F8.3,' MHz.')
112        CPS=SPEED*1.D+06
113        NSPCYC=1000.D0/SPEED
114        DO 7 L=1,MAXBIN
115            BINCYC(L)=0
116            BINCPU(1,L)=0
117            BINCPU(2,L)=0
118      7 CONTINUE
119        OLDTCC=-1
120        GO TO 8
121 C
```

The initialization stanza $\boxed{103\text{-}120}$ is familiar except that it now obtains the processor speed using GETMHZ, reports the value, and computes $\boxed{112}$ the number of cycles in a second and $\boxed{113}$ the duration of one cycle in nanoseconds. It is now $\boxed{115}$ BINCYC, rather than BINTOD, that we set to zero.

At statement 5 (below) we compute the time spent out in the instrumented code and $\boxed{125}$ add it to the appropriate bin count. This arithmetic with INTEGER*8 values can be done with ordinary assignment statements. Then $\boxed{129\text{-}130}$ we account for the time that was spent inside TIMER on the previous call.

On the next page we $\boxed{133\text{-}145}$ convert all of the INTEGER*8 cycle counts into CPU times as [sec,nsec] two-part values. In the g77 implementation of INTEGER*8 variables DFLOAT converts an INTEGER*8 to REAL*8, but to avoid the possibility of an overflow it is necessary $\boxed{140}$ to convert a REAL*8 quantity to INTEGER*8 by assignment rather than by using IFIX.

The remainder of the code is the same as in the other version of TIMER, except that here we use GETCYC $\boxed{153}$ to find the exit time TX.

```
122 C      accumulate processor cycles for bin NBIN (TCC=0,1...MAXBIN)
123      5 DELTA=TE-TX-TOH
124        IF(DELTA.LT.0) DELTA=0
125        BINCYC(NBIN)=BINCYC(NBIN)+DELTA
126        NTMEAS=NTMEAS+1
127 C
128 C      accumulate processor cycles used making timing measurements
129        DELTA=TX-TL+TOH
130        BINCYC(MAXBIN)=BINCYC(MAXBIN)+DELTA
131 C
```

```
132 C      convert the processor cycle counts into CPU times
133        DO 9 L=1,MAXBIN
134            NCYC=BINCYC(L)
135            SECS=IFIX(SNGL(DFLOAT(NCYC)/CPS))
136            BINCPU(1,L)=SECS
137 C
138 C          explicitly fixing this product can overflow a fullword
139 C          so convert to long integer implicitly by assignment
140            SECCYC=CPS*DFLOAT(SECS)
141 C
142            NCYC=NCYC-SECCYC
143            NSEC=IFIX(0.5+SNGL(NSPCYC*DFLOAT(NCYC)))
144            BINCPU(2,L)=NSEC
145      9 CONTINUE
146 C
147 C      if this is an update leave the bin number alone; else reset it
148        IF(TCC.EQ.0) GO TO 8
149        NBIN=TCC
150        OLDTCC=TCC
151 C
152 C      get cycle count upon returning to the instrumented code
153      8 CALL GETCYC(TX)
154        RETURN
155 C
156 C      handle errors
157      3 IF(STA.EQ.0) WRITE(0,903)
158    903 FORMAT('A call to TIMER')
159        IF(STA.NE.0) WRITE(0,904) STA
160    904 FORMAT('A call to TIMER at station',I10)
161        WRITE(0,905) TCC,OLDTCC
162    905 FORMAT('gives the illegal control code',I10/
163      ;        'the previous control code was ',I10/)
164        STOP
165        END
```

18.5.5   Finding Processor Speed

For the cycle-counting TIMER to convert counts to CPU time it needs to know the processor speed. Linux interrogates the processor at boot time and saves the clock rate in the file /proc/cpuinfo, so GETMHZ simply opens that file and reads the appropriate number.

```
 1 C
 2         SUBROUTINE GETMHZ(SPEED)
 3 C       This routine reads /proc/cpuinfo to find processor speed.
 4 C
 5 C       variable  meaning
 6 C       --------  -------
 7 C       SPEED     processor speed in MHz
 8 C       TEXT      input line read from file
 9 C
10         REAL*8 SPEED
11         CHARACTER*21 TEXT
12 C
13 C ----------------------------------------------------------------
14 C
15 C       open the file
16         OPEN(UNIT=99,FILE='/proc/cpuinfo',ERR=1)
17         GO TO 2
18       1 WRITE(0,991)
19     991 FORMAT('OPEN failed on /proc/cpuinfo')
20         STOP
21 C
22 C       read the "cpu MHz" line
23       2 READ(99,901,END=3,ERR=4) TEXT
24     901 FORMAT(A21)
25         IF(TEXT(1:7).EQ.'cpu MHz') THEN
26            READ(TEXT(12:21),*,END=3,ERR=4) SPEED
27            CLOSE(UNIT=99)
28            RETURN
29         ENDIF
30         GO TO 2
31 C
32 C       handle errors
33       3 WRITE(0,992)
34     992 FORMAT('cpu MHz not found in /proc/cpuinfo')
35         STOP
36       4 WRITE(0,993)
37     993 FORMAT('read error on /proc/cpuinfo')
38         STOP
```

GETMHZ begins [16] by opening the file; if this fails it [18-20] reports that fact and stops the program. The next stanza [23-29] reads lines of text from the file until it finds one that has the string cpu MHz in characters 1-7. Then [26] it reads SPEED from characters 12-21 of that line and [27] returns the value. If the end of the file is reached before finding cpu MHz or if there is an error in reading the value, an appropriate message is written [32-33,35-36] and [34,37] the program stops.

This routine uses [25-26] the character substring notation described in §13.10.3.

18.6   A Shell Script for Global Edits

In maintaining an application, as described in §14.4, it is sometimes necessary to make the same text substitution in several `.f` files. For example, it might be necessary to change the string `REAL*8 A(20)` to `REAL*8 A(30)` everywhere that declaration appears. It is possible to do this with a single UNIX™ command by using the shell script `changeall` listed below.

```
#! /bin/sh
# change all occurrences of $1 to $2 in the files listed after

# tell how to use the script
if [ $# -lt 3 ]
then
  echo 'usage: changeall "frompattern" "topattern" files'
  exit 1
fi

# escape any special characters in the old and new strings
was="$1"
old=`echo "$was" | sed -e 's/[\ \*\$\&\/]/\\\&/g'`
shift
now="$1"
new=`echo "$now" | sed -e 's/[\ \*\$\&\/]/\\\&/g'`
shift

# change all occurrences in all the files
for fyle in $*
do
  grep -s -q "$old" $fyle
  if [ $? -eq 0 ]
  then
    rm -f /tmp/$fyle
    mv $fyle /tmp/$fyle
    echo "changing  $was  to  $now  in $fyle"
    sed -e "s/$old/$new/g" /tmp/$fyle > $fyle
    if [ $? -eq 0 ]
    then
      echo "$fyle done"
    else
      echo "ERROR: nonzero return code from sed; stopping"
      cp /tmp/$fyle $fyle
      exit 1
    fi
  fi
done
exit 0
```

The code above will be mysterious if you're not a UNIX™ shell programmer, and I'm going to leave it that way because this book is about FORTRAN instead. But you can use the script even if you don't know how it works, and if you do then making the change I described earlier will be as easy as this.

```
unix[124] changeall "REAL*8 A(20)" "REAL*8 A(30)" *.f
changing  REAL*8 A(20)  to  REAL*8 A(30)  in main.f
changing  REAL*8 A(20)  to  REAL*8 A(30)  in subr.f
```

18.7   Caveats and Omissions

Because the routines of this chapter are directly useful in programs that do engineering and scientific calculations, it is reasonable for them to be written in FORTRAN like the code that will invoke them. On the other hand, because the operations they perform are mostly non-numerical it would not be *un*reasonable to code them in a language such as C instead, provided you have a way to link together object modules that are compiled from source programs that were written in different languages.

CPU timing is a notoriously dubious enterprise, especially in UNIX™. How well the first version of TIMER works for partitioning CPU time according to wallclock time measurements depends on how carefully ETIME and gettimeofday are implemented, which varies from one machine to another depending on the hardware timing facilities available and the internals of the machine's version of UNIX™. The second version of TIMER works only on Pentium processors running Linux and reports CPU time only in an empty-and-idle test environment. Either of these routines might be adequate for some uses, but both are poor substitutes for operating system functionality that allows precise and accurate *direct* measurements of problem-state CPU time. For better or for worse they are, alas, the best I know how to do in most versions of UNIX™ without resorting to special timing hardware [39].

I have omitted from this chapter the man pages from which I wrote the routines discussed here. Additional examples of man pages would perhaps have been useful to some readers, but they would surely also have been tedious and repetitive in view of the extensive discussion of each routine already given in the text.

Finally, it is easy to imagine two-part value operations other than those discussed, two part values in which the parts are not both integers, and multiple-part values, all of which are beyond our needs here.

18.8   Exercises

18.8.1   Write man pages for (a) BTD, (b) DTB, (c) INTINS, (d) STRINS, (e) GETFIL, (f) TPVADD and TPVSUB, (g) TPVNML, (h) TPV2R8 and R82TPV, (i) TPVSCL, (j) TIMER. In §12.3 I claimed that it is easier to code a subprogram *after* writing its man page. Is it also easier to write a routine's man page *before* writing the code, rather than figuring out what the code does and then writing the description?

18.8.2 What is printed by the following program? Explain how the code works.

```
      CHARACTER*1 STRING(10)/'N','=',8*' '/
      INTEGER*4 RC
      CALL DTB(' +51',5,N,RC)
      CALL BTD(N,STRING(3),8,RC)
      WRITE(6,900) STRING
  900 FORMAT(10A1)
      STOP
      END
```

18.8.3 Write a program that reads a character string `STR` and an integer `I`, uses subprograms discussed in this chapter to insert them in the message template below and remove any extra blanks, and prints the result.

```
      CHARACTER*1 TMPLT(23)/'V','a','l','u','e',' ','o','f',' ',
     ;                      5*' ','=',8*' '/
```

What gets printed if `I` has more than 8 digits?

18.8.4 Rewrite the `PROMPT` subroutine of §10.4 to use `INTINS` for inserting the number of characters to be printed into the object-time `FORMAT` string.

18.8.5 Rewrite the `DTB` routine of §18.1.2 to use Horner's rule for computing `N`, so as not to need exponentiation ⎡59⎤ for finding the powers of 10.

18.8.6 The `STRINS` routine listed in §18.2.2 calls `SHIFTL` in its final stanza ⎡58-59⎤ to adjust the spacing of the result string. Use an example to explain in detail how this processing works. What happens if `LS-L=1`? The `SHIFTL` routine was discussed in §10.3.

18.8.7 In §6.2 I recommended that when you invoke a subprogram you *don't pass the same actual parameter for two dummy parameters if either dummy parameter gets changed.* In §13.6.3 I conceded that although doing this is risky it is not *always* an error, and I mentioned the `INTINS` and `STRINS` routines of §18.2 as examples each of which can be passed the same actual parameter for its input and output strings or the same actual parameter for its input and output lengths. In `GETFIL`, some of the calls to `STRINS` (e.g., ⎡134⎤) do indeed pass the same actual parameter for both the input string and the output string. (a) Explain why `STRINS` can be called in this way even though other routines, such as the first version of `EXCH` in §6.2, cannot. (b) Why do you think I broke my own rule in this case? Should my original recommendation be rescinded, or is it still a good rule to follow at least most of the time? (c) Suppose the first stanza of executable code in `STRINS` is changed to read as follows.

```
      LR=0
      IF(LS.LE.0) RETURN
```

Would it still be possible to pass the same actual parameter for both `LS` and `LR`? Explain. (d) One way of making it impossible to pass the same actual parameter for two dummy parameters is to recode the routine to do its work in-place, as we did with `EXCH` in §6.2. Would there be any drawbacks to recoding `INTINS` and `STRINS` so that they worked in-place?

18.8.8   Code an invocation of GETFIL that will attach a file to unit 3 for reading only. Suggest that a file named input be used. What happens if the program's executable is run using this UNIX™ command?

```
[125] a.out 3=otherfile
```

18.8.9   GETFIL reports errors in its parameters with simple WRITE statements, making no effort to format them for readability. File attachment errors are reported by inserting information in a message template, which is then carefully formatted for ease of reading. Why do you suppose these two kinds of errors are treated differently?

18.8.10   What does GETFIL do if the filename given in response to the prompt has more than 65 characters? Suggest a revision to GETFIL that would permit it to detect responses longer than 65 characters. What should it do then?

18.8.11   Write a subprogram to search command-line parameters for a unit assignment, and modify GETFIL to use it. Your routine should detect an error if the same unit is assigned by two or more command-line arguments.

18.8.12   Improve the GETFIL routine of §18.3 as follows. (a) Add a parameter RC, an integer return code that will be 0 if all went well, 1 if the user sends an end-of-file in response to the filename prompt, or 2 if an error occurs. Instead of stopping the program in some situations, GETFIL should now always return to its caller. (b) If the suggested name is accepted but the file is only to be written and it already exists, and if the reply to the question asking permission to empty the file is no, then omit the suggested name in subsequent prompts for the filename. (c) Add parameters DIR, a string containing a UNIX™ directory name, and LD, the number of characters in DIR. GETFIL should then find or create the file in the specified directory, or in the current working directory if LD is zero or DIR is all blank. (d) Make the assumed display width in columns a PARAMETER constant and use it to calculate the dimensions of FILNAM and PAR. Does your compiler permit the use of a PARAMETER constant for the size of the CHARACTER*n variable ARG? (e) Return in SUGNAM the name of the file to which GETFIL actually assigns the unit (it might be different from the suggested name that is passed in). After this change, a literal can no longer be passed in for SUGNAM.

18.8.13   Normalize the two-part value [-78$, 123¢]. Why do TPVADD and TPVSUB prenormalize their operands?

18.8.14   If a two-part value is converted to REAL*8, can an overflow occur? What happens to the number of significant bits used to represent the value?

18.8.15   When a REAL*8 value is converted to a two-part value, can an overflow ever occur? If so, what value is returned by R82TPV?

18.8.16   Rewrite TPVSCL to scale the parts of TPV separately, rather than converting to REAL*8, multiplying by S, and converting back. Which approach yields a more accurate result?

18.8.17   Explain how it is possible to do exact integer arithmetic using values larger than 2147483647 by using two-part values in which the smaller part counts from 1 to 1000000000.

18.8.18   Angles are sometimes measured using whole-number degrees, minutes, and seconds of arc. (a) Write a subroutine ARCADD(ANG1,ANG2, SUM) to add angles stored in this way. Be sure to normalize the SUM returned. (b) Generalize your routine to work for arbitrary 3-part values. (c) Can your generalized routine also be used for adding quantities that are stored as 2-part values?

18.8.19 What does TIMER do if two successive calls give the same timer control code TCC? How does TIMER use the station number STA?

18.8.20 (a) What is a spin loop? Why does the first version of TIMER include one? (b) What is a stub routine? When is a stub routine necessary?

18.8.21 Write a calibration program for use in finding the value of TOH2 that should be set in TIMER to produce a zero elapsed time measurement when TIMER is used to time an empty code path.

18.8.22 (a) The first TIMER routine of §18.5 could be simplified if the measurements returned by ETIME were precise to the nearest microsecond rather than only to the nearest hundredth of a second. But even if ETIME could *measure* CPU time exactly, the result would still be returned as a REAL*4 value and could therefore usually not be *represented* exactly. If the measured time is 1 second, what time difference corresponds to a difference in the least significant fraction bit of the REAL*4 value? (b) The TIMER routine of §18.5.4 reads the Pentium clock-cycle counter to measure CPU time. If the processor runs at 1GHz, what time difference corresponds to a difference in the least significant bit of the 64-bit cycle counter? (c) In §18.5.4 we store the cycle count in a (signed) INTEGER*8. Exactly how many cycles can be counted before the counter overflows into its most significant bit and becomes (as understood by FORTRAN) a negative number? On a processor that runs at 1GHz, how long would the machine have to be on before that happened?

18.8.23 The routines of this chapter are written in Classical FORTRAN. In a few places they could be simplified and made clearer and more convincingly correct by using Fortran-90 features described in §17.1. For example, by using array operations the addition of one two-part value to another (as is done in TPVADD) could be written using fewer lines of code.

```
C     Classical Fortran          C     Fortran-90
      C(1)=A(1)+B(1)                    C=A+B
      C(2)=A(2)+B(2)
```

Write down all the other opportunities you can find to improve the code of this chapter by using the Fortran-90 constructs discussed in §17.1.

Bibliography

If you encountered a citation in the text and want to look up the reference, find the entry with the given number. For example, the citation [1] refers to the first entry below, Jon Bentley's book *Programming Pearls*.

If you have a particular work in mind and want to check whether it is used as a reference or find the number by which it is cited, scan for the author's name or for the title. To make this easy, the entries are sorted into three categories and are listed alphabetically by **author's name** within each category. Documents containing no attribution of authorship, such as most manuals, are listed at the beginning of each section and arranged alphabetically by the ***most significant words*** in the title.

Some of the entries include annotations in *slanting type*. The World Wide Web addresses and mailing list names that are given in a few of the entries (and elsewhere in the book) were valid when I used them but might have changed since then.

Suggested Reading

This category lists basic works that are relevant in a general way to computer programming, and which I recommend in their entirety for further study.

[1] **Bentley, Jon**, *Programming Pearls,* Addison-Wesley, Reading, MA, 1986. *The title says it all.*

[2] **Bentley, Jon**, *Writing Efficient Programs,* Prentice-Hall, Englewood Cliffs, NJ, 1982.

[3] **Brooks, Frederick P. Jr.**, *The Mythical Man Month: Essays on Software Engineering,* Addison-Wesley, Reading, MA, 1975.

[4] **Burden, Richard L.** and **Faires, J. Douglas**, *Numerical Analysis,* Seventh Edition, Brooks/Cole Publishing, Pacific Grove, CA, 2001.

[5] **Forsythe, George E.; Malcolm, Michael A.;** and **Moler, Cleve B.**, *Computer Methods for Mathematical Computations,* Prentice-Hall, Englewood Cliffs, NJ, 1977.

[6] **Golub, Gene H.** and **Van Loan, Charles F.**, *Matrix Computations,* Second Edition, Johns Hopkins University Press, Baltimore, MD, 1989.

[7] **Horowitz, Ellis** and **Sahni, Sartaj**, *Fundamentals of Data Structures,* Computer Science Press, Potomac, MD, 1976.

[8] **Kernighan, Brian W.** and **Plauger, P. J.**, *The Elements of Programming Style,* McGraw-Hill, New York, NY, 1974.

[9] **Knuth, Donald E.**, *The Art of Computer Programming: Volume 2 Seminumerical Algorithms,* Addison-Wesley, Reading, MA, 1981.

[10] **Knuth, Donald E.**, *The Art of Computer Programming: Volume 3 Sorting and Searching,* Addison-Wesley, Reading, MA, 1973.

[11] **Overton, Michael L.**, *Numerical Computing with IEEE Floating Point Arithmetic,* Society for Industrial and Applied Mathematics, Philadelphia, PA, 2001.

[12] **Press, William H.; Teukolsky, Saul A.; Vetterling, William T.**; and **Flannery, Brian P.**, *Numerical Recipes in FORTRAN: The Art of Scientific Computing,* Second Edition, Cambridge University Press, New York, NY, 1992. *An essential reference with an unfortunate programming style.*

[13] **Warren, Henry S., Jr.**, *Hacker's Delight,* Addison-Wesley, New York, NY, 2003. *Clever programming tricks in C, to provoke deep thinking about simple calculations in any language.*

Technical References

This category lists other references about computer programming and related technical subjects, which are cited in the text as authority for specific claims made there or as sources of additional information about particular topics. You might be interested in reading some of these books and articles in their entirety, but I have not cited them primarily for their tutorial value.

[14] *IBM Visualization* ***Data Explorer*** *User's Guide,* Seventh Edition, `SC38-0496-06`, International Business Machines, Almaden, CA, 18 Sep 1997. See `http://www.almaden.ibm.com/dx` also.

[15] ***Engineering and Scientific Subroutine Library*** *Guide and Reference,* Second Edition, `SC23-0526-01`, International Business Machines, Kingston, NY, Jan 1994 (3 volumes).

[16] *IBM System/360 and System/370* ***FORTRAN IV Language***, Eleventh Edition, `GC28-6515-10`, International Business Machines, San Jose, CA, May 1974 (revised by `TNL GN26-0891` of 18 Mar 1977).

[17] ***Harwell Subroutine Library,*** Release 11, Theoretical Studies Department, AEA Industrial Technology, Harwell Laboratory, Didcot, Oxfordshire, England, July 1993.

[18] ***High Performance Fortran Language Specification,*** *Version 1.1,* `CRPC-TR92225`, Center for Research on Parallel Computation, Rice University, Houston, TX, 1994.

[19] ***IEEE*** *Standard for Binary Floating-Point Arithmetic,* ANSI/IEEE Std 754-1985, The Institute of Electrical and Electronics Engineers, New York, NY, 12 Aug 1985.

[20] ***IMSL*** *Numerical Libraries Version 3.0,* Visual Numerics, Houston, TX, 1994.

[21] *IA-32* ***Intel*** *Architecture Software Developer's Manual,* Intel Corporation, Mount Prospect, IL, 2001. See Volume 3: System Programming Guide, Order Number `245472`, §14.7, page 14-22, "The Time Stamp Counter," and Volume 2: Instruction Set Reference, Order Number `245471`, page 3-673, "RDTSC."

[22] *LoadLeveler*™, G325-3496-00, International Business Machines, Kingston, NY, Apr 1996.

[23] *IBM System/360 Operating System FORTRAN IV Library – **Mathematical** and Service Subprograms*, Second Edition, GC28-6818-01, International Business Machines, New York, NY, Sep 1972.

[24] MIL-STD-1753, *FORTRAN, DOD Supplement to American National Standard X3.9-1978*, US Department of Defense, 09 Nov 1978 (cancelled 25 Mar 1996 because the features described were by then included in the FORTRAN-90 standard).

[25] *MPI: A Message-Passing Interface Standard*, Message Passing Interface Forum, University of Tennessee, Knoxville, TN, 1994.

[26] *NAG Fortran Library Manual Mark 17*, Numerical Algorithms Group, Downers Grove, IL, Sep 1995.

[27] *Numerical Computation Guide*, 819-3693-10, Sun Microsystems, Santa Clara, CA, 2008. *I used some values from this reference in the table of §4.7.*

[28] *Optimization and Tuning Guide for Fortran, C, and C++*, SC09-1705-00, International Business Machines, Armonk, NY, 1993.

[29] *AIX Versions 3.2 and 4 Performance Tuning Guide*, Fifth Edition, SR28-5930-04, sections on "Design and Implementation of Efficient Programs" and "Appendix C. Cache and Addressing Considerations," International Business Machines, Austin, TX, Apr 1996.

[30] *PGHPF Compiler User's Guide*, The Portland Group, Inc., Wilsonville, OR, 2007.

[31] *IBM 9076 Scalable POWERParallel Systems: General Information*, GH26-7219-00, International Business Machines, Kingston, NY, 1993.

[32] *SPARCompiler*™ *FORTRAN Version 2.0 User's Guide*, Revision A, 800-6552-11, Sun Microsystems, Mountain View, CA, Oct 1992.

[33] *ANSI/ANS-10.4-1987, American National Standard Guidelines for the **Verification** and **Validation** of Scientific and Engineering Computer Programs for the Nuclear Industry*, American Nuclear Society, LaGrange Park, IL, 13 May 1987.

[34] *Visual Fortran: The Gold Standard in Fortran Development for Windows Systems*, 4 Jun 2001. See www.compaq.com/fortran/visual for a description of various promotional enticements. *Despite the title of the article, versions of this compiler are available for* UNIX™ *and for the VMS operating system as well as for Microsoft Windows.*

[35] **Abromowitz, Milton** and **Stegun, Irene A.**, *Handbook of Mathematical Functions*, Dover, New York, NY, Dec 1972.

[36] **Amdahl, Gene M.**, "Validity of the single processor approach to achieving large scale computing capabilities," *AFIPS Conference Proceedings* 30:1 483-485, Spring Joint Computer Conference, 18-20 Apr 1967.

[37] **Anderson, E.; Bai, Z.; Bischoff, C.; Demmel, J.; Dongarra, J.; Du Croz, J.; Greenbaum, A.; Hammarling, S.; McKenney, A.; Ostrouchov, S.;** and **Sorensen, D.**, *LAPACK Users' Guide*, Second Edition, Society for Industrial and Applied Mathematics, Philadelphia, PA, 1995.

[38] **Anderson, Robert B.**, *Proving Programs Correct*, Wiley, New York, NY, 1979. *Some of the examples discussed in this book are* FORTRAN *programs.*

[39] **Black, David L.**, "The Mach Timing Facility: An Implementation of Accurate Low-Overhead Usage Timing," *Mach I Workshop Proceedings*, pages 53-71, UseNIX Association, Berkeley, CA, 4-5 Oct 1990.

[40] **Boettner, Donald W.** and **Alexander, Michael T.**, "The Michigan Terminal System," *Proceedings of the IEEE* 63:6 912-918, Special Issue on Interactive Computer Systems, Jun 1975.

[41] **Borenstein, Nathaniel S.**, *Programming as if People Mattered: Friendly Programs, Software Engineering, and Other Noble Delusions*, Princeton University Press, Princeton, NJ, 1991.

[42] **Bourne, S. R.**, *The UNIX System*, Addison-Wesley, Reading, MA, 1983. *The traditional* UNIX™ *culture in a nutshell.*

[43] **Colen, Larry**, "Code Reviews," *Linux Journal* :81 163-164, Jan 2001.

[44] **Crandall, Stephen H.**, *Engineering Analysis, a Survey of Numerical Procedures*, McGraw-Hill, New York, NY, 1956. *A golden oldie.*

[45] **De Boor, Carl**, *A Practical Guide to Splines*, Springer-Verlag, New York, NY, Dec 1978.

[46] **Decyk, Viktor K.; Norton, Charles D.;** and **Szymanski, Boleslaw K.**, "Expressing Object-Oriented Concepts in Fortran 90," *ACM Fortran Forum* 16:1 13-18, Apr 1997.

[47] **Dommel, Herman W.**, "Digital Computer Solution of Electromagnetic Transients in Single- and Multiphase Networks," *IEEE Transactions on Power Apparatus and Systems* PAS-88:4 388-399, Apr 1969.

[48] **Dongarra, Jack J.**, *Performance of Various Computers Using Standard Linear Equations Software*, CS-89-85, Oak Ridge National Laboratory, Oak Ridge, TN, 1999. See http://www.netlib.org.benchmark/performance.ps for the most recent version of this report.

[49] **Dongarra, Jack J.; Duff, Ian S.; Sorensen, Danny;** and **van der Vorst, Henk**, *Solving Linear Systems on Vector and Shared Memory Computers*, Society for Industrial and Applied Mathematics, Philadelphia, PA, 1990.

[50] **Dowd, Kevin**, *High Performance Computing*, O'Reilly, Sebastopol, CA, 1993.

[51] **Duff, Iain S.; Erisman, A. M.;** and **Reid, J. K.**, *Direct Methods for Sparse Matrices*, Clarendon, New York, NY, 1986.

[52] **Duke, Dennis W.; Green, Thomas P.;** and **Pasko, Joseph L.**, *Research Toward a Heterogeneous Networked Computing Cluster: The Distributed Queueing System Version 3.0*, SCRI, Florida State University, Tallahassee, FL, 02 Mar 1994.

[53] **Ecker, J. G.** and **Kupferschmid, Michael**, *Introduction to Operations Research*, Wiley, New York, NY, 1988 and reprinted with corrections by Krieger, Malabar, FL, 1991, 2001, and 2004.

[54] **Eisenstat, S. C.; Gursky, M. C.; Schultz, M. H.;** and **Sherman, A. H.**, "Yale Sparse Matrix Package I: The Symmetric Codes," *International Journal for Numerical Methods in Engineering* 18:8 1145-1151, Aug 1982 and *The Yale matrix package II: the non-symmetric codes*, Report 114, Yale University Department of Computer Science, 1977.

[55] **Etter, D. M.**, *Structured FORTRAN-77 for Engineers and Scientists*, Benjamin/ Cummings, Reading, MA, 1983.

[56] **Fagan, M. E.**, "Design and code inspections to reduce errors in program development," *IBM Systems Journal* 15:3 182-211, Jul-Sep 1976.

[57] **Fite, Matthew**, "First Look at an Apple G4 with the AltiVec Processor," *Linux Journal* :86 108-118, Jun 2001.

[58] **Gallivan, K.; Heath, M.; Ng, E.; Ortega, J.; Peyton, B.; Plemmons, R.; Romine, C.; Sameh, A.;** and **Voight, R.**, *Parallel Algorithms for Matrix Computations*, Society for Industrial and Applied Mathematics, Philadelphia, PA, 1990.

[59] **Geist, Al; Beguelin, Adam; Dongarra, Jack; Jiang, Weicheng; Manchek, Robert;** and **Sunderam, Vaidy**, *PVM: Parallel Virtual Machine – A User's Guide and Tutorial for Network Parallel Computing*, MIT Press, Cambridge, MA, 1994.

[60] **Gentleman, W. M.** and **Wichmann, B. A.**, "Timing on Computers," *ACM SIGARCH* 2:3 20-23, Oct 1973.

[61] **Ghezzi, Carlo; Jazayeri, Mehdi;** and **Mandrioli, Dino**, *Fundamentals of Software Engineering*, Prentice-Hall, Englewood Cliffs, NJ, 1991.

[62] **Greene, Daniel H.** and **Knuth, Donald E.**, *Mathematics for the Analysis of Algorithms*, Second Edition, Birkhäuser, Boston, MA, 1982.

[63] **Greenwood, Allan**, *Electrical Transients in Power Systems*, Second Edition, Wiley, New York, NY, 1991.

[64] **Gropp, William; Lusk, Ewing;** and **Skjellum, Anthony**, *Using MPI: Portable Parallel Programming with the Message-Passing Interface*, MIT Press, Cambridge, MA, 1994.

[65] **Gropp, William; Huss-Lederman, Steven; Lumsdaine, Andrew; Lusk, Ewing; Nitzberg, Bill; Saphir, William;** and **Snir, Marc**, *MPI – The Complete Reference, Volume 2, The MPI-2 Extensions*, MIT Press, Cambridge, MA, 1998.

[66] **Harris, Jonathan; Bircsak, John A.; Bolduc, M. Regina; Diewald, Jill Ann; Gale, Israel; Johnson, Neil W.; Lee, Shin; Nelson, C. Alexander;** and **Offner, Carl D.**, *Compiling High Performance Fortran for Distributed-Memory Systems*, High Performance Computing Group, Digital Equipment Corporation, Maynard, MA, 1997.

[67] **Harrison, David**, UNIX™ man page for xgraph, University of California, 01 Feb 1989.

[68] **Hatton, Les**, personal communication, 19 Mar 1997.

[69] **Heath, James R.; Kuekes, Philip J.; Snider, Gregory S.; and Williams, R. Stanley**, "A Defect-Tolerant Computer Architecture: Opportunities for Nanotechnology," *Science* 280:5370 1716-1721, 12 Jun 1998.

[70] **Heckel, Paul**, *The Elements of Friendly Software Design*, Warner, New York, NY, 1984.

[71] **Hill, T. P.**, "The First Digit Phenomenon," *American Scientist* 86:4 358-363, Jul-Aug 1998.

[72] **Hollingsworth, Jack**, *Hollingsworth's Documentation Rules*, class handout, Rensselaer Polytechnic Institute, Troy, NY, Feb 1979.

[73] **Jennings, Alan**, *Matrix Computation for Engineers and Scientists*, Wiley, New York, NY, 1977.

[74] **Kelley, Al** and **Pohl, Ira**, *A Book on C*, Third Edition, Addison-Wesley, New York, NY, 1995.

[75] **Kennedy, Ken; Koelbel, Charles; and Zima, Hans**, "The Rise and Fall of High Performance Fortran: An Historical Object Lesson," *Third ACM SIGPLAN History of Programming Languages Conference Proceedings*, pages 7-1 – 7-22, Association for Computing Machinery, San Diego, CA, 2007.

[76] **Kerrigan, Jim**, *Migrating to Fortran 90*, O'Reilly, Sebastopol, CA, 1993.

[77] **Knuth, Donald E.**, "An Empirical Study of FORTRAN Programs," *Software – Practice and Experience* 1:2 105-133, Apr-Jun 1971.

[78] **Knuth, Donald E.**, "Structured Programming with GO TO Statements," *ACM Computing Surveys* 6:4 261-301, Dec 1974.

[79] **Koelbel, Charles H.**, personal communication, 08 May 1997.

[80] **Koelbel, Charles H.**, *HPF Users Group Meeting, Porto, Portugal, 25-26 Jun 1998*, notes distributed to the hpff@cs.rice.edu mailing list, 09 Jul 1998.

[81] **Koelbel, Charles H.; Loveman, David B.; Schreiber, Robert S., Steele, Guy L., Jr.; and Zosel, Mary E.**, *The High Performance Fortran Handbook*, MIT Press, Cambridge, MA, 1994. *The definitive reference, but I found it exquisitely difficult to read.*

[82] **Kupferschmid, Michael**, *An Ellipsoid Algorithm for Convex Programming*, Ph.D. Thesis, Rensselaer Polytechnic Institute, Troy, NY, July 1981. *I apologize for the abysmal typesetting of this thesis.*

[83] **Liskov, Barbara** and **Guttag, John**, *Abstraction and Specification in Program Development*, MIT Press, Cambridge, MA, 1986.

[84] **Loukides, Mike**, *UNIX for FORTRAN Programmers*, O'Reilly, Sebastopol, CA, 1990.

[85] **Markstein, P. W.**, "Computation of elementary functions on the IBM RISC System/6000 processor," *IBM Journal of Research and Development* 34:1 111-119, Jan 1990.

[86] **Maron, Melvin J.**, *Numerical Analysis: A Practical Approach,* Macmillan, New York, NY, 1982.

[87] **McCracken, Daniel D.**, *A Guide to FORTRAN IV Programming,* Wiley, New York, NY, 1965. *The wonderful little text against which all subsequent FORTRAN books, including this one, must be judged.*

[88] **McCracken, Daniel D.** and **Salmon, William I.**, *Computing for Engineers and Scientists with FORTRAN 77,* Second Edition, Wiley, New York, NY, 1988. *An encyclopedic tome.*

[89] **Mohrmann, Kelley B.**, *Algorithms for Hard Nonlinear Programs,* Ph.D. Thesis, Rensselaer Polytechnic Institute, Troy, NY, 1993.

[90] **Nyhoff, Larry** and **Leestma, Sanford**, *FORTRAN 77 for Engineers and Scientists,* Third Edition, Macmillan, New York, NY, 1992.

[91] **Offner, Carl**, electronic mail to the `hpff@cs.rice.edu` mailing list, 20 Oct 1998.

[92] **Oram, Andres** and **Talbott, Steve**, *Managing Projects with* `make`, O'Reilly, Sebastopol, CA, 1991.

[93] **Ossanna, Joseph F.** and **Kernighan, Brian W.**, *Troff User's Manual,* Computing Science Technical Report No. 54, AT&T Bell Laboratories, Murray Hill, NJ, Nov 1992. This document can be downloaded from `http://www.cs.bell-labs.com/cm/cs/cstr/html`.

[94] **Parnas, David L.**, "On the Criteria To Be Used in Decomposing Systems into Modules," *Communications of the ACM* 15:12 1053-1058, Dec 1972.

[95] **Raymond, David J.**, "SISAL: A Safe and Efficient Language for Numerical Calculations," *Linux Journal* :80 190-195, Dec 2000. *The article begins "Back in the misty, early days of computing, famed computer scientist John Backus invented a programming language called Fortran. Given his other accomplishments, most computer scientists have probably forgiven him for this. After all, how was he to know that his invention would grow into a Frankenstein [sic], sweeping away all attempts to replace it with more pleasant and useful tools?" The SISAL project began at Lawrence Livermore National Laboratory in 1985 and was canceled in 1997, but the compiler is still available. It translates SISAL source text into either* FORTRAN *or C, but "[t]he Fortran interface is more developed."*

[96] **Ortega, James M.** and **Golub, Gene H.**, *Scientific Computing: An Introduction With Parallel Computing,* Academic Press, San Diego, CA, Jan 1993.

[97] **Ortega, James M.** and **Voight, Robert G.**, *Solution of Partial Differential Equations on Vector and Parallel Computers,* Society for Industrial and Applied Mathematics, Philadelphia, PA, 1985.

[98] **Redwine, Cooper**, *Upgrading to Fortran 90,* Springer-Verlag, New York, NY, 1995.

[99] **Salisbury, Richard A.**, General Editor, *The Michigan Terminal System Manual, Volume 3: System Subroutine Descriptions,* University of Michigan Computing Center, Ann Arbor, MI, 1982.

[100] **Scarborough, Randolph G.**, "Writing Optimizable Fortran," *SHARE 51 Proceedings,* Session S703, Boston, MA, 20-25 Aug 1978. *Inside information from an eminent compiler designer.*

[101] **Snir, Marc; Otto, Steve; Huss-Lederman, Steven; Walker, David;** and **Dongarra, Jack.**, *MPI – The Complete Reference, Volume 1, The MPI Core,* Second Edition, MIT Press, Cambridge, MA, 2001.

[102] **Stallman, Richard M.; Pesch, Roland;** and **Shebs, Stan**, *Debugging with gdb*, Ninth Edition, Gnu Press, Boston, MA, Jan 2002. Also available on-line at `http://sourceware.org/gdb/current/onlinedocs/gdb.html#SEC_Top`

[103] **Standish, Thomas A.**, *Data Structure Techniques,* Addison-Wesley, Reading, MA, 1980.

[104] **Terry, Paul; Shan, Amar;** and **Huttunen, Pentti**, "Improving Application Performance on HPC Systems with Process Synchronization," *Linux Journal* :127, 68-73, Nov 2004.

[105] **Weinberg, Gerald M.**, *The Psychology of Computer Programming,* Van Nostrand Reinhold, New York, NY, 1971. *Still interesting but now noticeably dated.*

[106] **Welsh, Matt; Dalheimer, Matthias Kalle;** and **Kaufman, Lar**, *Running Linux,* Third Edition, O'Reilly, Sebastopol, CA, Aug 1999.

[107] **Wilkinson, J. H.**, *Rounding Errors in Algebraic Processes,* Dover, New York, NY, 1994.

[108] **Williams, Thomas** and **Kelley, Colin**, *GNUPLOT: An Interactive Plotting Program,* Version 3.2, August 1990.
See `http://www.cs.dartmouth.edu/gnuplot/gnuplot.html` also.

[109] **Wirth, Niklaus**, "Program Development by Stepwise Refinement," *Communications of the ACM* 14:4 221-227, Apr 1971.

[110] **Wirth, Niklaus**, "On the Composition of Well-Structured Programs," *ACM Computing Surveys* 6:4 247-259, Dec 1974.

Other References

This category lists nontechnical references that are cited in the text as authority for specific claims made there or as sources of cultural context.

[111] See `http://www.cac.cornell.edu` *Clusters can also be built using computers that run Windows or MacOS.*

[112] ***Cray*** *Previews Next-Generation Vector Supercomputer* press releases, `hpcwire@tgc.com`, 27 Jun 2006.

[113] *The **Earth Simulator** Center* at `http://www.es.jamstec.go.jp`

[114] ***Elf90,*** *Essential Lahey Fortran 90,* Document 9267, Lahey Computer Systems, Incline Village, NV, 19 Jan 1999.

[115] See `http://www.facebook.com` *"Facebook is a social utility that connects you with the people around you. [sic]"* and `http://www.myspace.com` *"a place for friends"*.

[116] See `http://www.gnu.org`

[117] "**Honors**," *SIAM News* 26:8 4, Society for Industrial and Applied Mathematics, Philadelphia, PA, Dec 1993.

[118] ***ISO/IEC 1539-1:2004, COR1:2006, and COR2:2007, Information Technology – Programming Languages – FORTRAN – Part 1: Base Language** and **ISO/IEC 1539-2-1994, Information Technology – Programming Languages – FORTRAN – Part 2: Varying Length Character Strings**,* International Organization for Standardization/International Electrotechnical Commission, Geneva, Switzerland.

[119] ***NEC** Launches SX-8R* press release, Business Technology Network, 17 Oct 2006.

[120] *USA **Standard Fortran**,* Standard X3.9-1966, United States of America Standards Institute, New York, NY, Mar 1966.

[121] *USA **Standard Fortran**,* Standard X3.198-1992, United States of America Standards Institute, New York, NY, 21 Sep 1992.

[122] *Henessy: Vector **Supercomputers** Disappear in 5-10 Yrs,* press release, `hpcwire@tgc.com`, 27 Nov 1997.

[123] "**Trends**," *[Group]Computing* 2:2 14, Sep/Oct 1997. *The statistics were collected by ON Technology, later Elron Software Inc. As part of a sales promotion, companies contemplating purchase of an Internet monitor product collected data over a 3-day interval about web sites visited by their employees. ON chose 100 of the company responses at random. The percentages listed in the table are the numbers of reports out of that sample including at least one web site of the given type.*

[124] ***Zohar**,* part 1, page 183a; also see *Bereshith Rabbah* 18:5.

[125] **Anonymous,** *Creators Admit Unix, C Hoax,*
see, e.g., `http://www.ocean.ic.net/doc/comp/unix/unix.hoax`   *This widely-disseminated item of web humor claims to be excerpted from an April Fool's Day 1991 issue of Computerworld magazine; there was indeed an issue of that publication dated 01 Apr 1991, but it contains no such article. A version of this document also appears as Appendix B of [145].*

[126] **Anonymous**, communicated by **Chuck Somerville** and reported by **Stan Kelly-Bootle** in "Devil's Advocate: Readers' Footnotes," *Unix Review* 6:6 29, Jun 1988.

[127] **Alper, Joseph**, "From Army of Hackers, an Upstart Operating System," *Science* 282:5396 1976-1979, 11 Dec 1998.

[128] **Backus, John**, "The History of FORTRAN I, II, and III," *Annals of the History of Computing* 1:1 21-37, Jul 1979. *The first Programmer's Reference Manual, entitled* The FORTRAN Automatic Coding System for the IBM 704 EDPM, *is dated October 15, 1956 and refers to "the system which will be made available during late 1956." Its companion volume,* Programmer's Primer for FORTRAN Automatic Coding System for the IBM 704, *is* ©*1957.*

[129] **Bainbridge, William Sims**, "The Scientific Research Potential of Virtual Worlds," *Science* 317:5837 472-476, 27 Jul 2007.

[130] **Bernstein, Danielle R.; Stern, Joshua; Ehrich, William; Dunlavey, Michael R.; Zettel, Leonard; Herbert, Bruce B.; Nelson, Mark; Smyth, W. F.; Walker, Bruce W.; Gordon, Robert M.; Cole, Stephen N.;** and **Lightstone, David B.**, "Debatable," Letters, *Communications of the ACM* 33:3 264-271, Mar 1990. *Discussion on Dijkstra's advocacy of formal methods as the basis for teaching computer science.*

[131] **Billings, Josh** (Henry Wheeler Shaw), quotation #966 (page 185) in *Respectfully Quoted*, edited by Suzy Platt, Library of Congress, Washington, DC, 1989. *Shaw may have spoken the words quoted, but the closest he comes in print is "It is better to know nothing than to know what ain't so," in his 1874 book* Proverb. *Advocates for the conventional wisdom about* FORTRAN *programming style seem to know many things that I believe ain't so, but I do not think it would be better for them to know nothing at all.*

[132] **Campbell-Kelly, Martin**, "Obituary: John Backus (1924-2007)," *Nature* 446:7139 998, 26 Apr 2007.

[133] **Carroll, Lewis (Charles L. Dodgson)**, *Alice's Adventures in Wonderland*, D. Appleton & Co., New York, 1866. The quotation appears on page 89; the illustration is by **Sir John Tenniel** and appears on page 91.

[134] **Colburn, Timothy R.; Fetzer, James H.;** and **Rankin, Terry L.**, Editors, *Program Verification: Fundamental Issues in Computer Science (Studies in Cognitive Systems, Volume 14)*, Kluwer Academic, Mar 1993.

[135] **Cringely, Robert X.**, *Accidental Empires: How the Boys of Silicon Valley Make Their Millions, Battle Foreign Competition, and Still Can't Get a Date*, HarperCollins, New York, NY, Sep 1996.

[136] **Dagum, Leonardo; Kremenetsky, Mark; Schreiber, Robert; Bailey, David; Jespersen, Dennis; Levit, Creon; Saini, Subhash; Schuh, Michael; Serafini, David; Simon, Horst;** and **Vaziri, Arsi**, "An open letter to the parallel computing community from a group of users of parallel supercomputers," NASA Ames Research Center, early 1995.

[137] **Daves, Doyle**, personal communication, 1998.

[138] **Dijkstra, Edsger W.**, "GO TO Statement Considered Harmful," letters, *Communications of the ACM* 11:3 147-148, Mar 1968.

[139] **Dijkstra, Edsger W.**, "The Humble Programmer," *Communications of the ACM* 15:10 859-866, Oct 1972.

[140] **Dijkstra, Edsger W.**, "On the Cruelty of Really Teaching Computing Science," and **Denning, Peter J.; Parnas, David L.; Scherlis, W. L.; van Emden, M. H.; Cohen, Jacques; Hamming, R. W.; Karp, Richard M.;** and **Winograd, Terry**, "Colleagues Respond to Dijkstra's Comments," A Debate on Teaching Computing Science, *Communications of the ACM* 32:12 1397-1414, Dec 1989. *Dijkstra argues that formal methods should be the basis for teaching computer science.*

[141] **Ettles, Chris**, personal communication.

[142] **Foster, David; Ross, David E.; Bourgeois, Frederick J. III; Kuekes, Lawrence C.; Cohen, Norman E.; Weisert, Conrad; Rubin, Frank;** and **Dijkstra, Edsger W.**, "GO TO, One More Time," Letters, *Communications of the ACM* 30:8, 659-662, Aug 1987.

[143] **Galli, Peter**, from an article originally appearing in *eWEEK*, quoted in "Java to overtake C/C++ in 2002," Features and Commentary, hpcwire.tgc.com, 24 Aug 2001.

[144] **Gardner, Martin**, "Mathematical Games," *Scientific American* 198:4 118-122, Apr 1958 and 198:5 126, May 1958. *The original problem involves five people rather than three. Gardner cites an earlier source.*

[145] **Garfinkel, Simson; Weise, Daniel;** and **Strassman, Steven**, Editors, and **Klossner, John**, Illustrator, *The UNIX-Hater's Handbook*, IDG, San Mateo, CA, May 1994.

[146] **Gehrke, Wilhelm**, *The F Language Guide*, Springer Verlag, New York, NY, Oct 1997.

[147] **Glanz, James**, "Chain of Errors Hurled Probe Into Spin," *Science* 281:5376 499, 24 Jul 1998.

[148] **Hatton, Les**, "Does OO Sync With How We Think?" Focus, *IEEE Software* 15:3 46-54, May-Jun 1998.

[149] **Hoffman, Donna L.** and **Novak, Thomas P.**, "Bridging the Racial Divide on the Internet," *Science* 280:5362 390-391, 17 Apr 1998 and **Krueger, Joachim; Graves, Joseph L. Jr.; Bereano, Philip L.; Powell, Adam Clayton III; Globus, Al; Daniel, Hal J. III; Hoffman, Donna L.;** and **Novak, Thomas P.**, "Division on the Internet?," Letters, *Science* 281:5379, 919-923, 14 Aug 1998.

[150] **Hook, Audrey A.**, "A Survey of Computer Programming Languages Currently Used in the Department of Defense," *CrossTalk, The Journal of Defense Software Engineering* 8:10 4-5, Software Technology Support Center, US Department of Defense, Oct 1995.

[151] **Kahan, W.**, "Further Remarks on Reducing Truncation Errors," *Communications of the ACM* 8:1 40 Jan 1965. *The author remarks "The convenient accessibility of double-precision in ... FORTRAN ... compilers indicates that double-precision will soon be universally acceptable as a substitute for ingenuity in the solution of numerical problems."*

[152] **Kaiser, Jocelyn**, "NetWatch," *Science* 291:5506, 951, 09 Feb 2001; *also see* www.mathsoft.com/asolve

[153] **Keen, Andrew**, *The Cult of the Amateur*, Doubleday/Currency, New York, NY, 2007.

[154] **Kidder, Tracy**, *The Soul of a New Machine*, Little Brown, Boston, MA, 1981. *This true story is to computing what Tom Wolfe's The Right Stuff is to the space program.*

[155] **Kraut, Robert; Lundmark, Vicki; Patterson, Michael; Kiesler, Sara; Mukopadhyay, Tridas;** and **Sherlis, William**, "Internet Paradox: A Social Technology That Reduces Social Involvement and Psychological Well-Being?" *American Psychologist* 53:9 1017-1031, Sep 1998.

[156] **Lanier, Jaron**, *VR Pioneer Offers An Uninhibited And Idealistic Vision of VIRTUAL REALITY,* announcement of a lecture delivered at Rensselaer Polytechnic Institute, Troy, NY, 22 Sep 1997. *The lecture announcement includes an Abstract, which begins as follows: "The original goal of science and technology, beginning with the Renaissance, was to increase the power of mankind relative to nature. It is remarkable that this goal has largely been met in the twentieth century. We can proudly say, at this time, that we have more to fear from human behavior than from the rest of nature. The only areas of development in science or technology that are truly, objectively needed now are medicine and the study of natural disasters. All the rest we must honestly describe as being justified for cultural reasons alone."*

[157] **Lee, J. A. N.**, "Pioneer Day, 1982," *Annals of the History of Computing* 6:1 7-14, Special Issue: FORTRAN's Twenty-Fifth Anniversary, Jan 1984.

[158] **Le Guin, Ursula K.**, *A Wizard of Earthsea,* Bantam Books, New York, NY, 1968.

[159] **Lehrbaum, Rick**, "Here Come the Devices!" *Linux Journal* :88, 50-52, Aug 2001. *This article contains a description of the Sylvania Internet/TV appliance.*

[160] **Locke, John L.**, "No Talking in the Corridors of Science," *American Scientist* 87:1 8-9, Jan-Feb 1999.

[161] **Luecking, Daniel H.**, electronic mail footer appearing in the newsgroup `comp.lang.fortran`, 30 Aug 1995.

[162] **Mody, R. P.**, "C in Education and Software Engineering" *ACM SIGCSE Bulletin* 23:3 45-56, Sep 1991.

[163] **Moore, Donald; Musciano, Chuck; Liebhaber, Michael J.; Lott, Steven F;** and **Starr, Lee**, " 'GO TO Considered Harmful Considered Harmful' Considered Harmful?" Letters, *Communications of the ACM* 30:5 351-355, May 1987.

[164] **Muxworthy, David**, "Specialist Groups Development Funds Programme Project: Support for Fortran Standards Development," `http://www.fortran.bcs.org/2006/devrep06.php`, 31 May 2006.

[165] **Nettle, Daniel** and **Romaine, Suzanne**, *Vanishing Voices: The Extinction of the World's Languages,* Oxford University Press, New York, NY, 2000.

[166] **Norman, Donald A.**, "The Trouble with UNIX: The User Interface is Horrid," including **Lesk, Michael**, "Another View," *Datamation* 27:12 139-150, Nov 1981.

[167] **Norman, Donald A.**, *The Invisible Computer,* MIT Press, Cambridge, MA, 1998.

[168] **Oppenheimer, Todd**, "The Computer Delusion," *The Atlantic Monthly* 280:1 45-62, Jul 1997.

[169] **Plotkin, Kenneth**, "HOW to make Fortran attractive to UG?" `comp.lang.fortran` newsgroup, 05 Apr 1996.

[170] **Rabinowitz, Stan,** an untitled test code for the VAX FORTRAN compiler, Digital Equipment Corporation, Maynard, MA, circa 1984. *This program was designed to elicit one syntax error message from the compiler for which it was written, but contains many bizarre constructions that were regarded by that compiler as legal.*

[171] **Raymond, Eric**, *The Cathedral and the Bazaar: Musings on Linux and Open Source by an Accidental Revolutionary,* O'Reilly, Sebastopol, CA, Feb 2001. *Insight and inspiration about counterculture software development collaborations.*

[172] **Rogers, Edwin H.**, personal communication.

[173] **Rowe, Jennifer**, personal communication, 16 Jun 01. *This poem is widely attributed to John Harold Saxon [1923-1996] (see, for example, http://home.earthlink.net/~sealltlelite/Mathlim.htm, where his name is misspelled Jon). However, his textbook company (Saxon Publishers of Norman, OK) reports that they have never found the poem in any of his textbooks or other writings and that his family and associates do not recall his having composed it.*

[174] **Rubin, Frank**, " 'GO TO Considered Harmful' Considered Harmful," Letters, *Communications of the ACM* 30:3 195-196, Mar 1987.

[175] **Schatz, Bruce R.**, "Information Retrieval in Digital Libraries: Bringing Search to the Net," *Science* 275:5298 327-334, 17 Jan 1997.

[176] **Solomon, Daniel** and **Rosenblueth, David**, "Selecting a Programming Language Made Easy," *ACM SIGPLAN Notices,* 21:9 6, Sep 1986.

[177] **Stoll, Clifford**, *Silicon Snake Oil: Second Thoughts on the Information Highway,* Anchor, New York, NY, Apr 1996.

[178] **Struble, George W.**, *Assembler Language Programming: the IBM System/360 and 370,* Addison-Wesley, Reading, MA, 1975.

[179] **Strunk, W. Jr.** and **White, E. B.**, *The Elements of Style,* Third Edition, Macmillan, New York, NY, Jan 1979.

[180] **Talbott, Stephen L.**, *The Future Does Not Compute: Transcending the Machine in Our Midst,* 1st Edition, O'Reilly, Sebastopol, CA, Jan 1995.

[181] **Tolkein, J. R. R.**, *The Two Towers,* Being the Second Part of The Lord of the Rings, Ballantine Books, New York, NY, Sep 1970. *The wise old wizard was Gandalf, explaining palantiri to the young Peregrin Took. The closest thing we have to a palantir these days is a computer connected to the World Wide Web.*

[182] **Turkle, Sherry**, *Life on the Screen: Identity in the Age of the Internet,* Simon & Schuster, New York, NY, Sep 1997. *A convincing and thoroughly objective argument that the Web culture arises from, implements in practice, and helps to legitimize the philosophical system known as Postmodernism. The central theses of Postmodernism are that there is no such thing as objective truth, that everything we believe is the result of our cultural background, and that all opinions and beliefs are equally valid.*

[183] **Van Alstyne, Marshall** and **Brynjolfsson, Erik**, "Could the Internet Balkanize Science?" *Science* 274:5291 1479-1480, 29 Nov 1996.

[184] **Van der Wijngaart, Rob F.** and **Smith, Merritt H.**, "In defense of parallel diversity," electronic mail from NASA NAS, 24 Feb 1996.

[185] **Weinreich, Max**, *Bilder fun der Yidisher Literaturgeshikhte,* Tomor, Vilna, Lithuania, 1928 (4 volumes, Yiddish). **Liptzin, Sol**, *A History of Yiddish Literature,* Jonathan David, New York, NY, Nov 1990 (English).

[186] **Willard, Christopher G.**, "Technology Update: High-Performance Fortran," *Workstation and High-Performance Systems Bulletin,* IDC #12526, Volume 2, Tab 6, International Data Corporation, Framingham, MA, Nov 1996.

[187] **Wu, Shaun-inn; Katz, Andrew; Gintowt, George M.; and Harrison, Michael J.**, "A Funny Thing Happened on the way to the Forum," Letters, *Communications of the ACM* 30:7 632-634, Jul 1987.

Index

function	returns	name
`Y=DSQRT(X)`	$y = \sqrt{x}$	square root
`Y=DEXP(X)`	$y = e^x$	exponential
`Y=DLOG(X)`	$y = \log_e(x) = \ln(x)$	natural logarithm
`Y=DLOG10(X)`	$y = \log_{10}(x)$	common logarithm
`Y=DCOS(X)`	$y = \cos(x)$	cosine
`Y=DACOS(X)`	$y = \arccos(x) = \cos^{-1}(x)$	arc cosine
`Y=DSIN(X)`	$y = \sin(x)$	sine
`Y=DASIN(X)`	$y = \arcsin(x) = \sin^{-1}(x)$	arc sine
`Y=DTAN(X)`	$y = \tan(x)$	tangent
`Y=DATAN(X)`	$y = \arctan(x) = \tan^{-1}(x)$	$\left.\vphantom{\begin{array}{c}a\\a\end{array}}\right\}$ arc tangent
`Y=DATAN2(X,S)`	$y = \arctan(x/s) = \tan^{-1}(x/s)$	
`Y=DSINH(X)`	$y = \sinh(x) = (e^x - e^{-x})/2$	hyperbolic sine
`Y=DCOSH(X)`	$y = \cosh(x) = (e^x + e^{-x})/2$	hyperbolic cosine
`Y=DTANH(X)`	$y = \tanh(x) = \sinh(x)/\cosh(x)$	hyperbolic tangent
`Y=DERF(X)`	$y = \mathrm{erf}(x) = \frac{2}{\sqrt{\pi}}\int_0^x e^{-t^2}dt$	error function
`Y=DGAMMA(X)`	$y = \Gamma(x) = \int_0^\infty t^{x-1}e^{-t}dt$	gamma function
`Y=DABS(X)`	$y = |x|$	$\left.\vphantom{\begin{array}{c}a\\a\end{array}}\right\}$ absolute value
`J=IABS(I)`	$j = |i|$	
`S=DMAX1(X,Y)`	$s = \max(x,y)$	$\left.\vphantom{\begin{array}{c}a\\a\end{array}}\right\}$ highest value
`K=MAX0(I,J)`	$k = \max(i,j)$	
`S=DMIN1(X,Y)`	$s = \min(x,y)$	$\left.\vphantom{\begin{array}{c}a\\a\end{array}}\right\}$ lowest value
`K=MIN0(I,J)`	$k = \min(i,j)$	
`Y=DMOD(X,S)`	$y = x \bmod s$	$\left.\vphantom{\begin{array}{c}a\\a\end{array}}\right\}$ modulus
`J=MOD(I,K)`	$j = i \bmod k$	
`Y=DSIGN(X,S)`	$y = [\text{sign of } s] \times x$	$\left.\vphantom{\begin{array}{c}a\\a\end{array}}\right\}$ transfer of sign
`J=ISIGN(I,K)`	$j = [\text{sign of } k] \times i$	
`Z=DCONJG(W)`	$z = x - y\sqrt{-1}$ if $w = x + y\sqrt{-1}$	complex conjugate

name	purpose	§
ETIME	measure elapsed CPU time	15.1.3
EXIT	stop the program with a specified return code	14.2.6
FDATE	get the current date and time of day	14.2.1
FLUSH	cause an output buffer to be written	14.2.2
FSTAT	get information about a file attached to a given unit	14.2.2
GETARG	get command-line arguments as character strings	14.2.4
GETCWD	get the name of the current UNIX™ directory	
GETENV	get the value of a UNIX™ environment variable	14.2.3
IARGC	get the number of command-line arguments given	14.2.4
IDATE	get the current date	14.2.1
IOINIT	change FORTRAN I/O initializations from defaults	
IRAND	generate pseudorandom integers	
ITIME	get the current time of day	14.2.1
SLEEP	suspend execution for a given interval of time	
STAT	get information about a file having a given name	14.2.2
SYSTEM	execute UNIX™ commands from within the program	14.2.5
UNLINK	remove a file	14.2.2

quantity		hexadecimal	decimal
INTEGER*4	zero	00000000	0
	+1	00000001	1
	−1	FFFFFFFF	−1
	largest +	7FFFFFFF	2147483647
	largest −	80000000	−2147483648
REAL*4	+0	00000000	0.0
	−0	80000000	−0.0
	+1	3F800000	1.0
	−1	BF800000	−1.0
	largest	7F7FFFFF	3.4028235E+38
	smallest normal	00800000	1.1754944E−38
	smallest subnormal	00000001	1.4012985E−45
	infinity +	7F800000	$+\infty$
	infinity −	FF800000	$-\infty$
	NaN	7FFFFFFF	not a number
REAL*8	+0	0000000000000000	0.D0
	−0	8000000000000000	−0.D0
	+1	3FF0000000000000	1.D0
	−1	BFF0000000000000	−1.D0
	largest	7FEFFFFFFFFFFFFF	1.7976931348623157D+308
	smallest normal	0010000000000000	2.2250738585072014D−308
	smallest subnormal	0000000000000001	4.9406564584124654D−324
	infinity +	7FF0000000000000	$+\infty$
	infinity −	FFF0000000000000	$-\infty$
	NaN	7FFFFFFFFFFFFFFF	not a number